WALES AND THE REFORMATION

WALES *and the* REFORMATION

Glanmor Williams

UNIVERSITY OF WALES PRESS
CARDIFF
1999

© Glanmor Williams, 1997

Originally published in Hardback, 1997
Paperback Edition, 1999

British Library Cataloguing-in-Publication Data
A catalogue record for this book is available from the British Library.

ISBN 0–7083–1542–9

Published with the financial support of the Arts Council of Wales

DA
714
.W49
1999

Cover design: Neil James Angove
Cover photograph: Tintern Abbey by Jean Williamson, Mick Sharp Photography

Typeset at the University of Wales Press
Printed in Great Britain by Dinefwr Press, Llandybïe

To my students, colleagues and friends

Contents

Preface

If, as Macaulay recorded, Charles II hoped his courtiers would excuse him for having been an unconscionable time dying, I must certainly ask forgiveness of any readers I may have for having been an even more unconscionably long time bringing this book into existence. I began to collect material for it as early as 1950, but within two or three years I came to the conclusion that I ought first of all to write a book on the Welsh Church before the Reformation. After that study was published in 1962 I had hoped to produce, within a relatively short space of time, a sequel to it on Wales and the Reformation. Circumstances, however, obliged me to set aside such intentions for what I supposed would be a period of some five to ten years. In the event, I was not able to take the project up again until about 1988. Although during the intervening years I had tried to maintain my reading on the Reformation and even to write occasional essays on subjects relating to it, I found it difficult to pick up all the threads once more, and it has taken me some eight years to complete this volume. I hope it does not betray too many of those gaps and inconsistencies that seem to be almost inseparable from a book written with many interruptions over a period of more than forty years.

Such shortcomings, and others, would be more apparent had I not received help and encouragement over the years from many kind friends, to all of whom I am deeply grateful. A number of those to whom I was indebted in the early stages are now dead: Professors Henry Lewis, T. J. Morgan, T. Jones Pierce, Melville Richards, Glyn Roberts, David Williams, Griffith John Williams, and Gwyn A. Williams, and Messrs. E. D. Jones, William Greenway and J. D. H. Thomas. Others, like Professors D. J. Bowen, David Quinn, FBA, and J. E. Caerwyn Williams, FBA, and Drs J. R. L. Highfield and T. B. Pugh, are happily still flourishing. So, too, are Dr and Mrs David Walker, who have been close friends and very helpful in their interest in my work for over forty years. In more recent years I have also profited much from the advice, interest and help of friends and colleagues: Professors R. R. Davies, FBA, R. A. Griffiths, Ceri W. Lewis, and K. O. Morgan, FBA; Professor J. B. and Dr Llinos Smith, Professors J.

Preface

Gwynn Williams and J. Gwynfor Jones, and Drs Madeleine Gray, R. Brinley Jones, Prys T. J. Morgan, Nia W. Powell and Peter Roberts. I owe a great deal to kindnesses shown me by my former students; not only to those who are distinguished scholars in their own right, Professors Geraint H. Jenkins and Gareth E. Jones, and Drs W. P. Griffith, W. S. K. Thomas, Richard Welchman, and Barrie Williams, but also to many generations of undergraduates whom I had the pleasure of teaching at Swansea for nearly forty years and who, in return, taught me so much in the process. There are three friends to whom I am especially grateful: Dr F. G. Cowley, who has always been consistently helpful in drawing my attention to items of bibliographical and scholarly interest and discussing them with me; Professor R. G. Gruffydd, FBA, whose published studies have been very illuminating, but whose willingness to allow me to borrow his doctoral thesis for an extended period was even more valuable; and my oldest and dearest friend, Professor Ieuan Gwynedd Jones, who from the outset has been an unfailing source of assistance, encouragement and inspiration.

I should also like to thank the many librarians and archivists, especially those at the British Library, the National Library of Wales, the Public Record Office, and the University of Wales Swansea, who have made my life much easier by their kindness and courtesy.

The Leverhulme Trustees extended their generosity to me by the award of a Research Fellowship in 1956–7 and an Emeritus Fellowship in 1988–90, for which I thank them sincerely.

I am also deeply indebted to the staff of the University of Wales Press for the kindness and help they have consistently extended to me while the volume has been going through the press. I should particularly like to thank Ms Susan Jenkins, Senior Editor, Ms Ceinwen Jones, and Ms Liz Powell.

For over fifty years I have been happily married to my wife, Fay, who throughout could not have been more understanding, patient, or supportive. She and my children, Margaret and Huw, created a wonderfully contented home, which provided an ideal atmosphere in which to write this and other books. My debt to them is inexpressible and irredeemable.

Glanmor Williams
May 1997

List of Abbreviations

AC	*Archaeologia Cambrensis*
APC	*Acts of the Privy Council*
Augs. Procs.	*Records of the Court of Augmentations relating to Wales,* ed. E. A. Lewis and J. C. Davies
BBCS	*Bulletin of the Board of Celtic Studies*
BIHR	*Bulletin of the Institute of Historical Research*
BL	British Library
C1	Early Chancery Proceedings
C3	Chancery Proceedings, Series II
Carm. Antiq.	*The Carmarthenshire Antiquary*
Cath. Rec. Soc.	The Catholic Record Society
CCCC	Corpus Christi College, Cambridge
CPL	*Calendar of Papal Letters*
CPR	*Calendar of Patent Rolls*
CSP Dom.	*Calendar of State Papers, Domestic*
CSP For.	*Calendar of State Papers, Foreign*
CSP Rome	*Calendar of State Papers, Rome*
CSP Span.	*Calendar of State Papers, Spanish*
CSP Ven.	*Calendar of State Papers, Venetian*
Cymm.	*Y Cymmrodor*
DNB	*The Dictionary of National Biography*
DWB	*The Dictionary of Welsh Biography*
E36	Renunciations of papal supremacy
E112	Exchequer Bills and Answers
E117	Church goods
E163	Miscellanea of the Exchequer
E164	Exchequer miscellaneous books, series I
E301	Chantry certificates
E321	Proceedings of the Court of Augmentations
E322	Surrenders of the monasteries
EHR	*English Historical Review*
GCH	*Glamorgan County History*
GPC	*Geiriadur Prifysgol Cymru*
Hist. Journ.	*Historical Journal*

List of Abbreviations

HMC	Historical Manuscripts Commission
JEH	*Journal of Ecclesiastical History*
JHSCW	*Journal of the Historical Society of the Church in Wales*
JWBS	*Journal of the Welsh Bibliographical Society*
JWEH	*Journal of the Welsh Ecclesiastical History Society*
JWRH	*Journal of the Welsh Religious History Society*
KLlB	*Kynniver Llith a Ban*
LlC	*Llên Cymru*
LlCh	Llandaff Chapter Records
LP	*Letters and Papers of Henry VIII's Reign*
Mont. Colls.	*Montgomeryshire Collections*
NLW	National Library of Wales
NLWJ	*National Library of Wales Journal*
PCC	Prerogative Court of Canterbury
Penbrokshire	G. Owen, *Description of Penbrokshire*
PP	*Past and Present*
PRO	Public Record Office
Req.	Court of Requests
RHS	Royal Historical Society
SA/MB	St Asaph Miscellaneous Books
SD/BR	St David's Bishops' Registers
SD/Ch	St David's Chapter Records
SP	State Papers
STA C	Star Chamber Proceedings
Stat. Realm	*Statutes of the Realm*
SWMRS	*South Wales and Monmouthshire Records Society*
TAAS	*Transactions of the Anglesey Antiquarian Society*
TCHS	*Transactions of the Caernarvonshire Historical Society*
TCS	*Transactions of the Honourable Society of Cymmrodorion*
TMHS	*Transactions of the Merioneth Historical Society*
TRHS	*Transactions of the Royal Historical Society*
VCH	*Victoria County History*
WC	G. Williams, *The Welsh Church from Conquest to Reformation*
WHR	*The Welsh History Review*
W and R	G. Williams, *The Welsh and their Religion*
WRE	G. Williams, *Welsh Reformation Essays*
W 1415–1642	G. Williams, *Recovery, Reorientation and Reformation: Wales c.1415–1642*

Dates, punctuation and orthography have all been modernized.

CHAPTER 1

Wales before the Reformation

O N the eve of the Reformation, the more thoughtful among the Welsh, laymen and clerics alike, were profoundly conscious of their own primordial ecclesiastical heritage. In their eyes, it stretched back to apostolic times, when their ancestors, the Ancient Britons, had been converted to Christianity, they believed. It certainly went back to the very beginnings of their separate history as the *Cymry* (Welsh people) in the immediate post-Roman era of the fifth and sixth centuries AD. For them it was a Christian inheritance which had had a decisive share in shaping not only their religious beliefs and moral values but also their awareness as a people and their cultural identity. Like other European nations, they were intensely proud of their ancient and particular history; not least because, emphasizing as it did their alleged connections with Rome, its empire, civilization and church, it conferred upon them immense moral superiority over their Saxon neighbours who, for so long, had been unlettered heathen barbarians.

Such an understanding of their Christian past, like so much else in their history – real and imaginary – was based very largely on Geoffrey of Monmouth's *Historia Regum Britanniae*.[1] The existence of other early authorities on British history, like Gildas, Bede, Nennius, the *Liber Landavensis*, the lives of the saints, and the Welsh Triads, was well known to them; but much of what they derived from such sources had been filtered through Geoffrey's writings. His work proverbially exercised an irresistible fascination for the inhabitants of medieval Europe, and for none more than the Welsh. The latter's reaction was understandable when Geoffrey had furnished them with illustrious Trojan ancestors and a past more spectacularly glorious than that of almost any other people. Those early

---

[1] Geoffrey of Monmouth, *The History of the Kings of Britain*, ed. L. Thorpe (Harmondsworth, 1966); *Historia Regum Britanniae*, ed. Acton Griscom (London, 1929).

British heroes, as they appeared in Geoffrey's pages, were unsurpassed in the valour and brilliance of their exploits or the breathtaking success of their achievements. Moreover, he had recounted his story in entertaining and readable fashion unmatched by most other writers. Small wonder that he was one of Europe's most eagerly read authors; the excitement, if not the reliability, of his chronicle entitled him to his place of honour.

Geoffrey's *Historia* purported to narrate the history of the British from their arrival in the island as migrants from Troy to the death of their last king, Cadwaladr, late in the seventh century. The Christian strand in the story highlighted what its author regarded as a number of key individuals and episodes, most of which were entirely legendary, though a few had some foundation in fact. Accepted as authentic in its entirety, his account exercised enormous influence. It began soon after the death of Jesus Christ with the claim that Britain had first been converted to Christianity by none other than the keeper of the Saviour's grave, Joseph of Arimathea. This gave the Britons the *cachet* of apostolic conversion, a privilege coveted by a number of Christian peoples. Even more emphasis was laid on the role of a British 'king' as the effective founder of the Christian Church in Britain. Hopelessly improbable as that might seem, Lucius son of Coel was put forward as having 'ruled' in second-century Roman Britain. Impressed by what he had heard of Christianity, he wrote a letter to Pope Eleutherius requesting him to send missionaries for the purpose of converting the island. Eleutherius duly complied, and dispatched Fagan and Duvian, whose evangelizing efforts met with resounding success among the Britons. The seats of the pagan hierarchy of arch-flamens and flamens were transformed into episcopal sees, those of the arch-flamens at London, York, and Caerleon becoming archbishoprics – a point of the utmost importance for Wales, since the archbishopric of Caerleon was believed to have passed later to St David's.

Thereafter, the Britons were to remain steadfastly loyal to their Christianity, in spite of being rigorously persecuted for their beliefs by Diocletian and other idolatrous Roman emperors. British devotion found testimony in the heroic deaths of indomitable martyrs like Alban, or Julius and Aaron, whose names continued to be held in the highest honour. In due course the Britons claimed to have reared from their own midst two of the most illustrious Christian figures ever to have been associated with Rome: Constantine, the first Christian emperor; and his mother, Helen, to whom was attributed the supreme distinction of having been chosen to find the true cross, the most sacred relic of all. It was these alleged links that they could claim with two such pre-eminent personalities which gave the Britons no small part of their entitlement to be associated as a people with the life and Christianity of Rome.

Again, in the fifth century, in spite of the departure of the Romans and the advent of pagan Saxon invaders, the Britons continued true to their Christian heritage. Furthermore, in the teeth of the heresy being propounded by the followers of Pelagius who, sad to say, had been born in Britain, they remained constant. Their steadfastness owed much to the two missions of St Germanus of Auxerre. He and his associates, Lupus of Troyes and Severus, not only preached with candescent fervour and conviction but also won miraculous military success – the 'Alleluia' victory – over the Saxon enemies. During this same era, God had also called forth from among the Britons themselves a host of their own heroic native saints to preach and teach widely.[2] Dyfrig, Illtud, David, Teilo, Beuno, and many others were revered as holy men endowed with miracle-working powers, whose reputation remained a household word among their countrymen and whose deeds became inextricably interwoven into history and folklore. Their very names had been given to churches and parishes all over Wales and served as a ubiquitous reminder of their presence.

Throughout these early centuries the Britons remained devotedly Christian in contradistinction to their sworn enemies, the Saxons. The latter were not only heathens but were also deemed to be inveterately prone to deceit and treachery. They betrayed British rulers like the despicable Vortigern, who may have deserved what he got, and Aurelianus Ambrosius and Arthur, who certainly did not. Ambrosius appealed to his countrymen to restore the Christianity so damaged by Vortigern and his Saxon confederates. Arthur, mightiest of all British heroes, was depicted by Geoffrey in still more sympathetic light. He appeared in the *Historia* as a paragon of Christian kingship; a majestic ruler, crowned by Archbishop Dubricius (Dyfrig) at Caerleon, and an all-conquering general who won his triumphs battling in the name of Christ and bearing a likeness of the Blessed Virgin on his shield.[3]

Throughout the sixth century the embattled traditions of British Christianity and Saxon paganism maintained their uneasy coexistence in the island. Not until 597 AD did Pope Gregory the Great dispatch his emissary, Augustine of Canterbury, to convert the heathen Saxons. When Augustine got in touch with the Christians of the west, no common ground could be established between them. There opened up the lamentable conflict

---

[2] S. G. Baring-Gould and J. Fisher, *The Lives of the British Saints* (4 vols. London, 1907–12); E. G. Bowen, *The Settlements of the Celtic Saints in Wales* (Cardiff, 1954), *Saints, Seaways and Settlements in Celtic Lands* (Cardiff, 1977); N. K. Chadwick, *The Age of the Saints in the Early Celtic Church* (Cambridge, 1961); G. H. Doble, *The Lives of the Welsh Saints* (Cardiff, 1971); M. Henken, *Traditions of the Welsh Saints* (Cambridge, 1987); A. W. Wade-Evans, *Vitae Sanctorum Britanniae et Genealogiae* (Cardiff, 1944).

[3] *Hist. Kings of Britain*, pp. 216–17.

between the native British and the missionaries of Canterbury. Envoys of the pope though the latter may have been, they were unacceptable to the Britons. It was a clash of two traditions – that of Rome and that of Celtic Christianity, which for 150 years or more would remain unreconciled.

Geoffrey ended his narrative by relating the fate of Cadwaladr, the last independent king in Britain, late in the seventh century. It was an inglorious episode for the British people; punished for their iniquities by a dreaded troika of calamities distressingly familiar to the Dark Ages and medieval times – war, plague and famine. So ruinous was their impact that, in despair, Cadwaladr left for Brittany. Yet his harrowing experience did not end on a note of despair but, on the contrary, with a divine promise of a glorious future, delivered by an angel, no less, in a peal of thunder. 'As a reward for its faithfulness, the British people would occupy the island again at some time in the future, once the appointed moment should come.'[4] This was a prophecy that was much older than Geoffrey and was one that would be devoutly cherished by the Welsh descendants of the ancient British. It was all the more influential for having a religious as well as a secular connotation and would buoy them up in the darkest days of endless hardships and innumerable disappointments.[5]

Geoffrey's chronicle may have ended with the promise to Cadwaladr, but it encompassed all the essentials of the alleged ecclesiastical history of Britain which were enshrined in the Welsh memory. The main headings of the account related by him were to be what the medieval Welsh preserved as the core of their religious heritage. By the eve of the Norman Conquest the fundamentals of Christian practice and belief were the same in Wales as those found elsewhere in the Church. They constituted the same admixture of basic Christian belief and older customs, often suitably modified or glossed over to conform with Christian teaching. The most potent attraction offered by the Church was its promise to the faithful, beset by the hardships and uncertainties of brief existence on earth, of the reward of eternal life. Only the power of the Church and its sacraments, and the intercession of its holiest sons and daughters, could ensure salvation. It was the power of the saints, especially the native saints and the BVM, which tended to dominate popular religion. Relics associated with them – particularly their bones, real or reputed, but also their bells,

---

[4] Ibid., p. 283.
[5] M. E. Griffiths, *Early Vaticination in Welsh with English Parallels* (Cardiff, 1937); cf. A. O. H. Jarman, *The Legend of Merlin* (Cardiff, 1960); G. Williams, 'Prophecy, poetry and politics in medieval and Tudor Wales', in H. Hearder and H. R. Loyn (eds.), *British Government and Administration* (Cardiff, 1974), pp. 104–16.

croziers, altars, wells, or even books – were the objects of intense pride, veneration, and confidence.[6]

In addition, Welsh piety had some characteristics of its own. It recognized in some fashion the supremacy of the see of Peter, but though Rome was highly thought of as a place of pilgrimage,[7] the practical authority of the pope counted for little in Wales, as indeed in other parts of Europe that were distant from him. Nor did the Welsh bishops acknowledge the jurisdiction of Canterbury; and their associations with the Church in Ireland were as close as, if not closer than, with the Church in England.[8] The organization of the Welsh Church was markedly less territorial than that of the Church on the Continent, and the place within it of monasteries distinctive to Celtic peoples, with their *clasau* (chapters) of canons, much more pronounced. Admittedly, a great deal about its history and nature from Roman times to the Norman Conquest is still obscure, and likely to remain so, even though archaeologists and historians have added and keep adding enormously to our knowledge of it. Much – indeed, most – of what Geoffrey of Monmouth wrote about it with such sublime confidence has had to be abandoned as being very largely the figment of his endlessly resourceful imagination. In the Middle Ages, of course, things were very different. Many of the core themes which inspired him became firmly fixed in the Welsh folk memory and remained there for centuries afterwards.

Among the essentials of that recollection was first, the belief in a providential conversion to Christianity in the early days after Christ's death, which they interpreted as a token of the Welsh having been called out from the wilderness as a people chosen by God. Secondly, they had ever since maintained an independent tradition of their own secular and ecclesiastical history, their language, and their literature; an inheritance which they believed to be more ancient than and superior to that of other peoples within the island of Britain and one closely connected, in terms of Trojan origins and later associations, with the empire and civilization of Rome. Thirdly, they had, all along, despite sins and shortcomings on their part, remained loyal to the true faith; this in face of fierce persecution by Roman emperors, the savage hostility of heathen peoples, and the insidious wiles of heretics. Fourthly, God had further revealed his favour towards them by raising up from their midst a great company of their own

---

[6] For early Welsh Church history: L. Alcock, *Arthur's Britain* (Harmondsworth, 1971); M W. Barley and R. P. C. Hanson, *Christianity in Britain, 300–700* (London, 1971); W. Davies, *Wales in the Early Middle Ages* (Leicester, 1982); J. K. Knight, *GCH*, II (1984), chap. 9; S. Victory, *The Celtic Church in Wales* (Cardiff, 1972); H. Williams, *Christianity in Early Britain* (Oxford, 1912).

[7] G. H. Jones, *Celtic Britain and the Pilgrim Movement* (London, 1912), pp. 153ff.

[8] N. K. Chadwick, *Studies in the Early British Church* (Cambridge, 1958).

sanctified and miracle-working saints, many of whom had left among them sacred relics of supernatural power. Giraldus Cambrensis was in due course to testify that they 'paid greater respect than any other people to their churches' and 'the relics of their saints'.[9] Finally, they set great store by the prophecy of their future triumph, entrusted to them, as they thought, by a celestial messenger. True, they might have transgressed grievously and been justly punished for their wickedness, being deprived by their enemies of their former privileged status and much of their territory; yet they could take consolation from the promise of the future renewal of their earlier greatness. God, it appeared, had some profound purpose of his own, which he intended them to fulfil, and in preparation for which he was preserving them, their church, and their language. This kind of confidence was crystallized in the prophecy delivered to Henry II by the old man of Pencader, on which Giraldus set such store:

> My Lord King, this nation may now be harassed, weakened and decimated by your soldiers, as it has often been by others in former times; but it will never be totally destroyed by the wrath of men, unless at the same time it is punished by the wrath of God. Whatever else may come to pass, I do not think that on the Day of Direst Judgement any race other than the Welsh, or any other language, will give answer to the Supreme Judge of all for this small corner of the earth.[10]

In the centuries that followed the Norman Conquest all these convictions were to be subjected to severe erosive forces; yet, although in some respects weakened or modified, they survived largely intact, buckled but unbroken, to the age of the Reformation.

During the very century in which Geoffrey of Monmouth (?1090–1155) lived, however, profound changes were overtaking the Welsh Church.[11] This was the early period of the Norman Conquest which, in its effects upon the Church, wrought a transformation not incomparable in scale and magnitude to that later brought about by the Protestant Reformation or the Methodist Revival. From the end of the eleventh century onwards, when the Normans began to extend their rule over large areas of south and

[9] Giraldus Cambrensis, *The Journey through Wales . . .*, ed. L. Thorpe (Harmondsworth, 1978), p. 253.

[10] Ibid., p. 274.

[11] For the history of the early medieval Church: J. C. Davies, *Episcopal Acts relating to Welsh Dioceses, 1066–1272* (2 vols. Historical Soc. Church in Wales, Cardiff, 1946–8); R. R. Davies, *Conquest, Co-existence, and Change: Wales, 1063–1415* (Oxford, 1987); D. G. Walker, *A History of the Church in Wales* (Penarth, 1976); *WC*.

east Wales, it was to be expected that they should seek to exercise control over the Church in the interests of consolidating and expanding their authority. The Church they found in Wales was still closely similar to what it had been for centuries, differing markedly from the ecclesiastical institutions with which the Normans were familiar. This was a state of things which the intruders were unlikely to tolerate for long. Accustomed to a territorially organized church ruled over by their own aristocratic bishops and well-born abbots of Latin-type monasteries, all of whom had, to a greater or lesser extent, come under the inspiration of a reformed papacy, the Normans were eager to introduce comparable institutions and personnel into Wales. Brutal and materialistic as they often were, they were able to cloak their pugnacious instincts and their political need to dominate the Church with a sense that was comforting to themselves of a mission to introduce Church reform. Nor were the individual Norman lords who carried out piecemeal their conquest of the Marches of east and south-east Wales the only ones to appreciate the need for tightening their grip on the levers of ecclesiastical power. Behind them loomed the Norman kings of England and the archbishops of Canterbury, who were no less conscious of the strategic value of bringing the Welsh Church under their direction.

One of the primary stages in the process of subordination was to secure management of the choice of bishops and thereby to ensure their allegiance to the archbishop of Canterbury. Hitherto, bishops in Wales had not acknowledged his authority; but in 1107 Urban, the first Norman bishop of Llandaff, was induced to make a profession of obedience to the primate of England. It proved to be a fateful decision which set the pattern for the future. By the middle of the twelfth century the bishops of all four Welsh dioceses had been prevailed upon to make a similar submission. Thus had been accomplished the first and crucial stage in bringing the Church under the jurisdiction of king and archbishop; a shift pregnant with consequences for Church and people.

The new-style prelates introduced far-reaching modifications into the organization, possessions, and discipline of the dioceses. They replaced the earlier system, by which episcopal authority was exercised by the heads of 'mother' churches over the clergy in a series of 'daughter' churches affiliated to them, with territorially demarcated dioceses having fixed geographical boundaries. This was an arrangement not brought into being without heated disagreements over limitations and jurisdictions between rival bishops. Within the newly defined diocesan boundaries other ecclesiastical units were mapped out. Rural deaneries and archdeaconries came into existence; the former based broadly on civil administrative units, the commote (*cwmwd*) or cantref; the latter on earlier kingdoms or provinces, such as Meirionnydd (Merioneth) or Brycheiniog (Brecknock).

Parishes were also carved out for the first time in many parts of Wales; this proved to be a slow process that was not completed in north Wales until the fourteenth century. In upland Wales the parishes were generally large and sprawling; in heavily Normanized districts in the south and east, like Pembrokeshire or the Vale of Glamorgan, they tended to be small and compact, corresponding very often to knights' fees. For the maintenance of the clergy in these parishes tithes were now introduced for the first time.

As the Normans gradually took over much of the control of the Church, some of the most distinctive features of its previous existence were rudely uprooted. Dedications to native saints were strange and unacceptable to the alien intruders, who proceeded in many places to eradicate them and rededicate churches to saints with whom they were familiar. The earlier Welsh *clas*, or body of canons, usually hereditary and serving one of the more celebrated churches of ancient foundation, was destroyed where possible, and its endowments transferred to those monasteries in England or France specially favoured by the conquerors. Churches in south-east Wales, which came early and completely under Norman control, suffered particularly badly, The celebrated *clas* associated with the name of Illtud at Llanilltud Fawr (Llantwit Major), and that of Cadog at Llancarfan, for example, were both suppressed and their possessions made over to the abbeys of Tewkesbury and Gloucester.

Closely connected with such steps taken to break up the links between 'mother' and 'daughter' churches and to demolish the *clasau*, was the introduction of Latin-type monasteries into Wales.[12] The first to be founded were daughter priories of Benedictine houses which stood well with the conquerors. Hitherto unknown in Wales, the Black Monks were planted along the Normanized fringes and located mainly in the shadow of Norman castles in lordship capitals like Chepstow, Abergavenny, Monmouth, Cardiff, or Brecon. They were nearly as much of an instrument of conquest as the castle, borough, or lordship. Not one of their cells flourished in those parts of the country held for any length of time by Welsh princes. For most of the Middle Ages the monks who dwelt within them were generally recruited from a non-Welsh population.

Another of the intentions behind the new territorial organization was to pave the way for the implementing of stricter canons of ecclesiastical discipline, in enforcing which the archdeacons and rural deans were to be the key officers. Although these were usually men of Welsh origin, who were in close touch with priests and people, theirs was a delicate responsibility. Progress was slow, and compromises and failures were inevitable. One of the most intractable stumbling-blocks proved to be the

---

[12] F. G. Cowley, *The Monastic Order in South Wales, 1066–1349* (Cardiff, 1977).

celibacy of the clergy. Many of the medieval Welsh priests, in accordance with time-honoured custom and in defiance of the requirements of Canon Law, continued to take 'wives' right down to the Reformation.

One of the more beneficial results of the Norman Conquest was that it helped in bringing to an end the tendency on the part of the Welsh Church to be somewhat isolated from the rest of Christendom. Had the Normans never come to Wales there would no doubt have been closer integration anyway, but the price of earlier autonomy had been the risk of stagnation. In the outcome, the advent of the invaders helped notably in the process of throwing the Welsh Church open to fresh and invigorating streams of reform flowing in briskly from the Continent. The most momentous consequence of this was to bring clerics into a more intimate relationship with the fountain-head of medieval religion, the reformed papacy. To Rome the most active and zealous clerics, Welsh and Norman alike, turned for leadership and guidance; from Rome came much of the driving force underlying the transformation of ecclesiastical inspiration and government.

Yet, profound and wide-ranging as were the changes set in train by the Normans, they did not by any means entirely submerge earlier characteristics. That long-standing awareness of independent conversion, separate history and identity, heritage of native saintly champions, and belief in a special destiny in store for people and language, continued to flourish among the Welsh. Older ways were tenaciously defended and unwelcome novelties stubbornly resisted. The overlordship of Canterbury was not accepted without long and embittered struggles to maintain the autonomy previously enjoyed by Welsh prelates. In the northern principality of Gwynedd its princes, following a precedent set by Prince Owain Gwynedd (1137–70), regarded the diocese of Bangor as their own preserve, and were unwilling to allow the authority of Canterbury to be extended over the see. In south Wales, the claims of St David's to be recognized as an archbishopric were perennially an even more disputatious source of controversy. Paradoxically enough, it was Giraldus Cambrensis, himself three parts a Norman, who was to stand as the boldest champion of the alleged rights of St David's to be considered the metropolitan see of Wales. For a quarter of a century, from 1176 onwards, he fought a desperate, though ultimately vain, campaign to have these pretensions upheld, pleading his case in season and out of season, at royal court and papal curia, amid clergy and laity, with all the resources of one of the swiftest pens and most eloquent tongues known to the Middle Ages.[13] Nor,

---

[13] Davies, *Episcopal Acts*; M. Richter, *Giraldus Cambrensis: The Growth of the Welsh Nation* (Aberystwyth, 1972); R. Bartlett, *Gerald of Wales, 1146–1223* (Oxford, 1982).

when Giraldus disappeared from the scene, had the last been heard of the independent archbishopric of St David's.

Moreover, however much the Normans might have some of the upper echelons of the Welsh hierarchy at their command, they were simply too few in number to be able to dispense with the need for having to make extensive use of native-born clergy, on some of the more exalted planes within the Church as well as at grass-roots level in particular. Many Welshmen were keen to participate in developments which they recognized as being in the best interests of religion. They accepted papal leadership readily, but in the course of time showed no reluctance to bypass king and archbishop in order to reach the pope directly and thus enlist his support for Welsh claims to more sympathetic treatment. One of the more memorable examples of such an approach was a letter of 1274, signed by no fewer than seven Welsh Cistercian abbots and directed to Pope Gregory X, seeking with some success his sympathy on behalf of Prince Llywelyn ap Gruffudd.[14]

Again, in the face of attempts by the Normans to drive out or downgrade dedications to Welsh saints, the Welsh contrived to cling on to them with unyielding determination. St Andrew might have been introduced by the Normans to a place alongside St David in the dedications at the latter's cathedral, but it was the native hero, Dewi, who survived throughout the Middle Ages as the patron saint of Wales; a magnet for popular pilgrimage and the focus of patriotic loyalty, he almost completely eclipsed St Andrew in the people's devotion.[15] Similarly, at Llandaff – the cathedral and see which came most completely under Norman domination – the shrine which proved to be its most specific and enduring attraction was that of three Welsh saints: Teilo, Dyfrig, and Euddogwy.[16] While in north Wales, St Beuno continued greatly to exceed all others in the depth of affection and trust that he inspired.

Not even in the new kind of Latin-style monasteries introduced by them did the Normans have it all their own way. In contrast with the failure of the Norman-sponsored Benedictines to take root among the Welsh, the Cistercian order flourished prodigiously in their midst.[17] Although White Monks came to Wales first under the aegis of the Normans, and a minority of their houses, like Tintern or Basingwerk, always tended to remain

[14] *Councils and Ecclesiastical Documents relating to Great Britain and Ireland*, ed. A. W. Haddan and W. Stubbs (3 vols. Oxford, 1869–78), I. 499.

[15] H. James, 'The cult of St David in the Middle Ages', *In Search of Cult: Archaeological Investigations in Honour of Philip Rahtz* (Woodbridge, 1994).

[16] G. Williams, 'Poets and pilgrims in fifteenth- and sixteenth-century Wales', *TCS* (1991), 76.

[17] J. F. O'Sullivan, *Cistercian Settlements in Wales and Monmouthshire, 1140–1540* (New York, 1947); D. H. Williams, *The Welsh Cistercians* (2 vols. Tenby, 1983, 1985).

Anglo-Norman in sympathy, the Cistercians as an order were not associated in Welsh minds with the conqueror. Far from being timid henchmen who clung close to the skirts of Norman castle and borough, the sons of Cîteaux sought out the undeveloped solitudes of mountain and moorland, especially in *pura Wallia*, that part of the country not encroached upon by the Normans. Their emphasis on retreat into the wilderness, manual labour, pastoral farming, austere discipline, and rigorous self-renunciation seemed to the Welsh to be a reincarnation of the widely admired pristine ideals of ascetic early saints like Dewi or Beuno. Cistercian houses became havens of ordered prayer and worship, cradles of learning, pioneers in the arts of agriculture and stockbreeding, flock management and wool production, even embryonic industry and metal-working. Their close association with the princely families, national chronicles, and native literature turned them into active agents of patriotic aspiration, who made an essential contribution to keeping bright the flame of an independent Welsh ecclesiastical and secular heritage. Such a role won them a unique place in the hearts of princes and people. The very names of their houses – Strata Florida, Aberconwy, Valle Crucis, Margam, Neath, or Hendygwyn ar Daf (Whitland) – became some of the most hallowed talismans in the history of religion in medieval Wales.

The later orders of Franciscans and Dominicans, when they appeared in the thirteenth century, were likewise taken warmly to Welsh hearts.[18] Although towns were few and small in Wales, ten friaries were founded in widely scattered locations. From the friars' ranks sprang some of the foremost scholars and bishops of the age, and some of its greatest masters in the arts of preaching and literary composition. Typical of them was the Dominican bishop of St Asaph (1268–93), Anian Ddu. Scion of a royal line of rulers and warriors, he had no hesitation about proclaiming his own rights as a prince of the Church against Welsh abbots or English bishops, against Edward I no less than Llewelyn the Last. Another leading friar was the Franciscan, John Wallensis; a regent-master at Oxford and Paris, and a prolific author, whose sermon collections were among the most popular compendia of their kind in Europe. He was only one of a number of Welsh clerics burning with an insatiable thirst for knowledge. Members of religious orders and secular clergy alike, they found their way in small but growing numbers to the universities, to Oxford especially.[19]

A feature of the spread of learning among the clerical élite was that it was not confined to the Latin language and literature. One of the more

---

[18] R. C. Easterling, 'The friars in Wales', *AC*, VI/16 (1914), 323–56.

[19] G. Usher, 'Welsh students at Oxford in the Middle Ages', *BBCS*, XVI (1953), 193–8; R. W. Hays, 'Welsh students at Oxford and Cambridge Universities in the Middle Ages', *WHR*, IV (1968–9), 325–61.

impressive achievements of the Welsh Church was to produce a substantial body of religious literature in the vernacular,[20] which those among the clergy and laity who were less educated might also understand. The centuries-old links between religion and the native literary tradition were consolidated and extended during the medieval period. Parts of the Bible were translated into Welsh; so were the Creed, the more popular hymns and prayers, lives of the saints, and works of devotion and mysticism. These prose recensions were well known to the bards of Wales and left a pronounced impress on the poetic tradition which had, for centuries already, had a strongly religious element within it. The themes of the poetry were few and simple, and they recurred repeatedly. Chief among them were praise of the Trinity, especially the sufferings of Christ, and terror at the prospect of the four last things, which was perhaps the most persistent and awe-inspiring motif of all. It was accompanied by unrelenting emphasis on the brevity and brittleness of human life, and the vanity of mortals' preoccupation with fleeting worldly honour and material possessions. There were regular reminders of the need for timely confession of sins and the value of devotion to the BVM and the saints. Thus was the continuity between the pre-Norman age and post-Norman experience maintained largely unbreached in the expression of popular devotion.

From about the middle of the fourteenth century until well into the fifteenth, virtually the whole of Christendom passed through a long series of crises: a crisis of authority, a crisis of unity, a crisis in individual consciences, and a crisis in ecclesiastical finances and maintenance. Some of the most important causes of this 'time of troubles' affected the western Church as a whole and may be mentioned only briefly in passing. Among the most serious was the decline in the moral, spiritual, and practical authority of the papacy as the result of the Babylonish Captivity and the Great Schism. It was a lapse whose effects tended to spread downwards from head to members throughout the clerical hierarchy and thereby to increase the power of lay rulers relative to that of the clergy. Comparable weaknesses might be detected in the break-up of the thirteenth-century synthesis of philosophy and faith, and the emergence of deeply divisive controversies and heresies; the cooling enthusiasm of the religious orders; and the economic and social disruption caused by demographic crisis and economic decline.

---

[20] D. S. Evans, *Medieval Religious Literature* (Cardiff, 1986); *WC*, chaps. 2, 12; J. E. C. Williams, 'Welsh religious prose', *Proceedings International Congress Celtic Studies 1963* (Cardiff, 1966), pp. 65–97; *Canu Crefyddol y Gogynfeirdd* (Cardiff, 1977).

Other factors affected England and Wales more immediately.[21] First among them was Edward I's final conquest of Welsh independence in 1282–3. The tendency thereafter – much speeded up in the fourteenth century – was to subordinate the interests of the Welsh Church even more thoroughly to those of the English monarchy. The king was by this time recruiting most of his leading servants from among the academically trained clerical élite. He rewarded them with bishoprics and other valuable preferment in the Church. In the process they tended increasingly to become administrators and politicians, absent from their sees and far less capable of giving them pastoral care and direction. In Wales, discipline and morale were made all the worse by the king's exclusion of Welsh clerics from the most lucrative and influential benefices in their country. For a time this was partially offset by the popes' attempts to protect the native interest by promoting Welshmen by means of papal provisions. Before the end of the fourteenth century, however, papal influence had been effectively ruled out in practice, if not in name, as a result of the popes' need to appease the king of England in an attempt to ensure his support in the course of the Schism. This systematic elimination of Welsh clerics from the upper ranks of the hierarchy served to feed a rising sense of frustration and resentment, which later found an outlet in the Glyndŵr Rebellion (1400–15).

Another major source of discontent sprang from the seemingly endless campaigns fought in the course of the Hundred Years War with France. The king's need for money to pay for his military adventures led him to exploit clerical appointments and tap the financial resources of the Church still more rigorously in his own interest. The wars had a further damaging effect on some of the religious houses. Alien priories belonging to French monasteries were seized by the Crown while warfare was being waged; and the most prominent religious order in Wales, that of the Cistercians, was cut off for long periods from its mother houses of Cîteaux and Clairvaux in France, and thereby suffered serious disruption to its discipline and standards.

To accentuate the clergy's misfortunes came the outbreak of the Black Death (1348–50) and further visitations of epidemic disease in 1361, 1369, and later. The landed possessions and income of the clergy were hit hard. Even more grievous, the numbers of the clergy were sharply reduced as a consequence of high clerical mortality, and the replacements for them, hastily drafted in, were of decidedly mixed, not to say inferior, quality. The religious orders suffered very badly and, as the numbers of monks and friars fell drastically and afterwards remained well below their pre-plague levels, their contributions to scholarship and literature slumped alarmingly.

---

[21] Davies, *Conquest, Co-existence*, pp. 431–60; *WC*, part 1.

All these disasters aggravated the already severe economic difficulties of the age. By the end of the fourteenth century the Church and its clergy, by and large, had become much poorer, and there is widespread evidence of the severe financial problems and reduced resources with which they had to contend.[22] They had to resort to a variety of expedients, most of which were not in the best interests of the Church, even if they temporarily eased economic pressures. Pluralism and non-residence became increasingly common among the secular clergy, while the religious houses had little choice but to acquire appropriations of parishes and to lease out rectories and temporal estates to laymen, and at the same time to keep down their numbers. Clergy of all kinds found it increasingly necessary to depend on the more widespread and indiscriminate sale of indulgences to make ends meet. Like the laity, they found themselves under gruelling pressure from deteriorating social and economic circumstances. In consequence, many of the Welsh clergy were in as bitter and rebellious mood as their lay kinsfolk and, like them, were inclined to attribute their woes mainly, if not entirely, to their English overlords. Only a spark was needed to touch off a conflagration; tinder in plenty lay all around.

The flame was lit when Owain Glyndŵr[23] raised the standard of revolt in September 1400. In his approach to his countrymen, Owain could appeal to that volatile mixture of age-old expectant patriotism and current disaffection among clergy as well as laity and hope to find a ready response. In his so-called 'Pennal programme' of 1406 he resurrected claims to the autonomy of the Welsh Church and the role of a Welsh archbishop of St David's, Dewi's successor and independent of Canterbury. Such a primate would control all the higher clerical appointments in Wales in the interests of its prince and its native clergy. Owain also aimed at re-establishing earlier Welsh links with a sympathetic papacy – this time with the pontiff at Avignon – to use him as an ally against England in the creation of a separate province and archbishop; interestingly enough, just as Scotland would do. Like Scotland, too, he hoped for independent university institutions, one for north Wales, and one for the south, where would-be clerics could be educated. The success of his appeal to his principal allies among the clergy bound all the recognized upholders of Welsh traditions to him: frustrated higher clergy like Bishop John Trefor and Gruffudd Young, along with many of the parish clergy and university students, as well as their counterparts among the Cistercian and Franciscan orders. He won a measure of support, too, from an

---

[22] *WC*, chap. 4.
[23] J. E. Lloyd, *Owen Glendower* (Oxford, 1931); G. Williams, *Owain Glyndŵr* (Cardiff, 1993); R. R. Davies, *The Revolt of Owain Glyn Dŵr* (Oxford, 1995).

intellectual like Adam of Usk and from a vocal Lollard critic in the person of the Welshman, Walter Brut, who intriguingly proclaimed that the 'manifest destiny' so long foretold for the Welsh nation was the overthrow of the papal Antichrist.[24]

For a brief intoxicating year or two it looked as if Glyndŵr's heady and high-flying prospectus for an independent state and an autonomous church might be fulfilled, if only his French and Scottish allies would but help him pull his chestnuts out of the fire. Alas! by 1408 at the latest, his whole ambitious enterprise could be seen to be disintegrating rapidly towards extinction. Meantime, as the result of his rebellion, the Church was suffering untold losses. Its buildings and estates were severely damaged and in some instances destroyed; worship was badly disrupted, services discontinued or irregularly held, service books and other indispensable requisites irretrievably dispersed or vandalized; discipline shattered or interrupted; and learning and literature at their lowest ebb. The monastery of Margam, once the second-richest abbey of Wales, was described in 1412 as 'utterly destroyed so that abbot and convent are obliged to go about like vagabonds'.[25] As late as 1428 the bishop of Llandaff declared his church to be in total danger of desolation on account of the Rebellion and pestilences.[26] Such destitution was not untypical of the state of the Church when the insurgency ended. Even a century and a half later, its appalling consequences were still graphically recalled when Bishop Richard Davies, in the preface to the first Welsh New Testament of 1567, deplored in tones of acute distress the havoc inflicted as a result of the depredations of both Glyndŵr and his enemies: 'What destruction of books [i.e. manuscripts] Wales suffered from the destruction of townships, bishops' houses, monasteries and churches that were burnt throughout all Wales at that time.'[27]

Devastated as the Church was in the first quarter of the fifteenth century, it did not remain in that plight overlong. Before the end of the century it had been able to stage a remarkable resurgence.[28] Recovery was achieved, however, only at the price of seeing the hold of the Crown and powerful laymen over the Church becoming still more extensive than it had previously been. By 1500 the process of material recuperation was largely complete. Income from clerical possessions was more or less back to normal, but the adjustments needed to meet a changing age, already begun in the fourteenth century, had been taken still further. The choice of

[24] *WC*, pp. 205–9.
[25] *CPL*, VI. 282.
[26] Ibid., VIII. 65.
[27] *Testament Newydd...* (1567), introd.
[28] *WC*, chap. 7.

bishops and higher clergy was now almost completely under the control of the king and his ministers or favourites. Monasteries were content to lease out the bulk of their temporal and spiritual assets to surrounding laymen and to appoint influential figures from among them to manage their affairs and safeguard their interests. They appeared to have surrendered most of the initiative in economic as well as religious affairs to others. Monks themselves had few qualms about living in comfortable and relaxed fashion as *rentiers*. Their acts of prayer and worship, and their charitable functions, though still undertaken, were noticeably diminished in scale and enthusiasm. The friars, once so dedicated to itinerant preaching and hearing confessions, now appeared to be far less active and much more confined to their houses.

The revived material fortunes of the parishes and their populations found expression in that remarkable wave of expenditure on church-building in England and Wales which foreigners found so impressive. It characterized the period from the second half of the fifteenth century down to the Reformation, and took the form of extensions, refurbishments, and embellishments.[29] This activity was intended not only to beautify the churches but also to signify the people's piety and their pride in places of worship. It was further directed towards transmitting the teaching of the Church more effectively through ritual and image – through the eyes rather than the ears, although church music also seems to have gone through something of a renaissance at that time. This was an age of erecting new lady chapels, aisles, and towers; extending windows and adorning them with stained glass depicting sacred scenes and stories; and putting up statues and images. New images of saints seem, in the fifteenth century, to some extent to have replaced relics in the popular estimation.[30] Above all, perhaps, it was a time for installing in churches in all parts of Wales graceful and elaborate rood screens and lofts, with their figures of the crucified Christ surrounded by many saints.[31] Much of this activity was connected with the encouragement of pilgrims and financed by their offerings. Pilgrimages, though often criticized by the most devout, achieved an extraordinary popularity in the fifteenth century. The social composition of those who embarked upon them became more varied than ever before, particularly with the remarkable flowering of the shorter-distance domestic pilgrimages, old and new.[32]

---

[29] Ibid., chap. 12.
[30] E. Duffy, *The Stripping of the Altars: Traditional Religion in England, c.1400–1580* (New Haven, 1992), p. 167.
[31] F. H. Crossley, 'Screens, lofts, and stalls situated in Wales and Monmouthshire', *AC*, XCVII (1943)–CVII (1958).
[32] Williams, *TCS* (1991), 70ff.

The two cults into which most of the popular piety was directed were those of the Suffering Saviour and of the BVM. In the fifteenth century, it was the physical intensity of the sufferings of Christ rather than his spiritual or mental agony which were emphasized, to the point where his resurrection was almost forgotten. The anguish was portrayed with intense realism: the broken body hanging limp, the blood flowing profusely from his wounds, the sadistic crown of thorns, and the brutal spear-thrust. It was impossible to escape the universal emphasis on the Passion and its familiar emblems, carved everywhere in wood or stone within the churches and their precincts – the cross, ladder, nails, wounds, sponge, and spear. The rood screens and lofts came to dominate the appearance of a majority of Welsh churches. Even today, the little Breconshire church of Llanfilo, by means of its sensitively reconstructed roodloft gives an overwhelming impression of the kind of impact that was made on medieval worshippers. There were a number of roods which, for the first time in the fifteenth century, drew large numbers of devotees. The attraction of the stricken Saviour may well have sprung from contemporaries' deep awareness of the horror of death and the sense of their own culpability, for what could have been more awesome to the believer than the agony of his redeemer's crucifixion?

The popularity of the Virgin of the Sorrows may have derived from the same source. The widespread veneration for her is observable in the way in which a number of new images of her became exceptionally attractive to fifteenth-century pilgrims. Most celebrated of all was her famous statue housed in the remote shrine at Pen-rhys in the Rhondda, which had never previously been known to appeal to pilgrims but now inspired large crowds from many different regions, outside Wales as well as inside, to show their devotion. Other saints, though perhaps not capable of luring such crowds as the sacred roods or images of the BVM, could nevertheless draw many votaries to their newly established images, or even their ancient wells, some of which were given new and impressive buildings like the celebrated well-chapel of St Winifred at Holywell.

Another symptom of contemporary recovery was the revival of religious verse and prose. This was part of that astonishing renaissance of Welsh literature in general, in evidence from c.1440.[33] Given the place of honour anciently occupied by religious literature in the Welsh tradition, it was to be expected that it would share in the literary revival of the age. Not a great deal that was new appeared in the prose literature. Most of it consisted of the recopying and reworking of old favourites from an earlier period.[34]

[33] *WC*, chap. 11.
[34] Ibid., pp. 416–30.

New translations of well-loved prose texts like John Mirk's *Festial* or Henry Parker's *Dives et Pauper*, together with Welsh versions of the lives of the saints, appeared in manuscript. So, too, did Welsh recensions of popular plays, symptomatic of the desire of the period for instruction purveyed in the form of entertainment but an exciting new development in Welsh writing. The verse exhibited more vigour and innovation than the prose. Much of the contemporary poetry seems to have been designed to publicize the pilgrim attractions and the cults associated with them.[35] Poetry, like other art forms of the age, was closely connected with the Passion. It, too, focused on the humanity of Jesus and the agony of his sufferings on behalf of sinful and frequently ungrateful humankind. The same human touch was also to be traced in the approach to the BVM, whose womanly qualities of tenderness and affection, added to her compassion for sinners at the Last Judgement, were prominently featured. As much to the fore as ever, too, was the *mana* of the saints and their holy places, especially those associated with Wales. They were believed to have a special regard and concern for their own kith and kin. The saint was someone with power, and if approached with the appropriate rites and deference, could make it available to supplicants. A foremost Welsh bard, Lewis Glyn Cothi, steeped to the eyebrows in the history and lore of his country, could appeal to the saints of Wales to rule 'a second time, so that the present hope of Wales might rest in the saints of this island'.[36] But even the eminent humanist scholar, Richard Whitford, who spent his adult life in England, was nevertheless keen to add a number of saints of his native Wales to his *Martiloge in English after the Use of the Church of Salisbury* (1526).

To all outward appearances, therefore, the Church in Wales at the beginning of the sixteenth century was in much sounder condition than it had been a hundred years earlier in the havoc-laden days of the Glyndŵr Rebellion and its immediate aftermath. Behind the façade, however, lurked a number of perilous sources of weakness and decay.

[35] Williams, *TCS* (1991), 69–92.
[36] *WC*, p. 489.

CHAPTER 2

On the Threshold of Change

H OWEVER much the Church in Wales may have recovered by the eve of the Reformation, there were many aspects of its condition which left it, like the rest of Christendom, in a vulnerable state. It was subject to imperfections to which contemporary reformers like Colet sorrowfully drew attention, and which later sixteenth-century reformers, whether Protestant or Catholic by conviction, would recognize and seek in their own way to remedy. There were, first of all, obvious shortcomings among its clergy. The clergy in Wales might be said in a number of respects to be a living illustration of those four great evils which Dean John Colet singled out in his famous sermon of 1511: ambition for ecclesiastical office and pluralism; covetousness; moral laxity; and too great a concern with the secular world.[1]

Almost all the bishops of Welsh dioceses were servants or favourites of the king, owing their preferment to royal goodwill, and men who would hesitate to act in opposition to the sovereign's wishes, whatever they might be.[2] Customarily not Welsh by origin, and absent from their dioceses most of the time, nearly all of them were men of talent and good education; but most were graduates in law, not theology, and administrators rather than pastors of souls. Between them and a majority of their parish clergy, as well as between them and most of the population of their dioceses, there yawned a wide gap of wealth, interests, attitudes, culture, and language. To many folk, lay and cleric alike, the bishop of their diocese must have seemed nearly as remote a figure as the pope. Later in the sixteenth century, it was the widespread failure on the part of late medieval bishops truly to act as fathers in God to their clergy and people which was seen as one of the most disastrous defects of the pre-Reformation Church. The later Roman Catholic Church regenerated by men such as Cardinal Borromeo, or the Anglican Church under Archbishop Whitgift, would underline unmistakably the key role of the resident diocesan bishop, in whom pastoral headship and responsibility were to be firmly anchored.

[1] J. H. Lupton, *Life of Colet* (London, 1887), pp. 293–9.
[2] *WC*, pp. 298–314.

Most of the higher clergy[3] were very like the bishops, to whose ranks many of them aspired to be elevated in due course. They, too, for the most part were able and well-educated administrators in Church and State; but they were large-scale pluralists who absorbed a great deal of the wealth of the dioceses without performing anything much in the way of spiritual functions. They were mostly aliens and absentees from their cathedrals and men whose dioceses seldom if ever saw them. Like the bishops, they were widely separated from the rank-and-file clergy and the populace. So, oversight of the Welsh dioceses, whose poor, thinly populated, dispersed, and inaccessible parishes were spread over far-flung upland communities with wretched communications, became all the more fitful and inadequate. Even the minority of cathedral clergy who were Welsh by birth and resident in the dioceses left much to be desired. They tended to be men of upper-class origins, wrapped up in secular affairs, of indifferent morals, and self-seeking in attitude. Cardinal Wolsey's trusted confidant and one of the most influential of the higher clergy of Wales during the first decades of the sixteenth century, Robert ap Rhys, was a notorious pluralist, a social climber, and a married man with sixteen children, for all of whom he was inordinately ambitious.[4]

The parish clergy varied widely in aptitude, attainment, and attitude.[5] Some among them were men of good birth, with all the social instincts and cultural tastes of the lay *uchelwyr*; lavish housekeepers and generous patrons of the native culture. A minority were university graduates with many years of training behind them. The sad fact, however, was that Welsh parishes were generally too poor and out-of-the-way to attract many of the ablest and best-educated members of the clergy. A number of the latter, having proceeded to the universities of Oxford or Cambridge for their higher education, were tempted to stay there, or, more often, to seek lusher pastures in the larger towns and richer parishes of England than their native heath could offer them.[6] It was to be noticeable that when clerics came to stand up and be counted in the religious debates of the Reformation, most of the leading Welsh controversialists on both sides were to be found in the ranks of *émigrés* in England.[7] Most of the lower clergy, however, were sadly ignorant and under-educated. There were, almost certainly, far too many of them. The tendency to multiply the number of masses being offered led to a corresponding multiplication in

---

[3] Ibid., pp. 314–27.
[4] Ibid., pp. 322–6.
[5] Ibid., pp. 327–46.
[6] For a similar attitude on the part of Lancashire priests, C. Haigh, *Reformation and Resistance in Tudor Lancashire* (Cambridge, 1973), pp. 37–9.
[7] Below, pp. 48–9.

the number of mass priests and the ordination of an excess of them.[8] Even among the beneficed clergy of Wales a high proportion were badly remunerated: about a quarter of them (24 per cent) held benefices valued in *Valor Ecclesiasticus* (1535) at less than £5 a year, and nearly half (46 per cent) received £5–10 a year. That meant that virtually three-quarters of the beneficed clergy were near or below what was generally regarded as the clerical poverty-line. The result was that many of them supplemented their income by singing additional masses, or by other expedients not always appropriate to their calling. Another quarter held benefices worth between £10 and £20, and only 6 per cent received the £20 or more usually regarded as an income which could comfortably maintain its recipient in an adequate state.[9] Among this handful of more prosperous Welsh parish clergy it was not uncommon to find non-resident parsons. Archbishop Lee said of benefices in Lakeland counties, like Wales a poor and neglected area, 'many benefices be so exile [i.e. poor] of £4, £5, or £6, that no learned man will take them and therefore we be fain to take such as be presented'.[10] But if the beneficed clergy were badly paid and poorly prepared for their vocation, that was even more true of the small army of chantry and mass priests, curates, and stipendiaries, who were about equal in number to the beneficed clergy.[11] Dire poverty among the priesthood was, and would for centuries remain, one of the worst problems of the Church in Wales.

The other critical deficiency was that no facilities existed properly to educate the rank-and-file clergy. There were hardly any grammar schools available for them, and no seminaries. The average priest-to-be learnt his duties from a parish priest who agreed, in return for small services, to lodge him and instruct him in saying mass and the offices, hearing confessions, and performing other clerical functions. In Wales, where clerical marriage and priestly families were so usual, many boys probably learnt the clerical craft from their fathers. The outcome was that far too many among them were inadequately trained to perform their functions as they ought. Contemporaries tended to take a poor view of the attainments of the average priest. William Tyndale, who was brought up in Gloucestershire on the borders of Wales, complained that most of the clergy of his acquaintance knew 'no more what the Old or New Testament meant than do the Turks; neither know they any more than they read at mass, matins and evensong, which they understand not'.[12] A Scottish contemporary,

[8] *WC*, pp. 327–9.
[9] Ibid., pp. 284–97.
[10] S. M. Harrison, *The Pilgrimage of Grace in the Lakeland Counties* (RHS, London, 1981), p. 14.
[11] *WC*, pp. 290–1.
[12] *Doctrinal Treatises* (Parker Soc., London, 1848), I. 146.

Archibald Hay, was scathing on the standards of some of the ordinands in his country, who were probably no worse than many of their Welsh *confrères*. He described them as bringing with them 'utter ignorance, others false pretence of knowledge, some a mind corrupted by the greatest sins and trained to commit all the most scandalous excesses'.[13] Bishop Hooper was later scandalized to find in his diocese of Gloucester that over half the clergy could not repeat the Ten Commandments and some were unable to recite the Lord's Prayer or tell who its author was.[14] It was therefore hardly surprising that the outstanding pioneer of Catholic education and training for the clergy, Cardinal Allen, should later comment that the pre-Reformation clergy's 'want then in manner even of necessary knowledge' was notorious.[15] In these circumstances, it was to be expected that the average priest should be lax in the matter of instructing or catechizing his people, and still more inadequate as a preacher. His duties as a preceptor were largely neglected; it was the sacerdotal aspect of his calling which overwhelmingly seemed to matter.

Nor could it be said that most parish priests set their people any conspicuous example by their morals or their behaviour. Bishop Alcock even thought that their lives were 'vastly inferior' to those of the laity.[16] There was scant suggestion that the cleric was called upon to live on a higher plane than his flock, despite Chaucer's praise for his poor parson as a model of his kind. It was the priest's ordination as someone singled out to minister the sacraments and his function as a reconciler of quarrels that set him apart from other men. Neither were his morals improved by the understandable insistence of the Church that the efficacy of the sacraments was not impaired by any unworthiness on the part of the celebrant. Indeed, in one respect where they should have differed from laymen – in the matter of celibacy – many Welsh priests took wives or had *focariae* ('hearth companions') at their commandment. This custom, as widespread in Wales as it was in Ireland,[17] was regarded as perfectly normal and was so usual in Wales that the practice was popularly believed to have official approval. So, too, was the tendency for benefices to run in families. But priests were regarded as dispensers not only of the sacraments but also of quasi-magical powers. They enjoyed a reputation as cursers of thieves and healers of sick people and animals; powers that were attributed to them for centuries after

[13] D. H. Fleming, *The Reformation in Scotland* (London, 1909), p. 43.

[14] J. Gairdner, 'Bishop Hooper's visitation of Gloucester', *EHR*, XIX (1904), 98–121.

[15] T. F. Knox, *Letters and Memorials of Cardinal Allen* (London, 1882), p. 32.

[16] J. W. Blench, *Preaching in England in the Late Fifteenth and Sixteenth Centuries* (Oxford, 1964), p. 238.

[17] P. J. Corish, *The Catholic Community in the Seventeenth and Eighteenth Centuries* (Dublin, 1981), p. 9.

the Reformation.[18] In view of the way in which the Church, its saints, shrines, and holy wells were generally regarded as having available to them an inexhaustible treasury of supernatural powers and privileges, appropriate to provide for the temporal as well as the spiritual welfare of the faithful, it was hardly to be wondered at that the clergy should be esteemed as the chosen agents and instruments for the bestowal of that goodwill.[19]

The imperfections of the secular clergy were made all the more serious by the unmistakable decline in the quality of the regular orders, once the spearhead of devotion and learning. Friars, formerly so active in preaching, hearing confession, and promulgating religious literature in Latin and Welsh, and earlier regarded by Archbishop Pecham as being much the brightest hope for the Welsh Church,[20] had become, since the fourteenth century, much more inert and ineffective. The monks, too, for a century or more stringently reduced in numbers, had lost much of the zeal and vitality which had fired them in earlier centuries and appeared content to lead the leisurely, quiescent life of *rentiers*.[21] Far from being withdrawn from the world, they were too immersed in the secular society around them. Neither they nor the friars seemed any longer desirous or capable of awakening religious enthusiasm or setting a shining example to the laity. It was patently obvious that recent reforming movements among the religious orders had not succeeded in gaining a foothold in Wales. Neither the Carthusian monks, nor the Observant friars, nor the Brigittine nuns had exercised any influence within the country. Those of its sons and daughters who felt moved to respond to the call of such reformed orders had no choice but to cross into England to do so. This lessening of vision and dynamism among the clergy, regulars and seculars, had resulted in much of the creative drive in religious life and activity passing increasingly from them to a small minority of educated and pious lay men and women, some of whom might conceivably become more responsive to unorthodox and critical inclinations.

Whatever the failure and shortcomings of some of its ministers, the Church nevertheless continued to convey its message to the people by the same methods which it had employed for centuries.[22] Its principal means of impressing its teaching was through the media of ritual, word, and image. The most important element in medieval religion was the ritual of the

---

[18] D. E. Owen, 'Pre-Reformation survivals in Radnorshire', *TCS* (1910–11), 92–114; K. Williams-Jones, 'Thomas Becket in Wales', *WHR*, V (1970–1), 350–65.

[19] K. V. Thomas, *Religion and the Decline of Magic* (London, 1971), *passim*.

[20] *WC*, pp. 21–2.

[21] Ibid., chaps. 10, 11.

[22] For a general view of religious life and practice in late medieval Wales, ibid., chap. 13.

sacraments, being ministered by the priest on behalf of the whole community. Men and women were 'collective' Christians, for whom religion consisted chiefly in participating together in the rites of the Church and not in holding a body of conceptual beliefs. They seem not to have known much about Christian doctrine and to have understood little of what was going on in church services conducted in the Latin tongue. For the majority it was enough to have been present in the church at mass, or more often, outside it, then rushing in to see the host being elevated. They were community Christians, who accepted that the rites, being conducted by the celebrant in a language which hardly any of them understood, were being undertaken on behalf of them all. Receiving communion was called 'trading one's rights', i.e. claiming one's place in the adult community.[23] For all the seasons of the year and at all the great milestones in the ordinary individual's life – birth, marriage, and death – the Church and its ministers provided the appropriate sacraments and services. The drawback usually was, however, that no matter how carefully its leaders continued tó lay down the Church's teaching concerning the precise significance of its rites and sacraments, the way in which they were interpreted by the mass of the people might be very different. The attitude of most of the faithful towards the mass, the most important sacrament of all, for instance, tended to be mechanical and lacking in true understanding. Emphasis had shifted over the centuries from the mass as a communion of believers to the consecration and elevation of the host by the priest as a sacrifice for the living and the dead. Lay people had come to assume that they could increase the effect by the simple process of multiplying the number of masses sung, the magnificence of them, and the amount of offering made at each. So it became an increasingly common practice to leave in one's will as much money as could be spared for the singing of as many masses as possible.

Doctrine concerning penance and penitential discipline could become similarly distorted. The official line was careful and scrupulous, but this did not prevent its being badly wrenched out of context by the interpretation widely put upon it. In theory, when men and women had confessed their sins they were supposed to undergo temporal punishment for them, which might be undertaken on earth or in purgatory. But penitential discipline had been relaxed and it had become the practice to issue indulgences for the remission of those penalties. The sale and purchase of indulgences had become increasingly general, and more and more of a commercial transaction. They were regularly offered for sale in large quantities at most of the bigger churches and at all the main centres

[23] E. Duffy, *The Stripping of the Altars: Traditional Religion in England, c.1400–1580* (New Haven, 1992), p. 167.

of pilgrimage. The highest church authorities had found them such a convenient way of raising funds that they could not resist the temptation of issuing them for sale on a huge scale to meet the ever-growing demand. Inevitably, most people came to view the practice in the light of an easy means of buying relief from the consequences in the afterworld of sins committed on earth; 'pardwn rhag y purdan dig' ('pardon from savage purgatory'), as one Welsh poet put it.[24]

This kind of commercialization of the means of grace, selling it for money in effect, could be destructive in its consequences. There were widespread abuses in the sale of indulgences, which were often forged and sold by unscrupulous vendors. Even worse was the growing risk that it might come to be taken for granted that grace was more readily available for the rich than the poor; that only those who could afford to pay for it would obtain it. A Welsh poet, Phylip Emlyn (*flor.* fifteenth century), and he a cleric at that, sang blithely of the power of his purse:

> And God's pervading grace within me dwell,
> Strength for my body, Heaven for my soul,
> With many a pope's indulgence furnished well,
> So am I sure to assuage each enemy,
> My purse, for this, grammercy to be thee.[25]

It would doubtless be a mistake to take such satirical verse literally, yet the essential criticism made by the poet was not unjustified and was echoed by, among others, Christopher Columbus, who declared that gold not only enabled a man to buy whatever he wanted in this world but also to redeem souls from purgatory and call them to paradise.[26] Money was talking louder than official doctrine, and many besides Phylip Emlyn and Columbus were well aware of that. Such transactions tended gravely to weaken the connection between religion and morality. Erasmus observed how people 'calculated the time to be spent in purgatory down to the year, month, day, and hour, as if it were a container that could be measured according to a mathematical formula'.[27] The Church lessened the value of its own ideals and its own official teaching when it allowed, even encouraged, ordinary people to conclude that their own lack of virtue and Christian behaviour could be made good by a monetary exchange which enabled the merits of the truly good and holy to be applied to them.

[24] *WC*, p. 520.
[25] H. I. Bell, 'Translations from the *cywyddwyr*', *TCS* (1940), 241.
[26] Quoted in W. Raleigh, *The English Voyages of the Sixteenth Century* (London, 1910), p. 28.
[27] C. S. L. Davies, *Peace, Print and Protestantism* (London, 1977), p. 143.

Ritual was, in theory, supposed to be fortified and deepened by a good deal of instruction given by the clergy by word of mouth. They were enjoined to teach and expound to their people regularly four times a year the Lord's Prayer and the Ten Commandments in the common tongue, and also to instruct them in the twelve articles of the Creed, the seven works of mercy, the seven deadly sins, and the like. All the texts needed for the purpose certainly existed in Welsh and Latin, and were to be found in contemporary manuscripts.[28] There is reason to believe, all the same, that such indoctrination was not widely or effectively carried out. In addition to the general comments on the slackness and ignorance of the lower clergy, already referred to, there is the specific criticism made by Sir John Price, humanist scholar and author of the first Welsh printed book, to the effect that the clergy 'either cannot or will not reveal to their parishioners' those things which they ought to teach them.[29] To make good these deficiencies, Price had gone to the expense and trouble of printing in his book such items as the Creed, the Lord's Prayer, and the Ten Commandments, so that the clergy might conveniently have at hand all those materials with which they and their parishioners ought to be thoroughly familiar. It seems to have been clear from the outset that Price also intended his little book to be used in schools and households.[30] As to preaching, that had never been a strong point among the parish clergy, who had left it very largely to the friars. The latter had by this time become much less active and were no longer nearly as influential as once they had been. True, there were some Welsh translations of the sermons of popular preachers like John Mirk, and much of the religious poetry appears to be steeped in the conventional sermon themes of the period.[31] But overall, it seems that we must conclude that sermons were even rarer and more ineffectual in the early sixteenth century than they were later, in John Penry's time.[32] Even when a preacher delivered a sermon, it might have been less than welcome to his potential congregation, if the comments of Roger Edgeworth, a Welsh preacher of the early Tudor era, are to be believed. He complained that 'most will get themselves out of the church, feigning some business', or else would spend their time sitting in taverns, or gossiping with friends in the churchyard, rather than stay and listen to a sermon.[33]

[28] *WC*, pp. 84–96.

[29] [J. Price], *Yny Lhyvyr Hwnn . . .*, ed. J. H. Davies (Bangor, 1902), introd.

[30] P. R. Roberts, 'The Welsh language, English law and Tudor legislation', *TCS* (1989), 42–4.

[31] *WC*, pp. 420–1, 427–30.

[32] J. Penry, *Three Treatises concerning Wales*, ed. D. Williams (Cardiff, 1960), p. 36, who declared that 'for to that one parish where there is one ordinary quarter sermon, we have twenty that have none'.

[33] Roger Edgeworth, *Sermons Very Fruitful . . .* (London, 1557), p. xii.

The third element in transmitting religious teaching, the visual image, was of the utmost importance in an age when most of the population was illiterate. Their eyes were more receptive than their ears, and for centuries art had been accepted as a compelling means of communicating sacred truths. Paintings, frescos, stained-glass windows; carvings in stone, wood, or metal; roods and roodscreens; even the clergy's vestments, could simultaneously be homage to God and, for the believer, a direct and telling expression of the message of the Church.[34] The second half of the fifteenth century and the early decades of the sixteenth had witnessed a great surge of enthusiasm for beautifying the churches and at the same time making use of works of art as 'the poor man's Bible'. Even small, off-beat churches might acquire a wealth of quite striking and colourful wall-paintings, as did the church at Llandeilo Talybont, whose treasures were only revealed in recent years.[35]

No matter how diligently the Church had tried and was still trying to put across its teaching to the masses, it is difficult to escape the conclusion that most of them were no more than superficially Christianized. The insistence of some authors that the medieval Welsh adhered 'to the Old Faith as rigidly as Spain or Italy in the nineteenth century'[36] failed to take into account the effect of the devoted instruction to which Catholic people were subjected in the centuries after the Council of Trent. Like that of most of the denizens of Christendom at the beginning of the sixteenth century, the religion of the average Welsh man or woman was performed, and to a large extent believed, for them by the clergy. Christianity continued to be shot through with pervasive magical and pagan elements. Those responsible for the formal teaching of the Church exerted themselves to distance Christian doctrine from magic and superstition. Their predicament lay in not being able to overcome the instincts of a largely uninstructed population, beset by poverty, hardship, disease, and misfortune, who demanded that the Church should provide them with protection, comfort, and reassurance. Their world-view was one which envisaged them being surrounded by hostile ranks of devils seeking the destruction of body and soul, which only the Church could keep at bay. Even an educated churchman like Giraldus Cambrensis, as his writings reveal, was by no means wholly immune from the common belief in the quasi-magical powers of relics and holy wells, the supernatural properties attaching to dreams, divinations, prophecies,

---

[34] *WC*, chap. 12.

[35] The church fell into a ruinous state, and when it was being dismantled, a number of striking wall-paintings were discovered, expertly removed, and cleaned. They are now in the National Folk-Museum of Wales at St Fagan's, Cardiff.

[36] G. H. Jones, *Celtic Britain and the Pilgrim Movement* (London, 1912), pp. 2–3; cf. D. Mathew, *The Celtic Peoples and Renaissance Europe* (London, 1933), pp. 31–2.

soothsayers, and the like, and the machinations of evil spirits and incubi.[37] That the generality of the people should therefore look to the Church to exert its extensive range of other-worldly powers on their behalf was only to be expected. The inhabitants of the remoter, more sparsely populated, mountainous areas like Wales, Ireland, Scotland, or the north of England, were more than ordinarily likely to be somewhat primitive in their beliefs. As late as the reign of James I there were people in the north of England reported to be as 'ignorant of God as . . . the very savages among the infidels', who could not say the Lord's Prayer and had never learnt it,[38] just as John Penry declared that thousands in Elizabethan Wales knew nothing of Christ, 'yea, almost that never heard of him'.[39] Yet in this respect they were no different from people in the rural areas of northern Italy in the seventeenth century when the Jesuits came to their midst and found so large a proportion of them remaining at the stage of Christianity based on myths and legends that they sometimes had the impression they had been transported to India.[40]

It was precisely in localities of this kind, where the parishes tended to be unusually large, and communications very bad, that many of the poorer cottagers and squatters, living on the fringes of cultivated land and in other out-of-the-way corners, frequently found themselves at a long and awkward journey from the church. They rarely or never came to worship, and so were the people least under religious influences. Many of the upland parishes of Wales were well over 20,000 acres in extent and straggled over bleak hill and moorland. As late as 1851, when the Religious Census was compiled, there were many complaints about how difficult, sometimes impossible, it was for worshippers to get to church, especially during the winter months.[41] Yet even in a prosperous and urbanized area like Flanders much the same sort of backwardness was apparent. The Flemish were violent, superstitious, given to the excesses of the flesh and the table, often deserted the sacraments, frequently forgot Sunday mass, and either ignored, or were unaware of, the elementary dogmas of their religion.[42] The same shortcomings figured very largely in the 'confessions' rehearsed by Welsh poets in those poems in which they poured out an admission of their

---

[37] Giraldus Cambrensis, *The Journey through Wales . . .*, ed. L. Thorpe (Harmondsworth, 1978), pp. 78, 86, 87, 92, 99, 117, 120, 136, 144–7, 150–1, 154–5, 170, 246–7.

[38] Thomas, *Religion and Magic*, pp. 164–5.

[39] Penry, *Treatises*, p. 32.

[40] P. Chaunu (ed.), *The Reformation* (Gloucester, 1989), p. 158.

[41] I. G. Jones and D. Williams (edd.), *The Religious Census of 1851* (Cardiff, 1977, 1981).

[42] J. Toussaert, *Le Sentiment religieux en Flandre à la fin du Moyen Age* (Paris, 1965).

sins.[43] The truth was that it would be necessary for both Catholic and Protestant reformers everywhere to concentrate on teaching the basics of their faith to the populations at whom they directed their efforts.

Nevertheless, for all its lapses, the Church was accepted by most people as a necessary and inevitable part of their existence. There may, indeed, have been an urgent need for improvement and the raising of standards in the religious life of late medieval Wales, but there had been as yet little demand for reform. Earlier, at the turn of the fourteenth century and afterwards, the Lollard heresy had made no great impression on the country. It made some headway along the Marches between England and Wales in Herefordshire and Shropshire, and it could boast of at least one very notable Welsh convert in the person of Walter Brut.[44] On the Welsh population in general, however, it does not seem to have had much impact. Most of the propaganda on behalf of Lollardy in speech and in writing found expression in English, and that alone would seriously have restricted its circulation amid a mainly Welsh-speaking populace, although there is some indication of the Lollard Bible having left its mark on Welsh literature.[45] During the fifteenth century the Lollards continued their activity underground at Lydney in Gloucestershire, very near to the Welsh border, but there is no sign of any significant Welsh response in their favour.

Such awareness as there was of the need for stricter religious observance was expressed in urgings of a more traditional kind. The Glyndŵr Rebellion led to promptings by a 'Welsh Savonarola',[46] the abbot John ap Hywel of the Cistercian house of Llantarnam, that the successes of Welsh rebels on the field of battle would be continued only if they abandoned their evil living. The defeat of the insurgents caused some poets to infer that the adversity which had befallen them was God's punishment on their nation for its wickedness. The sternest prophet of woe, and the one who exercised a dominant influence on later poets, was Siôn Cent (*flor.* 1400–30), who has sometimes, though mistakenly, been suspected of Lollard convictions.[47] He voiced with a heightened eloquence the typical puritanical pronouncements of earlier religious poetry. He unsparingly denounced his contemporaries' pursuit of ephemeral vanities – wealth, fame, physical beauty, and luxurious living. He urged upon them that, instead, they should diligently attend at

---

[43] *WC*, pp. 418, 426–8, 502.

[44] Ibid., pp. 205–9.

[45] I. Thomas, *Yr Hen Destament Cymraeg, 1551–1620* (Aberystwyth, 1988), p. 24, for the influence of a Lollard Bible on an early Welsh translation of a scriptural passage.

[46] *WC*, pp. 236–7.

[47] Ibid., pp. 239–41.

church, scrupulously observe mass, and regularly remit tithes and other offerings. More graphically than any other poet he spelt out the fifteenth-century horror of death and decomposition, and its dread of the terrors of retribution that awaited sinners in hell and purgatory. He set the pattern for others who followed in his footsteps and aired his well-worn themes: resistance to the temptations offered by the world, the flesh, and the devil, and dutiful obedience to the teachings and sacraments of the Church. Much of the prose and verse of the fifteenth century was concerned to proclaim the merits of the saints and the benefits of going on pilgrimage to the shrines, wells, and other holy places associated with them.[48] The marked growth in the volume of religious literature and the increase in the number of manuscripts being copied[49] appear to be linked to some spread of literacy among the laity. Although the ability to read remained extremely restricted in scope, it was becoming somewhat more usual among lay people than it had been, but was insufficiently general to prepare more than a small proportion of the population to voice criticism of the existing Church or to welcome new ideas.

There was as yet little indication in Wales of the penetration of the new reforming trends observable in some parts of Europe. These were dependent to an enormous extent on the growing circulation of printed books, the increase in literacy among some sectors of the population, and wider development of the art of silent reading. Perceptible among them was the emergence of the pietistic and mystical approach, seen at its best in the *devotio moderna* and Thomas à Kempis's hugely influential book, *The Imitation of Christ*, translated into many languages, though not into Welsh.[50] It stressed the patient search for perfection by the sanctified individual, subjecting the soul to the imitation of Christ under the inspiration of immediate divine guidance. Rather more impression had been made among some of the Welsh by the newer trend of humanist learning. This was found principally among some university graduates, who had been fired by the ideal of making Renaissance scholarship the handmaiden of faith. They gave pride of place to the return *ad fontes*, to the sacred texts of scripture, and to giving due emphasis to the power of reason to bring about improvement. Among those whose pulses had been stirred by interests of this kind was a handful of young Welshmen educated at the universities. Most prominent of these was Richard Whitford[51] (*flor.*

---

[48] Williams, *TCS* (1991), 69–92.

[49] *WC*, pp. 416–30.

[50] Published first in 1418, it became the most influential work of its kind in the fifteenth century.

[51] G. Williams, 'Two neglected London-Welsh clerics: Richard Whitford and Richard Gwent', *TCS* (1961), 23–43.

1495–1540), bosom friend of Erasmus and Sir Thomas More. After a distinguished career at university, he had entered Sion monastery, where he became a prolific author of religious books in English. They set out an earnest plea on behalf of the sanctified life and the power of private prayer, worship, and meditation on the part of the individual. It was, however, to be all too rare and unusual for scholars of this kind – Whitford, or others like William Glyn, Edward Powell, or John Gwynedd – to apply their talents and learning specifically for the benefit of their fellow-countrymen in Wales. The most effective of those who were to do so in print were John Price and William Salesbury, both of them laymen, who were to pioneer the way with the publication of Welsh books.[52] Nor is it entirely easy to tell how far such graduates maintained contacts and exercised influence, other than by means of printed books, among those of their countrymen who had not had the benefit of a university education. But at least, among clerics and laymen, they formed a tiny minority which was alert and articulate, and in touch with new thinking. What was particularly interesting, moreover, was that a sizeable number of this minority had not only imbibed Renaissance ideals but had associated them firmly with the distinctive literary and historical heritage of Wales. This link was to be as stoutly maintained in the future among those who favoured Catholic reform as those who advocated Protestant changes.[53]

There were to be markedly fewer tokens in Wales of that crisis of the spirit which predisposed individuals in other parts of Europe readily to embrace the heresies which appeared in the second and third decades of the sixteenth century as a seemingly heaven-sent response to the deepest needs and uncertainties of their existence. Yet there may have been among Welsh people, too, some who were aware of uneasy misgivings. Sombre undertones of strain and anxiety could be detected in the religious poetry of the age: pessimistic doubts about what might happen at the Last Judgement and in the hereafter. Such forbidding speculations weighed heavily on the minds and hearts of grave and austere late medieval bards like the Glamorgan layman, Llywelyn ap Hywel, and were voiced in their poetry.[54] To what extent such poets were giving tongue to the perplexities of others besides themselves it is impossible to tell with any certainty. But the undoubted popularity of this kind of verse, taken together with the sudden changes of religious allegiance revealed later on the part of poets like Lewis Morgannwg or Gruffudd ap Ieuan ap Llywelyn, or the enthusiasm for

---

[52] Below, chaps. 6 and 7. For William Salesbury as a book-buyer in London on behalf of his relative, John Edwards of Chirk, H. S. Bennett, *English Books and Readers 1475 to 1557* (Cambridge, 1952), pp. 20–1.

[53] G. Williams, 'Iaith, llên a chrefydd', *LlC* XIX (1996), 29–40.

[54] *GCH*, III (1971). *The Middle Ages*, 155.

Tyndale's New Testament shown by its anonymous Welsh translator, and William Salesbury's pressing desire for a Welsh Bible,[55] all suggest that they may be symptomatic of wider dissatisfaction with existing religion and a slightly larger potential audience for Protestant doctrine than has sometimes been supposed. Yet, when all this has been taken into account, it would scantly be possible to argue for there having been more than a very small fraction of the populace which found itself prepared to welcome joyously the message of the Protestant reformers when it came to be proclaimed in Wales.

There were, in fact, all kinds of obstacles in the path of spreading any novel teaching which called for radical changes in the nature of the Church or religious belief. Wales was an upland country, whose rivers flowed outwards from a mountainous core, which itself acted as a barrier between the regions which impinged upon it and not as a focus for them.[56] Communications between the different parts of the country had always been, and still were, very poor. Travel was at all times difficult, but especially during the inclement winter months. To the Tudor Welshman a journey from one part of Wales to another, or to England, over the badly maintained roads and trackways was 'grievous and painful'.[57]

Such geographical conditions very largely determined the patterns of economic and social life. Only in a few favoured areas, around the fringes of the country, along the restricted coastal plains, the major river valleys, and the eastern border areas, was it possible to practise mixed or arable farming.[58] It was in these districts that most of such towns as had sprung up were to be found. Over the greater part of the surface area of Wales, however, the high relief, heavy rainfall, thin acidic soils, and a short growing season made a barely viable pastoral farming the norm. The outcome was a small population, thinly dispersed in little hamlets or isolated farms and crofts. Living near the margin of existence, dwellers within such communities were apt to be tenacious of their ancient ways and suspicious of innovation. The few towns that existed were small, and hardly bigger than villages, with a population ranging from 300–400 souls in the smallest, to the 2,000 to be found in Carmarthen, the largest. Yet it was in these little municipalities that there existed an English-speaking population, and this, together with a greater degree of literacy among the inhabitants, made them more responsive to changes in outlook and

[55] Below, chap. 7.
[56] E. G. Bowen (ed.), *Wales* (London, 1958), pp. 267–81; *W 1415–1642*, chap. 3.
[57] *Penbrokshire*, III, 15.
[58] *W 1415–1642*, chap. 3.

attitude.[59] Although there may have been a fair amount of movement on the part of Welsh traders, drovers, soldiers, seasonal workers, and pilgrims, and a certain degree of seaborne commerce and overland trade in cattle and wool, the economic life of the country was, in general, backward and underdeveloped. None of the great trade routes, along which ideas as well as commodities were exchanged, passed through Wales; nor had there consequently grown up any of the larger towns or cities, where printing-presses, or universities and grammar schools might become established, and whose populations were inclined to be more literate and correspondingly more open to new opinions. Among those ambitious Welshmen who wanted to make their mark in the learned professions it had long been a constant attraction to go to England for their education at university, or inn of court, or both. Those who aspired to rise at court, in the law, politics, church, or trade, migrated to London and the larger English urban centres – a tendency encouraged but certainly not initiated by the Tudor dynasty.[60]

The isolation created by geographical conditions was reinforced by political circumstances.[61] Since Edward I's defeat of the house of Gwynedd in 1282–3, the Welsh had had virtually nothing by way of independent institutions. There was no longer any native dynasty, court, or capital to attract men of ability. After the suppression of the ruling families, the Welsh clergy, secular and regular, had suffered a damaging loss of patronage and stimulation. The seculars found themselves being eased out of bishoprics and canonries, while Cistercian abbots lapsed into backwater insignificance. The absence of a native university was an even more grievous deprivation after 1283. In the fourteenth and fifteenth centuries Welshmen did not find it easy to proceed to universities and, having been there, came up against more daunting barriers on the road to advancement. Their ensuing frustration was a major factor in accounting for the Glyndŵr Rebellion, and helps to explain the formulation of a demand for an autonomous church and university. The absence of a university, and the fewness of wealthy households or large centres of populations, meant that there were hardly any foci around which the liveliest and best-trained minds among the Welsh could come together. The bardic schools admittedly offered a long and arduous apprenticeship, but their intellectual basis was narrow and unconducive to innovation. The kind of well-to-do and motivated household, like the *familia* of Bishop John Trefor of St

---

[59] For the Reformation in Carmarthen, *W and R*, chap. 4.
[60] G. Williams, *Religion, Language and Nationality in Wales* (Cardiff, 1979), chap. 8.
[61] R. R. Davies, *Conquest, Co-existence and Change: Wales, 1063–1415* (Oxford, 1987), parts 4 and 5.

Asaph[62] (1394–1410), where what was best in Welsh and cosmopolitan learning could happily blend together, was the greatest rarity.

The lack of intellectual liveliness and stimuli of this sort largely explains the failure of the printing-press, for a century after it had been discovered, to leave its mark on the Welsh language. Yet the value of the printed book in accelerating and transmitting the revolutionary intellectual and religious currents of the age can hardly be overestimated. 'The subtle science of printing books', thought Werner Rolewinck,

> was the art of arts, the science of sciences, by whose swift operation a desirable treasure of wisdom and knowledge, yearned after by all men through their natural instinct, hath leapt forth as from the depths of hidden darkness to enrich and lighten this world that is seated in darkness.[63]

Three out of every four of the books published between 1445 and 1520 were of a religious nature;[64] but the first printed book in Welsh – a religious primer – did not appear until 1546. Its author, Sir John Price, urged his readers to participate, as all Christendom had already done, in the printing of God's blessed words so that 'as good a gift as this should not be without fruit for us any more than for others ('val na bai ddiffrwyth rhodd kystal a hon yni mwy noc y eraill').[65]

But the investment of money in presses, the organization of production, the marketing of the finished article in the shops, fairs, and markets of bigger towns along the major trade routes, and waiting to recoup the initial outlay, made printing a capitalist industry, the resources for which did not exist in Wales itself. Printing Welsh books on presses in England was to prove a slow, inefficient, and expensive process. Nor were authors willing to publish in Welsh easy to come by; those Welshmen who were competent to write in English or Latin often preferred to do so in the hope of reaching a wider readership.[66] The potential market in Wales for books in any language was small, illiteracy was rife, and a number of those who could read Welsh were either reluctant to buy books or simply could not afford to do so.

Even so, closed to criticisms of the Church and to concepts of change and reform as Wales, like Ireland and many parts of England, might be, it

---

[62] *DWB*, s.n.; E. J. Jones, *Medieval Heraldry* (Cardiff, 1943).

[63] Quoted, G. G. Coulton, *Five Centuries of Religion* (4 vols. Cambridge, 1927–50), IV. 40–1; cf. E. Eisenstein, *The Printing Press as an Agent of Change* (Cambridge, 1980), chap. 1.

[64] J. M. Lenhart, *Pre-Reformation Printed Books* (New York, 1935); D. M. Loades, 'The press under the early Tudors', *Trans. Camb. Bibliog. Soc.*, IV (1964–5), 29–50.

[65] [J. Price], *Yny Lhyvyr Hwnn . . .*, ed. J. H. Davies, introd.

[66] G. Williams, 'Welsh authors and their books, c.1500–1642', in M. B. Line (ed.), *The World of Books and Information* (London, 1987), pp. 187–96.

is possible nevertheless to argue that, in the early stages of the Reformation at least, even in the more receptive milieu of the capital and the surrounding counties of the south and east of England, it was not the strength or coherence of opposition to the existing Church which brought about change. The success of the Reformation everywhere depended on how far it could insinuate itself into the contemporary structures of power. It was the rulers and the ruling classes who, in almost every instance, took it upon themselves to decide the fate of the Reformation. Thus, in England and Wales, just as in Sweden, Denmark, and parts of Germany, it was the impetus of political and social forces which set the Reformation on course when they backed up religious criticism. The two decisive factors in England and Wales were the king's anti-papal policies and the laity's willingness to co-operate with him, or at least not to resist him. Without this coalescing of the most dynamic secular forces of the age, such religious protest as there was would probably have been ignored or forced underground. The Reformation in England might possibly never have triumphed at all; it would certainly have been postponed. So it may matter less to the student of the Reformation in Wales that he should painfully scrutinize the contemporary scene for traces of heretical doctrine or overt criticism than that he should try to estimate the strength of royal authority in the country and the likelihood of its being given support by the laity in its ecclesiastical proceedings.

Even before the Act of Union between England and Wales of 1536/43 was passed, the power of the Crown was sufficiently weighty and unchallenged to impose far-reaching religious change on Wales with every show of confidence. That Welsh loyalty which Henry VII had been able to muster for his Bosworth campaign had been fortified by his victory and continued throughout his reign. It had been shrewdly underpinned by the rewards he had conferred on his Welsh followers and by the effectiveness of his measures.[67] The fidelity evoked by the first Tudor had passed undiminished to his son. It was symptomatic of Henry VIII's control of Wales that he was able to deal peremptorily with any signs of restlessness on the part of a Marcher grandee like the duke of Buckingham in 1521, or Rhys ap Gruffudd, one of the foremost figures among the native gentry, whom he executed in 1531.[68] Henry VIII, like his father, had at his disposal in all parts of Wales a reliable network of followers and dependants.[69] When, therefore, he came to pass the key statutes of 1529–34 against the papacy and the Church, he was able to apply them all to Wales and set

[67] G. Williams, *Henry Tudor and Wales* (Cardiff, 1985).
[68] R. A. Griffiths, *Sir Rhys ap Thomas and His Family* (Cardiff, 1994), pp. 88–111.
[69] *W 1415–1642*, pp. 246–50.

himself up as Supreme Head without meeting any serious opposition. The coercive power of the Crown was to be exhibited still more evidently in Bishop Rowland Lee's presidency of the Council in the Marches, 1534–43, and the enactment of the Act of Union.

What made it easier for this formidable royal power to find willing allies among the gentry were the deep-seated social changes that had been maturing in Wales for a century or more before Henry's reign.[70] In both the Principality and the Marches of Wales, there had emerged a class of landowning gentry who effectively controlled the countryside. In the course of the troubled times before and during the Wars of the Roses they had constituted an ambitious, self-regarding group, who had in general played the game of clientage in relation to king and aristocracy with considerable skill. As more and more of the Marcher lordships passed into the hands of the king, and in the frequent absences of many of the powerful officials who nominally exercised authority in the Principality, local gentry had increasingly acquired the right to rule in the name of others. They looked for the furtherance of their political and economic interests to the continued patronage of the Crown and the leading members of the nobility. Already, well before the Reformation changes ever began, they had gained a firm foothold in the affairs of the Church. They were substantial leaseholders of monastic, episcopal, and capitular estates;[71] they were influential office-holders as stewards and bailiffs, and as such were often able to manipulate the election of abbots and the choice of higher clergy to the advantage of their own kinsmen and clients.[72] Lay influence had penetrated deeply into the local management of ecclesiastical possessions, which appeared in the eyes of the gentry less like the inviolable patrimony of the Church than as valuable assets to be manoeuvred and exploited. Given a lead by the king, they were unlikely to be averse from extending their hold still further, or from translating *de facto* control into *de jure* proprietorship.

Attitudes of the kind were reinforced by the existence of a certain degree of anticlerical feeling among them.[73] This manifested itself in mockery and satire of the clergy for their shortcomings; dislike of the commercial privileges claimed by the monastic clergy; and the usual resentments against the payment of tithes and mortuaries, the jurisdiction of the clergy in the ecclesiastical courts, and in issues concerning wills and probate. Anticlerical sentiments of this nature were certainly to be found in Wales, but it has to be said that they were not particularly virulent and seem to

[70] Ibid., chaps. 3 and 4.
[71] F. Heal, *Of Prelates and Princes* (Cambridge, 1990), p. 42; cf. below, chap. 4.
[72] *WC*, pp. 320–6, 340–6, 408–9.
[73] Ibid., pp. 548–57.

have been perfectly compatible with orthodoxy in belief and a strong distaste for heresy. The adherence of the laity to the doctrine of the Church was still unshaken, but it was a shallow allegiance which, unreinforced, was unlikely to be able to withstand the force of powerful currents of change.

Among the landowning classes there was a tiny minority of intellectuals more susceptible to the notions of innovation and reform. Men who had undergone years of higher education at university or inn of court, they included, significantly enough, a number of trained lawyers, who would readily appreciate the importance of the sovereign's authority and the need to obey the law of the land. Among them figured men like John Price, Edward Carne, Ellis Price, William Thomas, William Salesbury, George Constantine, and the eminent London-Welshman, John Dee. All would be prepared willingly to defer to Henry VIII's wishes and to go along with his measures in relation to the papacy and the Church. Some, like Salesbury, Constantine, or Thomas, enthusiastically proceeded further along the road to outright Protestant reform. The Protestant revolution of Edward VI's reign, however, proved to be the parting of the ways; it was then that conservatives like John Price and Edward Carne pulled back, and were, by Mary's reign, confirmed Catholics once more. This kernel of alert and articulate educated gentry was to increase during the century as larger numbers of laymen made their way to grammar school and university. By the end of Elizabeth's reign, educated laymen of this kind were making an invaluable contribution to the life of the Established Church – and that of the opposition.

Nevertheless, in Henry VIII's reign, most of the gentry were neither equipped to address the finer points of politico-religious debates, nor were they unduly desirous of doing so. It seems highly unlikely that they would have appreciated the wider implications of Henry's revolt against Rome. The pope must have seemed to most of them to be a remote Italian prince, for whose interests they would not be prepared to put themselves out. Henry, by contrast, was much nearer at hand; the fount of patronage and profit, but also, if displeased, a source of sudden and unsparing retaliation. Nor could the dispute between pope and king have appeared in the light of a battle between the true faith and heretical error when most of them thought of their sovereign, as he envisaged himself, as a man of unimpeachable orthodoxy. That such an image should prevail was wholly understandable, when most of the bishops, abbots, and learned clergy hailed him as such. Certainly, the clerical ranks of Wales collapsed before the royal might and gave the laity no lead in opposition. There was indeed some restlessness among the clergy at grass-roots level and criticism of Henry's actions, but the only ones on a higher plane who would reject the supremacy were Bishop Athequa and Dr Fetherston, both non-resident foreigners without influence, and a handful of *émigré* clergy living in England. The laity were unlikely to take their cue from opponents such as these.

The gentry did what the law required of them, all the more willingly when this obedience involved them in no departure, seemingly, from their normal religious practices. Public opinion appeared to be applauding what the king was doing as the actions of a resolute monarch dealing determinedly with his external enemies (who included the pope) and his internal foes (who numbered among them the monks and 'traitors' like Bishop Fisher), if the comments of authors like John Price or William Salesbury, or poets like Lewis Morgannwg or Siôn Brwynog,[74] meant anything. What the leading laity wanted to see above all else was firm and stable control at the hub of government, and their own local leadership being confirmed and safeguarded. So it came as no surprise when, in the immediate aftermath of the religious changes, the regime made its choice of the first generation of Welsh justices of the peace and lesser officials in the 1530s, that it should find no difficulty in recruiting them, in spite of the censorious comments of the president of the Council in the Marches, Rowland Lee, concerning the gentry of Wales.[75]

The general willingness of the leading lights in Welsh society to defer to royal fiats was very useful to the Crown. Unlike other remote and conservative parts of the realm, Wales showed no disposition to rebel against the king in the early Tudor period. Whereas in Ireland, the north of England, and Cornwall before 1550 there were to be dangerous uprisings, in which religion was at least partially the cause, in Wales there was to be no such upheaval. On the contrary, it always seemed possible to recruit large contingents there to suppress insurgency elsewhere. This may have been partly due to the feelings of loyalty inspired by the Tudors being seen as a Welsh dynasty. Of greater weight, however, was the disappearance of an older Marcher aristocracy more willing to pit itself in opposition to the Crown. The newer families like the Somersets, the Herberts, and the Devereux, were only gentry writ large. They owed their advancement to the king's pleasure and were not inclined to challenge his will. Most of the Welsh gentry had built up their estates in the fluid conditions of the fifteenth century and were dependent on Tudor benevolence. They were hard-headed and realistic; of strongly dynastic bent, they had already gained advantages for themselves and their families since 1485, and they discerned the possibility of gaining many more by close co-operation with the king and his ministers. Order, stability, prosperity, and influence were

[74] See below, pp. 45–6, 107, 112–13, 153.
[75] *LP*, X. 453.

becoming synonymous in their minds with being *en rapport* with the Crown. This tacit alliance between an anti-papal sovereign and a mainly compliant gentry was what would ultimately ensure the success of the Anglican Church. It would, admittedly, be only a minority among the laity and the clergy who would be truly convinced of the truth of reform as a body of doctrine, just as only a minority would continue loyal to the old Church. Both would have to tow in their wake the inarticulate mass of the people; ignorant, illiterate, unconvinced, and not overconcerned about matters of religious principle.

CHAPTER 3

The Royal Supremacy Achieved

THERE was little sign during the first half of Henry VIII's reign of those dramatic changes that were later to convulse both Church and State. Henry's regime then appeared to be in many respects a continuation of that of his father but on a more grandiose and extravagant scale. It proved to be a relatively successful and prosperous era to which later generations looked back with nostalgia from the tempestuous uncertainties of the 1530s and 1540s. The young king himself – handsome, athletic, intelligent, and regal – was greeted with acclamation by courtiers, scholars, poets,[1] and commoners alike.[2] His preoccupations and pleasures were those thought to befit an early sixteenth-century monarch. He exulted in and excelled at the excitement of war, the subtleties of diplomacy, and the joys of existence in a Renaissance court: tournaments, hunting parties, sports, banquets, music, dancing, witty conversation, flirtation, and the like. His own religious attitudes owed much to his having been brought up under the tutelage of his devout grandmother, Margaret Beaufort, and his conventionally pious father, Henry VII. Added to these earlier influences was that of his wife, Catherine of Aragon,[3] a worthy daughter of the most celebrated of Europe's Catholic rulers, Isabella of Castile, who set her husband a notable example of punctilious religious practice and belief. It used once to be suggested that before the untimely death of his elder brother, Arthur, Henry had been intended for a career as a leading ecclesiastic. Although this now seems to historians to have been unlikely,[4] he had certainly been carefully educated and, for a layman, he had a sound knowledge of theology, on which he prided himself throughout his life. Even as a young man, he held an exalted view of his role as a Christian king and of the authority he claimed to exercise over his clergy.

[1] *W 1415–1642*, pp. 246–7.
[2] J. J. Scarisbrick, *Henry* VIII (London, 1968).
[3] G. Mattingley, *Catherine of Aragon* (London, 1950); A. Fraser, *The Six Wives of Henry VIII* (London, 1992).
[4] Scarisbrick, *Henry VIII*, p. 4.

The Church itself continued to exert its pervasive sway over many facets of contemporary life. Its clergy officiated at the three main events in most people's lives – birth, marriage, and death. They dispensed the sacraments, without the help of which people believed themselves to be doomed to an eternity of horrifying punishment. They also regulated those 'good works' thought to be essential for spiritual health in this world and the next – pilgrimages, cults of the saints, veneration of relics, indulgences, and all the other proliferations of popular devotion. In the ecclesiastical courts they controlled morality, enforced discipline, and disposed of bequests and property. As teachers in parishes, schools, and universities, they enjoyed a near-monopoly of instruction, education, and thought-systems – although laymen, becoming better educated and more literate, were increasingly infringing on these clerical preserves. Bishops, cathedral clergy, and abbots were amongst the most substantial landowners and wealthiest individuals in the kingdom, having in their care some of its largest and more beautiful buildings. Even in the humblest parish the church was usually its most important building and the priest one of its more influential inhabitants. Moreover, the intellectual capacity of the higher clergy and their prolonged training as university graduates made them indispensable as some of the king's leading administrators and civil servants.

Supreme among them during the years from 1514 to 1529 was the lord chancellor, Thomas Wolsey,[5] archbishop of York, cardinal, *legatus a latere*, and pluralist *par excellence*. Under the king, Wolsey combined in his own person supreme power in Church and State, much of whose widely ranging jurisdiction was derived by delegation from the pope as well as the monarch. That Wolsey was an immensely talented and hard-working individual is undeniable; just the man to meet the requirements of a sovereign who loved command but had no wish to be saddled with the tedious chores of a 'working king'. But the power Wolsey exercised and his personal traits of arrogance and a love of pomp and display were not calculated to endear him or his papal overlord to Henry's subjects – not even to the clergy, let alone the laity. Yet there were parallels in other European countries at this time for the concentration of secular and ecclesiastical authority in the hands of a cardinal-chief minister. Cardinal Ximenes occupied a similar role in the kingdoms of Spain, while Cardinal d'Amboise was perhaps a still closer counterpart to Wolsey in the French kingdom. What such a phenomenon symbolized, even so, was less the power of the Church over the monarchy than the hold of the king over his clergy.

Wales, like the rest of the king's domain, came under Wolsey's all-seeing surveillance. Down to the mid-1520s it remained, in terms of government

[5] A. F. Pollard, *Wolsey* (London, 1929).

and religion, in much the same state as it had done for half a century previously. It was still divided into Principality and March, though many of the arrangements for its government, now seriously outdated, were creaking ominously and in need of radical overhaul.[6] The shires, and the Marcher lordships especially, cried out for reform, even though most of the latter had become swallowed up in the possessions of the Crown. A further major step in the same direction followed in 1521, when the greatest of the surviving Marcher lords, Edward Stafford, third duke of Buckingham, was put to death and his lordships taken over by the king. What this episode established, if indeed such a demonstration were needed, was how powerful the Crown already was *vis-à-vis* the lords and with what terrifying force and suddenness Henry could react if his suspicions were aroused. Not even the mightiest and most highly born of subjects was proof against the wrath of such a prince!

In spite of the anachronisms attaching to the royal administration in Wales, Wolsey was able to exercise much authority in the king's name. He did so through the agency of a number of ambitious but trusted lieutenants. Chief among them was one who had held sway long before the cardinal ever came to power. He was Sir Rhys ap Thomas, KG, whose ability to raise large bodies of troops and lead them successfully in battle had served the Tudor dynasty consistently and well since 1485. Chamberlain of south Wales since 1485 and Justiciar since 1496, as well as holding many lesser offices, Rhys lorded it in vice-regal state at Carew Castle until his death in 1525.[7] In the south-east his opposite number was the king's favourite, Charles Somerset (1460–1526), earl of Worcester from 1513. He owed his position initially to his marriage to the Herbert heiress, Elizabeth, daughter of the earl of Huntingdon, and later to the king's favour, which conferred on him the stewardship of several royal lordships of the March. From *Twr Melyn Gwent* (Yellow Tower of Gwent), his splendid castle at Raglan, he was able to dominate much of the south-eastern and middle March.[8] In north-eastern Wales a miniature Wolsey had emerged in the person of Robert ap Rhys. Third son of that Rhys Fawr who made his fame and fortune at Bosworth Field,[9] Robert was a consumingly ambitious clerical lawyer. In spite of the ill feeling which existed between Wolsey and Bishop Henry Standish of St Asaph, Robert had wormed his way into the favour of both men and established himself

[6] *W 1415–1642*, chap. 11.

[7] D. B. Rees, *Sir Rhys ap Thomas* (Llandysul, 1992); R. A. Griffiths, *Sir Rhys ap Thomas and His Family* (Cardiff, 1993).

[8] See a series of articles by W. R. B. Robinson in *BBCS*, XX (1962–4), 421–38; XXI (1964–6), 43–74, 334–61.

[9] *W 1415–1642*, p. 226.

as one of the most powerful figures in north-east Wales.[10] In the north-west the position was rather more complicated. William Gruffydd of Penrhyn, resident chamberlain of north Wales, was the most influential of the local gentry. But his position was being strongly challenged by Richard Bulkeley, knighted in 1534 and the first major figure of the family that was to dominate Anglesey for so long.[11] Bulkeley seems to have won Wolsey's favour in spite of being at odds with William Gruffydd and with William Glyn of Glynllifon, the bishop of Bangor's main confidant.

Not that close links between Wolsey and his local agents always worked to the advantage of the Church, especially when the bishop of the diocese was a stranger and non-resident, as was usually the case in Wales. Wolsey himself farmed the diocese of Llandaff, along with Worcester and Salisbury, because all three bishops were non-resident foreigners.[12] The bishop of Llandaff since 1517 had been a Spanish friar, George de Athequa, who was normally attendant upon Catherine of Aragon as her confessor. To carry out Athequa's episcopal duties, Wolsey had installed John Smart, abbot of Wigmore and bishop of Pavada *in partibus*, as suffragan bishop. Smart created a great scandal in the 1520s by ordaining an excessive number of priests and deacons in return for money payments. He may not have been nearly as unscrupulous as was alleged, yet he was, all the same, 'an ambitious, dishonest and unworthy man'.[13] In the same diocese, Wolsey's ally, the earl of Worcester, was taken to the court of Star Chamber by the abbot of Tintern, who accused him of bullying and unprincipled conduct.[14] Even more outrageous behaviour was attributed to Sir Rhys ap Thomas by Clement West, commander of the Knights of St John at Slebech. He contended that Sir Rhys and his son had unlawfully cut down 2,000 or more oaks, had kidnapped some of West's servants, and been responsible for forcibly entering the premises at Slebech and removing goods and chattels.[15]

Bangor was another diocese which had an absentee bishop from 1508 to 1533. He was Thomas Skeffington, abbot of Beaulieu, Hampshire, whose enemies in 1529 avowed that he had not set foot in his bishopric for fourteen years.[16] In his absence he had farmed out his diocese to William Glyn, LLD, a member of the Glynllifon family, as his vicar-general. In

---

[10] *WC*, pp. 322–6.

[11] *DWB*, s.n. Bulkeley family.

[12] J. Guy, *Tudor England* (Oxford, 1988), p. 111.

[13] D. Knowles, 'The last abbot of Wigmore', in V. Raffer and A. J. Taylor (eds.), *Medieval Studies presented to Rose Graham* (Oxford, 1950), pp. 138–45.

[14] PRO, STA C, 2/29/61.

[15] PRO, Req., 2/10/76.

[16] A. I. Pryce, *The Diocese of Bangor in the Sixteenth Century* (Bangor, 1923), pp. xiii–xiv.

1524 Skeffington was in trouble with Wolsey and the Bulkeleys over the archdeaconry of Anglesey, held by one of the Bulkeley family, the announcement of whose death, like that of Mark Twain, had been much exaggerated. When Archdeacon Bulkeley did, in fact, die in 1525, Skeffington lost no time in naming Glyn, whom he described as a man 'right cunning, very virtuous and of very good fame and name', as his successor.[17] This promotion was regarded by Wolsey and Richard Bulkeley as a gratuitous snub to themselves which they did not forget. In May 1529 there were more altercations, when one Edward Johns, rector of North Crawley and one of Wolsey's men, was backed up by Richard Bulkeley in his attempts to push the cardinal's interests in opposition to those of William Glyn, who was said to have 'commissioners in every bush'. Johns urged Wolsey to be 'even with him [Glyn] to his pain. *Poena unius debet esse metus multorum*' (the punishment of one should be the cause of dread to many).[18] Glyn simultaneously came under the lash from Robert ap Rhys, who brought four articles against him. They accused him of securing the archdeaconry of Anglesey by false representation, of acquiring four benefices by gift from the bishop when they belonged to the king's patronage, of maintaining murderers who escaped punishment, and of receiving £60 over and above the amount due from the bishopric of Bangor for the king's subsidy. In the ensuing scuffles between the rival parties, 'some had broken elbows'. Bulkeley leaped in on Wolsey's side – with more zeal than discretion, even Edward Johns had to admit. Fortunately for Glyn, Wolsey's own disgrace in the autumn of 1529 saved him from further discomfiture, but the rancour between him and Bulkeley continued to smoulder.[19]

Wolsey's downfall in 1529, which saved William Glyn's bacon, brought near-disaster for Robert ap Rhys, the cardinal's right-hand man in St Asaph. Robert had benefited hugely from his association with Wolsey and Bishop Standish. He had become chancellor and vicar-general of the diocese, and had amassed a large number of benefices, some in his own possession and others under lease, though not as many as the eighteen attributed to him by his enemies. He had also profited handsomely from monastic estates; he farmed the Hospitallers' lands at Ysbyty Ifan worth £40 a year, together with extensive property belonging to the abbeys of Conwy and Strata Marcella.[20] His pride and his dynastic ambitions – he had a wife, twelve sons and four daughters, for whose worldly advancement he cherished lively expectations – aroused in the clergy and the laity of the

[17] *WRE*, pp. 36–7.
[18] PRO, SP 1/30, p. 291; 1/53, pp. 286–7.
[19] Ibid.
[20] *WC*, pp. 323–6.

44

neighbourhood profound resentment, which exploded into the open once his mighty patron had been disgraced. Among the gravest charges brought against him were that he had abused his powers as vicar-general, had seized Richard Griffith, parson of Cerrigydrudion, and had had him 'carried in irons from place to place among thieves and murderers'.[21] His bitterest lay opponent, John Salusbury, alleged that he had oppressed the inhabitants of the lordship of Denbigh 'with extortion and bribery' to the tune of 'four or five thousand marks without restitution or punishment', 'the greatest extortions in Wales for five hundred years'.[22] Salusbury's charges were doubtless infused with all the vindictive exaggerations of a mortal enemy; nevertheless, the acrimony with which the feuds were pursued gives an indication not only of the hostility which Wolsey himself and his henchmen aroused but also of the readiness of laymen and clerics alike to fight out their battles at the expense of the Church.

Yet some of the more enlightened among contemporaries were not unaware of the shortcomings of the Church or of the need for reform. During the early years of Henry VIII's reign there were moderate and thoroughly orthodox demands for improvement. John Colet, dean of St Paul's, for example, preaching to the Convocation of Canterbury in 1512, had assailed clerical abuses and called for the reform of the Church from within. Wolsey himself was not unmoved by some inclination towards reform. But despite his accumulation of powers, all he managed to achieve was the suppression of a few small monasteries, employing the proceeds to found his colleges at Oxford and Ipswich. The wave of Renaissance calls for renewal reached their crest with the arrival in England of Erasmus, brightest luminary of the Northern Renaissance and the hero of his English admirers like Sir Thomas More. The latter greeted with rapture the improved knowledge of the original languages of the scriptures and the great humanist's satirical demolition of the superstition widely prevalent in contemporary religion. Such trends left a profound impression on bright young men educated at the universities. In their midst were promising Welsh graduates like Richard Whitford, boon companion to Erasmus and Thomas More,[23] or Edward Powell, prebendary of Lincoln and Salisbury, and a court preacher much in favour with Henry VIII at this time.[24] Others like them were the laymen, John Price[25] of Brecon, or Edward Carne[26] of Glamorgan, both to have long and distinguished careers as lawyers and

---

[21] PRO, STA C 2/16/325.

[22] PRO, SP 1/76, pp. 196, 227.

[23] *WRE*, pp. 67–75.

[24] T. P. Ellis, *The Catholic Martyrs of Wales* (London, 1933), pp. 10–14.

[25] *DNB*; N. R. Ker, 'Sir John Price', *The Library*, V (1955), 1–24.

[26] *DNB, DWB*, s.n.

royal servants. It is noticeable, however, that all these men followed their *métiers* outside Wales. Whitford went to the Brigittine house at Sion; Powell held a range of preferments but not one in Wales; and Price and Carne made headway in legal and administrative circles in London. That was not in any way surprising since there was little or no opportunity within Wales itself to pursue interests of this kind, professional or intellectual; and for quite some time most of its ablest sons had been drained away to England.[27]

Another feature of the early part of Henry's reign was the upsurge of bad feeling between the clergy and the laity between 1514 and 1517. The occasion of it was the case of Richard Hunne, a London tailor who had been embroiled with ecclesiastical authority over a dispute about a mortuary and, as a result, imprisoned in the prison of Dr William Horsey, the bishop of London's chancellor. In December 1514 he was found dead from hanging in his cell in the Lollards' Tower. Laymen laid the blame for his death squarely on the ecclesiastical authorities. The episode provoked a furious outcry among the laity, not simply at the treatment of Hunne but also at the pretensions and privileges of the clergy in general. It sparked off a tremendous outburst in the House of Commons, which met in February 1515. The liberties of the Church were defended by the abbot of Winchcombe, to whom Henry Standish, warden of the Greyfriars, was put up to reply. Although Wolsey and his fellow-bishops were incensed by Standish's temerity, the latter was protected by the king.[28] A few years later, in 1518, in the teeth of intense intrigues by Wolsey on behalf of other candidates, Standish was rewarded by his royal patron with the see of St Asaph.[29] Anticlerical feeling on the scale of the Hunne affair never surfaced in Wales. Nevertheless, there were occasional signs of ill will and friction, especially in relation to monastic rights. There was chronic ill feeling between the monks of the Augustinian priories at Haverfordwest and Carmarthen and the neighbouring townsmen.[30] In 1520 a quarrel broke out between the monks of Margam and the burgesses of Afan over rights to common land, and in 1521 a particularly serious clash occurred between the merchants of Neath and the Cistercians at Neath Abbey.[31] Yet there is not much sign that such disagreements ever reached anywhere near the point where they were interpreted by clerics as a serious threat.

---

[27] G. Williams, *Religion, Language and Nationality in Wales* (Cardiff, 1979), pp. 171–99.
[28] A. Ogle, *The Tragedy of the Lollards' Tower* (Oxford, 1949), pp. 148–51, 154–7.
[29] *LP*, II, 4070, 4074, 4083.
[30] *W and R*, pp. 123–7.
[31] *WC*, pp. 501–2.

What did, however, constitute a challenge of the utmost gravity to the whole Church was the protest begun by Martin Luther in 1517. When this and other similar denunciations exploded onto the scene, some of the reverberations soon began to spread from Europe to England. Lutheran and other heretical books and teachings were imported through London and other eastern ports. They found favour, predictably perhaps, among the merchants of London and elsewhere and among the students at the universities, 'inexpert youth' as Archbishop Warham described them to Wolsey.[32] Others who may have provided an audience ripe for the reception of these new heresies were the underground remnants of the native heresy of Lollardy. It may indeed have been the danger that the old and new subversions would coalesce which alarmed the clerical establishment as much as anything. Wolsey and the hierarchy were deeply antagonized by the new opinions and, as early as May 1521, the cardinal presided over the first great bonfire of heretical books. The king himself entered the fray to contest Luther's arguments. So fired was he with pro-papal zeal that Thomas More counselled caution upon him. With unconscious foresight he warned that a 'breach of amity' might arise between king and pope and urged that the latter's authority might be 'more lightly touched upon'.[33] Henry was not to be restrained, however, and plunged with abandon into his book, *Assertio Septem Sacramentorum* (1521). It turned out to be an effective piece of anti-Lutheran propaganda and ran through a number of editions. A grateful pope bestowed upon its author the title of *Fidei Defensor*, and, by putting him thus on a par with his envied rivals, the 'most Christian' king of France and the 'Catholic kings' of Spain, gave him immense gratification. It was a book which enjoyed considerable kudos as the work of a ruling monarch, in Europe as well as at home. This growing weight of reaction against heresy drove some Protestants underground and forced others like William Tyndale or John Frith into exile. But little groups of believers continued to meet in secret, smuggled in books published on the Continent, and circulated them clandestinely. Much the most popular among them was Tyndale's New Testament in English, all the more joyfully received because England was almost alone among major European countries in not having available an officially allowed vernacular translation of the scriptures.[34]

Wales was remote from such ferment. It had neither universities, nor towns, nor centres of trade of any consequence. It lay far from the trading routes with northern Europe and most of its seaborne foreign exchanges

---

[32] H. E. Jacobs. *The Lutheran Movement in England during the Reigns of Henry VIII and Edward VI* (Philadelphia, 1908), p. 4.

[33] W. Roper, *Life of Thomas More*, ed. E. V. Hitchcock (EETS, 1935), pp. 67–8.

[34] *Cambridge History of the Bible*, ed. S. L. Greenslade (Cambridge, 1963), III. 141.

were directed towards the mainly, even staunchly, Catholic countries like Spain, France, and Portugal.[35] Little or no intellectual or religious effervescence was observable in such towns or larger households as existed. Nor was there any trace of the new stirrings to be seen in those manuscripts circulating in the Welsh language. Wales not having been even partially penetrated by printed books in the native tongue, most of its people were still cut off by the barriers of language from the volume of printed literature being produced elsewhere. In general, the only ones who came into contact with the novel trends in scholarship or religion were the privileged few who graduated at the universities or who participated in law or trade or other callings in London and other big towns.[36] An excellent example of the type was Edward Powell (?1478–1540), former fellow of Oriel College, a large-scale pluralist and a popular court preacher, who published his *Propugnaculum summi Sacerdoti Evangelici . . .* (1523), a fierce attack on Luther's heresies in the form of a dialogue between himself and the German heresiarch. The university of Oxford was sufficiently impressed by his work to applaud it as a 'chief and brilliant gem' and to commend Powell himself as 'the glory of the university'.[37] Another outstanding scholar, Richard Whitford (?1470–1540), former fellow of Queens' College Cambridge and friend of Erasmus and Thomas More, chose to enter Sion, a strictly observant monastic house of a kind not to be found in Wales. There he pursued a life of committed devotion and became the author of a series of highly influential books of impeccable orthodoxy.[38] On the other side, one of a handful of graduates irresistibly attracted to heretical doctrine was a young man from Pembrokeshire, George Constantine (1500–60), who graduated B.Can.L. at Cambridge in 1524 and there imbibed Protestant heresy. He later fled to Antwerp, where he assisted Tyndale and Joye with publishing the New Testament and other heretical literature. Subsequently, he became involved in smuggling such books into England and was eventually arrested in London.[39] An interesting feature of Constantine's career was that he kept up his contacts with his native area. In this respect he was typical of a number of gifted young Welsh graduates of various shades of religious opinion, like Richard Gwent,[40] John Price, Edward Carne, or Richard Davies,[41] who all maintained contacts with Wales. Tenuous those links may have been, but

---

[35] *W 1415–1642*, pp. 75–8.
[36] Williams, *Religion, Lang. and Nationality*, pp. 171–99.
[37] Ellis, *Catholic Martyrs*, pp. 10–14.
[38] *WRE*, pp. 67–75.
[39] *DWB*, s.n.
[40] *WRE*, pp. 75–89.
[41] G. Williams, *Bywyd ac Amserau'r Esgob Richard Davies* (Cardiff, 1953).

they may none the less have helped to encourage some penetration of the country by the religious and intellectual stirrings of the age.

In the 1520s, however, there were portents of the end of an era in Wales. One execution and three deaths which took place in fairly quick succession seem, in retrospect, to symbolize the passing of an older order in society, religion, literature, and politics. The first to go was the third duke of Buckingham, last of the great lords of the March. A grandee with the prolific Edward III's blood in his veins, related by kinship or marriage to a number of other notabilities, and reputedly the richest aristocrat in the kingdom, he may have found it difficult to adjust to the reduced role expected of him in Henry VIII's England. His incautious utterances and behaviour, and his partiality for the cloudy but grandiloquent predictions of astrologers, may well have aroused suspicions in a king acutely sensitive, even at this early stage, to the lack of a recognized male heir and successor. When in 1520 Buckingham sought permission to take a retinue of 400 men to Wales, it prompted fears that he might have it in mind to repeat his father's ill-fated *coup* of 1483 against Richard III. He was brought before a court, condemned, and executed. Wolsey was popularly held to have been to blame for the duke's execution, but he may have borne far less responsibility for it than his autocratic and easily offended master. Buckingham's fate was not only an object lesson to the foremost aristocrats but also meant that the king's position *vis-à-vis* the lords of the March was now quite unchallengeable.[42]

The next to disappear from the scene was Edward Vaughan, bishop of St David's who died in 1522. A Cambridge graduate, Vaughan had had a long and varied career, characteristically spent almost entirely in England, but he had been promoted to the episcopal bench as bishop of St David's in 1509. He was that rare phenomenon of the later Middle Ages, a Welshman elevated to be a bishop in Wales – one of four such appointed during Henry VII's reign.[43] Vaughan was the last of the great native-born medieval bishops of St David's, whose tenure of his see was noteworthy for the fact that he resided there. Like some of his distinguished predecessors, he also engaged in large-scale building projects at St David's and at his palaces at Lamphey and Llawhaden. He was buried at his cathedral in the charming

---

[42] *W 1415–1642*, pp. 249–50; B. J. Harris, *Edward Stafford: Third Duke of Buckingham, 1478–1521* (Stanford, Calif., 1986).
[43] *WC*, pp. 301–3.

and elegant Trinity chapel raised by him.[44] Thereafter, the story at St David's would be one of declining fortunes and considerable episcopal neglect.

If Edward Vaughan was the last of the Welsh-born princes of the medieval church, Tudur Aled was the last great *pencerdd* (master-poet) of medieval Wales.[45] For forty years before his death, *c*.1525, he had been acclaimed as the most accomplished exponent of the classical *cynghanedd* or strict-metre poetry, the crown of the Welsh literary art. Over most of his career he had looked to Sir Rhys ap Thomas as one of his most lavish patrons; as he did not compose an elegy to the old chieftain, it has generally been supposed that he must have died suddenly in Carmarthen about the same time as Sir Rhys. Like the latter, Tudur, too, was buried in Carmarthen friary, having taken a precaution in keeping with late medieval piety of being wrapped in a friar's habit to give him better hopes of safeguards for the hereafter. His death was greeted with an unprecedented outpouring of grief by his fellow-poets. The elegies of at least nine of them have been preserved for us: effusions by all the leading poets of the age. Among them was a line by Lewys Môn which serves as a fitting epitaph to the last of the really outstanding poets. In Tudur's grave, Lewys said, 'the muse will dwell for ever' ('y trig awen tragywydd').[46] No poet would again enjoy quite the same unalloyed assurance nor the air of undisputed mastery over his medium as Tudur, 'pen Taliesin', the last of the giants of the golden age of Welsh verse.

In 1525 the most powerful single individual among the native gentry also died. Rhys ap Thomas, head of the Dynevor family, had concentrated in his own hands a formidable accumulation of offices in south Wales and the March. After a long and sometimes turbulent life, he died in all the odour of medieval sanctity and was buried in Carmarthen Friary, bequeathing a more than usually lavish series of legacies to churches and religious houses with which he was associated.[47] Whatever might have been the expectations of his family and some of his fellow-gentry, it was not one of Rhys's own descendants, nor even a member of any other south Wales family, who was appointed to succeed him in the offices he held from the Crown. That may have been due to the relative inexperience of his youthful grandson, Rhys ap Gruffudd, or to the king's reluctance to countenance any impression that any one family had an indefeasible right to succeed to office in south-west Wales, or possibly on account of both reasons. Whatever the

---

[44] W. B. Jones and E. A. Freeman, *History and Antiquities of St David's* (London, 1856), p. 70.

[45] *Gwaith Tudur Aled*, ed. T. G. Jones (2 vols. Cardiff, 1926).

[46] *W 1415–1642*, pp. 162–3.

[47] *WC*, pp. 565–6; Griffiths, *Rhys ap Thomas*, pp. 76–9.

explanation, Henry made it evident that the old regime was over when, on 22 August 1525, he conferred for life on Walter Devereux, Lord Ferrers, the key office of justice of south Wales, and, on 25 May 1526, followed that up with the office of chamberlain of south Wales. This decision to appoint Ferrers was undoubtedly regarded as an affront by Rhys ap Gruffudd, his kinsfolk, and the men of the south-west, and was later to cause serious trouble for the Crown.[48]

These changes in the personnel of political and administrative authority were underlined by another measure taken at this time, one designed to instil new life into the Council in the Marches. During the years from 1523 to 1525 Wolsey had learned how resistant the populace could be to his plans for increasing the yield from taxes and had appreciated the need to attain further control over outlying areas and to delegate some of the responsibilities of Star Chamber to regional bodies. Thus, in 1526 he had set up a council in the Marches to attend upon Princess Mary, the steward of whose household was none other than Lord Ferrers. The new president of this council was John Veysey, bishop of Exeter, who was charged with improving 'good order, quiet and tranquillity' in the area of his jurisdiction, but whose lack of drive prevented him from achieving any significant results.[49]

All these relatively minor developments were soon to be completely overshadowed by the emergence of the issue that would dominate the affairs of the whole kingdom during the years after 1527 – the king's 'great matter', i.e. Henry's grave doubts about the validity of his marriage and his desire to have it annulled so that he could marry again. For some years after he had taken to wife Catherine of Aragon, the widow of his elder brother Arthur, the king had appeared to be happily married to this paragon among royal spouses: faithful, affectionate, intelligent, pious, and exceedingly helpful to him in his diplomacy. In the eight years after 1510 she had borne him six children, only one of whom, his daughter Mary, had survived. By 1518 Catherine was prematurely aged and Henry was tired of her. There seemed virtually no prospect of her now giving birth to an heir, and the possibility that his daughter might succeed to the throne filled Henry and his subjects with alarm. There was no certainty, even, that she *could* succeed, but if she did, there might be endless problems over her marriage, whether to one of her own subjects or to a foreign prince. The king had good reason to be alarmed about the succession, the central issue of politics. His acute anxiety on this score may earlier have triggered his savage reaction to Buckingham's aspirations. As early as 1522 or 1523,

[48] W. Ll. Williams, 'A Welsh insurrection', *Cymm.* XVI (1902), 1–93.
[49] C. A. J. Skeel, *The Council in the Marches of Wales* (London, 1903).

according to Bishop Longland,[50] Henry was voicing alarmist conscientious scruples to the effect that, by denying him an heir, God was punishing him for breaking the injunction in the Book of Leviticus against marrying a brother's widow. When in 1525 the Emperor Charles V threw over both the English alliance and his projected marriage to the Princess Mary, Henry's mixed reactions of rage and apprehension were vastly magnified. He seriously began to think of grooming the duke of Richmond, his bastard son by Elizabeth Blount, as heir to the throne.

What made an already delicate and complicated situation very much worse was that by 1525–6 Henry had become hopelessly infatuated with one of the ladies of his court, Anne Boleyn, daughter of the earl of Wiltshire.[51] She was a lively and intelligent young woman, with a mind of her own, though many of her contemporaries found difficulty in understanding quite what it was about her looks or personality that accounted for the extraordinary fascination she held for her royal lover. All the more remarkable, given the moral laxity of the average European court, was that Anne should be determined not to bestow her sexual favours upon the king outside marriage. Henry's obsessive desire for her fused with his intense concern over the succession and drove him into a position from which he convinced himself that he could escape only by means of divorce. He now believed that he had never been legally married to Catherine at all and that the original papal dispensation from Pope Julius II allowing him to do so had not been valid in the eyes of God. There was nothing for it but to turn the screw on the curia to annul the so-called 'marriage', the obvious agent for such an operation being Cardinal Wolsey.

The king's desire for a papal dispensation to dissolve his marriage did not necessarily mean that an irreparable breach between Rome and England was inevitable There were many precedents for such divorces being granted by the pope largely as a matter of convenience for royal personages. Louis XII of France had obtained one in order to marry the heiress of Brittany, and two such concessions were made to members of Henry's own family – his sister, Margaret, queen of Scotland, and his brother-in-law, Charles Brandon, duke of Suffolk. Nor was it inconceivable that the king might tire of his obstinate mistress or that she might yield to royal persistence; though, whatever the outcome between them, the succession problem would not go away. Wolsey, all the while, was in an acutely uncomfortable position. While he was under severe pressure to secure a divorce for his exacting master, ideally he wished to switch to a French alliance, to be confirmed by the king's marriage to a French

---

[50] Scarisbrick, *Henry VIII*, p. 162.
[51] E. W. Ives, *Anne Boleyn* (Oxford, 1986).

princess. He had no wish at all to clear the way for Henry's marriage to a young woman of dangerously heretical inclinations. What made his dilemma all the more painful was the capture of Rome by imperial troops in 1527, which put Pope Clement VII in the power of Catherine of Aragon's kinsman, Charles V. In 1528, however, Wolsey did manage to extract from the pope permission for the divorce case to be heard in London by himself and Cardinal Campeggio. What he did not know was that the latter was under strict instructions to play for time and to take no irrevocable decision.[52]

While Queen Catherine was being put under the harrow by the proceedings for the divorce, among those who were prominently associated with her cause were a group of clerics all of whom had connections with Wales. Standish of St Asaph was a conservative theologian appointed by the Crown to be one of her counsel. Her confessor, Bishop Athequa of Llandaff, throughout remained steadfastly loyal to her, as did Richard Fetherston, archdeacon of Brecon and her daughter's preceptor. One of those who came out most forthrightly on her behalf was Edward Powell. He pleaded for her in the legates' court and composed a Latin treatise entitled *Tractatus de non dissolvendo Henrici Regis cum Caterina matrimonio* (Treatise why the marriage of King Henry to Queen Catherine should not be dissolved), copies of which no longer exist. Both Powell and Fetherston were again to speak on the queen's behalf in the Convocation of Canterbury in 1529, when they were two out of only four who had the courage to defend her.[53] Another up-and-coming Welsh ecclesiastical lawyer, Richard Gwent, was also appointed counsel for Catherine, but he appears to have acted on her behalf with little conviction and certainly without imperilling his future career.[54] Athequa, Standish, Fetherston, and Powell seem to have been active members of the 'Aragon faction' grouped around Eustache Chapuys, the imperial ambassador. Another Welshman well known to Chapuys and with whom he sympathized warmly was Rhys ap Gruffudd, who became involved in a dangerous fracas with Lord Ferrers in 1529 and was executed in 1531. Chapuys was convinced that a major reason for Rhys's downfall was his regard for Catherine of Aragon and his intense dislike of Anne Boleyn.[55] There must have been other leading figures among Welshmen in Wales and in London who would surely have been well aware of the tension existing between the king and the queen but have left little or no indication of their attitude towards it. As

[52] G. Constant, *La Réforme en Angleterre: Henri VIII* (Paris, 1930), pp. 28–9.
[53] Ellis, *Catholic Martyrs*, pp. 10–11.
[54] *WRE*, pp. 76–7.
[55] W. Ll. Williams, *Cymm.* XVI, 1–93; Griffiths, *Rhys ap Thomas*, chap. 4.

for the mass of the Welsh people, it is even more difficult to assess what their reactions may have been. In general, however, there appears to have been a good deal of sympathy for Catherine as a dutiful and badly used wife and much hostility to Anne, who was regarded as a minx no better than she should have been. Most of the Welsh might have been forgiven if the whole crisis appeared to them as somewhat remote and unreal – the affair of a distant pope and a powerful, god-like sovereign which impinged but little on their obscure existence.

The impact of the rift between king and pope would, nevertheless, come home to all the king's subjects, including those in Wales, with much greater impact during the ensuing years. On 31 July 1529 Campeggio adjourned the divorce proceedings, which were now revoked to Rome. Later that autumn, Wolsey was dismissed from office, leaving his Welsh dependants like Rhys ap Gruffudd and Robert ap Rhys isolated and at the mercy of their enemies. Parliament was summoned to meet in November 1529, presumably in order to mobilize lay anticlericalism in support of the king, to intimidate the clergy, and to intensify the squeeze on the pope. The forces of lay resentment against the clergy were beginning to be unleashed, in Wales like everywhere else in the realm. They were less easily organized in Wales, which was unrepresented in the House of Commons and had a mere handful of resident peers and bishops who sat in the Lords. In spite of that, it is noticeable that, from the outset, the statutes passed in the Reformation Parliament were made applicable to Wales as though it were fully part of the realm.[56] Indeed, in one of the first of the statutes passed in 1529, that against mortuaries, a specific clause was inserted to ensure that no new mortuaries would be demanded in Wales.[57] On the other hand, in Convocation, because the four Welsh dioceses were part of the ecclesiastical province of Canterbury, each was represented by its bishop and members of the lower clergy. When that body assembled in November 1529 John Fisher's impassioned and historic defence of the queen was supported by Powell and Fetherston.

During the year 1530 royal pressure on the Church was stepped up. Henry's representatives solicited from a number of European universities views on the rightness of his case for divorce. Evidence designed to justify the historic rights of British rulers over the Church since the time of King Lucius (187 AD) and the Emperor Constantine was brought together in a document known as *Collectanea satis Copiosa*[58] (A sufficiently plentiful compilation). In the mean time, the young Welsh lawyer, Edward Carne,

---

[56] W. Rees, 'The union of England and Wales', *TCS* (1937), 27–100 argued that the Act of Union had been passed in 1536 in order to ensure that Reformation statutes applied to Wales, ibid., p. 45.

[57] I. Bowen, *The Statutes of Wales* (London, 1908), p. 50.

[58] G. R. Elton, *Reform and Reformation, 1509–1558* (London, 1977), pp. 135–6.

had been sent to Rome as the king's *excusator* to delay any judgement from being passed against his master for as long as possible, and he and his colleague, William Benet, contrived deftly to spin out the proceedings for eighteen months. Before the year was out Henry was thoroughly apprised from a variety of sources of the measure of supremacy he believed he ought to enjoy over his clergy. In December 1530 all the clergy were accused of having committed the offence of praemunire by recognizing Wolsey's legatine authority. When Convocation assembled in 1531, in order to gain pardon for its transgression, it was forced to offer the king £100,000, to which the bishop of Bangor made the large contribution, for one of the poorest sees, of £333. 6s. 8d.[59] What was more serious was that the clergy had to yield the unprecedented recognition that the king was 'protector and only supreme head of the English Church', 'as far as the law of Christ allows'.[60] The year 1531 further witnessed the emergence of the phenomenally resourceful and energetic Thomas Cromwell as the king's chief minister. Skilfully guided by this master of procedure and statute, Parliament would, over the next three years, pass a number of revolutionary statutes designed to hammer home the king's supremacy over the Church.[61] A number of bright Welsh clerics and laymen hitched their wagons to the rising star; among them Richard Gwent, John Price, Ellis Price, and Richard Bulkeley. In Wales itself, over and over again in the ensuing years, it became apparent that influential leaders of lay and ecclesiastical life thought it crucial to secure Cromwell's favour.

Henry was now moving to the stage of finally disencumbering himself of his first wife and acquiring a second one. In 1532 he at last began to cohabit with Anne Boleyn, and before the end of the year she was pregnant. It was essential that a decision over the king's divorce should be rushed through in England so that any child she bore should have no taint of bastardy hanging over it. Fortunately for the king, Archbishop Warham of Canterbury, who had been showing growing signs of obstinacy and even of hankering after martyrdom, had died in August 1532, so steps could be taken to secure a complaisant successor. In January 1533, Thomas Cranmer, a reformer and himself a married man, was chosen to succeed him; and papal approval, no less, was obtained for the choice. Cranmer hastened to give judgement against Catherine; and to ensure that no appeal to the pope would carry any weight the crucial Act in Restraint of Appeals of 1533 was passed. Effectively, the links with Rome had been snapped. The way was now clear for a series of antipapal statutes, culminating in the

---

[59] *LP*, V. 657. No other record of contributions by Welsh clerics seems to be available.
[60] Ogle, *Lollards' Tower*, pp. 324–30.
[61] A. G. Dickens, *Thomas Cromwell and the English Reformation* (London, 1959); G. R. Elton, *England under the Tudors* (London, 1954), chap 6.

Act of Supremacy of November 1534, which declared the king and his heirs to be 'the only supreme head in earth of the Church called *Anglicana Ecclesia*'[62] (which was deemed to include the Welsh dioceses). By means of these statutes a revolution had unquestionably been accomplished: it transferred to the Crown the authority exercised for centuries hitherto by the pope. Oaths of loyalty to the king's enhanced status would have to be extracted from his subjects with the minimum of delay.

During the summer and autumn of 1534, consequently, the clergy of the Welsh dioceses were required to swear such an oath of loyalty. In June and again in September the clergy of Llandaff were summoned to comply; in July and August those of St David's; and in August those of St Asaph.[63] No record exists of the clergy of Bangor doing so, but there is no reason to suppose either that they were not required to swear or that they refused. In all, the subscriptions of 758 clergy who took the oath in the three dioceses are extant. To these should be added the names of the friars, who were included in the special visitation of all the friars undertaken by Fathers Hilsey and Browne, and seventy monks, out of the 250 or so estimated to have been members of Welsh religious houses at this time. Two kinds of oath are known to have been administered. The one seems to have required the parish clergy simply to swear that the bishop of Rome had no greater jurisdiction given to him by God in the realm of England than any other foreign bishop.[64] The other, which was demanded of members of religious houses, was much longer and more elaborate. It called on them to be loyal to the king as head of the Anglican Church, the queen, and their heirs. They also forswore the authority of the pope as pontiff and promised never to pray for him except as bishop of Rome. They accepted that in the 'bidding prayer' the king's name should replace that of the pope. Finally, they promised to preach in a Catholic and orthodox way Christ and his words and works.[65] Two of the Welsh bishops renounced the papal jurisdiction very late in their lives: Henry Standish of St Asaph, earlier a supporter of Catherine of Aragon, took the oath on 1 June 1535, only a month before his death; and Richard Rawlins of St David's on 4 April 1535, less than a year before his death in February 1536.[66]

Among those who refused to swear was Athequa, bishop of Llandaff. Because he was one of the two clerics in Catherine's entourage who

---

[62] *Statutes of the Realm* (11 vols. London, 1810–28), III. 463.

[63] PRO, E 36/63; *LP*, VII, 769, 891, 1216–17, 14–16, 21 (Llandaff); 1121 (25) (St Asaph); 891, 1024, 17–21, 28, 34, 37, 1121, 4, 12 (St David's).

[64] Ibid., VII. 25.

[65] J. G. Jones, *Wales and the Tudor State* (Cardiff, 1988), pp. 221–2; G. E. Jones and T. Herbert, *Tudor Wales* (Cardiff, 1988), p. 119. For a list of all the houses, see *DK's Reports*, VII (1846), app. 2, pp. 219–306.

[66] *LP*, VIII. 803, 494.

understood Spanish, the language in which she always confessed, he was allowed to stay with her in her banishment at Buckden. Neither he nor Richard Fetherston would accept the validity of the divorce or the royal supremacy. When Fetherston was summoned along with Bishop Fisher and others to swear obedience to the statutes or else suffer the fate of the executed Carthusians he was given six weeks to change his mind. He replied he would not do so in six hundred years.[67] Edward Powell, another member of the group, had already found himself in grave peril on account of his opposition to the king's proceedings, uncompromisingly declared in a series of sermons preached at Bristol in reply to Latimer's reforming crusade there. He fearlessly announced that 'a king ought not to break the contract of his marriage when the Church will not and cannot dispense him. The authority of the Church is above that of the worldly ruler.' He further had the temerity to liken King Henry to King David who, 'with his adultery, sat also in the chair of pestilence'.[68] In 1534 he was put in gaol at Dorchester, whence he was transferred to the Tower. Richard Whitford was another who held out against the oath throughout 1534 and 1535 in spite of the heavy pressure put on him by persecutors who employed 'both fair words and foul'.[69]

The hostility aroused in Wales by the treatment of Catherine and her daughter and by the king's dealings with the Church led to grave concern being voiced about the possible outcome. As early as 1531 Chapuys had written to Charles V about Rhys ap Gruffudd's contempt for Anne Boleyn and the sympathy which the Welsh showed for him.[70] A Venetian emissary's comment that the king of Scotland was hoping for Welsh and Irish support in a war he was preparing against England[71] was taken up in similar reports from Chapuys and from Flanders in 1533.[72] Chapuys again noted in 1534 that, like the Welsh, people in Lancashire, another remote, conservative area similar to Wales, were disaffected by that 'which is done against the faith'.[73] The outbreak of the Kildare Rebellion in Ireland in 1534 greatly heartened the ambassador, who was quick to point particularly to the partiality of the Welsh for the Irish rebels.[74] He had high hopes of what might be achieved in Ireland by the notorious Welsh dissident, James ap Gruffudd ap Hywel, uncle to Rhys ap Gruffudd, who had recently crossed

---

[67] Ibid., p. 666.
[68] Ellis, *Catholic Martyrs*, p. 11.
[69] *WRE*, p. 70.
[70] *LP*, V. 563.
[71] *CSP Ven.* IV. 792.
[72] *LP*, VI. 902, 907.
[73] Ibid., VII. 1368.
[74] Ibid., 957, 1057, 1141, 1534.

over there from Scotland.[75] His views seemed to be confirmed by the reported conversation of May 1534 between two Middlesex clergymen, John Hale and Robert Feron. The former was alleged to have said, 'Ireland is set against him [the king] . . . and what think ye of Wales? The noble and gentle ap Ryce [Rhys ap Gruffudd] so cruelly put to death . . . they will join and take part with the Irish and so invade our realm.' And he concluded that they had cause enough for rebellion, 'and truly we of the Church shall never live merrily until that day come'.[76] Both Chapuys and Martin de Conoça considered that the treatment of the queen, the princess, and Rhys ap Gruffudd had thoroughly alienated Wales, and Chapuys claimed that it was freely being said that its people only waited for a chief to take the field.[77] In the light of all this it was therefore not surprising that when two Observant friars from Newark, an order whose members were particularly opposed to Henry's policies and were warmly devoted to Catherine, sought to escape from the kingdom, they should make their way to Wales. When they arrived in Cardiff, disguised in secular habit and pursued by Hilsey, they caused considerable perturbation. But these two found neither security nor sympathy, were promptly arrested by the bailiffs of the town and packed off to Westminster as prisoners. Cardiff, in fact, seems to have served as a place of detention, and two other Observant friars were incarcerated there.[78]

Symptomatic of widespread simmering discontent in Wales during these years were the many isolated voices of protest that made themselves heard. One Caernarfonshire priest, Sir William ap Llywelyn, was taxed with having said, on 4 July 1533, that 'he wished to have the king upon a mountain in north Wales called "Withvay" (Wyddfa), otherwise called "Snoyden (Snowdon) Hill", saying that he would souse the king about the ears until he had made his head soft enough'. He was promptly seized by the servants of Richard Bulkeley, who reported the whole matter to Cromwell.[79] On 26 October 1534 Lord Ferrers was ordered by Cromwell to send up one Owen Glyn, vicar of Jeffreyston in Pembroke, for seditious comments he had made.[80] The following year it was Philip ap David of Forden who was alleged to have burst out in exasperation, 'The Devil take the king and all his acts', for which he was committed to Montgomery Castle by Rowland Lee.[81] Richard Hale of Llangefni in Anglesey protested

[75] Williams, *Cymm.* XVI. 1–93; Rees, *TCS* (1937), 47–8.
[76] J. A. Froude, *The Reign of Henry VIII* (London, 1928), II. 56–7.
[77] *LP*, VII. 1040, 1368.
[78] Ibid., 939, 1607, p. 601.
[79] PRO, SP 1/77/203–4.
[80] *LP*, VII. 1310.
[81] Ibid., VIII. 509 (ii).

that they were all 'clean gone out of the faith',[82] and an unnamed Gower priest was reported to have spoken seditious words about the king in 1536 but he died before he could be brought to answer for them.[83] In December of that year Robert ap Robert Heuster, parson of Llanelidan in Dyffryn Clwyd, was accused by Piers Salusbury of giving it as his opinion that the king had left Holy Church and that the people ought to be prepared to die for the faith rather than let him despoil them further.[84] About the same time, Pyer Andre, a Portuguese by birth, was reported to Ferrers for declaring in Pembroke that the king was married to 'villain's blood'.[85]

These rumblings of dissatisfaction, plentifully recorded in Wales like other parts of the country,[86] suggest that many, especially among the clergy, were deeply offended by what the king had done. Nevertheless, there appears to be no suggestion of any conspiracy against the Crown, and royal officers like Bishop Lee and Lord Ferrers were quickly able to stifle what discontent there was. In particular, there was no sign of serious disaffection on the part of the greater gentry, whose leadership would be critical if there were to be any armed rising. Possibly they had learnt the lesson of the danger involved in opposition to the Crown from the fate which had befallen Rhys ap Gruffudd in 1531. Too many of them may have shared the apprehensions of Richard Bulkeley's servants, who had been appalled by the possibility that they might share in Rhys's downfall.[87] Richard Bulkeley himself certainly showed no illusions about Cromwell's capacity for retaliation when he confessed to him, 'I know right well it lieth in your hands to undo me for ever with a word of your mouth.'[88]

In addition to all these protests against the royal supremacy there had been worrying reports during the early 1530s that, under the slack presidency of Bishop Veysey, the Council in the Marches was functioning very ineffectively. Officials were censured for being corrupt and negligent, with the result that serious crimes and breaches of the peace were frequent and going unpunished. A stream of correspondents had drawn attention to the weaknesses and malpractices and had offered prescriptions for remedying them.[89] In 1534 the position had become especially disturbing. Although the king had been able to annul his marriage, marry Anne Boleyn, and reject papal authority, he remained profoundly concerned about how the major Catholic rulers, Charles V and Francis I, might react.

[82] Rees, *TCS* (1937), 50.
[83] *LP*, XII/i. 969.
[84] Ibid., XII. 1202.
[85] Ibid., XII/ii. 1057.
[86] G. R. Elton, *Policy and Police* (Cambridge, 1972), *passim*.
[87] D. Mathew, *The Celtic Peoples and Renaissance Europe* (London, 1933), p. 42.
[88] PRO, SP 1/112/201.
[89] *W 1415–1642*, pp. 257–9.

In spite of their incorrigible mutual mistrust, there could be no guarantee that they might not combine – temporarily at least – against England. If they did, then Scotland could be expected to abandon its flimsy truce with Henry and enter into war. Such a prospect made the dangers of rebellion in Ireland and upheaval in Wales all the more frightening. The king and Cromwell were aware that Wales, like the northern borders, Lancashire, and other distant parts of the king's domain, was far from the main seat of power, conservative by religious inclination, and royal power there was more tenuous and insecure than in the more settled and prosperous south and east of England. In his remembrances of 1534 Cromwell betrayed uneasiness about the state of Wales. He made a note that letters should be sent to officers to ensure the apprehension of any papists who preached to the advancement of the bishop of Rome.[90] In May 1534 he took the decisive step of appointing as president of the Council in the Marches one of his more trusted lieutenants, Rowland Lee, bishop of Lichfield, a tough and uncompromising disciplinarian. A few weeks later, on 3 June 1534, the king himself met the Marcher lords at Shrewsbury to draw up a series of ordinances for the stricter enforcement of law and order in the Marches. These measures, together with a series of parliamentary statutes passed in relation to Wales and the Marches in 1534–5,[91] brought the country more securely under royal control. They not only prepared the way for the Act of Union of 1536 but also helped smooth the path for the more effectual propagation of the royal supremacy, even if Lee himself, although a bishop, had to confess to Cromwell, 'I was never hitherto in the pulpit.'[92] Obligingly, he volunteered to venture into such unfamiliar territory if it were thought helpful that he should do so.

Cromwell himself had no illusions about the necessity for presenting the supremacy as widely and as effectively as possible.[93] Thus, for example, the Act against Appeals was printed, and copies of it were published on every parish church door and with them the king's appeal from the pope to a General Council.[94] In Wales such a procedure was likely to have had a limited effect, not only because many of the people, like those of England, were illiterate, but also because they only spoke Welsh and would have found it difficult to get hold of anyone who could read such material to them. More reliance was placed on the spoken word by means of sermons to reinforce the printed one, though the Welsh clergy were not famous for their preaching either. Consequently, the bishops and the more learned

[90] *LP*, VII. 48, 420.
[91] Bowen, *Statutes*, pp. 51–72.
[92] W. Ll. Williams, *The Making of Modern Wales* (London, 1919), p. 53.
[93] Elton, *Policy and Police*, *passim*.
[94] P. Hughes, *The Reformation in England* (3 vols. London, 1950–4), I. 264.

clergy were exhorted to do their utmost; and even more important, specially eloquent preachers and visitors were dispatched to the dioceses to enlighten the locals. In this respect, the government was unusually lucky in Wales, where all four of the dioceses fell vacant between 1534 and 1537. Previously, each of them had had a conservative bishop who had occupied his see for many years and all of whom, to varying degrees, had either been opposed to royal policies or, at best, but lukewarm in their attitude. These vacancies now provided an opportunity to install prelates who might be expected to be more receptive to royally imposed change.

First to fall vacant was the diocese of Bangor, whose old-fashioned and indolent bishop, Thomas Skeffington, had been there since 1509 but had resided for almost the whole of that time at his abbey of Beaulieu in Hampshire. He had died in August 1533. He was replaced by the abbot of the Benedictine abbey of Hyde, John Salcot alias Capon. Salcot was rewarded with Bangor for having hounded the king's influential critic, Elizabeth Barton, the nun of Kent,[95] in a violent sermon preached at the royal instigation. Bishop Standish of St Asaph went next in July 1535. Although originally advanced to St Asaph in 1518 as a result of royal favour for his defence of Henry VIII's position in the Hunne controversy, he had always been a highly conservative theologian. Among other manifestations of his attitudes he had hotly opposed Erasmus, who in turn contemptuously dismissed him as 'St Asse'.[96] Since 1529, at least, he had moved much nearer to Catherine of Aragon and her circle, and he was also in deep trouble at St Asaph on account of his heavy involvement in the accusations of praemunire made against Wolsey.[97] Standish had only lived long enough to take the oath of loyalty a month before he died in July 1535. Despite the manoeuvrings of the dean, Foulk Salusbury, who was eager to secure the diocese for himself, Standish was succeeded by William Barlow, one of the protégés of Anne Boleyn and Cromwell, and a brash young radical in the mould of Latimer and Shaxton. Barlow remained at St Asaph only a few months before being translated to the larger, wealthier, and strategically more significant diocese of St David's in April 1536. Here he took the place of his former antagonist, the aged and hidebound Richard Rawlins. At St Asaph Barlow was quickly succeeded by Robert Wharton, alias Parfew, in May 1536.

In the remaining diocese, that of Llandaff, Athequa was still nominally bishop, even though he spent all his time in attendance upon Catherine of

[95] The Welsh cleric, Richard Gwent, was also prominently involved in examining Elizabeth Barton, *WRE*, p. 78. For Salcot's sermon in summary, *LP*, VII. 72 (3).

[96] D. Knowles, *The Religious Orders in England* (3 vols. Cambridge, 1948–59), III. 54.

[97] D. R. Thomas, *The History of the Diocese of St Asaph* (3 vols. Oswestry, 1908–13), I. 73–5.

Aragon. In spite of being a timid man, he had refused point-blank to take the oath of loyalty and may effectively have been suspended.[98] He was with Catherine at her deathbed in January 1536 and officiated at her funeral. Once she was dead, he found the screws being turned on him. Henry charged him with not silencing those preachers in his diocese who criticized royal policy; Cromwell reminded him of his duty to ensure the elimination of 'such abuses as by the corrupt and unsavoury teaching of the bishop of Rome and his disciples' had crept into the people's hearts.[99] Athequa, defenceless and terrified, 'finding he could not live as a Catholic or preserve his soul in safety' and fearing that Bishop Fisher's fate might befall him too, made plans to escape to his native Spain. As he was on the point of boarding a Flemish vessel in disguise he was arrested after being unwittingly betrayed by a servant who addressed him as 'my lord'. Athequa was now confined to the Tower and remained there until he was released through the good offices of Ambassador Chapuys, who also financed his passage home.[100] He had already resigned his see or been suspended from it some time during the autumn of 1536 and was succeeded in March 1537 by an able Gilbertine monk, Robert Holgate.

These vacancies, fortuitously occurring in the Welsh sees within the space of three or four years, had provided a chance of replacing the whole bench with more pliable new men. But whatever their other qualifications may have been, at a critical time in the fortunes of the Reformation in Wales, none of these bishops was Welsh nor had any previous contacts with their clergy or their flock. The incalculable value of having bishops in Wales with Welsh connections would not be appreciated until the reigns of Mary and Elizabeth.

The Welsh diocese which first felt the force of the wave of propaganda being launched on behalf of the royal supremacy was St David's.[101] Here, the Protestant zealot, William Barlow, was sent to become prior of the Augustinian priory of Haverfordwest, through Anne Boleyn's patronage, in the summer of 1534, just in time to take his oath of loyalty to the Crown in July. It would seem that he had been sent to carry out the same task of Protestant evangelizing at Haverfordwest as another of Anne's dependants, Hugh Latimer, was undertaking in Bristol.[102] Haverfordwest was the chief town of south Pembrokeshire, one of the few parts of Wales where conditions were not entirely unpropitious for the reception of changes in

---

[98] Elton, *Policy and Police*, p. 244.
[99] *LP*, X. 45, 46.
[100] Williams, *GCH*, IV, 204; L. Thomas, *The Reformation in the Old Diocese of Llandaff* (Cardiff, 1930), pp. 3–12. Cf. *CSP Span, Supplem.* II. 234–5, 325, 375, 411.
[101] *WRE*, pp. 111–24.
[102] *DNB*.

religion. In Haverfordwest, easily the largest of the local seaports, there flourished a small, but vigorous, merchant class with contacts in Bristol and other trading centres. There also existed a community of English-speaking inhabitants open to the antipapal literature of the period, as well as to Barlow's fiery sermons. As early as 1535 one of Barlow's servants in the town of Tenby possessed an English New Testament and other similar books. Barlow himself had control of three pulpits out of four in Haverfordwest and others in the vicinity, of which he took full advantage to deliver himself of powerful antipapal orations.

Otherwise, Barlow found circumstances in the area distinctly uncongenial to an enthusiast of his persuasion. The neighbouring cathedral of St David's was one of Wales's most revered pilgrimage centres, the shrine of the national saint, and a hotbed of what Barlow deemed to be superstition and idolatry. The bishop, Richard Rawlins, though not an unlearned man, was old and stubborn. He and most of his clergy were fixedly conservative in their bent, and the laity, according to Barlow, were 'miserably ordered under the clergy'.[103] To strengthen his endeavours 'against Antichrist [i.e. the pope] and all his confederate adherents' and to prosper family fortunes, of which he was ever very tender, Barlow brought three of his brothers with him. John Barlow, also a cleric, was now converted to being a fire-eating antipapist, having been, on his own admission, 'sometime a fautor of the papistical sect'.[104] Roger Barlow, probably the ablest and most interesting of the brothers, was a Bristol merchant, explorer, and author,[105] while the most colourless of the three, Thomas, was another cleric.

Soon after his arrival, William Barlow's impetuosity for religious reform and his appetite for power led him to meddle in the affairs of the diocese in a way which was almost bound to give offence to the bishop and his clergy. His inflammatory sermons evoked the enmity of the Black Friars of Haverfordwest, belonging to the order which more than any other upheld the sacred duty of suppressing heresy. It was one of the friars who, at Bishop Rawlins's instigation, presented a series of articles against Barlow to the king's council.[106] Barlow himself stood too well with Anne Boleyn and Cromwell for his reputation to be damaged by these attacks, but his adversaries had been able to take it out on one of his servants by accusing him of heresy. They ransacked his house at Tenby, seized his English New Testament and other books, 'as if to have the Testament in English were

---

[103] T. Wright, *Three Chapters of Letters relating to the Suppression of the Monasteries* (Camden Soc., London, 1843), p. 77.
[104] *LP*, X. 19.
[105] B. G. Charles, 'The Records of Slebech', *NLWJ*, V (1948), 179–88.
[106] *LP*, XII/i. 93.

horrible heresy',[107] and had him imprisoned. In response, Barlow denounced in unmeasured terms the hostility shown towards himself and his brothers by the clergy. Among the latter, he declared, there was not one 'that sincerely preacheth God's word, nor scarce any that heartily favoureth it, but all utter enemies thereagainst'. Barlow condemned the backwardness of the diocese in general, with its 'enormous vices, fraudulent exactions, misordered living and heathen idolatry'. No diocese, he claimed, was 'more corrupted, nor none so far out of frame' or more in need of redress.[108] The redress which he badly wanted to bring about was the appointment of himself as suffragan bishop, and he succeeded in obtaining from Cromwell letters to that effect. He was soon to protest on 19 March 1535 that these missives were being studiously ignored or opposed by the bishop and his officers. A fortnight later, on 31 March, John Barlow wrote to Anne Boleyn's vice-chamberlain to explain how hostile the bishop and his coterie were towards William, 'whom of all men they most hate for his preaching'. He added that opposition was also being stirred up among gentry and commoners, and nowhere worse than in Anne's own lordship of Pembroke,[109] so dangerously situated in relation to Ireland.

It may very well have been the Barlow brothers who carried tales about the 'unsoundness' of Rawlins's views concerning purgatory. The bishop admitted that he believed it was meet to pray for the souls of the departed but without specifying any particular place where they might be. He firmly denied, however, any intention of reviving the popish purgatory or any suggestion that expiatory acts such as offering candles, buying indulgences, or saying Paternosters before an appointed altar could release souls from purgatory.[110] Ironically enough, a year or two later, William Barlow was himself to be denounced for the very advanced views he held concerning the non-existence of purgatory. In the early summer of 1535 he was removed from Haverfordwest to become prior of Bisham and later in the year was dispatched on an important diplomatic mission to Scotland. St David's had not heard the last of him, however. In the spring of 1536, having successfully survived the disgrace of his patronness, Anne Boleyn, he was to return there as bishop.

In the north-western diocese of Bangor its new bishop, John Salcot, was trying hard to 'accomplish the diligent setting forth and sincere preaching . . . of the royal supremacy'. In June 1535 he had to confess that he found himself gravely embarrassed because he had no knowledge of the language

---

[107] Wright, *Suppression*, pp. 77–80; *LP*, IX. 1091.
[108] Wright, *Suppression*, p. 79.
[109] *LP*, VIII. 412, 466.
[110] Ibid., X. 225. This document is dated 1536, but since Rawlins died in February 1536, it ought probably to have been dated in the previous year.

generally spoken in this, the most thoroughly Welsh of all the dioceses of Wales. Nevertheless, he thought that he might be able to attain his ends by making use of other preachers for the same purpose.[111] Among those he may have had in mind were the royal visitors, Adam Becansaw and John Vaughan, already active in his diocese proclaiming the supremacy and enforcing order. One of their major tasks was tightening up discipline in relation to clerical 'marriages' and concubinage. The outcome was that in January 1536 the diocesan clergy sent a petition to Cromwell admitting that they had recently been 'detected of incontinency . . . and not unworthily'. They begged for 'remission or at the least wise of merciful punishment and correction', and pleaded to be allowed to 'maintain and uphold such poor hospitality as we have done hitherto and most by the provision of such women as we have customarily kept in our houses'. Otherwise, they would not be able to relieve the poor because they would be driven to live in taverns and alehouses since there were no clerical residences attached to their benefices. They touchingly confessed that gentlemen and substantial honest men, 'knowing our frailty and accustomed liberty, will in no wise board us in their houses'.[112] Their other submission was that an alarming effect of the changes in religion had been that laymen seized upon them as an excuse for not rendering to the clergy their tithes and customary offerings. Some corroboration of this may be found in contemporary Chancery lawsuits.[113]

Another complication for Salcot was that the royal supremacy became an issue in faction contests which really had very little to do with religion. If rival factions were fighting for the king's ear at the centre of government,[114] on a local scale there were also parties engaged in power struggles which became identified with an apparent zeal for reform or an alleged reluctance to embrace new ways. That earlier feud between Bulkeley and Glyn, which went back at least as far as 1524, flared up more violently than ever in 1535–6. Bulkeley, formerly Wolsey's agent in Gwynedd, was now one of Cromwell's confidants. His enemies accused him of overbearing pride and ambition, saying that he would 'suffer no man to live in the country but himself'.[115] Chief among his opponents were Edward Gruffydd, descendant of the Penrhyn family which had long held major crown office in north Wales, and William Glyn, who, though a cleric, was described as a man of 'stirring spirit', having 'a hand in all the temporal affairs of the country as

---

[111] Ibid., VIII. 832–3.
[112] PRO, SP1/101/205–6.
[113] PRO, C1/1977/23–4; 952/60; cf. *WC*, p. 552.
[114] E. W. Ives, 'Faction at the court of Henry VIII', *History*, LVII (1972), 169–88.
[115] PRO, SP1/93/175–6.

well as spiritual'.[116] Glyn had embraced, or assumed, markedly anti-Romanist attitudes. He informed Cromwell in November 1535 that, in the diocese of Bangor, as a result of the royal visitors' efforts, the sale of indulgences and the 'mart of vice' were now 'greatly decayed and would be even more reduced if the great maintainer of them, the bishop of Rome, were expelled from men's hearts'.[117] It was Glyn who lay behind the protest of Richard Gibbons, Salcot's registrar, against the sale of indulgences by Robert Oking, the bishop's commissary (the post held by Glyn in Skeffington's episcopate). Such an allegation put Bulkeley on the spot, since it would not do for him to be suspected of propapal sympathies. He therefore testified warmly to Oking's loyalty by claiming that the latter 'spoke as much at all times in the annulling of the bishop of Rome's authority as any man that I know in these parts'.[118] He also hinted that the whole charge against Oking was a malicious conspiracy concocted by Glyn with the intention of recovering his former office. In further letters Bulkeley continued to complain to Cromwell of his enemies' antipathy towards him; ill will inspired, he claimed, by the fear of the serious charges he could bring against them.[119] By early 1536, however, both parties were in Cromwell's bad books. Glyn was summoned to London to answer charges of gross pluralism, of sixteen years of non-residence, and of assessing himself for being liable for only 10s. in taxation when he should have paid £20.[120] What brought Bulkeley into grave danger was a more serious conjunction of religion, politics, and royal matrimonial discord. On 2 May 1536 his brother Roland had written to him giving him news of Anne Boleyn's downfall and the complicity in her disgrace of Henry Norris, chamberlain of north Wales, with whom Richard Bulkeley had been closely associated. Roland Bulkeley urged his brother to repair to court without delay so as to safeguard his interests.[121] Although Richard managed to survive this crisis successfully, he was by no means out of the wood with regard to his relations with Glyn and Gruffydd.

Richard Bulkeley had also been tussling with Ellis Price, another of the royal commissioners, over the abbey of Conwy. Price was exerting himself to secure the election of his brother, Richard ap Robert, as abbot. Bulkeley protested to Cromwell that if Richard were chosen he would 'utterly destroy the said abbey within short space'. If, on the other hand, Cromwell were to support Bulkeley's favoured candidate, David Owen, 'an honest

---

[116] John Wynn, *The Gwydir Family*, ed. J. Ballinger (Cardiff, 1927), p. 65.

[117] BL, Harleian MS. 604, f. 69; cf. *LP* IX, 748.

[118] PRO, SP1/92/134–5.

[119] Ibid., 93/175–6.

[120] Ibid., 102/84–6; C66/667, m. 12.

[121] *LP*, X. 785.

man meet to be the ruler of such a house', he was promised £100 for his pains. Yet Ellis Price's influence proved to be too strong – or his purse too long – because it was his brother who was unanimously chosen as abbot.[122] Ellis Price and William Glyn had further busied themselves with discipline in another monastic house in the diocese, that of Penmon in Anglesey, a house right on Bulkeley's doorstep and of which he was steward. By shutting up the prior in his own monastery and requiring him to forward documents relating to its foundation, they had grievously displeased Bulkeley, who now offered Cromwell twenty nobles, to be followed by twenty marks, for his favour to the prior.[123]

From Bangor the visitors moved on to the diocese of St Asaph. Here they had another troubled monastic house to deal with. The abbot of Valle Crucis, Robert Salusbury, had already been found guilty of highway robbery and a successor to him had to be found.[124] The diocese itself was vacant as a result of the death of Henry Standish, the disposal of whose goods led to considerable wrangling.[125] When his body was barely cold, active canvassing for the succession was going on. Once again the key arbiter was Cromwell, for whose favour there was lively competition. The abbot of Wigmore, in spite of his dubious conduct as suffragan bishop of Llandaff, put himself forward as a suitable candidate, while the dean of St Asaph, Foulk Salusbury, who claimed to have been chaplain to Henry VII and Henry VIII for thirty-two years, offered to put his deanery at Cromwell's disposal in return for his help to become bishop.[126] In the event, neither was chosen and the prize fell to William Barlow. For his part, Adam Becansaw was more concerned to regale Cromwell with the shortcomings of his fellow-commissioner, Ellis Price. He had been obstructive over Standish's possessions; even worse, he was bringing his colleagues into disrepute by 'riding about openly with his concubine' and rejecting all admonitions that he should abandon 'such young touches'.[127] These reproaches by Becansaw, supported by Vaughan, led to Cromwell's ordering Price to give up the visitation, despite a plea from Rowland Lee on his behalf that he was young and 'no tree grows to be an oak at first day'.[128] Price himself wrote in contrite tones conveying his regret that he

---

[122] R. W. Hays, *The History of the Abbey of Aberconway 1186–1537* (Cardiff, 1963), pp. 160–1.

[123] *LP*, IX. 566.

[124] *WC*, p. 403.

[125] Thomas, *St Asaph*, I. 75.

[126] *LP*, VIII. 1073, 1015.

[127] Ibid., IX. 607, 608.

[128] Ibid., 841.

had ever 'meddled with the business, especially if you are displeased and I am brought to ridicule'.[129]

Becansaw and Vaughan, meanwhile, were proceeding briskly to reform such abuses as they found in St Asaph. The many priests who shamelessly kept women at their disposal were, like those of Bangor diocese, appropriately disciplined. The lay people, too, 'not only the good but also the bad', enlightened by preachers commissioned to denounce the pope and his errors, were said to be grateful for being called from 'their sinful living'. They assembled to hear sermons and repent their wickedness. The visitors maintained that at a sermon recently preached by a BD at Gresford no fewer than a thousand were present, and people everywhere were declaring that they had been 'deceived by priests in churches'. This led Becansaw and Vaughan to express the hope that they would soon bring Wales into as 'good a trade as any part of England';[130] sanguine expectations which could hardly be said to have been fulfilled.

The visitors now made their way to south Wales and were at Llandaff cathedral on 11 November 1535. There they found plenty to criticize. In the continued absence of Bishop Athequa, he and his archdeacon, John Quarr, had been guilty 'not only of great ruin and decay of their mansions but of other great faults as you will see by our registry of visitations' – which has, alas, long since disappeared.[131] The visitors took steps to remedy these shortcomings and, in the negligence of the bishop 'to declare to the people the word of God', to depute preachers to fulfil this duty.[132]

From Llandaff they proceeded to the diocese of St David's. Unfortunately, no reports of their proceedings in this the largest of the Welsh dioceses, covering three-quarters of south Wales, seem to have survived except for their comments on Carmarthen priory and Brecon priory. They had moved back eastwards and reached Brecon by 1 March 1536. Writing from there, they were sharply critical of some of the monasteries. By 28 April Vaughan was reporting to Cromwell that the visitation of Wales had been completed.

Along with the assertion and enforcement of the royal supremacy, plans could be prepared for the exploitation of its financial possibilities. Already, the Act in Restraint of Annates (1534) had decreed that annates (i.e. the first year's revenues of an ecclesiastical benefice) were no longer to be rendered to the papal curia, and the Act for First Fruits and Tenths (1534) provided for these payments in future to be made to the Crown. This Act

---

[129] Ibid., 843.
[130] Ibid., 608.
[131] PRO, SP1/99/35; cf. *LP*, IX. 806.
[132] Ibid., 102/142; cf. *LP*, X. 393.

also laid down that local commissioners under the Great Seal were to inquire into the true annual value of the amounts due. Some of Cromwell's memoranda of 1534 suggest that he was turning over in his mind schemes for making his master the richest ruler in Christendom by expropriating ecclesiastical resources.[133] Whatever measures might ultimately be adopted, an essential preliminary to them would be as comprehensive and accurate a report as possible on the property of the Church. So, on 30 January 1535, commissions of inquiry were set in train which were to produce that extraordinary Domesday Book of the Church in England and Wales – the *Valor Ecclesiasticus*.[134]

The membership of each commission consisted of the bishop of the diocese along with a number of prominent laymen. For the two northern Welsh sees, the same panel of commissioners, with the exception of the bishop, was appointed for each. The leading figure among them, Richard Bulkeley, regarded the responsibility as a more than usually demanding one, 'knowing how barbarous and ignorant I and the gentlemen of the country are'. He claimed that they had done their best to get the parson and four reliable persons in each parish to declare the true value of the benefice, but in some instances they found other people coming forward with evidence of higher value.[135] From Llandaff, too, there is evidence which suggests that difficulties were encountered in conducting the inquiry. In spite of the impressive list of commissioners for the diocese, including Herberts, Carnes, and Mathews, only one of them in fact seems to have done most of the work. He was Sir William Morgan, who appears to have completed his task in the astonishingly short space of four months, between June and October 1535. How this came about he explained in letters written to Cromwell in August and October. Because the bishop (Athequa) was non-resident and the other commissioners lived 'forty or fifty miles asunder', he wrote, 'I could not have them together and many of them did little or nothing in executing the effects of the commission.' He had often inquired after the two auditors but 'could have no knowledge of them',[136] so he had to perform his task as best he might without their professional help. He asked Cromwell whether he should send up the books as they were or would Cromwell wish to 'appoint some auditor to come to me for the engrossment of the said books after the auditor's fashion'.[137] No auditor came, and Morgan did his best, with the help of Archdeacon

---

[133] BL, Cleopatra E. iv. 174; cf. *LP*, VII. 1355.
[134] The returns for the Welsh dioceses are printed in *Valor Ecclesiasticus* (6 vols. Record Commission, 1810–34), IV.
[135] *LP*, VIII. 599.
[136] PRO, SP1/98/86–7.
[137] Ibid., 95/167–8.

Quarr. He performed his task uncommonly well for the Monmouthshire deaneries, which are much the best returns surviving from any part of Wales. He wrote to Cromwell with justifiable pride on 27 October,

> I have sent a book . . . in as perfect a manner as I and my friends could devise possible; which book I do not doubt but it shall amount above any 'presidens' [?precedents] that any bishop in the diocese of Llandaff could make, as Master Quarr, archdeacon of Llandaff, can inform your mastership the very truth of the same.[138]

Not all the returns in the *Valor* were as full and informative as those of William Morgan; nevertheless, it is a remarkably full, accurate, and valuable document, which for centuries afterwards was used as the basis of all estimates made of the value of church property.

During the first six months of 1536 there occurred two events which might well have brought Henry VIII's Reformation to an abrupt end, had it sprung from nothing more than the consequences of his troubled amours. Catherine of Aragon, after years of humiliation, had died in January. Only a few months later, in June, her rival Anne Boleyn, having failed to produce a male heir and disgraced by accusations of adultery, was executed.[139] Anne had never been popular in Wales, even though one of its leading aristocrats, the earl of Worcester, had taken a prominent part in her coronation and in the christening of her baby daughter, the future Queen Elizabeth.[140] A Welsh chronicler, Ellis Gruffudd, the soldier of Calais was also able to treat her downfall sympathetically in his chronicle – presumably on account of his sympathies as a reformer. But a more typical expression of the long-suppressed Welsh dislike of her may have found expression in a vitriolic attack by the poet Lewis Morgannwg, who castigated her as the reincarnation of Rhonwen and Alice, the classical symbols in Welsh verse of English treachery.[141] He denounced her as a woman of inferior birth, unworthy of the king's trust, who ended up by betraying him. Once Anne was dead, many observers, pre-eminent among them Charles V, were sure that the crisis was over and that the errant Henry might now be reconciled to the pope. They were abruptly disillusioned; the king was to show that much more had been at stake than the divorce of his

[138] Ibid, 98/86–7. There is a careful analysis of returns for Llandaff in Thomas, *Llandaff*, chap. 2.

[139] Ives, *Anne Boleyn*; G. W. Bernard, 'The fall of Anne Boleyn', *EHR*, CVI (1991), 584–610.

[140] E. J. Saunders, 'Gweithiau Lewis Morgannwg' (MA thesis, Wales, 1922), pp. 200–2.

[141] Traditionally, they were the daughters of Hengist and were responsible, along with their father, for bringing about the legendary massacre of the Welsh, 'Brad y Cyllyll Hirion' ('The Treachery of the Long Knives').

wife and a marriage to his mistress. He had not the slightest intention of backtracking from any of the immense gains in jurisdiction accruing to him as result of establishing his supremacy over the Church. On the contrary, the stage was set for the next major phase in the drama – expropriating a large part of the wealth of ecclesiastics.

CHAPTER 4

The Houses of Religion Dissolved

THE targets towards which the king's vice-gerent, Thomas Cromwell, was turning his eyes in 1534–5 were the houses of religion. In the *Valor Ecclesiasticus* of 1535, newly compiled at his instigation, they had been estimated to be worth £160,000–£200,00 per annum, to which those of Wales contributed just over £3,000.[1] Generously endowed by the piety of laymen over many centuries, these sixteenth-century monasteries were the descendants of an ancient tradition. In Wales, they went back a thousand years or more to the fifth century AD, when monasteries were first founded by the Celtic 'saints'.[2] Those early foundations had differed in a number of respects from the Latin-style institutions by which they were superseded from the eleventh century onwards with the advent of the Normans. The new Benedictine houses established by these intruders were small and poorly endowed cells, daughter houses of larger abbeys in France or England favoured by the conquerors. Throughout their history they had remained alien outposts having little contact with the native population. In any event, most of them were too small, both on account of the fewness of their monks and the slenderness of their possessions, to have made any significant contribution to monastic life in Wales. Some were hardly more than distant rent-collecting agencies for their mother house.[3]

They had been followed in the twelfth century by the far better-loved order of the Cistercians, in whose midst the largest and best-known monasteries of Wales were to be found.[4] Most of the fifteen Welsh Cistercian houses were the creation of a vigorous stream of missionary zeal which flowed into all parts of Wales during the twelfth and thirteenth

---

[1] *WC*, pp. 561–3.
[2] E. G. Bowen, *The Settlements of the Celtic Saints in Wales* (Cardiff, 1954); idem, *Saints, Seaways and Settlements in Celtic Lands* (Cardiff, 1977); W. Davies, *Wales in the Later Middle Ages* (Leicester, 1982).
[3] J. C. Davies, *Episcopal Acts relating to Welsh Dioceses, 1066–1272* (2 vols. Cardiff, 1946–8); F. G. Cowley, *The Monastic Order in South Wales, 1066–1349* (Cardiff, 1977).
[4] J. F. O'Sullivan, *Cistercian Settlements in Wales and Monmouthshire, 1140–1540* (New York, 1947); D. H. Williams, *The Welsh Cistercians* (2 vols. Tenby, 1983, 1985); Cowley, *Monastic Order*.

centuries. It not only served to elicit handsome gifts of land for the order from Welsh princes and aristocrats, many of whom sought to be buried within Cistercian precincts, but also endeared the order to their subjects. Cistercian houses had been universally venerated as centres of dynamic activity and inspiration in the religious, economic, cultural, and patriotic aspirations of the country.

Half a dozen houses of Augustinian canons and one Premonstratensian abbey (Talley) were founded in much the same period. Some of them, like Bardsey or Beddgelert, were old pre-Norman *clasau* refounded as houses of canons, while others, such as Carmarthen or Haverfordwest, were established in major Norman boroughs. Though nothing like as influential as the Cistercian foundations, they were, nevertheless, widely respected.

A fresh wave of spiritual activity, designed to bring the religious into closer contact with the world outside their cloisters, had led in the thirteenth century to the formation of the orders of friars.[5] The Dominicans succeeded in founding five houses, the Franciscans three, and the Carmelites and Austin friars one each. Although both the main orders were directed from England – the Dominicans from Oxford and the Franciscans from Bristol[6] – the friars were undoubtedly successful in Wales, where they became very familiar figures as preachers, confessors, scholars, and littérateurs. But because their existence was closely geared to a dependence on towns, both for their sites and their support, their expansion in Wales was hampered by the underdeveloped state of Welsh towns, which were small in size, few in number, and mostly scattered around the perimeter of the country.

There were in all about fifty houses of religion in Wales in their heyday during the twelfth and thirteenth centuries.[7] Nearly all of them were intended for men, with only three small nunneries for women – two Cistercian at Llanllŷr and Llanllugan, and one Benedictine at Usk.[8] Monasteries of all kinds were far thinner on the ground than they were in England; whereas there was one to every ten English parishes, in Wales they numbered one to about every twenty parishes. For Tudor England and Wales as a whole there were about 9,300 religious out of a population of *c.*3.5 million;[9] in Wales there were only about 250 religious out of a population estimated at *c.*250,000, i.e. one to every 1,000 as compared with one to 375 in England. Such estimates, of course, take no account of the wide differences in topography and prosperity between the north-west and

[5] Easterling, *AC* (1914), 323–56.
[6] W. Rees, 'The suppression of the friaries', *SWMRS*, III (1954), 7–19.
[7] There were forty-seven at the dissolution, but four had earlier been lost.
[8] Two Cistercian nunneries at Llanllŷr and Llanllugan, and one Benedictine at Usk.
[9] G. W. O. Woodward, *The Dissolution of the Monasteries* (London, 1968), p. 2.

south-east of Britain. A mere glance at the map of monastic Britain[10] at once reveals that in the upland region of England monasteries were about as few and far between as they were in Wales, although it remains true that there were more of them in the single large county of Yorkshire than in the whole of Wales. Within Wales itself, most of the religious houses were concentrated in the more fertile areas of the south and east, with twelve houses in the former county of Monmouthshire and seven in old Pembrokeshire. In the south-eastern diocese of Llandaff, the one best endowed with monastic foundations, four-ninths of the diocesan revenue went to the monasteries and no less than thirteen-fourteenths of that income was drawn from the lowlands of the diocese.[11] Even then, the Welsh houses were never remotely as wealthy as they were on average in England. The great majority of the Welsh houses would have been placed in the category of small ones (of less than £150 yearly income, with many less than £100); a handful would have scraped in at the bottom end of the category of middling to small ones (£750 a year to £150); and none at all would have figured in the group of large and wealthy ones (£750 a year and upwards).[12] The resources of all the Welsh houses as estimated in the *Valor Ecclesiasticus*, if put together, only came to £3,178 and were comfortably exceeded by those of a single great house like Westminster (£3,740) or Glastonbury (£3,511). A more meaningful comparison, however, remembering how much poorer most parts of Wales were than many regions in England, is to set the income of Welsh monks alongside that of typical Welsh ecclesiastical landowners. Several Welsh abbots enjoyed an annual income considerably larger than that of the three poorest Welsh bishops. Twelve of them were better off than his lordship of Bangor (£131), seven wealthier than Llandaff (£144) and two more comfortably placed than St Asaph (£187).[13] So that the gibe made by the poet, Lewys Môn, that mere bishops were only too eager to snap up rags belonging to a leading Cistercian abbot, Dafydd ab Owain, was not wholly without foundation.[14]

During the fourteenth and fifteenth centuries, the fortunes of Welsh monasteries, like those elsewhere, had changed for the worse. They had had to face long years of difficulty and even disaster. This was a trying period for landowners, big and small, secular and ecclesiastical. Many had had to give up their former practice of direct cultivation of their estates and been obliged to let out large portions to tenants. Such a trend had been

---

[10] *Map of Monastic Britain* (2 sheets, Ordnance Survey, 1950).
[11] L. Thomas, *The Reformation in the Old Diocese of Llandaff* (Cardiff, 1930), pp. 24–8.
[12] *WC*, pp. 345–9.
[13] D. H. Williams, *Atlas of Cistercian Lands* (Cardiff, 1990).
[14] *WC*, pp. 345–9; see the whole of chap. 10 for their economic circumstances.

particularly noticeable among the great pioneers of direct farming among the monks – the Cistercians. By the end of the Middle Ages their *conversi* or lay brothers, who had in earlier days worked most of their granges, were but a distant memory, and the land was being rented and worked by laymen, though the monks may still have kept a watchful eye on what was being done by their tenants. Again, the long-drawn-out wars with France brought further troubles in their wake. They led to heavy taxation, depreciation of the currency, and closer control of monastic life in his own interest by the king. Moreover, the wars, by cutting off Cistercians off from regular contact with their mother houses of Cîteaux and Clairvaux, adversely affected discipline. Those Benedictine priories whose mother houses were situated in France were particularly hard hit; the result was that in the fifteenth century, three of them, Llangenydd, St Clear's, and Goldcliff, were suppressed and their possessions forfeited to the Crown.

To add to the difficulties, the Black Death of 1348–50 and later outbreaks of plague, by sharply reducing the population, made it subsequently more difficult to recruit monks. From the later fourteenth century onwards the position was aggravated by what appears to have been a marked tendency towards reducing overheads by deliberately restricting numbers. Finally, between the years 1400 and 1415 had come the Glyndŵr Rebellion, with its accompanying devastation. When that hurricane of destruction had eventually blown itself out, it left most Welsh monasteries in pitiable plight. The tiny priory at Cardiff disappeared altogether and the larger Cistercian house at Cwm-hir never really recovered. Even the celebrated monastery at Strata Florida, burial place of a dozen princes and once proud home to *Brut y Tywysogyon*, the chronicle that recorded the deeds of Welsh rulers, was pillaged by royal troops and its monks expelled.[15] Margam, one of the largest houses in Wales, was described in 1412 as being utterly shattered, so that its abbot and monks were forced to wander about like vagabonds.[16] The effects of the Rebellion, coming on top of the protracted earlier tribulations, had reduced Welsh monastic life to its lowest ebb ever.[17]

In spite of everything, almost all the monasteries had survived and, during the fifteenth century, a number of them achieved a remarkable recovery. Not even all the alien priories disappeared; Monmouth, Abergavenny, Chepstow, and Pembroke all contrived to patch up new arrangements with English houses which enabled them to continue their existence. Gradually, additional monks were recruited in many houses,

[15] Ibid., p. 231.
[16] Ibid.
[17] Ibid., pp. 219–31.

services and worship were restored to something akin to normality, and buildings were repaired. In some instances, new work was undertaken, though usually for the less than wholly estimable practice of creating an abbot's residence.[18] Pilgrims in growing numbers were once again encouraged to visit famous shrines at monasteries or associated with them, like Llantarnam's shrine of Our Lady at Pen-rhys in Glamorgan or Basingwerk's well of St Winifred at Holywell. They were also attracted by the well-organized traffic in indulgences, now offered at most of the religious houses. One of the latter, Strata Marcella, in dire need of additional revenues, was enterprising enough to obtain a supply of printed indulgences in 1528,[19] and other houses may have done the same. The Cistercians, especially, enjoyed something of a late Indian summer. Two of their outstanding abbots, Dafydd ap Ieuan of Valle Crucis and Dafydd ab Owain of Conwy, were consecrated bishops of St Asaph during Henry VII's reign; while their young contemporary, Leyshon Thomas of Neath, became a prominent figure in his order as a visitor and reformer.[20]

Nevertheless, the monks had not fully recovered from the trials of an earlier period. They may be likened to an individual who, having survived a series of heart attacks, came through them but only to lead a distinctly more supine existence. By the sixteenth century, the only Welsh monastery certainly maintaining the twelve monks believed to be the minimum needed to maintain a full round of prayer and worship was Tintern; though Carmarthen may earlier just have come within that bracket.[21] Reduced numbers were bound to have a serious detrimental effect on conventual life. They led to the contraction of worship, the abandonment of aspects of the life in common, the inability to give novices all the training they needed, and the gradual emergence of complacency about a state of things which worked towards the negation of the life professed.[22] It was hardly surprising that an energetic Cistercian reformer should have complained how many of the Welsh Cistercians had 'digressed from the path of holy religion in habit and tonsure and in other usages'. By 'other usages' he may well have been referring to abbots who fathered children, as at least three of them are known to have done.[23] Though the smaller number of monks did not lead to the complete disappearance of praiseworthy activities previously associated with monasteries – the maintenance of scholarship

---

[18] Ibid., pp. 387–8.
[19] E. Owen, 'Strata Marcella immediately before and after its dissolution', *Cymm.* XXIX (1919), 1–18.
[20] *W and R*, pp. 86–90.
[21] *LP*, XII/ii. 277.
[22] P. Hughes, *The Reformation in England* (3 vols. London, 1950–4), I. 40–1.
[23] Williams, *Welsh Cistercians*, p. 50.

and learning, the provision of hospitality, and the distribution of alms and charity – all these things were less in evidence than they had been. Not a few houses were seriously encumbered with debts and financial difficulties.[24] A further source of weakness which had become evident as the monasteries sank deeper into the landscape around them was the growth of lay influence. The surrounding gentry, in their capacity as monastic stewards or bailiffs, and, not infrequently, as relatives or patrons of the abbot, exercised a degree of control over the monasteries which was not conducive to the latter's spiritual health and welfare.[25] Had there not been so painfully apparent a slackness and lack of inspiration among the religious, the government's case against the monks on the moral issue could hardly have carried such weight or won over so many of the laity when the dissolution came.

Yet there are risks in generalizing too freely about the condition of the Welsh monasteries in the early sixteenth century. The truth is that there is hardly any information available at all about many of them. There are no detailed records of episcopal visitations such as those which exist for the dioceses of Norwich and Lincoln. From Cromwell's visitors of 1535–6 only about a dozen letters have survived and some of those are not concerned with religious houses. The only evidence which exists in reasonably ample quantity is a body of Cistercian correspondence and the native poetry addressed to Welsh abbots.[26] Although that consists of the testimony of friends commissioned to praise their mentors for stock upper-class virtues, cautiously used, it can be of considerable value. Even the verse, however, is confined to a limited number of heads of larger abbeys, and all of what it says may not be applicable to other convents. So we are obliged to make the best use we can of such scraps of evidence as have come down to us.

A feature that becomes immediately apparent is that conditions might vary markedly as between one house and another. Thus, Neath abbey under its last abbot passed through a distinguished phase in its history. Leyshon Thomas, abbot from c.1509 to 1539, proved to be one of its most successful heads. Ordained at Hereford in 1509, he may have become abbot in that year before graduating BA and BCL at Oxford in 1510 and BD in 1512. He quickly became recognized by his order as the foremost abbot in Wales and in 1517 and 1518 acted as visitor on behalf of the chapter-general. Among his other duties he was obliged to remove his brother abbot, Dafydd, from neighbouring Margam for misconduct. High in the counsels of his order, Leyshon Thomas carried out further visitations on

[24] Ibid., pp. 108–9.
[25] *WC*, pp. 369–70.
[26] *WC*, chap. 11; C. T. B. Davies, 'Y cerddi i'r tai crefydd fel ffynhonnell hanesyddol', *NLWJ*, XVIII (1974), 268–86, 345–73.

its behalf in England, Wales and Ireland, and possibly France. When in 1532 the king wished to keep out of his realm Cistercian visitors from France, he chose Leyshon Thomas as one of the five abbots of the order deputed for the purpose of visiting all its houses in England, Wales, Ireland, and the Isle of Man.[27] Echoes of his widespread reputation and activity may be heard in Lewis Morgannwg's famous poem praising Neath as 'the admiration of England, the lamp of France and Ireland'. Even if some of the bardic extravagance of Lewis's encomiums is discounted, it cannot be denied that no other Welsh abbot of Henry VIII's reign comes anywhere near achieving the distinction which Leyshon Thomas enjoyed.[28]

The general condition of an Augustinian house, Carmarthen priory, was the subject of a report by royal agents. Its favourable tone may owe much to the good sense of Carmarthen's prior, Griffith Williams, who spared no pains in making his visitors welcome, furnishing excellent hospitality for them and generally being very co-operative. The report produced on his house was an unusually favourable one and much the most enthusiastic contemporary comment available on any Welsh monastery on the eve of the dissolution. Described as being very well built and in a sound state of repair, it boasted lodgings which were still in a fit state to receive royalty. Until just previously it was said to have had twelve canons, though at the time of writing there were only eight, all of whom were of good report. Eighty people were dependent on it for their livelihood; weekly charity was dispensed to another eighty poor people; and hospitality was daily offered to rich and poor of 'this notable market town and common thoroughfare'. Strangers and merchants were so warmly received there that the king of Portugal had gone out of his way to express his thanks for the treatment accorded to his subjects.[29]

In sharp contrast to the flourishing state of Neath and Carmarthen, the priory of Monmouth had seen its head being deposed in 1534 by the bishop of Hereford.[30] Conditions were no better when the visitors, Vaughan and Becansaw, visited the place in 1535. Writing to Cromwell about what he had discovered there, Vaughan was scandalized to find that there 'was no pot, nor pan, nor monk in the said house, except one who boards in the town. The prior is in sanctuary in Garway' (a Hospitallers' house just over the border in Herefordshire). 'It is of the king's foundation and all the country marvels that there is no reformation as it can spend £60 a year, all charges borne.' He went on to say, 'I intend to suppress the said

---

[27] *LP*, V. 978 (6).

[28] *W and R*, pp. 86–90.

[29] *LP*, X. 1246.

[30] K. E. Kissack, 'Religious life in Monmouth, 1066–1536', *JHSCW*, XIV (1964), 25–58.

house, for the voice of the country is that while ye have monks there, ye shall have neither good rule nor good order there; and I hear such saying by the common people of all the houses of monks that ye have in Wales.'[31] Vaughan may well have been laying it on rather heavily, secure in the knowledge that what he had to say in such a context would be sweet music in Cromwell's ears. But it has to be remembered that the visitors had already encountered three large, well-known Cistercian houses in north Wales – Conwy, Valle Crucis, and Strata Marcella – all of which were heavily encumbered with debt; they were to visit two others in the south – Brecon and Tintern – which they would censure as being 'greatly abused' and 'having transgressed the king's injunctions',[32] and a third, Margam, where two abbots had been deposed within a short period for various misdeeds. While it would be wise to take what the visitors said with a pinch of salt because they were known to be looking for immorality and shortcomings to justify a possible dissolution, it would be equally prudent not to suppose that this was all smoke without any fire.

It was not only as between houses that conditions could vary; they could also change dramatically within the same house over a short period. Valle Crucis provides a striking example of rapid deterioration of this sort. Earlier on in the sixteenth century, under the rule of capable abbots like Dafydd ab Ieuan and Siôn Llwyd (John Lloyd), it had been in prosperous condition. In March 1528, however, Robert Salusbury, one of the powerful local family of that name, had been placed there as abbot by Cardinal Wolsey – presumably as a result of the same dynastic influence which had contrived to put the deanery of St Asaph in the way of his kinsman, Foulk Salusbury, with comparably disastrous consequences. In August of 1534, Abbot Robert was accused by Leyshon Thomas, accompanied by the abbots of Aberconwy, Cymer, and Cwm-hir, of many 'crimes and excesses'.[33] He could offer no more convincing defence than charging his accusers with 'being informers and polluted with divers crimes, excesses, and enormities, so that by law they were not able to accuse him'[34] – a rebuttal which the visitors indignantly refused to accept. When Vaughan and Becansaw arrived on the scene in 1535 they found that Salusbury and some confederates had been involved in highway robbery, for which they arrested him and an apostate monk, and imprisoned them.[35]

Strata Marcella was another house in sharp decline in the 1520s. The abbot there was John Price, son of Robert ap Rhys, installed as head at his

---

[31] PRO, SP1/102, fo. 142; *LP*, X. 898.
[32] *LP*, X. 393.
[33] BL, Stowe MS. 141, fo. 23.
[34] Ibid.
[35] PRO, SP1/92, fos. 233–6; *WC*, p. 403.

father's prompting, no doubt. Price found his house deep in debt and in ruinous condition. In addition to commercializing the sale of indulgences, he found he had to borrow to meet his needs and virtually to put himself in pawn to Lord Powys.[36]

Basingwerk, too, had fallen under undue lay influence – in this instance into the hands of the Pennant family. Abbot Thomas Pennant would appear to have left the abbey to marry a wife, Angharad or Mallt, by whom he had a large family. He was succeeded as abbot by his son, Nicholas, who may have been illegitimate. He, in turn, was accused of having openly declared that he proposed to retain the vicarage of Holywell in order to hand it on to his own son, as his father had done before him.[37]

Strata Florida, illustrious as it had for long been, was also a monastery whose buildings were now not in a good state and where discipline again was lax. Here, the charge of counterfeiting was brought against one of its monks, Richard Smith. He himself claimed that he was an innocent man falsely accused, and, since he was still a monk at Strata Florida when the abbey was dissolved, that may well be so. However, as the historian of Strata Florida rightly observed, 'even if he was not technically guilty, a man who could, on his own showing, drink casually with a weaver at an alehouse and who was at least not uninterested in the art of coining was hardly a monk with the highest sense of vocation'.[38] More destructive of the spirit of true monastic life than the escapades of this silly and gullible monk was the continuance of those internal feuds which had often bedevilled Strata Florida in the past. In 1534 Rowland Lee once more had to intervene in a quarrel between the abbot and one of his monks. On instructions from Cromwell he put the abbot in 'quiet possession and swore the monk to obedience'.[39]

From what is known, therefore, of the monasteries on the eve of the dissolution it would appear that laymen had acquired too much opportunity to manipulate, and even coerce, the monks in their own interest. The greatest authority on English monasticism, David Knowles, drew attention to the corrupting influence of the gentry when he wrote that it was 'difficult to think of an age in which unselfishness, devotion to an ideal, faithfulness to a master or a friend were rarer in public life, or one in which lust for material gain was greater'.[40] Coupled with this materialistic outlook went a widespread submission to the king's will on the gentry's

---

[36] Owen, *Cymm*, XXIX, 1–18.

[37] *WC*, pp. 401–2.

[38] S. W. Williams, *The Cistercian Abbey of Strata Florida* (London, 1889), pp. 169–70, lxxvii–lxxix.

[39] PRO, SP1/86, fos. 50–1; *LP*, VII. 1264.

[40] D. Knowles, *The Religious Orders in England* (3 vols. Cambridge, 1954–9), III. 197.

part. In these matters, the gentry of Wales were no worse than their English counterparts, but they were certainly no better. It might reasonably be argued that their eagerness to discover Thomas Cromwell's wishes in the years 1535–6 and to secure his support for their own schemes to benefit themselves may have been typical only of the last months of the monasteries' existence. That may be true; but it would not explain away the overbearing attitude towards the monks at a much earlier stage on the part of dominant lay personalities like Sir Rhys ap Thomas or the earl of Worcester, nor the manœuvrings of almost completely secularized clerics like Robert ap Rhys or the Pennants, *père et fils*.

The process by which the religious had become *rentiers* living on rents derived from tenants among whom they had parcelled out their estates by lease or some other form of tenure had called for the appointment of lay officials to manage those lands. Although the monks did not necessarily lose all interest in the exploitation of their resources, they were overshadowed by their lay officials. The most imposing figures among the latter were the stewards, invariably powerful men who, it was hoped, would be able to advance the interests of the monastery in high places and protect it from external pressures. They were drawn from a group of influential families, among whom the Somerset earls of Worcester, the Devereux Lords Ferrers, and the ubiquitous Herbert family stood out.[41] Their position gave them a secure foothold of influence, which they did not hesitate to use to their own advantage. When push came to shove in 1535–6 several families of this kind were chiefly concerned to ingratiate themselves with the king and Cromwell so as to be in a favourable position to exploit the changes that were in the offing. Included among them were the Bulkeleys, Pennants, Gruffydds of Penrhyn, Salusburys, Breretons, and the family of Robert ap Rhys in the north, and the Somersets, Herberts, Devereux, Morgans, Mansels, Vaughans, and the Prices of Brecon in the south. Even Richard, son of Robert ap Rhys, after a difficult year as abbot of Conwy, when he had found it very burdensome to maintain charity and hospitality during a season of famine scarcity in 1536, was principally concerned to secure from Cromwell that one of his brothers (presumably Ellis Price) should be the farmer of his house if it were dissolved.[42] In general, the attitude of landowners and merchants seems to have been to protect their own interests and to be alert to seize any benefits that might accrue to them from the ending of monastic life.

Less is known, therefore, about the state of the monasteries in the last years of their existence than might have been desired. Best documented are

[41] *WC*, pp. 369–70.
[42] PRO, SP1/104, fos. 108–9.

the extent and nature of their property interests, thanks to that indispensable survey, the *Valor Ecclesiasticus*. Exceptionally useful as it is, however, and on the whole fairly reliable, its record of aggregate incomes is about 20 per cent lower than it should have been.[43] Carmarthen priory, for instance, was valued at £164 by the *Valor* in 1535, but soon afterwards in July 1537, the royal commissioner reported that its prior had 'put in a book' showing it to be worth £209.[44] Margam similarly, was valued in the *Valor* at £181, but in a minister's account of 1538–9 was revealed as having an annual value of £239.[45]

Far less information is to be gleaned from the scanty surviving reports – about a dozen letters in all – submitted by the other group of visitors for Welsh houses in 1535–6. Although the visitors employed in the exercise were not as unprincipled as they have often been depicted as being by those historians who are critical of the suppression of the monasteries, they were nevertheless typical of men used by Thomas Cromwell: heavy-handed in relation to the monks, but pliant and eager to please their master, and always with a sharp eye for their own advantage. Curiously enough, although Sir John Price was extensively employed in the course of this visitation and rewarded afterwards with a lease of Brecon priory, his services were not made use of in his native Wales. Neither were those of Richard Gwent[46] nor Sir Edward Carne, although both served elsewhere. The three visitors used in Wales were John Vaughan of Whitland in Carmarthenshire, Adam Becansaw, a canon of St Asaph, and Ellis Price, 'Y Doctor Coch' (The Red Doctor), whose relationship with a mistress led to his services being abruptly terminated. At the outset, although the king and Cromwell had seemingly still not finally decided how far they would proceed with the appropriation of monastic property, or even whether they would get rid of any monasteries at all, one of the main objects of the visitation was clearly to provide information which could be used to justify any subsequent suppression that might be decided upon. The visitors carried with them two documents: a list of 'instructions' and a set of injunctions. The former consisted of a series of questions not very different in character from those previously asked by the bishops or their representatives in the course of earlier visitations. The injunctions, which were to be reserved until the end of the visitation, were also similar to earlier ones; but they contained additional material reflecting some of the changes which had recently been introduced into the English Church. Thus, they drew attention to the monks' renunciation of papal authority

---

[43] Knowles, *Rel. Orders*, III. 247.
[44] *LP*, XII/ii. 277.
[45] PRO, Ministers' Accounts, Henry VIII, 5675.
[46] *WRE*, p. 79.

and their acceptance of the royal supremacy. They also called for regular Bible-reading and denounced 'unprofitable ceremonies'. Finally, they permitted any monk to denounce his superior if the latter defaulted on any of the injunctions.[47]

As far as the visitation of Welsh houses was concerned, the surviving returns were, unfortunately, very scanty and shed little light either on the visitors' activities or the condition of the houses they inspected. Nothing exists for Wales to compare with the *Compendium Compertorum*, that scandalous catalogue of the immorality alleged to have abounded in northern monasteries. The Welsh visitors' itinerary took nine months to complete, lasting from August 1535 until April 1536, though they almost certainly spent part of their time in London. First of all, at Conwy they received the resignation of the abbot, Geoffrey Johns, and replaced him with Ellis Price's brother, the youthful Richard ap Robert ap Rhys. This they carried out in the teeth of fierce opposition from Sir Richard Bulkeley, who viewed the visitors, and especially Ellis Price, with unconcealed distaste. Bulkeley pleaded the cause of another monk, Dafydd ab Owain, who was supported by Geoffrey Johns; but all in vain.[48] Bulkeley again wrote to Cromwell on 21 November on behalf of John Godfrey, prior of Penmon, 'shut up in his house by Dr Ellis Price'.[49] The visitors then dealt with the rogue abbot of Valle Crucis, Robert Salusbury. They are next heard of when they arrived in the diocese of Llandaff in November. Two letters from them concerning Monmouth, Brecon, Tintern, and Carmarthen are extant. A last communication from them was a letter of 28 April 1536 from John Vaughan to Cromwell, informing him that the visitation of both southern dioceses had been completed. Vaughan told of many supplications presented to him in which the people complained that they had had no law ministered to them in spirituality for many years. Very typically he asked Cromwell to let him have one of the abbeys to farm, for which he would pay the king as much as any other man and would be enabled the better to do the minister service.[50] His plea did not go unrequited in later months, when he obtained the lease of Grace Dieu, Whitland, and Pembroke.[51]

Slight though the visitors' testimony was and welcome as more information from them would have been, in the long run, perhaps, it makes very little difference because, long before their visitation was complete or

[47] Knowles, *Rel. Orders*, III. 246–7.
[48] R. W. Hays, *The History of the Abbey of Aberconway* (Cardiff, 1963), pp. 160–1; *WC*, pp. 406–7.
[49] *LP*, IX. 1291.
[50] Ibid., X. 746.
[51] Ibid., XIII/i. 1520. He was here described as John Vaughan, LLD of London.

its conclusions could be fully digested, the decision to dissolve the smaller monasteries had been taken. Cromwell had had far-reaching plans for a major raid on church property as early as 1534,[52] even if he was still undecided quite what to do about the monasteries in 1535. Many of the monks themselves had hitherto shown relatively little concern about what might befall them, and it was 'business as usual' in most of the religious houses.[53] In spite of that, there were significant precedents indicating the route that Cromwell might be tempted to take. Already, about a century previously, a number of alien priories had been suppressed by Henry V. Nearer in time, events in Europe since the outbreak of the Reformation, in some of the Protestant parts of Germany and Switzerland, in Gustavus Vasa's Sweden, and in Frederick I's Denmark, had indicated ways in which determined rulers might profit from suppressing religious orders. Even in fervently Catholic Spain that incarnation of orthodoxy, Cardinal Ximenes, had closed down houses in the interests of reform.[54] At home in England, Bishops Alcock of Ely and Fisher of Rochester, by suppressing small monasteries to finance Cambridge colleges, may have planted in Wolsey's mind the seeds of an idea for his closure in the 1520s of no fewer than twenty-nine houses to found his college at Oxford and his grammar school in Ipswich. In 1529 at least one Welsh house, Brecon priory, was fearful of what might be its fate at Wolsey's hands.[55] In carrying out these enterprises for the cardinal, one of his most efficient and energetic agents had been Thomas Cromwell, who was therefore not short of experience in abolishing religious houses and diverting their endowments to other uses, though in fairness to Wolsey it ought to be said that it was never his intention to plunder the monasteries in the interests of the State. Furthermore, when the royal supremacy was being asserted in 1534 it can hardly have gone unnoticed that some of its most intransigent opponents and most steadfast upholders of the papal authority were members of the reformed religious orders – Carthusians, Observant friars, and Brigittines. So, although most of the monks in England and Wales had admittedly taken the oath of loyalty to the Crown without demur, a growing number in their midst may well have viewed with acute misgiving the king's proceedings in 1534 and with still sharper apprehension the visitations of 1535.

Those who harboured such fears found them being confirmed early in 1536. Sometime between 4 February 1536 when Parliament reassembled and before 14 April when it dispersed – probably in March – it gave its

---

[52] BL, Cleopatra MS. E iv, 174; cf. *LP*, VII. 1355.

[53] G. R. Elton, 'The quondam of Rievaulx', *JEH*, VII (1956), 45–60.

[54] G. Baskerville, *English Monks and the Suppression of the Monasteries* (London, 1940), pp. 103–4.

[55] R. W. Banks, 'Brecon priory: its suppression and possessions', *AC* (1890), 209–33.

approval to an Act for the dissolution of all monasteries worth less than £200 a year and having fewer than twelve inmates. The preamble to the measure justified it on the grounds that 'manifest sin, carnal and abominable living' prevailed among these smaller houses. It drew a distinction between them and the 'great solemn monasteries' of the realm, where religion was said to be 'well kept and observed',[56] which led the chronicler Hall to suggest that this was the reason why the Act went unopposed by those abbots who sat in the House of Lords 'in the hope that their great monasteries should have continued still'.[57] There is, in truth, little reason for supposing that these lesser houses were necessarily in worse case than the larger ones, since reports from the king's own commissioners of 1535 had been as critical of some of the greater convents as of the lesser ones. Nor were there lacking, even at this point, clear-eyed observers who sensed which way the wind might eventually blow. 'These (lesser ones)', they maintained, 'were as thorns, but the great abbots were putrified old oaks and they must needs follow.'[58]

This Act of 1536 was presented as one intended to bring about religious and moral reform among the monasteries. It would be naïve, however, not to conclude that uppermost in the minds of king and minister were considerations of financial gain. Ever since the outbreak of the Irish rebellion in 1534 and the fear of possible attacks from European powers, the need for an increase in the king's revenue had been critical. One of Cromwell's documents of 1534 reveals his preoccupation with far-reaching proposals for the expropriation of the wealth of the Church.[59] In addition, within weeks of the earlier Act for dissolving the monasteries, the passage of another for setting up the Court of Augmentation of the Revenues of the King's Crown in order to deal with matters arising out of the dissolution gave an unmistakable indication of what was in prospect. Another, and rather different, incentive may have been the intention to suppress the pilgrimages, the sale of indulgences, and the veneration of relics so closely associated with the monasteries and with papal authority. Although formal action would not be taken against them until 1538, it was on abuses of this kind and on sexual misdemeanours that the monastic visitors sent out in 1535 had largely concentrated.

The Act of 1536 dissolving the lesser houses was inconsistent in implying that all houses worth less than £200 also had fewer than twelve inmates and

---

[56] For the text, J. Youings, *The Dissolution of the Monasteries* (London, 1971), pp. 155–9; for the dates of the dissolution, S. Jack, 'Dissolution dates', *BIHR*, XLIII (1970), 180; *JEH*, XXI (1970), 97–124.
[57] Woodward, *Dissolution*, p. 7.
[58] Knowles, *Rel. Orders*, III. 292.
[59] Youings, *Dissolution*, pp. 145–7.

ought to be wound up. It did not necessarily follow that a house valued at less than £200 had fewer than twelve monks. In Wales, Tintern was rated at £192 but it nevertheless seems to have housed an abbot and twelve monks; and it is possible that that was also true of Carmarthen. However, since all the Welsh houses except the Hospitallers' house at Slebech (which may not have had twelve brothers) had been valued at less than £200, all of them were included in the official list of those that were to be closed.[60] The only ones that were exempted and which managed to survive for two or three years, were some of the smallest priories, on the grounds that they were daughter houses of English monasteries and were not suppressed until their mother houses disappeared. All of them were worth well below £200 a year and none of them came anywhere near to having the minimum number of monks. Included among them were Cardigan (£13: one monk), Ewenni (£59: three monks), Kidwelly (£29: two monks), Pembroke (£57: ? monks), and Malpas (£14: two monks). Three cells which had once been alien priories but had managed to survive the suppression of such houses in Henry V's reign were Abergavenny (£129: five monks), Chepstow (£32: two monks), and Monmouth (£56: two monks); all three were now to be dissolved under the terms of the Act of 1536. An unusual arrangement was arrived at in Ewenni, a daughter house of the large and undissolved abbey of St Peter's, Gloucester. Although Ewenni was not wound up in 1536, it could hardly be said to have continued to enjoy an independent existence. On 28 February 1537 the distinguished lawyer, Sir Edward Carne, leased the priory and its possessions for the long term of ninety-nine years from the abbot of Gloucester at a favourable rent of £20. 10s. 0d. In return, he agreed to provide board and lodging for the prior, Edmund Wotton, and his two monks, and pocket money for the prior at £6. 13s. 4d. and the monks at £3. 6s. 8d. apiece.[61] This arrangement lasted until St Peter's, Gloucester, was dissolved in 1539.

Under the terms of the Act of 1536 the king agreed, 'of his most excellent charity', to provide a pension for the head of every house which was to be suppressed.[62] Such pensions varied in value, broadly speaking in accordance with the size and possessions of the house concerned and the length of service given by its head.[63] Some of the abbots of the larger convents were reasonably well provided for. Griffith Williams, prior of

[60] BL, Cleopatra MS. E iv, fo. 290b; *LP*, X. 1238.

[61] G. T. Clark (ed.), *Cartae et Alia Munimenta quae ad Dominium de Glamorgancia Pertinent* (6 vols. Cardiff, 1910), V. 1927–9; J. P. Turbervill, *Ewenny Priory*, (London, 1901), pp. 49–51.

[62] Youings, *Dissolution*, p. 158.

[63] *LP*, XII/i. 574–7; cf. W. A. Bebb, *Machlud y Mynachlogydd* (Aberystwyth, 1937), pp. 84–91.

Carmarthen, thanks perhaps to his tactful handling of the royal visitors, received £26. 13*s*. 4*d*., and Roderick Jones of Talley, £24. Richard Wych of Tintern, however, though abbot of the wealthiest house in Wales, did less well than might have been expected, getting only £23, the same as the abbot of Valle Crucis. Heads of smaller houses fared no more than moderately: Robert Holden of Brecon was allocated £16 and Jasper ap Roger of Llantarnam £15. Near the bottom of the scale were Lewis ap Thomas of Cymer (£6. 13*s*. 4*d*.), John Elyn of Cwm-hir (£5. 6*s*. 6*d*.) and John Gruffydd of Grace Dieu (£4). Keeping them company in their poverty were the two Cistercian abbesses, Elizabeth Benham of Llanllŷr (£4) and Rose Lewis of Llanllugan (£3. 6*s*. 8*d*.), though Eleanor Williams of Usk at £9 fared considerably better.

Ordinary monks and nuns were awarded no pensions. The former abbot of Tintern, Richard Wych, was later to complain in the Court of Augmentations that at least one of his monks pretended to be entitled to a pension or annuity from Tintern and constantly vexed and troubled him for its payment.[64] Instead of pensions, monks were allowed their 'capacities' (i.e. liberty) if they so chose and these would allow them to live 'honestly and virtuously' in the world outside,[65] it was claimed. Or else they were to be 'committed to such honourable great monasteries . . . wherein good religion is observed'. Those monks who had taken orders might expect, perhaps, to find employment as beneficed or stipendiary priests, chaplains, tutors, or in some other comparable occupation if they were fortunate. Nuns, barred from avenues of this kind, would have found it more difficult to find a comfortable niche, since their own families might not be particularly anxious to take them in. Nor had they a legal right to take a precarious refuge in marriage, at least until 1549, when those in orders were allowed to marry, by which time some of them might have been dead or too old for such a chancy venture. As there were probably less than a dozen nuns in the whole of Wales this was not, in terms of the numbers involved, an especially intractable problem.

Making provision for the inmates of dissolved monasteries to transfer to other houses would suggest that, at this stage, only a partial dissolution had been envisaged. Indeed, it has been argued that if Henry had proceeded no further, the whole episode might now conceivably be regarded as a commendable and necessary reform.[66] That might have held good for England, though not necessarily for Wales, where by far the greater part of its monastic establishment, including all its largest and most

---

[64] PRO, E321/20/40; *Augs. Procs.*, p. 137.
[65] Youings, *Dissolution*, p. 158.
[66] Woodward, *Dissolution*, p. 71.

celebrated houses, would have been swept away. It may, indeed, have been the impact of the wholesale nature of the dissolution in Wales which partly accounted for the decision to allow some monasteries to survive. For any monk to have to move from a monastery in which he had spent all his adult life to another unfamiliar house in strange surroundings was always likely to be a traumatic experience. For a Welsh monk to be obliged to move to an English house was likely to be still more disorientating. Since there were in Wales far more monks belonging to the Cistercian order than any other and therefore likely to be in need of alternative accommodation, it was only to be expected that it should be from among their ranks that appeals were entertained to prolong the life of monasteries that ought otherwise to have been dissolved.

Three Welsh Cistercian houses successfully petitioned against immediate closure: Whitland, Neath, and Strata Florida.[67] It is not known just why these three should have been spared. All three of them were in south Wales; two of them in the remoter south-west. Yet it might have been expected, on grounds both of familiarity and convenience, that one of the north Wales abbeys might have escaped, and Abbot Richard ap Robert of Conwy seems to have entertained some slight hope – obviously in vain – that his house might have been chosen.[68]

Whitland, on the other hand, was the mother house of Welsh Cistercian abbeys and its seniority might have counted for something. Neath, again, had the advantage of a very good reputation and its abbot, Leyshon Thomas, was the most eminent Cistercian in Wales and the one with most influence. Yet this might not have mattered at all, because the third house, Strata Florida, had a decidedly doubtful reputation before the dissolution. Perhaps what had chiefly counted was that all three houses had been willing to offer large sums for the privilege of being spared and possibly a fat bribe for Cromwell himself.[69] Strata Florida put up £66, Neath £150, and Whitland the enormous sum of £400, the largest offered anywhere.

These financial inducements were undeniably burdensome and must have taxed the resources of the houses very heavily. The dates of the surviving leases of all three monasteries reveal a remarkable concentration within the years 1536–7. Neath had eighty-eight leaseholders as against three tenants-at-will, and fifty-one of their leases are dated later than the end of 1535. All of Whitland's 151 leaseholders held leases later than 1535, and so did most of Strata Florida's 175.[70] A symptom of the pressure being put on monasteries to raise money urgently is evident in the record of a

---

[67] *LP*, XII. 31 (43 and 46).
[68] PRO, SP1/43, fos. 183–4; *LP*, XIV/i. 395.
[69] Knowles, *Rel. Orders*, III. 316–17.
[70] *WC*, p. 364.

lease by Strata Florida dated 1 August 1537 of the grange of Morfa Bychan, by which the tenant paid £80 sterling 'in the name of a fine' to be used 'for the redemption of that said monastery (Strata Florida) out of the king's hands'.[71] Similarly, when Neath abbey was on the point of being surrendered in February 1539, Sir John Price wrote to Cromwell, 'My lord abbot of Neath is contented to surrender his house', but, he added, 'he hath ever hitherto lived worshipfully and well, and also hath of late dangered himself and his friends very far with the redemption of his house. This should be considered in the moderation of his bill.'[72] Severe though the strain of raising money may have been for Leyshon Thomas and his fellow-abbots, their exertions availed them little. Within two or three years all three houses had been yielded up as part of a widespread process of induced surrenders. With them went also those small Benedictine cells which had earlier survived as daughter houses. The Act of Parliament which followed in May 1539 may not have been intended so much to dissolve the larger monasteries (most of which had surrendered anyway) as to legalize the process of surrender, to calm the fears of the monastic tenants, and to safeguard their future rights.[73]

A few fragments of information exist concerning the movement of monks from a dissolved house to a survivor. John Eastgate, a monk of Whalley, together with his brother Richard, a monk of Salley, appeared before the courts on a charge of having been implicated in the Pilgrimage of Grace. Richard was found guilty and executed, but John was acquitted and expressed his desire to be received at the abbey of Neath.[74] Since his name does not appear on the list of Neath monks who received pensions in 1539,[75] it is possible that he never actually migrated to south Wales. Conversely, one Robert Morreby, a monk from an unknown dissolved Welsh abbey, moved to Fountains in Yorkshire, where he testified to the abbot in 1538 that some in Wales had been 'in readiness to have taken your part if ye had been so happy to have come forward [i.e. rebelled]'.[76] There were also two former monks of Margam who received pensions along with their *confrères* of Neath in 1539, which would seem to indicate that they must have moved there when Margam was dissolved or they would not have qualified for such payments.[77]

[71] PRO, LR 232, fos. 155–6.
[72] PRO, SP1/143, fos. 153–4; cf. *LP*, XIV/i. 395.
[73] Youings, *Dissolution*, pp. 83–4.
[74] Baskerville, *English Monks*, pp. 166–7.
[75] *LP*, XIV/i. 602.
[76] Ibid., XIII/ii. 346.
[77] A. L. Evans, *Margam Abbey* (Margam, Port Talbot, 1958), p. 99.

The year 1538 had been a difficult one, with the threat of a possible invasion from Europe adding to the king's need for money. This not only put increased pressure on the remaining monasteries but also led to action being taken against the orders of friars. Four years earlier, in 1534, a visitation of the mendicants had been undertaken by two leading members of their order, John Hilsey and George Browne. Their principal object then had been to secure from each friar an oath of loyalty to the king and repudiation of the pope's authority, but all records of their visitation seem to have perished. By 1538 the ranks of the friars had already been perceptibly thinned and many more were now anxious to leave their houses, which were frequently in debt and decay. At best, the friaries would have had little to offer, since they owned only insignificant amounts of property in the immediate vicinity of their houses. Their urban locations were keenly sought, however; and both Richard Bulkeley and Edward Gruffydd wrote to Cromwell begging him to let them have the sites at Llanfaes and Bangor respectively. The Dominican friary at Bangor, according to Gruffydd, was an old building with no lead and little glass; all the same, he would like to have it as a dwelling-house and, for the favour, was willing to pay Cromwell whatever he thought fit and render him any service in his power.[78] Because the friaries were not possessed of any lands worth mentioning they had not been included in the statute of 1536 for the dissolution of the smaller monasteries, but the events of the two years which had elapsed since then must surely have given their inmates increasingly disturbing indications of the fate likely to befall them, and some had already begun to leave their houses. Yet in spite of the lengthening shadows that darkened their existence, the friars remained surprisingly secure in the public affection and their prayers were greatly sought after. Notabilities like Edmund Tudor or Rhys ap Thomas or Tudur Aled had wanted to be buried in their churches, and all the friaries in Wales were regularly remembered by testators in their wills. These bequests continued, strikingly enough, right up to the very eve of the dissolution. Two wills drawn up in May 1538 provided offerings for them; yet another, drafted as late as October of that year and not proved until after the dissolution was completed, left money for three friaries.[79]

On 8 February 1538 Cromwell appointed as visitor-general of the mendicant orders Richard Ingworth, suffragan bishop of Dover and a onetime friar. Ingworth at first moved so slowly that he was taxed with having too much fellow-feeling for his former brethren. To which he felt obliged to reply that the favour he had shown was not on account of his

[78] *LP*, XIII/i. 1289.
[79] *WC*, p. 357.

'friar's heart' but in order to be able to bring things 'with more quiet to pass'.[80] At the end of May he expressed his intention of proceeding to the West Country and Wales, where he felt sure that most of the friars would 'give up their houses for poverty'.[81] He reached Wales on 17 August 1538. Beginning at Rhuddlan, he proceeded smartly from there via Denbigh, Bangor, Llanfaes, Ludlow, Brecon, Carmarthen, Haverfordwest, and Cardiff to Newport, where he completed his itinerary by 8 September. It had taken him the surprisingly short space of three weeks to visit all the friaries in Wales.[82] His confident expectation beforehand that the friaries would cave in without a struggle had been borne out by events. He had perfected a subtle technique for dealing with them; one that was guaranteed to bring about undelayed surrender. Wherever possible, he took care to summon to the friary the bishop of the diocese and the mayor and aldermen of the town in which it stood. In the presence of these dignitaries he gave the friars an apparent freedom of choice. 'Think not that ye be suppressed', he was reported to have said disingenuously, 'for I have no authority to suppress you but only to reform you.'[83] Having thus ostensibly absolved himself of any hostile intent, he then obligingly offered to accept any voluntary surrender. The friars could either continue to live as religious under the injunctions issued in 1538, or else give up their houses to the king. This ingenious formula rarely failed to elicit the desired outcome. By now, most the friars were in a state of poverty and despair, resigned to their inevitable fate and willing to accept it without further protest. Only at Carmarthen did Ingworth find a friary in a fairly healthy state. It was the largest in Wales, boasting a double cloister and still having no fewer than fourteen inmates as late as 1538 – the largest number in any Welsh religious house. It also possessed a considerable quantity of vestments and furniture, though the reports that some of its possessions were 'abroad' in the town suggest that attempts had been made by the friars to alienate some of their goods before being suppressed.[84]

What happened at the two friaries in Cardiff was typical of events elsewhere and may serve as a model for the rest. By September 1538, left in no doubt of their imminent fate, the friars found themselves in dilapidated buildings, with many of their possessions in pledge and themselves deep in debt. First to be visited were the Dominicans. They owed a local victualler, Thomas Robert, £1 for provisions and were 7s. 6d. in arrears with their

---

[80] *LP*, XIII/i. 1484.
[81] Ibid., XIII/i. 1053.
[82] Ibid., XIII, where his movements can readily be traced.
[83] Knowles, *The Religious Orders in England*, III. 361; Hughes, *Ref. in England*, I. 325.
[84] *LP*, XII/ii. 277.

servants' wages. To meet these debts Ingworth sold some of the friars' meagre possessions and also took a chalice to defray his own expenses.[85] The friars' poverty had in part been brought about by their attempts to realize what little they had in the way of possessions before the house was suppressed. Vestments worth £7 once belonging to them were missing and there were 'gone many things of which they had no knowledge' because 'the prior was dead'.[86] Those of their bits and pieces still left – plate, vestments, furnishings and utensils[87] – together with the friary itself, they declared themselves content to surrender. Had they, it may be asked, any practical alternative? Ingworth then compiled an inventory and delivered it and the friary to the bailiffs of Cardiff for safe keeping on the king's behalf.

On the next day, 9 September, the same procedure was observed at the house of the Grey Friars. They, too, were in debt and had been forced to raise money by putting two of their chalices in pawn. A careful record was drawn up of what little remained that might be turned to the king's profit: alabaster, vestments, plate, candlesticks, organs, and bells in the church; cooking utensils, platters, tables, and various oddments in kitchen, hall, and chamber.[88] All told, it yielded no more than a meagre and worn-out collection. The visitation completed and the inventories compiled, it only remained to sign the deed of surrender. At the Dominican friary, seven remaining friars put their names to it – until a week or two previously they had been ten, but death had intervened to carry off prior, sub-prior, and one other friar. It is difficult not to speculate on whether or not their end had been hastened by the prospect of impending dissolution. Over at the Franciscans' house, nine were left to sign the surrender. That done, all were free to make the best of it in a difficult world without the cushion of any pension such as some of the monks had been allowed.

Only one monastic establishment was now left in Wales – the Knights Hospitallers' preceptory at Slebech, valued at £211[89] and the most valuable of all the Welsh houses. Even as late as 6 May 1540 the prior of England, William Weston, had been allowed to obtain licence in mortmain for lands to the value of £200. Just about a fortnight later, on 21 May, the revenues of the knights were being transferred to the king and they were compelled to resign the White Cross, the badge of their order. The procedure for their

[85] PRO, E36/115, fo. 35; cf. *LP*, XIII/ii. 294; Clark, *Cartae*, V. 1872–4; Rees, *SWMRS*, III. 7–19.

[86] PRO, E36/115, fo. 35; Clark, *Cartae*, V. 1873.

[87] Summaried inventories of other Welsh friaries are to be found in *LP*, XIII/ii, *passim*.

[88] PRO, E36/115, fo. 83; Clark, *Cartae*, V. 1874–7.

[89] G. D. Owen, 'Agrarian conditions and changes in west Wales during the sixteenth century' (Ph.D. thesis, Wales, 1935), p. 92.

dissolution seems to have followed the same lines as that for getting rid of the friars. The official visitor received the surrender of the house together with an inventory of the property, including money, plate, relics, and landed estates. In addition to the property belonging to the Slebech preceptory, the two border houses of the order, Dunmore and Garway, also owned valuable estates in Wales which now passed to the Crown.[90]

Once the monasteries had been dissolved, measures had to be devised for dealing with their inmates, buildings, and possessions. In the spring of 1536 instructions had been issued to groups of commissioners for each Welsh diocese, which served as the unit for the purpose and not the county as in England. They were required to visit every religious house within the diocese to discover the number of its monks and what they intended to do in the future, and were also to survey the lead and bells, plate and jewels, the leases entered into, and all other valuables belonging to each.[91] Most of the monasteries in Wales were dissolved between the summer of 1536 and the spring of 1537. Of the 250 or so religious within them, the former heads of houses came off best, as might be expected. All were given pensions, including the abbots of the three spared houses, each of whom was allocated £40. These former abbots were often able to acquire benefices as well; Leyshon Thomas became rector of Cadoxton near Neath, Lewis Thomas of Cymer suffragan bishop of Shrewsbury and rector of Llandwrog in Bangor diocese, John Price of Strata Marcella dean of Pontesbury, and his brother, Richard of Conwy, subsequently married, was deprived, and ended up as parson of Cerrigydrudion, where he died at a ripe old age in 1589.[92] None, however, succeeded in making it to the episcopate, unlike a number of former English abbots drafted in to fill Welsh sees: John Salcot in Bangor (1534–41), William Barlow and Robert Ferrar at St David's (1536–47; 1548–55), Robert Holgate and Anthony Kitchen at Llandaff (1537–45; 1545–63), and Robert Wharton at St Asaph (1536–55). Ordinary monks still remaining in monasteries after the dissolutions of 1536–7 were awarded very small pensions, usually £3–£4. This was no more than the remuneration of a poor chantry or stipendiary priest and could have provided only the barest subsistence for men who may in many instances have been too old to earn their living in any other way. Nevertheless, Tudor governments did honour their pledges, apart

---

[90] J. R. Rogers, *Slebech Commandery and the Knights of St John* (London, 1900); W. Rees, *A History of the Order of St John . . . in Wales* (Cardiff, 1947).

[91] *LP*, X. 721; Youings, *Dissolution*, pp. 161–3.

[92] D. R. Thomas, *The History of the Diocese of St Asaph* (3 vols. Oswestry, 1908–13), I. 243, II. 143; A. I. Pryce, *The Diocese of Bangor in the Sixteenth Century* (Bangor, 1923), p. 8.

from a temporary crisis in 1552–3.[93] Nearly twenty years after the dissolution at least twenty-one Welsh monks still figured on Cardinal Pole's pension list;[94] and in 1558, five out of seven pensioners formerly at Strata Florida were still alive and paid the clerical subsidy due in the diocese of St David's that year. (They included Richard Talley, the former abbot.) Of those religious who were turned adrift without pensions very little can now be discovered. They may, indeed, have acquired benefices or served as stipendiary priests. One of them, Richard Conway, the former head of Denbigh friary, seems to have become vicar of Llandinam;[95] but the general absence of episcopal registers for the dioceses of St David's, Llandaff, and St Asaph makes it impossible to trace these men in benefices, and if they were unbeneficed they would not have appeared in the registers anyway. There is, however, a strong suggestion that the fewness of ordinations late in Henry VIII's reign and during that of Edward VI was caused to a large extent by the influx into the ranks of the parish clergy of the displaced religious.

As for the considerable numbers of servants and labourers employed in each monastery, it seems reasonable to assume, in the absence of hard evidence, that many, if not all, of them would be needed by the new occupants or owners and could expect to be employed in the same way as before. The general supposition, however, is that outdoor servants were probably less affected by the change and fared rather better than those previously employed indoors. What little evidence there is available does not suggest that Welsh houses before the dissolution were 'overstaffed' with underlings.[96]

Overall, therefore, there appears to be little sign of serious material hardship having been caused to the monks and their servants. It is even possible that some of the monks who had no very strong sense of vocation may have welcomed the opportunity to turn their backs on the cloister.[97] Many of the inmates would probably have had little choice when entering the monastery and might have been handed over to the house as young boys to be brought up as monks. What it is quite impossible to measure, or even discover, is the degree of mental and emotional distress which may have been created by turning out into a very different, if not an unsympathetic, world men and women who had taken a vow to live all

---

[93] A. G. Dickens, 'The Edwardian arrears in Augmentations payments and the problems of the ex-religious', *EHR*, LV (1940), 384–418.

[94] Williams, *Strata Florida*; PRO, E163, p. 75ᵛ; cf. E164/31.

[95] Pryce, *Bangor*, p. 10.

[96] *WC*, p. 372.

[97] G. A. J. Hodgett, 'The unpensioned ex-religious in Tudor England', *JEH*, XIII. 195–202.

their lives according to the rule of religion. Of the subsequent destinies of the overwhelming majority of the religious after the dissolution nothing can with certainty be said.

Once the monastery had been dissolved, such of its contents as were movable or saleable were quickly disposed of. Jewels, plate, cash, valuable manuscripts, or relics, like Margam's 'garnished reliquary' and Brecon's 'silver of two relics set with crystal stones' and its 'silver of two tablets of wood with relics, four square garnished with crystal stone',[98] were dispatched to the royal treasury. Other assets such as glass, vestments, missals, candlesticks, organs, timber, and other furnishings were auctioned on the spot; and there exist receipts for £447. 8*s.* for the sale of gold and silver plate from Edward Waters, receiver for the dioceses of Llandaff and St David's, and for £41. 13*s.* 9*d.* from William Stump, receiver for the dioceses of Bangor and St Asaph.[99] Special attention was paid to the bells and the lead. Bells, made of a resistant alloy of copper and tin, were particularly prized for their usefulness in the manufacture of cannon. Six bells from Margam, Neath's four, and the single bells from Cardiff and Haverfordwest friaries were bought by a London merchant and transported to Bristol for him. Three bells from Strata Florida were sold to the neighbouring parish of Tregaron and Whitland's three to the parish of Whitland.[100] The burgesses of Brecon successfully contended in the Court of Augmentations that three of the bells of Brecon priory had always belonged to them, while their fellows at Abergavenny similarly made good their claim to all four in the priory there.[101] Lead was set great store by as roofing material. Margam was estimated to have yielded 9⅜ fodders, or nearly 100 tons, of lead; while much of Basingwerk's was delivered to Ireland for the repair of Dublin Castle and the rest to Holt to refurbish the castle there. Caernarfon Castle was repaired with lead, stones, and timber brought from Maenan; and in 1546 most, if not all, of the lead from Tintern was bought by the earl of Worcester to repair his castles at Raglan and Chepstow.[102]

After all these more valuable items had been attended to, the commissioners were required by their official instructions to 'pull down to the ground all the walls of the churches, steeples, cloisters, fraters, dorter, chapter houses, etc.'[103] But demolition cost money, and the commissioners were often happy enough simply to deface the buildings and render them

---

[98] Banks, 'Brecon priory', *AC* (1896), 209–33.
[99] Woodward, *Dissolution*, p. 135.
[100] J. C. Davies, 'Welsh monastic bells', *Wales*, XXIII (1946), 74–7.
[101] PRO, E321, 15/92; cf. *Augs. Procs*, p. 21; *WC*, p. 459.
[102] E. Owen, 'The spoils of Welsh religious houses', *AC* (1897), 285–92.
[103] Knowles, *Rel. Orders*, III. 384.

uninhabitable by removing roofs and stairs. The work was sometimes completed, or at least taken a good deal further, by the eager pillaging hands of local inhabitants. A notable predator of this kind was Nicholas Purcell, of the parish of Forden, agent to Lord Powys. He was alleged in an Augmentations suit to have sold three bells belonging to Strata Marcella to the parish of Chirk for £20, the organ to St Mary's, Shrewsbury, for 20 marks, and a quantity of lead to Oswestry Castle. He also conveyed enough stone to Montgomery to build a steeple and various chimneys, and considerable amounts of iron, glass, lead, and church plate and vestments.[104] Two comparable disputes concerning the Cardiff friaries ended up in the same court. In one, the farmer of the Grey Friars, John White, maintained that four local men had 'broken and pulled to the ground . . . and borne away the stones, timber, windows and tiles thereof'.[105] In the other, a Cardiff cleric, Lewis Johns, complained that a lease he had taken of a house belonging to the Black Friars was being ignored by the farmers of the friary who had wasted no time in plucking down 'the walls, windows and timber of the same house . . . and had carried away the same and taken it to their own proper uses'.[106]

In spite of the depredations, more Welsh monastic churches have remained to this day as places of worship than is usually realized. Those Benedictine churches which had for centuries been resorted to for worship by the inhabitants of the parishes in which they stood were reprieved at the dissolution and continue to fulfil their age-old function. Brecon's imposing priory has not only survived intact but has in the twentieth century achieved the status of a cathedral church – and one of the largest and most handsome of Welsh cathedrals at that. The smaller, but still magnificent church at Ewenni is used for parish worship today, as are the handsome structures at Chepstow, Abergavenny, Monmouth, Pembroke, Cydweli, and Cardigan. The abbey churches at Talley and St Dogmael's served for some two hundred years before being replaced. Margam was the only Cistercian church to be spared, and even in its much-truncated form, having lost its choir and transepts, still stands out as one of Wales's most appealing parish churches. The other Cistercian fanes are by this time at best only 'romantic ruins' like Valle Crucis, Cymer, or Neath. Gaunt and roofless as they might be, two of them at least – Strata Florida and Tintern – still preserved enough of their aura to quicken the genius of a Welsh and an English

---

[104] PRO, E321/43/63; 37/51; 516/25–7; *Augs. Procs.*, pp. 151–3.

[105] PRO, E321/12/91; *Records of the County Borough of Cardiff*, ed. J. H. Matthews (6 vols. Cardiff, 1898–1911), III. 32–4.

[106] PRO, E321/12/96; *Cardiff Recs.*, III. 35–7.

master-poet to address unforgettable lines to them.[107] A few churches have disappeared altogether, leaving virtually no trace behind them – Whitland, Strata Marcella, Maenan, and most of the friaries. Fragments from others still beautify present-day churches – the stallwork at Montgomery and Beaumaris, or the roofs at Cil-cain and Llanidloes;[108] but most of the treasures of monastic houses disappeared when they were dissolved.

An occasional monastic community sought to maintain a precarious existence after it had been officially disbanded. A little group of monks struggled to continue the life in common at Monks Bretton near Barnsley, as did a company of nuns at Kirklees.[109] Suggestions have been made that similar bodies of Welsh monks from Strata Florida and Llantarnam may have persevered with the cenobitic life in the desolate moorland east of Strata Florida and amid the bleak hills of north Glamorgan around Penrhys.[110] The evidence cited in support of this notion is tenuous and speculative, however; and it has to be noted that none of the postulated survivors ever emerged into the open during Mary's reign, when it was safe for them to do so and when they might have expected to be welcomed. The truth would appear to be that almost all the monks, as far as can be judged, accepted without protest or resistance the treatment meted out to them.

In the run-up to the dissolution it had often been suggested that the proceeds from a suppression would be applied to the reform of the Church. In practice, only a very small proportion of the ensuing profits was devoted to the improvement of religion or education. True, some parts of the estates formerly belonging to the monasteries of Tewkesbury, St Augustine's Bristol, and St Werburgh's Chester, which lay in Wales, were made over as part of the endowments of the new cathedrals founded at Gloucester, Bristol, and Chester in 1541. Grammar schools, too, were ultimately to be founded at former religious houses in Abergavenny, Brecon friary, and Carmarthen,[111] and the former Capel Dolwen belonging to Strata Marcella was also converted into a school. Most of the monastic possessions and the churches appropriated to monasteries, however, were immediately leased out to laymen.

---

[107] W. Wordsworth, 'Lines composed a few miles above Tintern Abbey', *Poetical Works* (Oxford, 1950), pp. 163–5; T. G. Jones, 'Ystrad Fflur', *Caniadau* (Wrexham, 1934), p. 192; cf. W. Coxe on Tintern in *Historical Tour through Monmouthshire* (Brecon, 1901): 'the door being suddenly opened, the inside inspection of the church called forth an instantaneous burst of admiration and filled me with delight, such as I have scarcely ever before experienced on a similar occasion'.

[108] *WC*, p. 439.

[109] Woodward, *Dissolution*, pp. 152–4.

[110] D. Mathew, *The Celtic Peoples and Renaissance Europe* (London, 1933), pp. 490–4; Williams, *Welsh Cistercians*, pp. 120–2.

[111] *W 1415–1642*, p. 289.

The greater part of this land had previously been occupied by tenants who held it by a variety of tenures – leasehold, copyhold, tenancy-at-will, and the like. The Crown, fearing that heads of houses who had good cause to suspect what might befall them would enter into all sorts of late leases and other suspect procedures with their kinsmen and friends, sought to forestall such manœuvres by strictly forbidding them in the Act of 1536. That did not prevent abbots from concluding many late leases, especially in houses like Conwy, Basingwerk, or Llantarnam, whose heads had depended for their election on pressures being exerted by family and friends.[112] Even so, most of the tenants had their tenancies confirmed by the Crown; and that, no doubt, was one of the prime reasons why the dissolution met with so little opposition from the laity.

The sites of the former monasteries and the demesnes they had kept in hand were soon leased out, which suggests that at this point the intention may have been to retain most of the land in the royal possession.[113] Among those quick to pick up bargains with which their experience had made them familiar were men who had themselves been engaged in the dissolution. John Vaughan, earlier so importunate with Cromwell for favours of this kind, leased Grace Dieu, Whitland, and Pembroke; John Price acquired Brecon, and Edward Carne Ewenni. Other lessees had had previous connections with the monasteries, or enjoyed links with the court, or both. The earl of Shrewsbury leased Basingwerk's lands in Glossopdale, Abergavenny priory was leased to William Herbert of the Household, Llantarnam to John Parker of the Stable, Margam to Rice Mansel, and Chepstow to Morgan Wolfe, the king's goldsmith. Lord Powys's interest in Strata Marcella was confirmed, though Rowland Lee felt it necessary to write on his behalf, praising him as a 'noble and circumspect man' but pleading for his further advancement on the grounds that his monastic gains did not sufficiently compensate him for his losses elsewhere.[114] But it was the king's favourite, the earl of Worcester, who acquired the richest pickings. Having once been steward of Tintern, he was in 1537 granted the site and demesnes there virtually as a free gift to make good the losses he had sustained when the Marcher lordships were abolished in 1536.[115]

Grants of this kind made to the earl of Worcester, although few in number, may none the less have been an indication that Henry and

---

[112] Williams, *Welsh Cistercians*, pp. 103–5; Owen, *Cymm.* XXIX. 227; *LP*, XI. 1130.

[113] *LP*, XIII/i. 1520 for many early leases; cf. H. A. L. Fisher, *Political History of England, 1485–1547* (2nd edn., London, 1913), pp. 499–501; see Woodward, *Dissolution*, p. 135, for accounts from north and south Wales.

[114] *LP*, XII/ii. 905.

[115] Ibid., XII/ii. 795 (16).

Cromwell had it in the back of their mind ultimately to dispose of much of the monastic land. From 1540 onwards, it became increasingly apparent that, whatever the king's original intentions may have been, his desperate need for money would lead him to sell monastic estates wherever buyers were eager to purchase and could find ready cash to do so. The outbreak of war with Scotland in 1542 and France in 1543 made it still more imperative to raise money quickly and increased the pressure to sell. In Glamorgan buyers came forward with very little delay.[116] In other parts of Wales, by contrast, the gentry were clearly more reluctant or less able to buy outright, and it has been shown that in Monmouthshire and south-west Wales they sometimes preferred to lease rather than buy if that were possible.[117]

The dissolution of the monasteries closed what had been a long and, at its best, an illustrious chapter in the history of religion in Wales. For all that, it is not easy to draw up any kind of balance sheet of what the losses and gains may have been when the houses of religion were swept away. No precise assessment is possible, nor is there one which will commend itself universally, irrespective of individual religious sympathy. On one issue, though, there probably need be very little disagreement: the loss to architecture and art. Admittedly, a number of fine monastic churches survived; but the largest and most striking of them either disappeared or were reduced to ruins. Some of the finest Cistercian churches, like those at Tintern, Margam, Neath, Strata Florida, Cwm-hir, and Valle Crucis, were more spacious and impressive than the Welsh cathedrals, with the possible exception of St David's. Strata Florida and Valle Crucis, moreover, have been shown to have evolved their own distinctive native architectural styles not unworthy to be compared with the Cistercians' superb achievements in Yorkshire.[118] Strata Florida's unique west doorway remains *in situ* to testify all the while to their incomparable mastery in west Wales. Lost with these churches were some of the most exquisite treasures in sculpture, wood-carving, jewellery, plate, glass, floor tiles, and vestments; a loss pointed up rather than offset by the almost accidental preservation of fragments in a handful of parish churches. Their claustral buildings have suffered equally badly if not worse, although buildings like Margam's chapter house or Neath's abbot's hall must at one time have been structures of peerless beauty. Now, there remain only those 'bare ruin'd choirs where late the

---

[116] *WRE*, pp. 99–103.

[117] M. Gray, 'The disposal of Crown property in Monmouthshire, 1500–1603' (Ph.D. thesis, Wales, 1985); cf. G. D. Owen, 'Agrarian conditions and changes in west Wales during the sixteenth century' (Ph.D. thesis, Wales, 1935).

[118] G. V. Price, *Valle Crucis Abbey* (Liverpool, 1952); D. Pratt, *Dissolution of Valle Crucis Abbey* (Penly, 1982); *Valle Crucis* (London, 1987); *Strata Florida Abbey* (London, 1992).

sweet birds sang'; the wind whistling a melancholy dirge among the sad ruins where Guto'r Glyn in an earlier age had gazed spellbound upon Dafydd ap Ieuan's White Monks of Valle Crucis as if they were the very harbingers of heaven itself.[119] For a country like Wales, not over-endowed with fine architecture or moving works of art, this must be accounted a grievous deprivation, only partly diminished by the reflection that later religious changes would almost certainly have wrought serious havoc anyway. Along with the visual arts, literature suffered too. Welsh poets had for generations revelled in the status of honoured guests at religious houses and had repaid their mentors with many a matchless *awdl* or *cywydd*. With the passing of abbots such as Dafydd ab Owain and his like they had lost some of their most munificent patrons ever,[120] even if one or two of the bards, like Lewis Morgannwg or Gruffudd ap Ieuan ap Llywelyn Fychan, turned to bite the hands that once had fed them.

Education, scholarship, and learning were also impoverished when the monasteries vanished. The monks may have done very much less for the teaching of youth in their vicinity than was once believed.[121] Even so, some of them maintained schools for their own novices and saw to it that promising young men from among them like Dafydd ab Owain or Leyshon Thomas pursued a university career. Others may have taken boys and girls into their households to instruct them in good manners and polite behaviour.[122] Whatever may have been the deficiencies of the monasteries in the sphere of education the king did very little to amend them. Of the handful of schools set up in Wales out of the proceeds of the dissolution, two proved to be very short-lived (Carmarthen and Capel Dolwen). The monasteries' golden days as compilers of chronicles or copyists of manuscripts, too, may have long been past; but when their libraries were dispersed many of their contents were lost.[123] In spite of all the labours of John Leland, 'the king's antiquary', who tramped the length and breadth of England and Wales[124] in an effort to catalogue the monastic feats of erudition, his hopes for a library in which most of them might be retained were never realized. Nor could the concern of interested new owners like Sir John Price or Sir Edward Carne or, above all, the Stradling family of St Donat's whose library there became the focus of lyrical acclaim by

---

[119] *WC*, p. 389.

[120] Dafydd ab Owain, a leading Cistercian abbot, was one of the most generous of all Welsh bardic patrons, *WC*, pp. 404–5.

[121] Ibid., pp. 394–6.

[122] Ibid.

[123] N. R. Ker, *The Medieval Libraries of Great Britain* (revised edn., RHS, London, 1964) provides the titles of books or manuscripts surviving from monastic libraries.

[124] *Leland's Itinerary in Wales*, ed. L. T. Smith (London, 1906).

Archbishop Ussher and other scholars,[125] do more than salvage a small part of the books and manuscripts once in monastic hands.

Economically and socially, the monasteries no longer had much to commend them. They had long since ceased to be the pioneers of estate management, stockbreeding, wool production, mining, and metallurgy that they had been in earlier periods. Having given up direct exploitation of most of their lands, mills, fisheries, woods, and mineral resources, they were content to have gentry, yeomen, and husbandmen as their tenants and to live on the rents that they paid them. Nor is there any evidence to suggest that as landlords the monks' methods were appreciably more enlightened than those of lay owners.[126] Conversely, there is little to point to the new proprietors who succeeded them having been unduly harsh or oppressive in their treatment of their tenants. The records of the great lawcourts reveal little trace of such behaviour and neither do such voluminous collections as the Margam archives of the Mansel family.[127] Many of the new owners, though not without an eye to business, seem to have been more concerned with the prestige than the profits accruing from their new estates. Besides, the Crown had leaned over backwards when appropriating monastic land to confirm the sanctity of tenants' agreements already entered into with their former landlords.

Nor could the monks be described as having been conscientious rectors of those parishes whose tithes they pocketed. They had looked upon the appropriated benefices first and foremost as a source of financial benefit and had a poor reputation either for fulfilling their obligations to maintain chancels in good repair or making adequate allowances in kind or cash for vicars and stipendiary curates.[128] The laymen into whose hands these churches passed were, admittedly, no better; but they could hardly be said to have fallen away from previously high standards. The major criticism in this context should be reserved for the State's failure to ensure that this appropriated tithe was returned to the parishes whence it had come and there applied to worthwhile religious or educational ends. The parish clergy of Wales, always poor for the most part, were rendered worse off still in the ensuing centuries by the grasping attitudes of their lay rectors.

If the monks were not conspicuously benevolent landlords or rectors, neither can they be said to have been fulfilling their social responsibilities

---

[125] G. Williams, 'The Stradling family', in R. Denning (ed.), *St Donat's Castle and Atlantic College* (Cowbridge, 1983), pp. 75–7; C. W. Lewis, 'Syr Edward Stradling', *Ysgrifau Beirniadol*, XIX (1994), 139–207.

[126] *WC*, chaps. 10 and 11.

[127] *Augs. Procs. passim*; W. de G. Birch, *Catalogue of Penrice and Margam Manuscripts* (4 vols. London, 1893–5).

[128] *WC*, pp. 348–52.

with the vision or energy that might perhaps have been expected. In fairness, it should be acknowledged that right to the end of their existence a number of monasteries were maintaining a handful of corrodians (people normally of advanced years who were given board and lodge in return for gifts or earlier services to the monastery) drawn from among the elderly and infirm. A bard like the pathetically blind and decrepit Guto'r Glyn came to Valle Crucis to end his days *c*.1493, Gutun Owain retired to Strata Florida and was buried there, and Lewis Môn also drew up his will at Valle Crucis. But of the monks' attention to the sick in the last phase of their history little or nothing is known. It may perhaps be significant that the mazer bowl once belonging to Strata Florida continued for centuries to be held in high esteem as a sovereign antidote to ill health by the peasantry of north Cardiganshire when it passed into the possession of the Powells of Nanteos. Similarly, even after the dissolution of Basingwerk, the sick went on flocking by their hundreds to Holywell to Winifred's miraculous well.[129] Both these, of course, were strictly speaking supernatural rather than monastic sources of healing, though such a distinction would have been meaningless to medieval folk. The monks had also continued to dispense charity and hospitality. Many of them fulfilled their legal responsibilities to give alms to the poor and needy, as is recorded in the *Valor Ecclesiasticus*,[130] like Neath's £3 a year in alms and 'our lady's loaf and half a bushel of wheat weekly'.[131] Carmarthen's good name for charity and hospitality has already been noted; Guto'r Glyn testified that Strata Florida fed many, rich and poor; and according to Sir Richard Bulkeley even a tiny house like Penmon maintained sixteen persons, some of whom may well have been poor people.[132] Yet it is difficult to avoid the conclusion that much of the monastic hospitality about which the poets went into raptures was more concerned with maintaining the abbot's reputation for keeping up a good table for influential kinsmen and neighbours than with meeting the needs of the travelling stranger or the indigent beggar.[133] Nor is it easy to determine how closely related to actual need were the alms and charity that were doled out, and how far they simply maintained a group of those 'abbey lubbers' regularly denounced by contemporary satirists. It is certainly true that the end of the abbeys did not create for the first time the problem of pauperdom; nevertheless, in a bare upland country like Wales the disappearance of the social functions of monasteries may have been more sorely felt than in more affluent communities.

[129] Williams, *TCS* (1991), 96–8.
[130] A. Savine, *English Monasteries on the Eve of the Dissolution* (Oxford, 1909), p. 328.
[131] *Valor Ecclesiasticus*, IV. 351.
[132] PRO, SP1/99, fos. 78–81; cf. *LP*, IX. 866.
[133] *WC*, pp. 380–2.

All these aspects of monastic life so far discussed, valuable as they may have been to contemporary society, were secondary to the essential purpose for which monasteries had come into being. They had been founded first and foremost to undertake the *opus Dei*; that unceasing cycle of worship and prayer, eight services every day, beginning about 2 or 3 a.m. and ending at 6 to 8 p.m. Primarily they were offered for the founders of the house, but also on behalf of all Christian souls – the living and, especially perhaps, the dead. Over the years they had encouraged the faithful to journey to them on pilgrimage in order that they might venerate, and make their supplications to, holy relics or representations of the sacred, and avail themselves of papal indulgences. It is as centres of religious and spiritual activity that they must crucially stand or fall. In this capacity it is difficult not to conclude that they now fell far short, not merely of the original ideals of the founders of their orders which were, after all, almost terrifyingly demanding and but rarely achieved or maintained anywhere in all their fullness, but also of an earlier achievement. By the sixteenth century they were not, and for a long while had not been, capable of exercising their onetime positive influence as the creative minority within the Church. Reduced in numbers, zeal, and morale, the religious were a shadow of their former selves, unable to give a lead or inspire devotion. There were no longer enough of them in most Welsh houses even to keep up the full round of service and supplication.

In spite of that, it is possible for those who sympathize with the monastic life to argue that the existence of the whole community was impoverished when this source of vicarious acts of worship and prayer, however attenuated, was lost from its midst forever. Sir Thomas More, replying to Simon Fish's arguments in his *Supplication for the Beggars* that the monks were parasites on the nation, certainly argued with conviction and eloquence in the *Supplication for Souls* the case for the value of their prayers. Some indications would suggest that similar opinions were cherished by his less sophisticated contemporaries among the Welsh. Many testators continued to leave bequests for monastic prayers right up to the end.[134] Furthermore, former tenants of Strata Florida complained bitterly to the Court of Augmentations of the loss of customary services and prayers when the lessee of that monastery discharged two priests who had continued to dispense sacraments and sacramentals in a chapel of the abbey for the benefit of the surrounding population.[135] The inhabitants of Churchstoke parish also refused to pay tithes they had previously rendered to the dissolved priory of Chirbury,[136] though it is not certain whether this

---

[134] Ibid., pp. 564–8.
[135] PRO, E321/17/35; cf. *Augs. Procs.*, p. 27.
[136] PRO, E321/165/67; cf. *Augs. Procs.*, p. 150.

was because they believed themselves to be deprived of spiritual benefits. The tenants of Llanthony, however, made it plain that they refused to yield their tithes because, when that priory had stood, 'they and their friends were there prayed for yearly and now it is dissolved they know not why they should pay to any farmer'.[137] That reluctance to pay may, of course, have been partly inspired by more mundane considerations of sparing their pockets.

The whole question of the nature and extent of the religious loss caused by the dissolution is an imponderable over which it may be unprofitable to dispute. What can perhaps be added is that Tudor laymen who were to prove some of the most loyal sons of the Roman Church did not appear to think that their fidelity to it ought to embrace the preservation of the monasteries in Henry VIII's reign or their revival in Mary's. Even men like Sir Edward Carne or Sir Thomas Stradling or the Morgan family of Llantarnam did not hesitate to participate in the dissolution nor to profit from it; neither were they willing to re-endow the monasteries in the 1550s. Quite apart from the widespread desire among the gentry to feather their own nests and to conform to the king's policies, it would have been difficult for them to have adopted a different posture towards institutions which, without being dens of vice or haunts of immorality, seemed so largely to have outlived the essential religious or social functions they had once so notably performed and to have lapsed into a lethargic complacency.[138] In four hundred years of existence the monasteries had made an immeasurable contribution to the spiritual and secular life of Wales; but for a long time before their extinction they had been a sadly dwindling asset. That is not to say that they could not, even in 1536–9, successfully have undergone the drastic reform they so badly needed, had the will to bring it about been present on the part of the monks themselves, the lay population, or above all the Crown. Of that there was never a whisper.

[137] PRO, E321/26/45; cf. *Augs. Procs.*, p. 137.
[138] *WC*, pp. 412–13.

CHAPTER 5

The Supremacy Enforced, 1536–1540

B Y the end of the year 1535, before even embarking on the greatest act of land nationalization in the history of England and Wales – the dissolution of the monasteries – Henry VIII and his servants had already afforded a remarkable demonstration of caesaro-papalism over the Church and religion within the realm. They had pushed through Parliament a number of statutes which completed the breach with Rome and set up the king's supremacy over the *ecclesia Anglicana*. Henry had also pressurized Archbishop Cranmer into granting him a divorce from his first wife in the teeth of opposition from pope and emperor and had married a second one. He had changed the succession to the throne and obliged all his leading subjects, lay and clerical, to swear oaths of loyalty to the new arrangements as well as to his supremacy. He had set on foot two visitations throughout the length and breadth of his kingdom to inquire into the state of the monasteries and to draw up a valuation of the property of the Church on the scale of Domesday Book. The overt critics of these policies had been few, and the most resolute among them, of whom Bishop John Fisher and Sir Thomas More were the most illustrious, had been given short shrift and executed for their resistance. These profound constitutional and religious changes had been applied to the outer extremities of Henry's domains just as intensively as to those parts which lay nearer the centre of power. The statutory provisions were extended to cover 'any person, subject or resident within this realm or elsewhere within the king's dominions'. They were drawn up so as to include the Channel Islands, for example, and were enforced there as a matter of course.[1] The same was no less true of the Isle of Man and even distant Ireland, where legislation backed by force secured outward acceptance of the changes.[2]

On the Principality and Marches of Wales, likewise, although they had not yet been integrated into the English realm, these far-reaching

[1] A. J. Eagleston, *The Channel Islands under Tudor Government, 1485–1642* (Cambridge, 1949), pp. 35, 171.
[2] R. D. Edwards, *Church and State in Tudor Ireland* (Dublin, 1935), pp. xlii–xliii.

modifications had the same impact as in the king's other outlying lands and regions. There was no need for any Act of Union to bring these changes into force; they had already been applied in Wales.[3] Not surprisingly, all of them had been promulgated in the English language, which was becoming increasingly used for all official and governmental purposes. Statutes, proclamations, orders, sermons, printed books, and pamphlets were all employed to declare and implement the will of the Supreme Head of the Church. Although English was either not known to the majority of the people of Wales, or barely understood by them, the king's officers seem to have had little difficulty in making their instructions intelligible to the people. Enough of the individuals among them who mattered understood the language sufficiently well to give effect to royal policy. Since 1534 especially, with the appointment of Bishop Rowland Lee as president of a rejuvenated Council in the Marches and the enactment in 1534–5 of legislation giving more power to his elbow,[4] the Crown had kept a tight hand in Wales and been active in suppressing disorder and lawlessness. Furthermore, the appointment in 1534–5 to three Welsh dioceses of bishops who were more amenable to the royal wishes and typical of their fellow-prelates in being more tamed, and better fitted to carry out the king's will than almost any other bishops in Christendom, had given the Crown additional executants on whom it could depend.

Early in 1536 a further step of the utmost importance was taken in reorganizing law and administration in Wales. As part of a general process of extending a more centralized royal authority within the king's dominions – in the north, Cheshire, Calais, and Ireland – an 'Act for Laws and Justice to be ministered in Wales in like form as it is in this Realm' (27 Henry VIII, c. 26), usually known as the Act of Union, was steered through Parliament.[5] It ordained that Wales should be 'incorporated, united and annexed' to the realm of England. It introduced English law and parliamentary representation, and it turned the whole of Wales into shire ground. It also laid down that anyone holding office in Wales could do so only if he were able to speak English, but the law did not go so far to suppress the native language as it did in Ireland, where an 'Act for the English Order, Habit and Language . . .' was passed in 1537 which, among other things, required the nominees to all benefices to take an oath to preach and teach in English.[6] A later and longer Act of 1543 relating to

---

[3] *W 1415–1642*, chap. 11; for the earlier argument, W. Rees, 'The union of England and Wales', *TCS* (1937).

[4] C. A. J. Skeel, *The Council in the Marches of Wales* (London, 1903); P. H. Williams, *The Council in the Marches of Wales under Elizabeth I* (Cardiff, 1958).

[5] I. Bowen, *The Statutes of Wales* (London, 1908), pp. 75–93.

[6] Edwards, *Tudor Ireland*, p. 79.

Wales would also put the Council in the Marches on a statutory footing and establish Courts of Great Sessions (assize courts) and Quarter Sessions in Wales.[7] Henry's government obviously had no qualms at this time about carrying through its policies in relation to Church and State in Wales through the medium of the English language.

A knowledge of English had gradually been becoming more widespread and less uncommon in late medieval Wales. As the language became more widely used for official purposes, more of the Welsh population came to know how to frame legal and other documents in English and how to conduct correspondence in that language. A difference in speech had in any case been regarded in the medieval era as only one of a number of characteristics that went to distinguish a people; Ranulf Higden, for instance, had mentioned particularities of dress, morals, diet, and an inclination to idleness as typifying the Welsh but had not said a word about language. Although literary Welsh exhibited noteworthy vigour and flexibility, documents written for official purposes were not an accustomed feature of the language, and the letters and wills which appeared from the fifteenth century onwards were all drafted in English.[8] There may, in fact, have been a wider acquaintance with the English language in Tudor Wales than has often been taken into account. Along those parts of south Wales which had been heavily Normanized, in places such as south Pembrokeshire, Gower, the Vale of Glamorgan or the plain of Gwent, or again along the eastern borders of Wales, especially those districts within fairly easy reach of major towns like Chester, Oswestry, Shrewsbury, or Hereford, there were a number of Welsh people able to speak English. In all the ports, market-towns, and former Norman and Edwardian garrison boroughs in Wales, English was said 'to be as rife as Welsh'.[9] The celebrated scholar and littérateur, William Salesbury, claimed that there was hardly a parish in Wales which did not contain a number of English speakers.[10] It would appear that among the better-educated sectors of the population – some of the gentry and the merchants – an acquaintance with English had been a much-prized asset for much of the later Middle Ages. Priests and lawyers, by the very nature of their vocation, were others who often had a knowledge of the language; priests in order to draw up wills and other formal writings, and lawyers for the execution of legal processes and

[7] Bowen, *Statutes*, pp. 101–33.
[8] Ll. B. Smith, *Cof Cenedl*, I. 1–34; *LlC*, XVIII. 179–91; P. Roberts, 'The Welsh language, English law and Tudor legislation', *TCS* (1989), 19–76.
[9] Penry, *Treatises*, p. 37.
[10] W. Salesbury, *A Dictionary in Englyshe and Welsh* (1547), introd. For a map of linguistic usage in early modern Wales, see *Y Gymraeg yn ei Disgleirdeb*, ed. G. H. Jenkins (Cardiff, 1997), p. 50.

documents. A small but growing number among them were proceeding to universities and inns of court for their education, and many more were accustomed to trade and travel in England to gain a livelihood.[11] A tiny handful of intellectuals like Richard Whitford, William Owen, John Gwynedd, or Edward Powell, had even aspired to publish books in English, Latin and French.[12] Among all such groups, in Wales as in Cornwall, there may, indeed, have existed considerably more bilingualism than has been supposed.[13] Eustache Chapuys, Charles V's ambassador, could draw attention to the opposition of the Welsh to changes in law and custom in their midst in the 1530s but he made no mention of resistance on their part to language change.[14] So, although it is quite clear that most of the Welsh knew only their native tongue, there existed among them a strategically placed and highly influential English-speaking minority on whom the Crown could depend to understand and carry out its wishes.

The importance for the king of being able to maintain a firm hold on Wales was further brought home to him by the impact of the Pilgrimage of Grace in the north, 1536–7.[15] This was certainly the most dangerous rebellion of Henry VIII's reign and possibly the most serious domestic threat to the monarchy during the whole Tudor period. Reverberations from it might be feared to spread to every part of the kingdom and particularly to its remoter and less settled localities. Some years before the rising broke out, the preamble to the first Succession Act of 1534 had been at pains to spell out the perils of the 'great effusion and destruction of men's blood' that might be expected to result from 'the sinister appetite and affection' of rebellious subjects.[16] Such fears were confirmed in menacing fashion by the risings of 1536–7 in Lincolnshire first, then Yorkshire, afterwards the Lake Counties, and finally Yorkshire again. What made them potentially all the more destabilizing was that many of the circumstances which gave birth to disobedience in the north were evident enough elsewhere. Some were economic: the disastrous harvests of 1535 and 1536 and the consequent dearth and inflation; the problems of enclosure and landholding; and the intense dislike of taxes and the Statute

---

[11] G. Williams, *Religion, Language and Nationality in Wales* (Cardiff, 1979), chap. 8.

[12] G. Williams, in M. B. Line, *The World of Books and Information* (London, 1987), pp. 187–96.

[13] A. L. Rowse, *Tudor Cornwall* (London, 1941), pp. 21–5.

[14] *LP*, VII. 1534.

[15] M. H. and R. Dodds, *The Pilgrimage of Grace, 1536–7, and the Exeter Conspiracy, 1538* (2 vols. Cambridge, 1915); C. S. L. Davies, 'The Pilgrimage of Grace reconsidered', *PP*, XLI (1968), 54–76; R. B. Smith, *Land and Politics in the England of Henry VIII: The West Riding of Yorkshire* (Oxford, 1970); S. M. Harrison, *The Pilgrimage of Grace in the Lakeland Counties* (RHS, London, 1981).

[16] 25 Henry VII, c. 22.

of Uses. There were unpopular political pressures, too: the centralizing tendencies of the king's government; the growing influence of the south; and the marked inclination to downgrade and devalue former ruling families. The recent religious changes had also provoked deep resentment and served to provide a cause, or at least a pretext, around which the rebels could unite; not for nothing did the pilgrims rally to the banner of the five wounds of Christ. It was not the casting off of papal jurisdiction, nor its replacement by royal supremacy, nor even the dissolution of the monasteries, which roused the bitterest opposition, but rather the rise to influence of heretics like Cromwell and Cranmer and the widespread reports of what the king was believed likely to do with the parish churches. Gossip and rumour ran like wildfire to the effect that he would leave only one parish church for every five miles, that parish plate and jewels would be confiscated by him, and a tax levied on every birth, marriage, and funeral. The newly issued royal injunctions of 1536, especially those directed against practices deeply rooted in the people's affections, such as pilgrimages, popular prayers, honouring the saints, and the veneration of images, were greatly resented. Admittedly, when the risings came they were more easily put down in 1537 than might have been expected. After they were over, 216 were executed for their part – small numbers, indeed, as compared with those involved in Charles V's vengeance on the Communeros of 1521 or the thousands slaughtered in Germany after the Peasants' Revolt of 1525 – but all the same enough to sound a clear signal of the alarm that had been awakened.

Not unnaturally, there had been fears that the rebellion might spread from the north country to Wales. Wales might indeed appear, on the surface, to be a possible theatre of disturbance. Like the north, it was a sparsely populated, remote, upland pastoral country, conservative in attitude and having a long previous record of willingness to rebel. Only a year or two beforehand, rumours of subversive plots linking Wales to Ireland and Scotland had been freely bruited. It was not the sort of country likely to welcome extensive religious changes, especially when they were being disseminated in what was for most of its populace a foreign language. Its common people might be described in terms similar to those in which Robert Aske referred to the northerners, as 'rude of condition and not well taught the law of God'.[17] They, too, had suffered from bad harvests and their consequences: a Catholic poet of south Wales, Thomas ap Ieuan ap Rhys, is thought to have been protesting against the extortionate prices for their staple diet of bread and cheese being exacted from the 'poor, weak, obedient ones' ('ufydd tlawd, wan') as a result of the

---

[17] A. G. Dickens, *The English Reformation* (London, 1964), p. 126.

nine months of rain in 1535, when 'the whole island lay under Satan's paw' ('ve aeth yr ynys yma athraw oll yn llaw satan') and 'Christ's church had lost its privileges' ('ve aeth yn ddifraint eglwys grist').[18] Nor did they view with any relish the disappearance of those monasteries which had at least fed some of the poor, and they actively disliked the moves to restrict pilgrimages, prayers, and the invocation of the saints and their images. Wales, too, had earlier seen representatives of some of its most prominent families brought low by the Tudors – Sir William Stanley (1495), Buckingham (1521), and Rhys ap Gruffudd (1531). Very recently, since 1534, the Welsh had felt the weight of stricter and more centralized royal administration, Even the main agent of such pressure, Bishop Rowland Lee, had had to admit in worried tones in 1537 that 'there was never more rioting in Wales than there is now'.[19]

St Asaph, being the Welsh diocese nearest to the north and having a former English abbot as its newly installed bishop in the person of Robert Parfew alias Wharton, was the area where serious trouble might be expected. Sure enough, the bishop had already had to expel one David ap John Billington, a priest, for not erasing the pope's name from the service books and other offences.[20] In December 1536 Robert ap Robert Heuster, parson of Llanelidan, was alleged to have proclaimed that the king was out of the faith of Holy Church and that it was better that men should rise against him and die rather than let him rob them. Parson Robert was later accused of having spread reports that Henry intended to pull down all the dozen or so parish churches in the lordship of Ruthin except those of Llanelidan, Llanynys, and Llandyrnog. This was precisely the kind of rumour which had provoked some of the worst troubles in the north of England. Nevertheless, when Rowland Lee came to inform Cromwell of these charges as late as May 1537 there was a serious conflict of testimony. Not only did the offending parson deny ever having said these things – perhaps he would, wouldn't he? – but he was also supported in his denials by one Llywelyn ap David ap Ieuan, who was regarded as 'an honest man' by Piers Salusbury, the steward of Ruthin.[21] If indeed the incumbent at Llanelidan had been guilty of such utterances, he obviously found few sympathizers of any consequence, since there is no record of any trouble having occurred in the district.

In the neighbouring diocese of Bangor, too, serious concern was expressed about the extent of disaffection. Sharp disagreements had long

---

[18] *Hen Gwndidau, Carolau a Chywyddau*, ed. L. J. Hopkin-James and T. C. Evans (Bangor, 1910), pp. 34–6.
[19] Rees, *TCS* (1937), 50.
[20] *LP*, XI. 1446.
[21] Ibid., XII. 1202.

marred relations between Sir Richard Bulkeley and his opponents; a feud made much more dangerous if Bulkeley was justified in his contention that his main antagonists, William Glyn and Edward Gruffydd, were openly rejoicing in February 1537 'that mortal war is likely to be in England, which words and comfort have caused many light heads to pick many quarrels and caused much mischief to be done in these quarters'. This had led one of Glyn's servants to boast that his employer was sure 'it would be war and then his master and he trusted to be revenged of such as were their adversaries'.[22] This again, however, may be another instance where words may have come more cheaply than rebellious actions.

Although the diocese of St David's was the part of Wales most distant from the northern seat of disaffection, upheavals might have been anticipated there. This was, after all, the home territory of Rhys ap Gruffudd and James ap Gruffudd ap Hywel, members of that house of Dynevor concerning which so many alarming reports and rumours had been voiced earlier in the 1530s.[23] Many of the clergy and laity of the diocese, notoriously old-fashioned in their religious sympathies, had been irreconcilably opposed since 1534 to Bishop Barlow, one of the most vocal heretics in the country. Barlow was known to be particularly close to Cromwell and Cranmer, the rebels' most detested *bêtes noires*, and had himself been singled out by the northerners for hostile comment.[24] Earlier in the summer of 1536 his brother, John Barlow, had found it necessary to imprison the vicar of Tenby, Robert Collins, in the bishop's gaol at Llawhaden Castle on the grounds that he had indulged in criticism of Anne Boleyn and that he had not thoroughly defaced the pope's name from the service books but had only crossed it through in ink.[25] During the critical months at the end of 1536 and early 1537, relations between Barlow and his chapter were more than ordinarily tense. In the course of their altercations the bishop accused one of the richest and most influential of his canons, John Lewis, treasurer of St David's, of having had in his possession letters from rebels against the Crown. When Barlow required him to deliver them up, Lewis 'made excuse that he had lost them'. What made the treasurer's alleged sympathy for the rebels all the more sinister was that he was described by the bishop as a 'valiant bearer' and 'sworn chaplain' to the most influential layman in south-west Wales, Lord

[22] Ibid., XII/i. 507, 655; cf. PRO, SP1/111, fos. 117–18; 117, fos. 10–11.
[23] R. A. Griffiths, *Sir Rhys ap Thomas and his Family* (Cardiff, 1994), chap. 4.
[24] *LP*, XI. 705, 828ᵛ, 1319; XII/i. 405, 409.
[25] Ibid., X. 1182.

Ferrers.[26] It is difficult to believe, though, that Ferrers was likely to be disloyal to a monarch to whose favour he owed so much.

In Llandaff diocese Bishop Athequa had been a member of the dangerous Aragon grouping and had been censured by Henry and Cromwell for failing to preach the royal supremacy; following his unsuccessful bid to escape to his native country, he was kept safely in custody during the critical months of 1536–7. In his diocese it was not so much members of the secular clergy as one or two monks with south Wales connections who were peripherally caught up in the rebellion. One John Eastgate, who was acquitted of complicity, subsequently took refuge in Neath abbey, though no previous connection of his with that house is known. Another monk from a south Welsh abbey, one Robert Morreby, was reported later to have told the abbot of Fountains that there had been those in Wales willing to have come forward in rebellion if they had been given a lead. A third person indirectly implicated in the uprising was a secular priest closely connected with Reading abbey. He was John Eynon, born in south Wales, who became a close friend and valued counsellor of Abbot Cook. He made a copy of Robert Aske's letter and proclamation, which were circulated, it appears, by a blind Welsh harpist, William More or Mawr, said to have been 'singing songs which were interpreted to be prophesyings against the king'.[27] Cook and his friends, all unyielding opponents of the king, were under grave suspicion from 1537 onwards and were eventually put to death. There was no evidence, however, to suggest that there was any link between Eynon or the harpist and dissidents in Wales, except, of course, that prophecies of the kind that the blind man was circulating were always extremely popular among the Welsh, and it may be significant that the chronicler Hall refers to them as being 'interpreted',[28] which could conceivably mean 'translated' from Welsh.

Whatever subversive tremors ran through Wales in 1536–7 no serious upheaval erupted out of the Pilgrimage of Grace. Neither the social and political dissatisfaction, nor the religious discontent provoked by the dissolution of the monasteries and other changes, proved sufficient to trigger off any armed opposition. Henry himself stood tall in the affections of his Welsh subjects, as is shown in three celebrated poems and an elegy by Lewis Morgannwg, premier Welsh poet of the age and one enjoying the

---

[26] Ibid., XII/i. 830. For the full text of the letter, T. Wright (ed.), *The Suppression of the Monasteries* (Camden Soc., London, 1843), pp. 87–9, where the date, however, is given by implication as 5 April 1538. This dating is upheld in *LP, Add.,* I/i. 1228. But as the letter refers to events which are known to have taken place in 1537, and as there is not a single mention of this episode in any of Barlow's many letters of 1538, I see no reason to date it other than 1537.

[27] T. P. Ellis, *The Catholic Martyrs of Wales* (London, 1933), pp. 5–9.

[28] Ibid., p. 6.

reputation of being the king's own bard ('bardd y brenin'). Profoundly impressed by the force and majesty of the king's person, Lewis greeted with awed rapture Henry's status as Supreme Head of the Church:

Llywiawdr, ymddiffyniawdr ffydd,
Penn dan Grist, penna dan Gred

('Helmsman, defender of the faith,
Head under Christ, chief in Christendom')

Penn eglwys d'ynys, pinagl ystynnaist,
Penn ffydd a ffaunydd yr amddiffynnaist.[29]

('Head of the church in thy island, the pinnacle hast thou attained,
Head of the faith and always its defender')

Complimenting Henry on the way he had dealt firmly with his enemies, internal and external (including especially the pope), the bard sounded exactly those notes which Henry himself might most have commended. But the king had also given the Welsh good reason to tremble lest they brought down on themselves any retribution from him for disobedience to his will.

Thomas Cromwell was another who had won himself a circle of deferential clients among the up-and-coming gentry and lawyers, who were eager to ingratiate themselves with him. In addition, his most trusted aide-de-camp in Wales and the Marches, Bishop Lee, had imposed his authority in those parts with an iron fist. No Lord Darcy or Hussey emerged to set himself up as the head of rebellious forces in the Welsh countryside;[30] those who, like these two aristocrats, had been linked with the Aragon faction and were also associated with Wales – Athequa, Fetherston, and Powell – were all clerics and none of them a political or military leader. The numerous denunciations of the king and his policies reported from Wales had nearly all emanated from disgruntled clerics too. But critical to the likelihood of there being an armed uprising would be the attitude of the leading resident nobles and gentry. In this context, it was symptomatic that two of the most influential in their midst, the earl of Worcester and Lord Ferrers, when involved in a bitter quarrel with one another in 1536, quickly

---

[29] E. J. Saunders, 'Gweithiau Lewys Morgannwg' (MA thesis, Wales, 1922), pp. 191–2, 206.
[30] Darcy and Hussey were the most experienced commanders among the rebels and took the initiative once the rebellion had broken out, G. R. Elton, *Reform and Reformation: England, 1509–1558* (London, 1977), pp. 260–9.

came to heel after being required to do so by Bishop Lee.[31] Many of the more outstanding figures among the gentry had already revealed their willingness to put themselves and their resources at the disposal of the king and his minister. They might have reservations about the religious paths their masters were choosing to tread, but there is no evidence of any opposition on their part, still less of any willingness to resort to armed insurgency. Lewis Morgannwg's poetry provides a useful yardstick with which to gauge their attitude towards the king. Without upper-class leadership, no matter how grudging was the response of most ordinary people to Henry's religious changes, there would be no insurrection.

In the mean time, having succeeded in establishing his supremacy over the Church and overwhelming his conservative adversaries, the king proceeded to exploit the financial advantages his new-found mastery opened up to him and also began defining what his subjects must believe and what they must reject. Henry's approach throughout the rest of his reign was based on a rational appraisal by him of what constituted his own interests and those of his Church. Like every other contemporary ruler, he had no doubt that nothing cemented his kingdom together more securely than unity of religious belief on the part of his subjects. As Supreme Head of the Church it must, therefore, be his chief duty to ensure that his subjects knew and obeyed God's will as expounded for them by their sovereign. Henry's enemies, said Lord Herbert of Cherbury, believed that 'he seemed to be of no religion. Howbeit, this was pure calumny, for Henry stood firmly to his own reformation.'[32] That religion, properly ordered in accordance with his dictates, could add enormously to the effectiveness of those political reforms within his kingdom which he and his ministers, especially Thomas Cromwell, were now setting in train, and the closer degree of unity which they hoped to achieve by means of them. It mattered crucially that all his subjects, including those of Wales, so recently made full citizens of his realm, should recognize him as 'only supreme head' of, and themselves as belonging to, his national Church, 'the church of England called *ecclesia Anglicana*' and no other.[33]

In matters of doctrine, Henry believed himself to be thoroughly orthodox. Had he not laid it down in the Act of Dispensations of 1534 that the king did not intend to 'vary from the congregation of Christ's Church in any things concerning the very articles of the Catholic faith of

---

[31] P. H. Williams, *The Council in the Marches of Wales under Elizabeth I* (Cardiff, 1958), pp. 18, 30; cf. *WC*, p. 558.

[32] Quoted G. Redworth, 'Whatever happened to the English Reformation?', *History Today*, XXXVII (1987), 36.

[33] 'Act for the King's Highness to be supreme head of the Church of England . . . ', 26 Henry VIII, c. 1.

Christendom'?[34] In the first of those formularies of faith which he promulgated – the Ten Articles of 1536 – he would retain most of the traditional theology and much of the organization and outward appearance of the Church. Yet he was percipient enough to appreciate that in overthrowing the papacy there were some features of heretical teaching which could be useful to him in buttressing his own power structures, however obnoxious they might be to the taste of his more conservative subjects. Among them were the greater insistence upon reading the English Bible, making more use of the vernacular language in worship, and attacking papal indulgences and traditional notions about purgatory. But his major advisers were by no means united in the way they interpreted Henry's best interests. A layman like the duke of Norfolk or a cleric like Bishop Gardiner rejected papal authority without demur and were stout in their acceptance of the royal headship, but would have no truck with heresy. Among those in Wales who were politically aware and articulate, they almost certainly had an overwhelming majority of sympathizers. On the other hand, an opposing party headed by Cromwell and Archbishop Cranmer were much more favourable to moving closer to Continental reformers; not merely accepting Erasmian trends but even some of the heretical tendencies of reformers like Luther. Their aim was to re-educate the populace, and to achieve that they were prepared to unleash a 'propaganda campaign without precedent', in the process giving the preachers, and the printing-press especially, free rein.[35] In consequence, the kingdom would oscillate uneasily between the two factions, sometimes swinging one way, sometimes the other. Henry himself, whatever concessions he might from time to time be obliged to make, as a result of internal pressures or those from European states, always tried to keep his eye constantly fixed on what he deemed to be his own concerns and the best interests of strength and unity within his kingdom.

The Ten Articles were published in July 1536 and followed up in August of the same year by Henry's first set of injunctions.[36] These documents represented a compromise after a struggle in Convocation between the traditionalists and the reformers. More by omission than positive statement, they moved some way towards accommodating Lutheran beliefs. Thus, for example, although most of the bishops believed in all seven sacraments, mention was made in the Articles of only three – baptism,

---

[34] Quoted S. Doran and C. Durston, *Princes, Pastors and People* (London, 1991), p. 15.

[35] J. J. Scarisbrick, *Henry VIII* (London, 1968), p. 392; cf. also D. R. Starkey, *The Reign of Henry VIII: Personalities and Politics* (London, 1985).

[36] C. H. Williams, *English Historical Documents, V. 1485–1558* (London 1967), pp. 795–808.

penance, and the sacrament of the altar. Or again, although the existence of purgatory was acknowledged and the 'merit of prayers for the dead' recognized, the people were strictly forbidden to cling to abuses which led them to believe that 'through the bishop of Rome's pardons souls might clearly be delivered out of purgatory'.[37] Popular customs like pilgrimages and the honouring of the saints were heavily downplayed and the liturgical year greatly simplified. More positive steps that were ordained took the form of encouraging the clergy to acquire English and Latin versions of the Bible and urging their people to read the 'English bible as the very word of God and the spiritual food of man's soul'.[38] Priests were also instructed to teach their parishioners to learn the Creed, the Paternoster, and the Ten Commandments in English and to expound to them the royal supremacy and the antipapal legislation. They were also expected to test their parishioners in the confessional to see whether they could say the Paternoster and the Creed in English and, if their knowledge proved to be imperfect, were to be warned that they might find their Easter communion denied them. Knowing how uncertain a quantity was a knowledge of English or Latin among a good many of the Welsh parish priests and how poverty-stricken many of them and their flock were,[39] not to mention how averse to change, it must be doubted whether many of them went to the trouble and expense of purchasing Bibles. Nor, judging by the criticisms voiced by Sir John Price a few years later (1546) of their instructional efforts in conveying the rudiments of the faith to their people, are there good grounds for believing that the injunctions were universally or conscientiously obeyed. Yet these were the first faltering phases, however lacking in conviction, in the process of weaning the people of Wales, as well as England, away from Catholic beliefs.

In the next year, 1537, a second formulary, *The Godly and Pious Instruction of a Christian Man*, was issued.[40] This document swung back somewhat from the unorthodox tendencies of the Ten Articles but it still represented a compromise. It was again the work of the Lower House of Convocation, of which by this time the prominent Welsh cleric, Richard Gwent, had somewhat reluctantly become prolocutor,[41] though behind that body loomed the formidable presence of Thomas Cromwell. Signed by all the bishops, and published in their name, with the king's official authorization being withheld – probably deliberately – it became known as

---

[37] Ibid., p. 805.

[38] Quoted Dickens, *Ref. in England*, p. 131.

[39] *WC*, chap. 8.

[40] The text of this document may be seen in *Formularies of Faith Put Forward by Authority During the Reign of Henry VIII*, ed. C. Lloyd (Oxford, 1825).

[41] *WRE*, pp. 79–80.

the Bishops' Book. Although it still gave priority to the three sacraments mentioned in 1536, the validity of all seven was now acknowledged. In the course of the subsequent year, 1538, further steps were taken to put pressure on the larger monasteries and the friaries to induce them to surrender to the Crown. By September 1538 a second set of injunctions,[42] which emphatically reaffirmed those of 1536, was issued. The king's subjects were still more strictly forbidden to 'repose their trust . . . in wandering to pilgrimages, offering of money, candles or tapers to images or relics, or kissing or licking the same, or saying over a number of beads not understood or minded on'. The burning of candles before images was also prohibited. Once again it was emphasized that a Bible 'of the largest volume' was to be acquired for each parish church, along with a register for baptisms, marriages, and burials. The stress laid on the duty of each individual to find his own way to the truth by reading the Bible was hardly likely to maintain Catholic unity or strengthen the role of the clergy as the interpreters of the word of God. One must, however, of necessity doubt how great was the impact of the injunctions, when a circular issued by Henry VIII to the bishops in December 1538 complained that many of the clergy read them so confusedly that 'almost no man can understand the true meaning'.[43] Nor can it readily be believed that either the preached or printed word made much of an impression in many parishes in Wales, where illiteracy was general and where the English language was scantly known. Bishop Gardiner said of many contemporary Englishmen that 'when they have heard words spoken in the pulpit they report they were good and very good and wondrous good . . . but what they were . . . they cannot tell'.[44] If this was true of England, how much dimmer must the congregations' understanding have been in most parts of Wales?

During the years from 1536 to 1538 in all the Welsh dioceses efforts were made, which met with varying degrees of success, to try to ensure that the king's policies were understood and implemented. The degree to which the injunctions of 1536 and 1538 were enforced among the people depended in no small measure upon the attitude of the bishop and his officers, but nowhere could they be said to have gained much more than a formal outward acceptance. In St David's diocese the impetuous and aggressive Protestant, William Barlow, took up again in 1536 where he had left off in 1535 and for the next two or three years raised great whirlwinds of proposed change, especially in relation to his cathedral chapter, though

---

[42] Williams, *Eng. Hist. Docs.* V. 811–13.

[43] E. Duffy, *The Stripping of the Altars: Traditional Religion in England, c.1400–1580* (New Haven, 1992), p. 167.

[44] T. M. Parker, *The Reformation in England* (Oxford, 1950), p. 95.

when the dust had once more settled, little seemed to have altered. Bishop Parfew of St Asaph was another keen, but milder-mannered reformer, who also sought to introduce reforms into his diocese, but without conspicuous success. In Llandaff, on the other hand, the conservative Athequa refused to co-operate, to such an extent that John Vaughan, a royal visitor, commented despondently that the people 'were never so far out of frame, by reason of naughty bishops and worse officers'![45] The luckless bishop was in prison for much of 1536 and was replaced in March 1537 by Robert Holgate. A Yorkshireman and a Cambridge graduate, Holgate, former master of the Gilbertine order, was a man of thoughtful and scholarly bent, with a long and thorough university training. His later career proved him to be an administrator of more than ordinary competence and, despite his lack of local connections, he might have made a good bishop of Llandaff had he not been whipped away in 1538 to serve on the Council of the North.[46] Thereafter, Llandaff saw nothing of him. Nor was the diocese any more fortunate in its suffragan, John Bird, who was sent on an embassy to Germany in 1539. In Bangor diocese, where Bishop Salcot seemed to count for considerably less than some of the leading lay figures there, little was achieved.

Bishop Barlow returned from Scotland to St David's about the end of June or early July 1536. Initially, both he and his brother John were full of foreboding about their own future in the wake of the disgrace of their powerful patron, Anne Boleyn. Before the end of the year, however, they had overcome their misgivings, and William Barlow had again taken up the cudgels against his conservative antagonists in the cathedral chapter. In an important letter to Cromwell he outlined his intentions for the diocese.[47] He told how he viewed with extreme distaste the state of his see and the size of the task which faced him in trying to reform it. He denounced once more what he interpreted as the inveterate 'superstition' of its people, sunk in that 'horrible blasphemy of God and his verity' which made St David's to Wales what Bethel and Dan were to Israel.[48] He put forward his plans for reorganizing and reforming the diocese, notably by moving the cathedral to Carmarthen and by founding grammar schools and endowing regular preaching. What he omitted to tell Cromwell was that he was also intent upon trying to force on the chapter an unconstitutional extension of his authority over it. This precipitated an immediate trial of strength between bishop and canons, when it became plain that the latter were at

---

[45] *LP*, X. 45–6, 481.
[46] A. G. Dickens, *Robert Holgate* (York, 1955), pp. 3–17.
[47] *LP*, XI. 1427.
[48] Ibid.

least as much opposed to his attempts to make himself undisputed head of the chapter as they were to his efforts to introduce reform.[49]

St David's was unusual in having no dean; and in the absence of such a dignitary, it was the precentor who had established a prescriptive right to be the head of the chapter. The bishop was ordinarily accorded very wide powers by his canons, but Barlow regarded these as insufficient for his role as a reforming pastor. When it became unmistakably his intention to go much further than any of his predecessors had done in subordinating the chapter to his will, the canons naturally resisted with some spirit. If their bishop was seeking to get his own way by denouncing their 'papist idolatry', they were equally determined to reply in kind by exposing the 'rank heresies' they alleged to be held by Barlow. The list of his erroneous opinions drawn up in January 1537 by one Roger Lewis, LLB, accused him of having said that in earlier times no one had preached the word of God truly, confession was inexpedient, reverence of the saints pure idolatry, and purgatory an invention of the bishop of Rome for lucre, since dead souls had no need of prayer. Moreover, he had also maintained that where two or three simple persons such as cobblers or weavers were assembled in the name of God, there was the true Church, and he had insisted that the king could make any learned layman a bishop.[50] Even allowing for a certain degree of exaggeration in the heat of controversy, it can nevertheless be understood what consternation such views must have caused in a slow-moving diocese, though they may have been expressed in somewhat milder and more temperate vein than Lewis had appeared to suggest. All the more offence may have been given when Barlow was regarded, not only in his own diocese but in many other parts of the kingdom, as one of the foremost heretics among the king's bishops.

A month or two later, the conflict took a new and more rancorous turn, when Thomas Lloyd, precentor at St David's and later to be the first founder of the grammar school at Carmarthen,[51] was accused by Barlow of complicity with pirates. He seized Lloyd's person, took possession of his house, and distrained his goods.[52] Lloyd was a greatly respected figure, who shared some of Barlow's own views about the desirability of making use of the possessions of dissolved monasteries in order to extend the 'new learning' and who had seemingly had professions of affection and favour from his bishop. He was taken aback by this sudden and violent attack, which seemed to indicate that Barlow was willing to seize upon any pretext

---

[49] For a study of this episode, *WRE*, chap. 5, pp. 111–24.

[50] *LP*, XII/i. 93.

[51] G. Williams, '"Thomas Lloyd his skole": Carmarthen's first Tudor Grammar School', *Carm. Antiq.* X (1974), 49–63.

[52] *LP, Add.*, I/i. 1225.

to disgrace the head of his insubordinate chapter. Lloyd, reputedly a man 'much esteemed at St David's' for his learning, liberality and kindness', promptly retaliated by bringing a Star Chamber suit against the bishop.[53] The records of this suit are tantalizingly incomplete, and neither they nor Lloyd's statement of his grievances give a precise indication of the nature of his quarrel with Barlow, but at least they make it clear that the real issue was a clash of jurisdiction between bishop and precentor as head of the chapter and that Barlow had exceeded his rights in acting so high-handedly.

A number of influential canons had in the mean time taken Lloyd's side and enlisted the weighty support of Richard Devereux, deputy-justice of south Wales and son and heir of Lord Ferrers.[54] Devereux was accused by Barlow of having come to the episcopal residence 'with brags and high words' and, contrary to Cromwell's directions, presumed to interfere with liberties granted to the bishop by the king. Two of the richest canons, Griffith ab Owen and John Lewis, described as close friends of the Devereux family, were at this time accused of sympathizing with the northern rebels and were said by Barlow to be opposed to him only because of the zeal and sincerity of his attempts at reform. Lloyd, for his part, continued to complain of shameful behaviour on Barlow's side and of having been excommunicated by the bishop's commissary on Low Sunday (8 April) 1537.[55] He must have made a favourable impression on Cromwell, who was clearly less convinced than Barlow of the justice of the latter's cause and who seems to have intervened to have Lloyd's goods restored. Thereafter, for the rest of the year 1537, the documents fall silent concerning the altercations over the headship of the chapter, though the dispute between the two parties had not by any means come to an end.

Bangor was another diocese where earlier struggles between local notabilities had become identified with religious differences ostensibly arising out of clashes over the royal supremacy. Here, the role of the bishop was overshadowed by the feuds between local magnates. One of the earlier protagonists, Sir Richard Bulkeley, was another who had been hard put to survive unscathed by Anne Boleyn's disgrace, but having come through that crisis he again found himself at loggerheads with his former adversaries. Friction broke out between them once more late in 1536. At this stage, Bulkeley's position was weakened when he found himself temporarily in bad odour with Cromwell. He had offended the great man by intruding his kinsman, Dr Arthur Bulkeley, into a valuable living previously held by William Glyn which Cromwell had intended for his own nephew, Gregory

[53] PRO, STA C 2/23/177.
[54] R. A. Griffiths, *The Principality of Wales in the Later Middle Ages: South Wales, 1272–1536* (Cardiff, 1972), p. 165.
[55] *LP, Add.*, I/i. 1225.

Williams. Sir Richard hurriedly withdrew and abased himself before Cromwell, pleading that 'though I be not very wise I am not so stark mad to contend in anything appertaining to your lordship'.[56] The turn of the year 1536–7 saw the quarrel between Bulkeley and his rivals enter a new and more perilous phase. According to Bulkeley, for a large part of the year 1536 Glyn and Edward Gruffydd had been in London, and while they were away from north-west Wales, peace and order had prevailed. 'Within two or three days after their coming home', however, assaults and affrays had once more broken out. Then, in the cathedral at Christmas time 1536, so Bulkeley's story went, there had been further conflict between them and Dr Oking, the bishop's commissary, and on 21 February 1537 yet another fracas in the cathedral, involving a hundred 'riotous persons'. What made the whole affair still more sinister was that Glyn and Gruffydd were purported to be rejoicing at the prospect of civil war in England, which they trusted would give them the opportunity 'to be revenged of such as their adversaries'. Bulkeley professed himself to be extremely apprehensive about the dangers that might arise in north Wales at a time when rebellion was rife in the north of England and discontent seething in Ireland. Unless stern measures were promptly taken, he warned, the king might have 'as much to do with his subjects here in north Wales as ever he had in Ireland'.[57] Not too much reliance should be placed on such accusations of a treasonable connection, which were freely bandied about at this time to blacken an enemy's reputation but often on a very slender basis.

Although a good deal of the heat went out of these feuds with the death of William Glyn in the summer of 1537, a possible indication of the tardiness with which the king's wishes were being carried out in Bangor diocese may come in a letter written to Bishop Salcot by Dr Arthur Bulkeley in 1537. Bulkeley maintained that Cromwell was dissatisfied with conditions in the diocese 'which was never visited but superficially by the king's authority and . . . not so ordered as other men's dioceses be throughout the realm'. He suggested that better discipline was needed in order to exclude 'idolatry' and the 'incestuous and abominable living' of priests as well as laymen. He therefore begged to be appointed the bishop's commissary for the diocese, in which capacity he believed he might do much good. Salcot remained singularly unimpressed by these representations. He replied that although his own visitation was taken in his absence, he trusted that 'condign punishment with due reformation' was imposed on all offenders 'as well as if I were there myself'.[58] It may well have been that

[56] PRO, SP1/111/89–90; 112/260–1.
[57] Ibid., 116/117–18; 117/10–11.
[58] Ibid., 122/250–1.

Bulkeley, like most of his family, was eager for personal advancement, but he had a point in hinting that a well-born cleric with influential local connections might well be able to discipline the diocesan clergy more effectively than strangers could. This was a suggestion which may possibly have carried some weight in 1541, when Arthur Bulkeley was himself appointed bishop of Bangor.

Ambitious plans for far-reaching reform and reorganization were mooted in two other Welsh bishoprics at this juncture. In the diocese of St Asaph Bishop Parfew, who spent most of his time at either Wrexham or Denbigh, proposed to Cromwell that his cathedral should be moved from the village of St Asaph to Wrexham, one of the largest and most prosperous towns in the diocese. Later, he wanted to transfer it to Denbigh and also to establish a grammar school there. The burgesses of Denbigh liked the design well enough to confer the freedom of the borough on Parfew as a reward, even though their borough never became a cathedral city. Later, in 1539, Cromwell himself suggested that St Asaph should be joined to the new bishopric which was to be founded at Chester;[59] but clearly the bishop was able to stave off such a proposal. It is not certainly known whether or not there was a grammar school at St Asaph during Parfew's time as bishop; but one undoubtedly existed there in 1548 when, interestingly enough, the duke of Somerset wanted it transferred to Denbigh.[60]

Intentions for St David's similar to those of Parfew for St Asaph were cherished by Bishop Barlow. To speed the progress of reform in his diocese, he wanted to move his cathedral to Carmarthen, to establish a grammar school for the better education of the clergy, and to endow regular preaching. His schemes for moving the cathedral were linked with a plan to move the county town from Pembroke to Haverfordwest. These notions have often been censured as the aberrations of a rash and insensitive iconoclast, motivated by an unworthy personal ambition to achieve a greater degree of mastery over his cathedral clergy. Yet in fairness to Barlow there was much to be said in favour of his proposal. Historical associations with the patron saint apart, Carmarthen was a much more appropriate site for the cathedral than the remote village of St David's, so inconveniently sited on an isolated Pembrokeshire promontory – 'the most barren angle' in the diocese, Barlow described it. Carmarthen, by contrast, was the busiest and most populous town in Tudor Wales,[61] the essential

---

[59] D. R. Thomas, *The History of the Diocese of St Asaph* (3 vols. Oswestry, 1908–13), I. 78, 223.

[60] G. M. Griffith, 'Educational activity in the diocese of St Asaph', *JHSCW*, III (1953), 66–7.

[61] *WRE*, pp. 116–22.

hub of communications in south-west Wales, and much the nearest thing to a natural centre that existed in this large, inconvenient diocese. If the new reforming doctrines were to be vigorously propagated, then systematic preaching in a large market-town and port was one of the best ways of doing so. Removal of the cathedral from St David's might also have done something to check the abuses of non-residence among the cathedral clergy, then and for centuries afterwards one of their most flagrant shortcomings. Paradoxically enough, what may, more than any other consideration, have saved the cathedral at this time was the removal in the opposite direction of the body of Edmund Tudor, the king's grandfather, from Carmarthen to St David's.[62] The failure of Barlow's plan did not prevent later bishops of St David's from living at Abergwili, just outside Carmarthen, or from centring much of their administration in the town; but the decision not to move the cathedral was one for which the Anglican Church paid dearly in terms of its effectiveness in the diocese during the next two or three centuries.

Barlow was a keen advocate of better education, on the grounds that, 'in the whole diocese is not one grammar school, by reason whereof the clergy is unlearned and the people ignorant'.[63] Furthermore, he added, 'the English tongue is nothing preferred' – a drawback which must have seemed to him to be little short of disastrous when the Reformation was being promulgated almost entirely through the medium of English. The most obvious place in the diocese to site any new grammar school would be Carmarthen, especially since Barlow was proposing to fund the new foundation by transferring to it a large part of the resources of the collegiate church at nearby Abergwili, dismissed by him as being 'so unprofitable to the diocese'.[64] But although he praised Carmarthen as 'the most frequented place and indifferently situate in the middle of the diocese' and urged the removal of the cathedral to the Franciscan friary there as early as 1536 and the establishment of a free grammar school in the town, he proposed to set up his own grammar school in the town of Brecon. Presumably, he already knew of the schemes of Thomas Lloyd, the precentor, for setting up a grammar school in Carmarthen back in 1536[65] and it may be that he had no wish to further any project which his enemy had proposed for Carmarthen. Or else, to do justice to him, it could equally well be that Barlow knew that Lloyd had support in Carmarthen and was

---

[62] J. W. Evans, 'The Reformation and St David's cathedral', *JWEH*, VII (1991), 1–16.
[63] *LP*, XI. 1428.
[64] Ibid.
[65] Ibid., X. 226 (13).

likely to be able successfully to establish his school anyway. In that event, the bishop had every reason to plump for Brecon as the site for a new school, since it was the largest town and most convenient centre in the eastern half of his diocese and, next to Carmarthen, the most populous town in Wales.[66] Whatever his reasons, it was at Brecon that he ultimately founded his school.

Barlow's plans for the promotion of preaching and the removal of his cathedral were closely linked. He was convinced that St David's was too remote and awkwardly placed not only for the effective administration of his diocese but also for the propagation of new doctrines. What was worse was that its fame as a centre of medieval worship and a magnet which attracted every year hundreds if not thousands of pilgrims had led to its always being esteemed, in Barlow's lurid and partisan phrases, as 'a delicate daughter of Rome, naturally resembling her mother in shameless confusion, and like qualified with other perverse properties of execrable malignity'. He had therefore concluded that the only way to extirpate the 'memorial monuments' of Rome's 'puppetry' was to move the cathedral to Carmarthen, praised by him as the 'best town and in the middle of the diocese, where also the king's justice is kept, by occasion whereof the gentlemen and commons of the country most resort'.[67] Barlow's plans for systematic preaching at Carmarthen had much to recommend them. In spite of Bishop Gardiner's derogatory comments quoted earlier about how little hearers grasped of the purport of sermons at which they were present, another contemporary, Robert Ferrar, a protégé of Barlow who was, with his blessing, to succeed him at St David's, had very different views about the value of sermons. He recounted with enthusiasm how eagerly congregations assembled in the clothing towns of the West Riding to hear Protestant sermons being preached; so much so that he even wanted his own priory of Nostell turned into a centre for such preaching.[68] Barlow's intended programme at St David's suffered from one cardinal defect: it never once seems to have occurred to him that however common English may have been in some areas of his diocese, most of its inhabitants needed preaching in Welsh far more urgently.

The most general aspect of the activity undertaken in the dioceses during these years, as well as the one attended with most success, was the widespread demolition of celebrated shrines, relics, and places of pilgrimage. Throughout the year 1538, as the dissolution of large monasteries and friaries proceeded apace, a sustained onslaught had been mounted on those

[66] R. R. Davies, 'Brecon', in R. A. Griffiths (ed.), *Boroughs of Medieval Wales* (Cardiff, 1978), pp. 47–72.
[67] Wright, *Suppression*, pp. 208–9; *LP*, XIII/i. 634.
[68] Dickens, *Ref. in England*, p. 192.

places of ancient devotion associated with cathedrals and houses of religion, to which devotees had been accustomed to swarm in large numbers. Some of the most famous and wealthiest shrines in the land, like St Thomas's tomb at Canterbury, St Cuthbert's shrine at Durham, or the reliquary of the Holy Blood of Hailes, had been set upon, not only to destroy relics and images which gave rise to 'superstition' but also to appropriate to the king's use the jewels, plate, and other treasures with which they had been endowed. In Wales, it was William Barlow, as might have been anticipated, who led the hue and cry. As early as 31 March 1538 he jubilantly reported to Cromwell how he had proceeded to Haverfordwest – presumably to the Dominican friary in the town – to seize a miraculous taper which was reputed to burn without wasting. While thus engaged he had heard of a taper with a similar reputation burning at the image of the Virgin in the little Benedictine priory of Cardigan, as yet undissolved because it was a daughter cell of Chertsey, and had confiscated that, too. In addition, he had admonished the canons of St David's that they were not to set forth 'feigned relics' of the saint on St David's Day, and he referred with unconcealed disdain to the 'two heads of silver plate enclosing two rotten skulls' and other relics.[69] He took the opportunity of pressing again for the removal of the cathedral. Yet, contemptuous as Barlow may have been of the shrine and its reputation, it may not have been he who was responsible for demolishing it, but some of his canons. Later, in 1540–1, the Privy Council charged the president of the Council in the Marches with finding out what jewels had been embezzled when the shrine was broken up. In 1544 the Court of Augmentations was informed that the price obtained for 'le shryne of St David' was £66. 13s. 4d.[70] In August 1546 a warrant was issued to the treasurer of that court to pay a reward of £40 to James Leache for his expenses incurred in recovering 'plate and jewels which did belong to St David's shrine in Wales'.[71] Still later, Bishop Ferrar was to accuse some of the canons of despoiling the cathedral of crosses to the value of 400–500 marks.[72]

Round about the same time that Barlow was laying hands on the tapers at Haverfordwest and Cardigan, another of Thomas Cromwell's agents accustomed to carrying out his edicts for strong-arm action, Dr Ellis Price, acting as commissary-general for the diocese of St Asaph, informed his master that he had done his duty by 'expulsing and taking away of certain "abusions", superstitions and hypocrisies' in that diocese but gave no

---

[69] Wright, *Suppression*, p. 184.
[70] Evans, *JWEH*, VII. 5.
[71] *LP*, XXI/i. 1536 (34).
[72] Evans, *JWEH*, VII. 5.

further details concerning them. The greater part of his letter[73] was taken up with communicating how he had also 'removed an image of "Darvellgadarn" [Derfel Gadarn] within the same diocese'. The people had such 'great confidence, hope and trust' in the powers of this early Celtic warrior-saint that 500 or 600 of them had resorted to him on pilgrimage the previous day, believing that he had power to fetch them 'out of hell when they be damned'. Ellis Price ordered the wooden image of the saint to be cut off from the animal on which it was mounted and transported to Smithfield. There it was burnt in May, together with Friar Forest, formerly a confessor to Queen Catherine and an obdurate Catholic opponent to the king, thus fulfilling with black humour an ancient prophecy that it would one day set a whole forest on fire! The chronicler, Edward Hall, recorded that the following verses were posted up in great letters on the gallows:

> David Darvell Gatheren,
> As saith the Welshmen,
>   Fetched outlawes out of hell.
> Now is he come with spear and shield
> In harness to burn in Smithfield,
>   For in Wales he may not dwell.

> And Forest the friar
> That obstinate liar . . .
> That wilfully shall be dead,
> In his contumacy doth deny
>   The king to be supreme head.[74]

Bishop Latimer preached a sermon which created a sensation long remembered; years later, in 1552, Bernard Gilpin, preaching before the court referred disparagingly to the 'monster, Darvel Gatheren, the idol of Wales' and the traitor Forest, burnt with him.[75] The remains of Derfel's wooden 'stag' or 'horse' were still left at Llandderfel church in Merioneth and in later centuries remained the object of a good deal of local respect.[76]

Though there appears to be no record of the dismantling of the shrine of St Winifred, which stood at Holywell on land belonging to the former abbey of Basingwerk, it was probably at this time, or soon after, that unseemly scenes took place at the famous well. Evidence given in a suit heard at the Court of Augmentations told how servants of the last abbot of

[73] Wright, *Suppression*, pp. 208–9; *LP* XII/i. 634.
[74] Ibid.; W. G. Evans, 'Derfel Gadarn: a celebrated victim of the Reformation', *TMHS*, XI (1990–3), 137–51.
[75] J. A. Froude, *The Reign of Edward VI* (London, 1926), p. 271.
[76] Thomas, *St Asaph*, III. 97.

Basingwerk, Nicholas Pennant, sought to take offerings from the pilgrims who continued to resort to St Winifred's Well. They boldly proclaimed to the faithful that 'such money as you offer into the said stock, going to the king, shall never be remedy for your souls, for there stands one of the king's servants who will soon take it forth'. They then offered their own boxes for oblations and took on that one occasion £5. 13*s*. 4*d*. and an ox valued at £1. 3*s*. 4*d*.[77]

An equally attractive shrine in Llandaff diocese was that dedicated to the Virgin Mary at Pen-rhys in the Rhondda Valley on a grange belonging to the former abbey of Llantarnam.[78] It was widely known outside Wales; and Latimer, writing to Thomas Cromwell in June 1538, referred to it as 'our great Sibyl', 'the devil's instrument to bring many (I fear) to eternal fire'. He spoke of it with coarse hilarity as one of a number of images dedicated to the Virgin located at Worcester, Walsingham, Ipswich and Doncaster that 'would make a jolly muster at Smithfield; they would not be all day in burning'.[79] Cromwell needed no second bidding. On 23 August he wrote to William Herbert and the chancellor of Llandaff diocese ordering them to have the image taken down. Evidently fearing that popular indignation, though apparently little moved by the dissolution of the monasteries, might react much more sharply to the desecration of so revered an object of pilgrimage, he gave instructions that the image should be taken down 'as secretly as might be'.[80] On 26 September the royal will was proclaimed at Pen-rhys and 'idolatry' denounced. The image was taken away to London, burnt with a number of others of like character, and the event celebrated in a ballad written by William Gray, one of Cromwell's servants. Meanwhile, back in Glamorgan, the once-flourishing tavern at Pen-rhys, which had entertained the former throngs of pilgrims, fell into decay.[81]

Another celebrated shrine in the same area also broken up at this time was that of St Teilo in the lady chapel at Llandaff cathedral. This was an elaborate and costly creation, containing the images of St Teilo, Dyfrig, and Euddogwy, the three saints especially associated with Llandaff and reputed to possess astounding powers which could be deployed on behalf of faithful votaries.[82] The shrine was made mostly of silver gilt and

---

[77] *Augs. Procs.*, p. 96; for the full text of this document see E. Owen, 'The monastery of Basingwerk at its dissolution', *Flints. HS*, VII. 74–89.

[78] *WC*, pp. 492–3; *AC* (1914), 357–406.

[79] J. Gairdner, *Lollardy and the Reformation in England* (4 vols. London, 1908–13), II. 141; H. Latimer, *Sermons and Remains* (Parker Soc., London, 1845), p. 395.

[80] *LP*, XIII/ii. 345; a number of images were removed from London churches by night, so as to reduce the risk of rioting.

[81] *Augs. Procs.*, pp. 141–2.

[82] Williams, *TCS* (1991), 69–98.

surrounded by a mass of gold and silver treasures of various kinds, included among them assorted relics like St Teilo's bell, book (presumably the famous *Liber Landavensis*), and comb.[83] Some of the Llandaff canons tried to forestall royal expropriation of their church's most prized possession by dismantling the shrine and parcelling out its treasures among themselves. This is customarily said to have happened in 1540–1;[84] but the true date must certainly be earlier than June 1540, when Thomas Cromwell, who was prominently involved in the episode, fell from power. The most likely year in which it could have happened was 1538, about the time of, or soon after, the general attacks on shrines like that of St Thomas at Canterbury, St David at St David's, or Mary's image at Pen-rhys. Whenever it occurred, the Llandaff canons did not escape with their spoils. The bishop's commissary reported their doings to his absent master, Robert Holgate, who in turn informed Cromwell. Holgate ordered his chancellor, John Broxholme, to recover the missing parts. Broxholme succeeded in gathering up the 'three saints' heads with their mitres in silver and double gilt' and 4,000–5,000 ounces of plate, but he had to admit that a 'great part of the shrine was conveyed away', including 'all the rest of the jewels and stuff seized by Dr Smith, the treasurer'. The ringleader of the canons, Henry Morgan, was more in awe of Cromwell than Holgate and delivered a large part of the spoils to him. He also gave him to understand that Holgate had unlawfully pocketed some of the plate himself. Cromwell was unimpressed by these tales, but Holgate felt impelled to present the cathedral with 'a pair of organs and divers suits of vestments' by way of compensation. Nor was that the end of the episode. Many years later, during Mary's reign, Miles Mathew, a member of the local gentry,[85] was commissioned to inquire into the fate of the treasures, and on 20 July 1558 Dr John Smith, the treasurer, was bound over in the sum of 500 marks to answer to the queen's commissioner for his part in the affair.[86]

It was not until late in August 1538, with the winding up of the last friaries in Wales, that some of the most famous relics in Bangor diocese were seized. Richard Ingworth, bishop of Dover and visitor of the friaries, wrote from Hereford to tell Cromwell that he had a bizarre relic, but not untypical of the unpredictable fancy that medieval piety could conceive for

---

[83] Ibid., p. 76.

[84] *The Records of the County Borough of Cardiff*, ed. J. H. Matthews (6 vols. Cardiff, 1898–1911), I. 372–80; L. Thomas, *The Reformation in the Old Diocese of Llandaff* (Cardiff, 1930), pp. 75–90.

[85] The Mathew family, having emigrated to Australia, decided in February 1994 to return 'Teilo's skull', which was reputed to have been in the family's possession since 1450!

[86] Thomas, *Llandaff*, p. 79.

some very unlikely objects for devotion – 'Malchus's ear that Peter struck off'.[87] He added that he also had a thousand relics

as true as that; but the holiest relic in all north Wales I send to you here; there may no man kiss that but he must kneel as soon as he sees it, and he must kiss every stone, for in each is great pardon. After that he hath kissed it, he must pay a 'meed' of corn, or a cheese of a groat, or fourpence for it. It was worth to the friars in Bangor, with another image which I have closed up, twenty marks by the year in corn, cheese, cattle, and money.[88]

Although it is not possible to compile a comprehensive record of all the holy places that were attacked or all the precious objects taken away, it nevertheless seems probable that a large number of the better-known shrines so deeply embedded in popular affection and piety – in super- stition, too, in many instances – were removed from the focus of the people's devotion. There is no sign of there having been any public protest or uprising against these proceedings, but their general unpopularity may to some extent be gauged from the instructions given to William Herbert to remove the image at Pen-rhys as secretly as possible, and also from the way in which people continued to venerate the saints and go on pilgrimage for decades to come.[89]

Of the more constructive aspects of the royal injunctions that were enjoined upon the populace we hear very little in Wales during these years. Apart from Bishop Barlow's efforts there is little evidence of systematic attempts at preaching. Nor is there much sign that the literature streaming from Cromwell's propagandists was having any significant effect. Above all, there is little indication that the campaign to induce people to read the Bible for themselves, which was having a dramatic impact in some parts of southern and eastern England, was making any marked impression in Wales. True, on 31 March 1538 Barlow had instructed the clergy in Cardigan to declare the gospel or epistle of the day in the mother tongue, 'expounding the same sincerely as far as their learning will extend', and to preach for several Sundays to come against the 'deceitful juggling' of their predecessors.[90] But it is not clear whether 'mother tongue' in this context meant English or Welsh, though given Barlow's prejudice against Welsh, it seems more than likely that he intended English to be used. It would have been more to the point if he had taken the same steps in Wales as Bishop

---

[87] Matthew 26: 51; Luke 22: 50.
[88] Wright, *Suppression*, p. 212.
[89] Williams, *TCS* (1991), 92–8.
[90] Wright, *Suppression*, p. 187.

Veysey did in Cornwall, when he ordered the gospel or epistle to be declared in Cornish, where 'the English tongue is not used'.[91]

During the latter half of 1538, however, circumstances in Europe turned perceptibly to Henry's disadvantage and cooled the encouragement previously given to reforming tendencies. In the summer the two rival Catholic rulers, Charles V and Francis I, made peace with one another – always a source of worry if not acute potential danger to Henry – and in December the pope excommunicated him. Fearing an invasion by Catholic powers on a massive scale, Henry was obliged to look urgently to his coastal defences, including those of Milford Haven.[92] The inherent risks in the situation led him on the one hand to conduct a diplomatic flirtation with Lutheran powers as possible allies, but on the other to set his face against further religious experiments and finally to close ranks behind a traditional exposition of religion. On 5 May 1539 the Lord Chancellor told the Lords and Commons that the king desired 'above all things that diversity of religion should be banished from his dominions'.[93] On 28 June an 'Act for Abolishing Diversity of Opinion' (31 Henry VIII, c. 14), better known to its supporters as the Six Articles Act and to its opponents as 'the whip with six strings', received the king's assent. It affirmed an unmistakably Catholic interpretation of the central theological issues which divided the Henrician standpoint from that of Protestants. It emphatically reasserted the doctrine of transubstantiation, communion in one kind, clerical celibacy, the validity of vows of chastity, private masses, and auricular confession. Even more significant, perhaps, were the 'whips' attaching to it which decreed death at the stake for denying transubstantiation, and imprisonment for those who spoke or acted contrary to the provisions of the Act, followed by death if they persisted in their disobedience.[94]

Among those who had expressed their undiluted opposition to the Act were Protestant bishops like Latimer, Shaxton, and Barlow. The two former resigned their sees; but Barlow who, throughout his career, revealed a rare faculty for surviving adverse Reformation changes, was able to cling to his. So, of course, did a more important reformer, his archbishop, Thomas Cranmer, who never forfeited the king's affection – even in the darkest days. Indeed, during the months immediately following the passage of the Six Articles Act, Cranmer was engaged in a large-scale heresy hunt, in which the Welshman, Richard Gwent, one of the archbishop's right-

---

[91] *Kynniver Llith a Ban*, ed. J. Fisher (Cardiff, 1931), p. xxi.

[92] J. F. Rees, *The Story of Milford* (Cardiff, 1954), pp. 5–6.

[93] L. B. Smith, *Henry VIII: The Mask of Royalty* (London 1971), p. 130.

[94] G. Redworth, 'A study in the formulation of policy: the genesis and evolution of the Act of Six Articles', *JEH*, XXXVII (1986), 42–67.

hand men, was well to the fore in helping him to search for Anabaptists and Sacramentaries, especially in Calais.[95]

While the king and the conservatives were pushing through the Six Articles Act in 1539, Cromwell had simultaneously been angling for a Lutheran alliance for England, to be sealed by Henry's fourth marriage – this time to a Lutheran princess, Anne of Cleves.[96] It was a manœuvre being hotly opposed and fatally undermined by Cromwell's sworn enemies, headed by Norfolk and Gardiner. For some months it appeared by no means certain which of the two conflicting parties would gain the upper hand. In April 1540, when Cromwell was created earl of Essex, he looked to be in the ascendant; but by midsummer, the king had undergone a violent change of mood. On 10 June Cromwell was arrested and on 28 July executed.[97] His enemies had brought about the downfall of the king's ablest servant; partly on account of Henry's revulsion against his most recent bride; partly as a result of Cromwell's own misjudged tactics; partly owing to the failure of his foreign policy; and not least because he had been too well disposed towards the reformers' cause. His eclipse marked the end of a decade of radical change in government and religion. The last six or seven years of Henry's reign were to be a period of conservative consolidation, characterized by ruinously expensive wars and intense infighting between rival factions at court.

[95] *WRE*, p. 81.

[96] M. A. S. Hume, *The Wives of Henry VIII* (London, 1905); A. Fraser, *The Six Wives of Henry VIII* (London, 1993), chap. 14.

[97] G. R. Elton, *Reform and Reformation: England, 1509–1558* (London, 1977), pp. 292–5; A. G. Dickens, *Thomas Cromwell and the English Reformation* (London, 1959), pp. 165–73.

CHAPTER 6

Henry VIII's Last Years, 1540–1547

THE last years of Henry VIII's reign were characterized by struggles for power between rival factions at his court and in his council chamber. They were contests for influence over the king in which the participants were *politiques* rather than men of principle; their religious inclinations tended to be as much an excuse for cloaking personal and political ambition as they were a matter of conviction, if not more so. At the centre of the web of intrigue and counter-intrigue, like some monstrous spider being preyed upon as well as preying, was poised the ageing king, who now seemed bent on denying that too great an accession of power should pass to any single individual or group. In pursuit of his own ends of maintaining the power of the sovereign, handing it on intact to his heir, and consolidating the unity of the kingdom, he was prepared to play cat and mouse with his servants, setting one faction or person against another in a classic display of *divide et impera*.[1] Over most of these years, too, he was obliged to keep a wary eye on war and diplomacy. The disturbed state of European relations threatened him with repeated dangers, but also dangled before him the temptation of once more playing the role so dear to his ambitions of cutting a masterful figure in France and Scotland. As a consequence, he was to embroil himself in a succession of extraordinarily expensive but largely futile campaigns.[2]

From 1540 to 1546 Henry was to be greatly preoccupied with the entanglements of international conflicts. The precarious peace arrived at between the Emperor Charles V and King Francis I was unmistakably breaking up by the end of 1540. Wooed by both parties, Henry could not resist the temptation to meddle. After long and tortuous negotiations, by early 1542 he had arrived at an understanding with Charles that they should jointly invade France. Before embarking on such a venture, prudence dictated that he secure the position at his 'postern gate' in

---

[1] L. B. Smith, *Henry VIII: The Mask of Royalty* (London, 1971), *passim*; J. J. Scarisbrick, *Henry VIII* (London, 1968), chaps. 13–14.

[2] R. B. Wernham, *Before the Armada* (London, 1966), chaps. 11 and 12.

Scotland.[3] In November 1542 his armies defeated those of his northern neighbours at the battle of Solway Moss, but his heavy-handedness only succeeded in alienating the Scots and ultimately landed him in war on two fronts. Nor was his grandiose and exceedingly expensive campaign of 1544 in France much more successful. Although he captured Boulogne, he was soon deserted by his imperial ally and in 1545 faced the prospect of a large-scale invasion from France. The total cost to England of these military adventures has been estimated at the astronomical sum of £2,134,784.[4]

To try to meet this enormous outlay Henry had no option but to squeeze money from all the sources of revenue open to him. In an era when princely expenditure almost always outran income, an age of inflationary prices and free-spending courts, outdated fiscal methods and haphazard emergency financing, there was never enough money to cope with all royal demands.[5] Large sums had to be raised by taxation, direct and indirect; and the Subsidy Act of 1543 was the first of Henry's reign to be applied to Wales.[6] The preamble to that Act specifically declared its purpose to be to enable the king to pursue his claim to the Scottish crown. The royal mint was also reorganized, and some £363,000 raised by the debasement of the coinage between 1544 and 1546. A further £100,000 were borrowed on the Antwerp money-market and the huge sum of £270,000 extracted in forced loans from his subjects.[7]

An even more important source was tapped when sales of monastic land began in 1540, though this could be regarded as a process of 'selling the family silver' in the long run. Hitherto, in spite of some occasional conflicting signals like the granting away of Tintern's estates to gratify the king's favourite, the earl of Worcester, it seemed as if the intention had been to retain the bulk of the monastic properties in the king's own hands and thereby more than double his income. However, the crippling financial demands imposed by Henry's conduct of external affairs led to a drastic revision of his plans, a process in which the elimination of Cromwell's influence may have increased the disposition to sell. The actual sale of monastic lands in Wales began in February 1540, when William Cavendish, one of the officials of the Court of Augmentations, bought the house and possessions of the tiny priory of Cardigan.[8] This was followed shortly afterwards by the sale of the house, site, and demesne of Dore to John

---

[3] J. D. Mackie, *The Early Tudors* (Oxford, 1952); J. Wormald, *Court, Kirk and Community: Scotland 1470–1625* (London, 1981).

[4] J. Guy, *Tudor England* (Oxford, 1988), p. 192.

[5] G. Mattingley, *Renaissance Diplomacy* (London, 1955), p. 231.

[6] W. R. B. Robinson, 'The first subsidy assessments of the hundreds of Swansea and Llangyfelach', *WHR*, II/2 (1964), 125–46.

[7] F. C. Dietz, *English Public Finance, 1485–1641* (2 vols. Urbana, Ill., 1921), I. 144–77.

[8] *LP*, XV. 282 (108).

Scudamore and of part of the possessions of Basingwerk in Holywell together with the house and site of Rhuddlan friary to Henry ap Henry of Llanasa and Peter Mutton of Meliden.[9] Rice Mansel, who was already leasing Margam, made the first of his four major purchases there in June 1540.[10] From then until 1544 only a handful of disposals followed, including Brecon friary in 1541 to Barlow for the foundation of his college and the greater part of Neath's possessions in 1542 to Sir Richard Cromwell alias Williams, Thomas Cromwell's nephew.[11] Activity remained generally sluggish until 1545. This may have owed something to a reluctance on the part of the Crown to sell and lack of ready capital on the side of local purchasers. By the years 1545 and 1546, however, with the king far more desperately in need of ready money, and potential buyers showing a greater willingness to risk investment, there was a flurry of sales. They included some quite substantial transactions. Sir Edward Carne, who had already acquired the Margam granges of Crwys Bychan and Llystalybont near Cardiff in 1542, and Colwinston, formerly belonging to the priory of Deptford in 1543, achieved his long-standing ambition in August 1546 when he bought, for £726. 6*s*. 4*d*., the priory and lands of Ewenni, the advowsons of Colwinston, St Bride's, and Llandyfodwg, and '200 oaks being timber of 100 years' growth'.[12] Rice Mansel made two further purchases of Margam land in 1543 and 1546, and Nicholas Arnold acquired the priory of Llanthony, of which he was already the lessee,[13] in 1546. It was at this time, also, that the townsmen of New Carmarthen asserted their rights over Old Carmarthen, John Vaughan bought Pembroke priory, and the Barlow brothers, Roger and Thomas, got their hands on Slebech, Haverfordwest priory and friary, and Pill priory.

Most of the properties which had been bought during these years lay either in the counties of the southern seaboard like Pembrokeshire, Carmarthenshire, and Glamorgan, or else along the eastern border, where many of the possessions of Basingwerk, Valle Crucis, Strata Marcella, Cwm-hir, Grace Dieu, and Abergavenny passed into new ownership.[14] It was in these localities, in any case, that the bulk of monastic possessions had been located; but it is noticeable that the estates of quite large houses lying in some of the counties of western Wales, like Strata Florida, Talley, Whitland, Cymer, or Bardsey, continued to be leased rather than purchased, in spite of some of the players at the board being such major

[9] Ibid., 613 (40).
[10] Ibid., 831 (62).
[11] Ibid., XVII. 220 (95).
[12] Ibid., XX/ii. 266 (13).
[13] Ibid., XXI/i. 1166 (47); i. 1537 (28); ii. 332 (83).
[14] Ibid., XVI. p. 576; XVII. 1154 (64); XVIII/ii. p. 56; XX, XXI *passim*.

figures as the Devereux family (Strata Florida and Whitland) and Sir Thomas Jones (Talley).[15] Even the gentry of the south-eastern county of Monmouthshire were distinctly slower to buy than their neighbours in Glamorgan. That has led the historian of ecclesiastical property there[16] to suggest that this was because Monmouthshire, being a more backward and intellectually remote county than Glamorgan, did not produce as many men of affairs and initiative in law, politics, and war, and so had fewer individuals of substance who could afford to lay out capital. The same may equally well have been true of the counties of west and north-west Wales, though it has been pointed out that leasing itself could give rise to serious difficulties. It became very competitive as the century went on, and leases often had to be renewed at relatively short intervals, while other landholders found the burden of managing leased estates to be too heavy for them to cope with.[17]

A minority of the purchasers came from outside the area itself, like John Bradshaw of Presteigne, a leading figure in the entourage of Bishop Rowland Lee, who bought St Dogmael's.[18] Three of them, at least, had their main residence in England but had earlier connections with Wales. Nicholas Arnold, at the time when he purchased Llanthony, lived fairly near at hand in Hinehan in Gloucestershire, but his ancestors originally hailed from south Wales.[19] Richard Cromwell, alias Williams, Cromwell's nephew, although his main seat lay in Huntingdonshire, was another whose family had come from Glamorgan; and Lord St John, despite living in Bedfordshire, had important interests in Fonmon and Barry in Glamorgan, which was what had spurred him into acquiring former Margam lands at Bonvilston.[20] Most of the buyers were drawn from local families of gentry. A number of them were individuals who stood high in the royal favour like Henry, second earl of Worcester, or had performed with distinction in the king's service, like Sir Rice Mansel, Sir Edward Carne, John Scudamore, John Vaughan, or William Barlow. They were very rarely drawn from 'new' families but were more usually younger sons, or cadet members of well-known families, or men of gentry origin who had made a success of their

[15] G. D. Owen, 'Agrarian conditions and changes in West Wales during the sixteenth century' (Ph.D. thesis, Wales, 1935), pp. 338–9.

[16] Dr Madeleine Gray, see below, n. 19.

[17] Owen, 'Agrarian conditions', pp. 365–73.

[18] D. G. Walker, 'Religious change, 1536–1603', *Pembrokeshire County History*, ed. B. Howells, III (1987), 103.

[19] M. Gray, 'The disposal of Crown property in Monmouthshire, 1500–1603' (Ph.D. thesis, Wales, 1985); 'Change and continuity: the gentry and the property of the Church in south-east Wales', in *Class, Community and Culture in Wales*, ed. J. G. Jones (Cardiff, 1989), pp. 1–38.

[20] *WRE*, pp. 100–4.

professional careers. Their ability to buy monastic land often emphasized the distinction between them and less successful families and tended to consolidate the position of the 'upper crust' of county families. Such a tendency is more than usually apparent in a county like Glamorgan, rich in monastic property, where only a small group of leading families – Carnes, Mansels, Stradlings, Herberts, and Lewises – chiefly benefited from the disposal of former monastic estates.[21] The same was nearly as noticeable over a longer period in Monmouthshire, where it was the Somersets of Raglan, Morgans of Llantarnam, Williamses of Usk, Herberts of Troy, and Gunters of Abergavenny, who were the main beneficiaries.[22] Nor did the acquisition of monastic land automatically create a vested interest among these families in maintaining the Protestant church settlement. Among the most prominent Roman Catholic families of Elizabethan Wales were Somersets, Carnes, Morgans, Gunters, and Barlows, all of whom had benefited conspicuously from the purchase of monastic estates.

Legal knowledge and contacts often contributed usefully to the success achieved by some of these purchasers. Not only on the part of men with distinguished academic and administrative careers like Sir John Price, who bought Brecon priory, or John Vaughan, LLD, who acquired Pembroke, or Sir Edward Carne of Ewenni, but also in the case of much lesser figures like James Gunter or Roger Williams. Gunter was of relatively humble origins and born in Abergavenny. He trained as a lawyer and settled for a time in London. He bought monastic land successfully on his own behalf and that of others. He also made handsome profits as a speculator, buying monastic land for £50 in Abergavenny in 1543, for example, and selling it to a very well-known lawyer, David Lewis, also of Abergavenny, for £300 ten years later.[23] Roger Williams, purchaser of Usk priory, was also the son of a lawyer and did very well for himself by entering the service of William Herbert, later earl of Pembroke. Williams, too, bought extensively for others as well as on his own account.[24]

Merchant interest, though less evident than that of the landed gentry and the lawyers, did not go entirely unrepresented. The burgesses of Abergavenny managed to secure possession of the priory there to use it as their parish church and thus give them the opportunity to turn their former parish church of St John into a grammar school, which was called King

[21] Ibid.
[22] Gray, *Class, Community*, pp. 8–20.
[23] Ibid., p. 14.
[24] Gray, *Class, Community*, pp. 12–13.

Henry VIII School in honour of the king and still bears that name.[25] Brecon, not many miles up the valley of the Usk, was another town whose worthies lent their support to Bishop William Barlow so that he might establish a grammar school in their midst. Barlow's own brother, Roger, who acquired much the biggest stake in Pembrokeshire's monastic lands, had earlier in life been a highly successful Bristol merchant, though the Barlows actually sprang from a gentry family of Essex-Hertfordshire, which had come down in the world as a result of disasters incurred in the civil wars of the fifteenth century.[26]

The outstanding Welsh instance of merchant and municipal interest in the fate of dissolved religious houses was that of Carmarthen.[27] There, as early as 1536, a leading cleric, Thomas Lloyd, a native of the town, had petitioned to be allowed to found a grammar school and had been given permission to do so. Following the surrender of the Franciscan friary in the town in 1538, the mayor and aldermen descried a splendid chance of helping Lloyd carry out his plans. They petitioned the king to allow the site and buildings of the friary, described as having fallen into ruin and decay, to be adapted for use as a grammar school at the costs and charges of Thomas Lloyd. Not until 1543 did the project come to fruition. On 30 January of that year a royal grant declared that it had been represented to the king by Thomas Lloyd and others that no place in Wales was more suitable for a school than the site of Friars Carmarthen and that the king now wished the school to be known as 'the King's School of Carmarthen of Thomas Lloyd's Foundation'. Lloyd was allowed to acquire the site of the friary and other properties, the profits of which were to be applied for the maintenance of his establishment.[28]

In the mean time, the burgesses of 'New' Carmarthen, as the borough was then known, had been flexing their muscles with the intention of bringing into line their rivals in 'Old' Carmarthen, the little settlement which in the course of time had grown up around the priory. Its inhabitants, hitherto safeguarded by the influence of the priors of earlier days, had for centuries been claiming what the burgesses of Carmarthen regarded as unfair trading privileges. The aggrieved townsmen now sought to put the privileged men of Old Carmarthen on the same footing as themselves and liable to pay the same contribution to the borough's annual fee-farm. As a result, there were ugly scenes of violence along the quay in

[25] T. J. Edwards, 'The disposal of the monastic property in the diocese of Llandaff' (MA thesis, Wales, 1929), p. 58.
[26] E. G. Rupp, *Studies in the Making of the English Protestant Tradition* (Cambridge, 1949), p. 63.
[27] *W and R*, pp. 117–37.
[28] Williams, *Carm. Antiq.* X (1974), 49–63.

Carmarthen, in the course of which the rulers of New Carmarthen tried to impose their authority by force on the denizens of Old Carmarthen, despite the latter's attempt to invoke the help of an ally no less calculated to overawe their enemies than Richard Devereux. Eventually, the dispute ended up in the Court of Augmentations.[29] No record exists of the verdict in this suit, but the final outcome of the quarrel was perhaps the only fair and rational one: Old Carmarthen was merged into New Carmarthen. On 28 April 1546 the town was given a royal grant of liberties and became a free borough. Old Carmarthen was to be separated from Derllys hundred, annexed to the borough, and the names Old Carmarthen and New Carmarthen were to be abolished. It was to be the end of an old dispensation and the beginning of a new one in more senses than one. The friction over commercial interests and activities between local merchants on one side and the monks and their tenants on the other was relatively common before the dissolution. The existence of such rivalry may help to explain the widespread absence of public protest against the suppression of the religious houses. Even in Carmarthen, where the priory was in healthier and more active condition than most Welsh monasteries, there is no sign of outcry against its disappearance. That may well have been because a majority of the town's leading citizens saw in the extinction of the priory a long-awaited opening to rid themselves of a greatly resented source of privileged commercial competition. Here was yet another local illustration of a universal reaction to Reformation change: that men's attitudes might be determined at least as much by their secular interests as their religious beliefs. It is also a reminder that merchants, as well as landed gentry, hoped to reap personal benefit from the disappearance of the monasteries. Carmarthen's burgesses had a keen eye for how the suppression of the priory and friary could be turned to the advantage of their town.[30]

It was not only from the former monasteries and their possessions that Henry was urgently seeking to raise ready money at this time. The very suppression of the houses of religion so closely associated in the popular mind with prayers for the dead may partly have prompted the king and his servants to turn their eyes upon the chantries. The extinction of monastic prayer, accompanied by the unremitting condemnation of the doctrine of purgatory and the intellectual justification for papal indulgences, had had the effect of undermining fatally the position of chantries as institutions endowed to offer prayers and masses for dead souls. But just as important at this juncture, and probably more pressing, was the king's desperate need for ready cash. Although the chantries and similar institutions were far

---

[29] PRO, E321/13/75; 37/6.
[30] *W and R*, pp. 117–37.

more modestly endowed than the monasteries had been, the seizure of their assets could nevertheless constitute a useful contribution to the every-gaping maw of the royal treasury. The Chantries Act of 1545, whereby the king was empowered to take into his hands all the chantries and other like institutions, was followed up in February 1546 by the setting up of commissions in all parts of the kingdom to inquire into 'all chantries, hospitals, colleges, free chapels, fraternities, brotherhoods, guilds, and the salaries of all stipendiary priests "having perpetuity" and all their possessions'. The commissioners were to take careful inventories of these goods and endowments so as to prevent embezzlement.[31] Two commissions were appointed for Wales; one for the north and another for the south. Personnel for each was much the same and included the bishops of the four Welsh dioceses and a number of prominent laymen. Although they carried out their survey as directed and a copy of the certificate for south Wales has survived,[32] the king did not in fact go on to confiscate to his own use the chantry possessions. It was not until 1547, during Edward VI's reign, that action was taken against them (see below chap. 7). What the preliminaries of 1545–6 had done was to offer the king's subjects in the parishes advance notice of what was likely to befall them. This gave a number of them an opportunity, of which they gratefully availed themselves, to conceal or dispose of their assets beforehand. At least one leading Welsh cleric, John Gwynedd, who was incumbent of the rich and historic collegiate church of Clynnog Fawr, hastily seized the opportunity to have representations made to the king on his behalf. In January 1546 he induced his influential brother-in-law, Stephen Vaughan, to approach Sir William Paget to be a suitor to the king that he might have permission to keep his church, on which he claimed to have had to spend over 500 marks to defend his title. He also expressed his fears that 'the Welshmen' (presumably local inhabitants with influence) would shortly sue against him to have the church for themselves.[33] About the same time, Bishop Bulkeley of Bangor, in a comparable defensive action, obtained a licence to grant the advowson of Llandegfan and its annexed chapel of St Mary, Beaumaris, to his relative, Sir Richard Bulkeley, in perpetuity.[34]

Another feature of Edward VI's reign foreshadowed during the last years of Henry's life was the growing tendency on the part of the king and his powerful subjects to put pressure on the bishops to part with their property. During the year 1545–6 no fewer than seventeen exchanges of

[31] *LP*, XXI/i. 302 (30).
[32] E. D. Jones, 'A survey of South Wales chantries', *AC* (1934), 134–55.
[33] *LP*, XXI/i. 26.
[34] Ibid., XXI/i. 1166 (49),

land, considerably more favourable to the king or the aristocracy than the bishops, have been traced, as compared with only five such transactions between 1541 and 1544.[35] The outstanding Welsh example of this occurred over the manor of Lamphey, the most valuable episcopal estate belonging to the diocese of St David's. Throughout the Middle Ages, this delectable manor had been the jewel in the crown of the bishops, as well as their favourite residence on the comparatively rare occasions when they spent time in the diocese. It was Bishop Barlow's alienation of Lamphey that provoked most criticism of him as an impoverisher of his see.[36] Early in 1546, at his own suit, he received the royal permission to grant, bargain, or give in fee simple, the lordship of Lamphey to Richard Devereux, eldest son and heir of Lord Ferrers. On 14 August, with the consent of the precentor and chapter, Barlow surrendered the lordship and manor to the Crown. On 16 October he received a grant of the advowson of the rectory and vicarage of Carew in return for the surrender of Lamphey, which two days earlier had been granted to Richard Devereux. After 1546 the bishops of St David's spent most of their time at Abergwili, just outside Carmarthen, whenever they were in the diocese.

The motives which impelled Barlow to alienate this valuable manor in return for distinctly inadequate compensation have never been satisfactorily explained and may always remain something of a mystery. It is true that bishops were coming under severe pressure from the Crown and the laity to part with their temporal possessions. Henry VIII's finances were, as has been seen, certainly in dire straits at this time. Yet it was not the Crown, but the Devereux family, that gained most by the surrender of Lamphey. While Barlow had wanted to move his cathedral from St David's to Carmarthen and although he was not always a careful husband of the resources of his diocese, it is not easy to imagine that he would agree to enrich his old enemies except under some sort of duress. According to one tradition, he was placed in a state of severe embarrassment by the Devereux because they had discovered he was keeping a concubine. This is not entirely out of the question; and there may have been some scandal involving the bishop, the details of which have long been forgotten; but it does not seem at all likely as an explanation for the exchange. What may be more germane is the apparent shift in the religious allegiance of the Devereux during these years. Whereas in 1537–8 they had been allies and patrons of some of the more conservative canons of St David's, by 1546 the records of the Privy Council reveal that Richard Devereux and one John Olde, chaplain to Lord Ferrers, were both summoned before it on charges

[35] F. Heal, *Of Prelates and Princes* (Cambridge, 1990), p. 119.
[36] *WRE*, pp. 121–3.

of heresy.[37] Such an accusation, coupled with the alignment of Lord Ferrers with the Hertford–Lisle party during Henry's later years, and his own and his son's rapid elevation under the Somerset regime in Edward's reign, suggest that the family had moved much closer to the group favouring reform. Whether this change of direction had brought about a *rapprochement* with Barlow it seems impossible to tell with certainty on the basis of the surviving evidence. However, an old tradition that Barlow alienated Lamphey to his godson, Walter, Richard Devereux's young son and the future first earl of Essex, may have relevance in this context. At least, it suggests that Barlow and the Devereux were on much friendlier terms, for him to have been invited to be godfather to the boy. It may also have been far more than coincidence that in the very summer when William Barlow was yielding up Lamphey, his brothers, Roger and Thomas, were acquiring by purchase from the Crown very substantial monastic estates in Pembrokeshire. Theirs was a dazzling prize to be picking up so near the heart of Devereux territory; and resentment felt earlier by the Devereux at the intrusion of the Barlows into their preserves had been well known. By 1546, however, each side may have modified its previous attitude and come to regard the other as a useful ally. The acquisition of Lamphey by the Devereux, besides being a highly desirable reward in itself, may also have served as a *quid pro quo* for their accepting undisputedly the Barlow claims to the Haverfordwest and Slebech estates. It is a possible explanation of what still remains a mysterious transaction, even allowing for all the pressure that the king and one of his prominent aristocrats on very friendly terms with a leading court faction could apply to a bishop.

All the while, during these years from 1540 onwards, the tone set in religious affairs by the Six Articles Act was cautious and conservative, and the encouragement earlier given to the more enthusiastic reformers much less in evidence. Yet, ironically enough, as far as the Welsh were concerned, the era of reaction ushered in by the Act at first led not to the execution of Protestants but of a number of brave and principled Catholics. All of them were men who had carved careers for themselves in England, and that was where they staged their resistance to the king. The first to be sacrificed was John Griffith, hanged, drawn, and quartered on 8 July 1539. A secular priest, Griffith, like many a Tudor Welshman, had found a congenial niche for himself in the household of a leading aristocrat; in his case in the retinue of Henry Courtenay, marquis of Exeter. Courtenay, a descendant of Edward IV and a relative of Reginald Pole, had been beheaded in

---

[37] *APC*, I (1542–7), 401, 479.

December 1538 on a charge of conspiring to put Pole on the throne. Griffith, closely associated with the White Rose too, had refused, like his master, to recognize the validity of the king's divorce or his supremacy, and was executed for his stubbornness.[38] The next to be proceeded against was that John Eynon who had earlier been so intimately linked with Abbot Cook of Reading. He also rejected the divorce and the supremacy and, in addition, was accused of collusion with Aske and the northern rebels. After being put on trial in October 1539 Eynon, together with Abbot Cook and John Rugg, was hanged, drawn, and quartered on 15 November 1539.[39] His friend, the blind harpist, William Mawr or More, was also executed in 1540. In that same year, on 30 July, two days after Cromwell was put to death, two members of the old Aragon group – Edward Powell and Richard Fetherston – were led to execution.[40] By an ironic twist of fate, one of the three Protestants put to death on the same day was, like Fetherston, a member of the chapter of St David's. He was the ardent reformer, Robert Barnes, prebendary of Llanboidy, installed there by Bishop Barlow in the hope of strengthening Protestant influence in his diocese.

The Six Articles Act may not have been as adverse in its effects on reformers as they might have dreaded; probably not more than about a dozen or so were put to death in all. The truth was that 'godly preachers' were still needed to decry papal pretensions and to uphold the royal supremacy, which 'otherwise might lie hidden in an Act of Parliament', or so Cranmer's secretary thought; and Sir William Paget had no doubts that the new faith, purged of its papal dross, 'was not yet printed in the stomachs of the eleven of the twelve parts of the realm'.[41] Besides, like all Tudor legislation, the Act depended for its success upon the rigour of the officials of local government and justice, who may have been lax or haphazard in enforcing it. An interesting example of such an attitude comes from Haverfordwest in 1540. In this Pembrokeshire town, a centre of Bishop Barlow's reforming influence since 1534, a priest called Thomas Tye sought to exploit a loophole in the law in his own interests. He was accused of seditious and slanderous teaching – possibly of a Protestant complexion; but the Herefordshire justices of assize, before whom he appeared, decided that they could not hear his case because he had spoken the offending words in Wales. They kept him in Hereford gaol until the matter could be clarified, then allowed him to travel home to Wales so that he could collect money for his own defence and later took him up to London. All this was done without any reference to the Council in the

[38] T. P. Ellis, *The Catholic Martyrs of Wales* (London, 1933), pp. 4–5.
[39] Ibid., pp. 5–9.
[40] Ibid., pp. 10–15.
[41] Smith, *Henry VIII*, p. 143.

Marches. Tye eventually turned up in 1541 at Calais, a notorious nest of heretics, but managed to secure a pardon for himself.[42]

In Wales open heretics would in any event be likely to have been few and far between. The only certain instance of the Act being strictly carried out anywhere in the country occurred in the town of Cardiff, where a certain Thomas Capper was burnt at the stake in 1542, presumably for denying transubstantiation. Nothing is known about Capper beyond the details of his ultimate fate, of which we learn simply because of the chance survival of the Cardiff bailiffs' accounts for 1542–3. They record the payment of 4*s.* 4*d.*, being 'costs and expenses sustained in burning Thomas Capper, who was attainted of heresy in Cardiff . . . being in prison there by the space of 130 days'.[43] He may have been no more than an isolated individual; but it is also possible that the decision to burn him was intended to terrify into orthodoxy a number of others who shared his heretical opinions. The Protestant tradition in Cardiff did not die out when Capper met his end. It was to show fresh signs of life in Edward VI's time and provided another martyr in the person of the fisherman, Rawlins White, during Mary's persecutions (see below, chap. 8).

While Henry was keeping the doctrinal orthodoxy of his church intact, he was still prepared to allow, and even to encourage, within certain well-defined limits, the use of the vernacular for religious indoctrination and also to support the foundation of grammar schools within the dioceses. Such postures on his part emboldened at least two of the bishops in Wales to embark on cautious reforms. These two exhibited a marked contrast in attitudes and methods. While William Barlow was a fervent eager beaver of the Protestant persuasion, Arthur Bulkeley was a cautious and conservative Henrician ecclesiastical lawyer. Barlow was critical, even contemptuous, of what he saw as the backwardness of the Welsh in his diocese and the obstacles to reform presented by their language. Bulkeley, having been reared in his own diocese, was markedly more sympathetic to the language spoken by most of his flock and aware of the importance of using it.

Barlow had long been advocating the need to raise the standard and frequency of preaching and to improve the educational facilities in his diocese. Undeterred by the disgrace of his mentor, Thomas Cromwell, and his former episcopal colleagues, Latimer and Shaxton, he continued to seek for opportunities to secure his aims. In January 1541 he was able to acquire from the Crown the dissolved Dominican friary in Brecon to house his new

[42] G. R. Elton, *Policy and Police* (Cambridge, 1972), p. 300–1.
[43] *Records of the County Borough of Cardiff*, ed. J. H. Matthews (6 vols., Cardiff, 1898–1911), I. 228; cf. *GCH*, IV. 215.

college in the town.[44] He also obtained permission to 'convert the yearly sum of £53 provided for the stipends and salaries of singers' at the collegiate church of Abergwili. The buildings of the dissolved friary and the finances of the former college would now be put to 'better uses' to found a *ludus literarius* (a school to teach reading and writing) at Brecon, for which schoolmasters and readers in theology would be procured. Their duty would be to instruct the youth of the district and also 'to elucidate the Gospel' to the king's subjects. Barlow's justification for founding this new institution harked back to themes he had been rehearsing for some years. The college at Abergwili was situated in an inconvenient place, where it could not offer hospitality. Its resources would be better employed in helping to maintain a new grammar school at the old Dominican convent at Brecon. Such a school was badly needed in south Wales, where the king's subjects, on account of their poverty, were unable to educate their sons, and no grammar school was available in those parts. The result was that both clergy and laity of every age and condition were rude and ignorant of their duty to God and the obedience they owed the king. They were even unacquainted with the common English tongue, so that they could not readily understand the obligations which the law imposed on them.[45] The college now set up in Brecon became known as Christ College, Brecon, and it has served the community well for 450 years or more. It may be more than a coincidence that the pioneer of university education for the Welsh in Elizabeth's reign, Hugh Price, founder of Jesus College Oxford, was himself a Brecon man.[46]

Arthur Bulkeley, a scion of the well-known Anglesey family of that name, had been active in the diocese of Bangor for some years before becoming its bishop in 1541, and had already shown himself anxious to exercise authority and improve diocesan administration. When he was chosen to succeed Bishop Bird, he was allowed to supplement the meagre income of his bishopric, one of the poorest in the kingdom, by holding *in commendam* three rectories and two prebends, an undesirable practice which became routinely followed and the subject of much criticism.[47] Bulkeley seems to have agreed with his predecessor who, when he moved to Chester, found that the people there, like those of north Wales, were 'much behind the king's subjects in the south' 'for lack of doctrine and

---

[44] *LP*, XVI. 503 (30). Cf. W. Dugdale, *Monasticon Anglicanum*, ed. J. Cayley *et al.* (8 parts, London, 1846), VI/iii. 1497.

[45] Ibid.

[46] G. Williams, 'Hugh Price, founder of Jesus College, Oxford', *Brycheiniog*, XXV (1992–3), 57–65.

[47] Heal, *Prelates*, p. 197.

preaching'.[48] In an effort to improve this state of affairs, Bulkeley quickly followed up the king's proclamation calling on all his subjects to learn the Creed, the Paternoster, the Ten Commandments, and the Ave Maria in the vernacular. In 1542 he ordered his clergy 'every second Sunday [to] read the Paternoster and the Ave Maria after the Creed, at Mass Time, in English or in Welsh, treatably and distinctly, and cause all their parishioners which can already say that in English or Welsh, young and old, to rehearse it and every article and part thereof, to the end, every one by himself, to the intent that they may perfectly learn their Paternoster, Ave, Creed, and Ten Commandments'.[49] He also gave orders to heads of households and schoolmasters to fulfil the same duty.[50] Bulkeley, though the descendant of an immigrant English family, had been brought up in Bangor diocese and must surely have appreciated that in this most completely Welsh of dioceses, instruction in English was likely to have been ineffective for most of its inhabitants. His injunction that Welsh should be used was the first episcopal requirement certainly known to have been issued in Henry VIII's reign that the language should be employed by the clergy and others. Welsh versions undoubtedly existed of all these items specified by Bulkeley, though just how widely they were known and used among the clergy and people it is impossible to tell with any accuracy.[51] Nor can it reliably be estimated how readily available manuscripts containing them may have been. All that can be said on this score is that contemporary manuscript coverage in general tended to be 'patchy and fortuitous'.[52] Bulkeley may have found it necessary to insist upon the Pater, Ave, Creed, and Ten Commandments being taught in the vernacular because many of his clergy, like those in other parts of England and Wales, left to themselves were reluctant to do so. Within a few years (1546) translations of the passages in question would appear in the first printed Welsh book, published to meet a most urgent need, according to its author, Sir John Price. Yet Bishop Bulkeley himself may have proved to be a very reluctant reformer, not perhaps too warmly committed to the use of the vernacular, since in 1544 one of that name was imprisoned and attainted for treason and 'papal affection'.[53] All the same, he remained bishop of his diocese and continued to act in that capacity throughout Edward VI's reign.

---

[48] E. Duffy, *The Stripping of the Altars: Traditional Religion in England, c.1500–1580* (New Haven, 1992), p. 433.

[49] R. G. Gruffydd, '*Yny Lhyvyr Hwnn . . .* (1546), the earliest Welsh printed book', *BBCS*, XXIII (1968), 110–11; cf. Jesus College, Oxford, MS 115, fos. 379–86.

[50] Duffy, *Stripping the Altars*, p. 433.

[51] D. S. Evans, *Medieval Welsh Literature* (Cardiff, 1986); *WC*, chap. 2.

[52] H. S. Bennett, *English Books and their Readers, 1475 to 1557* (Cambridge, 1952), p. 1.

[53] *LP*, XIX/i, no. 1035, grant 140.

At about the same time as Bulkeley was pressing for the use of the vernacular by the clergy of his diocese, or possibly some years earlier, an anonymous cleric in south Wales was engaged in translating into Welsh substantial extracts from the New Testament.[54] His work was probably intended to help the author himself and some of his clerical colleagues in the task of 'declaring' the sense of the epistles and the gospels as commanded by the king and the bishops. He may just possibly have hoped for a wider circulation of his work by means of additional manuscript copies or oral repetition of it, but would hardly have envisaged a printed edition of his text. His translation was not based on any original Greek version of the New Testament but on the Latin Vulgate and Tyndale's English translation. Since it was made illegal to use Tyndale's work as from 1543, it must be supposed that the Welsh translation was undertaken before that date. Its prose style was a mixture of the standard Welsh literary language of the medieval period and of looser and more colloquial modes of expression,[55] as may be seen from the following brief extracts:

> Y wraic a ddywad wrthaw yntav Syre dyrro y mi beth or dwfr hyny val na bo ssyched arnaf ac na bo raid y mi ddyfod yma yn ol dwr / yna jessu addywad wrthi hithav / kerdda di a galw dy wr a dabre yma / Y wraic addywad wrtho ynte nid oes y mi vn gwr[56]

The second extract is a translation of the Lord's Prayer. It will readily be seen how much less accomplished it is than the later translations made by William Salesbury and William Morgan.

> O yn tad ni yr hwn y ddwyd yny nef bendigedic yw denw / dyfrenhiniaeth di y myni / kyflawnhaer dywyllys di megis yddis nynef ar y ddayar hon / dyro y ni heddiw yn bara beynyddol / madde yn tresbas ywnaythom yth erbyn di megis ninay yn tre baswyr ywnaethyn yn erbyn ninay / nad yn harwain ni newn profydigaethay / ond ryddha oddy wrth bob ryw ddrwc ac aflendid amen poed gwir[57]

The dialectal forms employed by the translator show the text to have been clearly the work of an author of south Welsh origin. The suggestion has been made that he might well have been a cleric from the diocese of St

---

[54] H. Lewis, 'Darnau o'r efengylau', *Cymm.* XXXI (1921), 193–216; R. G. Gruffydd, 'Dau destun Protestannaidd cynnar o Lawysgrif Hafod 22', *Trivium*, I (1966), 56–66; I. Thomas, *Y Testament Newydd Cymraeg, 1551–1620* (Cardiff, 1975), pp. 52–9.

[55] Gruffydd, *Trivium*, I. 56–66.

[56] Lewis, *Cymm.* XXXI. 206.

[57] Ibid., 211.

David's, one Thomas Talley, known to have been responsible for a Welsh metrical version of the Ten Commandments.[58] Adding credence to that attribution is the fact that a number of parishes in the diocese, in Carmarthenshire and Breconshire – Llandovery, Nantmel, Llanafan Fawr, Llandybïe, and Llanwrthwl – were all acquiring English Bibles in 1541.[59] However, the manuscript into which these scriptural translations were copied, Hafod MS 22, was transcribed late in the sixteenth century by a Glamorgan scholar, Anthony Powel of Llangynwyd, and it appears to be associated with other translations produced by a very active Glamorgan school of prose-writers of the fifteenth and sixteenth centuries.[60] So there is reason to conclude that it might conceivably have been translated by a man from the diocese of Llandaff, especially when the enthusiasm of the *cwndidwyr* for making the content of scripture known to their contemporaries is taken into account.

The year 1543 saw Henry apply the brakes fairly stiffly on the progress of reform and Bible-reading. In May of that year a revision of the Bishops' Book was issued under the title of *A Necessary Doctrine and Erudition for any Christian Man*. Officially licensed by the Supreme Head, it was very much the king's work and not surprisingly became known as the King's Book. It was distinctly conservative in tone and appeared to mark the arrest of any further progress towards reform. A parliamentary Act of the same year 'for the advancement of true religion' also condemned Tyndale's translation and other 'crafty, false and untrue' versions of the English Bible. While allowing that the Bible might be read in church on Sundays, the Act laid down that it was not to be read by 'women nor artificers, prentices, journeymen, serving men of the degree of yeomen or under, husbandmen or labourers', lest it should lead to disputes and dissensions among them.[61] As far as Wales was in question, it was unlikely that many of the lower orders, even in the improbable event of their wishing to obtain a copy of scripture for private reading, would have been able to make much of the English version anyway.

Yet a scattering of surviving upper-class wills seem to indicate that a small minority of the Welsh population was being influenced by the gradual dissemination of reforming ideas and the growing habit of reading the English Bible. Between 1540 and 1544 three such testators may be traced in a bishop's register of the diocese of St Asaph.[62] On 10 October 1540 Master Geoffrey Ruthin employed the reformers' favoured opening

[58] Gruffydd, *Trivium*, I. 56–66.
[59] NLW, St David's Chapter Act Book, 1384–1661 (SD Ch/B/13), pp. 28–9.
[60] G. J. Williams, *Traddodiad Llenyddol Morgannwg* (Cardiff, 1948), pp. 176–81.
[61] A. G. Dickens, *The English Reformation* (London, 1964), p. 190.
[62] NLW, SA/BR 1 pp. 1, 42, 49, 52.

formula of bequeathing his soul to God only and was careful not to leave any money for prayers or masses to be said for his soul. Matthew ap John, bailiff of Welshpool, was another equally scrupulous not to include any bequests of that kind in his will dated 17 June 1544. Finally, Edward Lloyd, in his will dated 14 November 1544 bequeathed his soul to God, 'trusting by the merit of his passion to inherit the kingdom of heaven'. Among the surviving wills proved in the Prerogative Court of Canterbury is the one drawn up by Sir Thomas Gamage of Coety Castle in Glamorgan in June 1543 which was even more emphatic: 'I recommend my soul to Almighty Jesu, my maker and redeemer, to whose blessed passion is all my trust of clear remission and forgiveness of sins', with never a word said about prayers or masses being offered for him.[63] In four other wills of a comparable period we find the same kind of stipulation: Meredith ap Philip (1540), a burgess of Abergavenny; Edward Griffith (1540) of Bangor; John Griffith (1540) of London; and Dr Richard Gwent (1544) also of London. It is noticeable how many of these testators were townsmen.[64]

The Act of Succession of 1544, enacted because the king was about to lead his armies into battle in France and, in case he met his death on campaign, wished to clear up any possible doubts about the succession to the throne before he departed, contained provisions which had important implications for the religious beliefs of his subjects. It provided a new long oath which consisted of a profession of faith in the royal supremacy and an utter rejection of the 'pretended authority' of the pope.[65] All office-holders within the kingdom were to swear this oath whenever called upon to do so.

Once again, neither the King's Book nor the Acts of 1543 and 1544 proved to be as harsh in their consequences for the reformers as the latter might have feared, in spite of the heresy hunt which accompanied them. Archbishop Cranmer continued to persevere quietly with his work of reform, and in 1544 produced his English version of the Litany.[66] This, too, evoked enough interest in Wales for at least one assiduous translator to try his hand at a Welsh version of it, which was subsequently included in Hafod MS 22,[67] along with the translations of parts of the gospels quoted above. Interesting though it may be, it can in no way be said to have achieved the distinction of Cranmer's original. A further step forward in the publication of religious material in the vernacular came in 1545 when

---

[63] PRO, PCC, Spert, 222. For traditional and non-traditional wills, Dickens, *English Ref.*, pp. 191–3.

[64] PRO, PCC, Alenger, 32, 81, 83; Pynnynge, 89.

[65] M. Levine, *Tudor Dynastic Problems, 1450–1571* (London, 1973), pp. 73–5; pp. 161–2 (text).

[66] H. M. Smith, *Henry VIII and the Reformation* (London, 1948), pp. 403–5.

[67] Lewis, *Cymm.* XXXI. 193–216.

the King's Primer in English was published. Towards the end of the same year Henry made a bid for religious unity among his subjects in his so-called 'Golden Speech' to Parliament. Its central object was to deter his people from quarrelling violently with one another over religious issues and to exhort them to live in harmony. The strict restraints placed in the Act of 1543 on the social classes being allowed to read the Bible had not prevented the word of God from being what was described as 'disputed, rhymed, sung, and jangled in every alehouse and tavern'. 'Nor was God himself among Christians ever less reverenced, honoured or served.'[68] The king sternly criticized both the *mumpsimus* of those too attached to Rome and also the *sumpsimus* of their opponents who were only too eager to overthrow what had been sanctioned by earlier Christians.

The last year of Henry's reign, 1546, was marked by a development of the utmost significance for the religious and cultural life of Wales: the publication of the first book ever to be printed in the Welsh language.[69] The title-page has not survived and it is always referred to by its opening words, *Yny Lhyvyr Hwnn* . . . ('In this book . . .').[70] Its author would be unknown were it not for a reference made to him as Sir John Price of Brecon in the preface to the first Welsh New Testament (1567) by Bishop Richard Davies.[71] Price, a doctor of laws of the University of Oxford, had shaped a highly successful career for himself in the service of the king and Thomas Cromwell. He took part in the dissolution of the monasteries, was appointed secretary of the Council in the Marches and ended up as a Member of Parliament. Like other Welsh authors and littérateurs – Gruffydd Robert and Arthur Kelton among them – he looked to William Herbert, brother-in-law to the queen, Catherine Parr, and a rising figure in court circles, as his patron. He tells us that from his youth he had been much 'exercised in the old language and antiquities of the British' and an enthusiastic collector of manuscripts. A man deeply influenced by Erasmian ideals, he was greatly impressed by the value of scripture as a 'purifying agent' and whole-heartedly approved of the king's policy of circulating knowledge of it among his subjects.[72] He now perceived the opportunity to bring together his two major interests – Welsh literature and the dissemination of vernacular scriptures – by the publication of a primer for the benefit of his fellow-countrymen, many of whom were able to read

---

[68] J. J. Scarisbrick, *Henry VIII* (London, 1968), p. 471.

[69] A number of Welsh authors had already made use of the press to publish books in other languages, Williams, in Line, *World of Books*, pp. 187–96.

[70] *Yny Lhyvyr Hwnn* . . ., ed. J. H. Davies (Bangor, 1902).

[71] R. Davies, 'Epistol at y Cembru', *Testament Newydd* (1567); cf. G. H. Hughes (ed.), *Rhagymadroddion, 1547–1648* (Cardiff, 1951), pp. 24–5.

[72] Gruffydd, *BBCS*, XXIII. 110–11.

their own language but could make nothing of English or Latin. In the introduction to his book he underlined heavily the key importance of the printing-press for the future of religion and literature in his country and urged upon his fellow-Welshmen the need to take advantage of it, so that a 'gift as valuable as this should not be without fruit for us any more than for others'.[73] He praised the king's desire to see God's word become more widely known among his subjects, which showed that their sovereign was as eager for their spiritual as their temporal welfare. His own book was clearly intended for widespread use in churches, private households, and schools.

He was severely critical of the general failure of the clergy to teach their parishioners those things that were indispensable for the health of their souls, as elsewhere he had been reproving of their lax morals and the unwillingness of some of their number to have the Bible translated. He was convinced that it would be the greatest sin to allow so many thousands of souls in Wales to fall into perdition for want of instruction in the only language they understood. If presently they lapsed into ignorance and wickedness more often than other nations did, this was not because they lacked 'good gifts of sense and understanding given them by God' ('donyeu da o synwyr a deall gwedy y dduw y rhoi yddynt') but because they had not been properly instructed.[74] He had therefore thought it only proper to produce for their benefit a primer containing essentials like the Creed, the Paternoster and the Ten Commandments in their native tongue. Though these things were to be found in hand-written copies, those manuscripts themselves were nothing like freely enough available in their midst. Like most other translators of the age, Price was quick to emphasize that he was writing for the rude and unlearned. In common with English writers he justified his efforts on the grounds that he wanted to make texts available so that his countrymen might have what people of other nationalities enjoyed.[75] The content of his work may have been slight, but his recognition of the crucial need to publish religious literature in the Welsh language for the generality of the people if reform was to make headway constituted a vital contribution. So, too, did his perception of the enormous benefit that effective use of the printing-press could confer.

A much more important figure than John Price in the history of religion, literature, and publishing in Wales was to make a fleeting appearance in the records of the world of printing during the closing months of Henry VIII's reign. William Salesbury has strong claims to be regarded as one of the most important single individuals in the history of the Reformation in

---

[73] Price, *Yny Lhyvyr Hwnn*, introd.
[74] Ibid.
[75] Bennett, *English Books*, p. 56.

Wales, as well as its outstanding scholar in the Tudor age.[76] His most massive contributions were to be made during the reigns of Edward VI and Elizabeth (see below, chaps. 7 and 9); but in December 1545, together with the printer John Walley, he secured a licence from the king to print a 'Dictionary both in English and Welsh, whereby our well-beloved subjects in Wales may the sooner attain and learn our mere English tongue'.[77] When the volume actually appeared in 1547 it turned out to be a Welsh–English dictionary. This led some scholars to suppose that Salesbury was ambivalent in his attitude: whatever lip-service he might pay to the desirability of Welshmen's learning English, a Welsh–English dictionary was not likely to be much help for such a purpose and would probably tend more to enrich their understanding of their own native culture.[78] Dissenting from this view, others have held that Salesbury, impressed by the vast output of English books on all subjects embodying the New Learning, was sincerely desirous of helping Welshmen to master the English language.[79] It was, he thought, 'a language most expedient and most worthiest to be learned, studied and enhanced, of all of them that be subjects and under the obeisance of the imperial diadem and triumphant sceptre of England, even for the attainment of knowledge of God's word and other liberal sciences'.[80] It is worth noting that in his later introduction to the Dictionary Salesbury recognized, as did Price, that there were many Welshmen who could read their own language and who, if they made the effort, should find it comparatively easy to get to grips with English. All the more so, he believed, since it was a language which was more necessary for the Welsh to acquire than almost anyone. Salesbury's enthusiasm for the vernacular Bible led him to urge his compatriots to learn English since the scripture would then be far more readily available to them. Nevertheless he, like John Price, realized that most of them were likely to find the task to be beyond them.

Looking back over Henry's reign, it might seem surprising that stronger reactions against his policies were not forthcoming from the Welsh. That tiny minority among them who had shown themselves to be profoundly

---

[76] D. R. Thomas, *The Life and Work of Richard Davies and William Salesbury* (Oswestry, 1902); I. Thomas, *Y Testament Newydd* and *Yr Hen Destament*; A. Mathias, 'Astudiaeth o weithgarwch Llenyddol William Salesbury' (MA thesis, Wales, 1949); *WRE*, pp. 191–206; R. B. Jones, *William Salesbury* (Cardiff, 1994).
[77] *KLIB*, p. 170.
[78] W. J. Gruffydd, *Llenyddiaeth Cymru: Rhyddiaith o 1540 hyd 1660* (Wrexham, 1926), pp. 41–2.
[79] *WRE*, pp. 193–4.
[80] Salesbury, *A brief and a playne introduction* (1550), p. E.i.b.

aware of the issues at stake and were prepared to take an open stand on the matters in dispute were men who had, almost without exception, followed their careers outside Wales. Many of them, as might be anticipated, were intellectuals; university graduates or *alumni* of the inns of court, who would not have been expected to find much scope for their talents in Wales itself. Clerics, largely excluded from the more lucrative preferment in their native dioceses by non-Welsh bishops, sought their best opportunities in the richer pastures of English dioceses or the universities; lawyers made their way in the royal service or the great lawcourts. All of them, in order to obtain advancement, had been obliged to climb the ladder of promotion across Offa's Dyke. Those of conservative bent who stood loyally by Catholic patrons – Edward Powell in Catherine of Aragon's entourage, Richard Whitford in Sion monastery, John Eynon at Reading abbey, or John Griffith in Henry Courtenay's household – had been prepared to defy Henry to the last ditch. Others who depended for promotion on the service of the king or his leading servants – men like John Price, Edward Carne, or Richard Gwent – though sympathetic enough to cautious reform, found it perfectly possible to fall in with the king's ambitions and accept the royal supremacy. Even younger men, deeply attracted to reformed doctrines, like George Constantine, Richard Davies, Thomas Young, or William Salesbury, were not as yet prepared to step too far out of line. Admittedly, it is known that almost all of these men maintained close contacts with their kinsfolk and friends back home and could have been expected to exercise persuasive influence over their thinking; but there is little surviving evidence from Wales itself of their being able to evoke much in the way of the expression of determined religious loyalties one way or the other.

At first sight, it might appear a trifle odd that Henry's religious policies had been received in Wales without tougher and more open opposition. After all, before the Reformation the country had experienced little preparation for those upheavals it subsequently underwent. What criticism of the state of the Church and its clergy there had been was relatively muted, and led to no very real demand for improvement, even though much had been amiss. When Henry broke with the papacy and replaced it with his own supremacy, he imposed those changes on Wales, if not against its will, certainly without its full-hearted consent. Yet although there had been suggestions by a foreign envoy like Chapuys or a Protestant prelate like Barlow that dissatisfaction in the country might lead its people to associate themselves with rebels against the Crown in Ireland or northern England, no alarming trouble had erupted; and that in spite of many rumblings of discontent and opposition, voiced mainly by clerics. This may have been partly because Henry was popular in a land where the Tudors were regarded as a native Welsh dynasty. Undoubtedly, Tudor prose authors like John Price or William Salesbury, or poets such as Lewis Morgannwg or Siôn Brwynog, were eager in their praise of Henry and his actions. He also owed much to the strengthening of royal authority in Wales through the operations of the Council in the Marches under Bishop Rowland Lee as its president and to the enhanced powers conferred by the Act of Union, 1536–43. Moreover, those ruling gentry families to whom public office was entrusted under that Act were generally keen to continue on favourable terms with their sovereign, whom they regarded as a potential source of still further authority, possessions, and influence for themselves. Nor is it likely that any of the laity felt themselves especially attached to a Church greatly flawed by such deficiencies as a largely absentee higher clergy, unlearned parish priests, and indolent monks, hardly any of whom had given a lead in opposing the erastian tendencies of the king. Finally, however portentous the constitutional reverberations of displacing the pope and setting up the king as head of the Church, dissolving the monasteries and the shrines, or encouraging the translation of the Bible and parts of the service into English, a large part of the Church order had been preserved. Services were conducted in Latin, the medieval sacraments were retained and their validity insisted upon, the clergy were still not allowed to marry, and the parish churches and the activities that took place in them seemed surprisingly similar to what they had been before 1530. The structure and administration of the Church had changed very little: bishops, cathedral clergy, archdeacons, rural deans, and parish priests; ecclesiastical law and lawcourts and traditional methods of discipline; and the familiar boundaries of bishoprics, deaneries, and parishes, all remained very much as before. For the ordinary worshippers it might well seem that nothing much was different. Many of them might have believed that theirs was a powerful monarch who had dealt faithfully with all his adversaries, including a remote and barely known pontiff and his subversive minions.

Even so, there was a perceptible under-current of popular resentment at some of the things the king had done. His treatment of Catherine of Aragon and her daughter had been disliked and there were many who had regarded Anne Boleyn as a baggage no better than she should be. A number of ordinary clergy had not concealed their hostility to some of the king's acts of policy. The suppression of the familiar shrines, the attempted banishment of the saints from the popular imagination, the attacks on images, the prohibition of prayers for the dead and pilgrimages to holy places had all been thoroughly unpopular. They had appeared to the ordinary man and woman like gratuitous assaults on old and well-loved friends and sources of help and comfort in a world that was often harsh and distressing. Not many people in Wales had either understood or favoured the English language used to introduce and propagate the Reformation changes in sermon, book, statute, and proclamation. Seeds of incipient misunderstanding and hostility had already been sown and would germinate rapidly in Edward VI's reign.

After thirty-seven years of Henry's masterful rule the replacement of a mature adult monarch by a youthful and inexperienced boy ruler seemed to be approaching rapidly during the closing months of 1546. The old king's bloated hulk showed all the symptoms of fast-declining health,[81] and the imminent possibility of a child-successor was in the air. Such a prospect held out the likelihood that a regency council might not be far distant, though no one in Henry's immediate entourage dared mention the contingency to the savage old tyrant. It thickened the atmosphere with suspicions and intensified the jockeying for position among the king's leading advisers. The conservative faction among them still occupied a position of some strength; led by the duke of Norfolk, his son the earl of Surrey, and Bishop Gardiner, it had capable leaders, more experienced than almost any in the ways of court politics. Whatever their sympathies for Catholic usages and doctrines might be, there was no reason to doubt their fidelity to the king and the royal supremacy. They represented a point of view that was common enough among the political classes at large: that the king might have defeated the pope but had left behind much that was reassuring in popery. Politically and tactically, however, advantage had been passing to their rivals, headed by Edward Seymour, earl of Hertford, and John Dudley, Viscount Lisle.[82] Younger men, both had given proof of their loyalty and ability in the military and naval campaigns of recent years, and Hertford had the added advantage of being the young prince's maternal uncle. They were reputed to favour the reforming party in religion and enjoyed the sympathy of Henry's last queen, the reformist Catherine Parr, her brother-in-law William Herbert, and the king's devoted secretary, the resourceful William Paget. At midsummer they had a further accession of strength when the earl of Arundel, one of the most influential nobles of the realm, adhered to their party. It even began to look as if Henry himself might be coming down on the side of the reformers. The three tutors he appointed to look after Edward's education and upbringing were reformers, and their sympathizers could muster a majority in the council.

Yet, true to form, Henry may still not have made up his mind. He might all the while have been playing off one group against another. In addition, he may have been taking careful note of how military developments were

---

[81] Smith, *Henry VIII*, chaps. 10–12; Scarisbrick, *Henry VIII*, chap 14.
[82] M. L. Bush, *The Governmental Policy of Protector Somerset* (London, 1975); B. L. Beer, *Northumberland: The Political Career of John Dudley* . . . (Kent, OH, 1973).

likely to unfold on the Continent, where Charles V was mustering his forces to settle accounts with his Protestant adversaries. At the end of 1546, the exiled English Protestant, John Hooper, could write:

> There will be a change of religion in England (and Wales), and the king will take up the gospel of Christ, in case the Emperor should be defeated in this most destructive war [i.e. against the Schmalkaldic League]; should the gospel sustain a loss, he will then retain the impious mass.[83]

Like many other sixteenth-century rulers Henry put considerations of state ahead of theology; his religion was in large measure the outcome of political circumstance.

Events at home in December 1546, however, tipped the balance suddenly and positively against the conservatives. Gardiner was excluded from the council, eliciting the comment from Henry to his courtiers to the effect that he had been able to control him and use him 'to all manner of purposes as seemed good unto me; but so shall you never do'.[84] On 12 December the Howards, father and son, Norfolk and Surrey, were arrested and clapped in the Tower. Surrey, gifted but brash and overweening, was accused of uttering these dangerously presumptuous words, 'If the king die, who should have the rule of the prince but my father or I?'[85] Such sentiments emanating from a man who could claim royal blood in his veins could hardly fail to rouse the ire of so proud and suspicious a ruler as Henry. Surrey was executed on 20 January 1547, and only Henry's own death saved Norfolk from the same fate. It was not to be wondered at, therefore, that a few days beforehand on 24 December 1546, an envoy from the Netherlands, van der Delft, in a letter to the emperor's sister, Mary of Hungary, had written thus of Hertford and Lisle: 'The publicly expressed opinion, therefore, that these two nobles are in favour of the sects may be accepted as true, and also that they have obtained such influence over the king as to lead him according to their fancy.'[86] It may be doubted whether their control was as complete as van der Delft envisaged, but they were none the less in a strong position to act when Henry died on 28 January 1547. His death was kept secret for three days and the royal will was signed

---

[83] Hooper to Bullinger; the letter is undated, but as it mentions Norfolk's arrest, it must be later than 12 December 1546, *Original Letters* (Parker Soc., London, 1846), I. 39.

[84] J. Foxe, *Acts and Monuments . . .* , ed. S. Catley (7 vols. London, 1837–41), V. 691–2.

[85] *State Papers*, I. 265, pp. 891–2.

[86] *CSP Span.* V. 533.

with the dry stamp and may have been doctored.[87] But Edward had come to the throne, and his royal uncle, Hertford, was strategically placed to take over the young prince and the reins of power.

[87] H. Miller, 'Henry VIII's unwritten will', in E. W. Ives *et al.* (eds.), *Wealth and Power in Tudor England* (London, 1978).

CHAPTER 7

The Edwardian Reformation

W ITH the aid of the wily and experienced William Paget, Hertford almost immediately established himself as Protector on 31 January 1547 and surrounded himself with men who were favourable to his seizure of power in his own interest and theirs.[1] He proved a man of ambitious and autocratic temperament and soon succeeded in raising himself to the highest ranks of the peerage as duke of Somerset. Having earlier evinced sympathies in favour of Protestant change, he readily perceived that proceeding further along the path of moderate reform would best serve his own personal and political aspirations. For nearly three years he would rule the kingdom in the young Edward's name. In doing so, however, he failed to handle wisely the powerful and self-seeking individuals about him at court and in the council; nor did he cope effectively with the crop of rebellions provoked in 1549 by his religious and social policies. A *coup* engineered against him in October 1549 was led by the conservative earls of Arundel, Southampton, and Wriothesely; but it was John Dudley, earl of Warwick, who had long been secretly intriguing against Somerset, who ultimately contrived to come out on top early in 1550. Dudley, soon to be created duke of Northumberland, continued to exercise power for the rest of Edward's reign. Aware that there would be no significant role for him in any religiously conservative regime, Northumberland pressed even more swiftly than Somerset along the road to Protestant reform. He was anxious to keep the Princess Mary and her conservative friends out of a place of influence and so was obliged to convey the impression that Edward was old enough to rule in his own right.[2] The youthful king, a precociously intelligent adolescent, indeed increasingly revealed his own convincedly Protestant tendencies and his Tudor taste for authority. The six years of his reign, therefore, witnessed a landslide of religious reformation being launched on England and Wales.

[1] For Edward's reign: M. L. Bush, *The Governmental Policy of Protector Somerset* (London, 1975); D. E. Hoak, *The King's Council in the Reign of Edward VI* (Cambridge, 1976); W. K. Jordan, *Edward VI: The Young King* (London, 1968); *Edward VI: The Threshold of Power* (London, 1970).
[2] B. L. Beer, *Northumberland: The Political Career of John Dudley* (Kent, OH, 1973).

The changes were at first introduced cautiously and moderately, but with an unmistakable indication of the direction being set. An early warning came on Ash Wednesday 1547, when in a sermon preached before the court Nicholas Ridley denounced the images of the saints and the use of sacramentals like holy water, and was followed by Bishop Barlow of St David's preaching in similar vein at Paul's Cross on the following Sunday.[3] During the summer of 1547 a general visitation of the realm was ordered and a set of visitation articles, based on those drawn up in 1536 and 1538 but more radical in tone, was issued. The dioceses of England and Wales were divided up into six circuits, one of which was comprised of the four Welsh dioceses and the two Marcher dioceses of Hereford and Worcester. The visitors for this circuit began their work in September 1547, and included in their ranks were Robert Ferrar, within a year appointed bishop of St David's, and George Constantine and Hugh Rawlins, both preachers of Protestant inclination from the same diocese. King Edward noted in his diary that their injunctions took away divers ceremonies and that the visitors were instructed to 'take down images' and to set forth 'certain homilies' to be read in the churches.[4] Injunction 28 ordered the destruction of all shrines, paintings, images, and 'all other monuments of feigned miracles, pilgrimages, idolatry, and superstition', to which offerings were made or which had candles burning before them. No more of the customary processions were to be allowed when mass was being celebrated; and instructions were repeated that all parishes should buy Bibles, together with copies of Erasmus's *Paraphrases* as an aid to the study of the scriptures, and the newly issued Book of Homilies, which was distinctly Protestant in tone in places.[5] Parishioners often proved to be slack in performing their duty to obtain these works.[6] Nor was this altogether surprising when the content of the Book of Homilies must often have been over the heads of the ordinary members of the congregations; all the more so in Wales where, if and when the book was being read at all, it was being heard by largely monoglot Welsh speakers.

When the first Parliament of the reign convened in November 1547 it showed its reforming disposition by repealing the laws against heresy and the Six Articles Act. Restrictions on reading the English Bible were relaxed and communion in both kinds was allowed. It also launched another

---

[3] E. Duffy, *The Stripping of the Altars: Traditional Religion in England, c.1400–1580* (New Haven, 1992), p. 449.

[4] E. C. Messenger, *The Reformation, the Mass, and the Priesthood* (2 vols. London, 1936–7), I. 345.

[5] W. H. Frère and W. P. M. Kennedy, *Visitation Articles and Injunctions of the Period of the Reformation* (3 vols. Alcuin Club, London, 1910).

[6] R. H. Hutton in C. Haigh, *The English Reformation Revised* (Cambridge, 1987), p. 125.

attack on the endowments of the Church. The Chantries Act now passed was taking up a precedent set by Henry VIII in 1545 when he made a move against chantries, hospitals, free chapels, and kindred institutions but did not carry the exercise through to its conclusion.[7] In 1547, with guilds, fraternities, and services also being included, the total value of chantry property accruing to the Crown amounted to £610,000. Lay commissioners were appointed to carry out the survey in Wales, those in the north headed by Roger Williams, and those of the south by Sir Thomas Jones.[8] The purpose of each commission was to 'survey all and singular callings, chantries, free chapels, brotherhoods, guilds and salaries of stipendiary priests . . . also all manors, lands, tenements, hereditaments and possessions, with the goods and ornaments, plate and jewels to the same belonging'.[9] The commissioners also took it upon themselves to estimate the number of 'houseling people' (i.e. adults receiving communion) in the urban parishes.

The certificate for north Wales returned lands to the value of £87. 17s. 5d. and stocks of cattle and money worth £531. 7s. 5d., while that for the south returned property worth £116. 17s. 1d. together with plate and ornaments worth £20. 11s. 1d. and cattle and money valued at £203. 7s. Wales, as will be seen, was poorly endowed with chantries and fraternities, most of which were concentrated in parishes along the border with England and along the south coastal plain.[10] The estimates now compiled showed the possessions to be worth far less than those of the monasteries, though they were almost certainly returned at a sum considerably lower than they ought to have been. Even before the Reformation many guilds and fraternities had been short-lived and at the mercy of changing circumstances, but during the twenty years from 1527 to 1547 widespread criticism of the doctrine of purgatory, serious doubts about the validity of prayers for the dead, the dissolution of the monasteries, and fears concerning the future of parish churches and their possessions had all had the effect of grievously undermining the position of the chantries. Furthermore, there had been a general tendency to offset the effects of a possible dissolution by concealing chantry lands and possessions, taking surreptitious possession of them, disposing of assets beforehand, and undervaluing them to the commissioners. This becomes evident from a list of lands, plate, and jewels being detained from the king, which was probably

[7] Jones, *AC* (1934), 134–55.

[8] PRO, E301/74–6; extracts are printed in *Records of the County Borough of Cardiff*, ed. J. H. Matthews (6 vols. Cardiff, 1898–1911), II. 293–309; cf. also A. Kreider, *English Chantries: The Road to Dissolution* (Cambridge, Mass., 1979).

[9] L. Thomas, *The Reformation in the Old Diocese of Llandaff* (Cardiff, 1930), p. 97.

[10] *WC*, pp. 290–5.

nothing like complete, and from a number of suits being pursued in the Court of Augmentations,[11] not to mention the disputes which never got that far. The chantry commissioner for north Wales, Roger Williams, was particularly keen in his pursuit of the king's interests, hauling defendants from Ruthin, Rhuddlan, Hawarden, and Towyn (Mer.) before the court to answer for their alleged peculations.[12]

What remained of their possessions was now seized in the king's name and the chantries were treated in much the same way as the monasteries had been. Most of the dispossessed priests, many of whom were elderly men and living in semi-retirement, were given pensions of £4–£5. In one instance, John Pylle, former chantry priest at St Mary's, Cardiff, was obliged, because of the negligence of church wardens, to petition the Court of Augmentations for his pension, while another Glamorgan priest, John Auger, testified that the surveyor, John Bassett, had declared him to be a chantry priest and secured him a pension of £5 when, in fact, he had never served as such.[13] Readily realizable chantry assets like plate, vestments or jewels were either sold locally or sent to London. Some of the bigger institutions, such as the collegiate church of St Mary at St David's, or the church at Holyhead, or the hospital of the Blessed David at Swansea, passed into royal hands without dispute. But at least two collegiate churches, those of Clynnog Fawr and Llanddewibrefi, were the subject of prolonged and fierce litigation. The incumbent of the former was John Gwynedd, a former monk of St Alban's, an accomplished author and an eminent musician, who hotly contested in a number of suits the claim that Clynnog was a collegiate church.[14] There is no record of whether or not he won his case; but his fellow north Walian, Rowland Meyrick, was successful after a long legal battle in proving that Llanddewibrefi was not a collegiate church.[15]

Many of the local gentry again benefited in no small measure from the disposal of chantry property. Houses or land were leased or sold, with no shortage of takers for compact blocks of property. Sir William Herbert (later earl of Pembroke) was quick to avail himself of chantry land at Cowbridge and Llantwit Major, and his brother, Sir George Herbert, did remarkably well out of the large hospital of the Blessed David at Swansea.[16] Miles Mathew took possession of land at Llandaff belonging to

[11] PRO, E321/30/50; 30/50; 131/21–6; 28/60; *Augs. Procs.*, pp. 87, 99, 108, 123.

[12] *WC*, p. 293.

[13] Thomas, *Llandaff*, p. 101.

[14] PRO, E321/37/32; 38/9; 46/98; 46/42; *Augs. Procs.*, p. 61; *APC*, I. 140; Evans, *Cymm.* LII. 99–100.

[15] G. Williams, 'The collegiate church of Llanddewibrefi', *Ceredigion*, IV/4 (1964), 376–52.

[16] *W and R*, p. 106.

the former David Mathew chantry as his 'hereditary right'. In Monmouth-shire which, like Glamorgan, was one of the Welsh counties best supplied with chantries, this property was disposed of without much difficulty and no disturbance.[17] Urban properties, there and elsewhere, were not so much sought after and were leased only with some difficulty, partly on account of their frequently ruinous or decayed condition and partly because they were often already leased out for ninety-nine years. Not a little of this kind of property got lost in the general confusion, as is revealed in legal disputes and commissions of concealments appointed well into the seventeenth century.[18] Some Welsh towns managed to cling on to their former assets with considerable success. Tenby, for instance, so ingeniously organized the profits from its chantry and hospital lands as not to have to levy a poor rate until as late as the eighteenth century.[19]

Pious hopes expressed in the preamble to the Chantries Act that the proceeds of the dissolution would be used to found schools or be devoted to charity went unrealized. The three schools definitely known to be associated with Welsh chantries – John Walbeef's charity at Llanhamlach in Brecon, the choir school of the flourishing fraternity at Montgomery, and the one linked with the Mathew charity at Llandaff whose priest had been required to teach twenty children as part of his duties – all disappeared.[20] There may well have been others which came to a similarly abrupt end. Also forfeited were those parts of chantry income which had previously been diverted to maintain a parish clerk at Cardigan, the quay at Aberystwyth and at Tenby, the bridge at Newport, and towards the upkeep of town walls, quay, and Taff Bridge at Cardiff.[21] Because the former chantries and similar institutions had been much more closely interwoven with parish life and amenities than the monasteries, they were correspondingly all the more missed. We have, however, no means of assessing just how badly their loss was felt, any more than we can tell how much psychological or emotional damage was caused to sincere believers by the loss of prayers for themselves or their loved ones.

In February 1548 another blow at religious tradition was struck when four venerable and well-loved ceremonies were forbidden: the blessing of candles at Candlemas; the carrying of ashes on Ash Wednesday; the blessing of palms on Palm Sunday; and 'creeping to the cross' on Good

[17] M. Gray, 'The last days of the shrines and chantries of Monmouthshire', *JWEH*, VII (1991), 20–40, provides a detailed survey of the position in the county.
[18] *WC*, pp. 292–5.
[19] G. D. Owen, 'Agrarian changes and conditions in west Wales during the sixteenth century' (Ph.D. thesis, Wales, 1935), p. 287.
[20] *WC*, pp. 290–6.
[21] Ibid., p. 295.

Friday.[22] During the following month a major step was taken to replace part of the Latin rite with the vernacular, when a proclamation introduced an English order for receiving communion in both kinds. The new order could not have been intelligible to many people in Wales and we have an early indication of some earnest but unknown Protestant's wish to make it more widely understood in the shape of his Welsh translation of it preserved in Hafod MS 22.[23]

During the years 1547–8 Archbishop Cranmer had been fortified by the arrival in England of a number of Protestant *émigrés* from Europe, who were attracted to a sympathetic Protestant regime and encouraged by the archbishop. The most notable among them were the great Strasburg reformer, Martin Bucer, the two Italians, Peter Martyr and Bernardino Ochino, and the Pole, John à Lasco. In September 1548 Cranmer was emboldened to lay before an assembly of his suffragans his draft of a new English service book.[24] Based largely on the medieval Sarum Use, it combined within the covers of a single volume the essentials of four principal service books and three supplementary ones. It was authorized by the Act of Uniformity which passed both houses of Parliament on 21 January 1549 and was published in March as the first 'Book of Common Prayer and Administration of the Sacraments and other Rites and Ceremonies of the Church of England'. The new service book reduced the eight divisions of the Catholic daily office to two – Matins and Evensong, later to be known as Morning Prayer and Evening Prayer – and it turned the Missal into the Book of Communion. It included much that was familiar and left a good deal that was optional, such as kneeling, crossing, holding up hands, knocking on the breast, and other gestures. The two changes that might have been most evident to the average worshipper were the use of the vernacular and the saying aloud of the central Eucharistic Prayer or Canon. The change from Latin to English, as the Prayer Book itself declared, was intended to ensure 'that the people might understand and have profit from hearing', though many of the king's subjects, including the majority of the Welsh, would have found English less familiar and, in the popular mind, less sacred than Latin. But at every point in the service where there was a difference between the old and the new teaching there was a carefully ambiguous use of words, which allowed members of the congregation to interpret them in accordance with their own

[22] G. Constant, *The Reformation in England: Edward VI (1547–1553)* (London, 1941), pp. 46–8.

[23] Lewis, *Cymm.* XXXI. 193–216; Gruffydd, *Trivium*, I. 56–66.

[24] For a general history of the Book of Common Prayer, F. Proctor and W. H. Frère, *A New History of the Book of Common Prayer* (London, 1914); S. E. Morison, *The Prayer Books* (Cambridge, 1949).

convictions, whatever their religious sympathies, Catholic or Protestant. If the book was a 'great compromise' it was also a 'great comprehension'. That was what enabled as stalwart an upholder of traditional beliefs as Bishop Gardiner reluctantly to concede that he could 'with conscience keep it'.[25]

Nevertheless, the emphasis of the new book was on 'common prayer', on the concept of active participation by members of the congregation in a dialogue between priest and people which served to endorse the Protestant doctrine of the priesthood of all believers. The lay people no longer had reason to believe, as they had often been encouraged to do in the Middle Ages, that the service was essentially only a relationship between the priest and God,[26] at which they were present at best as devout and prayerful onlookers, and at worst as thoughtless and inattentive bystanders. The Prayer Book proved to be Cranmer's masterpiece: inspiring, serene, dignified, and mellifluous, and it has aptly been described as the 'most effective of all the possessions of the Anglican Church' (A. F. Pollard). Its use was enforced in all parishes from Whitsuntide 1549 by the Act of Uniformity, which also required all parishioners to attend the church services. Copies of the new book were bought in most parishes, judging by the evidence of such church wardens' accounts as have survived, but was not necessarily used everywhere.[27]

There were, of course, several parts of the king's domains where the Book of Common Prayer would not have been intelligible to the majority of the population. In Calais, the Channel Islands, Ireland, Wales, the Isle of Man, and Cornwall, English was not the first language of most of the people. The bishops and priests of Ireland refused to have anything to do with the new book,[28] and the Cornish people rose in rebellion against the new order, which they contemptuously dismissed as a 'Christmas game'.[29] As far as Wales was concerned, the introduction of the new book caused worrying uncertainty and not a little friction when English was not only a language strange to the majority but was also often disliked as a conqueror's tongue. In fairness to the government, however, it appeared to have no objection in principle to the possibility of providing translations of the book. The French version, *Livre des Prières Communes*, translated by François Philippe and printed in London by Thomas Goultier, was

---

[25] J. A. Muller, *Stephen Gardiner and the Tudor Reaction* (London, 1926), p. 188.
[26] C. S. L. Davies, *Peace, Print and Protestantism* (London, 1977), p. 271; cf. H. Davies, *Worship and Theology in England from Cranmer to Hooker* (Princeton, 1970), pp. 224–6.
[27] Hutton, in Haigh, *Reformation Revised*, p. 125.
[28] Proctor and Frère, *Common Prayer*, pp. 63–4.
[29] F. Rose-Troup, *The Western Rebellion of 1549* (London, 1913).

prepared for French-speaking subjects, and suggestions were made that there should be similarly distinct versions for Ireland and Wales. The right to print a recension for Wales was granted to John Oswen, a Worcester printer;[30] but this seems to have been envisaged as an English not a Welsh edition, and in any case there is no evidence that Oswen ever proceeded to print one. All the same, the publication of a vernacular service book must have brought home to the handful of enthusiasts for a Welsh text the crying need for a translation. Much the most ardent of their number, William Salesbury, discerned more starkly than ever the nature of the problem in his country and set himself in all haste to produce a translation of the epistles and gospels of the Prayer Book, which he published in 1551.[31] In the mean time, it must be wondered quite what was going on in many Welsh country parishes and how some of the priests and most of their congregations were coping with the responsibilities newly thrust upon them by the Act of Uniformity. If and when they were using the new Prayer Book the suspicion would seem to be that they were resorting to those same subterfuges adopted by some of their English counterparts, described by Hooper in a letter to Bullinger of 27 December 1549. He told how,

> although they recite the sacred words of Christ in the vernacular tongue, yet they take pains to recite them so indistinctly and confusingly that they cannot be understood . . . and not a few . . . exhibit Christ's holy communion as the popish mass, nor are the common people present with any other intention . . . and although they are compelled to give up the Latin idiom, yet they most diligently observe the same tone and chants, to which they were accustomed hitherto under the papacy.[32]

Members of the clergy, by a statute of February 1549, were now allowed to take wives. Such permission had the effect of destroying an essential distinction between the priest, hitherto vowed to celibacy, and the layman, allowed to marry, and thereby undermined the sacerdotal significance of the former as a man set apart from others to minister the holy sacraments. In practice, many of the medieval clergy had had illicit relations with women or kept *focariae* ('hearth companions'). In Wales the custom of clerical 'marriages' had been commonplace, and at least three eminent Tudor bishops, one Catholic (William Glyn) and two Protestants (Richard Davies and Rowland Meyrick), were the offspring of such unions.[33] Many

---

[30] Morison, *Prayer Books*, pp. 75–6.
[31] *KLIB*, ed. J. Fisher (Cardiff, 1931).
[32] C. H. Smyth, *Cranmer and the Reformation under Edward VI* (Cambridge, 1926), p. 14.
[33] *WC*, pp. 335–46.

of those Welsh clerics who already had 'wives' now took the opportunity to regularize the existing relationship; one such was Robert Salusbury, vicar of Llanrwst, who had had a companion for twenty years before marrying her.[34] Some of the newly married clergy of St David's diocese, indeed, were not slow to censure those of their fellows who were 'naughty livers and such as openly kept concubines'.[35] Possibly it was because the custom of taking a 'wife' had been so usual in Wales that an unexpectedly large number of clergy in the two Welsh dioceses for which bishops' registers survive can be shown formally to have entered into marriage at this time.[36] In St David's the bishop, Robert Ferrar, himself a married man, deemed it necessary to defend the practice over and over again in his sermons, to such an extent that some of his hearers complained that they were 'wearied with hearing one tale'.[37] When during Mary's reign priests were deprived of their benefices for marriage it would appear that about one in six of them had taken wives in St David's diocese and one in eight in Bangor.[38]

In January 1550 an Act was passed for defacing images of stone, timber, or alabaster[39] – graven, carved or painted – and for calling in old service books. In May 1550 Bishop Ridley ordered the pulling down of altars everywhere within his diocese and in November this instruction was extended by the Privy Council to cover the whole country. Altars had until now been the focus of the mass, the central act of worship, and having them taken down and replaced with communion tables was an outward reflection of one of the profoundest of all Reformation changes – the shift away from the concept of the mass as a propitiatory sacrifice offered by the priest on behalf of the congregation in the direction of a commemorative communion of all believers. One of the first places in the kingdom where the instruction is known to have been carried out was Carmarthen, where a group of reformers were so zealous for change that they provoked heated altercations, in the course of which the communion table was moved a number of times within a short space and was the subject of unseemly squabbles.[40] In many other places, it was evident that late in 1551 the work of destruction was far from complete. On 24 November the council, 'in order to avoid all matters of further contention and strife', gave

---

[34] G. Williams, 'Wales and the reign of Queen Mary I', *WHR*, X (1981), 343.
[35] J. Foxe, *Acts and Monuments . . .*, ed. S. Catley (7 vols. London, 1837–41), VII. 17.
[36] G. Williams, 'The episcopal registers of St David's, 1554–65', *BBCS*, XIV (1950), 45–54, 125–38; A. I. Pryce, *The Diocese of Bangor in the Sixteenth Century* (Bangor, 1923), *passim*.
[37] BL, Harleian MS 420, fos. 99, 111, 114; *W and R*, p. 133.
[38] *BBCS*, XIV. 45–54, 125–38.
[39] M. Aston, *England's Iconoclasts: Laws against Images* (Oxford, 1988).
[40] *W and R*, p. 133.

instructions to the bishops that every altar should at once be removed from all churches everywhere.[41]

Finally, in 1552, under pressure from the duke of Northumberland as well as some of the more radical members of the episcopate, Cranmer produced his Second Prayer Book and the Forty-two Articles of religion. More advanced reformers had been critical of the compromises and ambiguities of the first book when it appeared in 1549 and regarded them as only to be 'retained for a time, lest the people, not having yet learned Christ, should be deterred by too extensive innovations'.[42] The radical Hooper had gone to the extent of placing on record his view that the book was 'in some respects indeed manifestly impious'.[43] All those earlier concessions and deliberate imprecicisions which had given such offence in some quarters were removed from the Second Prayer Book, making it impossible to conceive of the communion service as a sacrificial mass. The notorious 'black rubric', hastily included, explicitly denied the real presence and explained that kneeling to receive communion did not mean 'thereby that any adoration is done, or ought to be done'.[44] The new book was given approval by the Second Act of Uniformity, which was passed in April 1552, but did not authorize the use of the book until the following November. So even if parishes acquired their copies of it punctually – and there is no certainty that all of them did – they would have had less than a year's experience of using it before Mary ascended the throne in July 1553 and abrogated it.

Cranmer rounded off his efforts to define belief with his Forty-two Articles of the faith, which received the royal assent on 12 June 1553. Many of these included doctrines acceptable to most Christian believers, but there were others which bore a distinctly Protestant, even Calvinist, tinge, like Article 17, which declared that 'predestination to life is the everlasting purpose of God'.[45] Although the Articles circulated for only a brief space during Edward's reign, they were to form the basis of Elizabeth's later Thirty-nine Articles. Cranmer had also hoped to reform Canon Law but was thwarted from doing so by lay opposition. He had, nevertheless, introduced so large a measure of reformation into the Church of England that the churchwardens of Stanford in the Vale in Berkshire were voicing the widely held view when they declared late in Edward's reign that the schism in England dated not from Henry VIII's reign but from the second

---

[41] *APC*, II (1547–50), 304; III (1550–2), 411, 433.

[42] *Original Letters relating to the English Reformation*, ed. H. Robinson (2 vols. Parker Soc., London, 1846), II. 535–6.

[43] Ibid., I. 79.

[44] *The First and Second Prayer Books of Edward VI* (London, 1949), p. 393.

[45] S. Doran and C. Durston, *Princes, Pastors and People* (London, 1991), p. 19.

year of Edward VI, when all 'godly ceremonies and good uses were taken out of the church'.[46]

In the mean time, for most of the reign, the two powerful laymen successively in authority over the kingdom had set others, great and not so great, a notably bad example in their attitude towards the material possessions of the Church. As one of their more influential colleagues, Sir William Petre, confessed in a rare moment of candour, 'We which talk much of Christ have left fishing for men and fish again in the tempestuous seas of the world for gain and wicked mammon', while the Venetian ambassador in 1551 summed up their activities as 'one enormous act of sacrilege'.[47] All the Welsh dioceses suffered grievously at the hands of such predators. From 1549 to 1552 the diocese of St David's was racked by quarrels over many of its possessions between its bishop and a clique of powerful laymen and their influential clerical allies.[48] Bishop Ferrar himself was a shrewd and hard-headed man of business, whose enemies accused him of covetousness, sharp practice, and even oppression. In his anxiety to capitalize the resources of his diocese he appears to have overstepped the bounds of episcopal decency and decorum. A number of witnesses agreed in testifying that when he was ostensibly engaged on an episcopal visitation of his diocese he, in fact, spent most of his time surveying its mineral resources, agricultural potentialities, and other 'commodities'. He was accused of bringing pressure to bear on tenants, especially Robert Birt of Llandygwydd, the farmer of the episcopal manor there. In justice to Ferrar, on the other hand, much of the trouble appears to have arisen from his understandable reluctance to maintain the disastrous consequences for his diocese of the agreements arrived at by his predecessor, William Barlow, with his brother Roger and with Dorothy Devereux, widow of Richard Devereux, whose family had acquired the prize manor of Lamphey.[49] Ferrar's attempts at recovery only succeeded in making further enemies for him, notably Gruffudd Dwn, one of the leading landowners in south Carmarthenshire, who was acting as Dorothy Devereux's attorney. Other ambitious laymen in Ferrar's diocese with whom he came into conflict were the Pembrokeshire bigwigs, Arnold Butler, William Owen of Henllys, and William Philips of Picton. To make matters worse, he also contrived to lock horns with some of his most influential canons, particularly Thomas Young, the precentor, and Rowland Meyrick, the chancellor. The quarrel

---

[46] Duffy, *Stripping the Altars*, p. 462.
[47] W. G. Hoskin, *The Age of Plunder* (London, 1976), p. 131; *CSP Ven.* V (1534–54), 347.
[48] *WRE*, pp. 124–39.
[49] Ibid., pp. 121–3.

ended with Ferrar being imprisoned as a consequence of the enmity of his opponents, lay and clerical.

The bishop of the neighbouring diocese of Llandaff, Anthony Kitchen, lost his London house when it was one of three bishops' houses in the Strand that were pulled down to make way for Protector Somerset's own sumptuous new palace.[50] At home in Llandaff Kitchen found himself in uncomfortable proximity to one of the most powerful and grasping noblemen in the kingdom, William Herbert, later earl of Pembroke. Another of the bishop's neighbours, George Mathew of Llandaff, had married into Pembroke's family and he exploited his influential in-law's favour with Northumberland to exert pressure on the unhappy Kitchen. The result was that, late in Edward's reign, on 10 May 1553, when it would have been clear that the king was dying, the most lucrative of the episcopal estates, the manor of Llandaff, worth £50 a year and accounting for over a third of the bishop's income, was leased in perpetuity at an accustomed rent, i.e. was virtually granted away, to George Mathew. Kitchen was often condemned for his actions by his successors, one of whom, Bishop Babington (1591–5), complained with rueful humour that he was left as bishop of Aff because all the land had gone![51] We should not be too censorious of Kitchen, however. There is no reason to suppose that he would willingly have parted with so valuable an asset as the manor of Llandaff, and there are grounds for thinking that Mathew's all-powerful patrons gave the luckless prelate little choice in the matter. Up in north Wales, in the diocese of St Asaph, one of the most influential of Denbighshire's gentry, Sir John Salusbury, had succeeded in gaining illegal possession of the chapter seal and, with the connivance of his kinsman, Foulk Salusbury, the former dean, had been busily forging advantageous leases in his own favour.[52] In the remaining diocese of Bangor, after Bishop Bulkeley died in 1552, the see was deliberately kept vacant until 1555, greatly to its loss.[53]

Wholesale pillaging also went on at the level of the parishes when church goods were seized in the king's name in 1552–3. As far back as Henry VIII's reign, alarming rumours had been circulating to the effect that the king intended to confiscate to his own use the treasures of the churches.[54] Again, in 1547, the duke of Somerset had ordered an inventory of them to be compiled, ostensibly in order to protect them from alienation and keep them out of the hands of would-be predators. On 3 March 1551

---

[50] F. Heal, *Of Prelates and Princes* (Cambridge, 1990), p. 137.

[51] Williams, *GCH*, IV. 217–18.

[52] Williams, *WHR*, X. 355.

[53] Browne Willis, *A Survey of the Cathedral Church of Bangor* (London, 1721), p. 101.

[54] Above, chap. 6.

Northumberland mooted a scheme to 'take into the king's hands such church plate as remaineth to be employed unto his Highness' use'.[55] When the Second Prayer Book eliminated all suggestion of the mass and simplified church use, this was seized upon as a further pretext for removing all plate and vestments beyond the minimum now considered necessary. But it was not until April 1553 that the process of seizure began in earnest in Wales. The only Welsh county for which the inventories then taken have survived in full is Glamorgan,[56] though there is no reason to doubt that much the same kind of procedure employed there was put into operation everywhere else in Wales. Glamorgan was divided up into four groups of hundreds: Swansea, Llangyfelach, and Neath; Newcastle and Ogmore; Cowbridge; and Caerphilly, Llantrisant, Dinas Powys, and Cardiff. Eight lay commissioners, drawn from leading families of county gentry, worked from Swansea, Newcastle (Bridgend), and Cardiff. They summoned before them representatives from each parish to present an inventory of its plate, ornaments, vestments, and other valuables. All these goods, except for a bare minimum allowed for parish worship, were confiscated. However, many of the possessions of the parishes had already been disposed of, either by voluntary sales or embezzlements, in an attempt to prevent seizure by the Crown. The richest haul, naturally, was obtained from the cathedral at Llandaff which, though it was just about the poorest diocese in England and Wales, nevertheless retained an impressive quantity of vestments, plate, metal work, jewels, and other treasures, including the priceless book of 'St Teilo wherein is the whole knowledge of the church', i.e. the *Liber Landavensis*.[57] Most of the country parishes were very slenderly furnished, though some of the towns, Cardiff, Swansea, or even Llantwit Major, suffered considerable losses. Ironically enough, the spoliation went on for some weeks after Edward VI had died on 6 July 1553. The cathedral's treasures were not removed until 17 July 1553 and were seized in the name of Queen Mary, to whom such practices were utterly abhorrent and who was later to conduct an inquiry into the whole sorry affair in Llandaff.[58] Possibly no aspect of the attack on the possessions of the Church was more thoroughly disliked by ordinary parishioners than this rape of treasured possessions belonging to the local communities, particularly when the purportedly religious motives for removing them proved to be only a very transparent cloak for personal greed.

---

[55] *APC*, III. 228.
[56] PRO, E117/12/17; extracts in *Cardiff Recs.* I. 379–86; Thomas, *Llandaff*, chap 7.
[57] PRO, E117/12/17.
[58] Below, chap. 8.

These changes in religious life outwardly implemented during the six years of Edward's rule had been rapid and sweeping; they might with justice be categorized as a religious revolution. As far as Wales was in question, in the absence of any pressing demand for reform from below, they had necessarily had to be imposed from above. The success with which the Tudor rulers were able to enforce their will depended everywhere to a large extent upon an effective liaison between the authority of the king and his council at the centre and the power and goodwill of their agents and allies in the localities. In Wales the machinery at the disposal of the Crown for achieving just such a possible harmonization of interests was, by 1547–53, decidedly more efficacious than it had been even in the early 1520s. True, the working-out of the Act of Union of 1536/43 was still in its early stages, but that legislation had at least set up a uniform system of administration and justice throughout the country, based on that which existed in England. Wales had been divided up into counties and into the assize circuits of the Court of Great Sessions, all staffed with their appropriate cadres of officials appointed by the Crown – justices of Great Sessions, sheriffs, justices of the peace, and the rest.[59] Supervising the whole was the Council in the Marches,[60] which had been given a new lease of life and vigour by its president from 1534 to 1543, Rowland Lee. The two presidents during Edward's reign were, for the first time, powerful lay aristocrats and not bishops – in itself a noteworthy change of emphasis. Both John Dudley, earl of Warwick and president from 1548 to 1550, and William Herbert, earl of Pembroke and president from 1550 to 1553, were autocratic individuals and hardened soldiers: appointees who could hardly have been improved upon as men guaranteed to take a firm, authoritative line. Moreover, each of them, and Herbert especially, had extensive landed interests and a powerful corps of kinsmen and clients in or near Wales. Admittedly, both men had a list of priorities in which overseeing religious change in Wales came relatively low, but it may be symptomatic of the degree of control that they exercised there that Warwick could arrange for Sir Edward Knevett to raise a large body of Welsh troops to help put down Kett's rebellion in Norfolk in 1549,[61] while Herbert could recruit an even larger contingent to suppress the very differently motivated rising in the West Country in the same year.[62] Having aides in its service who could with such ease raise soldiery on this scale was a godsend to a regime facing

---

[59] *W 1415–1642*, chap. 11.
[60] P. H. Williams, *The Council in the Marches under Elizabeth I* (Cardiff, 1958); C. A. J. Skeel, *The Council in the Marches of Wales* (London, 1903).
[61] S. T. Bindoff, *Ket's Rebellion 1549* (Historical Association Pamphlet, London, 1949).
[62] Rose-Troup, *Western Rebellion*, pp. 248 ff.

widespread disaffection without the benefit of a standing army. To reinforce the Lord President's military authority came the decision of 1551 which constituted William Herbert lord lieutenant for all the counties in Wales as well as the neighbouring English ones under his jurisdiction as president of the Council in the Marches.

Turning from lay control to that of the Church we find that when Edward came to the throne, only one of the Welsh bishops, William Barlow, was a confirmed and enthusiastic Protestant.[63] He did not remain at St David's long before being translated to Bath and Wells in 1548. He was to be followed by another Augustinian canon turned reformer, Robert Ferrar, who had worked closely with Barlow in Scotland and been recommended by him as his successor at St David's, though Ferrar owed his appointment chiefly to being a protégé of Somerset. The first bishop to be appointed by letters patent, which dispensed with the customary *congé d'élire*, and the first to be ordained according to the new English Ordinal in September 1548,[64] Ferrar was to be an eager but ill-fated protagonist of reform. The other three bishops were typically cautious, conformist Henricians, who disliked change but found it impossible to depart from their usual pattern of obedience to the royal wishes. Two of them, Kitchen of Llandaff and Wharton of St Asaph, were former abbots and conservative in outlook. In the debates on the eucharist which preceded the Act of Uniformity of 1549, Kitchen recorded his opposition to change of any kind.[65] Wharton also expressed conservative opinions on the mass in answer to questions put to him early in 1548, affirming it to consist 'principally in the consecration, oblation and receiving of the body and blood of Christ'.[66] In spite of that, he entrusted his proxy on the Act of Uniformity to two bishops who voted for it, and he also voted for the new Ordinal. Bulkeley of Bangor was the personification of the ecclesiastical trimmer. Absent from the House of Lords when votes were cast on the Book of Common Prayer, he entrusted one of his proxies to a bishop who favoured change and the other to a bishop who opposed it.[67] It was typical, perhaps, of Kitchen, Wharton, and Bulkeley that they should have absented themselves when the vote was taken in the Lords on the book of 1552. It seemed unlikely that any one of them would dare to oppose the royal will by taking an overt stand for the old ways; all appeared reluctantly to have outwardly accepted a series of innovations which they privately opposed.

[63] *WRE*, pp. 110–24.
[64] Lambeth Palace, Cranmer's Register, fo. 328.
[65] P. Hughes, *The Reformation in England* (3 vols. London, 1950–4), II. 106.
[66] Griffiths, *JHSCW*, IX. 36.
[67] Hughes, *Ref. in England*, II. 106.

The attitude of the bishops was in keeping with that of many of their clergy. Only in the diocese of St David's had Barlow made any serious effort to introduce reformed doctrine and to recruit Protestant clergy.[68] A number of his higher clergy were keen reformers; men like Thomas Young, or George Constantine and Hugh Rawlins, both royal visitors and preachers in 1547. Among the higher clergy elsewhere were deeply conservative figures who were nevertheless able to accommodate themselves to Edwardian changes, though all of them were to become influential supporters of Mary's regime. They numbered among them William Glyn (Marian bishop of Bangor), Morgan Philips (Marian precentor of St David's), John Gwynedd and Roger Edgeworth (both eloquent propagators of Catholic doctrine in the 1550s). Among the parish clergy, while there was no marked enthusiasm for doctrinal change, there were two sets of circumstances which predisposed them in favour of accepting the Edwardian regime. One was that the general shortage of clerics enabled unbeneficed curates to acquire livings much sooner than they could have expected in ordinary circumstances, if indeed they would ever have done so.[69] Hence, perhaps, Owain ap Gwilym's scornful dismissal of the 'inexperienced boys' he saw in neighbouring parishes. Having obtained promotion unexpectedly, they might well have been loath to relinquish it. Again, the fact that priests were allowed to marry and that any offspring which had resulted from previous liaisons were now legitimated, created a vested interest in favour of the changed arrangements.[70]

Yet in spite of the authority to implement change which rested in the hands of the Crown and its agents, the truth was that while Edwardian policies may have been carried through without serious opposition in Wales, they had been accepted by a minority of the population only, and reluctantly even by some of them. The majority of the people of Wales remained confused, apathetic, or hostile. In the diocese of St David's, the most likely springboard for a further leap forward to Protestant reform, relations became soured within the reforming party itself. Bishop Ferrar, a close friend of Bishop Hooper and himself a keen reformer, fell foul of an influential group among the leading Protestant members of his cathedral chapter, described by their bishop as his 'mortal enemies',[71] as well as prominent laymen. The petty quarrels and backbiting which ensued largely undid the efforts of both factions to bring about reform – to such an extent that Gruffudd Dwn maintained

[68] *WRE*, pp. 110–24.
[69] M. Bowker in C. Haigh (ed.), *The English Reformation Revised* (London, 1987), p. 93.
[70] Williams, *BBCS*, XIV. 45–54, 125–38.
[71] *WRE*, p. 130

that if reformation be not had and such means found that God's word may be sown among the people, and that shortly, they will think there is no God. For how shall men think there is such a one as is not worthy to be talked of.[72]

The dispute between them dragged on its unedifying way for two years, until in 1551 a group of clergy, nearly all of them sympathetic to reform, presented a lengthy document containing fifty-six articles against their bishop and grouped under the headings of abuse of authority, maintenance of superstition, covetousness, wilful negligence, and folly. Ferrar defended himself stoutly and effectively, but when his erstwhile patron, Somerset, was executed in January 1552, his enemies carried too many guns for him. His diocese ended up in the sadly paradoxical position of having its reforming bishop clapped in gaol at the instance of a hostile group of Protestant clergy. They were accusing a man who, early in Mary's reign, was burnt at the stake for his reforming opinions of unduly favouring Catholic beliefs and practices.[73]

It was some of the Welsh towns which, like those in other European countries, offered the best prospects for making Protestant converts. In the market-towns and ports of the south and the east existed sizeable nuclei of English speakers, some of whom were literate and open to the appeal of English Bibles, Prayer Books, and the torrent of religious literature in English now pouring from the printing-presses. Here, too, were to be found merchants, lawyers, and craftsmen frequently in touch with London, Bristol, Gloucester, Shrewsbury, and other centres where Protestant beliefs were burgeoning. The most interesting example of such a town in Wales was Carmarthen.[74] The largest Welsh town and the regional capital of south-west Wales, with a population of 2,000 or so, it had already been the recipient of Barlow's proselytizing attentions and there were in the town a number of landowners, merchants, and clergy attracted to the new doctrines. They listened eagerly to Protestant sermons, read their English Bibles and other religious literature, and were critical of Bishop Ferrar for his alleged slowness to promote reform. Unfortunately, the quarrels between them and their bishop seriously retarded the progress of their cause. Cardiff was another seedbed where Protestant ideas took root.[75] In Edward's reign the Cardiff fisherman, Rawlins White, ' a notable and open professor of the faith', according to Foxe, was one of a group of townspeople drawn to Bible-reading and the espousal of advanced beliefs.

[72] BL. Harleian MS 420, fo. 115.
[73] *WRE*, pp. 134–5; *W and R*, pp. 135–7.
[74] *WRE*, pp. 116–37.
[75] Williams, *GCH*, IV. 215–22.

Haverfordwest, in English-speaking Pembrokeshire, seems to have been yet another cradle for the reforming cause and, like Cardiff and Carmarthen, was to produce its Protestant martyr in Mary's reign.[76] It may well be that other municipalities which in the seventeenth century exhibited a markedly puritan trend were first evangelized for Protestantism in the Edwardian period, though we have no clear evidence for the existence of such beliefs at that time. Towns with possible sympathies of this kind may have been Swansea and Brecon in the south, and Wrexham and Denbigh in the north.

A number of leading landowners were others who went along with the tide of reform willingly enough as long as they saw the possibilities of benefiting from material gains at the expense of church property. They appeared not to be unduly concerned about the subtleties of belief or practice as long as the structure of authority at the centre and in the counties was maintained stable. This was certainly true of easily the most powerful aristocrat in Wales and a careerist who served four different monarchs with no compunction and much profit – William Herbert, created Master of the Horse and Knight of the Garter in 1548. He and his clientele were particularly well rewarded after siding with Northumberland against Somerset. He himself received Somerset's Wiltshire estates and was created Lord Herbert of Cardiff and earl of Pembroke in 1551. Another closely tied in with the Edwardian establishment in south-west Wales and suitably recompensed for his devotion was Lord Ferrers, created Viscount Hereford in 1550. So, too, but to a much lesser extent were the second and third earls of Worcester along the south-eastern border, Ellis Price in the north-east and Sir Richard Bulkeley in the north-west. Even men like Sir Rice Mansel[77] or Sir Thomas Stradling,[78] who were to display pronounced Catholic inclinations in Mary's reign, were willing enough to act for the government as chantry commissioners and commissioners for church goods in her half-brother's time.

There is evidence to suggest, though, that some leading laymen were seriously attracted to Protestant doctrine as well as being willing to avail themselves of gains accruing from the disposal of church property. Sir John Price of Brecon, certainly attracted by Renaissance aspirations for reform, also dabbled in the Protestant notions embodied in the famous will (1531) of the Gloucestershire gentleman, William Tracy, which he carefully copied into his commonplace book, although he appears to have reverted to orthodoxy under Mary.[79] But Sir John Perrot, who was made a Knight

[76] Williams, *WHR*, X. 351.

[77] G. Williams, 'Rhys Mansel of Penrice and Margam', *Morgannwg*, VI (1963), 33–51.

[78] G. Williams, The Stradling Family', in R. Denning (ed.), *St Donat's Castle and Atlantic College* (Cowbridge, 1983), pp. 23–9.

[79] Balliol College MS 353 is Price's commonplace book; cf. also *WC*, p. 541.

of the Bath by Edward and benefited from royal generosity when he was in financial difficulty, under the influence of his uncle, Thomas Perrot, Edward's tutor, became and remained a keen Protestant.[80] A handful of Welshmen published incontrovertible testimony to how deeply they had become attached to reform. Most notable among them were the gentleman-poet, Gruffudd ap Ieuan ap Llywelyn Fychan, and that most talented of all the energetic and resourceful Salusburys of Denbighshire, William Salesbury.

Gruffudd ap Ieuan (c.1488–1553) was a well-known littérateur and landowner from Llannerch near St Asaph, who had been one of the leading lights at the famous poetic *eisteddfod* of Caerwys in 1524–5.[81] Before the Reformation he had been responsible for a number of poems to saints and pilgrimages which conveyed no suggestion of anything but mainstream late medieval piety.[82] But late in life he seems to have embraced Protestant beliefs and composed a *cywydd* voicing his new convictions, the content of which is all the more striking because, as a gentleman-poet, he had no patron to please but himself. In his poem he sang 'against the power of images and in memory of Christ's death and his last words to his disciples on the night before his passion' ('yn erbyn braint delwau ac i gof marw Crist ai ymddiddanion diweddaf wrth ei ddiscublion y nos cyn ei ddioddefaint').[83] It was a short *cywydd* but it focused on some of the central themes of the Reformation. Negatively, the poet rejected the excesses of the old faith, denouncing the 'blindness' that attributed more importance to images than to God and gave on 'bended knees to a withered image the honour that should have been accorded to Christ' ('Rhoi arddoliant ar ddeulin, a ddylai Crist I ddelw grin') and venerated saints and roods. How foolishly the people had departed from the 'godly faith of the apostles' ('ffydd dduwiol y postolion')! They must abandon the vanity of candles, incense, holy water, rosaries, the 'golden-haired angels' ('angel penfelyn') and a host of saints, none of which, nor any mortal man, could avail sinners anything. More positively, he urged them to place all their trust in the sufferings of Jesus on the cross, that unique act of sacrifice undertaken for their salvation. 'Every time they received communion in both kinds, as bread and wine, they remembered his body broken for them and his blood shed on their behalf until he came again.'

---

[80] J. Phillips, 'Glimpses of Elizabethan Pembrokeshire', *AC* (1897), 309.

[81] *Detholiad o Waith Gruffudd ap Llywelyn Fychan*, ed. J. C. Morrice (Bangor, 1910); cf. T. Roberts, 'Gruffudd ap Ieuan ap Llywelyn Fychan', *BBCS*, XVI (1954–6), 251–3.

[82] Williams, *TCS* (1991), 69–98.

[83] *Gwaith Gruffudd ap Ieuan*, pp. 31–4.

Hyn im coffa cur,
Bob amser pan gymerir,
Bara a gwin, bur air gwir,
Y gur farwolaeth tan go
A ddeliwch oni ddelo.[84]

In Christ's passion lay their only hope of forgiveness for their sins and the grace that he bestowed on his elect ('ddewis wŷr') and their hope of heaven.

William Salesbury[85] (?1520–?1584), scion of a cadet branch of the Salusbury family of Lleweni, was brought up as an 'earnest papist' in his own words. Later, he spent some time at Oxford University and the inns of court, where he presumably first came into contact with those Renaissance and Reformation ideals which were to dominate all his later aspirations. Between 1547 and 1552 his literary output, even judged by the standards of the explosion of printed books published in those years, was astonishingly varied and prolific.[86] Four of his works, in particular, are relevant to our understanding of the period. The introduction to his second book, *Oll Synnwyr Pen Kembero Ygyd*[87] (The Whole Wisdom of a Welshman's Head, 1547) and the third Welsh book to be printed, has fittingly been described as the 'manifesto of Welsh Protestant humanism'.[88] Its author was convinced that the Bible had existed in Welsh in early Britain and been well known to the populace, and he pleaded impassionedly with his fellow-countrymen that they should restore the scriptures to their rightful place in the national life. He urged them, unless they wanted 'completely to abandon the faith of Christ' ('A ny vynwch ymado yn dalgrwn dec a ffydd Christ') and 'wholly to forget and ignore his will' ('tros gofi ac ebryfygy i ewyllys ef'),

> to obtain the scriptures in your own language as they once existed among your fortunate ancestors, the early Britons . . . Go on pilgrimage in bare feet to the king's grace and his council that you may petition them to have holy scripture in your language, for the sake of those among you who are unable to learn English and have no prospect of doing so.[89]

---

[84] Ibid., p. 33.

[85] D. R. Thomas, *The Life and Work of Richard Davies and William Salesbury* (Oswestry, 1902); *WRE*, pp. 191–205; cf. also T. Parry and M. Morgan, *Llyfryddiaeth a Llenyddiaeth Gymraeg* (Cardiff, 1976), pp. 129–31 for further details.

[86] R. B. Jones, *William Salesbury* (Cardiff, 1994), pp. 18–19.

[87] *Oll Synnwyr Pen*, introd.; cf. G. H. Hughes (ed.), *Rhagymadroddion, 1547–1648* (Cardiff, 1951), pp. 5–16.

[88] S. Lewis, 'Damcaniaeth Eglwysig Brotestannaidd', *Efrydiau Catholig*, II (1947), 36–55.

[89] *Oll Synnwyr Pen*, introd.

mynwch yr yscrythur lan yn ych iaith, mal ac y bu hi y gan ych dedwydd henafieit yr hen Uryttanneit . . . Pererindotwch yn droednoeth at ras y Brenhin ae Gyncor y ddeisyf cael cennat y cael yr yscrythur lan yn ych iaith, er mwyn y cyniver ohanoch or nad yw n abyl, nac mewn kyfflypwriaeth y ddyscy Sasnaec.

The next two short polemical works, published in 1550, *The Baterie of the Popes Botereulx commonlye called the High Altare*[90] and *Ban wedy i dynnu air yngair allan o hen gyfreith Hoel Da . . . A certaine case extract out of the auncient law of Hoel Da*,[91] were both linked to major ecclesiastical changes then being enforced by the State and offer unmistakable evidence of Salesbury's profound Protestant sympathies. The *Ban* attempted to justify the permission given to clerics to marry on the basis of an appeal to the provisions of ancient Welsh laws associated with the name of Hywel Dda (d. 950). The *Baterie* was an attack on papist altars and the doctrine of the mass as a sacrifice that was associated with them. Its publication followed hard on the widespread demolition of altars in the churches during the years 1549–50, but it is not at all clear how widely it was read or how much impact it had on Wales.

Unquestionably the most significant of this group of books was *Kynniver Llith a Ban* (1551), a translation into Welsh of the epistles and the gospels which the Book of Common Prayer of 1549 prescribed for reading at the communion service on Sundays and holy days. Dedicating his work in Latin to the bishops of Wales and Hereford,[92] Salesbury administered a gentle rebuke that none of those reverend fathers in God had themselves seen fit to require a Welsh translation. It had been left to Salesbury to 'free the word of God from the fetters' in which, for most of the Welsh, it was shackled. He had been 'touched to the quick by the misery of those born in the same country and of the same nation as myself – a people however ignorant of sacred knowledge yet burning more than most men with a fervent zeal for God'. He urged the bishops to authorize his book for public use and to depute the task of examining it to six learned men from each diocese. His request was passed over in silence by the bishops, not one of whom, with the possible exception of Bishop Bulkeley of Bangor, would in any event have himself been capable of passing judgement on the work. But the book was used and copies of it survived into Elizabeth's reign.[93]

---

[90] G. Williams, 'William Salesbury's *Baterie against the Popes Botereulx*', *BBCS*, XIII (1949), 146–50.

[91] C. James, 'Ban wedy i dynny . . .', *Cambrian Medieval Celtic Studies*, XXVII (1994), 61–86.

[92] *KLIB*, ed. J. Fisher (Cardiff, 1931).

[93] D. R. Thomas, *Davies and Salesbury*, pp. 72–3.

Kynniver Llith a Ban had its faults. It showed signs of haste, which was hardly surprising considering the pressure at which Salesbury as a lone translator had been working. In some instances he was content to translate from the Great Bible rather than directly from the Greek, as was his usual practice. His translations of the epistles were noticeably weaker than those of the gospels. Most serious of all, the book bore the marks of his decidedly idiosyncratic, not to say wrong-headed, views about language and orthography (see below, chap. 13). For all that, it represented a most remarkable achievement.[94] It contained incomparably the most extensive biblical translations into Welsh so far undertaken. Moreover, even at this early stage, it revealed Salesbury's mastery of the original languages of scripture and his accuracy and expertise as a translator. Large parts of it, like the translation of the parables of the lost sheep, the lost piece of silver, or the good Samaritan, were excellent as pieces of Welsh prose, as long as the quirks of spelling and mutation were disregarded.[95] Undertaking so ambitious an enterprise had been an eminently fruitful training for Salesbury and, still more important, had established an invaluable precedent for the future. It had not only underlined emphatically the need for a Welsh Bible and order of service but had also demonstrated convincingly the possibility of satisfying that need.

Even so, it was not isolated reformers like Salesbury who accurately represented the reactions of ordinary folk. The sentiments of many of them were almost certainly more faithfully mirrored in that poetry which was mordantly critical of the Edwardian innovations. Much of this verse is found in the form of *cwndidau* (religious free verse) of south-east Wales which, in the first generation, were hotly opposed to the imposition of Protestant belief and practice.[96] The severest critic was Tomas ap Ieuan ap Rhys,[97] a descendant of the best-known bardic family of Glamorgan. He was thoroughly imbued with the vigorous ascetic tradition of medieval religious verse in the county. His response to the Edwardian Reformation was that of an unrelenting opponent; staunchly conservative, though by no means obscurantist, and a man deeply concerned for the religious and moral health of the community around him. His hostility to the new order was so fierce and undisguised that it could hardly have been safe for a poet like him to allow his views more than a limited circulation among a

---

[94] For Salesbury's qualities as a translator, *KLIB*, introd.; I. Thomas, *Y Testament Newydd Cymraeg, 1551–1620* (Cardiff, 1976), chap. 3.

[95] *KLIB*, pp. xxxii–xxxiii.

[96] G. J. Williams, *Traddodiad Llenyddol Morgannwg* (Cardiff, 1948), pp. 122–6, 138–41; C. W. Lewis in *GCH*, IV. 521–74.

[97] For his poetry, L. J. Hopkin-James and T. C. Evans (eds.), *Hen Gwndidau, Carolau a Chywyddau* (Bangor, 1918), pp. 1–44.

sympathetic Catholic audience until after Mary had come to the throne, even though the tone of some of the poems suggests that they must have been conceived earlier. He rejected with righteous indignation the whole Protestant teaching as an alien English faith ('ffydd Sayson') inflicted willy-nilly on the Welsh. Its effects on the churches had been calamitous: God's temples had passed into laymen's hands and become deserted; their high altars had been cast down and replaced by tables that resembled 'widows' boards' ('gwrachïod gweddwon'). The country had been turned into a 'Sodom and Gomorrha' having no prayer or fasting, no penance or assoiling, no confession or absolution, no Catholic baptism or burial, no incense or holy oil, no pax, nor rood nor holy water. Above all, the poet lamented the loss of the mass:

> gwedy esbeilio duw ay dy
> pery y ddy weision gyddio y gorff e
> a galw r byd y gymeryd briwsion[98]

for after despoiling God and his house, they caused his servants to hide his body and summoned the people to receive mere breadcrumbs

'Wales, bereft of the body of Christ, was sad indeed without it', he went on. As for the new-style married clergy, he dismissed them as pusillanimous 'conceited goats', for whom he had nothing but contempt. All this depravity was associated in his mind with men's insensate craving after wealth and possessions, which had already brought down on their heads famine, high prices, crop failures, dearth of game and livestock, and might bring down direr punishments yet.[99]

At the opposite end of Wales, up in the north-west, denunciations were equally vehement. One anonymous poet claimed that it was impossible worthily to translate the Latin mass into English.[100] Another anonymous bard was responsible for a series of quatrains mourning the loss of external symbols and aids to faith,[101] while a cleric-poet, Owain ap Gwilym, vicar of Taly-y-llyn, was scandalized that only 'apprentices' were to be found among the clergy in many parishes, a crowd of inexperienced boys where formerly there had been men. He was scornful, too, of the women and young girls who were now setting themselves up as experts in divinity.[102]

---

[98] Ibid., p. 44.
[99] Ibid., pp. 43–4.
[100] NLW, Llansteffan MS. 133, fo. 318.
[101] D. J. Bowen, 'Detholiad o englynion hiraeth am yr hen ffydd', *Efrydiau Catholig*, VI (1954), 5–12.
[102] D. G. Williams, 'Syr Owain Gwilym', *LlC*, VI (1960/1), 179–93.

The most scathing critic of them all, however, was Siôn Brwynog,[103] who had spoken of Henry VIII in terms of warm admiration but who lambasted his son's measures with unrestrained contempt and vigour. He viewed with horror a world torn by conflicts between the old faith and the new, some boldly embracing heresy, others standing fast by the old and true. After some harsh words about the married priest who, he complained,

> Ni son am fferen y Sul
> Na chyffes mwy na cheffyl.
> Ni all ddeall a ddowaid,
> Yntau yn ffôl, eto ni phaid.

('speaks not of mass on Sunday, nor of confession, any more than would a horse. He understands not what he says; he is foolish but will not desist.')

he went on to deplore the sad condition of the churches and religion:

> Oerder yn yn amser ni,
> Yr ia glas ywr eglwysi.
> On'd oedd dost un dydd a dau
> I'r llawr fwrw'r allorau?
> Cor ni bydd cwyr yn y byd,
> Na chennad yn iach ennyd.
>
> Yr eglwys a'i haroglau
> Yn wych oedd ein hiachau.
> Yr oedd gynt arwydd a gaid,
> Olew yn eli enaid.[104]

(the bleakness of our times, with churches cold as ice. Was it not a bitter blow to have cast down altars within a day or two? There is no wax in the world, nor a single candle in any chancel for a moment to make us whole; in the church that with its incense used to heal us so splendidly, there was once oil as a symbol of balm for the soul.)

Two other Welsh publicists who spent much of their time in England and whose books were published in Mary's reign, reveal how opposed they had been to Edward's reign in a vein very similar to that of the home-keeping

---

[103] R. M. Kerr, 'Cywyddau Siôn Brwynog' (MA thesis, Wales 1960).
[104] Ibid., pp. 133–4.

poets. John Gwynedd,[105] a former monk of St Alban's, who had published his *Confutation of the First Part of Frith's Book* as early as 1528, issued his *Declaration of the State of Heretikes* in 1554, and Roger Edgeworth,[106] who seemed passively to accept the Edwardian order although he later preached forcefully against it, brought out his *Sermons* in 1557. Gwynedd contended that Edwardian Protestants were only able to defend their doctrines with the help of state power. Both he and Edgeworth abominated a married clergy and utterly deplored the destruction of the mass and the altars and the attacks on ceremonies and visual representations in the form of images and pictures. Overall, therefore, it seems clear that a majority of the people of Wales had deeply disliked the changes of the years from 1547 to 1553. Some indication of the grudging stubbornness with which people refused to change their ways under compulsion comes from interrogations which Bishop Bulkeley of Bangor conducted as late as 1551. He then issued articles intended to discover whether or not the clergy of his diocese had acquired English Bibles and Prayer Books, whether any of their flock still prayed on beads or said masses, and whether there were any images, tabernacles, shrines, or feigned miracles to be found in churches.[107] Such inquiries in themselves give a broad hint of how little even the externalities may have changed in many places and are reminiscent of Ferrar's observations on the conservative attitudes and practices of Carmarthen people.

The reasons why the Edwardian Reformation had failed to make a significant impact in Wales are not far to seek. Since Henry VIII's reign there had never been much in the way of popular pressure for reform, and such innovation as had been inculcated had always had to be applied from above by governmental decree. But those alterations which the Edwardian regime had sought to introduce had been much more drastic and less acceptable than anything associated with Henry. For instance, the clergy had had liaisons with women before 1549, but the officially married priesthood then sanctioned was strongly disliked. Again, the appearance and furnishings of parish churches had been modified almost beyond recognition with the removal of images, pictures, roods, stained glass, chantries, church goods, and other familiar features of the medieval scene. When the mass and the altars had been taken away, a mortal blow was struck at the traditional concept of the priest offering a propitiatory

---

[105] *DWB., s.n.*

[106] *DNB, s.n.*

[107] Frère and Kennedy, *Visitation Articles*, II. Cf. the old lady who complained to her neighbour, 'Alas! gossip what shall we now do at church since all the saints are taken away, since all the rights we were wont to have are gone?' H. Davies, *Worship and Theology*, p. 21.

sacrifice on behalf of the whole community. They had further been deprived of such old and well-loved practices as making the sign of the cross, beseeching the help of the saints, praying with rosaries, and employing ceremonies with candles, ashes, and palms, and 'creeping to the cross'.[108]

The very language of worship had changed from Latin to English and everyone had been compelled to conform to a single, strange new English Book of Common Prayer. Nor did the transformation end there; the old religion had conveyed its message not only through the spoken word but also by means of all the senses – sight, smell, and touch as well as hearing. Indeed, with the participation of the priest and congregation in symbolic gestures, ceremonies, and processions, when the celebrant elevated the host and the worshippers beat their breasts with cries of 'mea culpa', much of the secret of the appeal had lain in the effective use of body language; not merely in what the Church and its ministers had said but also in what they had done. Much of that teaching, it is true, had been conveyed in colourful, familiar, and sometimes dramatic external symbolism and presentation, so that reformers might, not without justice, complain that for many the emphasis on repetitive, mechanical activities and unthinking outward tokens had degenerated into a superstition which usurped the place of genuine conviction and sincere emotion. Thus might William Salesbury censure his own conduct as a 'holy papist' when he 'kissed and licked devoutly saints' feet (for so called they their images) and besprinkled myself well favouredly with conjured water and done the superstitious penance enjoined to me', 'I thought and assuredly believed I had done my full duty unto God.' 'If I had done the same vain works and such other no better, I was no more beholden to God than He was unto me.'[109] But ordinary worshippers, most of them illiterate and ill-instructed, could not be compelled to abandon the picturesque nature or the warmth and reassurance of the old ways so closely interwoven with the customary pattern of their existence as individuals and as a community and with the crucial events of their lives and their normal farming round,[110] without feeling an acute sense of loss and deprivation. When the Catholic poets condemned the lifeless 'coldness' of the new religion, meaninglessly played out in churches left bare and empty as barns, there seems no reason to doubt that they voiced the emotions of many of their less articulate

---

[108] Above, note 22.

[109] Williams, *BBCS*, XIII. 146–50; cf. a very similar account by the English reformer, Thomas Becon, quoted in J. J. Scarisbrick, *The Reformation and the English People* Oxford, 1984), p. 56.

[110] *WC*, chap. 13.

fellows,[111] though we still have no means of knowing just how many of them lay almost entirely beyond the reach of religion since they rarely if ever came to church.

The aim of the reformers was, as far as they could, to turn religion into that of readers of Bibles and Prayer Books and to seek to internalize it as a matter of individual acceptance and belief. Such a faith was, in theory at least, much more demanding than that of earlier centuries and expected more in general of the clergy and their flock. It required the former to be better educated and more capable of instructing their charges systematically and preaching to them regularly. It called on the latter to listen much more attentively, to follow the service from a Prayer Book, and, ideally, to fructify still further what they heard in church with domestic devotions and private study of the scriptures. Gruffudd Dwn of Carmarthen claimed that he read the scriptures and gave his time to those 'studies which he thought God had led him into and wished him to follow'.[112] Inevitably, there would be a great many others who would have neither Gruffudd Dwn's means, nor his leisure, nor his acquaintance with English to be capable of indulging in such meditations. Much would depend at this stage on how much knowledge people had of the English language and how literate they were in it. Wales, it need hardly be said, contrasted sharply with England in this respect. Yet even in England conditions were far from ideal; educated Protestants there were all too aware of popular ignorance of the groundwork of theological belief. A barely literate people found the abstract word far more difficult to absorb than a message conveyed through all the senses. The visual appeal, in particular, was sorely missed; 'Catholics', said Bernard Gilpin more than a little unsympathetically in 1552, 'come to church to feed their eyes and not their souls . . . because they see not in church the shining pomp and pleasant variety of painted cloths, candlesticks, images, lamps and tapers, they say, as good to go into a barn.'[113] Protestant teaching was far more successful among urban populations, with their higher degree of literacy, than in the countryside, and in the south and east of England than in the remoter and less populated north and west. But in England at least, the English language was generally known; there was a considerably higher proportion of literates in its larger and more numerous towns; and there were vastly more religious books and sermons available than in Wales.

However, as has already been seen,[114] there may have been more knowledge of English in Wales than has often been supposed. Along parts of the

---

[111] *Hen Gwndidau*, pp. 31–44.
[112] *W and R*, p. 133
[113] Davies, *Worship and Theology*, p. 356.
[114] *W and R*, pp. 166–7.

south Wales coast and the eastern borders of Wales,[115] in all the market-towns and former garrison boroughs English was said to be 'as rife as Welsh',[116] and among gentry, merchants, lawyers, and clerics, there was a good deal of bilingualism.[117] Yet when all this has been taken into account, there can be no question that the majority of the Welsh were not able to understand English, let alone read it. When Bishop Ferrar preached in English in the town of Carmarthen his congregation seems to have had no difficulty in understanding him; when he moved a mile or two out of the town to Abergwili all but three or four of his listeners out of a congregation of about 140 gazed at him in blank incomprehension.[118] Welsh Tudor scholars who struggled to publish books in Welsh had no hesitation in insisting that the spiritual needs of their compatriots could be met only in their own tongue. Sir John Price, a Renaissance savant, emphasized that there were many who could read Welsh but who knew not a word of English or Latin,[119] and Salesbury, the whole-hearted reformer, was convinced that his countrymen's most desperate religious need was a Welsh translation of the scriptures.[120]

So, although the Crown had extensive powers of coercion available to it in Wales and was able to engineer obedience to the religious settlement, it had not succeeded in winning over the allegiance of more than a small minority. Even in a town like Carmarthen, and other similar places, where conditions were most favourable to the government's intentions, it encountered a good deal of resistance, and the quarrels between Catholics and Protestants which bedevilled Carmarthen may have been paralleled in other places, where the evidence has not survived. Bishop Ferrar was taken to task by Carmarthen's notabilities for undue tenderness towards Catholic susceptibilities, but his policy of 'softly, softly' may well have been justified. Eager though he was for reform, he had nevertheless to admit that there was stubborn resistance to the new order and that papist practices at services and funerals continued almost unabated. What he described as the 'grudge of the people' against reform was so resentful that he feared that any precipitate moves by reformers would be likely to provoke 'tumult', and that at a 'time of rebellion in Devon and Cornwall threatening to come

---

[115] Cf. Gruffydd Robert's well-known satirical quip that as soon as many Welshmen saw the spires of Shrewsbury and heard an Englishman say 'good morrow', they promptly forgot all their Welsh.

[116] J. Penry, *Treatises*, p. 17.

[117] Ll. B. Smith, 'Pwnc yr iaith yng Nghymru', *Cof Cenedl*, I (1986), 1–34; 'Yr iaith yng Nghymru'r Oesoedd Canol', *LlC*, XVIII (1995), 179–91.

[118] BL. Harleian MS. 420, fo. 153.

[119] Price, *Yny Lhyvyr Hwnn*, introd.

[120] Above, note 89.

into Wales' (a reference to the West Country rising of 1549).[121] From 1549 through to 1552 there were persistent fears of uprisings in Wales. Religious opposition was not the sole, nor always the main, cause for alarm but was never far from the surface. In north-east Wales in 1549 some of the servants of Thomas Seymour, the Protector's rebellious brother, were accused of spreading false rumours and throwing the country into 'a great maze, doubt and expectation, looking for some broil'.[122] In April of the following year, 1550, 'to prevent the inconstant disposition of the commons', the earl of Bedford was sent to the West Country and William Herbert to Wales.[123] Yet again in 1551 a Spanish representative reported the danger of insurrection in Wales caused by the debasement of the coinage and the unpopularity of the established religion.[124] Also in 1551 the dispatch of itinerant government preachers to certain parts of the country gave a fairly reliable indication of what were considered to be the most disaffected areas in matters of religion; Wales was included, along with Devon, Hampshire, Lancashire, Yorkshire, and the Scottish borders.[125]

For much of the reign, therefore, there were reports of possible rebellion in Wales or apprehensions of it. That it never erupted may have been due to a number of reasons. First, the Welsh tended on the whole to show genuine affection and loyalty to the Tudor dynasty. Typical of the attitude in official circles towards Wales at this time was the verdict of Walter Cowley, clerk of the Crown in Ireland, when congratulating Sir Edward Bellingham on the success of his policies there. He gave it as his view that 'Ireland, in a little time, would be as obedient and quiet as Wales.'[126] Certainly, whatever the fears that may have been expressed about a possible uprising in Wales, there never seemed to be much difficulty about raising troops there to put down insurrections elsewhere. The decisive element in Welsh society, the bigger landowners, though appearing to have little stomach for Protestant opinions, had gained much from Tudor rule and stood to lose a great deal by setting themselves up in opposition to it. As long as their own local supremacy was assured they were unlikely to make any great fuss over the issue of religion. In Edward's reign, and Mary's likewise, they seem in general to have been prepared to stand by the form of religion established by the sovereign with the consent of Parliament. If they stood firm, then men of lesser status would, by and large, follow their lead, regardless of the

---

[121] *W and R*, p. 134.
[122] *APC*, II. 225–6.
[123] Ibid., III. 6.
[124] *CSP Span.* X. 365, 368.
[125] *Calendar Carew MSS*, I. 393; III. 306.
[126] J. A. Froude, *The Reign of Edward VI* (London, 1926), p. 255; cf. Also *LP*, XVII. 65.

fulminations of outraged poets. The bishops and the higher clergy, as has been seen, were mostly timid and cautious; loath to forsake their conditioned response of deference to the royal behest. Those like William Glyn, Gruffydd Robert, John Gwynedd, or Roger Edgeworth, who evinced the greatest dislike, were domiciled in England, almost to a man. Furthermore, Northumberland had made it plain that he conceived of the earl of Pembroke and Viscount Hereford as his viceroys in Wales. He had been careful to build up the Herbert interest there in such a way as to make it virtually unchallengeable. During the final months of Edward's life, as the deteriorating symptoms of the 16-year-old king's illness became increasingly apparent, Northumberland made feverish attempts to tighten up the nuts and bolts of his scheme to divert the succession to the throne from the Catholic Mary and to enmesh Pembroke and Hereford ever more inextricably into the web of his plots.[127]

Edward's reign, though short-lived, was not without its significance for Wales. Hollow as the efforts to convert the Welsh people to Protestantism may have proved, they had nevertheless revealed how effective the power of the Crown and its agents was – in outward guise at least – to carry through major changes in worship and doctrine, the appearance of the churches, the role of the clergy, and the ownership of ecclesiastical possessions. The closer integration of Wales into the kingdom, the imposition of the improved structure of local government, and the willingness of the gentry to participate in administration had all expedited the execution of royal policy, though by the same token a reversal of royal intentions as the result of a change of ruler might be put into effect with no more difficulty. Edward's reign had also brought into focus how much Parliament's authority had been reinforced. Most of the crucial policy decisions had had to be implemented by Acts of Parliament, most notably the Acts of Uniformity of 1549 and 1552. The royal supremacy had been shown more patently than ever to consist of a partnership between sovereign and Parliament, so much so that Mary I would only be able to rid herself of it, and Elizabeth I to restore it, by means of Acts of Parliament. Wales, since 1536, had had an established system for returning its representatives to both Houses of Parliament and was thereby the more committed to any decision made in their name.

The sharpening tone of religious debate over the years 1547–53, referred to by the poet Siôn Brwynog with such apprehension and dismay, had also had the effect of demarcating much more incisively the lines of difference between the two religious camps. Most of those conservatives who, in Henry VIII's lifetime, had been able to accept the royal supremacy while

---

[127] Below, chap. 8.

remaining orthodox in doctrine, no longer found it possible to swallow such ambiguities as once they had. Their leaders, like Bishops Gardiner and Bonner, were imprisoned for their refusal to do so, and their outstanding Welsh representatives, such as William Glyn, John Gwynedd, or Morgan Philips, found themselves being painted more and more into a corner of having to recognize that if they wanted to retain traditional doctrine that might also entail being obliged to accept the jurisdiction of the pope. Conversely, resolute Protestant converts like William Salesbury, Thomas Young, or Richard Davies were coming to regard the pope as Antichrist and firmly to reject his authority along with all other remnants of 'papist superstition'. There had come into being two conflicting groups, each consisting of a minority of hard-core believers, who would battle it out in the coming decades.

For the tiny minority of dedicated Welsh Protestants, the experiences of Edward's reign had also rendered it painfully clear that if the Reformation was to succeed in Wales, an English Bible and an English order of service, imposed on all Welsh parishes by the government's *diktat*, were going to be quite insufficient. As in other European countries where it had prevailed, it would have to be presented in the vernacular. Formidable as the task of providing the necessary literature might be, and, nearly as tall an order, the extension of literacy among the people, both would have to be undertaken with the minimum of delay. For, whatever the Edwardian regime might or might not have achieved in England – and there is still considerable debate on this issue[128] – it had emphatically not succeeded in making Wales a Protestant country. There was still a very steep mountain left for Elizabeth's Church to climb. But before that task could begin, Mary I would make a determined effort to ensure that the forces of the papal Church would return in triumph.

---

[128] Among those who believe that England had become a virtually Protestant country are A. G. Dickens, *The English Reformation* and Claire Cross, *Church and People, 1450–1660* (London, 1976). But for a 'revisionist' view that England was far from converted, see C. Haigh, *The English Reformation Revised* and J. J. Scarisbrick, *The English People and the Reformation*.

CHAPTER 8

The Marian Reaction

BY February 1553 Edward VI, a youth whose health had always been delicate and given cause for concern, became seriously unwell with tuberculosis; so ill that urgent thought had to be given to the question of his successor.[1] Under the terms of his father's will, the next heir to the throne was the Princess Mary.[2] The prospect that this devoutly Catholic believer might come to the throne filled not only the duke of Northumberland with foreboding but Edward VI also. The latter therefore drew up a draft will specifying a changed order of succession, just as his father had done. He bequeathed the Crown to the heirs male of the daughters of his cousin, Frances, duchess of Suffolk, a descendant of Henry VIII's younger sister, Mary. By May or June 1553 his condition had further deteriorated and an amended will was devised, leaving the Crown to Frances's eldest daughter, Lady Jane Grey, who a month or two earlier had married Northumberland's son Guilford Dudley.[3] The plan to divert the succession was open for all to see. On 6 July 1553 Edward died and, four days later, Lady Jane Grey was proclaimed queen.

For some months before the king's death, Northumberland had been making dispositions to safeguard his position in all parts of the kingdom. In Wales he appeared to have won two of the most powerful noblemen to his party. Much the more significant of the pair was William Herbert, earl of Pembroke, a seasoned soldier who was not just the most influential figure in south Wales but also the aristocrat who could probably raise more troops to follow him than almost any other in the kingdom. Earlier, in February 1553, Pembroke had been reported by the imperial ambassador to be on bad terms with Northumberland, and in April he was forbidden to

---

[1] *CSP Span.* XV. 9, 17; cf. *The Diary of Henry Machyn* (Camden Soc., London, 1848), p. 30.

[2] H. F. M. Prescott, *A Spanish Tudor: The Life of 'Bloody Mary'* (London, 1952); C. Erickson, *Bloody Mary* (London, 1978); D. M. Loades, *The Reign of Mary I* (London, 1979); idem, *Mary Tudor* (Oxford, 1989); R. Titler, *The Reign of Mary I* (London, 1983).

[3] H. W. Chapman, *The Last Tudor King* (London, 1962), pp. 273-4.

withdraw to his estates.[4] Northumberland, however, was prepared to bid high for Pembroke's support, and he succeeded in inducing him to allow his son, Lord Herbert, to be married to the younger Grey sister, Catherine, on 21 May, the same day that Lady Jane Grey and Guilford Dudley were wed.[5] The other prop for Northumberland's plans in Wales was Walter Devereux, Viscount Hereford, formerly Lord Ferrers, a man of extensive influence in south-west Wales and one so deeply committed to Northumberland's cause that he was to be kept in prison for some time after Mary had reached London in August.[6] There were other considerable personages among the resident gentry in Wales, like Sir Richard Bulkeley in Anglesey and Dr Ellis Price in Denbighshire, who were also loyal agents to Northumberland. Furthermore, in June 1553, musters were being held and troops raised in Wales, Cornwall, and other places.[7] So impregnable did the duke's position seem to be, with his control of the armed forces, the Treasury, and the Tower, that the imperial ambassador was gloomy in the extreme about Mary's overall prospects. In at least two places in Wales – Beaumaris and Denbigh, thanks to Richard Bulkeley and Ellis Price – and possibly others, Lady Jane Grey was declared queen and Mary a traitress.[8]

In the hour of crisis, none the less, Northumberland's grasp on authority proved to be as nerveless in Wales as elsewhere. People there had little cause to love him or his works; neither he nor his family had any secure hold on Welsh affections. Back in 1551 there had already been intense stirrings in Wales against the debasement of the coinage at a time of sickness and dearth;[9] and Northumberland's religious changes appeared to have been too radical and too much associated with greed and opportunism for many Welsh people. Pembroke, whom Northumberland had envisaged as his viceroy in Wales, having created him president of the Council in the Marches in 1550, had been a reluctant ally in the plans to divert the succession. In the moment of decision he proved to be the one who took the lead in getting the Privy Council to change sides. Following the earl of Arundel's lengthy harangue to the councillors on the necessity of respecting the principle of hereditary succession, Pembroke tersely commented, 'Either this sword shall make Mary queen or I'll lose my life.'[10] The others gave way and Pembroke took command of the troops that brought Mary

[4] *CSP Span.* XV. 46.

[5] Ibid., pp. 13, 35–6, 44.

[6] *Machyn's Diary*, pp. 39, 43.

[7] *CSP Span.* XV. 44, 67; P. S. Edwards, 'Cynrychiolaeth a chynnen . . .', *WHR*, X (1980), 47, 52.

[8] Jesus College MS. 18, fo. 53.

[9] *CSP Span.* XIV, 368; cf. C. Wriothesley, *A Chronicle of England* (Camden Soc., London, 1875–7), II. 13.

[10] Prescott, *Spanish Tudor*, pp. 172–3.

to the throne. Most decisive of all among the Welsh was their fidelity to the claims of hereditary right and Tudor legitimism, reinforced as they were by the absence of any male rival who had an acceptable claim to the throne. Sentiments of support for Mary proved stronger in Wales than almost anywhere in the kingdom. It was her birthright as a 'Welsh' princess, far more than her Catholic beliefs, which unmistakably decided the issue in her favour. Even Protestants recognized the strength of her title to the throne and feared that to oppose her claims might be tantamount to resisting God's will.[11]

At both Beaumaris and Denbigh Mary was proclaimed queen after she had originally been denounced as a traitress – the day afterwards at Beaumaris and the afternoon of the same day in Denbigh, so it was claimed. But that could hardly have been possible, since it would have taken some days for the news to have come from London of the reversal of the situation there.[12] Some Welsh poets greeted her with joyful affection. The Anglesey poet, Siôn Brwynog, denounced the 'lies of Beaumaris' and sang of a county that 'longed for its welfare', 'judging her to be queen'.[13] Another, Dafydd Llwyd, with the pardonable poetic licence of his effervescent patriotism, hailed 'the genial queen from the heart of Gwynedd with her fortunate face'.[14] Some of the authors of the popular religious verses of Glamorgan were no less ecstatic. Acknowledged by them as heiress of the Tudors, 'bearing the crown of the island', justly inherited from her father and mother', Mary was referred to with evident delight by more than one as having been spared from the 'Saxons' who would have robbed her of her inheritance, had they not been 'silenced' by the earl of Pembroke.[15]

The rejoicings with which she was received in Wales and elsewhere may well have had the disastrous effect of leading Mary to suppose that she had triumphed miraculously as the specially chosen instrument of divine Providence and been welcomed as the paladin of the Catholic Church,

[11] See Sir Nicholas Throckmorton:

> And though I liked not the religion
> Which all her life Queen Mary had professed,
> Yet in my mind that wicked notion
> Right heirs to displace I did detest.
>
> (W. K. Jordan, *Edward VI: The Threshold of Power* (London, 1970), p. 525.)

[12] Williams, *WHR*, X. 335, n. 7.

[13] R. M. Kerr, 'Cywyddau Siôn Brwynog' (MA thesis, Wales, 1960), pp. 183–4.

[14] D. J. Bowen, 'Y Gymdeithas Gymreig yn niwedd yr Oesau Canol' (MA thesis, Wales, 1951), p. 100.

[15] *Hen Gwndidau, Carolau, a Chywyddau*, ed. L. J. Hopkin-James and T. C. Evans (Bangor, 1914), pp. 43–4, 59–68.

when in reality she had been borne to power as Henry's elder daughter and her brother's rightful heir. Conversely, most of those who supported her did not yet realize how much store she set by Roman rather than Henrician Catholicism, nor how profoundly she valued her relationship with the Holy See and the royal house of Spain. Painful disillusionment for ruler and subjects on these counts lay some time ahead. No one doubted, however, that most, if not all, of the anti-Romanist Church and worship constructed in the two preceding reigns would be demolished; all that was in question was just how fast would it go. Bishop Ridley had already pessimistically foretold 'grave incommodities and inconveniences' if Mary became queen, and letters from other leading reformers were full of apprehension about the future.[16] By contrast, a devout Welsh Catholic like Thomas ap Ieuan ap Rhys linked with his welcome to Mary the confident anticipation that it was the Blessed Virgin herself who had been responsible for winning her throne for her so that she might take vengeance on those 'false heads' ('pene ffeilstion') who 'had treated the son of God as badly as his avowed enemies had done, by stripping him naked and leaving him thus' ('y vab duw ni allen waeth nog ywnaeth y elynion ond ysbeilo ay ado yn noeth').[17]

Mary's first pronouncement on religion, made on 12 August 1553, was conspicuously conciliatory in tone. Firm though she was in her faith, she declared it to be no part of her intention to 'compel or constrain other men's consciences other wise than God shall (she trusteth) put in their hearts a persuasion of the truth she is in'.[18] All the same, she left none of her subjects in any doubt of her wish for the restoration of what she regarded as the true religion: the faith as it had been in 1529 not 1547. Nor did they need to doubt that in the process she would show every intention of actively helping the Almighty to put that 'persuasion of the truth' into her subjects' hearts. In the course of the later summer and autumn of 1553, without any formal Act of Parliament or proclamation to sanction the process, Catholic worship and practice were increasingly reintroduced in piecemeal and haphazard fashion all over the country.

Of initial Welsh reactions to the restoration of the mass and the revival of Latin services we have very little evidence. But if the reactions of some of the poets are typical then the return of the old faith must have been warmly welcomed, in parts of Wales at least. Those attacks made earlier in Edward's reign by the Glamorgan poet on the innovations of those years were so ferocious that he could hardly have dared to allow them to circulate

---

[16] J. Foxe, *Acts and Monuments . . .*, ed. S. Catley (7 vols. London, 1837–41), VI. 359; *Original Letters relative to the English Reformation*, ed. H. Robinson (2 vols. Parker Soc., London, 1846), *passim*.

[17] *Hen Gwndidau*, pp. 43–4.

[18] *APC*, IV. 397.

until the reinstatement of Catholic doctrine was in full swing and generally accepted.[19] Most positive acclamation emanated from Siôn Brwynog's enthusiastic greeting of the 'return of the privilege of the old saints' – 'the old masses' – 'behold God's right hand able to make us whole' ('Wele fraint y saint yn neshau' – 'yr hen 'fferennau' – 'wele Dduw â'i law ddehau yn gallu oll yn gwellau').[20] Such poets may well have been voicing the unspoken reaction of numbers of the monoglot Welsh-speaking population. Nevertheless, it cannot but be wondered what was taking place in towns like Carmarthen and Cardiff where, within the few preceding years, some of the population had seen Catholic altars taken down and medieval religious customs abandoned, and heard Protestant doctrines preached and had been reading English Bibles, all with apparent delight.[21] For how many of the clerics and lay people of the diocese of St David's as well as himself, was Thomas Young, its precentor and leader of the Protestant clergy there, speaking when he was one of only six clerics to uphold his reforming convictions in Convocation in October 1553?[22] It cannot be said for certain; but what can be stated is that he was sufficiently in earnest about them to go into exile on the Continent for their sake a year or two later.

Nor can it safely be specified what the reactions of Welsh members of the House of Commons were to Mary's policy proposals when she brought them forward. The first Parliament of her reign was convened on 5 October 1553. It had clearly been important that it should be as sympathetic an assembly as possible, and with that end in view, the Privy Council had given the Council in the Marches instructions to secure the return of 'grave men and . . . specially of the Catholic religion' as members.[23] But subsequent Welsh membership of the House seemed surprisingly little changed. The issue weighing more heavily than any other on the minds of members was that of the queen's marriage. At the age of 37 it was essential that she should take a husband quickly and wisely; but her choice of Philip of Spain was widely disliked, especially in the south-east of England. Cardinal Pole described the match to the pope as 'more universally odious than the cause of religion'.[24] While it may not have aroused such bitterness in Wales as in the south of England, some Welshmen were fiercely opposed to the marriage. Most implacable among them was William Thomas,

[19] *Hen Gwndidau*, pp. 31–2, 33–4, 35–6, 39–41, 43–4; cf. Siôn Dafydd, pp. 59–60.

[20] Kerr, 'Siôn Brwynog', p. 184.

[21] *W and R*, chap 4.

[22] J. Strype, *Ecclesiastical Memorials . . . under King Henry VIII, King Edward VI and Queen Mary* (3 vols. London, 1721), III/i. 233.

[23] P. H. Williams, *The Council in the Marches under Elizabeth I* (Cardiff, 1958), p. 39.

[24] *CSP Ven.* V. 586; although a conservative Yorkshire cleric described it as a 'joy and comfort to all good people', A. G. Dickens, 'Robert Parkyn's narrative of the Reformation', *EHR*, LXII (1947), 69.

formerly a clerk of the Privy Council, a convinced reformer as well as being intensely anti-Spanish.[25] He was the original instigator of the plot which led to the Wyatt Rising in January 1554; and his plan to assassinate Mary shocked the other leaders, or so they afterwards claimed.[26] He was, however, an isolated individual who had no important backing in Wales.

Other more influential conspirators envisaged simultaneous risings in Devon, Leicestershire, Kent, and the Marches of Wales, the last-named to be led by Sir James Crofts.[27] To forestall the rebels, the Privy Council sent Pembroke to Wales, Bedford to the West Country, and the Warden of the Cinque Ports to Kent. No evidence exists of any particular anti-Spanish animus in Wales or the Marches; a rebellion was mooted there only because of the local influence of Crofts and Sir Nicholas Arnold and because of the general reputation of the area for being remote and not easily controlled. Although wild rumours of possible rebellion in Wales were alarmingly reported by foreign ambassadors,[28] Crofts made no move and no rising actually took place. A few individuals were taken into precautionary custody, but all that is known of them results from a chance reference made a year later.[29] Not only did Wales in general remain calm, but the earl of Pembroke was able to take a large contingent of troops from south Wales to London to defend the queen and, without them, he might have been hard-pressed to crush Wyatt's rebels. Later, Sir Thomas Grey, one of Wyatt's fellow-conspirators, fled to Wales and was captured at Oswestry; but there is no indication that he was seeking supporters or doing anything more than trying to escape to a wild and inaccessible part of the realm for asylum.[30] William Thomas was executed after an unsuccessful attempt to commit suicide, Sir James Crofts was imprisoned, and Sir Nicholas Arnold fled to France. Within a week of the rebellion further proof of Welsh loyalty was forthcoming, when Simon Renard, the imperial envoy, reported that Mary was raising troops in Wales to protect her council.[31] Later accounts purported to confirm that Welsh and northern vassals of the queen were happy about her betrothal to Philip and

---

[25] J. A. Froude (ed.), *The Pilgrim* (London, 1861); E. R. Adair, 'William Thomas', in R. W. Seton-Watson (ed.), *Tudor Studies* (London, 1924); Jordan, *Edward VI*, pp. 415–19.

[26] D. M. Loades, *Two Tudor Conspiracies* (Cambridge, 1965), p. 19.

[27] R. E. Ham, 'The autobiography of Sir James Crofts', *BIHR*, L (1977), 48–57).

[28] J. G. Nichols (ed.), *The Chronicle of Queen Jane . . . and Queen Mary* (Camden Soc., London 1850), p. 40; cf. pp. 63, 69, 75–6; cf. Loades, *Conspiracies*, p. 96.

[29] On 11 May 1555 the Privy Council sent a letter to John Walshe, the justice of Carmarthen, to inform him that William Penry, serving under Sir Rice Mansel, had caused one Mitchell and others unnamed to be apprehended during Wyatt's Rebellion. Mitchell had since sued Penry, but Walshe was to ensure that Penry was not molested for actions taken by him during the Rebellion, *APC*, V. 122.

[30] *Machyn's Diary*, pp. 56, 61.

[31] *CSP Span*. XVI. 97.

that Welsh gentlemen had voluntarily met to swear fidelity to Mary and Philip.[32] Mary and Renard had every reason to convince themselves as well as Charles V of the popularity of the marriage and might be prone to exaggerate any favourable portents. Nevertheless, it seems evident that Spaniards were less unpopular in Wales – perhaps because they were never seen there – than they were in the south and east of England.

Besides the queen's marriage to Philip the other major issue had been the reintroduction of Catholic belief and worship and the abrogation of Edwardian Protestantism. Prohibitions against the saying of mass were lifted, the Acts of Uniformity repealed, and the authorization for the Book of Common Prayer withdrawn. Mary also held married priests in abhorrence and early made plain her intention to discipline them. Having repealed the statutes allowing clerical marriage in her first Parliament, she followed this up with a decree of December 1553 ordering that

> no man should sing nor say English service nor communion after the xx day of December, nor no priest that has a wife shall not minister nor say mass; and that every parish to make an altar and to have a cross and staff and all other things in all parishes all in Latin, as holy bread, holy water, as palm and 'assesse'.[33]

The Wyatt Rebellion may have provoked no upheaval in Wales, but the changes in the spring of 1554 were to produce a widespread shake-up among those of the clergy who had earlier taken advantage of the opportunity to get married. Many of the clergy found the reapplication of an earlier clerical discipline more than a little embarrassing when the deprivations for marriage began in March 1554. Later in the year 1554, in the month of November, Mary summoned her third Parliament to meet. It coincided with the long-delayed arrived of Cardinal Pole, whom the Emperor Charles had been determined to hold back until Mary and Philip were safely married. In a touching ceremony, Pole absolved the nation for schism and reconciled it with Rome.[34]

The first Welsh cleric to be disciplined was Robert Ferrar, the only Welsh bishop who had taken a wife.[35] He had been in prison since 1552 and had not exercised his functions as a bishop during that time. On 13 March 1554, along with two other married bishops, he was deprived of his bishopric. He was replaced by a reliable Catholic successor, the distinguished ecclesiastical

---

[32] Ibid., pp. 88, 95.

[33] *Machyn's Diary*, p. 50; D. R. Thomas, *The History of the Diocese of St Asaph* (3 vols. Oswestry, 1908–13), I. 86.

[34] J. D. Mackie, *The Early Tudors* (Oxford, 1952), pp. 548–9.

[35] *WRE*, pp. 124–39.

lawyer, Henry Morgan.[36] A Pembrokeshire man, Morgan was an Oxford DCL, who became principal of St Edward's Hall in 1528, when he entered Doctors' Commons. The appointment at this time of a lawyer, as opposed to a theologian, was a little strange, but it may have been supposed that St David's had had more than its fill of theological disputes and alien bishops[37] and that this energetic lawyer, a native of the diocese, might be the very man to bring the errant married clergy to heel. His register shows that he wasted no time in doing just that:[38] during the critical period for deprivations of the married clerics, between April 1554 and March 1555, no fewer than 115 admissions and collations were recorded. Even this need not represent the complete total since at least one folio is missing from the register, and an additional fifteen names of men presented by the Crown may be extracted from the patent rolls. This altogether abnormal total, which of course takes no account of the large number of unbeneficed clergy, of whose fate nothing can be learned, was about four times the yearly average.[39] The explanation for it appears to be that perhaps as many as ninety of the recorded vacancies were caused by deprivations, most of them for marriage, but with some for heresy as well. Whereas the heretics would not normally be trusted to exercise their priestly functions again, marriage alone did not necessarily mean a dismissal from the priesthood. As long as the married priest was prepared to put away his wife and do penance, he was allowed to minister elsewhere. All over the country married priests were agreeing to part from their spouses[40] – cynics commented that a short experience of the married condition was enough to convince them of the folly of entering into it! Most of these repentant sinners were then quickly switched to different livings in a kind of general post. Doubtless this happened in St David's diocese too, though the brevity of the entries in the bishop's register, which does not specify the name of the deprived clergyman or the reason for his removal, is such as to make it impossible to trace the process. But without such exchanges the authorities would have found it impossible to replace the deprived clergy, and without the income the latter would have found it difficult to survive.

In Bangor, the only other Welsh diocese for which registers survive in any fullness, this shuffling around of deprived clerics certainly took place.[41]

---

[36] *DWB*, p. 645.

[37] *WRE*, pp. 111–39.

[38] Williams, *BBCS*, XIV. 45–54.

[39] Ibid., pp. 47–9. In pre-Reformation times, there had been nearly as many unbeneficed as beneficed clergy, *WC*, pp. 289–91.

[40] G. Baskerville, *English Monks and the Suppression of the Monasteries* (London, 1940), p. 265; cf. Lambeth Palace, Register Pole, for the oath taken by deprived clergymen.

[41] A. I. Pryce, *The Diocese of Bangor in the Sixteenth Century* (Bangor, 1923) for an abstract of the registers.

Here, though there was no bishop – a successor had not yet been appointed in place of Arthur Bulkeley, who died in 1552 – the ejection of married priests was as rigorously carried out as elsewhere. In Bangor, too, the number of vacancies was abnormally high, being at least twenty-eight out of a total of 120 benefices, or one in four, as compared with one in three at St David's. At least twenty out of twenty-eight vacancies were due to deprivations for marriage, though because a number of the incumbents were pluralists, only fifteen were actually ejected.[42] In two instances there was a straightforward exchange: between Peter Tuder, rector of Llanengan, and Robert Evans, rector of Llanllechid; and between William Griffith, parson of Llaneurgrad and Richard ap Ieuan, parson of Llanfaethlu.[43] Others played a kind of game of 'musical benefices', as when Thomas Hughes, Thomas Griffith, and Robert Evans were swapped around between the two portions of Llanelidan and the rectory of Aber.[44] Dean Robert Evans lost a good deal financially on the changes, although by 1557 he had regained his deanery (but presumably not his wife!).[45] Three out of five of the remaining clerics were deprived for heresy as well as marriage. Rowland Meyrick, an Anglesey man and a future bishop of Bangor (1559–65), was at the time a prominent canon of St David's. John Salusbury, archdeacon of Anglesey and suffragan bishop of Thetford, was normally resident at Norwich and would seem to have come under the influence of the pronounced Protestant opinions prevalent in East Anglia. The last of the trio, Hugh ap Robert, rector of Dolgellau and Newborough, was described in a Chancery suit as having been deprived for 'evil opinions against the Catholic faith'.[46] The two remaining parsons, Owen Pole and Griffith ap Llywelyn, may also have been heretics or, more probably, clerics who refused to part from their wives; but no further trace of them is to be found, either in the register or in a list of Bangor clergy of 1561.

A survey of the estimates of deprivations for English and Welsh dioceses based only on episcopal registers provides good reason to believe that they are too low,[47] and that the registers of Bangor and St David's present an incomplete picture of the deprivations. Nevertheless, the upheaval caused among the clergy in 1554–5 was considerably greater than that brought about by any other religious changes during the century. Furthermore, the number of deprivations in these two Welsh dioceses was unexpectedly large

---

[42] Ibid., pp. 12–14, 85.

[43] Ibid., p. 13.

[44] Ibid., pp. 13, 14, 85.

[45] B. Willis, *A Survey of the Cathedral Church of Bangor* (London, 1721), p. 126.

[46] Ibid., p. 138 (Salisbury); PRO, C1/1379/44 (ap Robert).

[47] W. H. Frère, *The Marian Reaction in relation to the English Clergy* (London, 1896), p. 43.

compared with those for English dioceses. In England, the proportion of deprivations varied in inverse ratio to the distance of the diocese from London. Thus, for the diocese of London and the two neighbouring dioceses of Rochester and Canterbury, the proportion of deprivations was one to every four benefices; for Salisbury and Chichester it was one to six; for Peterborough one to ten; for Exeter one to twelve, and for Oxford one to twenty. But for Bangor it was one to eight and for St David's it may have been as high as one to six.[48] So in the two Welsh dioceses furthest away from London, in a country less touched by Protestant influence, the proportion of deprivations was unexpectedly high. Part of the reason may be that clerical 'marriage' had been much more common in Wales before the Reformation. Edward VI's legislation may therefore have served to give official sanction to many long-standing liaisons in Wales as well as to offer new opportunities for marriage, even though John Bale maintained that some Welsh clerics preferred to stick to their concubines rather than take wives. Ironically enough, in Mary's reign, priests who maintained such companions were punished less severely than those who married, being subject only to a fine and not being removed from their benefices.[49] Consistory court records which survive from other dioceses provide evidence of clerics who had married being punished for frequenting their former partners.

Information available from the other two Welsh dioceses is much too scanty to be able to tell at all clearly what happened there. Two St Asaph documents might have provided such details;[50] but their entries, even by the unexacting standards of Tudor registrars, are extremely fragmentary and haphazard. For the crucial year 1554 only two entries are recorded, and for 1555 there is none. It is quite certain, however, that the dean of St Asaph, Richard Puskyn, and the archdeacon, John Pollard, were both deprived.[51] Four other clerics are also said to have been ejected; but of these one was almost certainly not deprived for marriage,[52] two more seem distinctly doubtful,[53] and for the fourth no certain evidence exists.[54] On the other hand, two others were deprived for marriage – William Parboy, vicar of

[48] Williams, *BBCS*, XIV. 48–9.

[49] H. E. P. Grieve, 'The deprived married clergy of Essex', *TRHS*, IV/22. 145. For the effect of a married bishop's example in leading his clergy to marry, see Robert Parkyn in *EHR*, LXII. 69.

[50] NLW, SA/14 (a record of collations and admissions, 1506–70) and SA/BR/1 (an episcopal act book, 1536–48).

[51] Thomas, *St Asaph*, I. 87, 248.

[52] Thomas Davies cannot be shown to have lost any livings in the diocese of St Asaph, and he definitely retained his chancellorship of Bangor and other livings there, *DWB, s.n.*

[53] Griffith ap Ieuan was described in NLW, SA/MB/14, fo. 5b, as having 'freely resigned' his living in October 1556; nor can I find any trace of John ap Madog.

[54] Lancelot Pydleston (*recte* 'Puleston'?), rector of Corwen.

Northop, quite definitely, and William Payne, vicar of Denbigh, very probably.[55] It has been suggested that there was slackness in dealing with the married clergy in the diocese because Bishop Goldwell found it necessary, as late as 1556, to issue an injunction that 'no priest having a woman at his commandment' should celebrate mass.[56] This has been taken to refer to marriage,[57] but it could equally well be a reference to another kind of relationship, just as intimate but less formal, and hitherto very common in Wales. Evidence for Llandaff, where no register or act book has survived from this period, is even more tenuous. The *cwndidau* (religious verses) were scathing about the widespread existence in the diocese of married priests and their gross behaviour;[58] but only two, John Lippington, rector of Bishopston in Gower, and Henry Morgan, parson of Newton Nottage, can certainly be shown to have been deprived.[59]

While the fate of the married priests has been fairly well established, the fortunes of their wives and children are much more obscure. Many of these deprived priests, it has been suggested, were indifferent to what befell their families.[60] But there must have been some who felt too strongly the normal ties of family affection to have been so unconcerned. A priest who, like Robert Salusbury of Llanrwst, had had his wife as a hearth companion for twenty years before legally wedding her after 1549, was hardly likely to turn her adrift unprovided for when he was deprived.[61] When the priest himself was unmoved, he may well have been urged by his wife into doing something for her and the children before losing his benefice.[62] Those who parted from their wives and were removed to another benefice could presumably find something from its income for wives and children if they chose to do so. But there were those who wished to stay with their wives, or whose heretical beliefs debarred them from another living, and quite how they and their dependants were sustained is altogether more uncertain. Some went into exile with their families; but the large majority stayed in the country, some living on their patrimony if they had one, others depending on the charity of kin and friends, and yet others finding alternative employment. Some fourteen Chancery suits relating to Wales reveal the more dubious devices employed by deprived parsons to safeguard their

---

[55] PRO, C1/1354/27; cf. *Early Chancery Proceedings concerning Wales*, ed. E. A. Lewis (Cardiff, 1937), p. 127; NLW, SA/M/14, fo. 9.

[56] D. Wilkins, *Concilia Magnae Britanniae et Hiberniae . . . 446–1718* (London, 1837), IV. 143.

[57] Thomas, *St Asaph*, I. 87.

[58] *Hen Gwndidau*, pp. 32–44.

[59] PRO, C1/1389/24–6; C3/122/70.

[60] Baskerville, *Suppression of Monasteries*, p. 265.

[61] PRO, C1/1325/16–19.

[62] Ibid., 1342/7–9.

future incomes.[63] It would be reasonable to assume that there were other instances of the same practices, which went unrecorded because the expense and harassment of lawsuits prevented their being brought to court. Where the kinsmen or patrons of deprived clerics were powerful laymen, many sharp practices went unchallenged at law. It was a brave man who, like Henry Johns, parson of Llanrwst, was willing to take on what he described as the 'well allied and friended' Salusbury family, whose influence in north Wales was such as to give 'little hope of any indifferent trial'.[64]

Parsons who were to be deprived usually knew beforehand when their ejection was likely to take place, and they tried to realize what assets they could from their livings. A number of the married canons at St David's, knowing in the spring of 1554 of their coming deprivation, tried to get their hands on the yearly dividend from the revenues accruing to the chapter before the annual pay-out in August; but the most they could manage was to draw up a bill of debt, which was subsequently rejected by the Elizabethan courts.[65] Other incumbents stripped lead from the roofs, cut down standing timber, despoiled orchards, and even removed carp from fishponds.[66] So severe were the depredations at Bishopston, Glamorgan, that the incoming parson claimed that it would cost him £20 to complete the repairs.[67]

The allegation most usually brought against the priests, however, was that they entered into a fraudulent compact with the lessees of their benefices with intent to deprive their successors and bind them by the force of illicit agreements. Thus, Valentine Dale, Marian rector of Llandysul, accused his deprived predecessor, Stephen Green, of having leased the rectory in such a way 'that a great part of the profits . . . might come to the relief of himself, his wife and children'.[68] Leases were often alleged to have been antedated to make them appear more authentic; and Morgan Phillips, precentor of St David's, accused Thomas Young of leasing his prebend of Lampeter 'after his deprivation and ante-dated of purpose'.[69] The lessees had to be trustworthy, and that normally meant leasing to friends or

---

[63] The Welsh suits are C1/1325/16–19; 1347/5–7; 1354/27; 1354/88–91; 1365/49–50; 1370/91; 1376/47–8; 1379/44; 1389/24–6; 1432/54; 1447/14–17; 1447/36–7; 1459/72; 1460/59–62; cf. *Early Chancery Proceedings* pp. 97, 40, 127, 9, 41, 73, 41, 10, 209, 130, 73, 11, 43 (*bis*). There are also about sixty suits relating to livings in England which present much the same picture as those for Wales.

[64] PRO, C1/1325/16.

[65] PRO, Req. 2/157/186.

[66] PRO, C1/1341/14; 1349/8; 1359/1; 1382/22–4; 1388/16–18; 1405/14; 1435/24; 1460/109.

[67] PRO, C1/1389/24–6.

[68] PRO, C1/1347/7.

[69] Ibid., 1460/59.

relatives who could be depended upon. Thomas Young made an apparently strange choice in George Lee, a Calais merchant; but George was a brother to one of Young's closest friends, Thomas Lee, and Young, if he was already thinking of going into exile, may well have wanted a man with continental connections.[70] Rowland Meyrick, deprived of Eglwysael in the diocese of Bangor, installed his own nominee, Thomas Johns, to succeed him; and the rights of Robert Grono, who claimed to have been appointed by the bishop, were fiercely resisted by Meyrick, his wife, and brother, though Thomas Johns was so obviously in collusion with them as to deny that Meyrick had been deprived, even when the facts of the deprivation were recorded in the Bangor register.[71] Yet such juggling with leases was only to be expected, when the Chancery records, even before the Reformation, are full of allegations of forgery, antedating, and the like. Reformation changes and repeated attacks on church property had taught men to anticipate disaster by encouraging those who knew they were likely to suffer to take measures in advance for their own protection.

Most of these deprivations that caused so much turmoil among the clergy were for marriage and only a minority for heresy, though there were more of the latter than used to be thought. They reveal that there was in every Welsh diocese a small hard core of priests who had been won over to the cause of reform and were prepared to stand by their principles at the cost of personal hardship. Most of the clergy, on the other hand, were able to comply with the Marian government's requirements with the same obliging pliability which they had shown in earlier changes. Some of them showed a readiness to conform which was more than a little surprising in view of their previous reactions. Anthony Kitchen, bishop of Llandaff, timid, humane, and undogmatic, though a sympathizer with moderate reforms at an earlier stage, was unembarrassed by marriage or an over-ardent espousal of Protestant doctrine. He now gave way readily and served on two commissions to inquire into married and heretical bishops; he would be the one bishop to swing back and accept Elizabeth's settlement.[72] His *confrère*, Robert Parfew of St Asaph (1536–54), had helped to draw up the Protestant Prayer Book, yet he was not only able to obtain absolution from Cardinal Pole but was also translated to Hereford.[73] Two future Elizabethan prelates, Thomas Davies, bishop of St Asaph (1561–74),

---

[70] There is no evidence which specifically proves that Thomas Young received these revenues on the Continent, but another deprived parson, John Falconer, who also went into exile (C. H. Garrett, *The Marian Exiles, 1553–58* (Cambridge, 1938), p. 152) was certainly supported by these means, PRO, C1/1411/47–82.

[71] Ibid., 1325/16–19; cf. Pryce, *Bangor*, p. 13.

[72] *CPR, 1553–4*, p. 175; cf. Williams, *GCH*, IV. 223–4.

[73] Thomas, *St Asaph*, I. 223.

and Nicholas Robinson, bishop of Bangor (1566–85), were no more resistant. Davies, attracted to reformed doctrine at Oxford, was by 1554 chancellor of Bangor and almost certainly married with children, and would be an active reformer again in Elizabeth's reign; but he was able to accept the Marian restoration and keep his preferments.[74] Robinson, made a fellow of Queen's College at the instigation of Edwardian visitors, nevertheless set his hand to a Romanist declaration of faith in 1555 and, thanks possibly to the favour of his friend and former patron, Bishop Glyn, was ordained by him on the strength of a special dispensation from Pole.[75] Another with a supple conscience was Ellis Price. Agent of Thomas Cromwell and later of Northumberland, he followed his father, Robert ap Rhys,[76] as chancellor of St Asaph and also became lay rector of Llanuwchllyn, Llandrillo, and Llangwm; yet he was in 1553 MP for Merioneth and sheriff in 1556, while in 1565 he would warmly be recommended to become bishop of Bangor.[77] Admittedly, in St David's diocese, where Protestant doctrine had been more energetically propagated than anywhere else, a number of canons stood fast and were deprived for heresy – Thomas Young, Rowland Meyrick, Thomas Huyck, Stephen Green, and others. But even here there were at least two notable exceptions. George Constantine had been an eager reformer and colporteur of heretical books in 1528, later a friend of Bishop Ferrar, and then a critic of him for his slowness to reform; but he retained his position as registrar under Bishop Morgan and took part in Ferrar's trial, only to return as an Elizabethan visitor in 1559.[78] His colleague, Thomas Huet, was a close associate of leading Protestants during Edward's reign, yet under Mary he survived unscathed and actually obtained further preferment; under Elizabeth, he was one of the translators of the Welsh New Testament with Richard Davies and William Salesbury.[79]

These and others like them were prominent figures among the higher clergy, university graduates who might have been expected to appreciate the issues, and who, on critical occasions, appeared to adopt a positive stance. If they could change course so readily, how many were there among the hundreds of poor and ill-educated beneficed and unbeneficed parish priests who accepted the government's demands and wisely kept their own counsel about the rights and wrongs of them? Erratic and incomplete

---

[74] His daughter was old enough in 1570 to be married and have children, *DWB*, p. 142.

[75] *DWB*, p. 887; cf. Pryce, *Bangor*, p. 51. There appears to be no justification for Strype's view that Robinson 'suffered much from the papists'.

[76] *WC*, pp. 322–6.

[77] *DWB*, pp. 805–6.

[78] *W and R*, p. 137.

[79] *DWB*, p. 370.

though the Bangor registers are, they record at least eleven benefices, the incumbents of which successfully survived all the changes of the most troubled generation in the Church's history, from Henry VIII's reign to that of Elizabeth, without finding it necessary to make a stand at any point for doctrine or conscience.[80] Among them were graduates, men of good birth and local eminence like Thomas Bulkeley[81] and William Roberts, though most of them were ordinary parish priests. In all the dioceses there were, no doubt, a number of others like Richard Price, vicar of Llandyfaelog in Breconshire, who in 1568 was over 80 years old and had been incumbent there since Henry VIII's time, and of whom, but for the merest fluke, we should never have heard.[82]

For the laity the restoration of Catholic faith and worship in general caused fewer problems than for the clergy. In the eyes of some laymen the Edwardian revolution had slighted the fabric of the faith with almost intolerable abruptness and lack of preparation. English services must have been for the majority neither as familiar nor as reassuring as the Latin rite, nor even more intelligible. There had been claims that the mystery of the mass defied any satisfactory English translation.[83] Moreover, the Edwardian Church had been stripped of its beauty and robbed of its possessions by greedy, pillaging hands acting under the pretext of reform. The reactions aroused by such sacrilege had been vividly expressed by poetic defenders of the old faith who sang with mingled indignation and contempt of the replacement of 'hallowed altars' by contemptible 'widows' boards' and lamented that temples, fallen into the hands of laymen, had become bare neglected corners.[84] Poets of this kind welcomed the Marian restoration with apparent delight, and their enthusiasm was shared by some of the gentry and other layfolk. Sir Thomas Stradling, squire of St Donat's, for example, was a great favourer of the old ways who, with his Arundel kinsmen, had been kept under strict surveillance in Edward's reign but was now rewarded for his constancy and entrusted with extensive responsibility by Mary's government.[85] His neighbour, Sir Edward Carne of Ewenni, was not only MP for Glamorgan and a member of the

---

[80] Pryce, *Bangor*, under the archdeaconry of Merioneth, Llanbedr, Llandwrog, Llandyfrydog, Llanddeusant, Llanfairpwll, Llanfachreth, Llanfairfechan, Llanfechell, Llangefni, and Llangynhafal, in the index.

[81] D. Mathew, *The Celtic Peoples and Renaissance Europe* (London, 1933), pp. 46–8, has a charming piece on Thomas Bulkeley. Unfortunately, it seems to owe more to imagination than evidence. Mathew's point that Robert Salisbury was at Llanrwst from 1537 to 1573 is quite wrong; Salisbury was undoubtedly deprived for marriage.

[82] He appears in a Chancery suit, PRO, C3/138/20.

[83] D. J. Bowen, 'Y Gymdeithas Gymreig', p. 100.

[84] *Hen Gwndidau*, pp. 44, 39.

[85] *APC*, II. 304; Williams, *GCH*, IV. 232–3.

commission which supported Bishop Bonner, but he was also appointed to the key embassy at Rome – a strange irony for a man who had been there in the early 1530s to sue for Henry's annulment of his marriage with Catherine.[86]

However, the general picture among laity and clergy alike, as elsewhere, was one of caution, apathy, confusion, or even demoralization, as a result of a rapid succession of changes. Most of the politically conscious gentry were not unwilling to conform to the Church 'by law established', rather than to the pope's revived authority, but on the tacit understanding that their obedience did not necessarily require anything more than outward acquiescence rather than deep conviction. The mass of the population, in so far as it had views at all, seemed content to follow their example. Foreign observers doubted whether any true Catholic revival was taking place during Mary's reign. Venetian envoys believed that good Catholics, where they existed at all, were to be found only among people of over 35 years of age. Most of the queen's subjects, they thought, were content to follow their ruler's example, either from respect or from fear rather than goodwill. Ralph Allerton, examined by Bishop Bonner in 1557, sized up the situation in the country remarkably well when he told him that there were two earnest and hotly opposed minorities and a faction of 'neuters', which was much larger than ever the government had supposed.[87] Most of the laity in Wales would seem to have been 'neuter', prepared to obey the government as long as their own vital interests were not sacrificed in doing so They signified their willingness to serve as MPs and justices of the peace, though they saw it as no part of their duty to become the instruments of an unpopular policy of persecuting heretics. One or two found it more difficult to be returned to the House of Commons because of earlier associations with Northumberland's regime: Sir Richard Bulkeley, for example, found himself ousted from his seat as member for Anglesey by the conservative Lewis ab Owain.[88] But for the most part the same sort of people were returned as members for Welsh constituencies and filled the cadres of local government and justice.[89] On one point of cardinal import- ance, all of them, including prominent supporters of the regime, were agreed: their allegiance did not extend to a willingness to give up former

---

[86] Williams, *GCH*, IV. 232.

[87] A. G. Dickens, *The English Reformation* (London, 1964), pp. 263–4; G. Alexander, 'Bonner and the Marian persecution', *History*, LX (1975), 383.

[88] Edwards, *WHR*, X. 56–8.

[89] W. R. Williams, *The Parliamentary History of the Principality of Wales, 1541–1895* (London, 1895); S. T. Bindoff, *The House of Commons, 1509–1558* (3 vols. London, 1982); J. R. S. Phillips, *The Justices of the Peace in Wales and Monmouthshire, 1541–1689* (Cardiff, 1975).

Church possessions, by which many had enriched themselves.[90] The earl of Pembroke was staunch in his loyalty to Mary and highly regarded by Philip, but made no move to surrender Wilton Abbey or any other comparable gains. Mary's ambassador to Rome, Edward Carne, gave no sign of offering up his Ewenni estates – he would, indeed, do his utmost to protect them after Elizabeth's accession by trying to return from Rome.[91] William Morgan of Llantarnam, head of a leading family of Elizabethan recusants, encouraged pilgrims to go once more to Pen-rhys,[92] a shrine formerly belonging to Llantarnam abbey, during Mary's reign; but he would not relax his grip for one instant on the abbey itself, now the nucleus of his family estates. His kinsman, Sir Thomas Morgan, was willing to set at naught the authority of Cardinal Pole himself, exercised via the archdeacon of Llandaff, in his determination to cling to Caldicot parsonage, which the monks of Llanthony had once enjoyed.[93] All of the proprietors of former church lands in Wales showed a comparable determination not to part with them. Only at Slebech, towards the very end of Mary's reign, did her efforts to restore monastic lands meet with any success, when in April 1558 she tried to revive the Order of St John and nominated Richard Shelley as 'preceptor of Slebech and Halston', making him a grant of the former estates of the order.[94] Even there, it appears doubtful whether the Barlow family was in fact deprived of these lands, which were certainly in their hands during Elizabeth's reign.[95]

In contrast to their determined refusal not to countenance the restoration of church property, nearly all the gentry were prepared to acquiesce in the revival of medieval statutes against heresy. Early in 1555, therefore, pressure was exerted on leading heretics either to bring them to trial or to drive them into exile. Bishop Gardiner was first responsible for this policy,[96] though he did not originally envisage a holocaust of victims. Primarily concerned with the authority and security of the Church, he believed that heretics were so few in number that by making an example of some of their leaders, he could easily intimidate the others, 'the people being terrified with the example of these great learned men condemned'.[97]

---

[90] Renard wrote to Charles V, 'The Catholics hold much more property than do the heretics', and were just as determined to cling on to it, J. A. Muller, *Stephen Gardiner and the Tudor Reaction* (London, 1926), p. 261.

[91] Williams, *GCH*, IV. 232.

[92] Ibid., pp. 213–14.

[93] PRO, C1/1469/51.

[94] NLW, Slebech Papers, no. 3141; cf. *CPR, 1557–8*, pp. 313–21; J. D. Davies, *History of West Gower* (4 vols. Swansea, 1877), II. 32–4.

[95] J. M. Cleary, *The Catholic Recusancy of the Barlow Family of Slebech* (Cardiff, 1956), pp. 10–13.

[96] Renard to Charles V, *CSP Span*. XVI. 52.

[97] Loades, *JEH*, XVI. 38.

He soon came to see the futility of the policy, and the Marian state's ill-advised persistence with it was due more to the influence of Mary herself, Pole, and, possibly, Philip and his Spanish advisers.[98] Two of the heretics burnt in Wales came into the category of exemplary executions and were among the earliest martyrs in England and Wales. In bringing them to trial and execution, the authorities appeared to be determined to spell out a severe warning to Protestant sympathizers in south Wales.

Robert Ferrar, the deprived bishop of St David's, was, in accordance with government policy, brought back to Carmarthen to stand his trial in the place where he had most recently laboured. St David's diocese in general and Carmarthen in particular might be thought to be in need of a stern example. It had been the scene of a good deal of Protestant activity, and reforming ideas had found acceptance among the gentry and merchants of the town, and among such influential neighbouring families as the Devereux, Perrotts, and Dwns.[99] Once Ferrar had been sent down to be examined, Bishop Morgan tried hard to get him to recant, in the belief that a repentant one-time reformer could be more useful than a martyr.[100] Or possibly it was that Morgan had enough humanity not to want to see his predecessor condemned to a cruel death. Whatever the reason, Morgan summoned Ferrar to his presence on six separate occasions between 26 February and 13 March. All in vain! Ferrar refused to retract any of what his judges denounced as his 'heresies, schisms and errors'.[101] So, on 31 March 1555, the townsfolk of Carmarthen were to witness one of the earliest Marian martyrdoms and the only burning for religion's sake to take place in the town during the sixteenth century. Brought to Carmarthen's most public open site, described by Foxe the martyrologist as being 'in the market-place on the south side of the market cross', Ferrar died with truly memorable courage. He was reported to have said beforehand to Richard Jones, second son of Sir Thomas Jones of Abermarlais, 'that if he saw him once to stir in the pains of his burning then he should give no credit to his doctrine'.[102] It was vitally important for the reformers, as most of them well understood, not to give in but to meet death bravely so as to encourage the faithful and impress the waverers; and Ferrar met his horrible fate unyielding to the end on 31 March 1555.[103]

---

[98] Dickens, *English Ref.*, pp. 265–7; Loades, *Mary I*, p. 331.

[99] *W and R*, chap. 4.

[100] e.g. Henry Pendleton, who recanted, then preached at Paul's Cross, contributed to Bonner's book of homilies, and examined other heretics, C. Haigh, *Reformation and Resistance in Tudor Lancashire* (Cambridge, 1973), p. 198.

[101] *W and R*, pp. 135–6.

[102] Foxe, *Acts and Mons.* VII. 96.

[103] *W and R*, p. 136.

Another heretic to be burnt soon after was the Cardiff fisherman, Rawlins White. Indications point to Protestant ideas having made some headway in south-east Wales. In 1542 Thomas Capper had been martyred in Cardiff, and later on, according to Foxe, 'God of his mercy had raised up the light of his gospel through the blessed government of Edward VI.'[104] White looks to have been a very typical artisan heretic of the age. Ever since the time of Mary's accession he had probably refused to attend church and never received the sacrament, and this had brought him into conflict with the authorities. Having been in prison for a little over a year before his execution in March 1555, he must have been regarded as a more than averagely dangerous and vocal heretic. Nevertheless, Bishop Kitchen was obviously deeply reluctant to make an example of him. Kitchen is easily dismissed as a trimmer and a turncoat, but in his dealings with White he showed a degree of humanity and compassion all too rare in that age of savage persecution. White was not easy to handle; he could be as opinionated and unamenable to persuasion as only a self-educated fanatic can be. When Kitchen insisted on praying for him, White was plainly moved by this charitable act but could not refrain from adding, 'Do you pray to your God, and I will pray to my God. I know that my God will hear my prayer and perform my desire.'[105] Even then Kitchen allowed him a certain amount of freedom, giving his friends permission to visit him and derive consolation from him. The bishop continued to make desperate efforts to save him but without success. As his end approached, White confessed to the human weakness of 'a great fighting between the flesh and the spirit, and the flesh would fain have his swing'; but his courage did not desert him and he died without recanting a word of his opinions.[106] Tradition gives two possible sites as the place of his burning – one in High St., near the opening of Church St., the other in St John's Square, just north of St John's churchyard.[107] To make the maximum impact, his execution, like Ferrar's, was given the utmost publicity. The aim of frightening other Protestants may well have been achieved, since neither Carmarthen, nor Cardiff, nor their immediate environs figure at all in the annals of heresy for the rest of Mary's reign.[108]

Indeed, the fires of persecution remained unlit in Wales until April 1558, when the third martyr, William Nichol of Haverfordwest, was burnt.[109] An obscure figure, who met his death in mysterious circumstances, Nichol may

---

[104] Foxe, *Acts and Mons.* VII. 29.
[105] Ibid., VII. 28–33.
[106] Ibid.
[107] Williams, *GCH*, IV. 222.
[108] *W and R*, pp. 136–7.
[109] Foxe, *Acts and Mons.* VIII. 462.

well have been a man of simple mind, who barely understood the beliefs for which he gave his life. Earlier, he may have been one of those who were protected by the influence of Sir John Perrott. In 1556, however, Perrott was under suspicion of having been concerned with Henry Dudley's conspiracy, along with Sir Nicholas Arnold and Sir Anthony Kingston, both of whom exercised great influence in Wales and the Marches. A year later, he was accused of harbouring the heretics, Thomas Perrott and Laurence Nowell, and was imprisoned in the Fleet for about a month. His influence in Pembrokeshire now went into eclipse and a number of his friends were glad to escape into exile.[110] The hapless Nichol may have been left behind, a convenient scapegoat who could be seized and executed with impunity.

Though the fewness of martyrdoms in Wales has often been cited as proof of the lack of Protestant sympathizers, it is easy to make too much of the point. The intensity of persecution varied widely in different parts of the country, with 85 per cent of the victims in London, Canterbury, Norwich, and Chichester dioceses, but only one in the north and only one in England west of Bristol.[111] It was, in itself, no certain guide to the degree of sympathy with heretical opinion – there were, for example, a number of Protestants in Yorkshire and the West Country, though martyrdoms were fewer in both places than in Wales. Persecution depended not only on the numbers of heretics but also on the retributory zeal of laymen and clerics. Sheriffs and justices of the peace were notoriously reluctant to pursue heretics – in conservative Lancashire no less than in radical Essex.[112] Many bishops were equally unmilitant, preferring to send their heretics to Bishop Bonner to deal with. Among the martyrs burnt in the south-east of England who were mentioned by Foxe were men with Welsh-sounding names like Apprice or Floyd. Others were called Philip Humphrey, John David, Henry David, Robert Samuel, John Gwynne, James Harris, and Robert Williams; and all have been cited as possible Welsh victims.[113] However, in spite of the tendency to send Protestants to the diocese of London for punishment and the large-scale sixteenth-century migration out of Wales to London and the Home Counties, there is nothing to indicate with any certainty that these victims were sent from Wales or that they were Welsh by origin.

---

[110] Phillips, *AC* (1897), 308–9.

[111] D. M. Loades, *The Oxford Reformers* (London, 1970), for a map of the persecutions.

[112] Haigh, *Ref. and Resistance*, p. 191; J. E. Oxley, *The Reformation in Essex* (Manchester, 1965), p. 232.

[113] D. Peter, *Hanes Crefydd yng Nghymru* (Carmarthen, 1816), p. 441.

Social distinctions counted, too, in explaining why a number of upper-class sympathizers with reformed doctrine escaped punishment. The Devereux and the Perrotts, whatever their views, were most unlikely to be brought for trial just for heresy, still less to the stake; while major figures among the county gentry, like Sir John Price or Ellis Price, no matter how prominent they had been as agents of earlier governments' reforming policies, were able to come to terms with Marian authorities without difficulty. Even the author of polemic antipapal pamphlets and translator into Welsh of large parts of the Prayer Book, William Salesbury, met with nothing worse than a spell of enforced retirement at Caedu, which he may possibly have turned to good use by continuing with his translations.[114] Some of the well-born clerics deprived for heresy, like Robert Salusbury or Rowland Meyrick, also went unmolested. It was the lesser people, men from yeoman or working-class origins, like Rawlins White or William Nichol, who bore the brunt of the persecution; a fact about which one of Bonner's correspondents had no illusions. 'The sworn inquest for heresies do most commonly indict the simple, ignorant and wretched heretics', he wrote to the bishop, 'and do let the arch-heretics go.'[115] It is probably true that the Welsh, having seen little or nothing of the furies of persecution, were much less horrified or sickened by it than the people of the south-east. Besides, remembering how hardened the population was by the not uncommon sight of barbaric capital punishment for ordinary crime following each assize in all parts of the kingdom,[116] care should be taken not to overemphasize the horror which sixteenth-century people may have felt at the burnings. If, as one English reformer averred in 1558, 'men were never so merry in England'[117] despite the persecution, they may have been even less dismayed in Wales, though that did not mean that they had no heretics in their midst.

Side by side with stamping out and silencing heretics at home, the government also intended that its persecution should have the effect of frightening others out of the realm altogether, and in all nearly 800 people went into exile.[118] Fewer than a dozen of them came from Wales or had Welsh connections. The most interesting was the future bishop and biblical translator, Richard Davies, who fled to Frankfurt from parishes in Buckinghamshire.[119] Another was Thomas Young, who may have escaped

---

[114] *WRE*, p. 197.

[115] J. Loach, 'Pamphlets and politics, 1553–8', *BIHR*, XLVIII (1978), 31–44.

[116] *W 1415–1642*, pp. 421–2.

[117] Bentham to Lever, Strype, *Eccles. Memorials*, III/ii. 134.

[118] Garrett, *Exiles*, p. 32; D. M. Loades, 'The Essex Inquisitions', *BIHR*, XXXV (1962), 87–97.

[119] *WRE*, pp. 156–63.

from Milford Haven to Wesel with his former bishop, William Barlow.[120] Young would return to become bishop of St David's and later archbishop of York. The only other Welshman known to have gone abroad in 1555 was the virtually unknown Geoffrey Jones.[121] Two years later, a small group of exiles, all of whom had connections with west Wales, joined John Knox's congregation at Geneva. They included Thomas Jhones (?of Fountain Gate, i.e. Twm Siôn Cati), who arrived in May 1557;[122] Thomas Johns of Steynton and William Chambers, both of whom had been involved in a quarrel of 1551 with Bishop Ferrar;[123] and a priest called John Evans.[124] Another exile who reached Geneva in 1557, Thomas Duwick or Huyck, DCL, a canon of St David's during Ferrar's episcopate, may also have been associated with them.[125] It is tempting to see this exodus as having resulted from John Perrott's association with Mary's enemies like Henry Dudley, his consequent loss of authority in Pembrokeshire, and the intensification of pressure on heretics in south-west Wales. Perrott himself thought it wise at this point to take service in France with the earl of Pembroke.[126]

To dwell only on the repressive aspects of Mary's regime is to do it less than justice, however. While Reginald Pole wanted to eliminate heresy, he thought it one of his lesser problems – indeed, he seriously underestimated its strength and tenacity in south-eastern England. His overriding concern was with the Catholic reform movement, of which he had been a distinguished representative since the 1520s, and his prime ambition was to see the fulfilment in his own country of the ideals of the *Consilium de Emendenda Ecclesia*. Its programme called for the rededication of the Church in obedience to the pope, the restoration of the comeliness of worship, and the improvement of piety and learning.[127] To achieve these ends, he summoned a synod to meet at Lambeth on 4 November 1555 and hoped to see it followed up by regular episcopal visitations. At this meeting of bishops and representatives of the lower clergy, which continued in session until February 1556, he hoped to introduce reforms in the liturgy, clerical manners and education, and the nature of episcopal supervision.

---

[120] PRO, C1/1447/14.

[121] Garrett, *Exiles*, p. 200.

[122] Ibid., p. 201.

[123] Ibid., p. 199.

[124] Ibid., pp. 151–2; cf. *BBCS*, XIV. 50, 132, 133, for other references to a St David's cleric called John Evans.

[125] Garrett, *Exiles*, pp. 149–50; C. Martin, *Les Protestants anglais refugiés à Genève, 1553–60* (Geneva, 1915), pp. 333–4.

[126] *DWB*, p. 248; Loades, *Tudor Conspiracies*, pp. 210–11, 223, 233; J. Loach and R. Titler, *The Mid-Tudor Polity, c.1540–1560* (London, 1980), p. 14.

[127] W. Schenk, *Reginald Pole* (London, 1950), pp. 60–1, 142.

All were improvements of a kind for which he had been responsible in Rome as far back as 1536.[128]

An essential step was to raise the quality of the episcopate and higher clergy, and within three or four years much was achieved. It was of critical importance to ensure that bishops were resident in their dioceses, since it was widely recognized that their absence had been 'the cause of almost all the evils that affect the church'.[129] True, in the diocese of Llandaff, the unmilitant Kitchen, who bent unresistingly before each fresh breeze, remained in post and held the dubious distinction of being the only one among Mary's bishops who did not seek the pope's absolution from schism. None of the rest of the bishops, however, owed his see to service rendered to the Crown. At St David's Henry Morgan had already replaced Ferrar. He was fortunate to have as his precentor the able and sincere Catholic, Morgan Phillips, former fellow of Oriel College, where he had been William Allen's tutor.[130] Phillips would again have a notable career in exile during Elizabeth's reign. Pole's first episcopal appointment in Wales was William Glyn, appointed in 1555 to Bangor, a see which had been vacant since Arthur Bulkeley's death in 1552. Glyn was a man of zeal and erudition who had been Lady Margaret professor of Divinity – though he was suspended from lecturing during Edward's reign – and president of Queens' College at Cambridge. At Queens' he had gathered about him a circle of promising young Welshmen: Nicholas Robinson, Thomas Davies, Thomas Yale, Humphrey Toy, and William Davies. To three of these – Robinson, Thomas Davies, and Yale (who was also dean of the Arches) – he gave preferment at Bangor.[131] Glyn was described by Sir John Wynn as 'a great scholar and a great Hebrician, as by quotation of his books do appear, being rare in that time – he was a good and religious man after the manner of that time'.[132] He was one of those sent to Oxford to dispute with Cranmer, Latimer, and Ridley, and was warmly complimented by Fuller for having 'pressed the argument with more strength and less passion than any of the papists'.[133]

But the spearhead of Pole's reform movement in Wales was his own close friend and confidant, Thomas Goldwell, chosen bishop of St Asaph in

---

[128] D. Fenlon, *Heresy and Obedience in Tridentine Italy* (Cambridge, 1972); cf. R. H. Pogson, 'Reginald Pole and the priorities of government in Mary Tudor's church', *Hist. Journal*, XVIII (1975), 3–20.

[129] H. O. Evennett, *The Spirit of the Counter-Reformation* (Cambridge, 1968), pp. 97–100.

[130] *DWB*, pp. 760–1.

[131] *DNB*.

[132] J. Wynn, *History of the Gwydir Family*, ed. J. Ballinger (Cardiff, 1927), p. 65.

[133] *Fuller's Church History of Britain*, ed. J. S. Brewer (6 vols. Oxford, 1848), IV. 193–4.

1556.[134] Pole and Goldwell had first met in 1532 and for twenty years subsequently their lives had been interwoven. From 1538 to 1547 Goldwell had charge of the hospice for English pilgrims at Rome. In 1547 he had become a member of the remarkably austere order of the Theatines, among whom he experienced the disciplined fervour and spirituality of the Catholic Reformation.[135] These values he exerted himself to introduce into his diocese of St Asaph. In a set of injunctions issued almost at once to his clergy he prohibited any priest 'having a woman at his commandment' from celebrating mass and required obedience to 'all Church laws and constitutions'. He further ordered all priests to keep away from 'dicing houses' or 'common bowling alleys' or other 'suspect houses or places'.[136] He prohibited the schools for the poor which had begun to be held in churches; and this, at first sight, appears to be 'a mark of retrogression', as Archdeacon Thomas described it;[137] but the explanation for it may be that Goldwell suspected that the literacy acquired in such schools had encouraged unregulated Bible-reading that led to the kind of heresy of which Rawlins White had been accused.

Towards the end of Mary's reign, two exceptionally gifted young men, unusually well-attuned to the needs of the Welsh-speaking population, Morys Clynnog and Gruffydd Robert, were made bishop-elect of Bangor and archdeacon of Anglesey respectively.[138] Both were young Oxford graduates and each was to have a long and distinguished career in the service of the Roman Church, most of it spent in exile during Elizabeth's reign. Clynnog, even before Mary's reign, had already spent much time in Italy at the university of Padua, where he came under Pole's influence, and later became his chaplain.[139]

Glyn, and especially Goldwell, made valiant efforts by means of synods to improve their parish clergy. To do so meant not only patient and regular instruction in the essentials of the faith for a clerical labour force, badly educated, sadly undermanned, and made cynical, heedless, or perplexed by rapid change, but also the restoration of some of the wealth and possessions of the Church. In this respect, Pole and Mary had already had to admit to a major defeat in their failure to induce the laity to give back their gains from monastic and other church property. In addition, they and the bishops were faced with a position in which many parishes were

[134] Schenk, *Pole*, pp. 145–6.
[135] H. Davies, *Worship and Theology in England from Cranmer to Hooker, 1534–1603* (Princeton, 1970), pp. 138–9.
[136] Wilkins, *Concilia Magna*, IV. 141–5.
[137] Thomas, *St Asaph* I. 87.
[138] *DWB*, pp. 79–80, 857–8; G. J. Williams (ed.), *Gramadeg Cymraeg gan Gruffydd Robert* (Cardiff, 1939).
[139] *DWB*, pp. 79–80.

2222222

impropriated and impoverished; inflation and the shortage of clergy exacerbated the problems of pluralism; and the pillage of goods and ornaments had made churches as bare as barns. Some attempts were made, however, to recover what could be won back.[140] In 1554 Henry Morgan of St David's succeeded in obtaining no less than £1,000 of the debts of his see remitted, and early in 1557 the archdeacon of Llandaff was required to give some of his surplus from the collection of first-fruits and paid-out pensions to ease the debts of St David's.[141] Not that Llandaff was at all well off; a report on the confiscation of church goods in that diocese told a sad tale of wholesale embezzlement and speculation, with cathedral and parish churches alike in lamentable condition: books, goods, plate, and ornaments appropriated; services irregular and incomplete; and the clergy downhearted and dismayed. Nor was there much hope of recovering the loot, much of which had found its way into the pockets of Sir George Herbert and Sir Rice Mansel, from which it was unlikely ever to be turned out.[142] At St Asaph, conditions were much the same; the cathedral church 'in great ruin and decay' and 'destitute of decent and convenient ornaments' needed for services. But Thomas Goldwell was much more energetic and resolute in seeking restitution than Kitchen was at Llandaff. He showed great courage and determination in fighting a series of lawsuits with considerable success, not merely against the deprived archdeacon, John Pollard, and the former dean, Richard Puskyn, but also against no less mighty a county notability than Sir John Salusbury, and his allies, Pierce ap William of Disserth, and the Conway family of Pantryfan, to whom the archdeaconry had been leased.[143] In the course of these legal actions Goldwell alleged that, among other grievous malpractices, Sir John Salusbury had obtained illegal possession of the chapter seal and was using it to draw up forged leases.[144]

Before the end of Mary's reign the work of men like Goldwell seemed to be bearing fruit. He was hailed by a native poet, Siôn Tudur, as a 'great fount of true learning and faith', while Siôn Brwynog welcomed William Glyn as a 'shepherd of souls' ('bugail enaid') and a 'pillar of faith' ('a philer ffydd').[145] This connection between the bishops and Welsh literature

[140] R. H. Pogson, 'Revival and reform in Mary Tudor's church: a question of money', *JEH*, XXV (1974), 249–65.

[141] *CPR, 1553–4*, p. 112; some effort was made at St David's to repair vestments and restore the traditional Catholic services, W. B. Jones and E. A. Freeman, *The History and Antiquities of St David's* (London, 1856), 383–5.

[142] Thomas, *Llandaff*, pp. 106–12.

[143] PRO, C1/1431/26; 1431/27–8; 1472/2–6; C24/29/22, 28, 42; NLW, Plymouth Deeds, 1656, 1659.

[144] PRO, C1/1472/3.

[145] W. A. Bebb, *Cyfnod y Tuduriaid* (Wrexham, 1939), p. 94.

suggests that it may have been under this kind of inspiration that the first attempt was made to provide Counter-Reformation literature in Welsh, when George Marshal's *Compendious treatise in metre declaring the first original of sacrifice* was translated into Welsh by a north Wales priest. He was Arthur ap Huw, vicar of Tywyn in 1555 and afterwards incumbent of Llanfair Dyffryn Clwyd, 1563–70. He was warmly praised by contemporary bards for his exceptional learning and his generosity.[146] Certainly, there were men like Morys Clynnog and Gruffydd Robert, two of the most gifted Welsh prose authors of the sixteenth century, who would, during Elizabeth's reign, show themselves keenly aware of the need to provide Catholic literature in Welsh for the benefit of their fellow-countrymen. In this, as in a number of other respects, the work of firmly grounding Catholicism had only just begun when Mary's death brought it to a premature end. Pole's own ambitious plans, announced at the synod of 1555–6, for organizing seminaries at all cathedral churches for the education of future members of the clergy, for a Catholic translation of the Bible, and for a vernacular prayer book had all ended in disappointment.[147]

Assessing the impact of Mary's reign on Wales is difficult. Perhaps it should be said first of all that it has become increasingly clear that the Welsh population of the Middle Ages had not been as effectively instructed in the doctrines of the Catholic faith or as deeply committed to them as has often been suggested.[148] They had started from a more insecure base than might have been supposed, and the changes introduced between 1529 and 1553 had thereafter brought about bewilderment and hesitation but had also left many virtually unconcerned. Earning a livelihood was more important for most than taking a positive stance, one way or the other, in religion. Almost all the clergy, even, had shown little inclination to do other than veer with the cross-winds of change. For the politically conscious and informed, the safest course had been to believe as their prince did, to conform to the Church that his law required them to attend, to leave theological subtleties to the few who understood and cared about them, and to take their profit from the changes as and when they could. Their lead was followed by the mass of the population who, so far as they were affected at all, may have markedly disliked some of the enforced reforms, like the pillaging and iconoclasm in the churches, and found others, such as the introduction of the English liturgy, largely beyond their comprehension. Without leadership, they were certainly not prepared to rise in protest on behalf of any issue.

---

[146] B. Rees, *Dulliau'r Canu Rhydd, 1500–1650* (Cardiff, 1952), pp. 130–1. C. Fychan, 'Y canu i wŷr eglwysig gorllewin Sir Ddinbych', *DHTS*, XXVIII (1979), 120–2.
[147] J. Guy, *Tudor England* (Oxford, 1988), p. 240.
[148] *WRE*, pp. 11–12, 17.

Nevertheless, the developments of the Marian era undoubtedly served to reinforce the impact of the Edwardian Reformation by intensifying still further the differentiation between the two small minorities of committed Catholics and Protestants. The Protestants, drawn mainly from a few clerics and laymen attracted at the universities or the inns of court by the new doctrines and from a handful of gentry and townsmen who were literate and open to heretical ideas, resisted – overtly or, more often, in secret – the restoration of papal authority and medieval worship. Convinced Catholics, clergy and laity alike, who wanted to preserve their faith intact, were now becoming ever clearer in their minds that they would have to do so in communion with Rome; compromise with royal supremacy was no longer an option. But the number of those who would be willing to stand up to be openly counted for the old church at the beginning of Elizabeth's reign proved to be remarkably small.[149] The pope was still for many an unloved foreign potentate whose pretensions were mistrusted and shunned; even more so, perhaps, as the result of his recent clash with Pole and Mary. Even the notions which people had of what constituted Catholic doctrine, always nebulous and ill-grounded as a result of spasmodic and indifferent teaching by an ignorant priesthood with usually little or no training for the task, were now, after years of change and change-about, decidedly hazy at the centre as well as around the edges. They were 'Catholic' enough not to want to be 'Protestant' or to change over with any enthusiasm; but they would not be 'Catholic' enough to offer serious resistance or make a protest when Mary's successor brought back Edward's Prayer Book. There had as yet been far too little sign of that active Catholic evangelizing that would be called for at the parish level if both priests and parishioners were to be won over to the reformed and lively post-Tridentine Catholic faith. The battle for the soul of the Welsh people had still to be fought and would be waged for decades to come.

At the end of Mary's reign, in Wales as in most parts of England, the large majority were not consciously pledged either to Catholicism or Protestantism. In all ranks of society there was a mass of uncertainty, time-serving, incomprehension, and inertia. Many in Wales were, indeed, conservative and wedded to customary practices and assumptions but from habit rather than conviction.[150] At this point they were conforming Catholics whose loyalty did not go far below the surface. The leaders of society wanted primarily to see the whole fabric of authority, local and central, preserved and were more concerned to maintain their interests –

[149] Ibid., pp. 141–50.
[150] *WC*, pp. 559–60.

economic, social, and political – than with any dogma. A legitimate government, whatever its religious complexion, which guaranteed them these would in general get their support. If Mary's reign had lasted longer, say another ten to fifteen years, it might have been a different story. With the advantages of a Catholic sovereign and establishment, bishops of the calibre of Goldwell and Clynnog, and exposure to the full inspiration of the Council of Trent and revived Catholicism, enough impression might have been made on clergy and people to have created a really powerful Catholic opposition, though there can, of course, be no guarantee that that would have happened. As it was, Mary's regime lasted only five years, with the last year of it being wrecked by the calamitous enmity of Pope Paul IV for Cardinal Pole.[151] Furthermore, the effects of disastrous harvests in 1555 and 1556, together with the appalling outbreak of influenza in 1557, and the unsuccessful war against France, all compounded the queen's failure in religion. Many of these disasters were inevitably interpreted in the sixteenth century in the light of divine judgement on ruler and ruled.

Yet Mary was by no means completely unsuccessful. The foundations of Welsh Catholic opposition to Elizabeth had been laid during her sister's reign; its leaders would be men brought forward by Pole – Goldwell, Clynnog, Robert, Phillips, and others – and its supporters some of the families which traced the origins of their militant Catholicism to Mary's reign. The key failure was not of Mary's own making, and that was her inability to guarantee a Catholic successor. Not to have the support of the Crown in the sixteenth century proved to be fatal; without a Catholic ruler, the Catholic opposition had virtually no hope of success. That is why the Marian regime, as events turned out, provided the Catholic Church with its last chance of success in Wales; an opportunity which, for a variety of reasons, it had been unable to turn to permanent advantage.

---

[151] Schenk, *Pole*, pp. 164–6.

CHAPTER 9

The Elizabethan Settlement, 1558–1567

BY the middle of the month of November 1558, both Queen Mary and her archbishop and chief adviser, Cardinal Pole, were in the throes of terminal illness. On the 15th of that month the cardinal received the last rites from his old friend and trusted confidant, Thomas Goldwell, bishop of St Asaph. When, two days later, on 17 November, Pole heard the news that the queen had died at 7 a.m. that morning, he murmured despondently to Goldwell that he had always observed a 'great conformity' between Mary's disposition and experience and his own. Within a few hours he, too, was dead.[1] Goldwell was subsequently allowed to pronounce the funeral oration over his friend and mentor; the last public act of any consequence he was to perform before fleeing into exile. Before her death, Mary, despite her grave misgivings about what the fate of religion under Elizabeth might be, had reconciled herself to acknowledging that her half-sister must succeed her. No sooner had the last breath left her body than messengers were riding post-haste to acquaint Elizabeth with the news. The new queen's accession was greeted with acclamation in most parts of the kingdom.[2] National feeling was strong, and it found its expression in devotion and loyalty to the ruler. Nowhere, perhaps, was she received more affectionately than in Wales, where there was a particular twist to the people's allegiance. Her Welsh subjects reserved a special warmth for 'one of their own'; the heiress of that Tudor line reputed to spring from Cadwaladr, last 'true' king of Britain, and even from Brutus, mythical founder of the ancient kingdom. Poets would hail her enrapturedly as 'Sidanen' ('the silken one'), 'Sidanen fawr o Frutus' ('great Sidanen, progeny of Brutus') and 'Sidanen Maelgwn Gwynedd' ('Sidanen, descendant of Maelgwn Gwynedd').[3]

However elated Elizabeth may have been at succeeding to the throne without having to fight for it, it was a *damnosa hereditas* which had been

---

[1] W. Schenk, *Reginald Pole* (London, 1950), pp. 155–6.
[2] J. E. Neale, *Queen Elizabeth* (London, 1948), chap 4.
[3] E. G. Jones, *Cymru a'r Hen Ffydd* (Cardiff, 1951), p. 1; W. A. Bebb, *Cyfnod y Tuduriaid* (Wrexham, 1939), pp. 136, 142–3.

bestowed on her. Mary had left a realm rancorously divided in religion and politics. The last years of her reign had, in addition, been dogged by inclement weather, disastrous harvests, inflated prices, widespread epidemics, and heavy mortality. If that were not enough, she had also bequeathed to her successor a ruinous foreign war, an exhausted treasury, and an insecure title to the throne, to which Henri II of France was prepared to present rival claimants in the persons of his daughter-in-law, Mary Queen of Scotland, and her husband, the dauphin of France.[4] Nothing was more urgent for Elizabeth than the satisfactory settlement of religion; but it must be one which would not offend susceptibilities, nor give foreign powers any excuse for intervention. For a ruler in a position as delicate as hers, if it was dangerous to delay, it might be fatal to act too precipitately. The queen herself was cool, moderate, and tolerant in religion, though she disliked papal pretensions to authority, and, in any case, as Anne Boleyn's daughter, could scarcely have swallowed them. More than any other Tudor ruler, possibly, she directed her own religious policy, and throughout her reign, there were to be two central principles from which she never departed. The one was that she wanted to make her Church as broad and as comprehensive as possible, to which the majority, if not all, of her subjects could subscribe. The other was to maintain a Church which she could control through bishops of her own choosing. During the early months of 1559, therefore, Elizabeth and her advisers were moving carefully and advisedly towards a settlement dictated by expediency rather than dogma. Changes from Mary's regime there must be, but they must be such as would alienate as few as possible. Elizabeth hoped to win over the majority who, though put off by some of Mary's actions, were by no means convinced Protestants, and certainly not in Wales.

The backbone of Catholic resistance came from the bishops, who refused to budge an inch from the position they had taken up in Mary's reign. Proof against threats and cajolery alike, their constancy was the marvel of Catholic observers.[5] The bench of bishops had, nevertheless, been seriously weakened by a number of deaths which had occurred in their midst and the failure of Pole to appoint successors quickly; 'That accursed cardinal (Pole)', complained the Spanish envoy, Feria, in exasperated tones, had left twelve bishoprics unfilled.[6] In Wales, the two southern bishops, Henry Morgan of St David's and Anthony Kitchen of Llandaff – at first anyway – stood out manfully. Unfortunately, from the Catholic point of view, the position of the two northern bishops was

[4] R. B. Wernham, *Before the Armada* (London, 1966), pp. 239–40.
[5] *CSP Ven.* VII. 94, 104–8; *CSP Span. Eliz.* I. 86.
[6] *CSP Span. Eliz.* I. 32.

distinctly unsatisfactory. Thomas Goldwell, ablest of the Welsh prelates, was to have been moved from St Asaph to Oxford, but that translation never took place. Goldwell's position was so indeterminate that he was not summoned to the House of Lords. In the diocese of Bangor, William Glyn had died earlier in 1558. The man chosen to succeed him was Morys Clynnog, chaplain to Cardinal Pole and appointed commissary to the Prerogative Court of Canterbury in 1558, which may have delayed his consecration at Bangor.[7] That meant that two of the Welsh dioceses were effectively leaderless at a critical time. On its side, the Protestant faction looked for leaders to the exiles returned from those sanctuaries on the Continent where they had spent Mary's reign. Dismayed by Elizabeth's caution, they found the process of waiting for reform 'very tiresome', yet never doubted that all would soon be well, since they had a 'wise and religious queen', 'favourably and propitiously disposed' towards them.[8] In Wales there were very few keen Protestants, and even fewer returned exiles. Two of their number, however, Thomas Young and Richard Davies, were to be assigned a leading part in enforcing the religious settlement in Wales.

While the proposed legislation to change the religious arrangements was going through Parliament and being discussed in Convocation early in 1559, it encountered stiff opposition from the bishops and their allies among some of the conservatively minded members of the lay aristocracy. The only bishop of a Welsh diocese to stand with the rest of his brethren in opposition was Anthony Kitchen, bishop of Llandaff, who voted twice against the intended changes. The bishop of St David's, Henry Morgan, is also known to have been a convinced opponent, but does not appear to have been present in the Lords. Had Thomas Goldwell been summoned to take his seat, it is certain that he would have been found among those most obstinately opposed to the royal policies: 'of all the occupants of the episcopal bench Goldwell was the least likely to accept any compromise'.[9] As he was to explain to Cecil, however, he had had no writ to attend Parliament, which he regarded as very strange, since he still looked upon himself as bishop of St Asaph and had no intention of accepting the diocese of Oxford.[10] The failure to summon him to the Lords may have arisen from accident or misunderstanding, but it may also have resulted from a deliberate intention to exclude a particularly intransigent opponent. The most influential Welsh layman of the period, the earl of Pembroke, was another who joined his fellow-aristocrats in opposing the legislation.[11]

---

[7] *DWB*, s.n. Morys Clynnog.
[8] *Zurich Letters* (2 vols. Parker Soc., London, 1842–3), I. 33.
[9] N. Jones, *Faith by Statute* (RHS, London, 1982), p. 78.
[10] PRO, SP12/1/52.
[11] Jones, *Faith by Statute*, p. 100.

Eventually, however, on 29 April 1559, the Acts of Supremacy and Uniformity were passed. In order to get them through, the queen had been obliged to offer concessions. She had abandoned the harsh laws against Catholics that were at one time envisaged. She had also chosen to be known by the title of Supreme Governor (suggested by the returned exile, Thomas Lever) instead of Supreme Head of the Church, in deference to the susceptibilities of those who disliked the notion of the royal supremacy but who particularly objected to a woman's being designated 'Supreme Head'. The Act of Uniformity restored the Prayer Book of 1552, but with some significant adjustments of a conservative nature. Along with the expunging of the notorious 'Black Rubric' of 1552, the most notable modification was the attempt to combine the formula used in the communion service of 1549 with that of 1552: 'The body of our Lord Jesus Christ which was given for thee preserve thy body and soul unto everlasting life; and take and eat this in remembrance that Christ died for thee, and feed on him in thy heart by faith and thanksgiving.'[12] In spite of these concessions, the Act of Uniformity scraped through with a majority of only three, without the approval of a single churchman, and over the protest of Convocation. From its inception, the Elizabethan settlement was unmistakably erastian and was to remain so throughout. Outwardly, the Church retained many of the characteristics of its medieval predecessor, which made it appear different from the Reformed churches on the Continent. It still kept its bishops and hierarchy; its cathedrals staffed with prebendaries; the diocesan, ruridecanal, and parish structure; and the ecclesiastical courts administering Canon Law. All this may have helped in ensuring the relatively smooth acceptance of the settlement at large in the country.

As far as Wales was concerned, the new arrangements resurrected the same problems that had been encountered earlier in Edward VI's reign. The Elizabethan Prayer Book of 1559 was just as unintelligible to most of the population as the Edwardian one had been, and there was as yet no sign of any effort being made to meet the distinctive problems of Wales by the provision of any literature in Welsh. Letters were received by the earl of Pembroke from the Welsh counties, according to a report sent by Feria to Philip II, threatening that if preachers were sent across the Marches, they would not return alive.[13] Once again, however, a Tudor government appears to have had no doubts that its power structures in Wales were firmly enough grounded to ensure the acceptance of the new statutes by the people, and their successful enforcement. The Marian president of the

---

[12] *Book of Common Prayer* (1559).
[13] J. A. Froude, *The Reign of Elizabeth* (5 vols. London, 1912), I. 190.

Council in the Marches was Bishop Bourne and, for a few months, Elizabeth made no changes; but by February 1559 it was evidently impossible for her to continue employing a Catholic bishop in this post and he was replaced by Lord Williams of Thame.[14] Williams's vice-president, Sir Hugh Paulet, the man effectively in charge, did not appear at all concerned with problems of religion in Wales but had much to report about the prevalence of crime and disorder there.[15] It would seem that loyalty to the old religion was not intense enough to give rise to overt opposition and that the governing element still preferred an ecclesiastical administration parallel in structure with secular administration, with an orderly hierarchy and clear lines of responsibility.

Measures had now to be taken to try to secure the acceptance of the new regime by the clergy and the laity. First of all, the existing bishops were required to take the oath of supremacy. On 23 May action was begun against a number of them, including Goldwell and Kitchen. The queen had hoped to win several of these prelates to her side, but in the outcome all except one proved to be immovable. Goldwell predictably refused to take the oath and, seeing no future for himself in Elizabeth's realm, made preparations to flee to the Continent. On 26 June 1559 he wrote to his brother, Stephen, confessing his intention of going abroad and requesting Stephen to clear up his affairs in Wales. This letter was conveyed to Cecil by 29 June, and steps were taken to prevent Goldwell from leaving the country.[16] But it was too late; the bird had already flown and before 15 July he was deprived of his see. Henry Morgan, bishop of St David's, along with the bishop of Exeter, was deprived in the second week of August. He withdrew to live in retirement with his family at Wolverton near Oxford, where he died in December 1559.[17] The remaining Welsh bishop, the aged Kitchen of Llandaff, had voted in the House of Lords with his brethren against the supremacy and uniformity; but he was either too weary or too timorous to persist. By midsummer his resistance was showing signs of crumbling. On 12 July, the Spanish envoy, de Quadra, reported that the bishop of Llandaff, 'an old, greedy and little-learned man is wavering and it is feared he may take the oath'.[18] De Quadra did his best to comfort him and to screw up his courage; but in vain. Six days later, Kitchen signed a pledge to 'set forth in my own person and cause . . . to accept and obey the

[14] P. H. Williams, *The Council in the Marches of Wales under Elizabeth I* (Cardiff, 1958), pp. 250–1.
[15] Ibid., pp. 249–50.
[16] PRO, SP12/4/70, 70 (1).
[17] E. Yardley, *Menevia Sacra* (*AC* Supplement, 1927), pp. 95–6.
[18] *CSP Span. Eliz.* I. 86.

whole course of religion now approved in her Grace's realm'.[19] With the see of Bangor vacant, all the Welsh bishops had now been accounted for.

At least three other leading figures among the cathedral clergy besides Goldwell escaped to the Continent in the summer of 1559. One was Morys Clynnog, chaplain to Pole and bishop-elect of Bangor, and fleeing with him was Gruffydd Robert, archdeacon of Anglesey. He and Clynnog may possibly have gone abroad with Goldwell. Another who withdrew to Catholic Europe was Morgan Phillips, 'Morgan the Sophister' as he had been known in Oxford, where he cut a figure of some standing in intellectual circles. Subsequently appointed precentor of St David's, he refused the settlement of 1559 and fled the country.[20] All three were to spend the rest of their lives in exile, where they began their Counter-Reformation activities early. In 1561 Morys Clynnog proposed that Elizabeth be overthrown by foreign invasion, protesting that he would prefer to see his countrymen 'attain eternal blessedness under a foreign lord than to be cast into the nethermost hell'.[21] Along with others at Louvain the Welsh exiles wanted the Council of Trent to declare Elizabeth worthy of excommunication.[22]

Meantime, back home, a royal visitation was planned in the summer of 1559 to plant the settlement firmly among the cathedral chapters and the diocesan clergy. Following closely the precedent set earlier in 1547 by Edward VI, the intention was to administer the oath to the clergy under the Act of Supremacy, enforce the use of the Prayer Book, and promulgate the royal injunctions for religion. To make the work of the visitors easier, episcopal authority was inhibited and the dioceses grouped into circuits. The Welsh bishoprics, together with those of Hereford and Worcester, formed the western circuit, covering in general the area that came under the jurisdiction of the Council in the Marches. On 18 July a royal commission was issued to a group of visitors, which included the names of a number of prominent laymen, among them the president of the Council, Lord Williams, and his deputy. They were not expected to take part in the day-to-day proceedings of the visitation but merely to lend the weight and dignity of their office to the group of three clerics and two lawyers who did the real work. The visitors were all reliable men of firm reforming sympathies, four of whom were Welsh by birth and had had close connections with Welsh dioceses. Two of them, Richard Davies and Thomas Young, were returned exiles; and a third, Rowland Meyrick, had been ejected from

[19] W. P. Haugaard, *Elizabeth and the English Reformation* (Cambridge, 1968), p. 38.
[20] Yardley, *Menevia Sacra*, pp. 130–1; *WRE*, p. 150.
[21] D. Williams, *A History of Modern Wales* (London, 1950), p. 68.
[22] *CSP Rome*, I. 135.

his livings during Mary's reign. Another, George Constantine, though an early reformer, had managed to cling on to his chancellorship of St David's under Bishops Barlow, Ferrar, and Henry Morgan, and had contrived to become archdeacon of Brecon in 1559. The fifth member was a well-known Gloucestershire lawyer, Richard Pate.[23]

The visitation was not to be undertaken lightly, and formidable opposition was anticipated. The mass of the clergy were thought to be watching events in sullen or resentful silence; 'the whole body remains unmoved', reported the returned exile, Richard Cox; and Edmund Grindal gave it as the general opinion that not only the bishops but also 'many other beneficed persons would renounce their bishoprics and functions'.[24] There survive only a few scraps of evidence on the basis of which to reconstruct the activities of the western visitors.[25] These suggest that they began work in Llandaff cathedral on 9 August, then proceeded to Hereford, Worcester, St Asaph, and Bangor, ending up at St David's by January 1560. They also held sessions at convenient centres such as Stratford-on-Avon and Wrexham. Most of those deprived by the visitors were drawn from the ranks of the higher clergy. Standing out among them were the three who were to figure so prominently among the Catholic exiles of Elizabeth's reign – Clynnog, Robert, and Phillips. Others were John Lloyd, dean of St Asaph, who was afterwards to become a well-known lawyer, Humphrey Edwards, archdeacon of St Asaph, John Blaxton, archdeacon of Brecon, and William Leveson, archdeacon of Carmarthen.[26] One of the higher clergy deprived by the visitors was Edmund Daniel, dean of Hereford. Years later, in the course of his deposition in the papal court during the process for the excommunication of Queen Elizabeth, he gave his own account of the methods they had employed. He told how four delegates (probably Davies, Young, Meyrick, and Pate) presented 'to all the priests of my church in which I was a dean, and to the whole chapter' documents requiring them to subscribe to the royal supremacy and to the 'forms which parliament had ratified for keeping the hours and ministering the sacraments'[27] (i.e. the Book of Common Prayer).

The articles issued by the visitors were mild and careful in tone; their phrasing suggested that the queen and her agents were moving slowly and cautiously, unwilling to offend conservative sentiments unnecessarily. Judging by the very small numbers of clergy who refused to take the oath –

[23] *WRE*, pp. 142–4.
[24] *Zurich Letters*, I. 27; II. 19.
[25] *WRE*, pp. 141–53.
[26] Ibid.
[27] R. W. Dixon, *History of the Church of England* (6 vols. London, 1878–1902), V. 168–9.

only about a dozen, drawn mainly from the ranks of the higher clergy, have been traced for the whole circuit – they seemed to have been largely successful in attaining their object.[28] Small wonder that their colleague in the south-west of England, John Jewel, could proclaim jubilantly towards the end of the year that the 'ranks of the papists had fallen almost of their own accord'.[29] This was all the more unexpected since the new Prayer Book, in spite of the concessions offered, was to all intents and purposes the markedly Protestant book of 1552, which one might have supposed was plainly distasteful to many of the Welsh clergy. Another of the visitors' articles asked about 'images . . . or other monuments of feigned or false miracles, pilgrimages, edicts, and superstition, especially as have been set up in churches'.[30] The authorities were much exercised in mind that no papal furnishings should be retained or hoarded in the hope of a swing of the pendulum back to Catholic ways. How far the visitors were able to bring their influence to bear to secure the removal of altars, mass books, relics, roods, images, paintings, and other survivals from the Marian 'wilderness of superstition'[31] it is difficult to tell. True, the churchwardens' accounts of the parish church of St Mary's, Swansea, recorded the taking down of two stone altars and their replacement by a wooden communion table, for which 4*d.* was paid. At the same time, 4*d.* was paid for the removal of the great rood, though the loft itself was retained as a singing gallery.[32] But the Swansea churchwardens' accounts are unique, and later episcopal reports reveal the wholesale survival of Catholic features in many Welsh churches, twenty-five years and more after Elizabeth came to the throne.

One of the most important duties the visitors were called upon to perform was to oversee the filling of vacant dioceses. These had been kept empty by the queen as long as possible so that their revenues might 'gloriously swell' the Exchequer;[33] but lists of candidates suitable for promotion had been drawn up earlier in the year by Cecil.[34] It seems possible that the bishops-elect knew in advance of their impending promotion – possibly as early as August 1559.[35] Not until 4 December 1559, however, did the chapter of St Asaph elect Richard Davies, *per viam compromissi* (by way of arbitration), as its new bishop. Although Davies as

[28] *WRE*, pp. 149–50.

[29] *Zurich Letters*, I. 145

[30] W. H. Frère and W. P. M. Kennedy, *Visitation Articles and Injunctions of the Period of the Reformation* (3 vols. Alcuin Club, London, 1910), II. 176–89; III. 1–7.

[31] C. Cross, *Church and People, 1450–1660* (London, 1976), p. 135.

[32] Williams, *GCH*, IV. 229.

[33] *Zurich Letters*, I. 55.

[34] PRO, SP12/4/38, 39.

[35] *Zurich Letters*, I. 9, 16.

a returned exile, had been singled out early for promotion by Cecil – for the diocese of Worcester in the first instance – he was not the undisputed choice of the canons of St Asaph. They may indeed finally have reached their decision only under official pressure, applied by the visitors of 1559, as certainly happened at Salisbury when Jewel was chosen as bishop.[36] In December, also, another of the visitors, Rowland Meyrick, scion of a family of Anglesey gentry, was elected at Bangor. By 10 January 1560 the visitors were at St David's, where Young was chosen bishop. The chapter were reported as having had to borrow the visitors' seal to authenticate Young's election to the queen, because their own could not be found![37] All three of the new Welsh bishops, in December 1559 and January 1560, had to be given licences to hold their other livings *in commendam* because the income from their sees was too meagre to maintain them adequately. Meyrick and Young were once more able to enjoy much of the preferment they had held in St David's diocese during Edward VI's reign; the former to the value of £80 a year and the latter to the value of £67. Davies was allowed to hold his two restored livings of Burnham and Maidsmorton in Buckinghamshire, together with a prebend and a rectory in St Asaph diocese.[38] This began an undesirable practice of episcopal pluralism, which was to have unfortunate consequences later. It also suggested little prospect of any serious attempt being made to grapple with the long-standing abuses of pluralism and non-residence in Wales; though Archbishop Parker defended the custom on the grounds that 'the inconvenience may be thought less than that the order of godly ministers in that function should be brought to contempt for lack of reasonable necessaries'.[39] A much more hopeful portent for the future arising out of the choice of new bishops was that three men of Welsh origins were appointed to Welsh dioceses. This was in sharp contrast to the usual practice during the late medieval period, when non-Welshmen were chosen, although in fairness to Mary and Cardinal Pole it should be remembered that they had, in the main, made a point of preferring Welsh clerics to the Welsh dioceses. This early precedent became the normal procedure during Elizabeth's reign, when thirteen out of sixteen bishops appointed were Welshmen, even if Archbishop Parker was not entirely convinced of the propriety of doing so.[40] The Elizabethan bishops of Wales, by and large, set a good example to their clergy. They

---

[36] J. Jewel, *Works* (4 vols. Parker Soc., London, 1845–50), IV, xv.

[37] *Register of Matthew Parker*, ed. W. H. Frère (Cant. and York Soc., London, 1907), p. 83.

[38] T. Rymer, *Foedera, Conventiones, Litterae, etc.* (20 vols. London, 1704–35), VI/iv. 89–92.

[39] M. Parker, *Correspondence* (Parker Soc., London, 1853), p. 208.

[40] Ibid., pp. 257–8.

were a learned, resident, preaching clergy, familiar with their dioceses, and well known to their parish priests.

How far the brief tour of 1559 had enabled the future bishops to acquaint, or reacquaint, themselves with the state of religion in the Welsh dioceses, it is difficult to tell. Not only was it of short duration but it was hardly concerned with the laity at all. In any case, it seems that most laymen were either too confused, or rendered too cautious, by the vicissitudes of the previous twenty years or so to have hard-and-fast opinions about religion at all. The same was probably true of many of the clergy as well. This indecision is the more easily understood when it is recalled that the whole aim of the government was to discourage its subjects from thinking of the settlement in terms of a clear-cut choice between Catholicism and Protestantism. Doubtless, the visitors viewed with mixed feelings the general acceptance of the oath and the articles by the clergy. While it was gratifying to observe the readiness with which allegiance to the pope was abandoned by almost all except the bishops and some of the dignitaries, the visitors must have had grave misgivings about the fitness of many of the parish clergy to minister in a Reformed Church. Nevertheless, the visitation had at least enabled them to weed out their most uncompromising opponents, to gain some insight into prevailing conditions, and to form an impression of the agents upon whom they would have to depend.

Before they had been in their dioceses very long, the new bishops were in 1561 asked to send a certificate of their clergy to Archbishop Parker 'for certain considerations conducent to the general reformation of the clergy of the province of Canterbury'.[41] Three of the Welsh dioceses had already had new bishops; but because it was judged essential that the northern archbishopric should not be left vacant any longer, Thomas Young was translated from St David's to York in 1561. Richard Davies had in turn been moved from St Asaph to take his place, and had been succeeded by another Welshman, Thomas Davies, a native of Caerhun, Caernarfonshire, a Cambridge graduate. Thomas Davies had earlier been chancellor of Bangor and a married priest, deprived at first by Mary, but later restored by Cardinal Pole as custodian of Bangor diocese after the death of Bishop Glyn. Davies had also served as archdeacon of St Asaph before being elected bishop there in 1561.[42] He, together with his brother-bishops of Bangor and Llandaff, duly returned their certificates, but none for St

---

[41] They are printed in Willis's *Survey of the Cathedral Church of St Asaph* (London, 1801), pp. 257 et seq.; *Bangor* (London, 1721), pp. 267–71; and *Llandaff* (London), pp. 194–211.

[42] J. G. Jones, 'Thomas Davies and William Hughes: two Reformation bishops of St Asaph', *BBCS*, XXIX (1980–2), 320–35.

David's has survived. They are, on the whole, careful and comprehensive reports, giving details of the pluralists and absentees, preachers, graduates, those who maintained hospitality, and those who were in orders and those unordained. They reveal the existence of serious abuses; although, generally speaking, they were no worse in Wales than they were elsewhere. Absenteeism and pluralism were common among members of the cathedral chapters, and not a few of the canons were laymen. At St Asaph, out of a chapter of fourteen, four were laymen, and two more were youths pursuing their studies and therefore not resident. Six out of the fifteen-strong Bangor chapter (including two out of the three archdeacons) were non-resident. Six others were resident on livings within the diocese, while one divided his time between Bangor and Oxford. Out of thirteen members of the Llandaff chapter, six were non-resident, of whom the sole archdeacon was one, and six more resided on their livings. The treasurer (William Evans, member of a Glamorgan gentry family) alone was resident at the cathedral. Only one of the Bangor chapter was not in orders. There were four laymen among the Llandaff canons, and two at St Asaph, where the archdeacon had not proceeded beyond deacon's orders. Absenteeism among the diocesan clergy was disturbingly prevalent, too; though it seems to have been less of a problem among the St Asaph clergy than in the other dioceses. Out of a hundred clergy mentioned in the St Asaph return, eighteen were absentees, but these included seven pluralists living in other parishes within the diocese. In Bangor there were twenty-three absentees (five of them resident on other livings) out of seventy; and thirty-six (eleven of them pluralists) out of ninety at Llandaff. On the other hand, far more of the clergy of Bangor and Llandaff maintained hospitality in their parishes. There were forty-six accustomed to doing so at Bangor, and sixty-five at Llandaff, but only twenty-four at St Asaph. No means exist of checking the bishops' figures, nor is it by any means certain that the standards they applied were uniform over the three dioceses. One of the most serious obstacles confronting all of the bishops was the shortage of those clerics who were able to preach. Llandaff and St Asaph could muster five apiece. Bangor could name only two; but the sanguine Bishop Meyrick appended a list of thirty names of 'such as be able to preach and may do good'.[43]

Unfortunately, these returns say nothing of the reactions of either clergy or lay people to the church settlement. However, it is difficult to avoid concluding that if the new regime was not cordially received, at least it met with little resistance. No doubt, the hesitancy of the pope, restrained by Philip II of Spain, helped many to accept. Others must have yielded with

[43] Willis, *Bangor*, p. 269.

all kinds of mental reservations. Above all, it seems unmistakable that the majority were as pliable as they had been throughout all the religious changes of the sixteenth century. Martyrs for conscience were as rare then as they are now. The number of clergy who refused to subscribe was very small. Even among the higher clergy it was only a handful who stood out, while the vast majority of the parish clergy accepted with no apparent demur. In all parts of Wales there were clergy who survived the latest change of direction just as they had weathered a number of earlier crosswinds. At Llandaff, all the clergy seem to have followed the example of their bishop.[44] It was not only Bishop Kitchen who had come through all the shifts in position since Henry VIII's reign, there were also a number of his clergy who kept him company, including, possibly, his successor as bishop, Hugh Jones, who may have been in the parish of Tredynog since 1535.[45] An even more remarkable survivor was that man for all seasons and every climate, Dr Ellis Price, who had held his own as successfully as any vicar of Bray in his capacity as the sinecure rector of three parishes in the diocese of St Asaph from 1538 down to Elizabeth's reign. He then became chancellor of Bangor in 1561, and was seriously mooted as a possible bishop of the diocese in 1565.[46] He lived on until 1594.[47] Two of his long-lived *confrères* were Hugh Puleston, vicar of Wrexham, 1520–66, and John Griffith, who soldiered on at Llysfaen from 1524 to 1587.[48] Others defying time and change were Thomas Bulkeley at Llanddeusant from 1543 to 1579, and Humphrey ap Robert at Newborough from 1544 to 1587.[49]

Some of those who continued in their benefices were notoriously conservative in sympathy, and made little or no attempt to conceal the fact. William Leveson, treasurer of Hereford and archdeacon of Carmarthen, although presented to the visitors as a Catholic in 1559, was not deprived by them and succeeded in hanging on to his livings until his death in 1583, in spite of being denounced by Bishop Scory of Hereford as one of the chief patrons of Catholic priests.[50] Possibly the most astounding case of all was that of Walter Powell, sometimes dubbed 'the bishop of Llandaff', who continued to minister in that diocese for forty years. As late as 1604 he was reputed to be 'a priest ordered in Queen Mary's days . . . And for many

[44] Williams, *GCH*, IV. 221.

[45] M. Gray, 'The diocese of Llandaff in 1563', *JWRH*, II (1994), 57.

[46] Parker, *Correspondence*, pp. 257–8.

[47] *DWB*, s.n. Ellis Pryse.

[48] D. R. Thomas, *History of the Diocese of St Asaph* (3 vols. Oswestry, 1908–13), I. 331; III. 226.

[49] A. I. Pryce, *The Diocese of Bangor in the Sixteenth Century* (Bangor, 1923), pp. 13, 38.

[50] M. Bateson, 'Original letters from the bishops to the Privy Council', *Camden Miscellany*, IX (1893), 11–23.

years he hath been accounted a common mass-monger.'[51] Powell was thoroughly typical of those Marian priests described by Nicholas Sanders as celebrating mass secretly in private houses – however shocked Cardinal Allen may have been to learn of some becoming 'partakers on the same day (oh! horrible impiety) of the chalice of the Lord and the chalice of devils'.[52] There must have been a number of parish priests who continued to undermine the Anglican settlement as far as they dared. In many parishes the issues were blurred, and a variety of old religious practices kept up. There were churches where altars, images, holy water, rosaries, signs of the cross, and other medieval features persisted. Judging by later bishops' reports, some of the old-fashioned clergy, the 'sort of blind and ignorant priests' denounced by Bishop Marmaduke Middleton for elevating the host and performing other customs 'after the use of popish superstition' which retained a 'memory of the idolatrous mass',[53] continued until well into Elizabeth's reign to make the Prayer Book service as much like the mass as they could.

Episcopal registers for the early Elizabethan era survive for only two Welsh dioceses:[54] those of St David's from 1559 to 1565, and Bangor from 1555 to 1603. Their evidence suggests that the Elizabethan settlement was bedded down with singularly little resistance. The registers of the first two Elizabethan bishops of St David's, Thomas Young and Richard Davies, give no indication of any widespread or determined opposition on the part of the clergy. Though the register ends in 1565, the six years from 1559 covered the crucial period for the acceptance by the clergy of Elizabeth's brand of reformed religion. It is true that after that date there were priests who believed they had erred in accepting in the first place, but there were very few who felt bound to give up their livings after 1565. By this time, the queen's intentions, the nature of her settlement, and the issues involved, were all defined fairly unmistakably. The longer the waverers clung to their benefices, inevitably, the less likely they were to resist.

Davies's register records a total of seventy-three presentations over the period between 16 September 1561 and 23 December 1565. This figure is so low as to suggest that some folios have been lost; a suggestion which gains added plausibility from the present confused arrangement of the contents.

---

[51] *HMC, Wells Cathedral MSS, 10th Report*, III. 249.

[52] H. Davies, *Worship and Theology in England from Cranmer to Hooker, 1534–1603* (Princeton, 1970), p. 152.

[53] W. P. M. Kennedy, *Elizabethan Episcopal Administration* (3 vols. Alcuin Club, London, 1925), II. 146–8.

[54] The registers of St David's, bound in a single volume, dating from 1554 to 1565, are kept in NLW (SD/BR/2). A calendar, with analytical introduction, will be found in *BBCS*, XIV. 49–54, 125–38. The Bangor registers of the sixteenth century were published by A. I. Pryce, *Bangor*.

The most usual cause of vacancies was the death of the incumbent, which accounted for forty-three. Only six priests were deprived by the bishop, and, of these, three seem to have had no marked Catholic sympathies – two of them were simply moved from one living to another. The other three are obscure, but they may have been papists. Closer scrutiny of the entries suggests that there may have been other priests who were turned out of their livings, or obliged to resign, because of their beliefs. There are fourteen resignations and one cession recorded. Of these, four may have been occasioned by religious scruple, but the others who resigned were either known Protestants or at least had been placed in their livings by Protestant bishops. There are a further seven vacancies described as being brought about lawfully (*de jure*). Four of these are very unlikely to have been caused by the removal of papist incumbents, with the rest remaining doubtful. There are two other livings where no reason at all was given for the vacancy. Both may have been voided by papists.[55] However, if all these doubtful cases, or even a large proportion of them, could be proved beyond all question to be the outcome of devotion to the Roman rite, it would hardly change the general picture of a docile clergy in the diocese of St David's. It is plain that there was no upheaval comparable with the wholesale displacement of the married clergy during Mary's reign.

The Bangor registers for these years present a very similar picture to those for St David's.[56] The editor of the Bangor registers has rightly concluded that the 'crisis which inevitably arose in the years 1559 and 1560 passed off with very little disturbance'.[57] During the years from 1558 to 1566, only thirty-five presentations were recorded there.[58] Of these, just one incumbent – John Herde, MD, rector of Llanddwywe – was said to have been deprived, and even he is not certainly known to have been removed on account of his religious beliefs. Twenty-six were caused by death, and two more as the result of the resignation of parsons who were quickly moved elsewhere. Three arose from resignations where the incumbents were not moved to another parish: one as the result of a cession, and two from unspecified causes. Even if it were accepted that all six were caused by opposition on religious grounds, which seems distinctly unlikely, it would hardly change the impression of a pliable clergy. Admittedly, the number of presentations recorded in both sets of registers is small enough to suggest that some were not recorded at all,[59] or possibly that some pages are missing from the

---

[55] *WRE*, pp. 170–1.

[56] Pryce, *Bangor*, pp. 17–19.

[57] Ibid., p. xxiii.

[58] Ibid., pp. 17–19.

[59] Dr M. Gray, while describing a 'real rush' at Llandaff in the early 1560s, has been able to trace no more than twenty between 1561 and 1563 (*JWRH* II. 59).

registers. Such mishaps are not at all unlikely but would more probably have resulted from 'carelessness in binding and registering' 'rather than deliberate tampering'.[60] So it would appear that nearly all the clergy accepted the Elizabethan church settlement, with or without mental reservations. Such ready compliance on their part was probably not received by their bishops with unalloyed delight. Bishop Jewel doubtless epitomized the reactions of most of his brethren when he commented guardedly that it would be 'no easy matter to drag the chariot without horses, especially up hill'.[61]

The bishops' sense of frustration was intensified by the lack of suitable candidates for ordination. They complained that at Oxford and Cambridge during Mary's reign there were 'scarcely two individuals there with Protestant sympathies; and they were so dejected and broken in spirit that they could do nothing'.[62] To add to the difficulties, the devastating outbreaks of influenza in 1557–8 had caused severe clerical mortality. So desperate was the shortage of potential clerics and so urgent the need that some bishops were driven to ordain 'mechanics' and other unsuitable candidates, for which they were sharply rapped over the knuckles by the queen.[63] The difficulties encountered by Richard Davies are reflected in the ordinations conducted by him between 1561 and 1565. At first, they were a mere trickle: from November 1561 to March 1562 there were only three; and from March 1562 to March 1563 there were twelve. However, it should be noted that a number of candidates from St David's diocese were ordained at Bangor during these years, and others may have been ordained in neighbouring dioceses like Llandaff, St Asaph, or Hereford, whose cathedrals were actually nearer than their own. At St David's itself, numbers picked up appreciably from March 1563 to March 1564, when there were twenty-four, and in the next year thirty-six, dropping to fifteen in 1565–6. Only two of these ordinands were graduates, though another was described as *scholaris* and two more as *literati*.[64] At Bangor, ordinations were either more satisfactory, or were more fully recorded. In 1560 there were twenty-seven; in 1561 twenty; in 1563 twelve; in 1564 fifteen; and in 1565 eighteen. Here again, though, graduates were depressingly few in number, only one being recorded.[65]

It was hardly likely that graduates would be recruited in any numbers to the Church in Wales when it remained as desperately poor as it had ever

---

[60] W. H. Frère, *The Marian Reaction in relation to the English Clergy* (London, 1896), p. 31n.

[61] *Zurich Letters*, I. 45.

[62] Ibid., I. 33; cf. pp. 11, 29, 40, 55, 77, 92.

[63] *WRE*, p. 171.

[64] *BBCS*, XIV. 125–38.

[65] Pryce, *Bangor*, pp. 52–4.

been, if not poorer, with a large proportion of its benefices being rated as worth less than £10 a year, and its unbeneficed clergy miserably remunerated. As a result, the old familiar deficiencies of pluralism and non-residence were still in evidence, and there was a continuing tendency for well-qualified graduates to emigrate to England to seek more satisfying rewards. The Welsh bishops themselves, by holding benefices *in commendam*, were hardly setting a good example, and many of their higher clergy followed in their footsteps. In 1563 all four of the archdeacons of St David's diocese were pluralists, and even Hugh Price, the treasurer, 'who by his office should always be resident, was allowed to dwell elsewhere by dispensation under the great seal'.[66] The treasurer of Llandaff was rector of St Fagan's and vicar of Llangatwg-feibion-Afel; and his colleague, the archdeacon, John Smith, was not only rector of Merthyr Tydfil but was normally resident at Exeter, where he was chancellor, and also held several livings in that diocese.[67] In 1567 most of the Bangor chapter were absentees, and only Dean Robert Evans preached.

Nowhere were the ill effects of impoverishment more apparent than in the shortage of preachers. Throughout England and Wales there was 'a great and alarming scarcity of preachers', 'especially those who had any ability'.[68] It was not unusual for a cathedral chapter to have few or no preachers, and as late as 1585 Archbishop Whitgift deplored a state of affairs which meant that out of 9,000 parishes in England there were scarcely 600 which could adequately maintain preachers.[69] In Llandaff, Bishop Hugh Jones declared that there were only two livings in Glamorgan and two in Monmouthshire capable of sustaining preachers, and for the rest he had to procure preachers from other dioceses at his own expense.[70] In Wales generally preachers were in very short supply, especially those who could preach in the native language, not only because of the poverty of livings but also because of the lack of a Welsh Bible and an apologetic literature in Welsh – a dire scarcity that is all too apparent in all the reports returned by the bishops in 1561. Yet preaching was regarded by Protestant reformers as critical; more essential even than the printing-press for spreading the word, especially amid the large illiterate sector of the population. The new reformed minister was no longer looked upon primarily as a priest offering a sacrifice, as his medieval predecessor had been, but a preacher expounding the word of God. Preaching was at the heart of

[66] PRO, SP12/66/26.
[67] Williams, *GCH*, IV. 229.
[68] *Zurich Letters*, I. 98.
[69] Haugaard, *Elizabeth and Reformation*, pp. 166–7.
[70] Williams, *GCH*, IV. 229; *The Stradling Correspondence*, ed. J. M. Traherne (London, 1840), pp. 83–7.

Protestant edification, on which the dissemination of the scriptures depended; and the shortage of preachers was a fatal stumbling-block to the progress of the Reformation.

It is doubtful whether the laity, by and large, were any more enthusiastic than the clergy about the nature of Elizabeth's settlement, although they may, overall, have been able to accommodate themselves more readily to it. Catholic opponents were very few among them, but there were two gentlemen from Glamorgan, cousins to one another, who openly flew the flag of opposition: Sir Edward Carne of Ewenni, and Sir Thomas Stradling of St Donat's. Carne, a distinguished lawyer and diplomat, had been Queen Mary's ambassador at Rome, the only English representative permanently maintained abroad at the time. He was to have been replaced by Thomas Goldwell, but Mary's death intervened, and Carne was instructed to remain at his post until a final decision was taken about relations with Rome. He remained loyal to Elizabeth's interests, writing to inform her about the friendly disposition of Rome and Spain as he saw it, but letting her know about the unsuccessful attempts of Henri II of France to win support for Mary Stuart's claims to the English throne. He was, however, reluctant – possibly even afraid – to return home in view of his adherence to the Roman faith and his failure to secure recognition by the pope of the queen's title to the throne. Yet when the pope conferred upon him the wardenship of the English hospital at Rome, he feared that to accept it would so irritate Elizabeth that she would deprive his wife and family of the monastic estates he had acquired at Ewenni. A state paper presented to the pope urged him to allow Carne to 'go whither he please, provided he do not return to England, in which case the queen will readily allow him to retain his revenue, so long as he lives elsewhere than at Rome'. Death soon intervened to relieve the pope and Edward Carne of their dilemmas. The squire of Ewenni was buried in the church of SS. Andrew and Gregory at Rome, though his will was successfully proved in England.[71]

Carne's cousin, Sir Thomas Stradling of St Donat's, had been imprisoned back in 1551 – probably for religious reasons.[72] In Mary's reign, restored to high favour, he was active in the punishment of heresy. At first, he accepted Elizabeth's settlement reluctantly, but in 1559 his Catholic inclinations were powerfully reinforced by what he interpreted as a clear token of divine approval for Catholics and disavowal of Protestants, when a great oak tree crashed down on his estates and left an impression of a cross thought to be miraculous. Sir Thomas sedulously fostered the belief

---

[71] *DWB*, s.n. Edward Carne; *CSP Rome*, I. 15–16; PRO, PCC Loftus 21; Williams, *Modern Wales*, p. 68; Williams, *GCH*, IV. 232.

[72] *CSP Dom., 1547–80*, p. 176; ibid., *Add., 1547–65*, pp. 510, 512.

in 'the miracle of St Donat's', and in 1560 had four pictures made of the cross. He sent one to his son, David, and daughter, Damascine, a nun, both of whom were living as Catholic exiles on the Continent. Among Sir Thomas's friends was Sir Edward Waldegrave, who was closely questioned about his connection with the 'miracle'. William Cecil, alarmed by the possibility of a wider Catholic plot, involving the possible arrival in England of a papal nuncio and the enlisting of English representatives at the Council of Trent, clapped Stradling and Waldegrave in the Tower in 1561 and kept them there for two years. When Stradling was released he was dropped from the commission of the peace and kept under close surveillance.[73]

Stradling was not the only prominent layman and justice of the peace under suspicion. Archbishop Parker's return of 1564 on the attitude of the justices of the peace in Wales survives only for the diocese of Llandaff;[74] but there is no reason to believe that the state of affairs there was markedly different from conditions elsewhere in the country. Parker was more than a little cautious over the soundness of the justices of the peace in the south-eastern diocese. All he would commit himself to concerning the eleven justices listed by him was, 'I know them not, and some times informers serve their own turn and gratify their friends.'[75] The archbishop's hesitancy was justified. Among the eleven he named were Thomas Lewis of Y Fan, who was afterwards known to employ a recusant priest as schoolmaster to his children, and Christopher Turberville, who belonged to what was to prove the most devotedly recusant family in Glamorgan.[76] It was hardly surprising that the laity in Llandaff diocese should be tepid, not to say hostile. They had had a very uninspiring start to the new regime, with the trimmer Anthony Kitchen as their first Elizabethan bishop. Nor had the situation in Llandaff been helped when he died in 1563, and Elizabeth left the unfortunate diocese vacant for three years. In a letter written to Parker in 1565 Richard Davies urged him to choose a bishop who might 'set forth the glory of God and show light in these places of extreme darkness', which had, of all dioceses, 'most lacked good doctrine and true knowledge of God and where, in matters of religion', there had been 'no reformation or redress' since the queen's accession.[77]

---

[73] D. Williams, 'The miracle at St Donat's', *The Welsh Review* (1947), 33–8; R. A. Griffiths, 'The Stradlings of St Donat's', *Morgannwg*, VII (1963), 34–7; G. Williams, 'The Stradling Family', in R. Denning (ed.), *St Donat's Castle and Atlantic College* (Cowbridge, 1983), pp. 23–9.

[74] Bateson, *Camden Miscellany*, IX. 11–23.

[75] Ibid., p. 51.

[76] Williams, *GCH*, IV. 223, 235–6.

[77] BL, Lansdowne MS. 8, pp. 193, 195, 199, 202; cf. Parker, *Correspondence*, pp. 257–61.

Of all the Welsh bishops none was more devastating than Davies in his attacks on the gentry and the justices of the peace, in his own diocese and elsewhere, for 'defending papistry, superstition, and idolatry'. He was also severe in his criticisms of the pressure brought on churchwardens and others to give advance warning to those who were in danger of being brought to book in times of visitation.[78] In Bangor diocese, Bishop Robinson in 1567 was similarly disapproving of the stubborn survival of Catholic practices in his diocese.[79] Such a state of affairs must have been brought about by collusion between members of the clergy and some of the influential laity. When the most powerful gentleman of Robinson's diocese, Sir Richard Bulkeley, was reported to have abstained from Anglican communion services for sixteen years, it was hardly to be wondered at that Catholic habits should flourish so freely.

Most of the laity and clergy were alike content to accept the State Church outwardly, though no doubt with all kinds of inward reservations. Father David Augustine Baker was later to present a vivid sketch of how essentially unmoved by the change of religion were the inhabitants of his native town of Abergavenny, and doubtless many other places too:

> after the said change made by Queen Elizabeth, the greatest part even of those who in their judgements and affections had before been Catholics, did not well discern any great fault, novelty or difference from the former religion . . . save only the change of language . . . in the which difference they conceived nothing of substance or essence to be. And so easily digested the new religion and accommodated themselves hereto; especially in Wales and other like places remotest from London.[80]

Among such conformers were those who still continued to be sincerely attached to the Catholic faith, but who had, nevertheless, to be sharply reminded by Laurence Vaux that true believers must keep away from the parish services:

> The pope cannot dispense any of the laity to entangle themselves with the schism . . . If ye associate yourselves at sacraments or service that is contrary to the unity of Christ His church, ye fall into schism . . . the

---

[78] *Funeral sermon preached at Carmarthen on the death of the earl of Essex* (London, 1577), no pagination.

[79] PRO SP12/44/27; cf. D. Mathew, 'Some Elizabethan documents', *BBCS* VI (1931–3), 70–8.

[80] A. H. Dodd, 'The Church in Wales in the age of the Reformation', *Welsh Church Congress Handbook* (1953), 31.

wrath of God hangeth over you, and dying in that state shall lose the everlasting life of heaven.[81]

The majority of the populace were confused, bewildered, ignorant, or apathetic; many of them were left so 'punch-drunk' by frequent change as to become unmoved by either Catholic or Protestant extreme. Some respected the church 'by law established'; others were unsure what the future might hold in the event of Elizabeth's marriage or death – and none of the Tudors had hitherto been long livers! A handful of the bigger landowners considered their possessions to be more secure under the erastian Elizabeth. Not a few were understandably cautious about revealing their position too boldly or precipitately. Most of all, perhaps, their reaction signified that people stolidly refused to allow decrees promulgated by distant London governments to make much practical impact on them. They continued to adhere to their long-established assumptions and observances, which offered a measure or protection and solace in face of the misfortunes and ups-and downs of the average person's existence. During the early years of the reign, particularly, there continued to be great clouds of uncertainty, ambivalence, mind-changing, uneasy compromise, and a mass of downright apathy or unawareness. There were some 'church papists', other lukewarm conformers, and a great many stolid and indifferent 'neuters' who had no very defined opinions at all. The initial response to Elizabeth's settlement may not have been at all unacceptable to her, since she was more concerned with political loyalty than religious zeal; but it did not bode too well for a Church whose adherents were required – in theory at least – to show an intelligent appreciation of its tenets and worship.

Even so, the most insurmountable obstacle to the progress of the Reformation in Wales was the absence of a Welsh Bible and Prayer Book. The word of God, as Salesbury had written in 1551, was 'bound in fetters',[82] or else, to quote Bishop Robinson, it was 'closed up in an unknown tongue'.[83] Just as the Danish kingdom had brought the 'cultural imperialism' of a Danish Bible to the Norwegians, or the Swedes a Swedish text to the Finns, so the English had done to the Welsh, not even allowing them the use of a Latin text as they had done with the Irish.[84] William Salesbury took up the cry once more in his home diocese of St Asaph. Here, he found a small, but intensely enthusiastic band of supporters responding to his appeal. The arrival of a new bishop there in 1560 may

---

[81] Dixon, *Church of England*, VI. 217–20.
[82] *KLIB*, ed. J. Fisher (Cardiff, 1931), dedication.
[83] PRO, SP12/44/27.
[84] R. D. Edwards, *Church and State in Tudor Ireland* (Dublin, 1935), pp. 134–5.

have given his hopes a fresh fillip. Richard Davies was a returned exile, a convinced Protestant, who had seen for himself in many parts of Europe the beneficial effect of scriptural translations.[85] He and Salesbury may have been joined by other enthusiasts like Humphrey Lhuyd,[86] Renaissance scholar and literary enthusiast, Gruffudd Hiraethog,[87] friend of William Salesbury and literary tutor of Richard Davies, and members of the influential Myddleton family.[88]

The effects soon became apparent. Davies and/or Salesbury were almost certainly responsible for the articles drawn up at this time which suggested, though without success, that it might be made 'lawful for such Welsh or Cornish children, as could speak no English, to learn the catechism in the Welsh tongue or the Cornish language'.[89] Among Davies' papers was an 'Appeal', written perhaps by Salesbury and directed to the Privy Council in 1561, drawing a distinction between those 'few' who, 'with their heart to the uttermost of their power teach and declare God's holy word unto the people in the vulgar Welsh tongue', and those who shirk their duty or actively oppose it.[90] The Privy Council was urged to empower a body of the 'godliest and best learned men in divinity or knowledge of the holy scripture or the Welsh tongue' to 'traduct the book of the Lord's Testament into the vulgar Welsh tongue', 'for the expulsion of such miserable darkness for the lack of the shining light of Christ's gospel'.[91] Later that year, at a St Asaph diocesan council on 12 November 1561, the new bishop, Thomas Davies, ordered his clergy that after 'the epistle and gospel in English the same should also be read in Welsh', together with the catechism read in Welsh every Sunday, and in English. The Litany was also to be sung or said on Wednesdays and Fridays.[92] The only available Welsh translation in print of the epistles and gospels was Salesbury's *Kynniver Llith a Ban*, and that of parts of the catechism by Sir John Price. There was as yet no translation of the Litany, but in 1562 Salesbury's old printing partner, John Walley, paid the Stationers' Company 4*d.* for a licence to print copies of it in Welsh. No copy of this work is extant, but it was, presumably, a translation by Salesbury.[93]

[85] 'Epistol at y Cembru', *Testament Newydd ein Arglwydd Iesu Christ* (Caernarfon, 1850), p. iii.

[86] D. J. Bowen, 'Cywyddau Gruffudd Hiraethog i dri o awduron y Dadeni', *TCS* (1974–5), 103–31.

[87] D. J. Bowen, *Gruffudd Hiraethog a'i Oes* (Cardiff, 1958).

[88] D. R. Thomas, *The Life and Work of Richard Davies and William Salesbury* (Oswestry, 1902), pp. 16–17.

[89] BL, Egerton MS. no. 2350, fo. 54.

[90] Thomas, *Davies and Salesbury*, pp. 3–5, cf. W. Pierce, *The Life and Times of John Penry* (London, 1923), p. 109.

[91] R. B. Jones, *William Salesbury* (Cardiff, 1994), p. 51.

[92] Thomas, *Davies and Salesbury*, pp. 72–3.

[93] Ibid., p. 71.

The group which had thus been pressing for scriptural translations would seem to have come to the conclusion that to attain their ends they needed the blessing of Parliament. It has cogently been argued that no Act of Parliament would be needed to allow the Bible to be translated,[94] nor indeed had Salesbury sought one before proceeding with *Kynniver Llith a Ban*. That is, indeed, perfectly true; but it is very unlikely that, without authorization from queen and Parliament, permission would have been given for a translation of the service book and its use in parish churches. Therefore, in 1563, when Parliament and Convocation were in session, this offered the Welsh group a convenient opportunity to press their claims. They had already directed appeals to the Privy Council and, fortunately for them, they were not without sympathizers in high places. Archbishop Parker was in close touch with Bishop Richard Davies and would later assign him a share in the translation of the English 'Bishops' Bible'. The archbishop was himself deeply interested in the early Christian history of Britain[95] and in Anglo-Saxon and other versions of the scriptures. He would remain in correspondence with Davies and Salesbury on the subject;[96] so on more than one score he could be regarded as someone likely to be open to any appeal for translating the Bible and Prayer Book and extending knowledge of them. If Parker was the queen's chief ecclesiastical adviser, William Cecil was her principal lay counsellor. He, too, was greatly fascinated by British antiquities, may well have had indirect contacts with Davies when the latter was in exile,[97] and would maintain links with him and Salesbury on scholarly topics. Cecil may, moreover, have been seriously perturbed by the possibility of conservative Wales becoming exposed to Catholic intrigues at this time. In mid-February 1563 he had sent a letter to Sir Thomas Smith expressing profound concern that Catholic traitors had planned to land forces in Wales with the intention of proclaiming Mary, queen of Scotland, as queen of England;[98] just as an even more serious threat from Spain was to speed up publication of the Welsh Bible in 1588. It has additionally been pointed out that Dr Ellis Price may have been able to exert some influence in this respect, since he was on terms of friendship and clientage with the earl of

[94] G. R. Elton, 'Wales in Parliament, 1542–81', *Welsh Society and Nationhood*, ed. R. R. Davies *et al.* (Cardiff, 1984), pp. 108–21.
[95] W. W. Greg, 'Books and bookmen in the correspondence of Archbishop Parker', *The Library*, XVI (1935), 247ff.; R. Flower, 'William Salesbury, Richard Davies, and Archbishop Parker', *NLWJ*, II (1941), 7–14; *WRE*, pp. 212–13.
[96] Flower, *NLWJ*, II. 7–14; idem, *NLWJ*, III. 11–14; G. Williams, 'Bishop Sulien, Bishop Richard Davies, and Archbishop Parker', *NLWJ*, V (1945), 15–19.
[97] G. Williams, *Bywyd ac Amserau yr Esgob Richard Davies* (Cardiff, 1953), pp. 21–4.
[98] T. Wright, *Queen Elizabeth and Her Times* (2 vols. Oxford, 1838), I. 127.

Leicester,[99] though there is no evidence that either was specially interested in a Welsh translation. The queen herself was singled out for special praise with regard to the part she may have played by a number of Welsh littérateurs, including among them Salesbury, Davies, and William Morgan.[100] They suggested that her particular affection for Wales gave her a personal interest in this matter of scriptural translation. One thing appears certain: in view of the lynx-eyed vigilance she maintained over the use of the Prayer Book, a Welsh version would hardly have been allowed without her specific consent.

Whoever may, or may not, have been well-disposed towards a Welsh version, it was not government policy to promote the Act of 1563 for rendering the Bible into Welsh. It has been shown that, on the contrary, the Act was a private one, whose sponsors were themselves obliged to meet the substantial fees for its passage through Parliament.[101] The identity of those responsible for a bill of such immense significance to Wales is not known for certain, but it seems inconceivable that anyone other than the small group around Davies and Salesbury would have taken it on. It was introduced into the House of Commons on 22 February, presumably by one of the 'St Asaph circle', Humphrey Lhuyd, MP for Denbigh.[102] It wound its way somewhat slowly through all its stages by 27 March. It then went on to the House of Lords, where Richard Davies was the only Welsh member of the House present at all its stages and must surely have overseen it in the upper chamber.[103] It was finally passed by both Houses on 5–6 April 1563.[104] Its preamble referred to the 'unspeakable joy' given to English-speaking subjects by the Prayer Book, but as English was not understood by the 'most and greatest number' of Her Majesty's subjects in Wales, they were 'utterly destituted' of the Word and remained in 'the like or rather more darkness and ignorance than they were in the time of papistry'. The Act therefore required the bishops of Wales and Hereford (whose diocese contained many Welsh-speakers) to take order among themselves that the whole Bible and Book of Common Prayer 'be truly and exactly translated into the British or Welsh tongue by 1 March 1565' and that it be subsequently used in all those places where the language was 'commonly spoken'. In the mean time, the clergy were to read the epistle and gospel in Welsh, and the Lord's Prayer, Thirty-nine Articles (agreed at

[99] C. Ashton, *Bywyd ac Amserau'r Esgob William Morgan* (Treherbert, 1891), p. 64.
[100] In the introductory material to the New Testament of 1567 and the Bible of 1588.
[101] Elton, *Society and Nationhood*, p. 119.
[102] R. G. Gruffydd, 'Humphrey Lhuyd a Deddf Cyfieithu'r Beibl i'r Gymraeg', *LlC*, IV (1956), 114–15.
[103] *Journals of the House of Lords* (London, 1846), I. 610–13.
[104] For the text of the Act, I. Bowen, *The Statutes of Wales* (London, 1908), pp. 149–51.

the Convocation of 1563), the Ten Commandments, and the Litany in Welsh. In the House of Lords an amendment put back the date of completion until 1567, and a further modification called for a copy of the English Bible and Prayer Book to be placed alongside the Welsh versions so that by conferring both together the people 'might the sooner attain to the knowledge of the English tongue' – a pious hope never fulfilled in practice! What gave rise to this clause relating to the English Bible and Prayer Book was the opposition to the use of Welsh in public worship voiced at that time in Parliament; opposition which was to continue for at least another twenty years afterwards.[105]

The Act was one of tremendous importance for Wales. For the first time it gave official sanction and a specific mandate for a Welsh Bible. That represented a major reversal of policy on the part of the government in relation to the language of public worship in Wales, and it promised to overcome what had hitherto been the biggest hindrance to the progress of the Reformation there. Its prime concern was to help convert the Welsh more speedily to the Protestant faith and thereby to achieve greater political cohesion, not to save the Welsh language, though in due course it would accomplish that as well.

But passing an Act of Parliament was only the beginning of the process, and there were other serious obstacles to overcome in the short and long term. Although the tasks of translation and the authorization of the completed texts were entrusted to the bishops, only one of them showed himself at all concerned with the responsibility; and it was the bishop of London, Edmund Grindal, and not Welsh bishops, who ultimately authorized the work. Furthermore, there were no printing-presses in Wales, so the books would have to be printed in London by compositors who did not understand the language and would make innumerable errors.[106] Salesbury first came to an understanding with his old ally, the printer, John Walley, in the hope of being able to get around the Bible-printing monopoly rights of Jugge and Cawood;[107] though in the end it was Henry Denham who printed 'at the costs and charges of Humphrey Toy'. For the privilege of entering the Prayer Book in the Stationers' register, Toy paid 12*d.*, and a further 12*d.* for the New Testament.[108] Printing in London inevitably made the process all the more burdensome financially, and the Act made no provision for financial assistance, though 1,000 marks had earlier been made available to help pay for the printing of the English

---

[105] M. Kyffin, *Deffynniad Ffydd Eglwys Loegr*, ed. W. P. Williams (Bangor, 1908), pp. xiii–xiv.
[106] *W and R*, p. 156.
[107] Elton, *Society and Nationhood*, p. 120.
[108] Ibid.

Bible.[109] If, as was originally intended, the translation was to be made from the text of the Great Bible,[110] that would have been a comparatively straightforward exercise. If, however, as Salesbury and Davies proposed, it was to be made from the best available original texts of the scriptures, that would call for a much higher degree of scholarly expertise and intellectual judgement on the part of the translators. Salesbury, for example, insisted on acquiring and making use of Beza's work on the New Testament, which did not appear until 1565.[111]

Moreover, the translators needed to have not only an excellent knowledge of the classical tongues but ideally also had to be men thoroughly imbued with an intuitive awareness of the genius of their own language; they needed to be writers as well as scholars. Although Welsh prose had a tradition that was centuries-old, the authors of the sixteenth century constantly complained about the paucity of Welsh texts to which they had access and the fewness of the patterns on which to base their own writings. Welsh, like many other European languages, was at this time going through a difficult transitional stage between its medieval and its modern form, and handling it effectively would be a delicate operation. If possible, the language ought to be freed from outmoded terms and usages; not overdependent on any one dialect; flexible and intelligible, yet dignified, resonant, and preserving the classic qualities of uniformity, strength, and purity associated with the old literary tradition. All this had to be achieved within three or four years in accordance with the exacting demands of the Act; it was setting a herculean labour to translate the Prayer Book, Psalter, and Bible in that space of time. The enterprise demanded of the men who proposed to embark upon it a daunting combination of virtues. They would need a clear vision, an unswerving dedication, and a readiness to commit themselves whole-heartedly to what they saw as the highest service of God and the greatest good of their countrymen. With the human resources of a small nation numbering not much more than a quarter of a million on which to draw, the Welsh were singularly fortunate to find that men of this calibre appeared at the right time. As Salesbury had earlier predicted, if the task were postponed for another generation, it would be too late.[112]

If the five bishops mentioned in the Act ever consulted one another at all about their joint responsibility for accomplishing the translation, they must quickly have delegated it to one of their number, Richard Davies. Fired up as he was with the prospect, it must almost immediately have dawned on

---

[109] Thomas, *Davies and Salesbury*, p. 102.

[110] I. Thomas, *Y Testament Newydd Cymraeg, 1551–1620* (Cardiff, 1972), pp. 140–1.

[111] Williams, *Richard Davies*, p. 105.

[112] *Oll Synnwyr Pen*, G. H. Hughes, *Rhagymadroddion, 1547–1648* (Cardiff, 1951), pp. 10–11.

him – if, indeed, he had not realized it before ever the Act was passed – that to make real progress he would have to enlist the help of William Salesbury. As Davies was himself to confess to the Welsh people in his prefatory letter to the New Testament: 'Your bishops, with the help of William Salesbury,[113] bring you in Welsh and in print holy scripture.'[114] Both Davies and Salesbury appeared at first to have been working individually and apart from one another. It is distinctly conceivable that Salesbury had been steadily beavering away at his translations after 1551 – even during Mary's reign, though there was then no hope of publishing them. Unless he had done so, it is difficult to see how he could have completed all he did by 1567. Davies, too, would seem to have started on his own. At his palace at Abergwili he maintained a stimulating and attractive household where clerics and men of affairs, bards and squires, lawyers and scholars, all rubbed shoulders with each other. It was a hive of Renaissance scholarship and a workshop of Reformation theology, which Davies found conducive to his own literary efforts.[115] Here he was to translate the books he had been given to undertake for the Bishops' Bible; here also he tried his hand at translating into Welsh a number of epistles – 1 and 2 Timothy, Titus, and Philemon. What he did was basically to turn them into Welsh from the English text of the Great Bible, and his efforts are still preserved in Gwysane MS 27.[116] But he found the process slow and unrewarding; so, to expedite progress, in 1564 he invited his coadjutor, Salesbury, down to Abergwili. The latter enjoyed his experience there; not merely working with Davies in congenial intellectual surroundings, but also visiting other scholars in the vicinity at Cydweli and Brecknock. Even with Salesbury at Abergwili, however, the going was hard. Davies was the bishop of a large and sprawling diocese, which made heavy demands on him, and he had also committed himself to translating part of the 'Bishops' Bible'. On 19 March 1566 he was writing disconsolately to Archbishop Parker, acknowledging receipt of a portion of the English Bible and promising, 'I am in hand to perform your request and will use as much diligence and speed as I can, having small help for that or the Welsh Bible. Mr Salisbury only taketh pain with me.'[117] Since there was no mention in the letter of any help from Huet, it may not be until this point, or even later, that he was drafted in to assist.

---

[113] *Testament Newydd* (1950), p. vii.

[114] 'I may dy Escopion trwy gynhorthwy William Salesbury yn dwyn yt yn Gymraeg ac yn brint yr yscrythur 'lan' ('Thy bishops bring thee with the help of William Salesbury in Welsh and in print the holy scripture').

[115] Williams, *Richard Davies*, chap 5.

[116] Thomas, *Testament Newydd*, pp. 141–7. D. R. Thomas mistakenly supposed that they represented translations undertaken after 1567, *Davies and Salesbury*, chap. 5.

[117] Parker, *Correspondence*, p. 265.

Before the end of the year 1566 it would have been plainly apparent to the translators that all the works which the Act had called upon them to produce by March 1567 were not going to be anywhere near complete by then. Translation of the Old Testament and the Apocrypha did not seem to have been started, so if at that late stage the translators were to succeed in getting even a part of the assignment in shape for publication in time, the manuscripts would need to be taken to London without further delay in order to enable the printers to begin their end of the operation. Salesbury therefore set off for London, complete with the manuscript of the Book of Common Prayer, the Psalter, and the New Testament. Since Davies would be there for sessions of the House of Lords and the Upper House of Convocation, and Huet for the Lower House of Convocation, it is not out of the question that some of the translation may actually have been undertaken in London as well as in Abergwili,[118] especially since the Prayer Book (wholly Salesbury's work) was the first volume to be published. Salesbury found lodgings at St Paul's churchyard with Humphrey Toy,[119] a merchant with Carmarthen connections, who was putting up much of the finance for the venture. Toy's printer, Henry Denham, seems to have modelled the Welsh Prayer Book on the English one of 1564 printed by Cawood, the queen's printer. It was a large handsome folio volume of some 200 pages,[120] evidently designed to be used mainly in churches rather than by individuals. It is not certainly known how many copies of it were printed at this time, but the Act of 1563 had required that there should be one bought by every church with a Welsh-speaking congregation; half the cost to be met by the incumbent, and the other half by the parishioners.[121] As there were about 800 parishes in Wales and some Welsh-speaking ones over the border in England, that suggests than an edition of not less than about 1,000 copies was issued. The accounts of the Swansea church-wardens recorded that for their copy of the Prayer Book (the 'Welsh communion book', they described it), they paid 6s. 8d., and their vicar a further 6s. 8d.[122] – though this is not specified.

The bishops had been called upon by the Act to 'view, peruse and allow' the text of the Prayer Book, which they may indeed have done before it was published on 7 May 1567, since all of them, except Hugh Jones of Llandaff, were in London at the time.[123] The Stationers' register, however,

---

[118] Gruffydd, *JHSCW*, XVII. 47.

[119] *DWB*, s.n. Humfrey Toy.

[120] For a photographic reproduction of the volume, see *Llyfr Gweddi Gyffredin 1567*, ed. G. M. Richards and G. Williams (Cardiff, 1966).

[121] Bowen, *Statutes*, p. 150.

[122] University College of Swansea, Swansea Churchwardens' Accounts, 1559–1626.

[123] Gruffydd, *JHSCW*, XVII. 45.

stated explicitly that the book had been 'authorized by my lord of London'[124] (Bishop Grindal). Unlike the English Prayer Books of the period, the Welsh one included a translation of the Psalter. Nowhere in the text of the Prayer Book was there any formal identification of the translator(s); but two well-informed Elizabethan commentators, John Wynn and George Owen, attributed the work to Richard Davies.[125] Until about forty or fifty years ago that ascription was generally accepted. But it has long since been contended that Salesbury was in truth the author, and that was confirmed beyond any doubt by the exceptionally rigorous analyses published by Dr Isaac Thomas in 1967.[126] The text on which the book was based was, as would be expected, the English Prayer Book, the non-scriptural parts of which were translated directly from the English into Welsh.[127] The scriptural extracts – the epistles and the gospels – were rendered into Welsh from the original Greek, Hebrew, and Latin sources, just as they had been for *Kynniver Llith a Ban*, between the text of which and that of the Prayer Book there is a close 'family' resemblance.[128] For this purpose Salesbury, with his customary precise and scrupulous scholarship, used the best texts that were available to him, including the work not only of pioneers like Erasmus, Luther, or Tyndale, but also that of the most recent scholars such as Estienne and Beza.[129] A close and accurate translator, and a master of his own language, Salesbury was thoroughly deserving of following in Cranmer's footsteps. His Prayer Book, whatever the faults of its orthography may have been (see below, chap. 13), has fittingly been described as 'one of the major triumphs of humanist prose in Welsh'.[130]

The New Testament, which appeared later in the year, apparently without having been subject to any acknowledged examination, was a composite work: the outcome of a decidedly unequal partnership between Salesbury, Davies, and Huet. Salesbury carried by far the greatest part of the burden. He was responsible for all the books of the New Testament except six – 1 Timothy, Hebrews, James, and 1 and 2 Peter, which Davies undertook, and the Book of Revelation, which fell to Huet's lot. Salesbury's unresting exertions in completing the great bulk of these translations of 1567 himself were quite staggering. No less striking were the

---

[124] Ibid., p. 47.

[125] Wynn, *Gwydir Family*, p. 65; Owen, *Penbrokshire*, I. 240.

[126] Thomas, *Testament Newydd*, chap. 5, especially p. 163; W. A. Mathias, 'Astudiaeth o weithgarwch llenyddol William Salesbury' (MA thesis, Wales, 1949); *Llyfr Gweddi 1567*, introd.

[127] *Llyfr Gweddi 1567*, pp. xxxi–xxxiv.

[128] Ibid., pp. xxiv–xxx.

[129] Thomas, *Testament Newydd*, p. 260.

[130] Gruffydd, *JHSCW*, XVII. 53.

range and precision of his scholarship. At the outset, it seems to have been intended that the translators should do no more than turn the text of the Great Bible into Welsh.[131] Salesbury, for his part, envisaged an intellectual enterprise far more ambitious and valuable than that. While he was certainly willing to make the most meticulous use of existing English translations, including the out-of-favour Geneva Bible, which the 'Bishops' Bible' was intended to replace, he also insisted on going to texts in the original languages of scripture and using them to the best advantage, being enough of a scholar to trust to his own judgement whenever that seemed necessary and not having to rely on anyone else's.[132] His three guiding principles were: fidelity to the words of the original text; variety of expression so as to ensure intelligibility; and a dignity of expression consonant with the majesty of the word of God. His weakness was that in his undue concern to create the appropriate impact on the literary and intellectual audience of the time, he tended to overlook the pressing necessity of making his text readily usable by the ordinary parish priest, and intelligible to the man and woman in the pew (see below, chap. 13). Richard Davies, on the other hand, although perhaps not as fine a scholar, was more sensitively attuned to the needs of the rank-and-file and, with them in mind, wrote in a simpler and more natural style. This difference in attitude between the two partners towards the presentation of their material may, in later years, have led to an irreconcilable rift between them. As for Huet, it was as well, possibly, that he was only given one book to translate. He was not a conspicuous scholar, and he clung very close to the text of the Great Bible. Even worse, his Welsh savoured far too strongly of the south-western dialect of Dyfed[133] – though Huet himself hailed from Breconshire – to be intelligible to natives of other provinces in Wales.

In addition to his translation of some of the epistles, Davies had another major contribution to make to the New Testament of 1567: his 'Epistol at y Cembru' (Letter to the Welsh Nation), with which he prefaced it.[134] In this he rehearsed those themes of Church history dear to the hearts of all Protestant reformers but gave them a distinctively Welsh texture. Like all his fellows, Davies was anxious to prove that the Reformation was no newly dreamt-up heresy but the restoration of the Church to the purity in which it had existed in the time of the Apostles.[135] He believed implicitly in the conformity of the Reformed Church to the scriptural model, referring with

[131] Thomas, *Testament Newydd*, pp. 140–1, 233.
[132] Ibid., pp. 260–1.
[133] Ibid., p. 299.
[134] 'Epistol at y Cembru', English translation in A. O. Evans, *Memorandum on the Legality of the Welsh Bible* (Cardiff, 1925), pp. 83–124.
[135] 'Gwae'r neb ailw hon yn newydd, o ba vodd bynnac y gwnel, ai o anwybod ai trwy

ineffable pride to the 'second flowering of the gospel' ('ail flodeuad yr Efengyl').[136] Like other leading Protestants, he had no doubts that the historical reason for the decline of the Church down the ages had been the corruptions introduced by successive popes and their agents as the result of their usurpation of authority. In Britain, ever since Tyndale's time, Reformers had been passionately interested in this aspect of Church history, which had become one of the burning topics of controversy between them and their Catholic opponents during Elizabeth's reign.[137] Both Davies and Salesbury were immersed in the subject and were especially eager to see how the Protestant revamping of history could be fitted into that framework of the British story laid out by Geoffrey of Monmouth. Davies referred lovingly to the conviction that Britain had first been converted to Christianity by Joseph of Arimathea, who had planted the faith in all its gospel immaculacy.[138] It had subsequently been maintained among the Britons intact and uncontaminated in spite of Roman persecution, Pelagian and other heresies, Anglo-Saxon paganism, and – most crucial of all – in face of that debased version of Christianity tainted by papal superstition which Augustine of Canterbury had brought to England as the emissary of Rome. Only as a result of being forced by their Anglo-Saxon enemies to accept adulterated papism at the point of the sword had the British and their descendants, the Welsh, eventually been dragged down into the mire of Roman superstition and idolatry. Now, after centuries of benighted ignorance and papalist corruption, Davies argued, the people of Wales were being led back to the realm of truth and light by virtue of the gospel once again becoming as freely available in their midst in their own language as it had originally been in the early centuries of their history.

This 'reconstruction' of their history proved to be compellingly persuasive and appealing to many of Davies's compatriots on three counts. It bonded the Reformation to some of the oldest and most venerable themes of their history. Again, it blunted the commonly made suggestion that the Reformation was an upstart heresy, lacking roots in earlier faith and history; it sought to show, on the contrary, that it was grounded in the earliest and most glorious phase of Christianity in Britain. Finally, it met head-on the criticism that the Reformation represented an alien, English

---

wybot, yw dwyllo y hun ac y hudo'r bopul' ('Woe unto him who calls this [Testament] new, howsoever he does so, whether from ignorance or knowledge, to deceive himself and to ensnare the people').

[136] Cf. Salesbury's reference to having heard at Oxford the tidings of 'Christ's second birth', Jones, *Salesbury*, p. 38.

[137] G. Williams, *Reformation Views of Church History* (London, 1970), chap 5.

[138] *W and R*, pp. 40–1.

creed, imposed on the Welsh by the insensitive *diktat* of an unsympathetic government; Davies's contention was that it was papist beliefs which had originally been imposed on the Britons by their Saxon enemies. Implicit in the whole tone and approach of the 'Letter' was the conception that it was the Reformation, and the translation of the scriptures, which constituted the great purpose for which God had been preserving the Welsh people and their language. This, indeed, was to be the fulfilment of their heavenly ordained destiny as a people. Davies's reinterpretation of British history was to be reprinted a number of times[139] and was to exercise a decisive influence on the outlook of Welsh intellectuals, giving them a new confidence in themselves, their language, and their religious future.

The translation of the Prayer Book and the New Testament had completed the first stage in bringing the reformed faith and the Bible to the Welsh in their own tongue. Even if it was to turn out less successfully than had been hoped, it was an epic breakthrough which demonstrated that it was perfectly possible for Welsh authors to make an excellent independent biblical translation. It also proved that the Welsh language could meet the additional demands being placed upon it by the new forces of the age. The translation would be the foundation for the improved versions that would appear at a later stage. The achievement may, however, have been too easily taken for granted by subsequent generations as an automatic outcome of the developments of the sixteenth century. What should be appreciated is that it could very easily never have happened at all. Many Welsh-born authors of the Tudor period had been attracted to writing in English with marked success, and Salesbury, early in his career, had been by no means the least effective of them. The prospects of publishing in English were attractive: a powerful literary tradition extending its scope with impressive speed and diversity; many influential patrons; the possibility of reaching a wide and growing public; and the likelihood of gaining fame and making money. As against this there were many disincentives to publishing in Welsh: no printing-presses in Wales and few patrons; a low level of literacy among the Welsh population; a public restricted in numbers and even more in means, many of whom were depressingly apathetic in relation to their language.[140] The temptation to yield to despair must at times have been almost overwhelming. In assessing the achievement of the pioneer translators, and that of Salesbury especially, the odds stacked against it ought not to be overlooked.

By the time that the translations of 1567 were beginning to be used in Welsh churches, Elizabeth had sat on the throne for close on ten years. A

---

[139] E. Rees, *Libri Wallie* (2 vols. NLW, Aberystwyth, 1987), I. 196.
[140] *WRE*, pp. 203–5.

letter sent to Sir William Cecil by Nicholas Robinson, recently appointed (1566) as bishop of Bangor,[141] provides an admirable summary of the reactions of the people of his diocese and, doubtless, of other parts of Wales to Elizabeth and her church after a decade. They were reported to be good, faithful, and peaceable subjects to the queen, who showed no signs of hostility or resistance to their ruler. But as to their reception of the reformed religion

> I find by my small experience among them that ignorance continueth many in the dregs of superstition, which did grow chiefly upon the blindness of the clergy, joined with greediness of getting in so bare a country, and also upon the closing up of God's word from them in an unknown tongue; though the one be remedied by the great benefit of our gracious queen and parliament; yet the other remaineth without hope of redress, for the most part of the priests are too old, they say, now to be put to school. Upon this inability to teach God's word (for there are not sixty can preach in the three shires) I have found since I came to the country images and altars standing in churches undefaced, lewd and indecent vigils and watches observed, much pilgrimage-going, many candles set up in honour of saints, some relics yet carried about, and all the country full of beads and knots [i.e. rosaries].[142]

Robinson's observations, which were in general to be confirmed by other bishops, disclosed how many of the population, including a number of the clergy, remained set in their old ways. The vestiges of medieval belief and custom still freely and unconcealedly existing among them, showed that many remained creatures of habit. Most of those who attended church were largely unmoved by what they heard there, but yet were not sufficiently conscious Catholics to heed the strictures of a handful of convinced believers who proclaimed that the pope expressly forbade attendance at heretical services on pain of eternal damnation. There was evidently still a long distance to go in raising the standard of the clergy and winning the hearts and minds of the people. A fierce and protracted battle remained to be fought out between the two small minorities of hard-core Protestants and Catholics for the allegiance of the conservative but largely inert masses.

---

[141] A. O. Evans, 'Nicholas Robinson, 1530?–1585?', *Cymm.* XXXIX (1928), 149–99.
[142] PRO, SP12/44/27; cf. Mathew, *BBCS*, VI. 70–8.

CHAPTER 10

The Romanist Challenge, 1568–1588

OUTWARDLY at least, the first ten years of Elizabeth's reign were a relatively quiet and untroubled period for Roman Catholics in England and Wales. In spite of the persecution of Protestants during the Marian years, under the new queen there was no retaliation, no persecution, and certainly no executions. While Elizabeth kept most of her sister's surviving bishops in confinement, she allowed some of her more determined opponents to withdraw to the Continent. The queen seemed content to try to win her subjects over by conciliatory means, demanding nothing more from them than external conformity. It was a decade during which Catholic adherents or sympathizers, even in deeply conservative areas like Wales, found it possible, by occasional conformity, to evade the fines theoretically payable under the law for non-attendance. There were only the mildest signs of recusancy, and it seemed that as long as the queen was patient, she and time would be a match for the Catholic religion. As the old-style priests died out, mass was likely to disappear. There was every prospect that the whole realm would gradually slide from outward compliance to worship in the Anglican Church into force of habit and possibly even conviction. However justified the Venetian envoy, Cardinal Bentivoglio, may have been when he expressed the view that four-fifths of the people were Catholic at heart and, given the chance, would become openly Catholic again,[1] the power of the royal will was very strong: *cuius regio eius religio* ('the ruler's religion is that of his subjects') was a principle as operative in England and Wales as in Germany or Spain.

Yet there were convinced believers, especially those who had fled into exile who, from the outset, had never failed to see the dangers inherent in the situation. They had sensed the threat presented to the faith by the gradual drift into conformity. They had no doubt that as the faithful were gradually deprived of the sustenance of the sacraments, they would slowly but surely perish from spiritual malnutrition. Had not Morys Clynnog years before warned that it was better to strive for eternal salvation under a

---

[1] H. Daniel-Rops, *The Catholic Reformation* (London, 1968), p. 202.

foreign lord than to be driven into the depths of hell by an enemy at home?[2] Again, Laurence Vaux had in 1566 emphatically laid down the papal injunction that good Catholics must not compromise by attending Anglican services.[3] True, there were many priests of the old inclination, most of whom had accepted the Anglican Prayer Book as well as a minority who had refused it, who continued to minister the sacraments in secret to their people. But there were not enough of them to meet the need and in any case they were slowly disappearing from the scene. Nor could there be any proper provision for ordinary replacements for them as long as the surviving Marian bishops were held in captivity, though the exiled Thomas Goldwell continued to ordain his countrymen on the Continent until the time of his death. Rome did not appear to have found a way of filling vacant sees, or providing ecclesiastical government or organization. Catholic lay people in England and Wales were left with insufficient pastors, guides, or instruction. Unless the faith was ultimately to wither on the stalk, drastic steps would have to be taken to give it new life.

The little group of Welsh and English exiles in the Low Countries could not but be aware of the new spirit of reform and initiative at work within the Catholic Church. The Council of Trent, which concluded its deliberations in 1563, did not give birth to that awakening but did co-ordinate the disparate elements around a reformed papacy and redirect its vital energies.[4] The reformed Catholic Church which emerged was surer of its beliefs, better fitted to govern souls, and more conscious of its duties and responsibilities. One, at least, of the company of exiles, Thomas Goldwell, could have given a first-hand account of his experiences at Trent, as he was the only English bishop to attend the council. Another member of the group, Gruffydd Robert, was in 1564 to come to the notice of Cardinal Borromeo, the very embodiment of the spirit of Catholic reform, and would become one of the most notable members of that saintly man's entourage. Amid this whole company of exiles, the spirit of the Counter-Reformation, with its burning desire for the recovery of lost ground, would be unceasingly active. If that in itself were insufficient inspiration, as refugees in Europe, they were growingly aware of the deadly threat from the best-organized and most militant corps of Protestants, the Calvinists, especially in parts of Switzerland, France, Germany, and the Low Countries.[5] There could no longer be any question of passively wringing their hands as the ship of faith

---

[2] A. O. Meyer, *England and the Catholic Church under Queen Elizabeth* (London, 1910), p. 241.

[3] Above, chap. 9, n. 81.

[4] H. Jedin, *The Council of Trent* (2 vols. Edinburgh, 1961).

[5] R. B. Wernham (ed.), *New Cambridge Modern History*, III (Cambridge, 1968), chap. 9.

in England and Wales slipped further and further away from its ancient moorings. Ironically, hitherto it had been less the attacks of enemies than the indifference of friends which had wrought the greater harm on that Catholic community; in the ensuing years the Church which had shrivelled under toleration would thrive in persecution. The 1570s would see a determined effort mounted to revive Catholic life, whatever the obstacles.

Three decisive trends would be discernible in the Catholic resurgence of the coming decades: the importance attached to the priesthood; the emphasis placed on instructional literature; and the involvement in intrigue and conspiracy. The most important single step taken by the exiles was the founding at Michaelmas 1568 of the seminary at Douai for the training of priests.[6] There were, already, a number of Marian priests and schoolmasters at work in the home country. A number of young Catholic students were even continuing to proceed to the University of Oxford, where they sheltered under the wing of well-disposed tutors. Without the efforts of men like these there would have been little basis of Catholic faith on which the products of the seminaries could have exercised their gifts in England and Wales; though by 1580 there were fewer of the old guard left who rightly exercised their functions.[7] The founders of the Douai seminary, however, in keeping with the spirit of the Council of Trent, saw that what was needed above all else was a new kind of institution for the recruitment, education, and eventual ordination of a more thoroughly and systematically trained priesthood than the medieval world had ever known. Douai has been ranked by one distinguished Catholic historian along with the Society of Jesus, the Roman Oratory, and the Carmelite Renaissance as one of the greatest achievements of the Counter-Reformation.[8] Its founder was a Lancashire man, William Allen, who was greatly assisted with advice and material encouragement by two Welshmen – his former tutor at Oxford Morgan Phillips, who eventually left all his property to the seminary; and Owen Lewis, professor of Civil Law at Douai University. The aim of the seminary was to 'train Catholics to be plainly and openly Catholics, to be men who will always refuse any kind of spiritual commerce with heretics'.[9] Like Protestants they steeped themselves in the history of the Church; but, in diametrical opposition to their adversaries, they emphasized the unbroken continuity of that Church throughout the ages under papal leadership.[10] The object of the founders of

[6] *The First and Second Diaries of the English College, Douai*, ed. T. F. Knox (London, 1878).

[7] W. Ll. Williams, *The Making of Modern Wales* (London, 1919), p. 205 n. 2.

[8] P. Hughes, *The Reformation in England* (3 vols. London, 1950–4), III. 282.

[9] T. F. Knox, *Letters and Memorials of Cardinal Allen* (London, 1882), p. 59.

[10] Contrast the difference in the treatment of the early British Church history in Richard Davies's 'Epistol at y Cembru' (1567) and in the introduction to the anonymous *Drych Cristianogawl* (1585).

Douai was unquestionably religious and not political, but their pupils would find it difficult on occasion not to dabble in the murky waters of conspiracy. A relatively high proportion of Welshmen was at first attracted to the seminary: eleven out of fifty-two students on the mission between 1574 and 1578 were Welsh, at a time when the proportion of the population of Wales was only about one-twelfth that of England.[11] Thereafter, the stream of Welsh entrants to Douai declined, and by 1589 had dried up, although they continued to go to other continental seminaries in considerable numbers.

One of the pre-eminent characteristics of the education given at Douai was Allen's recognition of the need to accustom the students to make 'use of the vulgar tongue', 'a thing on which heretics plume themselves exceedingly, and by which they do great injury to the simple folk'.[12] By the 'vulgar tongue' Allen undoubtedly meant the English language, and his and the other English leaders' failure to realize how important a different sort of vernacular tongue was in Wales constituted a serious weakness on the part of those who directed the Counter-Reformation towards England and Wales. An ardent young Welsh-speaking student like Robert Gwyn did his utmost to make amends for his leaders' lack of understanding. Gwyn himself complained of feeling lonely and neglected at Douai, however, having little time and, seemingly, no encouragement to write his letter 'Na all fod un ffydd onyd yr Hen Ffydd' (There can be no faith save the old faith) to his relations and friends back in Wales.[13]

Allen and the other exiles certainly appreciated the value of printed literature in the vernacular. Allen was later to claim that even before the foundation of the seminary at Douai 'books opened the way'. 'The books written in English by our people', he declared, '. . . did much to bring about the change in minds', because they were aimed at popular understanding.[14] What he had in mind were the forty-one books written by exiles on the Catholic side in the controversy between the papist Harding and the Protestant Jewel, of which 20,000 copies were said to have been smuggled into England between 1564 and 1567, according to Nicholas Sanders.[15] This was a remarkable achievement, and it is very likely that many educated Welsh Catholics benefited from reading books of this kind. A number of Welsh-born authors certainly wrote such books in English and Latin.[16]

[11] J. M. Cleary, *A Checklist of Welsh Students in the Seminaries* (Cardiff, 1958), pp. 3–4.

[12] Knox, *Letters*, p. xli.

[13] G. Bowen (ed.), *Gwssanaeth y Gwŷr Newydd: Robert Gwyn (1580)* (Cardiff, 1970), p. xxx.

[14] Knox, *Letters*, pp. 55–6.

[15] J. H. Pollen, *The English Catholics in the Reign of Queen Elizabeth* (London, 1920), p. 111.

[16] D. A. Thomas, *The Welsh Elizabethan Catholic Martyrs* (Cardiff, 1971), pp. 191–3; *W and R*, pp. 139–40, 169.

However, it was no less true of Catholic sympathizers in Wales than of their Protestant counterparts there that most of them were likely to be able to benefit only from instruction and literature in their own language. That was a point whose significance seems to have been lost on most of the exiles. It is noticeable that, apart possibly from Milan, not one of the nerve-centres of Catholic activity and training in sixteenth-century Europe – Douai, Rome, Valladolid, Lisbon, Seville, or Ghent – became a focus for the publishing of Catholic books in Welsh. Given the difficulties which lay in the path, that may not have been altogether surprising. Publishing Welsh Catholic books was a formidable task; no easier than producing Protestant works. Both sides, in fact, came up against many of the same obstacles: the illiteracy and poverty of the Welsh, most of whom were completely unaccustomed to the notion of buying or owning books, or reading for themselves. Catholics, just as much as Protestants, needed generous patrons to help them with the huge costs of printing, as Owen Lewis was to explain to Cardinal Sirleto in his touching letter of 1579 appealing for money to help publish three titles.[17] Printing was as expensive for Catholics as Protestants, and even more difficult because of the extremely tight governmental censorship of the printing-presses in England.[18] That made it necessary to print on the Continent and smuggle the finished products into the country.[19] This was done with Morys Clynnog's *Athravaeth Gristnogawl* (1568), the first, and indeed the only, Catholic work written in Welsh to appear as a book printed on the Continent in the sixteenth century.[20] In the absence of printed books, Catholic authors had no option but to fall back on manuscripts, which were regarded as being as valid a literary medium for an author as a printed book. Nearly all the Catholic writings in Welsh – in prose and poetry – which saw the light of day were published in this fashion and circulated secretly.[21] Some devotees went to extraordinary lengths and faced the dangers of persecution and imprisonment to copy these manuscripts and distribute them. Notwithstanding the courage of these men, manuscript publication was necessarily more haphazard and unsatisfactory than the issuing of printed books would have been.

Even so, Catholics had no doubt about the importance of books, especially for use in instructing the young. The Council of Trent, following a path already trodden by the Protestants, called for a brief but thoroughly

---

[17] R. G. Gruffydd, 'Dau lythyr gan Owen Lewis', *LlC*, II (1952–3), 36–45; G. Bowen, 'Canolfannau llenyddol y ffoaduriaid Catholig', *LlC*, III (1954–5), 229–33.

[18] D. M. Loades, 'The theory and practice of censorship in sixteenth-century England', *TRHS*, 5th ser. XXIV (1974), 141–58.

[19] A. C. Southern, *English Recusant Prose, 1559–1582* (London, 1951).

[20] *Athravaeth Gristnogavl* (repr. London, 1880).

[21] *W and R*, pp. 152–5.

orthodox account of the faith which should be within the grasp of all Christians and taught them by their pastors. Catholics and Protestants alike made a point of teaching young children; and catechisms first appeared independently about the same time in Spain and Germany.[22] Following along these lines, Morys Clynnog produced in Welsh his simple guide to the faith, a translation of the little catechism by Father Juan Alfonso de Polanco. The foreword, written by his friend, Gruffydd Robert, admitted to profound mortification at the thought of how many children in Wales were failing to follow the path of truth for want of being educated from an early age. It pronounced emphatically that 'the main cause of this was the lack of books' ('yr achos fwyaf o hynn yw diphyg llyfrau').[23] Clynnog urged that his work should be used in churches and also in households. The book seems to have met with no little success in Wales; at the very least it was deemed sufficiently influential for one Lewis Evans, an Oxford graduate and originally from Monmouth, to publish an English reply to it in 1571.[24]

Quite apart from what might be described as the spontaneous uprush of spiritual energies, finding expression in the founding of the seminary and the publication of literature, the exiles and their sympathizers at home were coming under acute pressure from changes in the international and domestic situation during the years from 1568 to 1572.[25] These made the overall position more complex and dangerous, yet at the same time offered new possibilities for action. The state of European affairs between 1558 and 1568 had often been tense and perilous, but on the whole Elizabeth had managed to keep the ambitions of Spain, France, Scotland, and the papacy in reasonable balance. After 1568 her position became decidedly more risky and exposed. Whatever the attitude of Catholics might be towards her as ruler of England, they could hardly avoid looking upon her and William Cecil as the most determined and dangerous enemies of their religion. They could not but recognize, either, that the survival of the Anglican settlement was synonymous with the survival of Elizabeth herself. Catholic hopes depended to a large extent on how long she ruled as queen and who succeeded her. The most obvious successor, though one whom Elizabeth herself steadfastly refused to recognize, was Mary Queen of Scots;[26] indeed, a few Catholic ultras might even believe that Mary, as a

[22] P. Chaunu (ed.), *The Reformation* (Gloucester, 1989), p. 273.

[23] *Athravaeth*, introd.

[24] *A Brief Answer to a Short Trifling Treatise . . . written by one Clunnock . . .* (1571); G. Bowen, 'Rhyddiaith Reciwsantaidd Cymru' (Ph.D. thesis, Wales, 1978), p. 140.

[25] R. B. Wernham, *England Before the Armada* (London, 1966), chaps. 22–3; W. T. McCaffrey, *The Shaping of the Elizabethan Regime* (London, 1969), parts 4 and 5.

[26] A. Fraser, *Mary Queen of Scots* (London, 1969), chaps 19–20.

good Catholic of unquestionably legitimate birth, already had a better claim to the throne than Elizabeth. In 1568 Mary fled from Scotland to seek refuge in England. This left Elizabeth, as Archbishop Parker put it, 'holding the wolf by the ear';[27] dangerous to hold but even more dangerous to let go. Mary would remain in England until her death nineteen years later, a focus – often involuntary – for the plots and intrigues of all the dissentients against Elizabeth. Later in 1568, relations with Spain, on whose uneasy neutrality England had long depended, deteriorated to the brink of open warfare. Cecil, whose own tenure of office was under extreme pressure, penned an extraordinarily pessimistic memorandum in which he depicted the kingdom as being surrounded by powerful Catholic enemies headed by Spain, France, and the pope.[28]

Within the realm in 1569 discontent boiled over in the alienated, inwardly-turned conservative north in the shape of the 'Rising of the Northern Earls', which proved to be the most dangerous rebellion of the whole of Elizabeth's reign. The insurgents' watchwords appeared to favour the Catholic religion and the Scottish queen. As was to be expected, grave alarm was aroused in government circles concerning those parts of the country notoriously known to favour the old ways in religion. Catholic commentators for their part looked hopefully to Wales. The Catholic publicist, Nicholas Sanders, thought that the 'most remote parts of the kingdom are the least inclined to heresy, such as Wales, Devon, etc. . . . not one hundredth part is tainted'.[29] Guerau de Spes, the Spanish ambassador, in the spring of 1569, was sure a majority of the Welsh, like the people in the north, were Catholic and supported Mary,[30] while the Irish rebel leader, Fitzgerald, on the eve of his own rising of 1569, was equally confident that most of the Welsh longed for nothing more than to see the sacraments of Christ restored again to their country.[31] When the Northern Rising was at its height the Protestant Bishop Sandys of Worcester described Wales as 'vehemently to be suspected'.[32] In 1570 a supporter of Mary Queen of Scots believed that among the influential people who upheld her cause were sixty-eight gentlemen, 'all of them Catholics in Wales'.[33] Even a year after the rebellion was over, some observer using the name Alessandro Fidel reported to the pope that Wales was 'the stronghold of Catholics',[34] and

[27] L. B. Smith, *The Elizabethan Epic* (London, 1969), p. 190.

[28] C. Read, *Mr Secretary Cecil and Queen Elizabeth* (London, 1955), p. 437.

[29] *CSP Rome, Eliz.* I. 68–9.

[30] *CSP Span. Eliz.* II. 147.

[31] *Carew MSS.* I. 398.

[32] J. Strype, *Annals of the Reformation and Establishing of Religion . . .* (4 vols. Oxford, 1820–40), I. 32.

[33] *Cath. Rec. Soc,* XIII. 86–142.

[34] *CSP Rome, Eliz.* I. 389.

the papal nuncio in Spain gave it as his opinion that the people in Wales 'would soon with one accord declare themselves for the Catholic faith'.[35]

The Welsh people might, indeed, be conservative in their religious attachments, but that did not mean they were disloyal to Elizabeth or prepared to rebel against her. Just how ill-founded had been the expansive Catholic hopes and alarmist rumours became plain when the Welsh showed no sign whatsoever of rebelling during the perilous years 1569 to 1571. Not that that had deterred the Privy Council and the Council in the Marches from instituting urgent inquiries in the localities to discover the state of public security and popular opinion. In December 1569 the leading Glamorgan gentry were required by the Council in the Marches to take an oath that they and their families would loyally observe the Act of Uniformity.[36] Fourteen justices of the peace duly subscribed but reported that one of their number, Sir Thomas Stradling, refused to do so. He had been imprisoned some years before for his Catholic principles and in 1569 was the only magistrate in Wales who refused to take the oath of loyalty. Six of his fellow-justices were dispatched to exact his allegiance but found him ill in bed with (?diplomatic) gout. Their report revealed a curious mixture of prevarication on Stradling's part and sympathy on theirs. It was said that 'when he is able to come out of his house there is no lay man in this shire that cometh oftener to church . . . and also he doth yearly receive the blessed sacrament at times usual'. Or else he causes divine service to be said regularly at home on Sundays and twice in the week 'as it is said in the Book of Common Prayer'. He was even willing to make his own wine available, if needed, for communion in local churches. Nevertheless, he obstinately maintained that he could not take the oath 'with a safe conscience, as the Privy Council well knew'.[37] In view of his being 70 years of age and in failing health, his colleagues urged the Privy Council not to press him as long as he observed the bond he had given earlier. Since there was clearly no danger of his being involved in any rising, the Privy Council agreed. Eighteen months later, Stradling was dead. Contrary to what might have been expected, the preamble to his will was distinctly Protestant in tone.[38]

Round about the same time, three of the Welsh bishops, at least, were subject to inquiries from Archbishop Parker concerning the state of religious observance and the public mood in their dioceses. On 6 November 1569 he wrote to Hugh Jones, bishop of Llandaff, potentially the most contumacious of the Welsh dioceses, for a report. In spite of the worries

[35] Ibid., I. 318.
[36] PRO, SP12/66/19.
[37] Ibid.; cf. Mathew, *BBCS*, VI. 70–8.
[38] PRO, PCC Holney 21.

expressed by the justices about Sir Thomas Stradling, Bishop Jones, on 26 January 1570, was able to give a reassuring reply about the state of his diocese. All the inhabitants came obediently to church service, with the exception of two unnamed men from Newport, who were of no great account socially.[39] Richard Davies, bishop of St David's the largest Welsh diocese, replied on 25 January 1570. He also seemed to have nothing very alarming to put on record:

> After diligent inquiry . . . I could not find that there is any person of any degree within my diocese within contempt of religion now established in the realm, or obstinately refuseth the church common prayer or the receiving of the sacrament at usual times and especially at Easter.

There were, however, many who were 'slow and cold in the service of God; some careless for any religion, and some that wish the romish religion again'.[40] Nothing was heard from the diocese of Bangor until May 1570, when Bishop Robinson wrote a long and disquieting account about the funeral of one Lewis Roberts, solemnized at Beaumaris, the county town of Anglesey. Those present at it had obviously observed many old-fashioned practices, with 'three singing boys in their surplices' and 'wax candles alight upon the hearse'. Scandalized by those proceedings, Robinson had severely reprimanded not only the singers but also the mayor and justices, and the august Sir Richard Bulkeley himself. In mitigation, the offenders had all pleaded ancient custom and their own ignorance. Robinson, however, expressed the hope that his public censures might have the effect of deterring others from indulging in such superstition.[41] It was only in the following November (1570) that Thomas Davies, bishop of St Asaph, was able to send in a more optimistic statement about his diocese. It was now more obedient in religion than at his first appointment, although there were still some who were of 'corrupt religion' and could not be apprehended.[42] Yet it was clear from what the bishops wrote that there was no serious apprehension on the part of any one of them, nor any suggestion of rebellion in Wales.

Hard on the heels of the Northern Rising, although too late to be of any assistance to the insurgents, came Pope Pius V's bull of excommunication of Queen Elizabeth. For some years there had been among the Catholic exiles those who wished to see the pope take this decisive step before he

[39] PRO, SP12/66/90–1; for the text of the letter, M. Gray, 'The cloister and the hearth', *JWRH*, III (1995), 29–32.
[40] PRO, SP12/66/26.
[41] PRO, SP12/69/14.
[42] Ibid., 74/37.

actually did so. Back in 1567 Morys Clynnog – of all people! – had written a letter to William Cecil to warn him, in veiled language, that moves were on foot to excommunicate the queen.[43] But it was not until December 1569 that the pope instituted a 'process' against her at Rome. Among the twelve witnesses who appeared before him to submit evidence against her were three who had some connection with Wales: Thomas Goldwell, Morys Clynnog, and Edmund Daniel. In February Pius excommunicated Elizabeth and deprived her of what he called her 'pretended' right to the throne. He thereby relieved all Roman Catholics of their allegiance to her and condemned to excommunication along with Elizabeth herself all those who obeyed her.[44] This was an unmistakable declaration of war on the part of the papacy, interpreted by all patriotic subjects as an act of hostility and treachery by Rome and its followers. In fact, it made very little difference to the attitude of the overwhelming mass of Elizabeth's subjects in England and Wales, who continued to regard her as their rightful queen, no matter what their religious loyalties might be. The Elizabethan government, too, was judicious: 'it did not dragoon the Catholics or press the question of the bull on them'.[45] Clearly, the queen was proving to be true to her assertion that she had no wish to make 'a window into men's souls'. Parliament did, however, in 1571 pass an Act making it high treason to bring in, seek out, or publish any document emanating from Rome.[46]

One of the earliest consequences of the bull of excommunication was the Ridolfi Plot.[47] The man responsible for 'organizing' it – if that is not too flattering a description of the inept and widely publicized manœuvrings involved – was Roberto Ridolfi, an Italian banker and a *gran parlaquina* ('great gasbag'), as Alva called him. The idea was that, with the aid of an internal rising and a foreign invasion, Mary Queen of Scots should be freed and married to Thomas, duke of Norfolk. The scheme collapsed disastrously and Norfolk was executed in 1572.[48] Involved in it, however, were two Welshmen who, for many years, would be some of the most prominent and incorrigible plotters against Elizabeth. The one was Hugh Owen of Plas-du in Caernarfonshire who, for a whole generation, was to be 'intelligencer-in chief'[49] to the Spanish monarchy. He had been secretary to

[43] The text of the letter is printed in Thomas Jones (ed.), *Rhyddiaith Gymraeg*, II (Cardiff, 1956), 21–4.
[44] Latin text, together with English translation, G. R. Elton, *The Tudor Constitution* (Cambridge, 1960), pp. 414–18.
[45] W. R. Trimble, *The Catholic Laity in Elizabethan England* (Cambridge, Mass., 1964), p. 63; cf. J. V. P. Thompson, *Supreme Governor* (London, 1940), pp. 95–6.
[46] *Statutes of the Realm* (11 vols. London, 1810–28), IV. 528–31.
[47] J. E. Neale, *Queen Elizabeth* (London, 1948), chap. 12.
[48] N. Williams, *Thomas Howard: Fourth Duke of Norfolk* (London, 1964).
[49] A. J. Loomie, *The Spanish Elizabethans* (London, 1963), chap. 3.

the Catholic earl of Arundel and, when he fled abroad, was denounced for
being implicated in Ridolfi's plot. Years later, in 1596, he was to be referred
to by the Archduke Albert as a 'man of great intelligence whom the king
(Philip II) has used and is using in many affairs. He is diligent, very discreet
and suitable for any business. The duke of Parma always put in writing his
great satisfaction in him.'[50] The other conspirator was Thomas Morgan,
originally of Monmouthshire, who was recommended to the earl of
Shrewsbury in 1569 when Mary Queen of Scots was a prisoner in the earl's
house. Morgan ingratiated himself with Mary and became mixed up in the
Ridolfi Plot. He was imprisoned for nine months and then fled to Europe.
At Paris he became secretary to Mary's ambassador, James Beaton,
archbishop of Glasgow, and for many years was one of her chief agents in
France.[51] Owen and Morgan, more than almost any other Welshmen,
would be involved in the multifarious plots and machinations against
Elizabeth.

The 1570s were to prove a decade of rising tension and conflict between
the Elizabethan regime and the powers of the Counter-Reformation. This
was to be in sharp contrast with the first years of her reign when Elizabeth
and her advisers had deemed it prudent on the whole to pursue a
conciliatory line, letting sleeping dogs lie, while all the time keeping a
watchful eye on them. As long as the old faith appeared to be on its
deathbed Elizabeth was content to let it slip away. Since the rising of 1569
and the papal bull of 1570, however, the risks of inaction by the English
government looked to be greater than those of intervention. All the more so
when both wings of Catholic activists – spiritual and political – were
intensifying their efforts. On the one hand, strenuous efforts would be made
to step up the recruiting and training of priests, and dispatching them 'on
mission'. Together with Catholic schoolmasters and laymen they would be
encouraged to publish and circulate books. Some pinned all their faith on
such methods; Gruffydd Robert would assure English visitors to Cardinal
Borromeo how reluctant the pope was to trust to invasion. The holy father,
he claimed, would much sooner see the people 'be secretly persuaded . . . by
the priests that be sent over daily'.[52] Yet a devout Catholic like Almaviva,
the Jesuit General, in 1584 was to regret this loss of so many good men
'which might injure many Catholics and do no good to souls'.[53] The
'politicals', by contrast, took a different line. It was not difficult to
understand why those like Hugh Owen should be drawn to the attractions

---

[50] Ibid., p. 59.
[51] L. Hicks, *An Elizabethan Problem: Some Aspects of the Careers of Two Exile
Adventurers* (London, 1964).
[52] W. Ll. Williams, 'Welsh Catholics on the Continent', *TCS* (1901–2), app. A.
[53] E. Waugh, *Edmund Campion* (Harmondsworth, 1953), p. 49.

of persuading Philip II to unsheathe the mighty temporal sword of Spain. Such a course, if successful, might, at a stroke, sweep away the hostile queen and replace her with a Catholic ruler and establishment.

Some enthusiastic exiles could not forbear from dipping a finger in virtually every Counter-Reformation pie. Morys Clynnog, for instance, had been advocating invasion as early as 1562 and would do so again in 1575. He was also one of the earliest to perceive the necessity for printing Welsh Catholic books. He testified against Elizabeth in the process for her excommunication; but would be best remembered for his role, however unsuccessful, in founding the college at Rome. Owen Lewis was another busy in many spheres. Allen's chief lieutenant at Douai, eager in the drive to secure Welsh books and patrons for them, deeply involved with Clynnog at Rome, he was later to set his hopes on becoming archbishop of York or at least bishop of St David's when Elizabeth had ultimately been conquered by Spain. Others served their church no less whole-heartedly but restricted themselves almost wholly to spiritual activities. Perhaps the most dedicated of all the Welsh *alumni* of Douai was Robert Gwyn, a devoted undercover priest and the most productive of all the Catholic writers in Welsh. Author certainly of three Welsh books, maybe four or five, and just possibly of the most effective of all the sixteenth-century Catholic books written in Welsh, *Drych Cristianogawl*, he gave himself up entirely to his labours as a missionary priest and writer.[54] Or Richard White, poet, schoolmaster, and martyr, whose sufferings on behalf of conscience are particularly familiar to us because his co-religionists were so anxious that his sacrifices should be widely known that they went to great pains in writing full-length memoirs of his life, trial, and martyrdom.[55]

Whatever the Welsh Catholics may have owed to the inspiration of the exiles and the men they trained, their original debt to the older priesthood should not be forgotten. The Marian priests, both those who had been ejected from their livings and those who managed to square their consciences with retaining their benefices and their Catholic principles, had done and would go on doing much to keep their faith alive.[56] They, too, went in for a good deal of secret activity, like that Roger Johns, who made use of an altar, said to have been erected by a Glamorgan gentleman 'in a wood'.[57] Nevertheless, it was widely recognized that the new emissaries were much more fired-up and better educated than their predecessors had been. Moreover, their contacts with European Catholics, and their links

---

[54] Bowen, *Gwssanaeth*, introd.

[55] Thomas, *Elizabethan Martyrs*, pp. 84ff.

[56] C. Haigh, 'From monopoly to minority: Catholicism in early modern England', *TRHS*, 5th ser. XXXI (1981), 129–47.

[57] PRO, SP12/118/11.

with the papacy in particular, were to make them all the more subversive and suspect in the eyes of the English authorities. From 1574 onwards the missionary priests began to infiltrate into England and Wales by stealth. Not all of the eleven Welshmen among the first fifty-two from Douai found their way back to Wales to minister.[58] Most of these came from north Wales; the diocese of St David's being conspicuously lacking in recruits. Oddly enough, though, the first Douai priest to arrive in England, Lewis Barlow, was a man from Pembrokeshire.[59] Among the earliest to come to Wales was Robert Owen, who was in Llŷn in 1576.[60] He was a member of one of Caernarfonshire's staunchest Catholic families, the Owens of Plas-du, and a brother to the conspirator, Hugh Owen. An equally early arrival – from Caernarfonshire, too, and also back by 1576 – was Robert Gwyn.[61] Young, ardent, and zealous to the point of being pig-headed, Gwyn was insistent that there could be 'no faith but the old faith'. He was adamant that Catholics must not compromise by consorting with the 'opiniadwyr' (his word for heretics), and was quick to persuade his friends and family not to do so. He was, in fact, somewhat critical of an older generation of fellow-believers like Morys Clynnog and Gruffydd Robert, and did not hesitate to compare the Welsh people unfavourably with Lancashire Catholics because they were so much more reluctant to admit priests to their houses. The reason for this, he thought, was the overfondness of the Welsh for money.[62] He may not have allowed nearly enough for how difficult it was to arrange for priests to come over from the Continent and to organize their passage within the country. Robert Parsons, the celebrated Jesuit, gave an indication of how it was done. He described setting up a small 'establishment' at Rouen, where 'some can make trips to the coast to arrange for boats to convey people across', and others 'take charge of the preparation and introduction of books into the country', and others 'perform many services for the priests working among them in secret'.[63]

In the case of Robert Gwyn, the literature he produced was an integral part of his work as a priest. Most of his writings, like those of nearly all the Catholic authors, were pastoral in tone and seem to have been intended to sustain the faithful rather than convert the unbeliever, though Gwyn and others never missed an opportunity to put the heretics firmly in their place. The priests from Douai may have had a far-reaching effect on some of the

[58] Cleary, *Checklist*, pp. 3–13; idem, 'The Catholic resistance in Wales, 1568–1678', *Blackfriars* (March 1957), 111–25.
[59] Cleary, *Checklist*, p. 15.
[60] Ibid.
[61] Bowen, *Gwssanaeth*, introd.
[62] Ibid.
[63] *Catholic Rec. Soc.* XXXIV. 236.

laymen with whom they came into contact. It was the appearance of these missionaries which inspired the young schoolmaster, Richard White, to take his stand so openly. Although he had been devoted to the Catholic religion from childhood, it was the arrival of men from Douai which finally decided his course of action for him.[64] He then became not only a Catholic schoolmaster at a number of places along the border in north-east Wales but also a considerable Catholic poet.[65] Like most of his fellow Catholic poets he was more combative and controversial in his approach than the prose authors were.[66] He may have been provoked by the utterances of some of the more determinedly Protestant, even Puritan, of his adversaries. Like all the poets, White depended on manuscript copying or oral declamation for the circulation of his poems[67] One of the most committed of these copyists, Llywelyn Siôn, was himself a productive poet.[68]

Neither poets nor littérateurs could achieve much without the active co-operation of sympathetic local gentry families. The Catholic religion, like much else in Tudor society, depended heavily on upper-class patronage, without which it was hardly possible to influence the bulk of the populace. Landlords with Catholic views were usually careful to ensure that their tenants and dependants shared their sympathies. What was said of the Monmouthshire tenant in 1628: 'His religion is part of his copy-hold, which he takes from his landlord and refers it wholly to his discretion',[69] had probably been true for half a century beforehand. A Catholic landlord not only applied pressure; he also offered protection. It was his house that provided a priest with a bolt-hole where he could minister the Catholic sacraments in secret to the faithful: say mass, marry them, baptize their children, instruct them in the faith, and organize their funerals. Recusant landowners exercised their authority over their dependants by reading Catholic manuscripts to them when they met for worship in the absence of a priest.[70] It was not usually the biggest landowners who performed such a role; they were too preoccupied with maintaining their contacts with the Elizabethan regime to imperil their position by dabbling with recusancy. It was not the Bulkeleys of Beaumaris or the Wynns of Gwydir, but families of the second rank – the Owens of Plas-du, Pughs of Creuddyn, or Edwardses of Chirk – who were involved in risk-taking on behalf of the old faith in north Wales. Not the Mansels of Margam or the Devereux of

---

[64] Thomas, *Elizabethan Martyrs*, pp. 48–9.
[65] T. H. Parry-Williams, *Carolau Richard White* (Cardiff, 1931).
[66] *W and R*, pp. 154–5.
[67] Ibid., pp. 152–3.
[68] G. J. Williams, *Traddodiad Llenyddol Morgannwg* (Cardiff, 1948), pp. 78–80.
[69] F. H. Pugh, 'Monmouthshire recusants in the reigns of Elizabeth I and James I', *SWMRS*, IV (1957), 60.
[70] Bowen, *NLWJ*, XIII. 177.

Lamphey in south Wales, but the Morgans of Llantarnam, the Barlows of Slebech, the Wolfs of Werngochyn, or the Turbervilles in the Vale of Glamorgan. In the course of time, these Catholic families would maintain close contact with one another and might often intermarry.[71]

As well as these indications of activity by the 'spiritual wing', there were also signs of interest on the part of the 'political activists'. The latter clearly conceived of Wales as a base of support for the Romanist cause. Thus, in 1574 some Catholic supporter optimistically listed the names of eight men from Anglesey who could be counted upon to rally to Mary Stuart's cause. With even rasher confidence he went on to claim that 'all the Bulkeleys were Catholics'.[72] Anglesey had long been well known as one of the two most notoriously vulnerable points in the Welsh coastal defences – the other was Milford Haven – and might therefore have been considered an admirable landing-place for invaders. In the following year, 1575, the year of the Jubilee, Morys Clynnog drafted a memorandum to Pope Gregory XIII in which he outlined his own plans for an assault on the island on Mary Stuart's behalf. His proposal was that the pope should raise 6,000 men, to which another 4,000 recruited in Catholic countries should be added. This force should sail to Anglesey, seize the Menai Straits, and launch its attack from there. Morys Clynnog adduced a number of reasons in support of his scheme: the fleet did not guard the western shores; there were fewer heretics in Wales than anywhere; Catholic sympathies were particularly strong there; memories of Henry Tudor's successful invasion were affectionately recalled in Wales; the prophecies of deliverance to come from Rome were popular among the people. The proposals may have said much for Clynnog's enthusiasm for Catholicism and for action, but little for his gifts as a strategist. They were dismissed as being altogether too far-fetched and impractical.[73] Gregory XIII, none the less, was clearly anxious to take action that might benefit Mary, if only because he viewed with growing anxiety the threat from militant Protestantism in the rise of Calvinism in Europe. In December 1575 he summoned William Allen to Rome to give his opinion on the joint expedition between the pope and Spain being mooted to free the captive queen.[74] But plans suggested for her release and her marriage to Don John, King Philip's half-brother and victor of Lepanto, were slow-moving and difficult to co-ordinate, especially in the year 1576, a particularly bad time for Spain in the

---

[71] Pugh, *SWMRS*, IV. 63. The earls of Worcester did later become zealous Catholics.
[72] *Cath. Rec. Soc.* VIII (1913), 109.
[73] T. J. Hopkin and G. Bowen, 'Memorandwm Morys Clynnog at y Pab Gregori XIII yn 1575', *NLWJ*, XIV (1965), 1–34.
[74] Williams, *Modern Wales*, p. 207.

Netherlands.[75] They were finally brought to naught by the sudden death of Don John in 1577, though Catholics in some parts of England and Wales had grown more restless as a result of news of the prince's schemes to win the two kingdoms (England and Scotland) for himself.[76] In the following year, 1578, the two Welsh leaders, Owen Lewis and Morys Clynnog, were among those taken in by the mercurial adventurer, Sir Thomas Stukeley, and eagerly backed his abortive expedition intended to rescue Mary Stuart but which foundered in Portugal.[77]

Although all these schemes came to nothing, the expectations they aroused in some quarters, taken together with the arrival of seminary priests and the bolder attitudes they evoked among Catholic believers, caused consternation among the Elizabethan authorities. The first extant list of recusants in Wales seems to be one compiled in 1574 by a Caernarfonshire Catholic, possibly Hugh Owen. He listed no fewer than eighty-eight for Wales, twenty of whom lived in his own shire.[78] The mounting tension caused by rumours of Don John's ambitions was reflected in the many anxious letters directed to Elizabeth's Secretary of State, Sir Francis Walsingham, one of which summed up the situation by declaring that 'those who are backward in religion grow worse and worse'.[79] The Privy Council's anxiety about Wales showed itself in the appointment as vice-president of the Council in the Marches of John Whitgift, bishop of Worcester, a strict disciplinarian and keen anti-Romanist.[80] In the absence in Ireland of the president, Sir Henry Sidney, who was in any case slack about persecuting recusants in Wales, Whitgift was stern in his strictures on the state of the country now under his jurisdiction. Papists were very active; mass was widely said; pardons were sold; Catholic baptisms and burials were ministered; and corrupt ministers connived at these activities.[81] What Whitgift had to say was far more condemnatory than the reports returned by the Welsh bishops to inquiries put to them on 15 October 1577 by the Privy Council. William Hughes of St Asaph had heard of no one in his diocese who refused to come to church,[82] even though the Well of St

[75] P. Geyl, *The Revolt in the Netherlands* (2nd edn. London, 1958), pp. 145–54; G. Parker, *The Dutch Revolt* (London, 1977), pp. 176–93.

[76] R. B. Manning, *Religion and Society in Elizabethan Sussex* (Leicester, 1964), p. 81.

[77] P. Hughes, *Rome and the Counter-Reformation in England* (London, 1942), p. 199.

[78] *Cath. Rec. Soc.* XIII. 86–142. The figures given for individual counties were Anglesey, 8; Caernarfonshire, 20; Denbighshire, 8; Flint, 5; Merioneth, 12; Montgomeryshire, 4; Radnorshire, 3; Cardiganshire, 0; Breconshire, 4; Monmouthshire, 6; Glamorgan, 10; Carmarthenshire, 5; Pembrokeshire, 3.

[79] PRO, SP12/111/45.

[80] P. H. Williams, *The Council in the Marches under Elizabeth I* (Cardiff, 1958), pp. 264–6.

[81] J. Strype, *The Life and Acts of John Whitgift . . .* (3 vols. Oxford, 1820), I. 165–6.

[82] PRO, SP12/118/8.

Winifred, widely resorted to by Catholics, lay within its boundaries.[83] Nicholas Robinson of Bangor could report only a feeble old priest in Conwy who objected; but he did admit to having had to reprimand some gentlemen and yeomen living in Llŷn and Eifionydd for having withdrawn themselves from church and confessed that he did not know whether they had responded appropriately.[84] More would be heard of their misdeeds a short time later.[85] Bishop Richard Davies, though confessing that some were Catholics at heart,[86] throughout his whole huge diocese of St David's found only one poor, insignificant man in Radnorshire who stayed away from church. There were so few recusants reported in these dioceses as to give rise to serious doubts about the willingness of justices of the peace and churchwardens to provide details about offenders. Only in the diocese of Llandaff did the bishop, William Bleddyn, have any sizeable number of recusants and recusant sympathizers with whom he reported having to cope. He listed thirteen in all: one justice of the peace, Thomas Carne; three priests; three gentlemen; three men of 'ordinary means'; and three women. Two of the recusants were runaways from elsewhere – George Catesby from Herefordshire, and William Wynslot from Devon. In addition to Thomas Carne, Bleddyn knew of a number of other justices in his diocese who secretly afforded help and hospitality to Catholic priests, of whom there were at least four in his diocese. He also criticized the sheriffs for their slackness in arresting those who had fallen under ecclesiastical censure and were excommunicated.[87]

Beneath the surface there was clearly a good deal more recusant activity in Wales than the bishops' reports had brought to light. Without impugning the bishops' sincerity it may be doubted whether their returns accurately reflected the condition of the country in 1577. Walsingham only allowed them a week in which to draw up their lists. That meant that they had to rely very largely on such information as they had gleaned in the course of their visitations; but it was well known that visitations were an unreliable instrument. They were few and far between, and in the course of them many churchwardens' voices were effectively silenced. In the event of a sudden danger, like a proposal to make a secret search of houses, their owners were very often given warning in advance by friends and relatives.

In Bangor diocese, there were four squires in the Llŷn peninsula who were suspected of dangerous links with Catholicism: Thomas Owen of Plas-du; Thomas Madryn of Madryn; John Griffith of Cefnamwlch; and

[83] T. Charles-Edwards, *Saint Winefride and her Well* (London, 1964).
[84] PRO, SP12/118/8.
[85] E. G. Jones, 'The Lleyn recusancy case, 1578–81', *TCS* (1936), 97–123.
[86] PRO, SP12/118/11.
[87] Ibid., 122/31.

Hugh Gwyn of Pennarth. The last three were bitter adversaries of the earl of Leicester in the long-running quarrel over Snowdon Forest.[88] Their hostility to the unrepentantly Protestant earl may explain, partly at least, their adherence to Catholicism. The most sinister among them from the government's point of view, however, was Thomas Owen, eldest brother of the exiles, Hugh and Robert Owen. Thomas Owen had maintained regular correspondence for seven years with his brothers over the water. During that time he had been responsible for easing the path of a number of priests who had visited Llŷn. Hugh Owen's influential position among the exiles and his resourceful mind aroused the fears of the Privy Council, prompting it on 2 March 1578 to dispatch Bishop Robinson and Dr Ellis Price to inquire into the state of affairs in Llŷn.[89] They had doubtless been sent with the intention of intercepting treasonable correspondence, but were thwarted because of a tip-off to the guilty families beforehand. It was suspected that the person responsible for this 'leak' was none other than a clerk of the Privy Council itself.[90] Three of the squires were, in any case, in gaol at Ludlow as the price of their opposition to Leicester. Thomas Owen was also away from home, at his son-in-law's house in Shropshire. When he did return, he was promptly arrested at Pwllheli by Richard Vaughan, the sheriff of Caernarfonshire. The latter was a man hated 'of all papists that know him for because he doth correct their errors and goeth about to bring them to amendment of life'.[91] Thomas Owen eventually had the temerity to take his enemies to Star Chamber, where a good deal of information concerning Catholic activity in Llŷn came out into the open. In the course of the testimony, paradoxically enough, Bishop Robinson was himself accused of having Catholic sympathies, to which he replied to Leicester and Walsingham in indignant repudiation of that 'heinous course'. He claimed that he and his four chaplains 'taught Christ's truth and impugned papistry, that chaos of false religion'. So earnest had he been that he had several times gone 'in danger of his life in suppressing superstition'.[92] The verdict in the Star Chamber suit is, unfortunately unknown, but the outcome is certain: the commotion caused by the litigation thoroughly frightened the Catholic squires of Llŷn. Nothing further was heard of serious Catholic activity in those parts. Nicholas Robinson, however, continued to be very troubled by the persistence of traditional practices among the people and the failure of Protestant opinion to make headway

[88] E. G. Jones, 'The Caernarvonshire squires, 1558–1625' (MA thesis, Wales, 1936), pp. 244–6; cf. idem, *TCS* (1936), 97–123.
[89] *APC*, XI. 179.
[90] Ibid., X. 203–4.
[91] PRO, STA C 5/07/22.
[92] PRO, SP12/118/8; 153/667.

in their midst; 'of the whole multitude, such which be under thirty years of age, seem to have no show of any religion, the others will nearly all dare to profess and maintain the absurdest points of popish heresy'.[93]

Caernarfonshire may have been the main focus of the Privy Council's attention, but that body was also concerned to bear down on recusants in other parts of Wales at this time. In January 1579 the council wrote to Whitgift enclosing examinations which had been pursued in relation to 'disorders touching papistry' in the house of a notorious recusant, John Edwards of Chirk.[94] In the next month this was followed up with a commission directed to the bishops of Bangor and St Asaph and the justices of assize to try certain unnamed persons within the counties of Flint and Denbigh detected in hearing masses and other practices contrary to the established state of religion.[95] Similarly, one Robert Blades was brought up from the Marches in January 1579 by the servants of Fabian Phillips and imprisoned in the Tower for recusancy, though he was later released when he showed his willingness to conform.[96] Meantime, two commissions had been dispatched to the diocese of Llandaff, one for Glamorgan and the other for Monmouthshire. The intended object of the exercise was to arrest two popish priests: George Morris, who had at one time been one of Bishop Bonner's priests, and another unnamed. Much to Bishop Bleddyn's vexation, however, he learnt that his fellow-commissioners among some of the gentry were altogether too sympathetic to the priests and had warned them beforehand. It was the conduct of Rowland Morgan of Machen which particularly incensed Bleddyn. Morgan had not allowed his office as a justice of the peace to prevent him from receiving George Morris into his house on Christmas Days and holy days, or from deliberately absenting himself from Easter communion.[97]

In the mean time, in 1579, the Welsh contingent among the Catholic exiles on the Continent had suffered a deeply damaging set-back arising out of the critical differences of opinion and sentiment between English and Welsh students at Rome. The troubles sprang from discontents at the newly founded college in the city.[98] When Gregory XIII had suggested the establishment of this college, the proposal was warmly endorsed by Owen Lewis, now much in favour in papal circles. There had for centuries

---

[93] T. P. Ellis, *Welsh Benedictines of the Terror* (Newtown, 1936), p. 48.

[94] *APC*, XI. 29.

[95] Ibid., X. 48.

[96] Ibid., X. 29, 103, 190; cf. C. A. J. Skeel, *The Council in the Marches of Wales* (London, 1904), pp. 101–2.

[97] L. Thomas, *The Reformation in the Old Diocese of Llandaff* (Cardiff, 1930), pp. 147–8.

[98] A. Kenny, *The English Hospice at Rome* (London, 1962).

beforehand been a hospital at Rome which, some maintained, had originally been founded by the English, while others claimed a Welsh origin for it. When Gregory had founded his college in 1578 he made use of the hospital to endow it. As rector of the college he appointed the warden of the hospital, Morys Clynnog. He had been persuaded to do so by Owen Lewis, who had given books, furniture, and some money to help endow the new foundation. Twenty-six students were sent there from Douai in 1578, and a year later, there were forty-two students, together with the rector, three Jesuit fathers as teachers, and six servants. It would generally be admitted that Morys Clynnog, good man as he was in many respects, was not an ideal choice as rector. He had no experience of managing students and was too inclined to favour his own countrymen. The English students, who outnumbered their Welsh colleagues by thirty-three to nine, resented his attitude and walked out in protest. Any Welsh rejoicing there may have been at this 'victory' was short-lived. The English students were soon readmitted, and Morys Clynnog was removed from the rectorship, though he was allowed to remain as warden of the hospital.[99]

It seems likely that the dissensions between the opposing factions may have gone deeper than the issue of nationality. They may well have turned, *au fond*, on the question of what it was the college was supposed to achieve. Clynnog, Lewis, the Welsh students, and the Roman establishment viewed it as an institution for preparing men to occupy benefices until such time as it would be possible for them to return to their own country. The Jesuits, the English students, and Robert Parsons envisaged it as a seminary to train men for the mission field.[100] The split, whatever its origins, went very deep. Morys Clynnog was so put out that he soon afterwards left Rome, and, taking a ship to Spain, was drowned in the course of the voyage.[101] Owen Lewis, filled with bitterness against the Jesuits, also left Rome. He made his way to Milan, where he came very much under the influence of Borromeo and the latter's concept of a church which stood for the hierarchy and the rights of bishops, and was deeply opposed to some aspects of Jesuit activity.[102] This quarrel at Rome had some unfortunate after-effects. It made Owen Lewis and others of the Welsh unduly suspicious of the Jesuit order, which seemed to them to be too much under Spanish influence. It may also have reduced Welsh influence at the crucial levels of decision-making among the exiles, thus lessening the impact of Welsh advice about the most effective ways of bringing Catholic influences

[99] Williams, *Modern Wales*, pp. 218–20.
[100] J. Bossy, *The English Catholic Community, 1570–1850* (London, 1977), p. 26.
[101] Williams, *Modern Wales*, p. 220.
[102] Bossy, *Catholic Community*, pp. 26–8; idem, 'The character of Elizabethan Catholicism', *PP*, XXI (1962), 39–59.

to bear on Wales. All the same, the long-term impact of the dispute on Welsh efforts at reconversion has almost certainly been overemphasized in the past. The Jesuits were not as unacceptable to the Welsh as has at times been postulated.[103] As early as 1580, for example, at the 'Synod of Southwark', a meeting of Jesuits, seminary priests, and recusant clergymen, which included some Welshmen among them, was able to decide to concentrate its energies on three areas: the north, Wales, and East Anglia.[104] In the same year, the Welshman, William Griffith of Llanfeuthin in Glamorgan, took upon himself the hazardous task of giving shelter to the two celebrated Jesuits, Campion and Parsons, at Southland, his mother's residence near Uxbridge.[105]

The arrival in England in 1580 of those two Jesuits, Campion and Parsons, short-lived as their mission proved to be, created tremendous agitation in government circles. Closely associated with the Jesuits were two Welsh Catholics at least: the seminary priest, Robert Gwyn, and the layman, William Griffith. Both gave strong backing to the Jesuit plans to circulate Catholic books and to set up secret presses on which more literature might be printed.[106] It may have been the near-panic induced by the Jesuits' arrival which led the Privy Council to press Sir Henry Sidney to seek out Catholics in Montgomeryshire and elsewhere along the Welsh border. Sidney, however, was notoriously lenient towards Catholics and dilatory about prosecuting them – to such an extent that one of his own friends at court, Francis Walsingham, felt obliged to deliver him 'a mild rebuke and an urgent warning': 'Your lordship had need to walk warily, for your doings are narrowly observed, and Her Majesty is apt to give ear to any that shall ill you. Great hold is taken by your enemies for the neglecting of this commission.'[107] The council also believed it essential that the Welsh bishops should take action against 'all schoolmasters, public and private'.[108] This order resulted in the arrest of the Welshman, Richard White, and his imprisonment in Wrexham. White was regarded as all the more of a menace because he was acting as the agent and organizer for all the Douai priests in the area.

It was in the aftermath of the stir caused by Parsons and Campion that Parliament passed the statute of 1581, which extended the law of treason to cover all those who withdrew the queen's subjects from their allegiance to

---

[103] Williams, *Making Wales*, pp. 220–4.

[104] C. Haigh (ed.), *The English Reformation Revised* (London, 1987), p. 196.

[105] F. H. Pugh, 'William Griffith of Llanvithyn: a Glamorgan recusant', *Morgannwg*, XXX (1986), 11. Two of his brothers, Hugh and Richard, his nephew, James, and an illegitimate son of his grandfather all became Catholics.

[106] Ibid.

[107] Williams, *Council in Marches*, p. 94; cf. *Mont. Colls.* IX. 382–3.

[108] *APC*, XIII (1581–2), 427–8; Thomas, *Elizabethan Martyrs*, pp. 87–8.

her Church.[109] It made the hearing of mass punishable by imprisonment and raised the fine for recusancy to the prohibitive figure of £20. It proved to be impracticable to collect the £20 fine regularly, though some lesser amount might be borne. But in any event the operation of the recusancy laws proved to be haphazard and ineffective. Recusants escaped punishment because officials were often corrupt or negligent; many offenders were 'well-favoured and friended'; others had possessions in more than one county; and some came to church but did not commune.[110] Had the fines been regularly or effectually levied, they would surely have crippled those Catholics brave enough to defy the statute. It has been calculated, however, that only a quarter of convicted recusants suffered any actual financial loss.[111] A letter of May 1582 sent by Bishop Robinson to Walsingham seems to suggest that at first the pressure on Catholics was not as severe as it might have been. 'I am termed by letters from my countrymen beyond the seas [i.e. the Catholic exiles] a persecutor', he wrote,

for that of long time I have laid wait for their massing priests and such as hear them, and do make inquisition twice every year through every parish of such, whereby though some times there were many that did withdraw themselves from the Church, yet now in my whole diocese there be but six.[112]

In the same month of 1582 the Privy Council had complained that the number of recusants in Wales had greatly increased because of the slackness of justices of the peace.[113] This seems to have stirred the Council in the Marches into greater activity and, as the teeth of the penal legislation began to bite and the machinery of persecution ground more finely, the numbers of recusants brought before the courts increased. In 1582, John Bennett, the first seminary priest to be arrested in Wales, was seized near Sir Thomas Mostyn's house at Gloddaeth, imprisoned, and condemned to be hanged. Bennett appears to have been the principal target of the prosecutors, but fortunately for him, the sentence was changed in 1585 to banishment for life.[114] Richard White, imprisoned first in 1580, fared much worse. He was summoned before eight different assize sessions

---

[109] *Statutes Realm*, IV. 657–8.
[110] K. R. Wark, *Elizabethan Recusancy in Cheshire* (Manchester, 1971), p. 64.
[111] Pugh, *SWMRS*, III. 51.
[112] Evans, *Cymm.* XXXIX. 180.
[113] *APC*, XIII. 427.
[114] Cleary, *Blackfriars* (1957), pp. 113–14. Bennett also figures prominently in the accounts of the martyrdom of Richard White, Thomas, *Elizabethan Martyrs, passim*.

in all and subjected to almost unendurable pressure in order to get him to recant. Finally, in 1584 he and two other recusants appeared at Wrexham before Sir George Bromley, justice of assize, Dr Ellis Price, and others. White was questioned with exceptional severity about his loyalty to the queen in the light of the bull of excommunication of 1570. He was reputed to have replied, 'notwithstanding the bull (the which I never saw) I believe and confirm she (Elizabeth) is our lawful queen'.[115] Condemned by the court, he died a barbarously cruel death on 17 October 1584. Brave and unyielding as he was to the end, it has to be admitted that he could be stubborn and somewhat violent. His execution was deliberately designed to be a dreadful example to others. As such it may partly have served its purpose, since John Edwards of Chirk, one of the leading Catholics in north Wales, created a sensation by recanting publicly after White's execution.[116] On the other hand, the long and eloquent accounts of White's sufferings were certainly intended by those who compiled them to proclaim to his fellow-countrymen 'his patience and constancy for the faith of the old Britons, their dear progenitors'.[117]

The prosecution of Richard White, John Bennett, and others was part of a general drive against priests and recusants launched during 1583–5 in a thickening atmosphere of plot and hostility. In 1583 Francis Throckmorton was caught bringing over an incriminating letter to Mary Queen of Scots from her representative in Paris, Thomas Morgan, and was put to death in 1584 for his complicity.[118] In July 1584 William of Orange, Protestant leader of the Netherlanders' fight for independence, outlawed by Philip II and a price put on his head, was assassinated. A wave of unreasoning panic concerning the queen's safety flooded over England and Wales. It was intensified in Wales by the tone and content of a poem in Welsh bitterly attacking William, *Cywydd Marwnad yn Llawn Cabledd i'r Prins o Orens* (An Elegy full of Calumny against the Prince of Orange).[119] Once rejected as the work of Richard White, its attribution to him is now regarded as more possible.[120] To mobilize public opinion in defence of the queen, the so-called Bond of Association was circulated among all the leading gentry and was signed by hundreds of Welsh gentlemen regardless of their religious views.[121] About half of the forty who signed it in Monmouthshire, the most Catholic county in Wales if not in the whole

[115] Ibid., p. 99.
[116] Ibid., pp. 247, 289.
[117] Ibid., pp. 124–5.
[118] *Correspondence of Robert Dudley, Earl of Leycester . . . in the Years 1585 and 1586*, ed. J. Prince (Camden Soc., London, 1844), p. 342.
[119] Parry-Williams, *Carolau*, pp. 5–6.
[120] Thomas, *Elizabethan Martyrs*, p. 49
[121] *CSP Dom. Add., 1580–1625*, p. 130.

kingdom, were either Catholic recusants or Catholic in sympathy. They swore, none the less, to defend Queen Elizabeth, 'by whose life we do enjoy an unquestionable benefit of peace in this land'.[122]

At this very time, hysteria was raised to an even higher pitch by the knowledge that a Member of Parliament of Welsh origins, William Parry, born at Northop in Flintshire, was being accused of plotting to assassinate the queen. Parry was an enigmatic figure whose intentions are not easy to fathom. He had earlier been a spy on behalf of Cecil but had converted to Catholicism while in Europe. He may have been one of those double agents so common in the shifting sands of the religious loyalties of the age, or possibly somewhat unhinged mentally, or even both. He was clearly a very convenient scapegoat for those who wanted to make an example by ostentatiously executing an alleged Catholic plotter. If, however, he was in truth guilty of what was alleged against him he seems to have been acting as a lone individual without confederates in Wales.[123] Another Welshman, Thomas Crowther from Montgomeryshire, a priest who left Douai in 1578 and was later imprisoned in the Marshalsea, died in gaol in 1585.[124]

Enraged by the assassination of William of Orange, the excitement over the Bond of Association, and the discovery of the Throckmorton and Parry Plots, Parliament, in a fury of anti-papist feeling, passed the statute of 1585 against Jesuits, seminary priests, and other disobedient persons.[125] The Act made it unlawful for any Jesuit or seminary priest to enter the realm, or remain within it after forty days. Those who aided or sustained them were to be adjudged felons and put to death. Of the 189 Catholics executed during Elizabeth's reign, 123 of them (ninety-six being priests) were executed under the terms of this Act.[126] A much closer watch was henceforward kept on recusants in Wales and the Marches. Nine Catholic gentlemen, among them William Griffith of Llanfeuthin and Lewis Turberville of Llancarfan, were brought before the Great Sessions in 1585. In the next year, nineteen recusants were indicted after a violent and unseemly altercation over the issues of burying a dead Catholic according to the form and ceremonial of the Anglican Church.[127]

On 19 October 1586 an intriguing letter had reached the Privy Council from an anonymous correspondent in Pembrokeshire concerning one John

[122] Pugh, *SWMRS*, IV. 63.
[123] BL, Harleian MS. 4060, fo. 85; E. P. Roberts, 'Dr William Parry a'i gefndir', *LlC*, V (1959), 193–207; L. Hicks, 'The strange case of Dr William Parry', *Studies*, XXXVII (1948), 343–62.
[124] Cleary, *Checklist*, p. 115.
[125] *Statutes Realm*, IV. 706–8.
[126] Thomas, *Elizabethan Martyrs*, p. 14.
[127] *Records of the County Borough of Cardiff*, ed. J. H. Matthews (6 vols. Cardiff, 1898–1911), II. 145, 158–61.

Bowen, parson of Tenby.[128] It contained the somewhat startling accusation that this cleric of the Established Church was befriending Richard Benson, gentleman, of Martletwy, 'a notable papist and one vehemently suspected of being scarce the queen's friend'. It is even more surprising to discover Bowen being further alleged to have at his disposal 'a notable surrypost'[129] that 'often flies to London and suddenly back to Pembrokeshire, and so from papist to papist'. The papists were not only said to maintain close contacts with one another over wide distances but also to rejoice greatly in the 'young imps' of their religion lately sprung up, especially at the inns of court. Moreover, pilgrimages were reported as still being carried on in Pembrokeshire, as at 'St Mogans' (Capel Meugan) on Corpus Christi Day,[130] and at Cardiganshire to St 'Kyrryck' (Curig). In the following year, Benson and two others were brought before the justices of assize for recusancy.[131]

On 25 May 1586 the Privy Council expressed its profound disquiet at news from Wales and the Marches of the falling away of many of her majesty's subjects in religion and the bold and unlawful meeting of papists at masses, etc.' and contempt for the laws in general. All of this was attributed to the 'negligence and faction' of the justices of the peace.[132] As if to confirm his own apprehension of what was happening in Carmarthenshire, one Rees Lewis expressed his grave concern that a certain David William Delahaye of Llanegwad, who had not received communion for four years and was suspected of harbouring papist sympathies, was likely to be made sheriff of Carmarthenshire.[133] Edward Dwn Lee, presenting John Penry's *Aequity* (1587) to the House of Commons, reported the 'great idolatry' begun again in Wales to an 'idol' of a service, 'said in neither Welsh nor English' and of the 'superstition they use to a spring-well' and 'what ignorance they live in for lack of learned and honest ministers'.[134] Had the Privy Council been aware of what the Spanish ambassador, Bernardino Mendoza, was writing to his master in August 1586, it would surely have been even more perturbed: 'in south Wales and north Wales the gentry and common people are much attached to the Catholic religion and the queen of Scotland'.[135]

---

[128] PRO, SP12/183/27.

[129] I am not clear what the significance of 'surrypost' is here. *OED* (2nd edn.), however, under 'post' cites the chronicler Hall (1548) as saying that the earl of Surrey laid posts every way, which posts stretched to the Marches of Wales. I take it, therefore, to mean some rapid method of distributing news.

[130] F. Jones, *The Holy Wells of Wales* (Cardiff, 1954), pp. 59–62.

[131] *Pembs. Co. Hist.* III. 114.

[132] *APC*, XIV (1586–7), 123.

[133] BL, Harleian MS. 6994, fo. 40.

[134] BL, Harleian MS. 7188, fo. 93b.

[135] *CSP Span.* III. 610.

Whatever tremors of apprehension may have rippled along the nerves of Catholic sympathizers in Wales as a result of the executions of Richard White and William Parry, they were far less significant than the agitation aroused by the outcome of the Babington Plot of 1586. Anthony Babington himself had been introduced to Mary Stuart by Thomas Morgan who, as a result of representations made by the English government, was subsequently imprisoned in the Bastille by the French authorities.[136] Moreover, involved in the conspiracy were not only such prominent exiles as Hugh Owen, William Allen, and Robert Parsons, but also on the outer fringes of it in England were two leading young Denbighshire squires. They were Thomas Salusbury, head of the house of Lleweni, described by Babington as a 'comely personage, valiant, and extreme lover of his nation',[137] and his friend, Edward Jones of Plas Cadwgan. The conspirators' object had been to assassinate Elizabeth, release Mary, and encourage a foreign invasion. But details of the plot were thoroughly familiar to Walsingham, who was confident that, if the affair were well handled, it would 'break the neck of all dangerous practices'.[138] He was right; the plot was exposed, and the young Welshmen fled to their native Wales. There they were captured and later executed on 21 September 1586. The Babington Plot also proved to be the last twist in the winding road to Mary Stuart's own downfall and execution. The fate of Salusbury and Jones fatally shook the faith of many Catholic waverers. Taken with the growing threat of military and naval action, it was in 1586–7 that many of those who had been in danger of drifting from the Catholic religion finally abandoned it. One such was Sir Richard Bulkeley, reported to the Privy Council by his old enemies, Lewis ap Owen and Owen Wood for having 'secret conference with Salusbury',[139] and bound over in the enormous sum of £5,000 not to depart without special licence from the council.

Looking back on the years from 1583 to 1587 there is good reason for thinking that these plots against the queen proved a major obstacle to the evangelizing efforts of the priests. They had rendered suspect to many of Elizabeth's subjects all attempts to fortify the morale of Catholics, as subversive ploys designed to eliminate the queen, replace her by the Catholic Mary, and invite foreign papist troops in to rule the kingdom. John Penry was typical in his excoriation of 'these insatiable bloodsuckers, Babington and his adherents, who might have brought disaster on the queen and her subjects'.[140]

[136] *DNB.*
[137] D. Mathew, *The Celtic Peoples and Renaissance Europe* (London, 1933), p. 67 n. 2.
[138] *Correspondence Robert Dudley*, p. 342.
[139] *APC*, XVI (1588), 23–4.
[140] J. Penry, *Three Treatises concerning Wales*, ed. D. Williams (Cardiff, 1960), p. 27.

In spite of the intense and growing pressure on the recusants in the summer and autumn of 1586, a small group of Welsh Catholics embarked on the daring experiment of setting up their own secret printing-press.[141] Six years had gone by since it had been agreed at the Uxbridge conference of 1580 to establish Catholic presses. Although the times were anything but propitious for such an enterprise, the group went ahead with it. At the heart of the venture was a Caernarfonshire landowner, Robert Pugh, squire of Creuddyn on the eastern fringe of the county. In a cave on his own land at Rhiwledin on the Little Orme near Llandudno he gathered a group of friends about him. Besides Pugh himself they included his cousin, Hugh Thomas, from Watford; a seminary priest, William Davies; another priest called Roger Thackwell;[142] and four other anonymous persons. They occupied the cave for six months and, during that time, set up the first printing-press in Wales. They were engaged in printing the first part of *Drych Cristianogawl*, the most effective piece of Catholic writing produced in Welsh during the sixteenth century. Then, in February 1587 the cave and the little company were discovered by the servants of Sir Thomas Mostyn of Gloddaeth and a watch set on them. Nevertheless, the group managed to escape; possibly because Mostyn, according to the disdainful statement made about him by his fellow justice of the peace, Dr William Griffith, was 'a man not very rigid against Catholics, but one that complied with the times'.[143] That was a verdict applicable to many of his Welsh colleagues. Excavations conducted in the cave during the 1960s revealed nothing of any significance, except perhaps that it had two entrances, which may have been what facilitated its occupants' escape. No one has been able to show who the author of the work they were printing was, though it is evident that he depended heavily for his material on the text of Robert Parsons's *Christian Directory*.[144] The full three parts of the text were later copied in manuscript by Llywelyn Siôn *c*.1600.[145] Its object undoubtedly was to bolster the faith of Catholics; to encourage them to stand forth boldly as believers; to get them to realize the eternal punishment awaiting them if they failed to do so; and to seek to remove the worldly temptations which lured them into concealing their true belief and led them to temporize with the Anglican Church. The denunciation by John Penry of the volume and its printer, 'the knave Thackwell . . . which printed popish and traitorous

---

[141] R. G. Gruffydd, *Argraffwyr Cyntaf Cymru* (Cardiff, 1972), pp. 4–11.

[142] D. M. Rogers, '"Popishe Thackwell" and early printing in Wales', *Biographical Studies, 1534–1829* (Bognor Regis, 1952), XI/1. 37–54.

[143] Gruffydd, *Argraffwyr*, p. 9.

[144] Dr. G. Bowen believes it was Robert Gwyn; but Prof. R. G. Gruffydd thinks that Siôn Dafydd Rhys deserves at least part of the credit.

[145] Williams, *Tradd. Llen. Morg.*, p. 178.

books in Wales'[146] gives an indication of the mixture of the dread and anger which its publication awakened in Protestant circles. A seventeenth-century priest-poet, Gwilym Pugh, on the other hand, spoke with patent fellow-feeling of the sufferings of those who were the target of the angry search, inspired from Ludlow, of the watch set on the whole countryside, the shattering of gates, and the rampage through Penrhyn in the hunt for offenders.[147]

Difficult as it may be to believe, within a short space of time after the débâcle in Creuddyn, the Catholic group was courageous or rash enough to tempt fate with another try. This time the scene of its operations was the house of Siôn Dafydd Rhys at Brecon.[148] Dr Rhys was a fascinating individual; born in Anglesey in 1534, after a short stay in Oxford he spent many years in Italy between *c*.1565 and *c*.1570. He graduated in medicine at Siena in 1567 and became an accomplished Renaissance scholar. Throughout his time in Italy he was presumably a Catholic; but by 1576 or 1577, when he joined his uncle, Bishop Richard Davies, at Carmarthen, he had become a Protestant and now experimented with translating Protestant texts into Welsh at his uncle's request. After the bishop's death in 1581, Rhys moved to Cardiff and thence to Brecon. About this time, presumably under the influence of seminary priests, he reverted to Catholicism. In 1587 a Catholic group, organized by Robert Gwyn and his brother David, had been printing a book in Rhys's house at Brecon, according to the evidence given by Roger Thackwell, who was captured very late in that year.[149] When the house was searched, although nothing was found, Rhys was taken first before the Council in the Marches and later to the Court of High Commission. There he was examined by Archbishop Whitgift and, before being released, was forced to take an oath of loyalty to the queen. The book that was being printed at Brecon remains a mystery. It has aptly been suggested that it was the second part of *Drych*, although no copy of it has survived.[150]

All the while, Philip II's naval and military preparations for the invasion of England were proceeding apace. John Penry feared that they might be used the instrument of God's wrath to punish the Welsh nation for its sins. A major stumbling-block had been removed from Philip's path, ironically enough, by the execution of Mary Stuart in February 1587. Elizabeth had been justified in her conviction that Mary dead might be more of a

---

[146] Gruffydd, *Argraffwyr*, p. 9.

[147] J. G. Jones, *Wales and the Tudor State* (Cardiff, 1988), p. 105.

[148] Gruffydd, *Argraffwyr*, pp 11–20; 'The life of Dr John Davies', *TCS* (1971), ii. 175–9; 'Dr John Davies: the old man of Brecknock', *AC* (1992), 1–13.

[149] Gruffydd, *Argraffwyr*, pp. 15–16.

[150] Ibid., pp. 18–19.

threat to her than Mary alive. Philip no longer had any reason to fear that all his expenditure of blood and treasure to conquer England might simply end up in making Mary queen, thereby advancing the interests of France and Scotland at the expense of Spain. Nor were all his preliminaries concerned merely with strategic questions; plans were also afoot for the restoration of religion and the government of the Church after it had been brought back to the holy Catholic faith from whoring after damnable heresies. William Allen was created a cardinal in 1587 in the expectation that he would become archbishop of Canterbury once the Armada had triumphed. Owen Lewis was made bishop of Cassano in Naples, in preparation for being elevated to the archbishopric of York. Allen and other firm supporters of Spain were opposed to this proposal. Possibly they still recalled Lewis's pan-Celtic outburst to Mary Stuart's envoy, the bishop of Ross, 'my lord, let us stick together, for we are the old and true inhabitants of the isle of Britain. The others be but usurpers and mere possessors.'[151] Allen ruled out the archbishopric of York for Lewis and suggested instead that he be given St David's, 'the best bishopric in Wales or the Marches . . . with some occupation to keep him in play at a distance from Rome and London also'.[152] Alas! Both Allen and Lewis were destined to die in exile and neither was ever to see his homeland again. The defeat of the Armada led to the failure of the 'physical force' plans for the Church as well as for the rest of Elizabeth's kingdom.

The severe set-back caused by the defeat of the Armada did not, by any means, signify the deathblow of recusancy. Between the years 1570 and 1588 the patterns of recusancy in Wales had been firmly laid down and would remain in place with surprisingly little change from generation to generation until well into the seventeenth century. These years formed a crucial phase in the history of the Roman Catholic religion, when its adherents evolved a new and sturdier fibre of resistance, bred in them to a considerable extent by the advent of seminary priests, with their steely training and their inextinguishable confidence in the resurgent Catholicism of the Counter-Reformation. Francis Bacon described the product of the seminaries as the 'priest of sedition' and the old-style priest as the 'priest of superstition'.[153] The poet Spenser was justified in the contrast he drew between the 'zeal of popish priests' coming out of Spain, Rome, or Rheims 'by long and dangerous travel' to a land where they knew well that the peril of death awaited them and there was no hope of reward or riches to be

---

[151] Knox, *Records*, II. 82.
[152] G. Bowen, 'Llenyddiaeth Gatholig' (MA thesis, Liverpool, 1966), p. 30.
[153] A. Morey, *The Catholic Subjects of Elizabeth I* (London, 1978), p. 173.

found, and the 'idle and uncommitted priests' of the old-fashioned kind.[154] Robert Parsons, too, criticized the latter for being content with a 'stage-play where men do change their persons and parts, without changing their names or their affections', whereas the newcomers, by contrast, were less concerned with doctrine and more preoccupied with 'interior conversion and godly discipline'.[155] The self-sacrifice of devoted priests – and laymen, too – encouraged a considerable number of 'Nicodemuses' to embrace their faith openly and to reject the ministrations of the State Church. The recusants had, of necessity, to keep their doings under cover and as secret as possible, and so have managed to elude the attentions of subsequent historians as well as those of contemporary officers of justice. But the numbers of recusants arrested by the authorities increased dramatically between 1585 and 1588 and were recorded in contemporary sources: gaol files and calendar rolls of the Great Sessions, and the Recusant Rolls. Partly this owed much to the efforts of Catholic missionaries; but the increase recorded in the statistical record was also a product of sharper scrutiny by the agencies of persecution. Gravely perturbed by the mounting threat of subversion and invasion, the Privy Council and the Council in the Marches were exerting more and more pressure on the justices of assize and the local officers of justice and administration to search out more rigorously many of those recusants who had earlier been left unharried. Thus, for instance, in the most strongly recusant county, Monmouthshire, there was an extraordinary surge reported in the numbers of 'refuseniks'. Between 1581 and 1587 only seven seem to have been reported in no more than five parishes, whereas in the year 1588 288 from thirty-seven parishes are to be found in the sources.[156] It seems highly improbable that there were that number of converts in so short a space of time; it is much more likely that panic over the threat of the Armada applied a spur of unwonted efficiency to the search for offenders.

The geographical location of the main centres of recusancy and the families chiefly associated with it had also emerged during these years. The two westernmost dioceses of Wales – Bangor in the north and St David's in the south – were the least affected by it at this time. This may have been partly explained by the much greater fear felt in both dioceses of the possibility of invasion from Ireland and Spain, since the really vulnerable points in the coastal defences were to be found in the north-west and south-west.[157] It may also have been due to the fact that both these dioceses

---

[154] C. Haigh, *Reformation and Resistance in Tudor Lancashire* (Cambridge, 1973), pp. 242–3.
[155] Bossy, *Catholic Community*, p. 17.
[156] Pugh, *SWMRS*, IV. 66–7.
[157] *W 1415–1642*, chap. 15.

were remote from the main thoroughfares in England and along the border that were used by Catholic priests. Each contained its 'hot spots' of Catholic devotion, like Creuddyn in Bangor[158] and Slebech in St David's,[159] but neither of these dioceses was a particular stronghold. The most formidable redoubts of Catholic loyalty were to be found in the diocese of St Asaph in the north-east and Llandaff in the south-east. In each instance the liveliest and most vibrant centres of recusant activity were to be found on the borders between dioceses and counties. Thus, in St Asaph diocese they flourished near the border with the Catholic strongpoints in the diocese of Chester and the county of Cheshire. They were located in places like Holywell, whose Well of St Winifred was still one of the most magnetic foci of Catholic worshippers anywhere in the north;[160] Wrexham, with ten recusants recorded as early as 1581; Erbistock, where at least three priests were busy in Richard Lloyd's house in 1579; and Chirk, whose mainstays were John Edwards, senior and junior.[161] It was in this area that Richard White the martyr had dedicated himself with such effect. It was possibly the repercussions following his martyrdom and the execution of Salusbury and Jones that led to the fall in the numbers of recusants noted in the county of Denbigh from thirty-eight in 1581 to thirteen in 1587.[162] John Edwards, senior, was known to have shocked many of his fellow-believers by his recantation at White's trial.[163] Llandaff, too, may have owed much of the impressive strength of its recusant numbers to its proximity to England and the diocese of Hereford. Centres like Abergavenny, Raglan, or Monmouth lay conveniently near the border, and it has been calculated that 70 per cent of Monmouthshire's recusants were to be found within the valleys of the adjacent rivers of Usk, Monnow, and Afon Lwyd.[164] The Vale of Glamorgan also had easy communications by water with Gloucestershire and the west of England. The great Morgan family clan in Monmouthshire and the Turbervilles in the Vale of Glamorgan proved themselves to be pillars of recusancy from generation to generation. In the lists of recusants the names of the same families and identical parishes kept on recurring year after year. The habits of religious loyalty and resistance were becoming ineradicably ingrained.

It was, in the main, men and women of at least a modest economic competence who felt able to stand their ground in this way. The leaders of

---

[158] E. G. Jones, *Cymru a'r Hen Ffydd* (Cardiff, 1951), pp. 18–21.
[159] J. M. Cleary, *The Catholic Recusancy of the Barlow Family of Slebech* (Cardiff, 1956).
[160] G. H. Jones, *Celtic Britain and the Pilgrim Movement* (London, 1912), pp. 391, 408.
[161] Jones, *Hen Ffydd*, pp. 24–6.
[162] Ibid., pp. 25–6.
[163] Thomas, *Elizabethan Martyrs*, pp. 96–7.
[164] Pugh, *SWMRS*, IV. 61.

recusancy, as has been referred to, were the heads of gentry families. Alongside them were ranged their wives, relations, and servants, and those yeomen, tenants, and labourers who were dependent upon them.[165] One of the noticeable features was the high incidence of women in their midst, possibly because women tend to be more responsive to religion than men. What Richard Hooker had to say of the role of women in relation to Puritanism would be equally applicable to Roman Catholicism. Their courage and persistence were such as to draw children, servants, friends, and allies to worship with them.[166] On occasions also, a Catholic husband, in order to protect the family resources from fines and levies, might go through the motions of conformity while his wife kept the flag of family loyalty flying by pointedly staying away from the parish church. One of these Catholic ladies, a young Welsh woman called Elizabeth Orton, born in the border parish of Owyrtyn Madog (Overton), created a great sensation in the surrounding districts by putting her 'feigned visions' in writing and circulating them among the people. They were an 'invention' attributed to a 'Jesuit' or some other 'devilish seducer' 'to abuse the vulgar and ignorant sort'. The priest thus uncomplimentarily referred to by his enemies may well have been Edward Hughes.[167] Whatever the origins of her visions may have been, they created sufficient of a stir for Elizabeth herself to be apprehended and sent up to the Privy Council.[168]

In 1588 there still existed a mass of tenacious traditional beliefs and practices in Wales. Yet comparatively little of it crossed the frontier into open and conscious rebellion against the Established Church in the form of principled refusal to have any truck with Anglicanism. Those Catholic observers who continued to buoy up their own hopes of the existence of a large body of Welsh people prepared to take up arms on behalf of the pope and the old religion had misread the posture of those who were unaffected by Protestant doctrine and remained addicted to traditional practices. For the most part, theirs was a non-militant Catholicism, if indeed it could be called Catholicism at all. When push came to shove, nearly all of them were prepared to acknowledge, as indeed did most of the Catholic sympathizers even of Monmouthshire, that it was through Elizabeth's continued existence that they enjoyed 'an unquestionable benefit of peace in this land'.

---

[165] For the lists of parishes and the names of recusants within them, Pugh, *SWMRS*, III. 49–67; IV. 57–110.

[166] Wark, *Cheshire*, p. 84.

[167] Cleary, *Checklist*, p. 17; Thomas, *Elizabethan Martyrs*, pp. 41–4.

[168] T. M. Cahill, 'Thomas North at Chester', *Huntington Library Quarterly*, XIII (1949–50), 93–9, gives an account based largely on Barnaby Rich, *The True Report of a Late Practise Enterprised by a Papist with a Young Maiden in Wales* (1582).

CHAPTER 11

The Church by Law Established: I. The Clergy

THROUGHOUT all these years, from 1568 to 1589, those responsible for guiding the destinies of the Anglican Church in Wales could not but be painfully conscious of the challenge of Rome; or what Bishop Richard Davies denounced as the 'kingdom of Antichrist';[1] the devout clerical author, Rowland Puleston, as 'the open enemies of Christ, the papists';[2] and the Puritan John Penry as the 'lifeless and brutish stock of Rome'.[3] Even so, it was not the growth of open recusancy that was the main cause of worry to the Welsh bishops and other devoted Protestants. As became evident from their reports, the number of avowed adherents of Rome was not so great as to occasion them their most serious concern. In spite of the insufficiencies of the machinery for detecting recusants and all the covering up of offenders that went on, the degree of control exercised by lay and ecclesiastical authority, and the general willingness of the population to submit to it, were, broadly speaking, reassuring enough.

A much more intractable problem was the great mass of earlier belief and practice of every kind which survived in varying degrees among that huge majority of the population who were, in name, members of the Established Church. Many of these customs – vigils for the dead, veneration of relics and holy wells, pilgrimages, and the like – were the remnants of folk religion which had been handed down for centuries.[4] The more thoughtful churchmen of the Middle Ages might have deplored the grosser practices of the rank and file but had found them impossible to uproot.[5] Bishop Richard Davies was obliged to reproach his countrymen for clinging to the 'superstition, charms and incantations' of the former religion;[6] his successor, Marmaduke Middleton, described the people of his

---

[1] R. Davies, *Funeral Sermon preached at Carmarthen on the Death of the Earl of Essex* (London, 1577), no pagination.

[2] *Rhyddiaith Gymraeg*, II. *Detholion o Lawysgrifau a Llyfrau Printiedig*, ed. T. Jones (Cardiff, 1956), p. 54.

[3] J. Penry, *Three Treatises concerning Wales*, ed. D. Williams (Cardiff, 1960), p. 30.

[4] S. Victory, *The Celtic Church in Wales* (Cardiff, 1972), *passim*.

[5] *WC*, chap. 13.

[6] Ibid., p. 463.

diocese as 'having been for the most part trained up in erroneous opinions, idolatrous amity and wicked superstition'.[7] While Penry, with his invariable vehemence and exaggeration, declared that most of the Welsh people were either 'plainly mere atheists, or stark blinded with superstition'.[8] Not that conditions would seem to be any better in many parts of England, where a Puritan document of 1584 claimed that 'three parts at least of the people were wedded to their old superstitions still'.[9] As late as 1598 an Essex minister alleged that 'the poor people do not understand as much as the Lord's Prayer'.[10]

The Elizabethan era remained an age when, for most people, custom went on being king. It continued to be unthinkable not to cherish in the memory what one had heard, seen, and absorbed since childhood, and to transmit this inheritance to subsequent generations. For the majority, this culture was not derived from formal instruction or private reading but was an oral one. Literacy, though making progress among the better-off, was making little or no headway among ordinary folk. A contemporary account of the state of Wales told of the 'extreme poverty of its inhabitants . . . its thefts, ignorance of God's word' and its dire need for more schools.[11] A recent estimate by the most thorough student of education in Tudor and Stuart Wales has calculated that by 1640 there can hardly have been more than 20 per cent of the Welsh population who were able to read in English or Welsh.[12] For much of Elizabeth's reign there may have been no more than half, or at best three-quarters, of that proportion. That meant that religion continued to consist of those ingrained habits of thought and feeling and a body of traditional practices mostly picked up from ancestors and the surrounding community. There was still a prevailing tendency for the majority to look upon religion as a body of collective rites practised by the inhabitants of the parish as a community; activities to a large extent conducted on behalf of the layfolk by their parish priests. These customs were closely aligned with the seasons of the year, agricultural operations, and the *rites de passage* of the ordinary person. They were designed less to instruct the individual in a body of religious belief and moral conduct than to offer to the community's members, together with their crops, livestock, and property, some safeguard from harm and misfortune in this world and the next. The eminent Puritan, Thomas Cartwright, was convinced that

[7] W. P. M. Kennedy, *Elizabethan Episcopal Administration* (3 vols. Alcuin Club, London, 1926), III. 145.

[8] *Treatises*, p. 32.

[9] K. V. Thomas, *Religion and the Decline of Magic* (London, 1971), p. 73.

[10] K. Wrightson, *English Society, 1580–1680* (London, 1982), p. 204.

[11] J. Fisher, 'De presenti statu totius Walliae', *AC* (1915), 237–52.

[12] W. P. Griffith, 'Schooling and society', in J. G. Jones (ed.), *Class, Community and Culture in Tudor Wales* (Cardiff, 1989).

'heaps' of his contemporaries had, at the bidding of their ruler, cast aside much of their old religion without discovering the new.[13] One early seventeenth-century commentator thought it possible that only one part in twenty was 'Christian indeed', 'the greatest part being the worst'.[14] The more remote and less urbanized the region, the truer this was. Lancashire, being a distant upland county, was stubbornly conservative; holy water was widely in evidence, church bells were tolled for the dead, and rosaries most commonly used of all; as late as 1590 there was a very caustic description of survivals there.[15] Cumbria and Northumbria were no better, although, unlike Lancashire, survivals in those areas did not give rise to a comparably stubborn recusancy.[16]

The same went for large parts of Wales. John Penry described the Welsh as 'in very deed stark atheists . . . since the time you came out of the den of idolatry and popery, you were not made partakers of the power of God to salvation'.[17] The Elizabethan settlement may outwardly have been accepted, but infused into it were all kinds of ancient habits; frequent crossings of oneself, regular invocation of the saints, resort to wells, and persistent use of rosaries. The poet, Edward ap Raff, may have decried the old superstition and applauded the superiority of Elizabethan religion, but his plaudits, and others like them, fell on deaf ears as far as most of the people were concerned.[18] They seemed bent on adapting the Established Church and its worship into something as familiar to them as they could make it, and in doing so they were oftentimes helped by their clergy, many of whom were equally traditional and old-fashioned. This was all the easier for them because, in many respects, the priest's duties appeared to be much the same in Elizabeth's reign as they had been during her father's. They were still expected to baptize, bury, and marry their people; to visit the sick and console the dying; to offer hospitality to the poor; and to minister the sacrament of holy communion. It was possible for the conservatively minded among priests and people alike to add to the Prayer Book services many superstitious, even 'idolatrous', customs from an earlier age.

This picture of ignorance and inertia among the population is one that regularly emerges from a series of comments on the state of religion in Wales throughout the 1570s and 1580s. It comes out very clearly at the beginning of the period in one of the fullest episcopal reports on the

[13] S. Doran and C. Durston, *Princes, Pastors and People* (London, 1991), p. 82.

[14] P. Collinson, *The Religion of Protestants* (London, 1982), p. 191.

[15] C. Haigh, *Reformation and Resistance in Tudor Lancashire* (Cambridge, 1973), pp. 86, 219–22.

[16] D. MacCulloch, *The Later Reformation in England* (London, 1990), pp. 138–49.

[17] *Treatises*, p. 67.

[18] G. H. Hughes, *Rhagymadroddion, 1547–1648* (Cardiff, 1951), p. 52.

Elizabethan Church in Wales.[19] This account of his diocese was written on 25 January 1570 by Richard Davies, one of the most conscientious and hard-working of all the Welsh bishops of the Tudor age. At this time, as bishop of St David's he had pastoral care of the greater part of south Wales. His comments had been occasioned by the alarm felt by the Privy Council about the possible impact of the Northern Rising of 1569 on Wales. Davies, however, could allay the fears of the council by assuring them he had no open recusants or opponents of the regime within his see. What did grieve him sorely, though, was the 'great number' who were 'slow and cold in the true service of God. Some careless for any religion. And some that wish the romish religion again.' After examining what he considered to be the principal causes of the lamentable state of religion, he went on to refer dejectedly to widespread 'pilgrimages to wells and watchings in chapels and desert places . . . supporters and bearers of superstition and idolatry', and ended with a stirring call for the 'preferment of God's glory, true religion, and virtuous life'.[20] At about the same time Bishop Hugh Jones of Llandaff reported that his diocese was quiet and obedient and gave him little cause for alarm. The only aspect of its life which troubled him was that extensive lay impropriations of livings within its borders had led to an acute shortage of preachers.[21] In the light of earlier criticisms of how backward the state of religion was in the diocese and how little progress had been made by the Reformation, Jones's complacent observations may have reflected his own somewhat placid and uncritical disposition rather than the true state of affairs in his diocese. Shortly afterwards, in May 1570, Bishop Robinson of Bangor drew the Privy Council's attention to the disturbing features of a funeral at Beaumaris, but added, 'I am in very good hope that the public example [which he had given] commended also by your honourable authority, will be a wholesome means to stay the ignorant from other relics of superstition against which I travail.'[22] The remaining bishop, Thomas Davies of St Asaph, writing in November 1570, considered that his diocese, although now more obedient in religion than it had been, still harboured too many of 'corrupt religion' who could not be apprehended. For this he blamed both the civil and ecclesiastical authorities.[23]

Bishop Jones' successor at Llandaff, William Bleddyn (1575–90), was an altogether more forceful personality than his predecessor. He found his

[19] PRO, SP12/66/26, 26 (i); cf. D. R. Thomas, *The Life and Work of Richard Davies and William Salesbury* (Oswestry, 1902), pp. 41–3.
[20] Ibid.
[21] PRO SP12/66/29.
[22] Ibid., 69/14.
[23] Ibid., 74/37.

cathedral and diocese in very poor and run-down plight. Bent on thoroughgoing reform, in 1576 he condemned his cathedral as 'derelict and destitute of pastoral care', 'untidy, full of dirt and almost beyond repair';[24] a horrifying depiction which was in large measure confirmed by the Glamorgan antiquary, Rice Merrick, who described the canons as non-resident 'and their houses almost in utter decay'.[25] Bleddyn exerted himself strenuously to improve the state of the cathedral and the close, tighten up discipline, and insist on increased residence and more preaching. He castigated his canons for their scandalous negligence in allowing all the treasures of their cathedral to be wasted.[26]

At much the same time, in 1575, Sir Richard Price of Brecon, son of Sir John Price, was writing to Lord Burghley to inform him of the poor state of Wales. In addition to the serious shortcomings in the secular life of the country, he complained of the pitiful lack of preachers,

> whereby the common people are so rude and ignorant in the most necessary parts of the Christian faith that many of them cannot as much as say the Lord's Prayer and Articles of Belief in any language that they understand. And therefore it is no marvel that they are very injurious one to another and live in contempt both of the laws of God and man.[27]

Similarly, a traveller having passed through Wales in 1578 was horrified by the 'ignorance of God's word, petty thefts, idleness, and extreme poverty' which prevailed so widely. He had been especially shocked by the state of the upland regions, which he found in deep darkness 'with neither college nor free school, neither any bishop or prelate which with his authority of fatherly love offereth one prebend to a foundation'.[28] A few years later (1586) came a sharp reprimand for the college of Brecknock (Christ College) which had no preachers at all. The people in the surrounding countryside were 'fain to bury the dead themselves'. How the sick were visited, and what counsel and comfort they received 'in their greatest extremity' could only be conjectured. The ignorance of the population in things spiritual was appalling and 'hardly can any child or aged body be found that doth utter any speech without great oath'.[29]

[24] J. A. Bradney, 'The speech of William Blethin, bishop of Llandaff', *Cymm.* XXXI (1921), 240–64; cf. J. G. Jones, *Wales and the Tudor State* (Cardiff, 1988), pp. 231–3.

[25] R. Merrick, *A Book of Glamorganshire Antiquities*, ed. B. L. James (Cardiff, 1984), p. 102.

[26] Bradney, *Cymm.* XXXI. 240–64.

[27] BL, Lansdowne MS. 64, fo. 56; cf. H. Ellis, *Original Letters illustrative of English History . . .* (11 vols. London, 1824, 1827, 1846), III. 141–4.

[28] Fisher, *AC* (1915), 237–52.

[29] 'A brief collection of the state of Brecknockshire', PRO, SP12/191/17.

The most amazing exposé of the state of religion over a large area of Wales appeared in the visitation articles and injunctions issued by Bishop Middleton of St David's in 1583.[30] Following up a long series of inquiries into the widespread survival of papist and immoral practices of many different kinds, the bishop found it necessary to publish for his diocese one of the most severely critical sets of injunctions for its clergy and people known to have come from the pen of any Elizabethan bishop. He condemned outright an 'infinite number of popish ceremonies and other things contrary to the laws of God' and the queen's 'most godly proceedings'. These things flourished, he insisted, because the people had never been weaned away from their traditional errors and superstitions. Therefore, his clergy were strictly forbidden to maintain a whole crop of traditional practices surrounding the ministration of communion, 'whereof hath ensued horrible idolatry and religious adoration of the sacraments themselves', 'as by kneeling, knocking of the breast, lifting up of hands, closing of the eyes with the finger and thumb'. They were also to desist from anything that 'doth retain a memory of the idolatrous mass', though many of these practices had been officially forbidden as early as the reign of Edward VI. Nor were they to retain any ancient usages relating to baptism, such as putting the chrism on the head, or the churching of women, which in Wales continued to be regarded as a charm against witchcraft until late in the seventeenth century.[31] Funerals were not to be accompanied by the ringing of bells, the use of candles, or offering prayers for the dead. Images, altars, and roodlofts, still widely surviving, were to be banished; and pilgrimages, observance of holy days, and other similar customs, were all to be abrogated. Ministers were no longer to play at dice, cards, tables, or bowls, nor to keep taverns, and were to perform all their duties sincerely and honestly.[32] In a report to the Privy Council, probably of 1583,[33] Middleton added further depressing details about many 'unworthy members of the ministry' whom he had to endure; 'the gospel was hindered through such ignorant persons, the people perish through want of food'. In the same year, the earnest north Welsh cleric-author, Rowland Puleston, had no doubt that the end of all things was at hand, so numerous were the 'unchristian, unbelieving, careless, worldly, fleshly and ungodly men and false prophets' he saw all about him ('angristnogion, angredwyr, diofalwyr, bydolwyr, cnawdwyr ac eraill gav proffwyti').[34]

---

[30] Kennedy, *Eliz. Episc. Administration*, III. 139ff.
[31] Thomas, *Religion and Magic*, pp. 38–9.
[32] Kennedy, *Eliz. Episc. Administration*, III. 145–52.
[33] PRO, SP12/162/29.
[34] *Rhyddiaith Gymraeg*, II. 53–4.

Two Welsh Catholic authors were, in their own way, even more condemnatory of the general state of belief and attitude among the people. Robert Gwyn, in three manuscript works composed by him during these years, was devastatingly critical of his compatriots not only for deserting the Catholic faith and frequenting the Anglican Church but also for their worldliness and indifference. The three works were 'Nid Oes iawn Ffydd ond Un' (1574); 'Lanter Gristnogawl' (1574); and 'Gwssanaeth y Gwŷr Newydd' (1580).[35] In his introduction to the second of these works he described the Welsh 'living in so ungodly a fashion, gathering and congregating together so as to collect worldly wealth by means of swearing oaths and wronging poor people, full of anger, envy and malice towards one another . . . full of greed, never showing the slightest fear for God or love for man' ('sydd yn byw mor aniwiol / yn ym dyrry / ag yn ymgasgly y geisio mwnws y byd / drwg dyngy llyfe / a gwnythyr kam a ffobol dlodion / yn llawn dig / kynfigen / a malais vn yr llall . . . yn llawn kebydd dra / heb fod ofyn yny byd y dduw / na chariad y ddyn').[36] In the third work he expressed his wish to 'draw them if he could, from that addiction to love of the world, the flesh and the devil rooted in their hearts' ('i dyny, os gallwn, chwant y byd, y knawd, ar kythrel sydd gwedy griddio yn ych Calone').[37] The anonymous author of *Drych Cristianogawl* (1585) held that it was the Welsh gentry 'who set an example to the poor commons to be without faith or conscience' ('yn rhoi sampl ir tylodion cyphredin, fod heb na Phydd na Chydwybod') and would one day have to give account 'not only for their own sins but also for those of many of the common people . . . who lead their lives after the pattern set them by the gentry' ('nyd yn vnic am eu pechodae i hunain ond am lawer or cyphredin . . . yn dwyn eu buchedd ar ol sampleu'r bonneddigion').[38] Both these authors had no doubt that the cause of all these deficiencies was the removal of the Catholic faith from the midst of the people. What they seemed unable or unwilling to recognize was that the same ignorance and corrupt practices had been general in the Middle Ages, too, and were currently being denounced in Catholic countries by Catholic reformers.

The most forthright condemnation of all emanated from the fiery Puritan, John Penry. In his three pamphlets on the state of Wales published in 1587–8, he sketched a thoroughly depressing picture of the 'spiritual misery wherein we now live in the Country of Wales'.[39] Most people 'never think of any religion, true or false'.[40] 'All the misery, all the ignorance, all

---

[35] This last-named has been edited by G. Bowen (Cardiff, 1970).
[36] W. A. Mathias, 'Rhai sylwadau ar Robert Gwyn', *LlC*, III (1954), 73.
[37] Bowen, *Gwssanaeth*, p. 29.
[38] *Rhagymadroddion*, pp. 52–3.
[39] *Treatises*, p. 11.
[40] Ibid., p. 32.

the profaneness in life and conversation [behaviour] hath been for the most part by means of our bishops and other blind guides'.[41] There were two sovereign remedies for this heartrending plight, Penry believed. One was that the 'swarms' of unworthy ministers, those 'dumb dogs' who never preached, must be replaced by 'godly learned ministers' who would regularly preach the gospel and who should, therefore, be able to count on being adequately maintained.[42] Secondly, the task of completing the Welsh translation of the Bible must be 'set upon incontinently'.[43]

Finally, in 1589 a visitor to Clynnog in Caernarfonshire recorded his impressions of what he saw and heard there. He was scandalized by the 'abominable idolatries': the sacrifice of bullocks to St Beuno; pilgrimage-going; open carrying of rosaries to church by people who claimed to read upon them 'as well as others can upon their books'; calling on saints or 'idols' (after which the church was named) to help in all extremities; and 'above all, the sign of the cross [was] most superstitiously among them abused' – when closing windows, leaving livestock in the fields, and burying their dead. If anything ill befell them or their beasts, they attributed it to not having crossed themselves properly.[44] Yet conditions were little or no better in the archdiocese of York and the dioceses of Chester and Hereford, where bishops in the 1580s were still inquiring into those who used beads and primers, and retained Marian vestments and books.[45]

There can be no doubt that, overall, religious reform, whether of the Catholic or the Protestant variety, made dishearteningly slow headway in Wales, and that, on both sides, ardent upholders of their cause were pessimistic about their prospects – in the short run at least. Robert Gwyn, the Catholic writer, despondently contrasted the fortunes of Catholicism in Lancashire with the outlook for it in Wales; in the former there were many gentlemen who enthusiastically welcomed Catholic priests into their houses, while in the latter there were remarkably few.[46] John Penry, on the other hand, thought that the tiny handful of true Protestant worshippers in Wales had arrived at the truth either by means of private reading or else as a result of having lived in some part of England where the gospel was preached.[47] In the eyes of both these opposing groups Wales was one of those 'dark corners' of the land to which the truth had scarcely

[41] Ibid., p. 62.
[42] Ibid., pp. 27–9, 39–41.
[43] Ibid., p 41.
[44] PRO, SP12/224/74.
[45] E. Duffy, *The Stripping of the Altars: Traditional Religion in England, c.1400–1580* (New Haven, 1992), p. 579.
[46] Bowen, *Gwssanaeth*, p. xlviii.
[47] *Treatises*, p. 32.

penetrated.[48] Yet even in Wales not all parts were equally benighted. Besides the variations between social groups and individuals, there were marked differences between one region and another. There was no single Welsh religious or cultural attitude common to the whole country; Wales was a patchwork of different regional traditions and values. Persons moving some distance from one district to another felt themselves to be aliens in their new home and were usually looked upon with suspicion and prejudice by their neighbours. When, for instance, a man from Coety in Glamorgan appeared in a Denbighshire court, he was described by a local witness as a deceitful south Wales man, whose 'countrymen were desperate and wild fellows'.[49] English incomers were still more unpopular: 'it was an ill time', said a man from Castell Caereinion in Montgomeryshire who had killed his English neighbour, 'when an Englishman should master or control us'.[50] It has already been pointed out that there were marked disparities between east and west, as well as north and south.[51] By and large, the two western dioceses of Bangor and St David's were remoter, less touched by currents from outside Wales, and more reluctant to change than the eastern dioceses of Llandaff and St Asaph. Similarly, the upland, inland districts, separated by wide, empty stretches of hill and moorland, with their large, straggling, sparsely populated parishes, were less open to extraneous influences and more conservative than the valleys and the towns. But probably the key difference as far as the Reformation was concerned was that, along the south coast of Wales and the eastern border districts, the population was more exposed to the English language, printed books, trading contacts, and movement of ideas. It was here, among those social groups and individuals who were educated, literate, and had some knowledge of the language in which Reformation issues had chiefly been propagated and debated hitherto, that the new ideas penetrated most quickly and had the greatest impact. 'Iron whets iron' ('haearn a hoga haearn'), says a Welsh proverb, and this was validated in some of the main centres of population. Towns like Wrexham or Denbigh in the north, or Carmarthen, Brecon, or Cardiff in the south, tended to be the centres where advanced Protestant and Catholic opinion took root. Wrexham, the largest town in north Wales, was the scene of clashes between Richard White, the Catholic poet-martyr, and his Puritanly

---

[48] C. Hill, 'Puritans and the "Dark Corners of the Land"', *TRHS*, 5th ser. XIII (1963), 77–102.

[49] N. Powell in J. G. Jones (ed.), *Class, Community*, pp. 269–70.

[50] G. D. Owen, *Elizabethan Wales: The Social Scene* (London, 1962), p. 71.

[51] For the contrast between buildings and the general standard of living, P. Smith, *Houses of the Welsh Countryside* (HMSO, London, 1975); cf. E. G. Bowen, *Wales* (London, 1957).

inclined antagonists.[52] The prosperous market-town of Denbigh was the power-base in north Wales of the Puritans' patron, the earl of Leicester, where he hoped to establish a new cathedral and a focus of Protestant preaching; yet it was at the same time a prominent centre of recusant activity.[53] Brecon not only housed the collegiate church of Christ and became the residence of Bishop Middleton, but was also the scene of an attempt by Siôn Dafydd Rhys and his friends to establish a Catholic printing-press. Cardiff was home to citizens who strictly punished sabbath-breakers and others who sought to maintain Catholic practices at funerals.[54] If we are really to understand the development of religion, perhaps what are needed, in spite of the dire shortage of sources, are more studies of contrasting localities within Wales and, indeed, of contradictory trends within the same area.

The responsibility for implanting reformed doctrine among the people fell chiefly to the bishops. With one or two exceptions, the bishops of Elizabethan Wales were a well-chosen body of men. Thirteen (possibly twelve) out of the sixteen appointed were Welsh in origin, were conscious of the need to instruct their flock in their native language, and did much to establish Welsh as the language of religion in all those parishes where it was the one most commonly in use. Two out of the three main translators of the Bible into Welsh during the Elizabethan era were themselves bishops. All these prelates were graduates and were, in the main, conscientious reformers: one of the noticeable features of the episcopate was the strongly marked influence of reforming Cambridge men, including Archbishops Parker and Whitgift, in their midst.[55] All were resident in their dioceses; a number of them for upwards of fifteen to twenty years – Richard Davies at St David's from 1561 to 1581; Nicholas Robinson at Bangor from 1566 to 1584; William Hughes at St Asaph from 1573 to 1600; and William Bleddyn at Llandaff from 1575 to 1590. Such tenures as these enabled the bishops to get to know their dioceses well and establish a measure of continuity within them. They themselves were enthusiastic preachers and no less keen to encourage others, especially their chaplains, to preach. Richard Davies in

[52] D. A. Thomas, *The Welsh Elizabethan Catholic Martyrs* (Cardiff, 1971), pp. 50–1. Nearby, the large regional centre of Chester was a centre of considerable Puritan and Catholic activity.

[53] L. A. S. Butler, 'Leicester's Church, Denbigh: an experiment in Puritan worship', *Journ. Brit. Arch. Assoc.* (1974), pp. 46–63; E. G. Jones, *Cymru a'r Hen Ffydd* (Cardiff, 1951), pp. 22–6, 45.

[54] *Records of the County Borough of Cardiff*, ed. J. H. Matthews (6 vols. Cardiff, 1898–1911), II. 156–8; III. 58–67.

[55] Williams, *WHR*, XIV. 363–77.

1570 besought the Privy Council to ensure that the 'small patrimony of the Church . . . may so still continue to the sustentation of preachers and teachers',[56] and in 1576 he was one of the eight bishops who supported Archbishop Grindal's stand on behalf of the 'prophesyings' which were designed to remove clerical ignorance and provide a form of 'in-service' training for the clergy.[57] Bishop Hugh Jones of Llandaff, acutely conscious of the need for preaching in his neglected diocese, paid out of his own purse for preachers to come from other dioceses to fulfil the duty.[58] His successor, Bleddyn, could claim that, 'more than all others I have laboured and toiled for years, travelling about, according to the pressing need, that I may preach the gospel'.[59] So anxious was he to ensure, as far as he could, an adequate supply of preachers that he pressed lay patrons to confer upon them the better livings within their gift. He thus urged Sir Edward Stradling to present Andrew Veyn, 'being a public preacher, lawfully authorized', to his parsonage of Sully, 'which was able to maintain a preacher'.[60]

The bishops, from the outset, had no doubt that one of the main keys to extending reform within their dioceses was to improve the quality of the clergy.[61] During the first decade of Elizabeth's reign, diocesans had very largely had to take whatever they could get. The number of clergy had fallen steeply during Edward VI's reign and only very partially recovered during Mary's, so the recruits available to the early Elizabethan bishops were insufficient in number and of distinctly inferior quality. However convinced the bishops might be of the desperate need to move towards an all-graduate clergy that regularly preached to their people and instructed them, such a goal remained very remote. Bishop Davies in 1570 expressed the hope that it might be possible to appoint 'preachers and teachers after that the incumbents, now being no preachers, shall happen to depart'.[62] What he and his brethren clearly wanted was to be able to recruit clergy sufficiently well educated to fulfil their pastoral mission. Yet the queen's government had itself earlier put a brake on preaching. Fearing that some of the clergy might be disaffected in their attitude towards the settlement, it had insisted that only those who had a licence from their ordinary to preach might do so. The result may very well have been not only to reduce

---

[56] PRO, SP12/66/26.

[57] D. Wilkins, *Concilia Magnae Britanniae et Hiberniae . . . 446–1718* (4 vols. London, 1737), IV. 237, 268, 293–4.

[58] PRO, SP12/46/29.

[59] J. D. H. Thomas, *A History of Wales, 1485–1660* (Cardiff, 1972), p. 108.

[60] *The Stradling Correspondence*, ed. J. M. Traherne (London, 1840), pp. 83–7.

[61] Collinson, *Religion Protestants*, chap. 2.

[62] PRO, SP12/66/26, 26(i).

the number of preachers[63] but also to create a situation in which the content of many sermons passed unheeded and uncomprehended over the heads of those who heard them. As far as Wales was concerned, it is difficult to be sure on the point, since only a handful of the notes of sermons delivered there has survived from this period. Some were preached on formal occasions, like Bishop Davies's *Funeral Sermon* of 1577 to the earl of Essex, or William Morgan's sermon of 1587 in memory of Sir Yevan Lloyd of Bodidris, a follower of the earl of Leicester in the Netherlands, who died in London in February of that year.[64] But the surviving manuscript sermon notes in Welsh of two clerics which have come down to us suggest that they may have been far beyond the grasp of the average member of the congregation,[65] even assuming that they were listening intently – and that in itself would be a very big assumption, since Tudor congregations tended to be notoriously inattentive to sermons. The indications are that many of such sermons as were preached in Wales were delivered in English.[66] Certainly, the Book of Homilies, which was intended to provide ready-made sermons for those who were unlicensed to preach their own, was not translated into Welsh until 1606.[67] If and when it was used in Wales in its English form, its contents would not have made much sense to many hearers. William Morgan, in the dedication to his Welsh Bible of 1588, drew attention to the serious problems caused for preachers by the

long disuse of the [Welsh] language in the Church and the absence of a complete translation of the Bible, the proper terms having become either so forgotten or obscured that neither those who teach can explain with sufficient clarity what they wish, nor those who listen understand with sufficient readiness what is explained.[68]

Conditions remained so unsatisfactory that John Penry went so far as to hint broadly that laymen might be given permission to preach.[69]

[63] For the fewness of preachers, and the unpopularity of sermons, C. Haigh (ed.), *The Reign of Elizabeth I* (London, 1984), pp. 206–9; idem, *English Reformations: Religion, Politics and Society under the Tudors* (Oxford, 1993), pp. 268–9.

[64] Davies, *Funeral Sermon* (1577); Morgan, *A Sermon preached by Master Dr Morgan at the Funeral of Sir Yevan Lloyd, Knight* (1587); E. J. Jones, 'The death and burial of Walter Devereux, earl of Essex', *Carm. Antiq.* III (1945–57), 184–201.

[65] G. Morgan, 'Pregethau Cymraeg William Griffith ac Evan Morgan' (MA thesis, Wales, 1969).

[66] L. Owen, 'A seventeenth-century commonplace book', *TCS* (1962), 16–47, at p. 22.

[67] G. Williams, 'Edward James a llyfr yr Homiliau', *Tafodau Tân*, pp. 180–98.

[68] D. R. Thomas, *The History of the Diocese of St Asaph* (3 vols. Oswestry, 1908–13), I. 89.

[69] *Treatises*, p. 38.

Not the least of the bishops' difficulties arose out of the pronounced tendency for many of the abler and better-educated of Welsh-born clerics, like those of Lancashire,[70] to migrate to the more bountiful rewards in the vicinity of the universities or the richer cathedrals and dioceses in the south-east of England. Notable examples of the trend were Gabriel Goodman, born in Ruthin but dean of Westminster for forty years; Thomas Yale, a north Walian who held preferment in north Wales but lived in Canterbury, where he was Archbishop Parker's chancellor and right-hand man; Hugh Price, Brecon-born but first prebendary of Rochester, where he spent much of his time (although as treasurer of St David's he was supposed to be permanently resident there); or Thomas Roberts, a native of Wales who spent all his clerical career as a leading Puritan in Norwich diocese.[71] Some of the Welsh bards commented sardonically on the readiness of Welsh clerics to succumb to the monetary rewards England had to offer:

> Ag o medre un ddarllen Saesneg
> Ef a fynnai urddau ar redeg,
> Ag âi i gerdded y gwledydd
> I ddoedyd efengyl newydd.[72]

And if anyone among them can read English, he runs to seek orders and goes wandering the lands to preach a new gospel.

Trying to raise the level of the clergy in Wales was a formidable operation, as every Elizabethan bishop found to his cost. Even among the cathedral clergy, where the bishops achieved their greatest measure of success, there were a number of less than satisfactory brethren to be found. At St David's Richard Davies discovered that his vicars choral were particularly wild and insubordinate. Vicars choral had always tended to be unruly, and after the Reformation their behaviour seems to have deteriorated still further.[73] Their misdeeds at St David's found their way into the chapter records on a number of occasions during Davies's episcopate.[74]

---

[70] Haigh, *Lancashire*, pp. 41, 43.

[71] E. P. Roberts, 'Gabriel Goodman and his native homeland', *TCS* (1989), 77–104; Thomas Yale, *DWB*, s.n. Yale family; G. Williams, 'Hugh Price, founder of Jesus College', *Brycheiniog*, XXV (1992–3), 57–66; Thomas Roberts, P. Collinson, *The Elizabethan Puritan Movement* (London, 1967), pp. 127, 141, 203–4.

[72] W. A. Bebb, *Cyfnod y Tuduriaid* (Wrexham, 1939), p. 141.

[73] R. B. Manning, *Religion and Society in Elizabethan Sussex* (Leicester, 1964), pp. 170–1, for the situation in Chichester.

[74] NLW, SD/Chapter Records, I. 52, 57, 89, 114, 241; II. 1. Cf. also W. B. Jones and E. A. Freeman, *The History and Antiquities of St David's* (London, 1956), pp. 348–51.

They appear to have found drinking, gaming, and madcap pranks much more to their taste than pursuing their studies. Their unseemly behaviour often had to be reprimanded by the precentor, Thomas Huet, and the chapter; but the vicars choral listened with scant respect and were disconcertingly frank, not to say impudent, in their rejoinders. When Chancellor David Powell had lectured one of them, Thomas Lloyd, for keeping a tavern, the offender promptly rounded on his admonisher and charged him with acting 'more of malice than any good reformation', and then proceeded to upbraid him in turn for keeping a woman of ill-fame in his house! Also at St David's, under the very noses of the bishop and chapter, the sexton of the cathedral, one Ellis ap Howel, was discovered to have hidden certain 'ungodly popish books; as mass books, hymnals, grails, and such like (as it were looking for a day)', when he hoped, presumably, they would be needed again.[75] Yet when Davies's friend, Archbishop Grindal, went to York in 1574 he was horrified to find the same conditions prevailing there.[76]

Bishop Bleddyn of Llandaff was another who was at odds with his vicars choral. So much so that in 1576 he came to the conclusion he had no option but to propose a drastic reduction in their numbers. Still more scandalous was the behaviour of his canons, whom their bishop denounced for 'having wasted everything, sweet-toned bells, precious vestments, golden vessels, unknown treasures; to nothing are all things reduced'.[77] At St Asaph the dean, Thomas Banks, was censured for never having 'kept house in all his life' and for 'being unfit for the place'. He was excommunicated and sequestered for refusing to carry out the bishop's order for the repair of the chapter house. Nevertheless, he contrived to survive as dean until 1634.[78]

The parish clergy were frequently the subject of complaints on account of their indifferent morals and unedifying behaviour. Officially, they were supposed to be strictly banned from resorting to those notorious nurseries of vice, the alehouses, still less keeping them, or from playing at cards, dice, tables, or other unlawful games. Nor were they to take up unsuitable by-employments or casual pursuits unbecoming to a clergyman. But drink was, and would remain for centuries to come, the solace – and the downfall – of many a Welsh parish priest. Poverty, too, drove several of them into all sorts of inappropriate, even unlawful, devices for making money. The most shameful indictment of Welsh clergymen on account of licentious

[75] NLW, SD/Chapter Records, I. 236.
[76] D. M. Palliser, *The Age of Elizabeth* (London, 1992), p. 392.
[77] J. G. Jones, 'The Reformation bishops of Llandaff, 1558–1601', *Morgannwg*, XXXII (1988), 49–50.
[78] Thomas, *St Asaph*, I. 320.

behaviour in the Elizabethan age occurred in a Star Chamber record. It accused two Caernarfonshire clergymen, Richard Kyffin and Richard ap Howell, and their wives, sons, sons-in-law, and daughters, of excessive indulgence in drink, of cheating at cards and dice, of 'taking no order' in their churches, and being at evensong too drunk even to walk. It further charged them with abducting wealthy minors and forcing them to marry their daughters.[79] It would be dangerous to take these accusations too literally, when Star Chamber documents were proverbially *ex parte* and excessive in their wording. Even so, damaging allegations against the Elizabethan clergy were not uncommon; nor is it altogether surprising that in a litigious age, when clergymen were so widely involved in the drafting of legal documents, especially wills, they should have often been implicated in fraud. Hugh Price, clerk of Llywel in Breconshire, was charged with having forged the will of Philip Thomas ap Rees and subsequently proving the false document in the registry at St David's.[80] Bishop Bleddyn himself and one of his clergy, Thomas Jones, were similarly accused of tampering with the will of one Prichard in order to defraud his brother, Charles, of his rights of patronage.[81] In another case of a fairly common type, Griffith Evans, clerk of Hay, was said to have abducted the daughter of William Watkin of Hay, who was under 16 years of age and illegally attempting to marry her to one Thomas Jenkins.[82] Commenting on the behaviour of parish clergy, John Penry, with the severity characteristic of Puritan criticism, was unsparingly hard on the moral turpitude of the 'rogues and vagabonds', 'spendthrifts and serving-men', 'known adulterers, drunkards, thieves, roisterers, most abominable swearers' admitted to the ranks of the clergy by the bishops.[83]

No doubt there were inadequacies among the clergy, but they were in no small measure caused by the acute problems of poverty with which the Church was beset. A later bishop of Bangor was sadly to confess that 'by reason of the poverty of the place, all clergymen of hope and worth seek preferment elsewhere'.[84] In part this was the inescapable consequence of a relatively poor economy and was a legacy of the medieval period. It had since been made worse by the distressing effects of laymen's rapacity and clerical weakness or connivance to which Reformation changes had given rise. Permission for clerics to take wives had added to the economic

---

[79] PRO, STA C 5/J22/2.
[80] Ibid., D26/38; D16/38. Cf. P. H. Williams, *The Council in the Marches under Elizabeth* I (Cardiff, 1958), p. 100.
[81] Ibid., P18/24.
[82] Ibid., W27/16.
[83] *Treatises*, p. 63.
[84] W. Laud, *Works* (London, 1853), V. 359.

pressure on them. The consequences were plain to see in the insufficient income of churchmen. Most of the bishops, even on the reduced scale on which they were now expected to subsist as compared with their medieval predecessors, found it difficult to manage. Bishops, especially, and the upper clergy generally, were squeezed between two conflicting images of how they were supposed to conduct themselves. On the one hand, they were expected to be hospitable, to live in a style befitting their station, and to see their families appropriately provided for. On the other hand, it was also assumed that they would comport themselves as men of God and reformed pastors, employing their resources for the maintenance of learning and the relief of the poor, in order to accomplish which it was taken for granted that they would be sober and restrained in dress, diet, and mode of living. Four successive bishops of Llandaff, one of the poorest sees in the kingdom, found it to be a thankless and unending contest with dire poverty, in which each of them came off the loser. Bishops Jones (1566–75), Bleddyn (1575–90), Babington (1591–5), and Morgan (1595–1601) all complained in turn, with justice, of their grossly inadequate income.[85] But Richard Davies, although he was bishop of the wealthiest Welsh diocese, 'died poor, having never had regard to riches';[86] and his successor, Marmaduke Middleton (1582–93), was accused of having embezzled diocesan funds to keep his shaky finances afloat.[87] All the Welsh bishops were obliged to hold livings *in commendam* in order to maintain their status; and one of them, William Hughes of St Asaph (1575–1600), had an unusually shady reputation in this respect.

Their cathedral clergy, finding themselves in similar straits to their bishops, were no less eager to secure possession of a number of commendams. Some of the distinguished scholars and preachers among them were handsomely rewarded. In Bangor diocese, Edmwnd Prys, former college fellow, scholar, preacher, and poet, was archdeacon of Merioneth, parson of Ffestiniog and Maentwrog, rector of Ludlow and of Llanenddwyn. St Asaph's David Powel, DD, preacher and historian, held Ruabon, Meifod, and Llansanffraid ym Mechain, as well as two successive prebends. Thomas Huet, precentor of St David's and translator of part of the New Testament of 1567, found ample acknowledgement. In addition to his precentorship he was rector of Cefnllys, Llanbadarn ym Maeliennydd, and Diserth, prebendary of Llanbadarn Trefeglwys and canon at St David's, and prebendary of Ystrad and Llandegla in the collegiate church of

---

[85] Williams, *GCH*, IV. 225–6.
[86] J. Wynn, *The History of the Gwydir Family*, ed. J. Ballinger (Cardiff, 1927), p. 65.
[87] R. O'Day and F. Heal, *Continuity and Change* (Leicester, 1976), p. 117.

Brecon.[88] Plurality of this kind, probably the best if not the only way of keeping the ablest Welsh graduates in the Welsh chapters, led to the same kind of unfortunate consequences wherever it was practised. Churches and vicarages tended to fall into disrepair; the curates who took over the parish duties of the non-resident clergy were usually men of indifferent calibre, paid miserable stipends; and the nominal pastors of souls were unknown to their people. Yet, by the beginning of the seventeenth century Wales was still, in Dr Thomas Richard's words, a 'land of pluralism and non-residents'.[89]

In order to enhance their income, many of the upper clergy were prone to resort to doubtful practices. Scandalous reports were spread abroad about many of the Elizabethan bishops and upper clergy. They leased out Church lands to relatives or friends, liberally granted rights of advowson to kinsfolk or dependants, and placed sons, nephews, or clients in valuable preferment. The bad habits of the Llandaff chapter have already been referred to. In 1573 and 1574 Bishop Bleddyn brought grave allegations in the high court against two people, one of them a cleric, for fraudulent use of seals. The first action was brought against a widow, Grace Morgan, for having forged a document purporting to show her rights to tenancy of lands belonging to the bishop of Llandaff in Bishopston, Monmouthshire.[90] The second accused a clerk formerly of Wells diocese, John Badham, and others of counterfeiting the seal of the bailiff of Llandaff and wrongfully appointing ministers on the strength of documents sealed with it.[91] Bleddyn also laid down strict conditions for the leasing of capitular estates, but he himself can hardly have contributed much towards their implementation when he leased Bassaleg for a term of one hundred years or the manor of Undy for three lives. He also conferred prebends on his two sons, Morgan and Philemon, and made the latter vicar of Caerwent and rector of Shirenewton.[92] Richard Davies, too, provided amply for his own offspring. His son Peregrine was created archdeacon of Cardigan in 1563, when just a child, and Davies's youngest boy, Gerson, was given the prebend of Clydai and the vicarage of Penbryn at the age of about 16. Before his father's death he had also acquired the prebend of Llanbister.[93] Richard Davies's successor, Marmaduke Middleton, accused his predecessor of leasing all the episcopal lands, granting the advowsons of all livings worth more than £10 within his

[88] *DWB*, s.n. For Parker's defence of commendams, *Correspondence* (Parker Soc., London, 1853), p. 208.
[89] T. Richards, *The Puritan Movement in Wales, 1639–1653* (London, 1920), chap. 1.
[90] PRO, STA C 5/L/43/5.
[91] Ibid., L25/12.
[92] Williams, *GCH*, IV. 226.
[93] *WRE*, pp. 174, 179.

gift, and allowing the bishop's residences to fall into ruin. He also quoted Davies's brother-in-law to the effect 'that he never gave any living within his own gift, nor admitted any to other men's gifts without consideration, alleging he had not otherwise been able to live'.[94] Middleton was not the most trustworthy of witnesses, being the worst of contemporary bishops and one of the few Anglican diocesans ever to be dismissed from his see for his misdeeds; but the chapter records of St David's nevertheless show that there was some truth in his assertions. Advowsons granted to Davies's family and those of his precentor, Thomas Huet, accounted for well over a third of those conceded. Davies's sons and his wife's family also profited handsomely from leases of episcopal estates and parish tithes.[95] Huet was further accused by the treasurer of the diocese of unlawfully retaining the three seals of the chapter in his possession and using them to lease valuable estates for his own benefit.[96] Leading clerics like Bleddyn, Davies, or Huet, no less than squires, felt the pull of dynastic interests. They knew the pinch of having to provide for relatives out of reduced revenues, and in the process were inclined to forget that they were trustees of an entailed inheritance and not the proprietors of a landed estate.

The parish clergy were also vulnerable to the pressures of poverty. The main inducement with which graduates and other men qualified to preach could be tempted to Welsh dioceses was the offer of two or more of the better livings, as has been seen with the cathedral clergy. Another method of tempting a preacher was to ensure him a handsome augmentation to his income by encouraging him to preach their sermons on behalf of non-preaching incumbents – in return for an appropriate fee, of course. In this way, Morris Price, vicar of Nantmel in Radnorshire, worth £12 a year, doubled his annual remuneration.[97]

The unbeneficed clergy were in a worse plight. Some of them were young men awaiting preferment to a worthwhile benefice. Others already held unremunerative livings and were obliged to serve the cure of another parish whose parson was an absentee. Not a few were destined to remain as curates all their lives and had to make shift as best they could by taking one or more stipendiary cures. In his report of 1570 Richard Davies sought to explain to the Privy Council the nature of one of the most debilitating causes of 'disorder, contempts of godliness and service' and 'continuance of superstition and blindness'. It arose because many benefices had previously been appropriated to the houses of religion. In the Middle Ages their vicars had had their maintenance provided by the monasteries, as well

---

[94] PRO, SP12/162; fo. 29; 165, fo. 1.
[95] NLW, SD/Chapter Records, I. 71–2, 144–6, 163–4, 229–31, 213–14; II. 60–3.
[96] PRO, C3/57/6.
[97] Thomas, *Davies and Salesbury*, p. 38.

as the profit 'from the superstitious offerings then made'. Now, however, only the 'bare pension' (i.e. stipend) was left, and it was too poor to attract any incumbent, not to mention a cleric of quality. Other appropriated benefices had never had endowed vicarages, and they were in woeful condition. Because their impropriators offered only starvation wages, these parishes did not 'have whole service once in a year', but 'upon Sundays and holy days the Epistle and Gospel or suffrages only', 'making shift with a priest that shall come hither galloping from another parish', for which he was lucky if he received '40s., 4 marks [£2.13s. 4d.] or £4 at best'.[98] Davies's criticisms were confirmed by his successor and were particularly applicable to the two southern dioceses, which had by far the greatest number of appropriated benefices.[99] As a result, a number of important centres of population like Carmarthen, Haverfordwest, or Swansea, were either inadequately served or had no incumbent at all. The chancels of many appropriated churches, of which Davies was able to enumerate at least ten, were also falling into a dilapidated state.[100]

Nevertheless, Davies had integrity enough to admit that the blame did not rest wholly with the lay farmers of these livings. He drew attention to the corrupt bargains made by clergy, who obstinately resisted all attempts to discipline them. He reported sorrowfully,

some against all injunctions to the contrary taking upon them to serve three or four, yea sometimes five cures; but never one aright, being supported by gentlemen, farmers of the said churches and cures, who do procure the favour of the sheriff, so as they neither regard any interdiction nor can be brought to observe any good order.[101]

Middleton, in his turn, likewise condemned the impropriators and the clergymen, 'for simony hath been so common a custom with them that they are neither afraid nor yet ashamed to make public bargains thereof'.[102] A Glamorgan cleric, William Fleming, had no doubt about the widespread existence of simony amongst the clergy. Writing to Sir Edward Stradling, he explained that the 'door which leads men to any preferment be it never so mean can not be opened without the silver or golden key'; and if his key did not 'weigh ten pounds in silver, I shall have no entrance'.[103]

[98] PRO, SP12/66/26; although the wages of a stipendiary curate had been fixed in 1414 at £5. 6s. 8d.
[99] Walker, *Pemb. County Hist.* III. 117–19.
[100] PRO, SP12/66/26.
[101] Ibid.
[102] PRO, SP12/165/1.
[103] *Stradling Correspondence*, p. 331.

In justice to the bishops, however, confronted as they were by a sea of troubles and hardships, they continued to soldier on to the best of their ability. They may have been bitterly opposed to their Romanist adversaries, but for all the profound differences between them in aims and attitudes, interestingly enough, they also had a great deal in common.[104] Both groups believed profoundly in the necessity for regular preaching, catechizing, and teaching. Each was conscious of the need to make the paterfamilias in his Christian household the key to its efforts. Neither could neglect the importance of the appeal in the vernacular by speech and writing if it was successfully to present its message to the majority of the people of Wales. Both were convinced of the need to extend literacy and to improve the quality of educational opportunity, especially for the clergy.

One of the features of Tudor Wales was the encouragement of education.[105] In spite of the losses caused by the dissolution of the monasteries and the chantries, the connection with religion 'appears to have dominated the most important endowments in Wales for schools, mostly of the grammar type, before 1600'.[106] Clerics were naturally associated with the grammar schools at St Asaph and St David's[107] and also with the founding of new grammar schools at places like Bangor (1557) or Ruthin (1574) in the north, and Brecon (1541) or Carmarthen (1576) in the south.[108] Quite apart from these grammar schools established in Wales, there were others sited conveniently just over the border in England, at neighbouring cathedral cities like Chester or Hereford, and especially in a town like Shrewsbury, to which Richard Davies, Nicholas Robinson, and other notabilities sent their sons. In addition to these endowed grammar schools there were lesser schools like those referred to by Bishop Thomas Davies in 1561, to which he wanted the stipends of former 'lady priests' devoted, so that 'the idleness of youth may be avoided' and the pupils brought up 'in love and fear of God and knowledge of their duties'.[109] There must have been a considerable number of parish, town, or private-venture schools up and down the land; most of them kept by clerics, some of whom were men of scholarly distinction like Gervase Babington, future bishop of Llandaff and Exeter. In Glamorgan alone there were eight schools of this kind, according to the antiquary, Rice Merrick.[110] Not all of the schoolmasters were licensed by Anglican bishops – witness the school kept by Richard

---

[104] J. J. Scarisbrick, *The Reformation and the English People* (London, 1984), chap. 8; P. McGrath, *Papists and Puritans under Elizabeth I* (London, 1967), chap. 13.
[105] *W 1415–1642*, chap. 18.
[106] Griffith in J. G. Jones (ed.), *Class, Community*, p. 84.
[107] Griffith, *JHSCW*, III. 64–74.
[108] L. S. Knight, *Welsh Independent Grammar Schools to 1600* (Newtown, 1926).
[109] Thomas, *St Asaph*, I. 90.
[110] *W 1415–1642*, pp. 429–30.

White, the Catholic martyr-poet.[111] Some of the wealthier gentry families maintained private tutors for their own families and the children of some of their tenants. The Wynn family kept a school at Gwydir, which seems to have provided an educational springboard for the youthful William Morgan. The recusant Lady Lewis of Y Fan employed a Catholic priest, William Bylson, in order to educate her children and bring them up in the Catholic faith.[112] George Owen of Henllys hired Lewis Thomas to instruct his children and other pupils, while Thomas Pierson, chaplain to Sir Robert Harley and a fine scholar, prepared many gifted youths from the border districts for the universities.[113]

This general progress in educational provision was very slowly – almost imperceptibly down to the end of the 1580s – being reflected in the growth of the number of graduate incumbents amongst the clergy. The Canons of 1571 may have laid down the need for a fully graduate clergy, beneficed, resident, and preaching; but this was an ideal well beyond the reach of virtually all the dioceses, certainly those of Wales. It is difficult to know with certainty what was happening there, since Welsh episcopal registers for most of the period survive only from Bangor.[114] If, however, the Bangor documents are typical – and there is good reason for thinking that the situation was distinctly better there than in the southern dioceses – then they show only a very gradual improvement during the 1570s and 1580s. Out of some 115 presentations recorded, just forty-nine (43 per cent) are of graduates and sixty-six (57.7 per cent) are of non-graduates. The registers, of course, tell us nothing about how many of those non-graduates had attended at university for some time without completing their course, though it is likely that there were a number in that category. Nor do they provide any information concerning the unbeneficed clergy, though it must be supposed that a majority of the latter had not graduated. Moreover, the Bangor registers also reveal that a number of the graduates and non-graduates ordained within the diocese did not seem to have acquired benefices there.[115]

One of the main objects of increasing the number of graduates was to strengthen the preaching and teaching function of the clergy. On the basis of the somewhat slender evidence available to us, it appears that not much progress was being made in this respect. The bishop of the largest diocese, St David's, had only ten preachers (including himself) at his disposal in

---

[111] Thomas, *Elizabethan Martyrs*, pp. 47–8.
[112] Pugh, *SWMRS*, III. 64.
[113] *W 1415–1642*, p. 429.
[114] A. I. Pryce, *The Diocese of Bangor in the Sixteenth Century* (Bangor, 1923), *passim*.
[115] W. P. Griffith, 'Welsh students at Oxford, Cambridge, and the Inns of Court . . .' (Ph.D. thesis, Wales, 1981).

1570, and thirteen years later his successor could muster only fourteen.[116] At Llandaff, Bishop Bleddyn took drastic steps to try to increase preaching in his diocese by arranging a rota, which fixed their preaching days for the thirteen canons of his diocese. In the event of any one of the canons not being himself capable of delivering a sermon, he was required to find some one else able to fulfil his duty for him and to pay him 5*s.* for his pains.[117] The growing tendency for sermons to be preached was indicated by the gradual installation of seats and benches in the cathedrals and some parish churches. The congregations evidently wanted to be able to sit more comfortably if they were expected to pay attention to lengthy disquisitions from the pulpit; but the introduction of pews could lead to other consequences besides attentive listening. They were often the scene of unedifying quarrels and disturbances over place and precedence.[118] So put out was Bishop William Hughes at the 'perturbationes et malefacta' (perturbations and misdeeds) occasioned in St Asaph cathedral by the installation of seats that in 1576 he ordered the removal of the offending furnishings.[119] At Llandderfel parish in 1588 the contentions reached such a pitch of intensity as to be taken to the Court of Star Chamber, where the complainant deposed that he was afraid to allow the quarrel to go to arbitration by the justices of the peace because the defendants had worked themselves into such a furore.[120]

Clashes of this kind markedly increased in number and violence during the 1590s.[121] Nevertheless, sermons in Wales were nothing like frequent enough for the liking of the dissentient John Penry. In 1587 he fulminated against the disgraceful failure of the Church in Wales to provide a preaching ministry: 'We have preaching. How often? Quarterly. It is not so. For that one parish where there is one ordinary quarter sermon, we have twenty that have none.'[122] The evidence of Penry was unquestionably biased; but the more orthodox layman, George Owen, who took him to task for his comments may, on his part, have been going too far in defence of the Church when he claimed that he knew of as many preachers in the single county of Pembrokeshire as 'that shameless man (Penry)' had said were to

---

[116] *WRE*, p. 124.

[117] Thomas, *Llandaff*, p. 139.

[118] C. Hill, *Economic Problems of the Church from Archbishop Whitgift to the Long Parliament* (Oxford, 1956), pp. 176–7. *The Carmarthen Book of Ordinances, 1569–1606*, ed. J. Davies (Carmarthen, 1996), pp. 5, 27.

[119] Thomas, *St Asaph*, I. 291–2.

[120] PRO, STA C 5/E16/14; cf. E3/27; E5/37.

[121] I. ab O. Edwards, *Catalogue of Star Chamber Proceedings relating to Wales* (Cardiff, 1929), pp. 69, 72, 84, 88, 117.

[122] *Treatises*, p. 36.

be found in the whole of Wales.[123] Owen's evidence did not square with that of Bishops Davies and Middleton, or with that of his clerical neighbour, Robert Holland. Most Protestants would have agreed that Wales was still in need of very much more preaching and exposition of the word.

One of the most seasoned and percipient observers of the Welsh religious scene at this time was William Morgan, the biblical translator. He was concerned to emphasize how much Welsh preaching had already benefited from wider use of the translations of the New Testament and the Book of Common Prayer of 1567. Many of the population had acquired a better knowledge of English as a result. Yet he, too, would have conceded that much remained to be accomplished, especially as a result of a complete and revised translation of the Bible.[124]

Preaching was not the only form of exposition of the faith that was open to parish priests. In addition, those who could not preach and even those who could, found the question-and-answer drill of the catechism an effective medium for instruction, especially of the young and illiterate. A further advantage of the catechism was that it could conveniently be used at home by the literate and pious householder to indoctrinate children and servants. In the Injunctions of 1559 those with cure of souls had been enjoined to teach the Ten Commandments, the Articles of Belief, the Lord's Prayer, and the catechism set forth in the Prayer Book every holy day and second Sundays. We do not, however, have any means of knowing how regularly they did so. In any case, these materials were not readily available in Welsh until 1567. Thereafter, the independent translation of the Ten Commandments and of three separate versions of the catechism into Welsh besides that offered in the Book of Common Prayer give some indication of an eagerness on the people's part to avail themselves of the catechism.[125] None the less, in 1583 Bishop Middleton believed it to be necessary to insist upon the ministers teaching the catechism to the youth of their parishes, a practice which he declared to be 'now altogether neglected'.[126]

Given the limited impact being made by any variety of Protestant belief in Wales, it is hardly to be wondered at that the more advanced Puritan interpretations of it should be even more halting in their progress. The terms 'Puritan' and 'Puritanism' were very elastic in their usage. Broadly speaking, they referred to all those groups of widely differing kinds who wished to see the features which they regarded as the 'dregs of popery' being removed from the belief and worship of the Church of England. Their enthusiasm in the cause of religion was such as to mark them off

---

[123] Owen, *Penbrokshire*, III. 99.
[124] Morgan, *Beibl Cyssegr-lan*, dedication.
[125] Gruffydd, 'Religious prose', pp. 33–8.
[126] Kennedy, *Eliz. Episc. Administration*, III. 151.

from their more tepid and worldly contemporaries. Such views might be perfectly compatible with complete loyalty to the structure of government and discipline in the Church and acceptance of the episcopate. Equally, they could range to a decidedly more radical attack on the existing organization of the Church and demands for much more thoroughgoing reform.

In Wales there were no well-organized forms of protest, no moves towards the quasi-presbyterian or classis system as seen in parts of the south-east of England, certainly no call for such root-and-branch reconstruction as the establishment of separatist congregations.[127] Yet there seem to have been more manifestations of a mildly Puritan character on the part of individuals than has often been supposed. Returned Marian exiles like Thomas Young and Richard Davies sympathized with the reforming tendencies tinged with Puritanism exhibited by other bishops who, like themselves, had spent some years in Protestant cities in Europe. Davies, long after becoming a bishop, maintained his contacts with the Puritan group associated with Archbishop Grindal and the poet Edmund Spenser.[128] Bleddyn, too, was a bishop with ardent evangelizing inclinations.[129] Surprisingly enough, William Hughes of St Asaph, although the subject of much criticism, was closely associated in his younger days with the earl of Leicester's group and had been Lady Margaret preacher at Cambridge.[130] Another Cambridge graduate, Thomas Roberts of Christ's College, was typical of the gifted students who never returned to Wales after graduating. He settled in Norfolk, where he became 'president' of the Puritan ministers in Norwich diocese.[131]

Two notable examples of convincedly Protestant graduates who returned to Wales after a university career and spent all their lives there were William Morgan and Rowland Puleston. Morgan had kept aloof from the Puritan party as an undergraduate and was later to become bishop, first of Llandaff and then of St Asaph. As vicar of Llanrhaeadr ym Mochnant he was an enthusiastic preacher and showed distinct Puritan tendencies without ever once dreaming of rejecting episcopal authority.[132] Puleston was the author of an interesting prose work called 'Llefr o'r Eglwys Christnogedd' (Book of the Christian Church) which never found its way

[127] Collinson, *Eliz. Puritanism*; M. M. Knappen, *Tudor Puritanism*; P. G. Lake, *Moderate Puritans and the English Church* (Cambridge, 1982),
[128] *WRE*, p. 182.
[129] Thomas, *Llandaff*, pp. 132–52.
[130] W. P. Griffith, 'William Hughes and the "Decensus Controversy" of 1567', *BBCS*, XXIV (1987), 185–99.
[131] Collinson, *Eliz. Puritanism*, pp. 127, 141, 203–4.
[132] N. W. Powell, 'Dr William Morgan and his parishioners at Llanrhaeadr ym Mochnant', *CHST*, XLIX (1988), 98–101.

from manuscript into print.[133] The text reveals his many sources, all markedly 'leftish' in complexion, such as the Geneva Bible, John Foxe, Thomas Becon, and others. Having outlined the origins of papal primacy and the 'damnable ceremonies' which sprang from it, he condemned the sin and ignorance which grew up after the abandonment of earliest ecclesiastical discipline and went on to recount the state of the Church from the patriarchs to the Reformation and from the Reformation to his own day. It was not an impressive book in style or content and its range of readers was probably extremely restricted. It is of interest on account of its eloquent calls for more preaching and because it shows the profound influence moderate Puritanism could exercise over an otherwise little-known parish priest.[134]

Puritan opinions left their mark on isolated individuals among laymen, too. William Salesbury had long been one of the most zealous and active of Welsh Protestant laymen; but, inspirational as his trailblazing had been before 1567, he very largely disappears from view afterwards. In south-east Wales a number of the popular poets, or *cwndidwyr*, were convinced reformers and employed their verses to make Protestant views and scriptural knowledge more familiar among the people. Such verse, written in popular measures and colloquial language, sometimes set to well-known airs, was well adapted for its purpose, and it prepared the way for the still more popular compositions of Edmwnd Prys and Vicar Prichard.[135] The most notable figure among these *cwndidwyr* was Thomas Llywelyn of Rhigos (*flor. c.*1560–1610) in Glamorgan. He became the subject of the most remarkable stories, freely embroidered by Iolo Morganwg, to the effect that Thomas was an ardent Protestant reformer, an appealing lay preacher, licensed by Archbishop Grindal himself, and the founder of a number of early Nonconformist churches in the uplands of Glamorgan.[136] While it would be foolhardy to accept all that the imaginative Iolo had to say about him, it would be equally unwise to dismiss it without recognizing the nub of genuine fact embellished by so much fancy characteristic of many of Iolo's writings. There may be no reason to believe that Thomas preached in or founded any churches, but there were unmistakable Puritan traces in many of his verses.[137] He may have been typical of others in Glamorgan and elsewhere.

One layman in Wales who represented a more extreme strain of Puritan sympathy than any of those discussed so far was Edward Dunn (or Dwn)

[133] NLW, Plas Power MS. 1; cf. *Rhyddiaith Gymraeg*, II. 53–5.

[134] Gruffydd, 'Religious prose', pp. 41–50.

[135] *W and R*, pp. 164–6; Lewis, *GCH*, IV. 526–35.

[136] Williams, *Tradd. Llen. Morg.*, pp. 126–8, 153–4.

[137] Williams, *Tafodau Tân*, pp. 164–79.

Lee, a Member of Parliament for Carmarthen Boroughs in the Parliament of 1587, 'noteworthy as possibly the only Puritan among the Welsh members of parliament during Elizabeth's reign'.[138] His father was a Buckinghamshire landowner, who may well have been influenced by the religious radicalism of that county; but his mother was the co-heiress of Sir Thomas Johns of Abermarlais, Carmarthenshire, and his grandmother the heiress of Sir Edward Dwn of Kidwelly. It was Edward Dunn Lee, together with Job Throckmorton, MP, who presented John Penry's *Aequity* to the House of Commons in 1587. Speaking in the House, he rehearsed Penry's favourite theme: indictment of the idolatry and superstition so universally prevalent in Wales on account of the lack of learned ministers. For his pains, he was removed from the commission of the peace in Carmarthenshire, an indignity which he attributed to his sponsorship of Penry's petition.

Much the most celebrated of all Welsh Puritans was John Penry (1563–93),[139] whose education, interests, and willingness to preach all suggest that he was originally intended for the priesthood. He was never ordained, however, – possibly because of mutual antipathy between himself and the bishops – and remained a layman to the end of his short life. He was born on the northern slopes of the Epynt mountains in Breconshire, probably on a farm known as Cefn Brith, which still stands. The son of a minor gentleman called Meredith Penry, he was educated mainly at Peterhouse, Cambridge, where he came strongly under the influence of Puritan ideas, and later at Oxford. His religious inclinations were fortified by his early connection with Northamptonshire Puritans such as Job Throckmorton. Penry launched into print at the youthful age of 24 and made a name for himself with three pamphlets on the state of religion in Wales, published in rapid succession during 1587–8.[140] They are uniquely valuable in presenting Elizabethan Wales through the eyes of a left-wing Puritan. Yet to consider them in isolation, as being solely or even mainly concerned with the state of Wales, is probably a mistake. Almost certainly, they are best understood if regarded as part of a wider programme being organized by leading Puritans and intended to prepare the ground for drastic Church reform.[141] The first of these treatises, *The Aequity of an Humble Supplication*, was completed in haste so that it might be presented

[138] *Treatises*, p. xiv.

[139] Pierce, *John Penry*; D. J. McGinn, *John Penry and the Marprelate Controversy* (Rutgers UP, 1966); *Treatises*, introd.; G. Williams, 'John Penry: Marprelate and Patriot', *WHR*, III (1967), 361–80.

[140] *Treatises* provides a valuable modern reprint expertly edited by David Williams.

[141] J. E. Neale, *Elizabeth I and Her Parliaments, 1559–1581* (London, 1953), pp. 60–4, 146–65; Collinson, *Eliz. Puritanism*, pp. 273–8, 303–16.

to the Parliament of 1587. It was one of a series of accounts rendered by Puritans on the state of religion in various parts of the realm, including one on the county of Cornwall, in tones reminiscent of Penry, claiming to come from four score and ten thousand souls which, for 'want of the word, were in extreme misery'.[142]

Penry's own work was presented in the House of Commons by two Puritan members, Dunn Lee and Throckmorton. The publication of so cutting an attack on the Church establishment landed its author in hot water with Archbishop Whitgift and the Court of High Commission; not so much because of anything said specifically about Wales as for the radical tone of his criticisms in general, especially about the government of the Church of England. He may, however, have had powerful protectors – the earl of Leicester has been suggested as one – who were able to secure his speedy release. Not that this first clash with the archbishop prevented Penry from proceeding to publish two more highly critical tracts in undelayed succession: *An exhortation unto the Governors and People of Her Majesty's Country of Wales* and *A Supplication unto the High Court of Parliament*.

In these three works Penry issued a series of trenchant strictures on the existing state of the Church in Wales. He laid most of the blame for the poor condition of religion and Church life at the door of the bishops.[143] In attributing so much of the responsibility to them, Penry was less than just to many of their number who, as has already been seen, laboured long and hard to improve matters. However, two of the contemporary bishops may have justified some of the caustic things that were said of them. One was William Hughes of St Asaph.[144] He had a bad reputation for paying miserable stipends to curates and was also accused of sending unfit curates to the parish of Llandrinio, where the parishioners claimed to have desired a Welshman, John Williams, a scholar of Oxford and 'well seen in the Welsh tongue'.[145] He was further alleged to have sold livings in his own gift, leased manors for long terms to his wife, children, and other relatives, and compelled the dean and chapter to do the same. He was said to allow his chaplains corruptly to hold the chapter seals, to neglect hospitality and charity, and to have become involved in a series of unsavoury legal disputes over property. His most notorious failing was the gross pluralism in which he indulged. Said to have been the most disgraceful pluralist ever known in the Anglican Church, he was reputed to have held sixteen livings at various times in order to make up the income of £150 he was permitted to receive

---

[142] Ibid., p. 304.
[143] *Treatises*, p. 62.
[144] Jones, *BBCS*, XXIX. 320–35.
[145] PRO, STA C 5/A19/31.

in commendam.[146] Nevertheless, it may well be that Hughes has been excessively criticized for his shortcomings and insufficient allowance made for some of his better points.[147] There is less to be said on behalf of Marmaduke Middleton, bishop of St David's (1582–93), the ultimate black sheep of the whole Elizabethan bench. Eventually, he was found guilty of a number of heinous offences and removed from his see in 1593. Already, by 1587 he was on very bad terms with a number of laymen and clerics in his diocese and was accused of several misdeeds, including treason, murder, bigamy, and thefts. As Middleton spent much of his time in Brecon, Penry might well have been familiar with his miscreancies, although it is noticeable that it is not any personal blemishes on the part of a bishop which Penry pilloried so much as the failures of the episcopal system as a whole.[148]

In particular, he castigated them mercilessly for their imposition of an unworthy clergy on the country, accusing them of having admitted into their sacred function rogues and vagabonds, gadding about the country under the name of scholars, 'swarms of ungodly ministers', who kept out 'a learned and godly ministry'. The result was widespread non-residence and pluralism: 'non-residencies have cut the throat of our church. Some that never preached have three church livings.'[149] These publications, it should be remembered, were propaganda documents which markedly overstated their case against the prelates. The Puritan position was characterized by an emphatic statement of the ideal and by a constant stream of criticism of the bishops for failing to meet this counsel of perfection.[150] So, too, were Penry's onslaughts on the clergy for failing to preach the gospel; a charge more than ordinarily serious, since for Penry preaching was 'the ordinary means of salvation', without which none could come to the truth. His brethren, by contrast, 'for the most part know not what preaching meaneth, much less think the same necessary to salvation . . . they think it sufficient to have one sermon perhaps in all their life'.[151] Along with the absence of preaching what had caused the people's deplorable ignorance was the failure of the Church to ensure the translation of the whole Bible into Welsh. It was this lack of an adequate translation that led to the

---

[146] Thomas, *St Asaph*, I. 98–100; F. O. White, *The Lives of the Elizabethan Bishops* (London, 1898), pp. 197–8; Strype, *Annals*, III/ii. 471–5.

[147] Griffith, *BBCS*, XXIV. 185–99.

[148] *APC* (1587–8), 339–40; 1589–90, 337, 379; White, *Eliz. Bishops*, pp. 197–8; R. E. Head, *Royal Supremacy and the Trials of the Bishops, 1558–1725* (London, 1962), pp. 23–8.

[149] *Treatises*, p. 63, 27, 40.

[150] C. H. and K. George, *The Protestant Mind of the English Reformation, 1570–1640* (Princeton, 1961), p. 335.

[151] *Treatises*, p. 7.

appalling contrast which Penry saw between the favoured condition of the ancient British and the desperate state of his contemporaries, their descendants. He eagerly accepted the beliefs of Salesbury and Davies that the forefathers of the Welsh, the 'Cymbrubrittons', had, many centuries before, enjoyed as their 'possession and inheritance' the scriptures in their own tongue.'[152] He passionately advocated that this treasure should be restored. Yet, eloquently as Penry voiced his opinions concerning his own people, it seems very doubtful whether many of them were influenced by his writings. Only a minority would have been able to read English and fewer still could have been expected to sympathize with the content of his books. Indeed, in spite of his undeniably intense patriotism, it has to be wondered whether Penry was writing primarily for a Welsh public. His tracts were much more likely to have been attuned to appeal to Puritan readers ranged widely across the kingdom and it was at such an audience that they were directed. In spite of his impassioned appeals and the courage with which he faced martyrdom for his convictions in 1593, within months of returning from exile in Scotland, so little impact did he have on his native country that after his death his name passed into virtual oblivion.[153]

---

[152] Ibid., p. 30,
[153] G. Williams in *Gwanwyn Duw*, ed. J. E. W. Davies (Caernarfon, 1932), pp. 88–108.

CHAPTER 12

The Church by Law Established: II. The Laity

HOWEVER much the bishops required the support and co-operation of their clergy to implement the Elizabethan church settlement, they knew that to carry the day they would also need the goodwill and assistance of the laity. The Church depended heavily on the power of the main administrative and judicial executants of the Crown, such as the Privy Council,[1] Parliament, Star Chamber, Court of High Commission, or superior judges, not only to back up its own authority, but also, when necessary, to intervene on its behalf. Up to the 1580s the Privy Council included some confirmed Protestants among its members and did not hesitate to meddle with matters of religion when it considered such a course of action desirable. It was reluctant to allow the Church or the clergy any additional powers, and was, indeed, somewhat suspicious of the prerogatives they already claimed; but none the less, it did recognize the need to uphold the authority of the sovereign as it was manifested in religion.

The two main concerns of the Privy Council in this respect were the enforcement of the Act of Supremacy and the suppression of recusancy. In Wales it often acted directly on its own initiative but more usually operated through the agency of its daughter-institution, the Council in the Marches,[2] particularly since the president of that body was *ex officio* lord lieutenant of all the Welsh counties. For most of Elizabeth's reign its president was Sir Henry Sidney (1560–86). Although he was a conciliatory and well-meaning man, religious affairs were not his *forte*.[3] He was dilatory in his pursuit of recusants, as has already been seen, and in 1577, when Bishop Whitgift was appointed vice-president, a marked difference of approach and temper was

---

[1] G. R. Elton, 'Tudor government: points of contact', *TRHS*, 5th ser., XXIV. 183–200; XXV. 198–212; XXVI. 201–28; P. Williams, *The Tudor Regime* (Oxford, 1979).
[2] C. A. J. Skeel, *The Council in the Marches of Wales* (London, 1903); P. H. Williams, *The Council in the Marches of Wales under Elizabeth I* (Cardiff, 1958).
[3] Williams, *Council in Marches*, chap. 4. Cf. R. Flenley, *Calendar of the Register of . . . the Council in the Marches . . .* (London, 1916), p. 5. where he comments on the fewness of references to religion in the register.

immediately observable. During the last years of Sidney's presidency he had wanted to exercise greater control over the bishops, a move that was resolutely opposed by Whitgift. The final four years of Sidney's tenure of office, in consequence, were not good ones for religion.[4]

From about 1580 onwards, there existed a tribunal popularly known as the Court of High Commission, sitting in London and exercising wide powers of jurisdiction in ecclesiastical matters. It fulfilled two principal functions: it implemented the royal supremacy by means of commission, and it also acted as a court of justice similar to Star Chamber in Church matters.[5] It was empowered to equip the Council in the Marches with temporary commissions to hear ecclesiastical issues.[6] As it seems to have been mainly taken up in dealing with causes relating to Puritans like John Penry, it was not especially active in matters concerning Wales, although a prominent recusant like Siôn Dafydd Rhys was hauled before it to answer to the charge of having established a secret Catholic printing-press in his house at Brecon.

The assize judges were another major instrument of royal authority in Wales. They were regarded as having a conspicuous role to play in the maintenance of the established religion. Their attitude was carefully noted by the people, who were said to be the 'readier to draw forward or backward as they shall perceive the temporal magistrate to be affected'.[7] Thus, the appointment of Sir George Bromley, a staunch Protestant, as chief justice of the north Wales circuit of the Court of Great Sessions was reported to have stimulated the justices of the peace there to be more forward in stamping out religious subversion. It was significant that in 1579 Bromley should be commissioned, along with the bishops of St Asaph (Hughes) and Bangor (Robinson) to inquire into recusancy. This procedure led Bishop Robinson to declare that the people showed 'some better countenance to the gospel', 'by the godly zeal of the Chief Justice, whose counsel and aid . . . God . . . will turn . . . to the salvation of his people'.[8] In sharp contrast, the Catholic author of the account of Richard White's martyrdom castigated Bromley's attempts to win himself more favour and authority with that 'sponsor of legal butchery', the earl of Leicester, 'by the death of Catholic men'.[9]

However, the relationship between governmental agencies and the bishops was a two-way process. The bishops automatically sat not only in

---

[4] Williams, *Council in Marches*, p. 90.

[5] G. R. Elton, *The Tudor Constitution* (Cambridge, 1960), pp. 317–33.

[6] Williams, *Council in Marches*, pp. 88ff.

[7] PRO, SP12/66/24.

[8] J. G. Jones, *Wales and the Tudor State* (Cardiff, 1988), p. 100.

[9] D. A. Thomas, *The Welsh Elizabethan Catholic Martyrs* (Cardiff, 1971), pp. 229, 251.

the Upper House of Convocation but also in the House of Lords. They certainly looked to the Privy Council for help, but the council for its part was keen enough to enlist their assistance as members of the Council in the Marches, and as justices of the peace and members of special commissions, as well as to enforce the church settlement and search out recusants. Bishop Richard Davies's talents as an administrator were called upon by the Council in the Marches in a variety of ways: for supervising musters, inquiring into the exactions and bribes of sheriffs, checking on the misappropriation of army victuals, recovering stolen cattle, and overseeing the activities of tanners.[10] He was also employed several times in the task of suppressing piracy along the south-west coast of Wales, where it was a more than usually thorny problem.[11] Dealing with piracy was always an unpopular chore with those bishops called upon to undertake it,[12] and, judging from Davies's experiences, one can readily understand why. For although bishops, indeed the clergy in general, were widely regarded as having a traditional role as peacemakers and conciliators, in the context of trying to settle questions of piracy, Davies fell foul of two of the most prominent laymen of the area – Sir John Perrott and Richard Vaughan.[13] Another layman and fellow-member of the Council in the Marches with whom he quarrelled irreconcilably was the lawyer, Fabian Phillips.[14] Davies's brother-bishops, William Hughes and Nicholas Robinson, on the other hand, were very closely associated with Sir George Bromley and Dr Ellis Price in hounding down John Bennett and Richard White, and all of them closely co-operated in the general hunt for recusants.[15]

The bishops inevitably looked hopefully for the support of the leading aristocrats with influence at court. Bishop Hughes was alleged to have gained his bishopric of St Asaph on account of his undue influence with the earl of Leicester and to have made unworthy promises of favours in return.[16] All the same, prelates regarded these grandees with mixed feelings: while they appreciated their power and influence, they viewed with deep misgivings the eagerness, even ruthlessness, with which the great men pushed their desire for authority and possessions at the expense of the Church. Comparatively few of these major figures resided in Wales or had interests there. Among those that did were the earls of Leicester, Essex, Pembroke, and Worcester. To these might be added Sir Henry Sidney – not

---

[10] Flenley, *Register*, pp., 109, 126, 137–9, 190.
[11] *W 1415–1642*, pp. 374–80.
[12] R. B. Manning, *Religion and Society in Elizabethan Sussex* (Leicester, 1964), p. 96.
[13] *WRE*, pp. 167–8.
[14] Ibid., pp. 169–70.
[15] Thomas, *Eliz. Martyrs*, pp. 22–3.
[16] PRO, STA C 5/F25/12.

a member of the nobility, it is true, but president of the Council in the Marches and, withal, an influential figure at court and a leading member of the earl of Leicester's faction. Leicester himself had large-scale territorial interests in north Wales and was regarded as the patron of the Puritans there, and in Lancashire and the nearby cities of Chester and Shrewsbury. Among those who solicited his favour and worked assiduously on his behalf were Bishop Hughes, Dr Ellis Price, the Wynns of Gwydir, and Sir John Perrott ('an inward favourite of the earl').[17] In south-west Wales it was the earl of Essex who exercised a dominant influence until his relatively early death in 1577; though both he and his son, the second earl, were to encounter a good deal of opposition from major gentry in the area. Essex was an enthusiastic Protestant, whom Richard Davies applauded for his 'fear of God' and his ability to discern 'betwixt true religion and the hypocritical false religion', 'betwixt the right worshipping of God and idolatry, betwixt the traditions of men and God's word', which the bishop regarded as the essential characteristic of the genuine nobleman.[18] Small wonder, then, that in 1576 both should have been closely associated with each other in founding one of the new seminaries of Protestant and humanist teaching in the shape of the Queen Elizabeth Grammar School at Carmarthen.[19] In Glamorgan and Monmouthshire the first and second Herbert earls of Pembroke were men of the highest standing, despite now having their chief residence in Wiltshire; but rivalry prevailed between them and the third and fourth earls of Worcester. This intensified when the second earl of Pembroke became president of the Council in the Marches and a keen upholder of the Established Church, while the fourth earl of Worcester developed into a 'stiff papist'.[20]

In addition, the interests of the laity below the ranks of the greatest landowners necessarily called for careful attention from the leading members of the clergy. The success of Tudor government in town and country depended on the goodwill and co-operation shown by the 'political nation', i.e. that minority of the queen's subjects sufficiently propertied, educated, informed, and interested to participate in the tasks of government. They comprised about a quarter or a fifth of the adult male population (women were largely, though not wholly, excluded). From their ranks was recruited a bureaucracy of unpaid officials, on whose services the government of the country rested: deputy-lieutenants, sheriffs, justices

---

[17] Thomas, *Eliz. Martyrs*, pp. 22–3, 34; for Perrott, see J. Wynn, *History of the Gwydir Family*, ed. J. Ballinger (Cardiff, 1927), p. 64.

[18] R. Davies, *Funeral Sermon preached at Carmarthen on the Death of the Earl of Essex* (London, 1577), no pagination.

[19] G. Williams, *Bywyd ac Amserau yr Esgob Richard Davies* (Cardiff, 1953), pp. 91–2.

[20] *DWB*, s.n. Somerset.

of the peace, coroners, constables, churchwardens, and the like.[21] Such officers were moved less by a concern for religious conformity than for social stability Regardless of their own private opinions, they were more or less willing to acquiesce in Elizabeth's religious arrangements as long as her government maintained order and protected property; but they were apprehensive about any developments that might upset their supremacy in local affairs, their patronage, or their economic benefit. They were inclined to put the interests of self, family, friendship, clientage, or alliance ahead of what might be described as public duty. Within their own districts, gentry of the first rank, or even the second grade, tended to wield an uncontested supremacy. It was hardly surprising, perhaps, that it should be said of a Caernarfonshire magnate like Sir John Wynn that he could prove anything against a lesser adversary 'though the same was never so untrue' and that he was 'able to make these stones to be green cheese if he list'.[22] Even a man of considerably lesser status, Piers Holland of Abergele, could be described in the following terms: 'He is all in all and ruleth and commandeth all men, as he listeth, using his will for law and his affection for reason.'[23]

The gentry varied widely in their religious loyalties, as for that matter did the clergy. A minority of laymen were well disposed towards Protestant convictions, even enthusiastic in their espousal of them. Richard Vaughan, a Caernarfonshire justice, was hated by papists 'because he doth correct their errors and goeth about to bring them to amendment of life'.[24] Others, however, hankered after the old ways; and some were even confirmed Catholics, like Sir Henry Jones of Carmarthenshire, a would-be sheriff of the county but blacklisted by the earl of Essex in 1572 as 'an earnest papist'.[25] There were a number of well-known figures who were havering so uncertainly that serious doubts existed where their true allegiance lay. It was not at all clear whether that eminent scholar and public man, Humphrey Llwyd, MP, was a Catholic or a Protestant.[26] The author of a pedestrian Welsh prose translation of a Protestant apologetic tract, Sir John Conway, had a notoriously Catholic wife.[27] The Bulkeley family were uneasily suspected of nurturing warm Catholic predilections down to the 1580s. Sir Edward Stradling of St Donat's in Glamorgan was the son of a staunchly Catholic father, married into a leading Catholic family of Sussex,

---

[21] *W 1415–1642*, chap. 14.
[22] PRO, E134, James I, Mich. 3.
[23] NLW, Great Sessions, Gaol Files, Denbs. 5/1.
[24] PRO, STA C 5/07/22.
[25] Mathew, *BBCS* VI. 167.
[26] *W and R*, p. 145.
[27] G. Jones, 'Siôn Conwy III a'i waith', *BBCS*, XXII (1966–8), 193–207.

was a client of the conservative earl of Arundel, extended patronage to two avowed Catholic authors, Thomas Wiliems and Siôn Dafydd Rhys, and yet was a deputy-lieutenant, a justice of the peace, and was on terms of close friendship with a rigid Protestant like Sir Francis Walsingham and leading Anglican clerics.[28] Many of the gentry, however – probably the majority of them – were greedy, lax, and devoid of serious religious principle of any sort.

A feature of the officials of local government that was adversely commented on by contemporary observers was their corruption. The well-known Welsh judge, David Lewis, complained in 1576 that many of those appointed to be sheriffs and justices of the peace were men of little substance or credit, who made their living by 'polling and pilling' their neighbours. He would have wished to see them being chosen only from those 'best disposed to justice and godliness' and the number of them reduced to eight in each shire as prescribed in the Act of Union.[29] What struck Bishop Richard Davies was the contrast between the willingness of officials to oppress the poor while slavishly fawning on the great; 'void of all religion and fear of God', they used their authority to 'pill and poll the country and to beggar their poor neighbours'.[30] Elsewhere, in his introduction to the New Testament of 1567, he maintained that these were the sort of men who regularly gave sanctuary to criminals: 'Often in Wales, though the law takes no note of it, the gentleman's hall is the refuge of thieves . . . So I say that were it not for the arm and wing of the gentleman, there would be but little theft in Wales.'[31] John Penry, predictably, went to extremes in his condemnation:

> The seat of judgement in our common courts is turned into wormwood . . . It is irksome to think how hardly a poor man can keep anything from thieves of great countenance. Though he seeth his own sheep or other cattle feed within two miles of him in some men's pastures, he dareth not ask them.[32]

---

[28] C. Davies, *Latin Writers of the Renaissance* (Cardiff, 1981), pp. 105, 113; G. Williams, 'The Stradling Family', in R. Denning (ed.), *St. Donat's Castle and Atlantic College* (Cowbridge, 1983), pp. 17–53.

[29] D. Lewis, 'The court of the president and the council', *Cymm.* XII (1897), 1–64.

[30] *Funeral Sermon*, no pagination; cf. the complains made by 'Diggon Davie' (almost certainly Richard Davies) in Spenser's *Shepherd's Calendar* concerning the aggression shown in relation to weaker men by those powerful members of the gentry whom he likens to 'big bulls of Bashan', W. L. Renwick, *The Shepherd's Calendar* (London, 1930), pp. 118–19.

[31] G. H. Hughes, *Rhagymadroddion, 1547–1648* (Cardiff, 1951), pp. 32–3.

[32] J. Penry, *Three Treatises concerning Wales*, ed. D. Williams (Cardiff, 1960), pp. 35–60.

Some of the best-known Welsh poets of the age – Tomos Prys, Edmwnd Prys, Simwnt Fychan, or Siôn Tudur – were caustic in their strictures on the usury of the gentry, and their pride, avarice, and oppression of their tenants.[33]

From those gentry who constituted the official class, the queen looked in matters ecclesiastical for docility and obedience, not enthusiasm or militancy, since the delicate balance of her settlement, with its prime concern for national unity, might all too easily be wrecked by zealots of any persuasion. Her bishops were naturally inclined to think and speak rather differently. Richard Davies, having experienced exile in the reformed city of Frankfurt during Mary's reign, lashed out furiously at those gentlemen in his diocese who applied 'all their power to further and continue the kingdom of Antichrist'. He found it wholly lamentable that in a 'blessed time of light and knowledge of the gospel', they would 'neither themselves enter into the kingdom of heaven, nor suffer them that would'.[34] It was because he did not wish to give this opposition, already formidable enough, any further encouragement, that he deplored the attempts by his adversary, the lawyer Fabian Phillips, to provoke a quarrel with him.[35] But widespread attachment to old loyalties and slowness to accept change survived Davies in his diocese. In 1583 his successor, Middleton, deprecated, as Davies had done, the slackness of lay officials. They would not apprehend obstinate papists or reprimand the indifferent, and he could not.[36] Attention has already been drawn to Bishop Bleddyn's unhappy experiences in 1579 when he found the justices of the peace among his fellow-commissioners undoing all his efforts. They sabotaged the whole inquiry into recusancy in Glamorgan and Monmouthshire by informing the offenders in advance of what was afoot. A few years later, in 1582, the Privy Council itself had cause to rap Welsh justices over the knuckles for their laxity in allowing the numbers of recusants to increase,[37] and again in 1586 it sharply censured those same officers for their 'negligence and faction'.[38]

The relationship of the justices of the peace and other influential members of the gentry to the churchwardens was critical in determining the success or failure of the Elizabethan settlement. In theory, it was the churchwardens who bore the essential responsibility for enforcing the Act

[33] J. G. Jones, 'The Welsh poets and their patrons, c.1540–1640', *WHR*, IX (1979), 245–73.

[34] *Funeral Sermon*, no pagination; cf. C. H. and K. George, *The Protestant Mind of the English Reformation* (Princeton, 1961), p. 249, for clerical criticisms of the magistracy in general.

[35] *WRE*, pp. 169–70.

[36] PRO, SP12/162/29.

[37] *APC*, XIII. 427–8.

[38] Ibid., XIV. 124.

of Uniformity in the parishes. That statute required all Elizabeth's subjects to attend church on Sundays and holy days, morning and evening. If, without good reason for their absence, any of them failed to do so, they were to be fined 12*d.* They were also to be admonished by the church-wardens and, if they still did not mend their ways, were to be reported by the wardens to their ordinary. A brief summary of churchwardens' duties occurs in an entry in the St David's chapter records.[39] On 5 April 1575 the bishop, Richard Davies, chose eight men to be churchwardens in the parish of St David's, two for each *cylch* (district). They were charged with detecting, and presenting to the bishop, 'all vices, faults and misdemean-ours' within the limits of their responsibility. They were to report all parishioners who were negligent in coming to church or who failed to bring their children to be catechized; all 'filchers' (petty thieves), talkers in church, etc.; and generally to present 'all such matters as churchwardens are bound to present by virtue and commandment of the Queen's Majesty's most dreaded injunctions'.[40] Absence from church might be due to principled refusal, but much more usually it sprang from carelessness, indifference, or a preference to spend the time in alehouses, at recreations, or even at home. Churchwardens, therefore, had a highly responsible task to execute in reporting the absentees, especially, perhaps, in the larger, more sparsely populated parishes. They were, however, ill-equipped to fulfil it, and particularly to withstand pressure from powerful local notabilities, they being 'weak persons . . . loth to offend their betters or neighbours'.[41] Possibly the only body that might adequately have dealt with such men of influence was the Court of High Commission; but the laity in Parliament and in the secular courts were very reluctant to allow that body any significant increase in power or activity. Hence, as Richard Davies himself pointed out, the mouths of churchwardens might effectively be stopped by their influential neighbours; all the more so at times of visitations, when offenders were commonly either tipped-off or con-cealed.[42] So onerous and unappealing were many aspects of the church-wardens' duties that there were numerous instances of men trying to evade the responsibility altogether or else carrying it out very indifferently.[43]

The chapter at St David's had been well advised to draw the attention of churchwardens to their function of keeping a check on all vices, faults, and

---

[39] NLW, SD Ch, Reg. I, pp. 254–5.

[40] Ibid. For a fuller account of their duties, see J. S. Purvis, *Tudor Parish Documents* (Cambridge, 1948), pp. 182–3.

[41] *The State Papers and Letters of Sir Ralph Sadler*, ed. A. Gifford (2 vols. Edinburgh, 1909), II. 545.

[42] PRO, SP12/118/8, 10, 11 11 (i).

[43] F. G. Emmison, *Elizabethan Life* (Chelmsford, 1970), p. 231; Purvis, *Parish Documents*, p. 92.

misdemeanours committed in the church and its precincts. Church attendance was not always the peaceable and Christianly pursuit that might have been supposed. There were constant reports of irreverent and disorderly behaviour in places of worship;[44] this in spite of orders like that of Richard Davies to his parsons in the diocese of St Asaph as early as 1561 that they should appoint 'three or four honest, sage, and discreet persons to keep good rule and order in the churches in the time of divine service'.[45] The Elizabethan period was a turbulent age when weapons were customarily carried, and men and women were not loath to resort to violence to get their own way. The church and churchyard were places where they often gathered in numbers and came face to face with their enemies; could, indeed, plan to confront them there. There were plenty of opportunities to settle old scores, or initiate new ones, in or near the church. An extraordinary number and variety of disturbances and quarrels broke out during or immediately after divine service.[46] Again and again, the courts dealt with cases of laymen assaulting or insulting each other, churchwardens, or even clergymen. They were rows about seatings, burials and burial places, precedence, and status in places of worship; fierce squabbles over tithes, leases of church lands, and rights of advowson; and many quarrels which had originated in extraneous feuds and rivalries that had nothing to do with the Church or religion.

Reference to such outbreaks is not uncommon in the Quarter Sessions records for Caernarfonshire,[47] the only ones of their kind which survive for Wales, and is even more common in those of the Great Sessions and Star Chamber. If it would be wrong to conceive of these disputes as the norm, it would be equally mistaken to think of them as the kinds of events which rarely if ever happened in the experience of the average churchgoer. The court records probably represent the visible tip of the iceberg over the ocean into which most of the disputes of the period are now plunged.

Violence offered to a cleric was regarded as a most serious offence, but it nevertheless seems to have occurred many times. In at least two cases that subsequently ended up in Star Chamber, there are accounts of clerics fighting with one another inside the churches over which they were in contention. Humphrey Robinson, clerk, nephew to Bishop Robinson, was engaged in a furious struggle with David Robert, clerk, over their respective

---

[44] K. V. Thomas, *Religion and the Decline of Magic* (London, 1971), p. 161.

[45] W. P. M. Kennedy, *Elizabethan Episcopal Administration* (3 vols. Alcuin Club, London, 1926), III. 112–13.

[46] Emmison, *Elizabethan Life*, p. 112; cf. *The Carmarthen Book of Ordinances, 1569–1606*, ed. J. Davies (Carmarthen, 1996), pp. 8, 27.

[47] *Calendar of the Caernarvonshire Quarter Sessions Records*, I. *1541–58*, ed. W. O. Williams (Caernarfon, 1956), pp. 9, 21, 59, 84, 134, 136, 178.

rights to the church of Llanbedrog, Caernarfonshire. As is usual with Star Chamber suits, establishing precisely what happened is extremely difficult, but it is quite evident from the documents relating to the action and counter-action that, on Good Friday and Easter Monday 1584, of all days, the contestants and their allies on both sides became caught up in disgraceful brawls in the church, in the course of which each faction frantically wrestled with the other for possession of the Book of Common Prayer belonging to the parish.[48] A not dissimilar dispute broke out in the same year between the clerks William Vaughan and Thomas Gutto and their respective supporters, in the church at Llansanffraid in Radnorshire, where again physical assaults were alleged to have occurred during divine service, and also at an induction to the vicarage.[49] Examples of violence being offered to a cleric were fairly common. The celebrated translator of the Welsh Bible, William Morgan, when he was parish priest of Llanrhaeadr ym Mochnant, Montgomeryshire, was involved in a series of heated clashes with one of his most influential parishioners, Ifan Maredudd of Lloran Uchaf. Morgan was accused of wearing armour to church and carrying a pistol under his vestment, to which he replied that he was obliged to do so in self-defence because he and his curate had been set upon and went in fear of their lives.[50] In a comparable but less well-known instance, David ap Ieuan Lloyd, vicar of Llangernyw, Denbighshire, accused some of his parishioners of yelling opprobrious words at him in the course of the services and of assaulting him as he was leaving the church. He, too, claimed that he dared not attend divine service without a bodyguard of some of his parishioners.[51]

Numerous instances of alleged violence in churches are found in Star Chamber records.[52] A few of the more interesting examples from widely scattered parts of Wales may give an idea of the kinds of violent outbreaks which took place. In some of them, justices of the peace, whose duty it was to maintain peace and good order, became unashamedly embroiled in fights and scuffles. In the town of Carmarthen in 1567 there was an outrageous instance of the involvement of some of the leading officials of local government in a serious eruption of misbehaviour in St Peter's

---

[48] PRO, STA C 5/R9/27; R24/7; R9/26; R38/14.

[49] Ibid., V3/1.

[50] A detailed account of this quarrel, together with a full transcript of the relevant documents, is to be found in I. ab O. Edwards, 'William Morgan's quarrels with his parishioners', *BBCS*, II (1926–7), 298–339.

[51] PRO, STA C 5/L15/3; L34/1.

[52] I. ab O. Edwards, *A Catalogue of Star Chamber Proceedings relating to Wales* (Cardiff, 1930), pp. 22, 23, 26, 27, 28, 29, 33, 35, 42, 45, 46, 48, 50, 51, 56, 58, 59, 60, 61, 62, 63, 64, 65, 67, 68, 69, 72, 73, 76, 84, 85, 88, 92, 94, 98, 99, 100, 102, 104, 108, 110, 113, 116, 122, 126, 129, 136, 140.

church, when the mayor and aldermen of the town, together with a large congregation, were present. William Parry, JP, sheriff of the county, accused his opponents, Ieuan ap Philip, JP, and a supporting cast of about thirty others, of physically assaulting him and other justices of the peace and civic dignitaries when they were celebrating communion at Whitsuntide 1567. The origins of the dispute appear to have lain in Parry's refusal to allow his daughter to marry the defendant.[53] The beautiful parish church of Gresford, Denbighshire, was in 1574 the scene of riots involving two well-known justices of the peace, John Salusbury of Rug and Dr Ellis Price. It arose out of an irreconcilable land dispute between them, which had earlier been taken to the Council in the Marches and had not been resolved.[54] In the course of a burial service at the parish church of Knighton in Radnorshire, an affray involving the coroner, the parson, and churchwardens was stirred up by a group of townsmen, so their fellow-citizen, Pierce Bull, maintained.[55] A dispute over lands formerly belonging to the monastery of Strata Marcella led to alleged onslaughts in the church by servants of Edward Gray, Lord Powys, on John Jones, a citizen of London. It was not unusual for friction to arise between 'outsiders' like Jones and some of the local inhabitants in these matters.[56] The county of Monmouthshire was intensely divided over religion and one where faction fights between Protestants and Catholics waxed hot and frequent. In 1574 one Ieuan ab Ithel accused a number of men of assaulting him in revenge for his prosecution of recusants, at the celebration of communion at Llanddewi church, which he suspected of being papistical in character.[57] At Llanmartin in the same county, in 1587, Thomas Prichard accused the high constable of laying violent hands on him in the parish church and forcing the minister and parishioners to leave. Intriguingly enough, the defendants retorted that they were doing no more than executing a high sheriff's warrant, which they claimed to have read to the complainant in Latin, English, and Welsh![58] Andrew Vaen, archdeacon of Llandaff, averred that he had been appointed by the archbishop of Canterbury to hear ecclesiastical disputes in the diocese of Llandaff but that in the process he had been reviled and taunted by John Morgan Philip, a Catholic yeoman from Tredunnock, at the church of Caerleon and forced to abandon his inquiry.[59]

---

[53] PRO, STA C 5/P60/3; P53/29.
[54] Ibid., L21/24.
[55] Ibid., B75/14; B44/7.
[56] Ibid., J1/27; Addenda 13/7.
[57] Ibid., J1/40.
[58] Ibid., P23/31; P17/17; P31/37; P59/29.
[59] Ibid., V5/14; V8/35.

It seems evident from the nature of the quarrels and assaults which broke out in the churches, and the general expectation that if a man wanted to catch up with his enemy, then the church, like a fair or a market, was as likely a place as any to be sure of doing so, that the church was a place of resort, on high festivals at least, for many people. For the majority of the population – with the exception of the poor and vagrants, perhaps – Christianity continued to play a central part in their lives. Yet it is not at all clear how many attended church regularly on Sundays. It is generally accepted that in pre-Reformation times there were a number who either did not go to church at all, or went very rarely.[60] Attendance may actually have become worse after the Reformation. In that very nerve-centre of reforming doctrine and discipline, Calvin's Geneva, for example, it is known that traditional superstitions and 'ungodly' practices persisted among the peasantry who lived around the city. They continued to indulge in proscribed games, profane songs, dancing, resort to magicians, and the like.[61] Very similar habits flourished in England and Wales, where the Anglican Church encountered many rival attractions which lured men and women away from its precincts. True, it has been estimated that between 80 and 85 per cent made their Easter communion, but at other times in the year, attendance was well below that level.[62] One historian has gone to the extent of arguing that the Elizabethan era was the 'age of greatest religious indifference before the twentieth century'.[63] That may perhaps be going too far; all the same, the anonymous author of the Welsh Catholic book, *Drych Cristianogawl*, insisted in 1585 that there were whole shires in Wales

without a single Christian in them, living like animals, most of them knowing nothing of morality, but only keeping Christ's name in their memories, without knowing more about him than animals do.

heb vn Cristiawn ynddynt, yn byw mal anifeiliaid, y rhann fwyaf o honynt heb wybod dim oddi wrth ddaioni, ond ei bod yn vnig yn dala enw Crist yn ei cof, heb wybod haychen beth yw Crist mwy nag anifeilieid.[64]

---

[60] J. J. Scarisbrick, *The Reformation and the English People* (London, 1984), p. 163.

[61] P. Chaunu (ed.), *The Reformation* (Gloucester, 1989), pp. 245–6.

[62] P. Collinson, *The Religion of Protestants* (London, 1982), pp. 210–20.

[63] Stone, *EHR*, LXXVII (1962), 328; M. M. Knappen, *Tudor Puritanism* (London, 1965), p. 380.

[64] *Rhagymadroddion*, p. 52.

Writing a year later or two later, the Puritan John Penry could affirm that there were thousands of people in Wales who knew nothing of Christ 'yea, almost that never heard of him'.[65]

It is clear that in Wales, as in England, the particular object of the authorities in Church and State was to try to ensure that heads of households attended church regularly, bringing their families and servants with them. Securing the loyalty of each paterfamilias was regarded as the key to the religious conformity of the parish; and when Archbishop Grindal issued his injunctions for the province of York in 1571 he instructed all lay people, but 'especially householders', to come to church.[66] Amongst the heads of households were to be found a relatively broad range of social types – gentry, freeholders, lawyers, traders, and others of the same kind. Also included were the more prosperous tenant farmers: men of sufficient substance to bear the responsibility of holding minor offices such as those of parish constable and churchwarden. All these were not only expected to be 'sound' and 'healthy' in the faith themselves but also had the duty of enforcing religion and morality on those who came under their authority: wives, children, servants, apprentices, tenants, labourers, the poor, and the beggars.[67] Nevertheless, a large proportion of all social groups readily allowed themselves to be enticed away from the parish church at service time. One in five of the people of Kent, many from among the poor, it has been estimated, never attended at all.[68] It is also perhaps not surprising that younger members of the community were greatly attracted by the seasonal games, dancing, and celebrations that were arranged in most parts of the country. In the Wrexham area, the Puritans of the neighbourhood were so outraged by the worldly entertainments arranged on Sunday at service time that they summoned the organizers all the way to Star Chamber to prosecute them. In court they testified to the songs and the dancing (always sure to provoke intense indignation among the stricter Protestants) carried on at Llwynonn Green; the hiring of pipers by the maidens of Abenbury; and, most pagan of all, possibly, the setting-up of a maypole there.[69] There were similar disturbances at Shrewsbury in 1588, when several people were imprisoned for resisting attempts by the magistrates to pull down a maypole.[70]

[65] *Treatises*, p. 32.

[66] *The Remains of Edmund Grindal*, ed. W. Nicholson (Parker Soc., London, 1848), p. 438.

[67] G. Williams, *Grym Tafodau Tân* (Llandysul, 1984), pp. 161–3.

[68] P. Clark, *English Provincial Society from the Reformation to the Revolution* (Hassocks, 1977), p. 32.

[69] PRO, STA C 5/R10/8.

[70] S. Doran and C. Durston, *Princes, Pastors and People* (London, 1991), p. 80.

Taverns were the prime source of temptation for many others. A moralist like Bishop Pilkington was deeply dismayed by the fact that in England on an average Sunday the parish church was empty and the tavern was full.[71] In Wales the position seems to have been at least as bad. The Council in the Marches tried to run a stern rule aimed at reducing what it described as the 'excessive number of alehouses' within the area of its jurisdiction. That number was still increasing, with the result that 'felonies are increased, thieves, murderers, and women of light conversation (behaviour) are harboured, rogues and vagabonds maintained, whoredom, filthy and detestable life much frequented, unlawful games as tables, dice, cards, bowls, quoits, and such like commonly exercised'.[72] The Glamorgan poet, Thomas Llywelyn, like Bishop Pilkington, contrasted the emptiness of the church with the crowds thronging the tavern. The inevitable outcome, as he saw it, was drunkenness, gluttony, whoredom, swearing, cursing, bawdy songs, gambling, violence, quarrelling, and lawless behaviour. Such vices tended to be much more in evidence on Sunday than any other time, since that was the day when most people were at leisure. Christian festivals, too, were the chief occasions for fairs, revels, and debaucheries. The tavern, in the eyes of the popular poets, was a highly successful rival centre of a culture counter to that of the Church.[73] Yet a vicar choral at St David's himself kept an alehouse, and a bishop of the diocese in 1583 believed it to be necessary to forbid his own clergy from becoming tavern-keepers. At least one of the poets, Thomas Llywelyn, associated the tavern with the survival of Catholic beliefs as well as with immorality and ungodliness, although medieval poets, too, had frequently condemned taverns for luring people away from church.[74]

Nor was it only worldly pleasures that drew folk away from worship. Many small farmers and labourers, having perpetual care of crops or livestock, particularly at busy seasons of the year like harvest or lambing, found themselves obliged to work on Sundays. One of the sins most regularly admitted in Welsh confessional literature was that of labouring on Sundays.[75] The minor court rolls of Cardiff in Elizabethan times not only record convictions for playing unlawful games and selling beer on Sundays, but also for working on the 'Lord's Day'.[76] Yet another reason for

[71] *The Works of James Pilkington*, ed. J. Scholfield (Parker Soc., London, 1842), p. 6; cf. J. W. Blench, *Preaching in England in the Late Fifteenth and Sixteenth Centuries* (Oxford, 1964), pp. 313–14; *Carmarthen Ordinances*, pp. vi, 22.

[72] Flenley, *Register*, pp. 102–3; cf. pp. 145, 151; cf. also Williams, *Tafodau Tân*, p. 175.

[73] Ibid., pp. 159–61, 170–1.

[74] *WC*, pp. 195, 241.

[75] Ibid., pp. 502, 511.

[76] *Records of the County Borough of Cardiff*, ed. J. H. Matthews (6 vols. Cardiff, 1898–1911), II. 158–63.

absence from church was occasioned by the long distances and rough trackways to the parish church in many of the enormous Welsh parishes, which sometimes sprawled over an area of 15,000–20,000 acres and upwards. As late as 1851, when the Religious Census was taken, there were many complaints about the obstacles which difficult geography, poor communications, and inclement weather presented to church attendance in Wales, especially during the winter months.[77]

A surprisingly large number stayed away from church because they had been excommunicated. Interestingly enough, there exists at least one reference in court records to an excommunicate bringing an action against a churchwarden, who was alleged to have refused to allow the curate at his parish church of Llansanffraid yng Nglyn, Denbighshire, to administer communion to the offender. The churchwarden, in his own defence, maintained that the complainant had been excommunicated and that he, as a churchwarden, was simply carrying out his duty.[78] The main cause of the numerous excommunications was sexual delinquency, for which the people of Wales and the border shires were notorious. 'What a hand we have had in adultery and fornication, the greater number of illegitimate and base-born among us do testify. I would our Princes and Levites had not been chief in this trespass,' bewailed John Penry.[79] The large number of children born out of wedlock and openly avowed by gentry families bears out his comment. The inhabitants of north Wales were reputed to be more 'inclined to those offences than those in other parts', this lasciviousness being attributed to the bracing effects on them of mountain air.[80] But the climate of south Wales cannot have been much less stimulating, judging by the large number of 'vicious livers' reported in the diocese of St David's. In the absence of consistory court records we have to depend on the bishop's report of 1570, which acknowledged that there were 200 excommunicates in his diocese. Some of these offenders remained unrepentant after being excommunicated for more than four years because the sheriffs could be bribed into not delivering the writ *de excommunicatu capiendo* (the initial excommunication).[81] The consistory courts in Wales, as elsewhere, although they remained the principal weapon in the bishop's judicial armoury, had lost much of their terror, with the result that many of those excommunicated made no attempt to be reconciled. To quote the irrepressible Penry once more, 'The punishment hereof in our bishop's

---

[77] I. G. Jones and D. Williams (eds.), *The Religious Census of 1851* (2 vols. Cardiff, 1977, 1981), *passim*.

[78] PRO, STA C 5/M13/33.

[79] *Treatises*, p. 35; cf. also Williams, *Council in Marches*, pp. 100–2.

[80] Ibid., p. 101.

[81] PRO, SP12/66/26; cf. Bishop Bleddyn, above, chap. 11.

court is derided of our people. For what is it to them to pay a little money or to run through the church in a white sheet?'[82]

One of Bishop Davies's most relentless opponents, Fabian Phillips, accused him of allowing widespread immorality to go unchecked in his diocese;[83] accusations to some extent sustained by the Privy Council, which charged Davies that 'bigamy and whoredom are too frequent in your diocese and not punished'.[84] Davies retorted hotly that he had never tolerated evil living 'in any respect of any manner of gain, money, or any other commodity'. He admitted that sexual delinquency was rife in his diocese, but argued that he could not be held responsible for that any more than lay justices could be blamed for the 'felonies and other enormities that happened to be committed around them'. As evidence of his forwardness in detecting and punishing offenders he claimed that the enormous total of 500 persons were excommunicated in St David's diocese every year.[85] It may have been the very large numbers of those against whom excommunication processes were pursued, coupled with the inability to enforce penalties and a scant respect for corrupt and extortionate courts, of which Whitgift himself was critical,[86] that bred in contemporaries a contempt for them and a feeling that they could be ignored with very little peril. It may well have been the ineffectuality of these consistory courts, together with the desire of the Council in the Marches to profit from the fines it could hope to levy, which led that body to take a much closer interest in the punishment of delinquency.[87] Even so, the immorality itself continued to flourish unabated in the early Stuart era, as Vicar Prichard's poems revealed.[88]

Another significant reason for the reluctance of a large number to come to church as frequently as their ancestors had done may have been the erosion of the supernatural or quasi-magical powers attributed to the medieval Church and its clergy.[89] In the Middle Ages the Church had had at its disposal a vast reservoir of resources of this kind, and in spite of the anti-magical tenor of its official teaching, it had tended to pander to the popular appetite for the other-worldly and spectacular. Its central sacrament, the mass itself, in which the bread and wine were believed to be

---

[82] *Treatises*, p 35.

[83] *WRE*, pp. 169–70.

[84] PRO, SP12/131/42.

[85] Ibid., 120/42 (i). This may seem to be an inordinately large number of excommunicates; but one-sixth of the population of York was excommunicated (R. O'Day and F. Heal, *Continuity and Change, Personnel and Administration* . . . (Leicester, 1976), p. 245) and 10,000 in Essex (Doran and Durston, *Princes, Pastors*, pp. 175ff.).

[86] C. Hill, *Puritanism and Society* (London, 1964), pp. 318–19.

[87] Williams, *Council in Marches*, pp. 100–2.

[88] N. Lloyd, *Cerddi'r Ficer* (Cyhoeddiadau Barddas, 1994); R. B. Jones, '*A Lanterne to Their Feet*' (Llandovery, 1995).

[89] *WC*, pp. 333–5.

miraculously transformed into the body and blood of Christ, was thought to possess supernatural qualities. So was the priesthood which ministered it; 'the role of priest and magician were by no means clearly distinguished in the popular mind',[90] however much the medieval church might condemn the practice of magic. From the time of Giraldus Cambrensis, at least, we have evidence of those among the Welsh clergy who were popularly believed to be endowed with exceptional attributes, men like Dafydd Ddu Hiraddug or Siôn Cent.[91] In the sixteenth century they found successors among the celebrated Catholic physicians, Siôn Dafydd Rhys and Thomas Wiliems,[92] and John Davies of Mallwyd and Edmwnd Prys among the Protestants. A remarkable priest of this kind was 'Sir' Walter, incumbent of Usk, described by one historian as a 'miracle worker'. His powers as a charmer were graphically described by two poets, Maredudd ap Rhosier and Siôn Mawddwy. The latter has an exciting account in verse of how the priest was able to rout a devil who threatened to drown the town of Usk.[93] The Catholic practitioners, however, were held in greater esteem than their Protestant counterparts, just as in later centuries Anglican priests were thought to be more potent than Nonconformists.

Furthermore, many of the trappings associated with the Catholic Church – its saints, relics, images, charms, incantations, prayers, and exorcisms, not to mention its holy wells, water, bread, and oil had all contributed to the aura of exceptional power. When these things had either disappeared altogether, or were sadly diminished in scale, their place was filled, as Reginald Scott observed, by the 'wise men and women' of the countryside.[94] Even if the superhuman faculties which had been called upon to cope with the problems of daily living might have vanished, those difficulties themselves loomed as menacingly as ever. People still needed help in dispelling the anxieties caused by ill health or disease in humans, animals, or crops; they continued to tremble at the prospect of the havoc that minions of the devil, goblins, apparitions, or evil omens could wreak; they wanted to ward off the malign effects of spells or curses, or possibly to direct them against others; and they went on wishing to know how to detect thieves of livestock or household goods in the present, or to learn what the future held for them in the way of wealth, weather, or wedlock. So when the Reformed Church and its clergy seemed reluctant or unable to assist them in these matters, or had nothing more effectual than prayers or

---

[90] Thomas, *Religion and Magic*, p. 234.
[91] *DWB*, s.n. Dafydd Ddu Athro and Siôn Cent.
[92] Gruffydd, *TCS* (1971), II. 175–90; J. E. C. Williams, 'Thomas Wiliems y Geiriadurwr', *Studia Celtica*, XVI–XVII (1981–2).
[93] D. Davies, 'Siôn Mawddwy' *LlC*, VIII (1965), 225–6.
[94] Thomas, *Religion and Magic*, p. 265; *WC*, pp. 334–5.

sermons to offer, they turned increasingly to those places, objects, or persons who had a reputation for being able to secure the desired results. Sacred wells were assumed to possess the miraculous therapeutic efficacy almost of miniature pools of Bethsaida and Siloam.[95] Bells combated the wiles of evil spirits, were widely used in funerals, and the *bangu* (corpse bell) survived in Aberystwyth until late in the nineteenth century.[96] Most potent of all, perhaps, were those men and women who, in every district, had for centuries exercised their astounding gifts, but whose help was increasingly sought in Elizabethan Wales. The long list of Welsh names for such wonder-workers of both sexes in itself gives an indication of the variety of skills that were on offer: *brudiwr* (predictor, soothsayer, 1450–80);[97] *consuriwr* (conjuror, sorcerer, 1567); *cyfareddwr* (enchanter, 1567); *daroganwr* (foreteller, fourteenth century); *dewin* (wizard, magician, thirteenth century); *dyn hysbys* (wise man, 1740); *gwiddon* (witch, thirteenth century); *gwrach* (witch, twelfth–thirteenth century); *hudolwr, hudoles* (charmer, sixteenth century; enchantress, sixteenth century); *planedydd* (astrologer, 1588); *rheibiwr* (bewitcher, curser); *swyngyfareddwr, swynwr* (charmer, magician).[98] They were confidently believed to be able to cure a variety of common ailments, foretell the future, detect thieves, and ward off the effects of spells, curses, and evil spirits. In spite of the statutes passed against them in 1542, 1563, and 1603, the Elizabethan injunctions forbidding them, and a whole series of sermons and tractates against them, they were increasingly in vogue in Elizabethan and Stuart Wales.[99]

It was out of such a background that John Penry believed there sprang

---

[95] W. Howells, *Cambrian Superstitions* (London, 1831), pp. 92–3.

[96] J. C. Davies, *Folk-lore of West and Mid Wales* (Aberystwyth, 1911), p. 49.

[97] These dates are taken from *GPC*, which notes the earliest occasion on which the word is known to have been used in Welsh. The Dictionary does not as yet go beyond the letter 'p'.

[98] S. Baring-Gould and J. Fisher, *The Lives of the British Saints* (4 vols. London, 1907–12); Davies, *Folk-lore*; J. H. Davies, *Hen Ddewiniaid Cymru* (London, 1901); M. Henken, *Traditions of the Welsh Saints* (Cambridge, 1987); Howells, *Cambrian Superstitions*; E. Isaac, *Coelion Cymru* (Aberystwyth, 1933); T. G. Jones, *Welsh Folklore and Folk-custom* (London, 1930); W. Sykes, *British Goblins* (repr. Wakefield, 1973); E. Owen, *Welsh Folk-lore* (repr. Wakefield, 1976); J. Rhys, *Celtic Folk-lore* (Oxford, 1901); M. Trevelyan, *Folk-lore and Folk-stories of Wales* (London, 1909).

[99] D. S. T. Clark and P. T. J. Morgan, 'Religion and magic in Elizabethan Wales', *JEH*, XXVII (1976), 31–46; G. H. Jenkins, 'Popular beliefs in Wales from the Restoration to Methodism', *BBCS*, XXVII (1976–8), 440–62; J. G. Jones, 'Y "Tylwyth Teg" yng Nghymru'r unfed a'r ail ganrif ar bymtheg', *LlC*, VIII (1964), 96–9; G. D. Owen, *Elizabethan Wales: The Social Scene* (Cardiff, 1962); B. F. Roberts, 'Rhai swynion Cymraeg', *BBCS*, XXI (1964–6), 440–62; J. G. Williams, 'Witchcraft in seventeenth-century Flintshire', *Flints. Hist. Soc. Trans.* XXVI (1973–4), 16–38; XXVII (1975–6), 5–35.

our swarms of soothsayers and enchanters, such as will not stick openly to profess that they walk on Tuesdays and Thursdays[100] at night with the fairies, of whom they bring themselves to have knowledge . . . We call them *bendith u mamme*, that is, such as have deserved their mothers' blessing . . . Hence proceed open defending of purgatory and the real presence, praying with images &c., with other infinite monsters.[101]

The populace did, indeed, tend to make indiscriminate use of the purveyors of magic and what remained of the Roman Catholic rites. Penry again: 'If they meet with any who can write and read, they will demand of him whether he can teach them a good prayer against such a disease in man or beast. Ungodly Welsh books are fraught with these idolatries.'[102] Similarly, Thomas Powell, the rector of Hirnant in Montgomeryshire, bringing an action against a group of his own parishioners for forcible entry and assaults, threw in for good measure the accusations that they were 'seekers unto charms, invocators of saints, and common offerers unto wells'.[103] In neighbouring Denbighshire, Hugh Brychan of Pentrefelin confessed in the Court of Great Sessions that he had inherited from his uncle a crystal stone, which he employed to detect thieves, but the intriguing feature was that when using the crystal he always pronounced certain mystic formulas in the name of the Father, the Son, and Holy Ghost and made a sign of the cross above the stone.[104] In Carmarthenshire, one Margaret David effected her cures with a mixture of water and earth 'from Jerusalem'.[105]

Some fascinating aspects of the nature of witchcraft in Wales emerge from the only contemporary tract on the subject written in Welsh – 'Ymddiddan Tudur a Gronw' (The conversation of Tudur and Gronw).[106] This was the work of a Cambridge graduate, Robert Holland, a north Walian by origin, who became a parson in Pembrokeshire.[107] It consisted of a dialogue between Gronw, a learned man, and Tudur, a simple country fellow. There was never a shadow of doubt in its pages that there existed in Wales men and women who trafficked in the black arts and entered into compacts with the devil, having their familiars in the shape of cats, mice,

---

[100] It may be worth noting that the tradition of meeting with fairies on Tuesday and Thursday nights continued well into the seventeenth century, Jones, *LlC*, VIII. 98.
[101] *Treatises*, p. 33.
[102] Ibid., p. 34
[103] PRO, STA C 5/P11/2.
[104] Owen, *Eliz. Wales*, pp. 62–3.
[105] Thomas, *Religion and Magic*, p. 57.
[106] The text is printed in *Rhyddiaith Gymraeg*, II. 161–73. For a commentary on its significance, Clark and Morgan, *JEH*, XXVII. 31–46.
[107] Ibid., pp. 31–3.

rats, toads, or even fleas.[108] Some of these magicians were reputed to have acquired their arcane knowledge through study and from reading astrological books, some of which have survived in manuscript form from this period;[109] but others were simple, unlearned folk who picked up their skills from their family and by their own experience and cunning. The author drew a distinction between benevolent 'white' magic and the sinister intentions of 'black' magic; and his character Tudur pointed out that some individuals derived healing and foreknowledge of the future from 'white' magicians, who were held in high esteem even by the gentry, and who performed much good. His companion, Gronw, was unmoved by this argument. He denounced the whole business as devil's work and cited a host of texts from scripture which anathematized all magic and taught that every enchanter should be burnt. He urged his companion to listen to God's word being read, to read it himself, and to pray earnestly and fruitfully. Tudur, obviously impressed by the weight of scriptural learning, nevertheless maintained that magic flourished because lax clergy did not take any pains to read and reveal the word of God; and as for sermons, he had never heard one in his parish church. The problem about reading the Bible seemed to him to be less that people could not read than that the Bible was too expensive for an ordinary man to buy a copy and keep it at home. 'God knows how dire is the condition of the poor commoners',[110] he concluded. Their plight remained unaltered until well into the seventeenth century, judging by the comments of contemporary observers.[111]

One of the common aspirations of those who sought the help of the occult was to amass large sums of money. One of the characters in Holland's dialogue referred to the possibility that it might have been as a consequence of serving the devil that one of his neighbours became so wealthy, since his background was humble and his origins obscure. Yet he had now very quickly become 'an emperor for wealth', and no one in the district was a finer gentleman than he.[112] Few can have hoped to prosper in quite such spectacular fashion as this; but, without question, sermons and popular literature depicted the age as unusually acquisitive. They pilloried the usury, covetousness, and extravagance in diet and apparel so prevalent in all quarters. Welsh poets were as denunciatory of greed as their fellows in other countries. Leading strict-metre bards flayed the well-to-do classes for usury, pride, avarice, oppressive behaviour to tenants, dishonest land

---

[108] He makes no mention of the hare, an animal particularly favoured by the devil in the time of Giraldus Cambrensis.
[109] Clark and Morgan, *JEH*, XXVII. p. 42.
[110] *Rhyddiaith Gymraeg*, II. 172.
[111] Jenkins, *BBCS*, XXVII. 440–62; Jones, *LlC*, VIII. 96–9.
[112] *Rhyddiaith Gymraeg*, II. 163.

transactions, shady business deals, and corruption in office.[113] The poets of the free metres were still more scathing in their judgements. They saw society disintegrating as individuals and social groups engaged in merciless competition with one another. The underlying reasons for this free-for-all may have been the pressures caused by the growth of population and the inflation of prices, but the preachers and the poets attributed the 'rat-race' solely to religious and moral causes. They believed that faith and charity had perished from the earth, and that pride, greed, and selfishness had everywhere taken their place.[114] Bishop Richard Davies in his prefatory letter to the New Testament of 1567 was in despair at

> the excessive greed in the world today for land and possessions, gold, silver, and wealth, which means that rarely do we find trust in God and his promises. Violence and theft, perjury, deceit, falsehood and arrogance; with these, as though with rakes, does every manner of man collect and draw money in his own direction.[115]

Even the poor, lamented one poet, had not been able to refrain from joining in the desperate scramble for worldly possessions.[116] Clearly, however, it was easier for the powerful and the wealthy to seize the lion's share in the universal catch-as-catch-can.

No small part of the gains was made at the expense of the Church, whose property the influential looked upon as highly marketable propositions, to be acquired outright or leased on favourable terms for as long as possible. Recalling this rapacity on the part of the laity makes it easier to understand, if not to overlook, some of the less savoury tactics of the clergy. The most powerful among the laity had been set an unfortunate example by the Crown ever since the reign of Henry VIII. In Elizabeth's time the Church, in spite of the losses it had suffered as a result of the dissolution of the religious houses, the disappearance of the chantries, and lay pressure on episcopal and other possessions, still offered a store of capital wealth, to which the queen and the patriciate who served her might help themselves. As early as 1559 Elizabeth herself showed the direction in which she was likely to proceed, when a statute was passed empowering the Crown during the vacancy of any bishopric to survey its property and propose the exchange of its manors in return for tithes and spiritual revenues of ostensibly the same value. She continued along that path for

[113] Jones, *WHR*, IX. 270–1.

[114] Williams, *Tafodau Tân*, pp. 157ff.

[115] A. O. Evans, *A Memorandum on the Legality of the Welsh Bible* (Cardiff, 1925), p. 107.

[116] Williams, *Tafodau Tân*, pp. 158.

most of her reign, and would deliberately keep bishoprics vacant for some years in order to benefit from their revenues.[117] Her example of plundering the Church was followed by many of her lay subjects wherever they could. Those who had long battened on the Church's patrimony were not likely to desist now, still less to restore those gains on which they had already laid their hands. The leading aristocrats had their deferential followers and clients among the more prominent gentry. Dr Ellis Price, for instance, himself a lay rector in the diocese of St Asaph, addressed his patron, the earl of Leicester, in these sacrilegiously ingratiating terms, 'In thee, O Lord, do I put my trust.'[118] In 1575, John Whitgift, then Master of Trinity College, Cambridge, declared that 'every man seeketh to pull from the clergy, how also the temporality does envy any prosperity in the clergy . . . the temporality seek to make the clergy beggars'.[119]

Nor did his colleagues among the Welsh bishops cherish any delusions on the subject. Richard Davies referred witheringly to the 'insatiable cormorants' within his diocese, 'greedy for church spoils and contemptuously intolerant of the church's rulers'.[120] He may well have had in mind, among others, Sir John Perrott, one of the most powerful lay figures in south-west Wales, described as 'by nature very choleric' and 'unable to brook any crosses, nor dissemble the least injuries, although offered by the greatest personages'.[121] Davies was said to have 'stoutly confronted' Perrott when that testy knight became embroiled in 'private quarrels' and 'public contentions' with the bishop's friend, the first earl of Essex.[122] Davies's successor, Marmaduke Middleton, likewise became engaged in head-on collision with Perrott and a number of other leading laymen. Perrott had, it appears, 'divers times solicited the bishop for all his temporalities in exchange, or at least, for the stewardship of the lands'. According to Middleton's account, which no doubt is unlikely to have erred on the side of objectivity, Perrott and Alban Stepney had put themselves at the head of a body of men, 'evil affected in religion, drunkards, rioters, and pluralist priests' to concoct 'odious and scandalous libels' against him.[123] This was admittedly part of a large-scale campaign of opposition against an

---

[117] G. Donaldson, *The Scottish Reformation* (Cambridge, 1960), p. 172, for bibliographical details.

[118] A. G. Edwards, *Landmarks in the History of the Welsh Church* (London, 1913), p. 106.

[119] D. Wilkins, *Concilia Magnae Britanniae et Hiberniae . . . 446–1718* (4 vols. London, 1737), IV. 203.

[120] PRO, SP12/65/1.

[121] *The History of Sir John Perrott*, ed. R. Rawlinson (London, 1728), p. 20.

[122] Ibid.; Wynn, *Gwydir Family*, p. 64.

[123] *HMC, Salisbury MSS.*, IV. 279–81.

unworthy diocesan, but that did not necessarily absolve Perrott of all blame for bullying prelates to gain his own ends.

In north Wales the resourceful and ambitious Mostyn clan was the subject of protests by Bishop Henry Rowlands of Bangor. He complained that, over the episcopal estates of Gogarth, the Mostyns had been 'very cunning, and lightly would counterfeit divers things, and might prevail with the Registrar that was here . . . for copies of anything that he might make for them'.[124] William Morgan, when he was bishop of St Asaph, denounced Sir John Wynn of Gwydir as a 'sacrilegious robber of my church, a perfidious spoiler of my diocese'.[125]

The extent to which dominant members of the laity could benefit by exploiting their opportunities of acquiring land has been brought out in a careful recent analysis of the fate of Crown lands – lay and ecclesiastical – in the county of Monmouthshire during the sixteenth century.[126] By far the greater part of the spoils had fallen to the lot of the two foremost aristocratic stocks – the earls of Pembroke and Worcester – and a large part of the rest to three or four major gentry families. Descendants of the earls held over half the former Crown possessions by 1603, and a half of the remainder was in the hands of four families: the Morgans of Llantarnam, the Arnolds of Llanthony, the Williamses of Llangybi, and the Gunters of Abergavenny.[127]

It was the diocese of St David's which, in spite of its earlier losses, still remained much the wealthiest Welsh diocese at the beginning of Elizabeth's reign. But in succeeding years it was to be deprived of considerably more of its assets than the remaining Welsh bishoprics, and by the seventeenth century was not very much better off than the other three. The chief source of loss was the well-endowed church of Llanddewibrefi.[128] It became vacant in January 1566 as the result of the death of its incumbent, Rowland Meyrick, bishop of Bangor, who held it *in commendam*. Bishop Davies collated his own chancellor, Lewis Gwynn, in succession to Meyrick, only to find himself pitted against a pair of formidable opponents in the earls of Pembroke and Leicester, who were presenting a rival candidate.[129] The bishop regarded the presentation made by the earls as a manifest forgery and, in his predicament, wrote to Archbishop Parker

---

[124] A. D. Carr, 'The Mostyn family and estate, 1200–1602' (Ph.D. thesis, Wales, 1976), p. 282.

[125] J. G. Jones, 'Bishop William Morgan's dispute with John Wynn of Gwydir', *JHSCW*, XXII (1972), on pp. 67–8.

[126] M. Gray, 'The disposal of Crown property in Monmouthshire, 1500–1603' (Ph.D. thesis, Wales, 1985).

[127] Ibid., p. 237.

[128] Williams, *Ceredigion*, IV/4. 336–52.

[129] *WRE*, pp. 177–8.

for advice. The archbishop's reply was vague and guarded, but Davies seemed to derive much comfort from it.[130] The final outcome of the dispute is not known, but the bishop may very well have been victorious, in the short term at least.

It seems likely, however, that the two earls continued the feud through the agency of one George Cary, a groom of the queen's chamber. This individual shortly afterwards obtained a commission to inquire into concealed lands, i.e. Church lands being unlawfully withheld from the Crown. Such a commission was a favourite device of the speculating landsharks and covered a multitude of fraudulent and unjust dealings from which many dioceses suffered.[131] Cary now took advantage of his commission to get his claws into what he alleged to be the concealed collegiate church of Llanddewibrefi.[132] The idea of founding a college on the site of the historic synod of Llanddewibrefi, where legend had it that St David himself had preached and performed miracles, went back to 1287, when it had first been mooted by Bishop Thomas Beck. He endowed the church with a number of prebends situated in Carmarthenshire and Cardiganshire. Two and a half centuries later, when the colleges and chantries were dissolved in 1549, a chantry commissioner reported that there was serious doubt whether or not a true college had in fact been established there, and Rowland Meyrick remained in undisturbed possession. Later, Richard Davies insisted that the college had never come into existence, and that the Court of Augmentations had given judgement to that effect in Edward VI's reign.[133] Cary was undeterred by the bishop's opposition and proceeded to inform the queen that Llanddewibrefi was a concealed college. For his pains, Elizabeth allowed him to lease its lands for £40 a year – a very happy bargain, since he was able to sublet them to the Vaughan family of Trawscoed at an annual rent of £140.[134]

Success whetted Cary's appetite. His next step was to bring a writ of intrusion against the incumbent of Llanddewibrefi, Lewis Gwynn; but he was at first rebuffed by the decision of a jury of 'substantial gentlemen out of Herefordshire' who, in 1567, found judgement against him and declared the church to be 'no college nor concealed'.[135] Juries could, however, as Bishop Davies contended, be brought to 'swerve from the truth' by 'racking

[130] Parker, *Correspondence*, p. 104.
[131] J. Strype, *Annals of the Reformation and the Establishment of Religion* . . . (4 vols. Oxford, 1820–40), II/i. 312, 313; E. Grindal, *Remains* (Parker Soc., London, 1843), p. 344, for his condemnation of them. Leicester and his servants were past masters at the technique in Wales, BL, Lansdowne MS. 45, fos. 190–2.
[132] Williams, *Ceredigion*, IV/4. 336–52.
[133] PRO, SP12/49/35, 35 (i).
[134] Ibid.
[135] Ibid.; cf. Strype, *Annals*, III/ii. 226–7.

of evidence' and also 'by affection, fear, or favour', and in the following year another jury gave a verdict in Cary's favour. This brought not only Llanddewibrefi into his net but also thirteen other parish churches as parts and members of the supposed college. From the incumbents and farmers of these he was claiming arrears of rents and tithes amounting to the enormous sum of £3,420 and, in addition, £2,000 from the bishop himself in respect of the parsonage of Llanarth and Llanina. Litigation concerning the dispute dragged on its tedious course until after the bishop's death in 1581.[136] The vindictive Cary was still not content; typically insatiable, he now sued Davies's widow for arrears of rent. Even allowing for serious financial mismanagement on the part of the next bishop, Middleton, the diocese of St David's had already suffered a crippling loss to its income which left it badly impoverished for centuries to come. By the end of the sixteenth century its value had been reduced from £457 to £263 per annum.[137]

The possessions of the cathedral chapters, although subject to less pressure than those of bishops, none the less presented desirable acquisitions to the eyes of watchful lay landowners. Even before the Reformation it had long been the practice for them to be leased out by clerics to lay tenants for long terms of years. Such arrangements were obviously more damaging to the interests of the Church in an age of inflation like the sixteenth century, if rents remained static over a long period when prices were rising rapidly. The chapter records of Llandaff and St David's reveal the eagerness of laymen to enter into leases of episcopal and capitular property in both glebe and tithe.[138] Most of the lessees were local gentry, although there was also a sprinkling of lawyers and merchants and clergy, especially among those who appear to have been related to the lessors. Leases of Llandaff capitular possessions were dominated to a large extent by the families of Herbert and Morgan, but those of St David's, with its much wider geographical spread, show a greater variation. The records themselves, of course, tell us nothing much about the pressures exerted, or the inducements offered, to obtain such leases. It may be significant, though, that the registrar of St David's diocese noted in 1563 that he had no record of any lease before 1559, 'such hath been the alteration and disorder in these later days of our predecessors', and it is certainly noticeable that before 1571 a number of St David's leases had been entered into for terms ranging from thirty to seventy years.[139]

[136] PRO, SP12/49/35, 35 (i).

[137] Strype, *Annals*, III/ii. 226–8.

[138] NLW, Ll. Ch; SD Ch. I. and II. The chapter records survive only for the dioceses of Llandaff and St David's.

[139] NLW, SD Ch, Reg. I, *passim*.

Some attempt was made to put a brake on the process in 1571 with the passing of a statute forbidding the clergy from leasing their possessions for a term of more than twenty-one years or three lives. Ten years later, however, Elizabeth showed her scant respect for this enactment by putting pressure on Bishop Bleddyn of Llandaff to lease her the manor and rectory of Bassaleg for a term of no less than a hundred years. She, in turn, wasted no time in leasing them for sixty years to Sir William Herbert of Cardiff.[140] Belated attempts at reform made by the Llandaff chapter were not wholly successful. However, in 1593, Bishop Babington did succeed in ensuring that the manors of Bishton, Dewstow, and Llanddewi were leased to Thomas Lewis of Y Fan for a term of no more than twenty-one years and in return for an entry fine of £100. In 1598 the chapter decreed that its leases should no longer run for more than twenty-one years and, for some years afterwards, its records seem to indicate that the policy was moderately successful. During the first decades of the seventeenth century, however, the chapter continued to meet with serious difficulties in its leases to leading tenants.[141]

It has already been seen that in St David's diocese the families of Richard Davies and Thomas Huet did well for themselves out of capitular leases, despite the barbed comments Davies had to make about the 'insatiable cormorants' of his diocese.[142] Bishop Middleton also had cause to complain that all the best prebends in his diocese were leased out for long terms, and there were comparable grievances aired in other Welsh dioceses.[143] Parsonages impropriate to the bishop and chapter, 'the chiefest part of the revenues of the see', were all leased out so that 'almost none' would return for fifty years to come. Middleton is not the most reliable of witnesses and his statements cannot safely be taken at face value. Yet there is corroborative evidence from his own chapter's records and those of Llandaff, and from other sources, that such endowments were regularly leased, usually resulting in the long-term loss of income by the clergy.[144]

By Elizabeth's reign almost all the surviving Crown leases of former monastic possessions relate to rectories and tithe.[145] Examined decade by decade over the whole period they reveal some interesting trends. During the years 1558–70 profits anticipated from such leases seem to have been sufficient for the Crown to try to offset the effects of inflation by exacting

---

[140] Williams, *GCH*, IV. 225.

[141] NLW, Ll Ch 4; Badminton MS. 1463; cf. Williams, *GCH*, IV. 243–4.

[142] PRO, SP12/65/1.

[143] G. Williams, in C. Clay (ed.), *Rural Society: Landowners, Peasants and Labourers* (Cambridge, 1990), p. 155.

[144] Ibid., pp. 155–6.

[145] Ibid. pp. 151–2; *Augs. Procs.*, part 2.

high entry fines, averaging about three years' rent and rising to as high as six years'. Between 1570 and 1580 entry fines were still fairly high, averaging about three years' rent. During the whole period down to 1580 the term of a lease was invariably twenty-one years. In the decade between 1580 and 1590 the market hardened against the Crown; entry fines were down to an average of about two years, and leases for three lives began to appear, though those for twenty-one years were still more usual. By the time of the agricultural crises of the 1590s, leases for three lives began to predominate and entry fines were down to an average of about one year. The lessees continued to be local gentry for the most part, although it was comparatively rare for a family to maintain an unbroken lien on the lease of any rectory. Where urban tenements, notably parcels of the former chantries, were still being leased, complaints of their decayed and ruinous state were not infrequent.[146]

On the subject of lay impropriations Welsh bishops were outspokenly critical. The bishops looked upon many of these livings as 'the very best in all the diocese', but they were regarded by the impropriators almost solely as a source of profit to themselves. Where there was an endowed vicarage they squeezed the incumbents hard, by trying to cut down on their income and making no allowance in lieu of former oblations and other 'superstitious offerings' which had formerly accrued to them. The parish of Llanbadarn Fawr affords an interesting example of the methods to which they resorted. In this enormous parish of 180 square miles, with its 2,400 communicants, the farmer's issues were alleged to be worth over £1,000 a year, while his rent amounted to no more than £120 a year. He paid the vicar £20 but also allowed him £40–£50 in tithes to make up for the loss of former oblations. To maximize his own profits, however, the farmer had withdrawn this concession and, as a result, the vicar sued him in the Exchequer Court in an effort to recover his losses.[147] Where there was no vicarage endowed and no vicarial tithes, but only a stipendiary curate, the farmer could do even better. In these instances, it was usual for the rent to remain at its customary level when a lease was renewed, and in so far as the Crown reaped a profit at all it did so by means of entry fines. The customary stipend, meagre enough in pre-Reformation times, was grossly inadequate for a married clergy in an inflationary age, and was maintained unchanged from decade to decade, while the impropriator stood to gain handsomely from rising prices. In a return for St David's diocese made in 1583 by Bishop Middleton, out of seventy-nine curates' stipends listed,

---

[146] Ibid.
[147] *Exchequer Proceedings concerning Wales in Tempore James I*, ed. T. I. Jeffreys-Jones (Cardiff, 1955), pp. 103, 119, 224.

eleven only were worth £10 or more, and thirty-three were worth £5 or less.[148] Things were no better in Llandaff as late as 1603.

The sort of exigencies to which these circumstances could give rise were vividly depicted by the parishioners of Churchstoke, Montgomeryshire, in an Exchequer suit. Situated in one of the most fertile parts of north Wales the parish was said to yield an annual revenue of £160 in return for a rent of £6 or £7. The farmers of the living, however, paid their stipendiary curate the princely sum of twenty nobles (£6. 13s. 4d.) a year. The outcome was that their ministers were always 'unlearned, poor, bare, and needy fellows', 'forced to leave their wives and children to the mercy of the parish'. Such 'a mischief and inconvenience happened in those parts of Wales so often' that the complainants urged their lordships of the Exchequer to give their undelayed attention to the problem.[149] Furthermore, the chancel of the church there, like so many others in the grasp of impropriators, was in a ruinous condition on account of their unwillingness to spend money in fulfilling their obligations as rectors to maintain the chancel in good repair.[150]

Appropriations had given laymen extensive, even excessive, rights of patronage and control within the dioceses. They frequently made use of their power to present ill-qualified men, whom they could buy in at the cheapest rate. In addition, they missed few opportunities of adding to those privileges by securing from the bishops rights of advowson *pro hac vice* (for the next vacancy), whenever and wherever they could. A record from the diocese of St Asaph for the years 1538–40 shows that the practice of wholesale granting away rights of next presentation to livings within the bishop's gift was prevalent at least as early as Henry VIII's reign.[151] Later records from Llandaff and St David's showed that it remained usual throughout the Elizabethan period.[152] Bishops rarely parted with these valuable rights except for a consideration. Laymen's motives for getting hold of them were usually self-interested, too; either they wished to place relatives or clients in employment, or else they intended to extract a favourable lease or some other simoniacal agreement from the incumbent they presented. Protests against abuses which arose as a result of these practices were widespread, especially from Puritan quarters. Attempts were made to curb the misdeeds of patrons, but with little success. The tenth canon of 1571 instructed the bishops to exhort the patrons and proprietors, in their presentations 'to consider the need of the Church and to hold

---

[148] Williams in Clay, *Rural Society*, p. 156.
[149] PRO, E112/62/40, Montgomeryshire.
[150] Ibid.
[151] NLW, SA/M/21, part 2; cf. *WC*, pp. 310–11.
[152] NLW, Ll. Ch 4; SD Ch. Reg. B, 1–4.

before their eyes the final judgement'. They were ordered carefully 'to watch for simony and collusive agreements' and 'to expel from the priesthood and the ministry' those clergy implicated in them.[153] But the malpractices continued largely undiminished. In the diocese of Norwich it was said that 'Gehazi and Judas had a wonderful haunt', 'simony so widely prevailed in selling and buying benefices, fleecing parsonages and vicarages that *omnia erant venalia* (everything was for sale)'.[154] Llandaff diocese seems to have been in hardly better case if the testimony of two of its clerics, Andrew Vaen and William Fleming, is to be believed. George Owen of Henllys, a landowner on a considerable scale in St David's and, on many counts, an articulate champion of gentry interests, none the less had abundant cause to voice his disapproval of those 'scarred consciences' that allowed men in their hunt for gains 'to search any part of the Church livings, yea the Church itself, if we see it but hang loose'.[155]

Yet, destructive of the best interests of the Church as were the poverty of the clergy and the transgressions of the laity, it may be doubted whether they were the most telling factors in accounting for the slow progress of the Reformation in Wales. The crucial reason for its failure to win the hearts of the people continued to be the absence of an intelligible translation of the whole Bible into Welsh.

[153] Kennedy, *Eliz. Episcopal Admin.*, p. cxlv.
[154] Ibid., pp. cxlvii–cxlviii.
[155] Owen, *Penbrokshire*, III. 85.

CHAPTER 13

The Welsh Bible

THE Act of 1563 for the translation of the Bible into Welsh had, without question, been a decisive turning-point in the history of religion in Wales, and its outcome – the Welsh versions of the New Testament and the Book of Common Prayer – a splendid achievement. That Act had, nevertheless, required that the whole Bible be translated; furthermore, the needs of Church and people pressingly called for it. But managing even to complete the Welsh versions of the Testament and Prayer Book by 1567 had been a tight squeeze for the translators, who had been obliged to leave the Old Testament untranslated, apart from the Book of Psalms. This decision had been regarded by both translators merely as a postponement, certainly not an abandonment. William Salesbury, in his dedication of the New Testament to the queen, expressed the hope, 'would to God that your Grace's subjects of Wales might also have the whole book of God's word brought to like pass'.[1] His colleague, Richard Davies, went further and declared with some confidence, 'Here is the one part ready, that which is called the New Testament, while you wait, (through God's help that should not be long), the other part, which is called the Old Testament.'[2]

If Sir John Wynn's testimony is to be accepted, the two friends at first applied themselves with enthusiasm to the task, and Salesbury again took up residence with Davies for some time to expedite the work. According to Wynn, they were 'very far onward with the Old Testament, and had gone through with it, if variance had not happened' between them

for the general sense and etymology of one word, which the bishop would have to be one way and William Salesbury another, to the great loss of the old British and mother tongue, for being together, they drew homilies, books, and divers other tracts in the British tongue and had done far more, if that unlucky division had not happened.[3]

---

[1] A. O. Evans, *A Memorandum on the Legality of the Welsh Bible* (Cardiff, 1925), p. 82.

[2] Ibid., p. 101.

[3] J. Wynn, *History of the Gwydir Family*, ed. J. Ballinger (Cardiff, 1927), p. 64.

This difference of opinion between the two translators was dated to about the year 1575. Wynn tells us that 'the bishop lived five or six years after, and William Salesbury about twenty-four'.[4] Davies is known to have died on 7 November 1581; but 'an inexplicable silence' envelops the date of Salesbury's death, which may have taken place in 1584, though it has been more usually dated to 1594, or c.1594–1600.[5]

It was not until many years after the alleged quarrel occurred that John Wynn set down his account of it.[6] He was not always accurate in detail in his recollections of past events; for example, he recorded that Richard Davies spent his exile in Geneva, but the Genevan records reveal no trace of Davies's having been there, whereas there are Frankfurt sources which show that he spent most, if not all, of his time in that city.[7] Wynn could have been just as mistaken in what he said about the relations between Davies and Salesbury with regard to the translation of the Old Testament. Certainly, no indication has been found in print or manuscript of any joint work undertaken by them at this time. A letter from Salesbury to Gruffudd Hiraethog, written some time between 1567 and 1575, explicitly says, in somewhat huffy tones, that he would publish no more and that 'for good reasons' ('iawn achosion'); although Thomas Wiliems, in 1574, was much more hopeful of the prospects: 'we shall yet have (if God sees fit to grant him life) many notable pieces of his [Salesbury's] work' ('e geir eto (os gwyl Duw vod yn iawn gael ono einioes) lawer o bethau arbenic oi waith').[8] Wiliems's confidence may have sprung from his having seen a manuscript version of the *Llysieulyfr* (Medical Herbal), which Salesbury was engaged in writing between 1568 and 1574.[9]

All the same, it is perfectly possible that Wynn was right, and that the two men did quarrel irreconcilably over a single word. Remembering how embittered theological disputes could be in the sixteenth century, and how fine the hair-splitting between disputants could become, that is by no means out of the question. Yet, considering how harmoniously they had collaborated previously and how convinced each was that a translation was imperatively necessary, it does seem surprising. One might have expected

[4] Ibid.

[5] Alun Mathias argues for 1584 in *DWB*, s.n.; cf. 'Astudiaeth o weithgarwch llenyddol William Salesbury' (MA thesis, Wales, 1949). But for an earlier view, see D. R. Thomas, *The Life and Work of Richard Davies and William Salesbury* (Oswestry, 1902) who comments on the 'inexplicable silence' which 'envelops his end', p. 79.

[6] J. Ballinger, introd. to Wynn, *Gwydir Family*. Cf. also, J. G. Jones, *Sir John Wynn: History of the Gwydir Family and Memoirs* (Llandysul, 1990).

[7] *WRE*, pp. 156–61.

[8] Ibid., pp. 200–1.

[9] *DWB*. The 'Llysieulyfr' was published in Cardiff in 1916 in an edition by E. S. Roberts.

the New Testament rather than the Old to have been productive of such disagreements. On the other hand, Sir John Wynn would seem to have had no obvious reason to invent such a quarrel, although he might have misunderstood the real nature of it. If the two men did actually fall out, the rift between them is likely to have been occasioned by something more fundamental than a clash of opinions over one word. The basic cause may have been a dispute over Salesbury's views about orthography. His quirks in the matter of language were very curious indeed. His excessive admiration for the classics, his love of 'copiousness' in language, his Latinized spellings, his disregard of mutations of the initial consonants, and other peculiarities, had made the publications of 1567 distinctly puzzling to those who had to decipher them. This was all the more unfortunate because Welsh poets and prose-writers of the Middle Ages had preserved not just a single literary language but also, by and large, a common orthography, as Sir John Price had pointed out earlier.[10] It would not have been surprising if Davies, acutely aware as a bishop of the importance of the translations being intelligible to the parish clergy and easily used by them, had urged on his partner the need for making concessions in the interests of 'user-friendliness'. If he did, he was likely to have found Salesbury to be stiff and touchy in these matters, and unlikely to have given way with any grace or willingness. Differences of opinion between the pair may have been smouldering threateningly for a long time before they finally flared up into an open quarrel over a single word. On the other hand, if indeed they did disagree, they may have parted company over something else quite different – perhaps over the perennial problem of money.[11] The financing of a new venture would be costly, and the finished work would hardly be made any more saleable by Salesbury's idiosyncrasies over language. There may, of course, have been no quarrel at all; the two may just have drifted apart. All we can be sure of is that no joint publication by them ever appeared again.

The parting of the ways, whatever its cause, had a very different effect upon the two men. Salesbury, for one reason or another, became something of an Achilles sulking in his tent.[12] He, who had earlier been so prolific as an author, published nothing more. Davies, in spite of his multifarious responsibilities as a bishop and an administrator, appeared to be keen to find a new partner with whom to continue his efforts. If the break with Salesbury really took place in 1575, as Sir John Wynn suggested, then soon after, Davies invited his kinsman, the Italian-educated Siôn Dafydd Rhys, to help him in the task of producing Welsh books. Siôn Dafydd Rhys was,

---

[10] Ker, *The Library*, 5th ser. X (1955), 1–24.
[11] *WRE*, p. 201.
[12] Ibid., pp. 186, 200–1.

at the time, the chief schoolmaster at Friars' Grammar School, Bangor, and willingly accepted the bishop's invitation to come to his palace at Abergwili. Rhys himself claimed to have worked on four sets of translations in the ensuing years.[13] Two of them were Welsh versions of English catechisms – the one by Dean Nowell, and the other by Gervase Babington.[14] More significantly, he claimed also to have been engaged on a translation of the Book of Homilies, over a quarter of a century before the published translation by Edward James.[15] All that survives of this work is a fragment of his version of the homily, 'Against the peril of idolatry'.[16] Nothing remains of any translation which he and Davies may have made of parts of the Old Testament. This is hardly surprising; by this time the bishop was ageing and was in his late sixties at least, if not, more probably, well into his seventies.[17] He had a very large diocese to oversee; recusancy was on the increase; he had lost his most influential friend, the earl of Essex; and his other friend, Archbishop Grindal, was in disgrace with the queen; he was being called upon to cope with complex and trying administrative problems like that of piracy; and he was ensnared in the toils of damaging quarrels with powerful laymen like John Perrott, George Cary, and Fabian Phillips (see chap. 12).

In circumstances like these, it was understandable that Davies should be looking for younger men to whom he could entrust part, at least, of the responsibility for biblical translation. The need was undoubtedly pressing; whatever the merits of the publications of 1567 may have been, they were not really adequate to satisfy the requirements of the average man and woman in the pew. Salesbury biased his texts too heavily in the direction of the scholarly public for them to be of as much benefit to priest and parishioner as might have been hoped. While Bishop Robinson may have expressed his satisfaction at hearing everything done in the Welsh language and William Morgan in his dedication to the Bible of 1588 would pay glowing tributes to Salesbury's contributions, there would be others who would be far more critical, and not without cause. John Penry in his *Aequity* (1587) would be deeply concerned that

[13] Gruffydd, *TCS* (1971), 182–3; idem, 'Catecism y Deon Nowell yn Gymraeg', *JWBS*, VII (1950–3), 114–15, 203–7.
[14] Gruffydd, *TCS* (1971), 183. The text of the translation of Babington's catechism is printed in *Rhyddiaith Gymraeg. I. Detholion o Lawysgrifau, 1488–1609*, ed. T. H. Parry-Williams (Cardiff, 1954), pp. 52–3.
[15] R. G. Gruffydd, 'Religious prose in Welsh from the beginning of the reign of Elizabeth' (D.Phil. Oxford, 1952–3), pp. 130–60; G. Williams, *Grym Tafodau Tân* (Llandysul, 1984), pp. 180–90.
[16] Gruffydd, *TCS* (1971), 183.
[17] The date of his birth cannot be given with greater precision than the first decade of the sixteenth century, but it was probably nearer 1500 than 1510, G. Williams, *Bywyd ac Amserau yr Esgob Richard Davies* (Cardiff, 1953), p. 1.

the Old Testament we have not in our tongue, therefore the first lesson is read in English unto our people in many places that understand not one word of it. This reading is taken to be the blasphemous mass, and they give it the name of the mass, 'Y mae yr offeiriad ar y fferen' (say they, when the first lesson is read); that is 'the priest is at mass'.[18]

In his next tract, *An Exhortation* (1588), he was yet more severe: 'A few psalms, a few prayers, with one chapter of the New Testament in Welsh (for the Old never spake Welsh in our days) . . . most pitiably evil read of the reader, and not understood of one among ten of the hearers.'[19] Penry was so eager to see the whole Bible translated that it made him incautiously sanguine in his estimate that it need take no more than two years to complete.[20] He actually gave a broad hint that he himself had translated the minor prophets, though there are no surviving remains of any such translation.[21] Maurice Kyffin was another unsparing critic of Salesbury's translations: 'yr oedd cyfled llediaith a chymaint anghyfiaith yn yr ymadrodd brintiedig, na allai clust gwir Gymro ddioddef clywed mohono'n iawn' ('there was such a broad "accent" and so much that was strange in the printed version that the ear of a true Welshman could not bear to listen to it').[22] Dafydd Johns of Dyffryn Clwyd[23] also made an impassioned plea for the translation of the whole Bible. He, like Penry, had been profoundly distressed by the devastating famine conditions of 1585–6, which each of them interpreted as God's punishment on the Welsh for their sin and ignorance.[24] The one thing which had given Penry some heart in 1588 was the knowledge that the translation of the Old Testament had been undertaken and that he understood it was 'all ready to be printed'.[25] He was referring to the work of a Welsh country parson, William Morgan 1545–1604), who was to prove the single most important figure in the history of the Reformation in Wales.

Morgan[26] was born at some time between 19 December 1544 and 14 April 1545 at Wybrnant in the parish of Penmachno, Caernarfonshire. He

[18] J. Penry, *Three Treatises concerning Wales*, ed. D. Williams (Cardiff, 1960), p. 40.

[19] Ibid., p. 56.

[20] Ibid., p. 40.

[21] R. G. Gruffydd (ed.), *Y Gair ar Waith* (Cardiff, 1988), p. 34.

[22] *Deffynniad Ffydd*, p. x.

[23] G. H. Hughes, 'Cyfieithiad Dafydd Johns, Llanfair Dyffryn Clwyd', *NLWJ*, VI/2 (1949), 295–6.

[24] *Treatises*, pp. 40–1.

[25] Ibid., p. 56.

[26] Among the more useful biographical studies are: C. Ashton, *Bywyd ac Amserau'r Esgob William Morgan* (Treherbert, 1891); W. Hughes, *The Life and Times of Bishop Morgan* (London, 1891); G. J. Roberts, *Yr Esgob William Morgan* (Denbigh, 1959); R. T. Edwards, *William Morgan* (Ruthin, 1988). Among the celebratory publications which

was the second son of a moderately prosperous farmer on the Wynn estates. Both his father, John ap Morgan, and his mother, Lowri, were of gentle stock and were clearly ambitious for their son. The young William may have received some of his early education and his first introduction to Welsh literary culture at the house of Gwydir. Its master at this time was Morys Wynn, father of the more celebrated Sir John, who said of Morgan that it was at Gwydir 'he was brought up in learning'.[27] Others may also have taught him, but at all events he learnt enough to enable him to proceed to St John's College, Cambridge, in 1565. His decision to study at Cambridge was to be of crucial importance to his future.[28] The renown of the university as a centre of scholarship, particularly of those linguistic and theological studies central to the Renaissance and Reformation, had grown enormously in the sixteenth century. Of all its colleges none was better known than St John's, which had an outstanding reputation for the study of Latin, Greek, and Hebrew.[29] In the 1560s the college also became a hotbed of Puritan sympathies; but Morgan, though an ardent Protestant, was never drawn to embrace Puritan tenets. He remained an intensely loyal Anglican all his life. He took his initial degree of BA in 1568, his MA in 1571, and DD in 1583.

His education in Cambridge firmly implanted in him the key doctrines of the Renaissance and the Reformation. He avidly imbibed the notions of the central importance of the Bible as the unique and sovereign revelation of God's purposes for humankind and the absolute necessity for restoring it as the supreme fount of religious truth and authority. His career at the university also gave him a circle of friends who were, later in life, to be of considerable help to him. Among his contemporaries at St John's were two gifted north Walians, Richard Vaughan and Edmwnd Prys, both destined to become distinguished figures in the Church; Vaughan as bishop successively of Bangor, Chester, and London, and Prys as archdeacon of Merioneth and translator of the Psalms into Welsh metrical verse. Others at university with him were Gabriel Goodman, dean of Westminster, 1561–1601; William Hughes, bishop of St Asaph, 1573–1600; and Hugh

---

appeared in 1988 were: I. Thomas, *William Morgan a'i Feibl: William Morgan and his Bible* (Cardiff, 1988); R. G. Gruffydd, *Y Beibl a Droes i'w Bobl Draw: The Translation of the Bible into the Welsh Tongue* (Cardiff, 1988); idem, *William Morgan Dyneiddiwr* (Swansea, 1989); idem (ed.), *Y Gair ar Waith*; P. T. J. Morgan, *Beibl i Gymru: A Bible for Wales* (Aberystwyth, 1988); G. Williams, 'William Morgan's Bible and the Cambridge connection', *WHR*, XIV (1989), 363–79; G. Williams and T. M. Bassett, *Beibl William Morgan: William Morgan's Bible* (WEA, 1988).

[27] *Gwydir Family*, p. 65.

[28] Williams, *WHR*, XIV, 366–71.

[29] J. B. Mullinger, *The History of the University of Cambridge* (London, 1888); M. H. Curtis, *Oxford and Cambridge in Transition* (Oxford, 1959); H. C. Porter, *Reformation and Reaction in Tudor Cambridge* (Cambridge, 1958).

Bellot, bishop of Bangor, 1585–95. All of these were to be of help to him when he came to translate the Bible. Another who gave him crucial assistance was John Whitgift, master of Trinity College in the 1570s and virtual ruler of Cambridge,[30] with whom Morgan may have come into contact for the first time then. The influence of Cambridge on the Reformation in Wales is nothing like as well known as its influence on the English Reformation, nor was it as great. Even so, nine out of the sixteen bishops appointed to Welsh sees during Elizabeth's reign were Cambridge graduates,[31] although the Welsh students there were outnumbered by seven to one by those studying at Oxford.[32] Hardly less significant was the leadership afforded by three archbishops, Parker, Grindal, and Whitgift, all of them Cambridge men, and by William Cecil, another *alumnus* of the same university. Elizabeth herself may have had a soft spot for Cambridge graduates. Speaking to the students there in 1564, she had adjured them to remember 'that there will be no directer, no fitter course, either to make your fortunes or to preserve the favour of your prince than . . . to ply your studies here diligently'.[33]

Morgan was ordained at Ely cathedral as early as 1568. The declaration he made at the time of his ordination struck notes which were to be in keeping with the whole tenor of his later carer as priest, preacher, and biblical translator. He expressed his wish to be a deacon out of 'zeal to God his word', and proclaimed his faith that 'Evangelium Christi est potentia Dei ad salutem omni credenti' ('the gospel of Christ is the power of God unto salvation to everyone that believeth', Romans 1: 16).[34] Interestingly enough, William Salesbury had earlier given pride of place to the identical text on the title-page of his *Kynniver Llith a Ban* in 1551. Twenty years after being ordained, Morgan was to reaffirm his belief in the same verse by giving it a position of honour on the title-page of the New Testament in his Bible of 1588.

Morgan's first recorded benefice was the vicarage of Llanbadarn Fawr, Cardiganshire, in the diocese of St David's, to which he was collated at the age of 27 on 29 December 1572. The bishop of the diocese was Richard Davies, a Caernarfonshire man whose home had been located only a few miles away from where Morgan was born and bred. Davies was reputed to have favoured his fellow north Walians with preferment in his diocese, one

---

[30] P. M. Dawley, *John Whitgift and the Reformation* (London, 1955); V. J. K. Brook, *Whitgift and the English Church* (London, 1951).

[31] Williams, *WHR*, XIV. 363 n. 2.

[32] W. P. Griffith, *Learning, Law and Religion . . . c.1540–1642* (Cardiff, 1996).

[33] Curtis, *Oxford and Cambridge*, p. 7. For the influence of Cambridge on Elizabeth's own education, W. S. Hudson, *Cambridge and the Elizabethan Settlement* (Duke UP, 1980).

[34] A. O. Evans, 'Edmwnd Prys, archdeacon of Merioneth . . .', *TCS* (1922–3), 126–8.

of his favourite sayings being, 'I will plant you north Wales men, grow if you list.'[35] Morgan was one of those whom he planted, though he was not to grow in the diocese. At the very time when Davies collated Morgan to Llanbadarn, he may conceivably have been looking for young scholars to help with the work of translating the Old Testament into Welsh. Was it he who, if not the first to awaken in Morgan's mind the idea of translating the Bible, was perhaps the first in a place of authority to encourage him?

However, in 1575, the year when Davies and Salesbury were said to have quarrelled, and when a young assistant might have been more than ordinarily useful, Morgan moved to the diocese of St Asaph. On 8 August 1575, he was presented to the vicarage of Welshpool and the sinecure rectory of Denbigh by his Cambridge contemporary, Bishop Hughes.[36] The bishop, who had earlier been Lady Margaret preacher at Cambridge and was newly arrived at St Asaph, was keeping his eye open for gifted preachers, of whom his diocese was in dire need. What could be more natural in the circumstances than that he should seek to entice this young Cambridge graduate there? It proved to be an inspired choice on his part, for Morgan throughout his life proved to be a preacher of exceptional prowess. Towards the end of his career he was paid a remarkable tribute by the poet, Huw Machno:

> I bregethu, brig ieithoedd,
> Ugain llu, y gannwyll oedd.[37]

Pinnacle of languages, in preaching to a score of congregations he was the candle.

By conferring on him lucrative preferment Hughes may also have had it in mind to help finance his further studies at Cambridge. It was not until 1 October 1578 that Morgan assumed the responsibilities of a full-time parish priest, when he gave up his living at Welshpool and took up residence at the vicarage of Llanrhaeadr ym Mochnant, Montgomeryshire, which he held with neighbouring Llanarmon Mynydd Mawr. Here he was to spend the next sixteen years, and Llanrhaeadr is the benefice above all others with which his name is associated. In an appealing poem entitled 'Llanrhaeadr ym Mochnant', the contemporary poet, R. S. Thomas, himself a country parson for many years, suggests

[35] *Gwydir Family*, p. 63.
[36] D. R. Thomas, *History of the Diocese of St Asaph* (3 vols. Oswestry, 1908–13), I. 97–100.
[37] Gruffydd, *Beibl a Droes*, p. 83.

> This is where he [Morgan] sought God,
> And found him? The centuries
> Have been content to follow
> Down passages of serene prose.[38]

It was not only the divine presence that Morgan encountered there but human enmity as well. For much of his ministry he was to be enmeshed in long-running quarrels with some of his parishioners, most notably with the truculent barrister, Ifan Maredudd, of the house of Lloran Uchaf.[39] Vexatious and costly for Morgan as these altercations were to prove, he was sufficiently single-minded to persevere with his self-imposed task of rendering the Bible into his native tongue.

By 1578, having completed his study of Hebrew at Cambridge, he would be equipped to translate the Old Testament. It may have been as early as this that he took up the responsibility – possibly with Bishop Davies's blessing, since the latter knew only too well that the Act of 1563 had imposed upon the Welsh bishops the duty of taking order amongst themselves for ensuring that the translation was taken in hand. Davies might just possibly have been one of those unnamed 'good men' later mentioned by Morgan as having persuaded him to embark on the work in the first place.[40] Morgan might even have enjoyed the advantage of having sight of any translations which Salesbury and Davies (and possibly Siôn Dafydd Rhys) had themselves been able to undertake. If he did, that would help to explain John Wynn's sardonic and biased quip that earlier pioneers had done most of the work, for which Morgan took all the credit: 'he had the benefit and help of Bishop Davies and William Salesbury's work, who had done a great part thereof, yet he carried the name of that all'.[41] A tradition which owes its origins to a remark by Charles Edwards in his *Hanes y Ffydd Ddiffuant* (1674)[42] suggests that it was in 1579, while engaged in litigation with his parishioners in the Council in the Marshes, that Morgan came into contact – not necessarily for the first time, since he may have known him at Cambridge – with John Whitgift, then bishop of Worcester and vice-president of the Council in the Marches. It may have been that that was the occasion recalled by Morgan in his dedication to the Bible of 1588 when, having conveyed to Whitgift his despair at the prospect of being unable to do more than complete the translation of the Pentateuch, he was given the latter's warmest encouragement to persevere with his version of the whole.

---

[38] *W and R*, p. 188.
[39] Edwards, *BBCS*, II. 298–339.
[40] Dedication, *Y Beibl Cyssegr-lan* (1588).
[41] *Gwydir Family*, p. 66.
[42] *Y Ffydd Ddiffuant*, ed. G. J. Williams (Cardiff, 1936), p. 201.

Dr Isaac Thomas, however, suggests a different timetable. He considers it to be more likely that Morgan did not begin translating until after Davies's death on 7 November 1581. He then submitted his work to Bishops Hughes of St Asaph and Robinson of Bangor and obtained their approval for his efforts. Later, between 1583 and 1585, he was given Whitgift's encouragement.[43] The difficulty about such a suggestion would seem to be that it hardly allows enough time for Morgan to have completed all he had in hand. In most countries the Old Testament took far longer to translate than the New. It took Luther ten years to complete his translation of the German Bible; the team of twelve responsible for producing the Bishops' Bible spent from 1559 to 1568 over the task.[44] Morgan, however, on top of the translation of the Old Testament, had to translate the books of the Apocrypha, and thoroughly revise Salesbury's translation of the New Testament and the Psalter. To have expected him to encompass all this in the short space between 1583 and 1587 would appear to have been asking the impossible. Even supposing that he was working flat out between 1579 and 1587, what he was able to achieve was little short of phenomenal.

If, however, Morgan was recognized during these years as the successor to Davies and Salesbury, there remains a major mystery. Why was it that in 1586 a new printing of the Welsh Prayer Book, virtually a reissue of the book of 1567 but printed this time by John Windet at the costs and charges of Thomas Chard, was sanctioned, and who was responsible for seeing it through the press?[45] The explanation might be that a new edition of the Prayer Book was badly needed, but that at this point there was no hope of William Morgan's being able to find the time to undertake the thorough revision of Salesbury's text that was patently necessary. Salesbury himself may by this time have been dead, but in any case there is no indication of his having had a hand in the venture. There may, therefore, have been no alternative but to reprint the edition of 1567 virtually unchanged. It would not be until 1599 that Morgan was able to find the time for preparing and publishing the much-needed revised version.

Morgan gratefully acknowledged the help he received from a number of Cambridge friends in the course of translating the Bible. One of the most valuable of them was Edmwnd Prys, a notable scholar, former fellow of St John's, and a fine Welsh poet and writer. Prys was singled out by a contemporary Welsh author, David Rowlands, for his part in the translation, and he was probably better fitted than any of the others to advise Morgan not only on the original languages of the Bible but on the

[43] Thomas, *Morgan's Bible*, pp. 42–6.
[44] C. L. Cross (ed.), *Oxford Dictionary of the Christian Church* (Oxford, 1957), p. 175.
[45] G. M. Richards and G. Williams (eds.), *Llyfr Gweddi Gyffredin 1567* (Cardiff, 1967), pp. xliii–xliv.

particular problems of turning them into Welsh.[46] Richard Vaughan also helped Morgan; and so did two unnamed bishops. whom he acknowledged as having lent him books and examined his translation and approved it.[47] One was the much-maligned Hughes, Morgan's patron at St Asaph; the other may have been Nicholas Robinson, a fine scholar known to have advocated the translation of the Bible into Welsh, or, just possibly, it may have been his successor at Bangor, Hugh Bellot, closely associated with the translation of the Bishops' Bible but not thought to have had any great knowledge of Welsh.[48] Gabriel Goodman, dean of Westminster, helped in a number of ways. He allowed Morgan to borrow books from him, gave him the benefit of his opinion when the translation was read to him, and extended hospitality to Morgan while the Bible was going through the press in London. He may also have been instrumental in encouraging Whitgift to authorize publication of the finished text.[49] The friend and mentor whose intervention was quite indispensable, though, was John Whitgift. By 1583 Whitgift was archbishop of Canterbury, had the ear of the queen, was a leading member of the Privy Council, and from 1586 onwards exercised such control over the press that no books might be published without authorization from him and the bishop of London.[50] If any man was in a position to override public opposition to the publication of a Welsh Bible, it was he. His contribution to encouraging and expediting the translation, helping to meet its printing costs, and authorizing and enforcing its use in Welsh-speaking parishes was invaluable.

Nevertheless, however well-disposed his friends may have been, it was Morgan himself who clearly had to bear the brunt of the burden. It was an awesome, even daunting, assignment for a parish priest, living far from well-stocked libraries and centres of scholarship, having only very modest funds at his disposal, and constantly being distracted by worrying and expensive litigation with fractious parishioners. Yet Morgan was undoubtedly impelled by deep and weighty motivation to persist with his mission. He tells us that he had been profoundly impressed by what the translations of 1567, whatever their limitation and deficiencies, had achieved. He believed that they had extended the knowledge of English as well as Welsh (an object cherished by many sixteenth-century authors); they had made preaching in Welsh more widespread and effectual; and they had enlarged

---

[46] G. A. Williams, *Ymryson Edmwnd Prys a William Cynwal* (Cardiff, 1986), pp. civ–cvi.

[47] Dedication, *Beibl 1588*.

[48] F. O. White, *The Lives of the Elizabethan Bishops* (London, 1898), p. 295.

[49] *W and R*, p. 204.

[50] G. R. Elton, *The Tudor Constitution* (Cambridge, 1960), pp. 179–84.

knowledge and understanding of the scriptures.[51] They had not, admittedly, included the Old Testament, and their orthography and presentation had caused grievous difficulties. But Morgan might be forgiven if he were confident that it lay within his power to remedy these defects. At the same time, he was distressingly aware of strong currents of opinion that ran contrary to the whole idea of providing a Welsh Bible. Influential voices were advocating that, in the interests of uniformity, the Welsh should be made to learn English and be forbidden a Bible in their own tongue. Such opinions were even echoed within Wales itself by Welsh clerics,[52] possibly on account of their disillusionment with the translations of 1567. Among these critics at one stage appears to have been Bishop William Hughes, according to the historian David Powel,[53] though in the light of the generous patronage he extended to William Morgan, he must later have changed his mind. In response to such opposition Morgan pleaded eloquently that religion must take priority over political expediency, and that countless thousands of his countrymen ought not to be allowed to sink into eternal perdition from ignorance of the sacred word. Besides, he argued, a common religious faith was a stronger bond of potential unity between the English and the Welsh than a common language would be; an argument advanced by almost all of even the most enthusiastic proponents of the Welsh language until this century. If that appears to be an unconvincing proposition nowadays, it may be worth recalling what the contemporary French statesman, Michel L'Hôpital, who spared no effort to preserve the precarious unity of Catherine dei Medici's strife-torn France, had to say to the States-General of his country: 'We see that an Englishman and a Frenchman, whose religion is the same, have more affection and friendship for one another than two French citizens who belong to the same city and are subject to the same overlord, but who adhere to different religions.'[54]

Morgan may have had other more personal sources of inspiration, of which he has left no record. He may have been moved by the ambition of a younger son to make his mark in the world, by the enthusiasm of a Renaissance linguist, and by the awareness of the revolution that the printed book had wrought in language and communications. As compelling as any of these driving forces, if not more so, may well have been his immense pride in, and affection for, his native language and its glorious literary heritage, which in him could best find expression and fulfilment as

[51] Dedication, *Beibl 1588*.
[52] Kyffin, *Deffynniad Ffydd*, p. xiv.
[53] Gruffydd, *Gair ar Waith*, p. 30.
[54] H. Daniel-Rops, *The Catholic Reformation* (London, 1968), pp. 164–5.

the writer of sacred books. His translation of the Bible may thus have been the realization of an objective towards which he was driven on partly by concern for the public good, and partly by more personal, but honourable enough, private ambitions. It was this felicitous conjunction of Morgan's *pietas* towards his faith and his people with his genius as a writer and scholar that his contemporaries were to hail with unprecedented rapture when his Bible appeared.

The year 1587, in which Morgan completed his text, was one of acute crisis for the whole kingdom. The preceding years, 1585–6, had been a time of severe famine, which some Welshmen had interpreted as God's punishment on their people. In 1586 the Babington Plot, in which leading Welshmen were implicated, led to the execution of Mary Stuart and brought Spain and England to the brink of all-out war. A Puritan like John Penry feared that Spain might be the chosen instrument of divine vengeance for the waywardness of the Welsh.[55] These alarming events were bound to intensify governmental concern about those parts of Elizabeth's realm like Wales, where Protestantism had lagged far behind. Adding to the worries about increasing Catholic activity since 1580 had been the two attempts to establish secret Catholic printing-presses. In view of a crisis of these proportions it is not surprising that Morgan had been impelled to refer so effusively in his dedication to the merits of Elizabeth and her archbishop and their exceptional concern for the welfare of the Welsh people. This all suggests that he had a particular target in mind. The mark at which he may have been aiming, though never mentioned by him, was John Penry, author of the *Aequity*, presented to the House of Commons in February 1587. Whitgift had been incensed by the audacity of its attacks on him and the rest of the hierarchy, and obliquely, on the queen. In March 1587 he had the author brought before the Court of High Commission to answer for his writings.[56] Penry's onslaught on the episcopate may have had a far-reaching effect. It can hardly have been just a coincidence that in a matter of months, if not of weeks, Whitgift was pressing Morgan to stay with him at Lambeth Palace to speed up work on the Welsh Bible. It could conceivably have been Penry's deadly shafts, added to the other perils of the time, which spurred Whitgift to a greater sense of urgency and forced him to realize the desperate need to counter-attack Penry and other Puritans on the one hand, and the Catholics on the other, by publishing a Welsh Bible.

Morgan came to London in 1587 to supervise the progress of his manuscript through the press. On this occasion, contrary to the usual

[55] *Treatises*, p. xviii.
[56] W. Pierce, *The Life and Times of John Penry* (London, 1923), pp. 174–6; D. J. McGinn, *John Penry and the Marprelate Controversy* (Rutgers UP, 1960), pp. 81–2.

practice,[57] he was to act as proof-corrector as well as being the author of the volume. He stayed not with the archbishop at Lambeth on the south bank of the Thames, as originally suggested, but at Westminster with Dean Gabriel Goodman, which obviated the need for frequent crossings of the river to consult with his printers. On 22 September 1588, the Privy Council, with Whitgift present, and doubtless playing a directing role, issued instructions that letters be dispatched to the four Welsh bishops and the bishop of Hereford. These were to inform them that the 'translation of the Bible into the Welsh or British tongue, which, by Act of Parliament should long since have been done, is now performed by one Doctor Morgan and set forth in print'.[58] The diocesans were ordered to ensure that churchwardens in each parish should, by the ensuing Christmas-tide, have provided 'one Bible and two Psalters' of the same translation. They were also enjoined to keep the English Bible safe 'to the end that such as will confer them together may have the same ready'.[59] Incorrigible defaulters within any diocese were to be reported to the archbishop. Many parsons acquired a copy almost at once, and so did many parish churches, like Swansea's St Mary's.[60] Yet in one parish, at least, that of Bodfari in St Asaph diocese, no Bible was recorded as having been bought until November 1592, at a cost of 20*s*.[61]

A quarter of a century had elapsed since the Act of 1563 had been passed, and because Parliament was not in session in 1588, it was an obvious advantage for the Privy Council to have authorized a new translation and issued instructions for the provision and use of the texts in parish churches. Seen against this background, Morgan's dedication to the queen, his respectful deference to the Established Church, its archbishop, and hierarchy are all readily explicable as being, in part at least, a stern riposte to Penry's criticisms. Yet it remains one of the exquisite ironies of Welsh history that Penry, so often rightly likened to a voice crying unanswered in the wilderness,[62] may have had a decisive share in moving Whitgift and Morgan to hasten the consummation of a project as dear to Penry's heart as it was to Morgan's.

The Welsh Bible of 1588 was a handsome, if bulky, folio volume of 1,122 pages,[63] containing the Old and New Testaments and the books of the

---

[57] W. Thomas, 'The Trinity College, Carmarthen, copy of William Morgan's Bible', *Carm. Antiq.* XXIV (1988), 110–13.

[58] *APC*, XVI (1588), 283–4.

[59] Ibid.

[60] M. Walker, 'Welsh books in St Mary's, Swansea, 1559–1626', *BBCS*, XXIII (1968–70), 397–402.

[61] Thomas, *St Asaph*, I. 96.

[62] *Treatises*, pp. xxvi–xxvii.

[63] A facsimile edition of the Bible of 1588 was published by NLW in 1988.

Apocrypha. It was bound in leather on a wooden base, with the text printed in black letter on paper imported from either Normandy or Champagne, and printed in ink also imported from France.[64] The printing was entrusted to the queen's printer, Christopher Barker, who delegated the work to George Bishop. He printed it at his press at the sign of the Bell in St Paul's churchyard.[65] The edition must have run to at least 1,000 copies, and possibly more, each copy being sold at £1, the cost to be jointly borne by the incumbent and the parishioners in the case of parish churches. Whitgift may have shouldered a considerable share of the outlay involved in printing the volume, although Morgan himself may have been at great expense, since the poet, Siôn Tudur, refers feelingly to the 'heavy cost' ('mawrgost') which he had incurred.[66]

Of the excellence of Morgan's translation much has been written.[67] Three qualities have been especially singled out for commendation: his talents as a scholar; his revision of Salesbury's New Testament and Prayer Book; and his gifts as a writer of Welsh. Morgan proved himself to be a consummate scholar, who made use of the best Hebrew and Greek texts available to him with exceptional skill and discernment. He set out to translate the original wording as faithfully and accurately as he could, but without in any way sacrificing intelligibility in the process. Much as he admired the fine scholars who had preceded him, he was not afraid to choose his own path and back his individual judgement. He was rarely wrong and, in some instances, he offered translations which anticipated the mature scholarship of the Revised Version of the English Bible of 1882.[68] He was a singular master of the rare art of turning the 'spare, muscular, direct language of the Hebrew original into Welsh that is distinguished by the same qualities'.[69] Even John Wynn, exasperated by Morgan's stubborn opposition to him and reluctant to pay him any compliments, grudgingly admitted that he was 'a good scholar, both a Grecian and Hebrician'.[70]

Morgan was only too conscious of the infelicities of earlier Welsh versions. Although he accepted about three-quarters of Salesbury's actual translation of the New Testament, he comprehensively revised its whole text, as far as orthography and vocabulary were concerned. In relation to

[64] Thomas, *Carm. Antiq.* XXIV. 110.
[65] Gruffydd, *Dyneiddiwr*, p. 17; Thomas, *Carm. Antiq.* XXIV. 110.
[66] Gruffydd, *Beibl a Droes*, p. 37.
[67] All previous work on the subject has been completely superseded by Dr I. Thomas's magisterial studies: *Y Testament Newydd Cymraeg* (Cardiff, 1972) and *Yr Hen Destament Cymraeg* (Aberystwyth, 1988). Cf. also his *William Morgan* for a useful summary of his main conclusions.
[68] *W and R.*, p. 211.
[69] Thomas, *William Morgan*, p. 67.
[70] *Gwydir Family*, p. 68.

vocabulary he showed his preference for living words rather than the less familiar archaisms; he rejected many of Salesbury's loan-words, derived either from English or Latin; and he cut down drastically on those excessive variations in the text and margin so beloved of Salesbury in his quest for 'copiousness'. Throughout, he aimed at fidelity to the original texts, consistency, and regularity. In short, he made a point of eliminating Salesbury's archaisms, Latinizations, and other idiosyncrasies, which had caused the versions of 1567 to be so difficult to understand and so badly read. There would, in future, be no reason for the scriptures to be 'so pitifully evil read', in Penry's words.

Finally, and most commendable of all, perhaps, Morgan's handling of the Welsh language bore all the hallmarks of a superb writer as well as an erudite scholar. He had the instinctive sureness and intuitive grasp of a man to whom his native tongue was an heirloom to treasure as well as a tool to use. Not without good cause was he hailed by the poet, Huw Machno, as 'clo'r iaith'[71] ('the lock of the language'). He was, it is true, capable of some unfortunate errors of judgement. The worst of these was his fondness for using the abnormal sentence, that is, putting the subject before the verb, instead of the normal Welsh fashion of placing them the other way round. Even that, curiously enough, may have conferred upon his Welsh an added air of dignity consonant with that of the sacred text which he was translating. At a fateful juncture for the language, when the bards, hitherto the guardians and exponents of its classic strength and purity, had entered on a period of irreversible and accelerating decline, Morgan embodied in his translation all that was best and finest in their tradition. Yet he did so in a way that was neither obscurantist, nor esoteric, nor inflexible. The pre-eminent living authority in Wales on the Celtic languages has commented admiringly on how much simpler, more natural, and closer to the spoken idiom Morgan's Welsh was, as compared with that of most of the contemporary Welsh humanist writers.[72]

The following extracts from two well-known Psalms are designed to illustrate how favourably Morgan's versions compare with those of Salesbury:

Salesbury: Prayer Book of 1567. Psalm 1
Gwyn ei vyd y gwr ny rodiawdd yn cyccor yr andewolion, ac ny savodd yn
    ffordd pechaturieit, ac nyd eisteddawdd yn eisteddfa yr ei gwatwrus.
Eithyr bot ei ewyllys yn Deddyf yr Arglwydd, ac yn ei Deddyf ef bot yn
    mevyrio ddydd a' nos.
Canys ef vydd mal pren wedy'r blanny yn-glan dyfredd yr hwn a ddwc ei

[71] Gruffydd, *Beibl a Droes*, p. 52.
[72] J. E. C. Williams in *Gair ar Waith*, p. 152.

ffrwyth yn ei dempor: a' ei ddalen ni wywa: a' pha beth bynac y wnel ef, a lwydda.

Nyd velly [y bydd] yr ei annuwiol, eithr mal y man vs, yr hwn a chwal y gwynt ymaith.

Am hyny ny saif yr andewiolion yny varn, na'r pechaturiait yn-cynn-ulleidfa yr ei cyfion.

Canys yr Arglwydd a edwyn ffordd yr ei cyfion, a' ffordd yr andewiolion a gyfergollir.

Morgan. Psalter 1588. Psalm 1

Gwyn ei fyd y gŵr ni rodiodd yng-hyngor yr annuwolion, ac ni safodd yn ffordd pechaduriaid, ac nid eisteddodd yn eisteddfa gwatwar-wŷr:

Onid [bod] ei ewyllys ef yng-hyfraith yr Arglwydd: a mefyrio o honaw yn ei gyfraith ef ddydd a nôs.

Canys efe a fydd fel prenn wedi ei blannu ar lann dyfroedd, yr hwn a rydd ei ffrwyth yn ei brŷd: a'i ddalen ni ŵywa, a pha beth bynnac a wnêl, efe a lwydda.

Nid felly [y bydd] yr annuwiol, onid fel mân vs yr hwn a chwâl y gwynt ymmaith [oddi ar wyneb y ddaiar.]

Am hynny yr annuwolion ni safant yn y farn, na'r pechaduriaid yng-hynnulleidfa y rhai cyfiawn.

Canys yr Arglwydd a edwyn ffordd y rhai cyfiawn, a ffordd yr annuwolion a ddifethir.

Salesbury. Prayer Book of 1567. Psalm 23

Yr Arglwydd [yw] vy-bugeil, ny bydd diffic arnaf.

Ef a bair ym' orphwys mewn porva brydverth, ac am tywys ger llaw dyfredd tawel.

Ef y adver vy eneit, ac am arwein i rhyd llwybrae cyfiawnder er mwyn ei Enw.

A' phe rhodiwn rhyd glyn gwascot angae, nyd ofnaf ddrwc: can y ty vot gyd a mi: dy wialen ath ffon, hwy am diddanant.

Ti arlwyy vort gar vy-bron, yn-gwydd vy-gwrthnepwyr: ireist vy-pen ac oleo, [a'] m phiol a orllenwir.

Sef ddaoni a' thrugaredd am canlynant oll ddyddiae vy-bywyt, a' phreswiliaf yn hir amswer yn-tuy yr Arglwydd.

Morgan. Psalter 1588. Psalm 23

Yr Arglwydd [yw] fy mugail: ni bydd eisieu arnaf.

Efe a bar i'm orwedd mewn porfeudd gwelltoc: efe a'm tywys ger llaw dyfroedd tawel.

Efe a ddychwel fy enaid, ac a'm harwain ar hŷd llwybrau cyfiawnder er mwyn ei enw.

A phe rodiwn ar hŷd glynn cyscod angeu nid ofnaf niwed, o herwydd dy [fod] ti gyd â mi; dy wialen a'th ffon a'm cyssûrant.

Ti a arlwyi fort ger fy mron, yn erbyn fyng-wrthwyneb-wŷr: iraist fy mhen
ag olew, fy phiol [sydd] lawn.
Daioni a thrugâredd yn ddiau a'm canlynant oll ddyddiau fy mywyd: a
phresswyliaf yn nhŷ'r Arglwydd yn dragywydd.

It would, of course, be less than just to Salesbury not to take full account
of most readers' long familiarity with a version of the Psalms and a biblical
orthography which are basically Morgan's original. Yet, even when all
such allowances have been made for the almost irresistible predisposition
in favour of the 1588 version, there is no gainsaying the vast improvement
in Morgan's text as compared with that of Salesbury. Gone from
Morgan's Psalter are the Latinized garb of Welsh words like 'tempor' for
'tymor', 'oleo' for 'olew', or 'llwybrae' for 'llwybrau', the archaisms of
vocabulary and spelling, and that characteristic Salesburian trampling on
the initial nasal mutation in such horrors as 'vy-pen' ('fy mhen') or 'yn-tuy'
('yn nhŷ'). Salesbury's unpredictable inconsistencies and variations have
also been tidied up and regularized, and his innumerable marginal glosses
and alternatives – omitted here, but peppering his own text – have also
disappeared. It was not that Morgan's prose rendering as such was always
much better than Salesbury's; more often than not, indeed, he found
himself in agreement with the earlier version when stripped of its
peculiarities. It was in terms of its insight into what was needed, its good
sense, clarity, and consistency that the uniform excellence of Morgan's
version scored so heavily over the idiosyncrasies and irregularities of
Salesbury's.

Morgan often appears at his best in the more prophetic and poetic
passages of the Bible, having an unmatched certainty of instinctive feeling
for sonority, rhythm, and balance in his writing. The fine biblical scholar
of our own century, C. H. Dodd, went so far as to describe Morgan as 'a
Hebrew poet of genius'.[73] Two short extracts will have to suffice in
illustration of this point. Both are taken from the Old Testament; not
because there is any shortage from the New, but simply because in
translating the Old Testament Morgan had few or no precedents to guide
him. The extracts given below once again serve to remind us, if such a
reminder were needed, how very much the Bible known to generation after
generation of Welsh people was Morgan's Bible.

---

[73] Gruffydd, *Dyneiddiwr*, p. 122.

Proverbs 12. 1–9

Mwy dymunol yw enw da na chyfoeth lawer; a gwell yw grâs nag arian ac nag aur.

Y tlawd a'r cyfoethog a gyd cyfarfuant; ond yr Arglwydd yw gwneuthydd y rhai hyn oll.

Y call a genfydd ddrwg, ac a ymgudd; ond y ffyliaid a ânt rhagddynt, a hwy a gospir.

Gobr gostyngeiddrwydd, ac ofn yr Arglwydd yw cyfoeth, anrhydedd, a bywyd.

Drain a maglau ŷnt yn ffordd y cyndyn; y neb a gadwo ei enaid a ffŷ ymhell oddi wrthynt hwy.

Hyfforddia fâb ym mhen ei ei ffordd; a phan heneiddio nid ymedu â hi.

Y cyfoethog a arglwyddiaetha ar y tlawd; a gwâs fydd yr hwn a gaffo fenthyg i'r gŵr a roddo fenthyg.

Y neb a heuo anwiredd a feda flinder; ac a balla trwy wialen ei ddigofaint ef.

Yr hael ei lygad a fendithir; canys ef rydd oi fara i'r tlawd.

Isaiah 40. 7–15

Gwywodd y gwelltyn, [a] syrthiodd y blodeun, canys Yspryd yr Arglwydd a chwythodd arno, gwellt yn ddiau [yw]'r bobl.

Gwywodd y gwelltyn, syrthiodd y blodeun, a gair ein Duw ni a saif byth.

Dring rhagot yr efangyles Sion i fynydd vchel, derchafa dithe dy lef trwy nerth ô efangyles Ierusalem: derchafa nac ofna, dywed wrth ddinasoedd Iuda, Wele eich Duw chwi.

Wele'r Arglwydd Dduw a ddaw'n erbyn y cadarn, ai fraich a lywodraetha arno ef, wele ei obrwy gyd ag ef, ai waith oi flaen.

Fel bugail y portha ef ei braidd, âi fraich y cascl ei ŵyn, ac [ai] dŵg yn ei fonwes, ac a goledda y mamogiaid.

Pwy a fessurodd y dyfroedd yn ei ddwrn? ac a fessurodd y nefoedd âi rychwant, ac a gymhwysodd bridd y ddaiar mewn messur, ac a bwysodd y mynyddoedd mewn pwys, a'r brynnau mewn cloriannau?

Pwy a gyfarwyddodd Yspryd yr Arglwydd? ac yn ŵr oi gyngor ai hyffordd-iodd ef?

A phwy'r ymgynghorodd efe, ie [pwy] ai hyfforddiodd ac ai dyscodd mewn llwybr barn? ac a ddyscodd iddo ŵybodaeth, ac a gyfarwyddodd iddo ffordd deallgarwch?

Wele'r cenhedloedd a gyfrifwyd fel defnyn o gelwrn, ac fel brychewyn oddi wrth gloriannau: fel brychewyn y bwrw ef ymaith yr ynysoedd.

The translation of the scriptures into the vernacular was one of the foremost linguistic and cultural developments of sixteenth-century Europe. Wales was but one of a number of countries where the Bible had been rendered into the mother tongue and set forth in print before 1600. Following the publication of the New Testament in Germany in 1522 and the Bible in 1534, the New Testament had appeared in France in 1523 and the Old in 1530, in the Low Countries in 1523 and 1527, in English in 1524 and 1535, in Danish in 1524 and 1550, in Swedish in 1526 and 1541, in Finnish in 1529 and 1548, in Icelandic in 1540 and 1584, in Hungarian in 1541 and 1590, in Spanish and in Croatian in 1543, in Polish in 1552–3, in Slovenian in 1557 and 1582, in Romanian in 1561–3, in Welsh in 1567 and 1588, in Lithuanian in 1578 and 1582, and in Czech in 1579 and 1593.[74] Wales had, admittedly, had to wait half a century or so longer than England and some other countries for its Bible, but, bearing in mind some of the particular disadvantages which its translators had to overcome, they had succeeded in a comparatively short space of time. Of all the Celtic-speaking countries, Wales was the only one which successfully achieved the feat within the sixteenth century. The year 1588 had proved to be one of destiny for the kingdom of England and for Wales. England had safeguarded its political independence by defeating the Spanish Armada; Wales had ensured the future autonomy of its language and culture by the publication of Morgan's Bible. Nor was the Bible the last of his contributions to Wales. There was more to follow in the shape of his revised edition of the Prayer Book in 1599, and also in the new version of the New Testament which he completed but which, unfortunately, was destroyed in a fire at his publisher's premises before it could appear in print (below, chap. 14).

Unlike many prophets, Morgan was not without honour in his own land and lifetime. Many of his contemporaries were sufficiently educated and experienced to appreciate that the potential value of the Welsh Bible to Wales could bear comparison with what a vernacular Bible had done for England and other countries. Some of the earliest and most ecstatic in their reception of it were the Welsh poets.[75] Not only were they the public voice of Wales, but they were also quick to point out what the translator of the Bible had done for the language and literature of Wales as well as its religion. Following the lead given by Davies and Salesbury in 1567, poets may further have sensed Morgan's contribution to its history and national tradition, too. As might have been expected, they eulogized Morgan's conventional virtues, though these might have been applicable to almost any prominent Welsh cleric – his learning, his ability as a preacher, and his hospitality and charity. But it must have given him unbounded satisfaction to discover how they all valued his unique contribution as the translator of the Bible, the man who had conferred upon his people the most precious

---

[74] Williams in *Gair ar Waith*, p. 24; *The Cambridge History of the Bible*, ed. S. L. Greenslade (Cambridge, 1963), III, chap. 3.

[75] For a splendid collection of the relevant poems, see Gruffydd, *Beibl a Droes*.

gift the Reformation had to offer: the word of God in their own tongue and intelligible to every Welsh man and woman.

One of the earliest and most intriguing of the poems which greeted the Bible was that by Thomas Jones, a poet-parson of Llandeilo Bertholau in Monmouthshire, whose muse gave tongue at Christmas-time 1588,[76] within weeks of the publication of the work. Jones was not writing within the patrician milieu of the *canu caeth* (fixed-metre poetry) but in the more informal free-verse genre of the *cwndid*, designed for a popular and broad-based audience. He had evidently savoured with relish that Protestant interpretation of early British Church history outlined by Richard Davies in his preface to the New Testament of 1567. Jones had been cast down by what he saw as the long ages of neglect and darkness, during which the papacy and its minions had succeeded in suppressing the Welsh scriptures and the learning associated with them, which he believed had once been universal among the Welsh. But now, a new dawn had broken with the publication once more of a Bible in their own language. In a succession of metaphors designed to pinpoint in the people's memory the merits of Morgan's Bible – a 'treasure', 'pearl beyond price', 'jewel', 'sword of the spirit', 'shield of faith', 'manna from heaven', 'bread of life', 'sovereign remedy', 'fount of truth', 'column of fire', 'heavenly candle' – new hope and assurance were proffered to all. There was no mistaking the insistence and warmth which Jones infused into his appeal to the Welsh. Perhaps the most striking feature of the poem was that it envisaged laymen being able to buy copies of the Bible, and Jones pleaded with them, a generation before Vicar Prichard's more celebrated exhortation in the same vein, to sell their shirts in order to buy a Bible:

> Er mwyn prynu hwn rhag trais,
> Dos, gwerth dy bais, y Cymro.[77]

(In order to buy this and be free of oppression, go, sell thy shirt, thou Welshman.)

Thomas Jones may have been a trifle optimistic in supposing that many of the public would be able and willing to buy copies of the Bible at that time; but it was symptomatic of his enthusiasm for Morgan's work that he could urge upon them so earnestly to try.

---

[76] *Hen Gwndidau Carolau a Chywyddau*, ed. L. J. Hopkin-James and T. C. Evans (Bangor, 1914), 187–92. Jones was described by the Catholic poet, Mathew Turberville, as a 'great Puritan' ('Pywritan mawr'), NLW, Brogyntyn MS. 6.

[77] *Hen Gwndidau*, p. 189.

The Welsh Bible

A number of the classic *cynghanedd* poets, among them Huw Machno, Siôn Tudur, Owain Gwynedd, Ieuan Tew, Siôn Mawddwy, and Rhys Cain, were equally complimentary, though in metre and diction more difficult to absorb than Jones's more direct and less sophisticated verses. Huw Machno,[78] like Jones, deplored the long-drawn-out tribulations to which the Britons and their language had been subjected as a result of papal subterfuges of every kind. He attributed the upward turn in their fortunes to the wisdom and benevolence of a ruler of Welsh descent, Elizabeth ('Cymraes o hil Cymro' – a Welshwoman of the race of a Welshman), and the learning of William Morgan, whom he likened to Moses leading his people from the land of captivity to one of light and freedom. Probably the most interesting of the classic poets, however, was Siôn Tudur. He referred acidly to the way in which the papal church had confined the people by treachery to darkness and ignorance

> The enmity of the Church of Rome
> For us was a terrible anguish,
> She played a dirty game with us –
> Sour nurse that she was – a mumming game.
> Playing yesterday – we realize now –
> At keeping us as a blind nation,
> Shutting our heads inside a sack
> With our eyes behind a mask.[79]

He, too, could now welcome the substitution for the pope's vaunted but 'false pardons from blazing purgatory' ('pardwn Pab rhag purdan poeth') of the truly 'effectual pardon of the blood of the Lamb to save the soul' ('Gorau pardwn . . . gwaed yr Oen i gadw'r enaid'). He greeted ecstatically the authentic source of religious truth now opened to them, 'the Word of God that scares the devil' ('Gair Duw yw'r arf a darf diawl').[80] All the poets were unanimous that Morgan's master-stroke had been to offer his countrymen the key to unsullied religion and true illumination in the shape of God's own word in their native language. Owain Gwynedd rejoiced that all which had previously been shrouded in darkness had now been flooded by Morgan with light:

> Hyn oedd yn dywyll inni
> A lanwech o oleuni.

(That which was dark for us, you have filled with light.)

[78] Gruffydd, *Beibl a Droes*, pp. 51–4.
[79] Morgan, *Bible for Wales*, p. 14.
[80] Gruffydd, *Beibl a Droes*, pp. 37–8.

He hailed Morgan as 'porth a phen puriaith ffydd' ('gate and head of the pure language of faith').[81] The poets were the more transported with delight because they recognized instinctively that Morgan's Bible had simultaneously resolved what a contemporary scholar has described as the twin dilemmas confronting sixteenth-century Wales – those of religion and culture.[82]

Prose-writers, no less than poets, cordially acclaimed the new Bible. George Owen, the most famous antiquary of Tudor Wales, wrote with gratification of the benefits that might be expected to flow from the translation.

> And now, not three years past, we have the light of the gospel, yea, the whole Bible in our native tongue, which in short time must needs work great good inwardly in the hearts of the people, whereas the service and sacraments in the English-tongue were as strange to many of the simplest sort as the mass in the time of blindness.[83]

A few years later, Maurice Kyffin, in the introduction to his translation of John Jewel's *Apologia*, alluded to Morgan's Bible as 'an indispensable, masterly, godly, learned work, for which Wales can never repay and thank him as much as he deserves' (gwaith angenrheidiol, gorchestol, duwiol, dyscedig; am yr hwn ni ddichyn Cymru fyth dalu a diolch iddo gymaint ag a haeddodd ef').[84] About the same time, another Welsh prose author, Huw Lewys, referred to the 'truly excellent and most learned man, Dr Morgan' ('y gwir ardderchawg ddyscedicaf Dr Morgan'), to whom Wales was indebted for 'so notable a treasure, the true and holy word of God, giving light freely to all' ('y cyfryw drysawr, sef gwir a phurlan air Duw, i oleuni yn gyffredinawl i bawb').[85]

The passage of time served only to justify still further the raptures with which the Bible of 1588 was initially greeted. Over the ensuing four centuries it left its imprint deep and irremovable on the life of succeeding generations of Welsh men and women. Its power to shape the distinctive characteristics of Welsh life was, arguably, stronger than that of the English Bible in England. Among those responsible for giving it to Wales, William Morgan stands foremost; only William Salesbury comes anywhere near him in deserving a share of the credit for what has aptly been described as 'the most important book in the Welsh language'.[86]

---

[81] Ibid., p. 63.
[82] Gruffydd, *Dyneiddiwr*, pp. 5–8.
[83] Owen, *Penbrokshire*, III. 56–7
[84] Kyffin, *Deffynniad Ffydd*, pp. ix–x.
[85] Williams in *Gair ar Waith*, p. 151.
[86] W. J. Gruffydd in *Gair ar Waith*, p. 151.

CHAPTER 14

The Reformation Ensured, 1589–1603

THE final twelve to fifteen years of Elizabeth's reign witnessed the gradual decay of her regime. It had reached its climax with the defeat of the Armada, but that was not by any means a decisive victory. It had signalled the beginning, not the end, of the struggle between Spain and England for supremacy at sea. For the remainder of Elizabeth's reign, and beyond until 1604, warfare continued between them, along the sea-lanes, on the Continent, and in Ireland. On more than one occasion in the 1590s, and especially in 1596 and 1599, there were further ominous threats of a Spanish sea-borne invasion. Hostilities with Spain were accompanied by a long war of attrition in Ireland, fought in appallingly adverse circumstances and one to which Wales was obliged to make a disproportionately onerous contribution.[1] Between them, these campaigns took a devastatingly severe toll in men, equipment, and money. To add to the distresses of the population, the 1590s were a time of economic and social adversity. Harvests were poor, especially between 1594 and 1597; food shortages, high prices, and unemployment were universal; and outbreaks of famine, infection, disease, and high mortality endemic.[2] There was also evidence of political decline. Most of the older generation of statesmen who had served queen and country devotedly were now dead; only Burghley was left, and he was in failing health and would be gone by 1598. The position was complicated further by the problem of the succession to the throne, which the execution of Mary Stuart in 1587 had critically opened up. There was no shortage of rival claimants, though the queen, in spite of her age and increasing frailty, adamantly refused to recognize any one amongst them. The succession was closely linked to the issue of religion, in view of the decisive jurisdiction which the sovereign exercised over the beliefs of his subjects,. In effect, rivalry became narrowed down to three candidates: James VI, king of Scotland; Lady Arabella Stuart; and Philip II of Spain

---

[1] *W 1415–1642*, chap. 15; J. J. N. McGurk, 'A survey of the demands made on Welsh shires . . . for the Irish wars, 1594–1602', *TCS* (1983), 56–68.

[2] *W 1415–1642*, chap. 16.

(or, in practice, his daughter the Infanta).[3] Catholic and Protestant subjects eyed the position with growing apprehension. Neither side could remain unaware that victory for the 'wrong' candidate might mean disaster for the unsuccessful faction. By this time, both the Catholic and Puritan groups were leaderless and divided. The sharp edge of the challenge from each had been blunted as a result of determined governmental action waged against them, though both were capable of fighting on, and neither was prepared to yield to its adversaries. Paradoxically, each side looked hopefully to James VI for more favourable treatment, only to have their teeth set on edge by the bitter flavour of disillusionment.

As far as the recusants were concerned, the defeat of the Armada had made less difference to them than might perhaps have been expected. Before the Spanish fleet had ever set sail, most of the Catholics in England and Wales had looked upon Elizabeth as their rightful ruler and viewed Spanish plans with anxious suspicion. They had continued loyal to the queen in face of intense pressure on her from external Catholic forces. In Ireland, by contrast, there was a significant group among the Gaelic element in that country which was prepared to switch its loyalty to Spain, partly on account of Mary Stuart's bequeathal of her rights to Philip and partly because of the favour shown him by the pope, whose right to the overlordship of Ireland was claimed on the basis of the alleged donation of it by Pope Hadrian IV to Henry II.[4] Nearly all the English and Welsh Catholics contrived harmoniously to combine loyalty to the queen with conformity to their faith. Many heads of Catholic households were able both to keep the authorities at bay and square their consciences by the practice of occasional conformity. They left it to their wives and other female relatives stubbornly to keep away from church. However, there were a few Welsh Catholics whose faith in Spain had been shaken by the defeat of the Armada. As devout a believer as William Griffith was so taken aback by the débâcle of 1588 as to offer Francis Walsingham his services as a spy on his fellow Catholics. Writing from Venice on 10 June 1589, he claimed to know 'the very grounds of some men's undutiful proceedings abroad' and offered to reveal from time to time all the plots which he might discover against the Church and the 'quiet of the realm'. Although Griffith thus volunteered to spy on other Catholic exiles, having been allowed to return home, he was himself again convicted of recusancy in 1592, 1593, and 1594.[5]

[3] J. Hurstfield, 'The succession struggle in late Elizabethan England', S. T. Bindoff *et al.* (eds.), *Elizabethan Government and Society* (London, 1961), pp. 369–96.

[4] R. D. Edwards, ibid., p. 331.

[5] Pugh, *Morgannwg*, XXX. 15–16.

Overall, for the same reason that very few of Griffith's co-believers had supported the Armada, correspondingly few of them were put off by its defeat. In the years that followed 1588, the hard-core recusant minority continued to maintain the congregations of its faithful in what had become over the years its customary sources of vitality. To do so doubtless taxed its resources to the utmost. Nevertheless, it speaks volumes for the devotion not only of priests and seminarists but also of lay devotees, men and women, as well as of the cohesiveness of families and households, that they were able to cling to their beliefs so steadfastly. This in spite of the relatively tight control exerted over them by the authorities of central and local government for many years, and the position of inferiority and stigmatization to which most of them were reduced. In face of ostraciza- tion, fines, and imprisonment, they contrived to soldier on from year to year and from generation to generation. In some instances they raised the banner of resistance in parishes where they had not been detected before.[6] In the county of Denbigh the number of recusants rose from thirteen in 1587 to twenty-six in 1590 and forty-eight in 1592.[7] In Glamorgan, they were uncovered in the 'new' parishes of Pyle, Kenfig, and Cornelly in 1590, and Cadoxton-juxta-Neath in 1596, as well as being reported in Colwin- ston, Llancarfan, Llysworney, St Bride's, Newcastle, and other strong- holds where they had been traced some years before.[8] It may be doubted, though, whether these were new recruits to the faith so much as offenders being newly brought to light as a result of intensified persecution.

It was the familiar foci that still served to attract the recusants and hold them together. They included the homes of sympathetic members of the gentry; earlier holy sites such as chapels, wells, or shrines; and former sacred buildings like monasteries or monastic chapels. Some religious houses had actually been acquired by landed families who either were, or soon became, Catholic in conviction and who transformed the former monasteries into dwelling-places. The abbey of Llantarnam in Monmouth- shire was now the home of the Morgans, one of the most loyal and influential recusant families in the whole of Wales.[9] What had once been Ewenni priory housed the Carne family, whose head, Thomas Carne, was the only justice of the peace prosecuted for recusancy in the diocese of Llandaff, though this did not prevent his being appointed sheriff of his county of Glamorgan on three separate occasions.[10] Slebech in Pembrokeshire, once a house of the Order of St John, was the residence of

---

[6] E. G. Jones, *Cymru a'r Hen Ffydd* (Cardiff, 1951), p. 26.
[7] Pugh, *SWMRS*, III. 51.
[8] Ibid., pp. 54–5.
[9] *DWB*, s.n. Morgan of Llantarnam; cf. Pugh, *SWMRS*, IV. 60–1, 108.
[10] Williams, *GCH*, IV. 234.

the Barlows who, ironically enough in view of their rabidly Protestant origins, had become zealous Catholics.[11] Other dwellings, like Creuddyn in Caernarfonshire, or the Edwards home in Chirk, or the residences of the Herberts in Montgomeryshire, although without earlier monastic connections, continued to offer hospitality to peripatetic priests and the faithful of the locality.[12]

Wells, not surprisingly, were an ongoing source of attraction, not to recusants only but also to many others who were conservative by inclination and habit. In addition to their religious connotations and their long-standing reputation as places of pilgrimage, they still went on performing their traditional functions in the popular mentality as focal points of healing, divining, vow-taking, and other quasi-magical exercises. In north Wales the times fixed for pilgrimages to wells were given out by poets known as *pencars* (an Anglicization of the Welsh term, *pencerdd* ('head poet')), 'who, at the direction of some old gentle woman, do ordinarily give the summons of the time certain for such meetings'.[13] The Protestant cleric-historian, David Powel, denounced a number of wells still being frequented in his own time by many superstitious people 'vt fons diuae Venefredae sacer; fons Dyfnoci in strata cludensi; fanum Aenoe regis in aruonis; fanum Davidis in Demetia' ('such as the well of the holy maiden Winifred; the well of Dyfnog in Dyffryn Clwyd; the shrine of King Owen in Arfon; the shrine of David in Dyfed').[14] A letter written c.1590 testified that Welsh people still went 'in heaps on pilgrimage to the wonted wells and places of superstition', and to chapels or the former sites thereof.[15] Other celebrated wells were those of Beuno, Trillo, Meugan, and Curig; but much the best known of all was St Winifred's Well at Holywell. Not only was it associated with countless medieval pilgrimages, whose fame still endured, but it was also linked with Basingwerk abbey, possessed its own elegant well-chapel, and went on enjoying the reputation of being the most celebrated place of Catholic worship in north Wales, drawing large numbers of pilgrims from neighbouring English counties as well. A manuscript written in Welsh during Elizabeth's reign recounted the innumerable ailments that Winifred was claimed to have cured, even during those wicked days since the new faith had come to the country.[16]

[11] J. M. Cleary, *The Barlow Family of Slebech* (Cardiff, 1956); cf. B. G. Charles, 'The records of Slebech', *NLWJ*, V (1947–8), 179–88.
[12] Jones, *Hen Ffydd*, pp. 18–23, 27–8.
[13] BL, Lansdowne MS., 111, fo. 10.
[14] D. Powel, *Giraldus Itinerarium*, quoted F. Jones, *The Holy Wells of Wales* (Cardiff, 1954), pp. 61–2.
[15] Jones, *Holy Wells*, p. 62.
[16] G. H. Jones, *Celtic Britain and the Celtic Movement* (London, 1912), p. 406, quoting an unspecified Cardiff manuscript.

Devotees took advantage of the convenience as well as the holiness of some of these sites to solemnize christenings, marriages, or burials according to the Catholic rites. The well of St Trillo near Llandrillo in Denbighshire was a favourite place of resort by Catholics and one warmly recommended on religious as well as medical grounds by the Catholic physician, Siôn Dafydd Rhys.[17] Here, at least one secret marriage between Catholic communicants was performed in Latin in 1590 by a priest who preferred to remain unknown to the bridal pair.[18] Doubtless there were other Catholic weddings among those clandestine marriages which so frequently took place in Wales throughout this period.[19] Similarly, the judges of the Carmarthen assize court were informed that in the year 1591, at an old monastic chapel near the house of David ap Ieuan in Margam, a large congregation estimated at some eight score (of whom six score were said to have been women) had assembled to hear mass sung by Morgan Clynnog, nephew of Morys Clynnog.[20] Those attending had clearly been notified of the gathering beforehand, since David William Delahay from Llanegwad in Carmarthenshire had travelled there for two days to take the opportunity of having his child christened. The infant had been carried in his nurse's arms and the ritual had been duly performed.[21] Burials were not infrequently accompanied by Catholic rites and often took place at night to ensure greater secrecy.[22] There were quarrels over such interments in Cardiff; a burial of that kind caused a fracas at Caerleon in 1603;[23] but the most sensational of all was the one that provoked a serious riot just over the Herefordshire border in James I's reign in 1605.[24]

It was evident that if Catholics were to keep up their numbers and their morale, they would be crucially dependent on the zeal and loyalty of their priests, whether drawn from what was left of the Marian priesthood or recruited from the younger generation educated in the Catholic seminaries. In the absence of adequate arrangements for ordaining priests in England and Wales, or effectively directing the activities of those who were available, the ranks of both groups were becoming conspicuously thinner. Death was markedly depleting the numbers of older priests in the 1590s. Although a rare Methuselah like Walter Powell might be able to maintain his presence

[17] Gruffydd, *TCS* (1971), part 2, p. 189.
[18] NLW, Great Sessions, Gaol Files, Denbighshire, 8/2.
[19] 'Godwin's Injunctions . . . 1602', K. Fincham (ed.), *Visitation Articles and Injunctions of the Early Stuart Church* (Church of England Record Soc., London, 1994), p. 2; cf. 'Robert Parry's diary', *AC* (1915), 109–39.
[20] BL, Harleian MS. 6998, fos. 3–16.
[21] Ibid.
[22] L. Owen, 'A seventeenth-century commonplace book', *TCS* (1962), 29.
[23] J. Bossy, *The English Catholic Community, 1570–1850* (London, 1977), p. 141.
[24] R. Mathias, *Whitsun Riot* (London, 1963).

on the scene until 1604, most of his fellows were dead by the end of the sixteenth century. Recruits to the seminaries were also becoming notably fewer on the ground. The contrast between the numbers who were active in Elizabeth's reign and those of the early Stuart era was painfully apparent. Eleven students went from the diocese of Bangor during the former period; only two between 1603 and 1642. St Asaph's numbers dropped from twenty in the former to six in the latter; and Llandaff's from sixteen to four.[25] Not all those recruited were Welsh-speaking; but several even of those who were, were not returned to Wales on the mission, yet non-Welsh speakers would be decidedly less effective there. Others were diverted by the temptations of working in London and south-east England. Thus, of the six or seven Welsh-born Catholic martyrs traced between 1589 and 1598 by T. P. Ellis, all but one of them were detected and executed in or around London.[26]

A number, however, came back to Wales to conduct their activities. They tended to fall into three groups, though they were not so sharply differentiated for there to be no overlap between them. Some were household chaplains or tutors in major aristocratic establishments, of which that of the earl of Worcester at Raglan was the most significant example in Wales. Others migrated between the households of lower-ranking gentry like the Turbervilles of Pen-llin, who gave shelter to two priests in 1595–6, or the Pughs of Creuddyn, where the martyr, William Davies, found a temporary berth. A third group led a more itinerant existence, wandering from place to place between small groups of recusant believers. Thus did Roger Cadwaladr tramp the hills of Monmouthshire for sixteen years, or Morgan Clynnog peregrinate among Catholic centres in Wales for no fewer than thirty-seven years between 1582 and 1619.[27] It was a thankless task, trudging the countryside in disguise, in constant fear of traitors, government agents, and informers, evading the unwelcome attentions of justices and constables, being interrogated and examined, in and out of prison, with the shadow of persecution and even death constantly hovering over them.[28] Given the fewness of the priests and the pressures put upon them, it becomes difficult not to wonder how regularly they were able to conduct services and administer the sacraments, especially to the smaller and more remote Catholic groups.

Between the sometimes haphazard and infrequent visits of priests, their congregations must have had to look to the untiring labours of the

[25] Cleary, *Blackfriars* (1957), 117.

[26] T. P. Ellis, *The Catholic Martyrs of Wales* (London, 1933), pp. 44, 67.

[27] J. M. Cleary, *A Checklist of Welsh Students in the Seminaries* (Cardiff, 1958), pp. 17, 21.

[28] For a remarkable account of such an existence, written by the priest himself, *John Gerard: The Autobiography of an Elizabethan*, tr. P. Caraman (London, 1951).

The Reformation Ensured, 1589–1603

littérateurs and manuscript copyists in their midst. Such enthusiasts certainly continued their efforts unflaggingly during these years. Pre-eminent among them was Llywelyn Siôn, poet and scribe, a yeoman of the parish of Laleston in Glamorgan.[29] The contemporary gaol files of the Great Sessions records leave us in no doubt that he was only too well known to the persecuting authorities and regularly summoned to appear before them during the years 1587 (twice), 1590 (twice), 1591, and 1593.[30] None the less, he persisted in diligently copying his manuscripts, and it is to his fluent pen that we owe a large body of medieval religious texts, not to mention the only complete copy of the sixteenth-century Catholic classic, *Drych Cristianogawl*, which is in existence. He was also the author of a number of poems which have come down to us. Though the content of most of them is non-controversial, there is one in which he sharply contrasts the truth proclaimed by the four evangelists with the rank heresies purveyed by Luther, Zwingli, Calvin, and Beza.[31] Other Catholic poets of these years whose work has survived were William Davies, the martyr of Anglesey, Mathew Turberville, Siôn Morris, and Edward Dafydd. These literary effusions were greatly treasured and widely circulated among the Catholic faithful. The Turbervilles cherished such texts in their home, John Games of Brecon was accused in Star Chamber of reading them, and John Edwards of Chirk is known to have read them to his tenants when priests were not available. Even John Penry had been obliged to admit that they were among the very few effective popular sources of religious instruction available to ordinary people.[32]

All the while, the Privy Council found it difficult to control the recusant population, especially in more inaccessible areas such as Wales. In spite of the regular reporting of recusants to the authorities, the executions and imprisonments imposed upon them, and even the martyrdoms of priests, it proved to be impossible completely to trample down the stout defences which Catholics had been able to put up in the counties. The greatest handicap was the sheer remoteness of the more distant shires from London – or even Ludlow – and the inability of the Privy Council to keep a tight enough hold on the justices of the peace and other officials. In 1591 the council found it necessary to alert its daughter-body at Ludlow that many recusants were escaping over the border from England into Wales and the

[29] G. J. Williams, *Traddodiad Llenyddol Morgannwg* (Cardiff, 1948), pp. 157–60; 176–8; Lewis, *GCH*, IV. 550–4.

[30] Pugh, *SWMRS*, III. 53–5, where he appears as 'Llywelyn John'.

[31] *Hen Gwndidau, Carolau a Chywyddau*, ed. L. J. Hopkin-James and T. C. Evans (Bangor, 1914), pp. 98–9.

[32] John Penry, *Three Treatises concerning Wales*, ed. David Williams (Cardiff, 1960), pp. 34–5.

Marches. It warned in sombre tones of 'great backsliding in religion in these parts, and especially in the confines of the shires between England and Wales, as Monmouthshire and the skirts of the shires of Wales bounding upon them' and that 'there are many runners abroad and carriers of mass books, super altars, all kinds of massing apparel, singing bread, and all other things used at or in the singing of mass'.[33] These reports were borne out in a number of Monmouthshire parishes by the returns of the Exchequer Recusant Rolls in 1592–3, when the lands of nineteen inhabitants of the county were seized for their inability to pay fines imposed upon them. Another thirty-eight were threatened with the same punishment unless they paid the fine. Here then, within the same year, fifty-seven fairly substantial landowners were singled out in the single county of Monmouthshire.[34] The Council in the Marches, on its part, reported in 1592 that people in Carmarthenshire still repaired to places where in the past there had been pilgrimages, images, and offerings.[35]

This same year (1592) saw the Privy Council embark on a process of clamping down on recusants. In the following spring, Parliament enacted a new law declaring that every individual over 16 years of age converted to recusancy was to be confined to his residence and to a five-mile radius around it. Any violation was, theoretically, to lead to the sequestration of all the offender's goods and chattels and, during his lifetime, the sequestration of his lands.[36]

Particular pressure was applied by the Privy Council on the two sensitive nodal points in the defences of Wales – Anglesey and Milford Haven. Strange as it may seem, although Anglesey was regarded as being so vulnerable to invasion, there was not much evidence of recusancy there before the 1590s. In March 1592, however, a Catholic priest, William Davies, together with four would-be student companions, and Robert Pugh (a member of the recusant family of Creuddyn), were arrested at Holyhead. Davies, the grandson of Dafydd Nantglyn, the most famous Welsh harpist of his day, was himself referred to by a seventeenth-century poet, Gwilym Pugh, as 'seren ei wlad' ('star of his country').[37] He may earlier have been a student at Oxford, but had certainly studied at Douai between 1582 and 1585.[38] Following his return to Wales in 1585, he had been very active in missionary work and in recruiting potential priests. He had also been involved in setting up the secret press at Rhiwledin in

---

[33] *HMC, Hatfield MSS.*, XI. 466.
[34] Pugh, *SWMRS*, IV. 59–65.
[35] *W 1415–1642*, p. 327.
[36] *Statutes of the Realm* (11 vols. London, 1810–28), IV. 843–6.
[37] D. A. Thomas, *The Welsh Elizabethan Catholic Martyrs* (Cardiff, 1971), chap. 5.
[38] P. J. Crean, *Sir William Dai* (Dublin, 1958).

1586–7. His later arrest was brought about by an ardent Anglesey Protestant, one Foulk Thomas, in the teeth of a good deal of local resistance. Davies was brought for trial in July 1592 before Hugh Bellot, bishop of Bangor, two assize judges, and others, and found guilty.[39] No sentence was immediately pronounced on him – possibly because the government was at that time in two minds over the desirability of executing Catholic priests.[40] He was, therefore, kept in prison, 'a dark and stinking place', but he still contrived to maintain a regular round of worship and devotion. It obviously made a highly favourable impression and was later described in a memorial to Davies as being such a way of life that 'all of them felt that theirs was not a life lived in the sadness of a gaol but one lived in the joy of heaven'.[41] During his imprisonment Davies also managed to compose Catholic poetry, including the celebrated 'Carol Santaidd i'r Grawys' (Holy Carol for Lent).[42] His second trial, in July 1593, was carried out on the orders of the Privy Council, which now appeared to have decided to give it as much adverse publicity as possible in the surrounding area. Davies was found guilty and was executed with the usual gruesome accompaniments. This was in sharp contrast to an earlier decision of 1587 which had condemned the Welsh priest, John Bennett, to a term of imprisonment only. Leading Catholics from north Wales, like Robert Pugh and John Edwards, made determined efforts to secure bloodstained relics of the dead martyr.[43] The fate of William Davies, like that of Richard White in 1584, was evidently envisaged as a dreadful warning to all Catholic sympathizers in Anglesey and the nearby mainland. It may conceivably have fulfilled the purpose for which it was intended, since no further instances of recusants were recorded in Anglesey. Some indication of the impression that Davies's death created among those sympathetic to the old religion may be derived, however, from the diary of a Welsh lawyer, Robert Parry. The only occasions on which he revealed his Catholic proclivities were when he recorded the martyrdoms of White and Davies.[44]

The loyalty of the inhabitants of those shires adjoining Milford Haven was also something of a doubtful quantity and was the subject of close scrutiny by the Privy Council. The Council's nerves were already on edge as a result of the long-running feuds between Bishop Marmaduke Middleton

[39] Ibid., p. 30; Thomas, *Catholic Martyrs*, pp. 61–2.
[40] Hurstfield in Bindoff, *Elizabethan Government*, p. 382.
[41] Thomas, *Catholic Martyrs*, p. 283; cf. the Welsh priest who gained access to recusant prisoners in Chester gaol and said mass to them, W. R. Wark, *Elizabethan Recusancy in Cheshire* (Manchester, 1971), pp. 71–3, 106.
[42] R. G. Gruffydd, 'Carol Santaidd i'r Grawys o waith y Tad William Davies', *TCHS* (1967), 37–46.
[43] Thomas, *Catholic Martyrs*, p. 64.
[44] Parry, *AC* (1915), 114, 119.

and some of the most prominent local gentry. Concerned that recusants might take heart from such rifts among leading Protestants and worried about the maritime threat from Spain and the hostilities in Ireland, the council ordered in 1592 that much stricter control should be exercised over those who repaired by night and day unto 'certain places where in times past there have been pilgrimages, images, or offerings . . . in great numbers, both of men and women, a thing intolerable to be permitted after so long time preaching of the gospel'.[45] In July it issued orders to a company of men to proceed to the widely renowned well at Capel Meugan in Pembrokeshire and pull it down completely, stone by stone. They were utterly to forbid any resort to it thereafter, 'by night or day . . . in superstitious manner'.[46] At much the same time a commission was issued to John Gwyn Williams to suppress pilgrimages and 'idolatrous places', and particularly Ffynnon Gwyddfaen at Llandeilo Fawr. At least one of the local justices of the peace, Morgan Jones of Tre-gib, was described as a 'man very backward in religion, not having received the sacrament for ten years and a harbourer of recusants and seminary priests'.[47] Jones was clearly reluctant to take action against those who, according to him, 'had gone to the well, hoping by the help of God thereby to have their health', and he discharged them. No fewer than two hundred people in all had been involved in what appeared to be a well-organized pilgrimage, and, two years later, in 1594–5, Jones ended up in Star Chamber to answer for his sympathies with the Catholics.[48]

While all this was going on, the earl of Pembroke, president of the Council in the Marches, had written to the queen in 1593 to inform her that the inhabitants of the shires around Milford Haven were 'in religion generally ill-affected, as may appear by their use of popish pilgrimages, their harbouring of mass and priests, their retaining of superstitious ceremonies and the increase of recusants'.[49] Round about the same time, in 1594, a foreign commentator also described 'most of the inhabitants from the coast of Wales' as being 'in religion Catholics', and added, 'this country is strongly Catholic'.[50] Morgan Jones, JP, certainly maintained his partiality for the old faith without being removed from the commission of the peace on account of it. Some years later, in 1600–1, he was again brought to Star Chamber on a charge of sympathy for recusants.[51] On this

---

[45] *APC*, XXII (1591–2), 544–5.

[46] NLW, Vairdre Book.

[47] PRO, STA C 5, G45/3.

[48] Ibid.

[49] *HMC, Salisbury MSS.*, XIII. 478.

[50] Jones, *Pilgrim Movement*, p. 3.

[51] PRO, STA C 5, V5/20.

occasion it was Sir John Vaughan who brought the accusations against him, though it has to be admitted that they smack as much of local political feuds as they do of religious antipathy. In spite of these alarmist reports the main sources of our knowledge of recusants – the Recusant Rolls and the Great Sessions Gaol Files – reveal the presence of only a very few recusants in south-west Wales.[52]

The year 1596 was another when the threat of a possible Spanish invasion made the ranks of officialdom distinctly uneasy. The county of Monmouthshire reported a prevalence of recusancy within its borders which severely limited the choice of officials.[53] In neighbouring Breconshire there was already a violent quarrel raging between the influential local gentry family of Games and the municipal authorities of the borough of Brecon.[54] To add weight to allegations being made against John Games, JP, he was further accused of being 'evil disposed' in religion, of reading Welsh 'superstitious' books, repeating 'vain songs and rhymes' of a recusant nature, and creating disturbances in church by playing with little children.[55] In the same year, the presence of two active seminary priests, Morgan Clynnog and one Fisher, at the Pen-llin home of the notorious Glamorgan recusant family of Turberville, was reported to the Privy Council. It led to the instant dispatch of two justices of the peace there to search out 'by secret and discreet plans' not only the two priests but also 'treacherous books and correspondence'.[56] No fewer than ten members of the Turberville family were brought before the Great Sessions as a result. Two of them, Jenkin Turberville and his son Lewis, were to be incarcerated in the Tower for some time, Jenkin being rigorously examined while in custody, a process which may have hastened his death. Two other members of the family, James and Lewis, died of gaol fever at Cardiff in 1598.[57] Many other recusants were similarly confined to prison at a time when a gaol sentence was sometimes not far removed from a death penalty, so pestilential and overcrowded were gaols like the one at Cardiff, or that at Beaumaris, where William Davies was imprisoned, in the 1590s.

Late in the decade, as it became apparent that the queen was unlikely to have much longer to live, the question of the succession to the throne necessarily loomed larger in men's minds. Catholics inevitably hoped for a

[52] H. A. Lloyd, *The Gentry of South-west Wales, 1540–1640* (Cardiff, 1968), pp. 189–94.

[53] W. R. Trimble, *The Catholic Laity in Elizabethan England* (Cambridge, Mass., 1964), p. 168.

[54] PRO, STA C 5, W38/27; W64/3.

[55] Ibid., W69/19.

[56] *APC*, XXVI (1596–7), 310–11, 378.

[57] A. L. Evans, *The Story of Sker House* (Port Talbot, 1956), pp. 15–16; *Records of the County Borough of Cardiff*, ed. J. H. Matthews (6 vols. Cardiff, 1898–1911), II. 166–72.

Catholic successor or, at the very least, for one who might be tolerantly disposed towards their faith. They were, however, irreconcilably divided over the choice of a potential candidate. The majority tended to favour Philip II's daughter, on grounds both of religion and because Mary Stuart had in her will bequeathed her own claims to the Spanish king.[58] It is interesting to observe that the Spaniards, backing her claim, sought to persuade the Welsh that when they (the Spaniards) conquered the kingdom the Welsh should be 'lords as they were before and revenge themselves of all the injuries' they had received at the hands of the English, 'by whom they were kept in tyranny and despised and scorned, that it is wonder that such valorous and noble people of truth and antiquity can endure it'.[59] Such propaganda seems, however, not to have made much impression on the majority of Welsh Catholics.

A smaller but articulate faction argued in favour of James VI's claim but would also have wished to arrive at some understanding with him which would have allowed them a position of tolerance not unlike that achieved by the Huguenots in France. That the majority should favour the Spanish claim was understandable. The opinion expressed by so eminent a Catholic as Sir Francis Englefield as early as September 1596 was that

> without the support and troops of Spain it is scarcely probable that the Catholic religion will ever be restored and established in that country [England and Wales]. Even the seminaries, powerful as they are in preparing men's minds for a change, must fail to complete their object without the aid of temporal force.[60]

To complicate matters still further, the dissensions over the succession became bound up with the feud between the earl of Essex and Sir Robert Cecil. Essex could command a considerable measure of support in Wales, and among his backers was an influential Catholic coterie in Monmouthshire. This group was opposed both to Cecil and the earl of Pembroke, president of the council in the Marches and opponent of Essex.[61] Evidence of the group's support for Essex comes from a remarkable Welsh ode (*awdl*) written by a Monmouthshire Catholic, Edward Dafydd.[62] It called on the Welsh to rise in open rebellion and was circulating freely among the

---

[58] Hurstfield, *Elizabethan Government*, pp. 372–3.
[59] PRO, SP 99, Bundle 2, 117.
[60] A. O. Meyer, *England and the Catholic Church under Queen Elizabeth* (London, 1910), p. xiv n. 3.
[61] *W 1415–1642*, pp. 346–7.
[62] R. G. Gruffydd, 'Awdl wrthryfelgar gan Edward Dafydd', *LlC*, V (1958–9), 155–63; VIII (1964–5), 65–9.

numerous body of Catholics in the county. The poem was regarded by William Morgan, bishop of Llandaff, as being sufficiently threatening for him to send a copy of it to Archbishop Whitgift who, in turn, sent it on to Cecil. The poet flatly rejected the pernicious new doctrines of the 'Ammonite destroyer' and appealed unashamedly to the Cymric pride of the Welsh in their ancient Catholic religious inheritance. It did not hesitate to play upon the strings of their age-old prejudice against the 'traitorous Saxons' and ended with a rousing appeal that they take up arms for 'the holy mysteries of the mass' and thereby win an 'unfading crown' in the battle against the 'loathsome heretics'.[63] All to little avail, however, when the die came to be cast! Although Essex was not without supporters in Wales, they were nothing like influential enough in numbers or weaponry to carry the day.[64] Even if they had been, it is doubtful whether the earl himself would have wished, or been able, to do much for the recusants. As it was, when his rebellion proved disastrous, a spy reported that its failure made it somewhat easier to impose religious conformity in Wales. It removed an influence which had previously been employed to ensure immunity for some of the gentry, allowing them to use their homes for the celebration of mass and the administration of the Catholic sacraments.[65] When the critical moment of Elizabeth's death arrived in March 1603, the Welsh Catholics, like their fellows elsewhere, were found wanting in power, organization, and unity, and were unable effectively to press their point of view.

The truth was that by 1603 the exertions of toiling for more than a generation against a mountain of difficulties had taken their toll of recusant energies and morale. Even the most zealous among them – men of the calibre of Sir Thomas Tresham or Edward Morgan of Llantarnam – cherished a profound respect for established order and a notable dread of public anarchy or foreign domination. Yet recusancy could be propagated only in secret and outside the law. It was smeared with suggestions of disloyalty, subversion, and conspiracy. It tended to debar men from positions of authority and brought them in danger of raids by pursuivants, damaging fines, and long imprisonments, even if the evasions of the recusants themselves, the favours of their friends, and the inadequacies of the fining system were responsible for alleviating much of the rigour of the penal statutes. Recusant couples who married outside the Anglican Church according to the Catholic rite had reason to fear for the validity of their

---

[63] For extensive translations of the poem, G. D. Owen, *Elizabethan Wales: The Social Scene* (Cardiff, 1962), pp. 218–19.
[64] A. H. Dodd, 'North Wales in the Essex revolt of 1601', *EHR*, LIX (1944), 348–70.
[65] Trimble, *The Catholic Laity in Elizabethan England*, p. 173.

marriages and the legitimacy of their offspring if the latter's births were not recorded in the parish registers. They also had difficulty in educating their children as they grew up. What was more serious was that by 1603 there was a worrying shortage of Catholic priests. Nearly all those ordained in Mary's reign or earlier were dead, and out of 804 seminarists, perhaps no more than 471 were active during Elizabeth's reign, and more than a quarter of these were executed.[66] There were too few to be able to take their message beyond existing recusants and crypto-Catholics to the broad masses. Most of the priests at work were confined very largely to gentry houses, and the Catholicism they ministered had become a seigneurially structured affair. Its impact was confined very largely to the well-to-do, leaving any others ticking over gently at a level suited to a preliterate mentality. The illiteracy of many believers was nearly as serious a problem for recusants as it was for Protestants. Without an active role by priests in their midst, there was little more than vestigial superstition left amongst the masses.

As far as Wales was concerned, there were additional difficulties created by the complications of language and nationality. Although a number of recusant priests were proud of their 'British' antecedents and eager to exercise their ability to communicate in the Welsh language, few were directed back to Wales on mission. The Welsh, moreover, had little or no part to play in the planning of Counter-Reformation activity in England and Wales. The ablest of the Welsh exiles in this respect, Owen Lewis, was held in some suspicion by Cardinal Allen and others, and largely excluded from the direction of affairs. Even the Jesuit, Robert Parsons, complained that in many parts of Wales and the north, where the people, in spite of or because of their 'spissa ignorantia' ('dense ignorance'), were most likely to respond, not enough seminary priests had ventured.[67] Furthermore, as has already been seen, the number of priests in Wales had fallen drastically by the early Stuart era.

In spite of all these difficulties and disadvantages, however, the Catholic population succeeded in keeping up its numbers remarkably well in those districts recognized as its centres of strength. In 1603 a return for all the Welsh dioceses gave a total of 808 avowed recusants, as opposed to a nominal churchgoing population of 212,450.[68] Broken down as between dioceses the statistics were: Bangor 38,840 communicants, 32 recusants (0.082 per cent); St Asaph 53,188 and 250 (0.470 per cent); Llandaff 37,100 and 381 (1.026 per cent); and St David's 83,322 and 145 (0.174 per cent).

---

[66] J. Guy, *Tudor England* (Oxford, 1988), p. 301.
[67] Bossy, *Catholic Community*, p. 223.
[68] BL, Harleian MS., 280, fos. 162ᵛ–64.

The figures given for objectors probably need to be multiplied by about four or five in order to obtain something like an accurate impression of the real numbers of recusants. In addition to those recorded, there were likely to have been a comparable number of Catholics who did not communicate or were church papists. Additionally, it would not be unreasonable to allow another 50 per cent for inefficiency or neglect on the part of those compiling the return, and a further 40 per cent for children.[69] That would give in all about 3,500 for Wales. Such a figure may seem very small as the proportion of open Catholic objectors in relation to the total population in a proverbially conservative country like Wales. It is important to notice, however, that as compared with all the dioceses in England and Wales, the two Welsh dioceses of Llandaff and St Asaph were third and fourth behind Chester and Durham in relation to the number of recusants per parish. The diocese of Llandaff had a higher proportion of recusants to Anglican churchgoers than any other diocese in England or Wales, while the county of Monmouth, in relation to its area, was perhaps the most strongly recusant shire in the kingdom, having one convicted recusant to every 50 Anglican communicants, and 117 convicted recusant households in every 1,000, as compared with Lancashire, which came next, with 112 convicted households in every 1,000.[70]

The largest concentrations of Welsh recusants were still to be found in the long-standing strongholds of the north-east and the south-east. The high figures for Flintshire and Denbighshire owed much to the fabulous esteem in which St Winifred's Well was held and to the proximity of the strongly recusant centres in the diocese of Chester. Together, they formed a single area of activity, within which priests moved fairly freely. The even higher figures for Monmouthshire similarly owed much to the Catholic bastions over the border in Herefordshire, as well as to the stout protection offered by the families at Raglan and Llantarnam. The recusants enjoyed the advantage of having antiquity and precedent on their side; of sustaining an earlier tradition and not having to create a new one. But, without a Catholic sovereign on the throne, they had virtually no hope of re-establishing their Church within the kingdom, or reversing the slowly rising tide of Protestantism. When eventually such a ruler emerged in the person of James II, he came far too late to produce the desired effect. In the mean time, however, as an embattled and disadvantaged minority, they had succeeded surprisingly well in holding true to their faith. For much of the first half of the seventeenth century, they repeatedly awakened nightmares of alarm in the imagination of the Protestant population, who could never forget that

[69] Bossy, *Catholic Community*, pp. 191–2.
[70] Pugh, *SWMRS*, IV. 60.

domestic recusants represented what they saw as only the native stalking-horse of the formidable external powers of the pope and the great Catholic kingdoms in Europe. It took the effects of Puritan persecution during the Civil Wars and Commonwealth and the Anglican suppression of the Restoration to succeed in effectively reducing the hardy Catholic minority. As late as 1717, nevertheless, a list existed giving the names of no fewer than 440 Catholics in the single county of Monmouthshire.[71]

Whatever the hardships confronting the recusants may have been, the Anglican Church, too, faced some grave problems during these years. The worst scandals were those associated with the downfall of Bishop Middleton of St David's. When he had first arrived in south-west Wales from Ireland he had come bearing warm commendations from Archbishop Loftus and the Lord Deputy as to his 'worthiness' and his 'zeal and honest conversation'.[72] His earliest actions seemed to bear out these encomiums. His report and injunctions of 1583 were courageously outspoken in their condemnation of superstition and ignorance in his diocese and fervent in their attempts at reform. Within a few years, none the less, relations between him and the clergy and laity had become strained to the point where physical assaults were made on him and discreditable charges laid against him in the Court of High Commission.[73] In the Martin Marprelate Tracts of 1588 he was listed among the episcopal 'dunces' and accused of ignorance and bigamy.[74] Middleton himself retorted that all the enmity shown against him had been whipped up by those who had cause to fear his attempts to reform them.[75] But further allegations were brought against him in the Court of Star Chamber in 1590–1. Although he counter-attacked indignantly, he was convicted of contriving and publishing a forged will.[76] He was once more brought before the Court of High Commission and this time was found guilty of dilapidation and the embezzlement of church property. A commission entrusted to Edmund Price to inquire into the matter found that Middleton had committed fraudulent behaviour at St David's, and especially at Brecon.[77] So serious were his misdemeanours that he was formally degraded from his episcopal office and died soon after.[78]

[71] Ibid.
[72] F. O. White, *Lives of the Elizabethan Bishops* (London, 1898), pp. 253–9.
[73] Ibid., p. 257.
[74] W. Pierce, *The Mar-Prelate Tracts, 1588, 1589* (London, 1911), pp. 90, 95, 186.
[75] *HMC, Hatfield MSS.*, II. 526.
[76] PRO, STA C 5, S3/15; 3/29; G15/23; G2/8.
[77] White, *Eliz. Bishops*, pp. 257–8.
[78] Ibid., p. 259.

The fundamental hindrances to reform, however, went much deeper than the failings of an unworthy individual. They remained what they had been since the beginnings of the Reformation: the poverty of the Church in Wales and the inequitable distribution of its resources; the inadequacies of many of the lower clergy; the slowness of the publication of Welsh books; the illiteracy of the population at large; and the obdurate persistence of indifference, superstition, and Catholic residualism in their midst.

The changes associated with the Reformation had led to far less money being spent on the fabric of the churches, which in many instances were in a deplorable state of repair. There were no longer any chantries, religious guilds, or fraternities to contribute towards the upkeep of churches and services; nor were there any shrines, paintings, images, or relics to attract the offerings of throngs of pilgrims. The officially ordered removal of many of the most attractive features of medieval worship – vestments, lights, plate, jewellery, roodlofts, and the like – had encouraged a general attitude of negligence towards the maintenance of ecclesiastical structures. Bequests in wills, though they still continued,[79] were much less munificent than they had been; in 1603 Bishop Godwin of Llandaff believed it to be desirable to exhort his clergy, 'so often as you are called upon to any sick person of ability, especially when they shall make their wills', to 'put them in mind . . . of how acceptable a thing it shall be to Almighty God to contribute towards the sustentation of his house'.[80] The lay patrons into whose possession those churches formerly appropriated to religious houses had passed, were oftentimes reluctant to spend money on the fulfilment of their responsibility for maintaining chancels. The outcome was that 'many churches and chancels lie unrepaired'.[81] Even the cathedrals were in a dilapidated state. In 1594 Bishop Babington and his canons, deeply distressed by Llandaff cathedral's 'ruinous and decayed state', 'more like a desolate and profane place than like a house of prayer', gratefully accepted William Mathew's offer to have the north side paved and the windows repaired.[82] Just ten years later, however, Bishop Godwin's injunctions in 1603 referred to the cathedral as 'fallen into such decay as 500 marks will not repair the same, that it must needs fall to the ground without some extraordinary relief'.[83] The state of the cathedral and its finances continued to be a source of deep anxiety to the chapter for some generations to come.[84]

[79] W. K. Jordan, *Philanthropy in England, 1480–1660* (London, 1959).

[80] *Visitation Articles and Injunctions of the Early Stuart Church*, ed. K. Fincham (Church of England Record Soc., London, 1994), p. 2; cf. Gruffydd, *JHSCW*, IV. 19.

[81] *Visitation Articles*, p. 1; Gruffydd, *JHSCW*, IV. 18.

[82] Williams, *GCH*, IV. 226–7.

[83] Fincham, *Visitation Articles*, p. 2; Gruffydd, *JHSCW*, IV. 19.

[84] *Cardiff Recs.* V. 8–10.

At St David's it was the episcopal residences which gave rise to the greatest concern. When Middleton went there in 1583, he reported 'all his houses, except one, down to the ground; and that one in most extreme ruin . . . so that neither could he live with credit, nor keep hospitality'.[85] He spent much time away from his diocese and seems to have done nothing to improve the state of the buildings. When Anthony Rudd took over from him, he complained that he found the bishop's palaces so 'ruinous and decayed for want of reparation that they were not fit for any man, especially a bishop, to dwell and keep hospitality in'.[86]

The sole bishop's palace at St Asaph was in such a tumbledown condition that the bishop could not live in it and was forced to take up residence in Plas Gwyn, the archdeacon's house in the parish of Diserth.[87] It was to William Morgan's credit that, although a relatively poor man, he not only began the work of restoring the palace but also renovated the cathedral roof at his own expense.[88]

Bangor cathedral seems to have been in no better state than that of St Asaph. Early in the seventeenth century (1611), a letter from Bishop Henry Rowlands referred to the 'lamentable ruin' there and called upon a number of his clergy to assist him with financial contributions in the task of reroofing the building.[89]

In spite of the poverty of the Church, the higher clergy, who were nearly always pluralists, usually managed to live fairly comfortably. Those who farmed their own glebe and who were able to collect all the tithe due to them, or had leased out these resources at competitive rates, may not have found the pressures of contemporary inflation bearing too heavily upon them. The value of such livings was estimated to have increased three- or fourfold during the period, which was about in line with the rise in prices generally.[90] The income of their incumbents was, consequently, elastic enough to offset the worst effects of inflation, though they had always to contend with the reluctance of the laity to pay tithe and their continual attempts to encroach upon glebe lands. Bishop Godwin complained that as a result of this, much land was 'daily embezzled from the church'.[91] Some of the incumbents of the better livings were men of means. Hugh Price, treasurer of David's, died a wealthy man, who was able to leave money to

[85] E. Yardley, *Menevia Sacra* (*Arch. Camb.* supplement, 1927), p. 399.
[86] P. Hembry, 'Episcopal palaces, 1535 to 1660', in E. W. Jones *et al.* (eds.), *Wealth and Power in Tudor England* (London, 1978), p. 150.
[87] *W and R*, p. 196.
[88] Ibid., pp. 196–7.
[89] NLW, Bangor Misc. MSS., 23. p. 71; M. L. Clarke, *Bangor Cathedral* (Cardiff, 1969), p. 24.
[90] Williams, *Rural Society*, p. 187.
[91] *Visitation Articles*, p. 2; Gruffydd, *JHSCW*, IV. 19.

found Jesus College, Oxford.[92] Morgan Nicholas, who ended his days as archdeacon of Llandaff, when he died in 1598, was in a position to bequeath to his wife, sons, and other relatives valuable landed interests and livestock, goods and chattels worth £143, including household possessions worth £35, and books and apparel valued at £5.[93] Lewis Philip, parson of Michaelston-super-Ely (d. 1611) never became a member of the cathedral clergy, but he must have lived and farmed on the scale of a wealthy yeoman, if not a member of the minor gentry, with his sixteen kine, thirty-four head of cattle, fifty-nine sheep, five horses and mares, household goods worth £10 and total assets of the order of £100.[94] Robert Wall, rector of Port Eynon (d. 1587) left an unusually lengthy and detailed introduction to his will, in which he bequeathed his soul into the

> most sacred hands of Almighty God, my good creator, firmly believing to be saved by the precious blood shedding of our most sweet Lord, redeemer and only Saviour, Jesus Christ, the Second Person in the Trinity, and by no other merit or means whatsoever besides him and his most holy ordinance, who said, John xiv, 6, 'Nemo venit ad patrem nisi per me' [No one cometh unto the Father but by me].[95]

He, like a number of contemporary Welsh clerics, left books in his will but without specifying their titles.

The real economic squeeze came on those who were vicars of poor livings or, worse, stipendiary curates hired by lay impropriators or even tight-fisted clerics. Llandaff had a higher proportion of such members of the clerical proletariat than any other Welsh see. As it happens, there survives an episcopal return of 1603 for that diocese,[96] which provides a graphic snapshot of the sort of conditions which prevailed in livings of the kind. There were thirty-four impropriations listed for the county of Glamorgan, twenty-four of them endowed vicarages and ten of them stipendiary vicarages, making up in all about one-third of the livings of the diocese. Their total value to impropriators (£1,185. 10s. 0d.) was worth two and a half times the share received by the incumbents (£455. 16s. 0d.). The list of impropriators reads like a roll-call of leading gentry families: Herberts, Mansels, Carnes, Stradlings, Lewises, Mathews, and the rest.

---

[92] G. Williams, 'Hugh Price, founder of Jesus College, Oxford', *Brycheiniog*, XXV (1992–3), 57–66.

[93] *Cardiff Recs.* III. 112–15.

[94] NLW, Llandaff PR, 1611.

[95] NLW, Brecon Probate Index, II. 492; cf. also E. J. L. Cole, 'Radnorshire wills', *Trans. Rads. HS*, XXXVII (1967), 47–50; 'Border priests', *JHSCW*, IX (1959), 23–31.

[96] BL, Harleian MS., 595, fos. 1–8; *Cartae et Alia Munimenta . . .*, ed. G. T. Clark (6 vols. Cardiff, 1910), VI. 2144–8.

Heading the list was Anthony Mansel, impropriator of St John's and St Mary's Cardiff, Llantrisant, Llanblethian, Cowbridge, Penmark, and St Mary Hill, worth in all £269 a year. Close on his heels came Sir William Herbert, with Cadoxton-juxta-Neath, Eglwysilan, Penarth, Lavernock, and Llanedern, worth £258 a year. Half of the vicars had incomes worth one-third and more of the value of the living. In many others the disparity between the impropriator's share and the incumbent's was very wide. The Cardiff livings were worth £100 to Anthony Mansel but the vicar received only £20. Eglwysilan brought William Herbert £120, leaving £15 for its parish priest; and Henry Dodington raked in £100 from Margam and paid its curate £10. In one instance, at Uchelolau (Highlight), Christopher St John would not pay a curate at all, 'so the parish hath been without service these thirty years and more, and the church almost fallen down'.[97] What made the situation still more worrying was that the impropriated livings were among the best in Glamorgan, in market-towns and centres of population like Cardiff, Cowbridge, Llantwit, Neath, Aberafan, and Swansea, and ought to have been supporting an able and well-educated clergy. Nor do the figures given above tell the whole story, for they reveal nothing about those unfortunates who were entirely dependent on the miserable pittances they usually received in the way of stipends only.

Poverty continued to prevail among the lower clergy in all parts of Wales. Consequently, the long-familiar deficiencies remained unremedied and all too plainly apparent. A number of the most talented Welsh graduates never returned to their home country. The miserable remuneration on offer for the poorest livings was quite insufficient to attract men of education and ability. John Penry, of course, sweepingly dismissed all Welsh incumbents as 'known adulterers, drunkards, thieves, "roisters", most abominable swearers'.[98] The unlearned curates of north Wales have already been referred to, as have Huw Lewys's criticisms of those of the north-west, and Middleton's of his problem children. Sir William Meredith of Stansty declared that he could not remember a 'learned or godly minister at any time in Bromfield and Yale'.[99] If and when wretched curates could be induced to accept such poverty-stricken livings, they ordinarily found it necessary to take on more than one at a time, with the usual results for the unfortunate parishioners over whom they euphemistically exercised 'cure of souls'.

When Bishop Godwin came to issue his injunctions in 1603,[100] he obviously had in his diocese those 'dumb dogs' with whom Huw Lewys and

[97] Ibid.
[98] J. Penry, *Three Treatises concerning Wales*, ed. D. Williams (Cardiff, 1960), pp. 63, 66.
[99] *W 1415–1642*, p. 326.
[100] *Visitation Articles*, pp. 1–2; Gruffydd, *JHSCW*, IV. 17–20.

John Penry were familiar and had to insist on quarterly sermons being preached – though with what effect it is impossible to tell. He also tried to ensure that the widespread practice of allowing excommunicates to attend divine service was stopped and the common practice of performing clandestine marriages ended. No doubt the fault for parents being lax about bringing their children to be catechized lay largely with them, but part of the blame may well have been attributable to the idleness of clergymen. In these circumstances, it is hardly surprising that Godwin should believe it essential to condemn the outrages frequently committed against the clergy in his diocese, not only by means of 'reproachful and contemptuous speeches' but also in the form of physical assaults.[101] Although the bishop made no mention of recusants in his injunctions, the large numbers of them who continued to flourish in his diocese were unlikely to be weaned away from their 'errors' or be attracted to their parish churches by inadequate Anglican clergymen of the sort he describes. Nor were those careless semi-pagans in his diocese who, in his words, everywhere 'horribly prophaned' the sabbath by playing unlawful games at the time of divine service, often in the churchyard itself, likely to be susceptible to appeals from clergy for whom they had minimal respect.[102] A whole generation later, *c.*1630, reforming authors like Vicar Prichard, Robert Llwyd, Rowland Vaughan, or Oliver Thomas, would still be lamenting those vestiges of medieval practice and belief they found it so difficult to uproot and the widespread apathy and ignorance of their congregations.[103]

The failure of church services to make much impact was made worse by the acute scarcity of Welsh books which might have helped in the process of domestic instruction and devotion. In the Breconshire parish of Talachddu, for example, out of twenty-five books available for the parishioners to read, only three were in Welsh for the largely monoglot Welsh population.[104] The keynote of the sponsors of the first popular edition of the Welsh Bible – the 5*s.* one of 1630 – was that it must be a familiar friend in the home: 'it must dwell in thy chamber, under thine own roof – as thy friend, eating of thy bread like a dearest companion and chief adviser' ('mae'n rhaid iddo drigo yn dy stafell di, tan dy gronglwyd dy hun . . . fel cyfaill yn bwytta o'th fara, fel annwyl-ddyn a phen cyngor it').[105] That was the cherished ambition of all those Welsh authors who strove so hard to publish books in Welsh. As things stood, progress continued to be

[101] Ibid.
[102] Ibid.
[103] *W and R*, pp. 158–61.
[104] W. P. Griffith, *Learning, Law and Religion . . . c.1540–1642* (Cardiff, 1996), p. 305.
[105] Dedication to the reader, *Y Bibl Cysegr-lan* (1630).

painfully slow among the mass of the people in face of the stubborn persistence of long-standing handicaps: the poverty and inadequacy of many of the clergy; the conservatism, illiteracy, and apathy of isolated pastoral communities; the fewness of towns and the smallness of urban populations; the sluggishness of communications in terms of the movement of people and the circulation of ideas; and the scarcity of sermons and Welsh printed books. Ignorance, swearing, drunkenness, adultery, and gambling were the most prevalent failings; inertia, residualism, adherence to old ways, and neglect of church services the most common attitudes. They remained ever-present and were the despair of earnest moralists and critics.[106]

However unresponsive to improvement many aspects of the Elizabethan Church may have been, the year 1588 opened a decidedly more promising phase in the development of Protestantism in Wales. William Morgan's Bible met with almost instant recognition as an outstanding milestone on the road to reform. It was rapturously welcomed by the literate elements of the Welsh population and by many who were not. It would be a great boon if more evidence had survived to enable us to tell just how the Welsh Bible was received by the parish congregations and by the typical household, but those who have left their opinions on record were universally enthusiastic. It seems fairly safe to assume that it led to a marked improvement in the communication of the faith to the Welsh-speaking population. The central position allotted to the scriptures in Reformation belief and teaching had been acknowledged in all Protestant countries as requiring, as an inevitable consequence, a vernacular version of the Bible if the Reformed religion was to succeed in taking root among the people at large. That held good for Wales no less than elsewhere; but not until Morgan published his translation was it fully achieved. The success of his efforts was to lead in the ensuing thirty to forty years to the appearance of a growing number of books of a religious nature.

The first to appear were two major prose works published in 1595. One was *Deffynniad Ffydd Eglwys Loegr*,[107] a highly accomplished translation into Welsh by Maurice Kyffin of John Jewel's *Apologia*, a classic defence of the Anglican Church. Kyffin in his youth had been a pupil of William Llŷn, the greatest Welsh poet of the mid-sixteenth century. He had,

[106] *W and R*, pp. 42–3.
[107] *Deffynniad Ffydd* (1908); W. J. Gruffydd, *Llenyddiaeth Cymru: Rhyddiaith o 1540 hyd 1660* (Wrexham, 1926), pp. 86, 97; R. G. Gruffydd, 'Religious prose in Welsh from the beginning of the reign of Elizabeth I to the Restoration' (D.Phil. Oxford, 1952–3), pp. 66–76.

however, spent most of his adult life outside Wales, and he admitted that it might have been easier for him, and might have added more to his literary reputation, if he had written in some language other than Welsh.[108] As the friend of such contemporary authors as Spenser, Camden, John Dee, David Powel, and William Morgan, and himself author of *The Blessednes of Brytaine* (1587) and an English translation of Terence's *Andria* (1588),[109] he had good reason to appreciate the force of his own comment. He nevertheless pressed on with his Welsh translation because he was painfully aware of how pitifully scarce were appropriate reading materials in the language. He dismissed such religious writings as had earlier appeared in Welsh as old wives' tales, drawn mostly from the *Legenda Aurea*, a work he thought might more suitably have been entitled 'The Treatise of Lies'.[110] He himself wrote with exceptional smoothness and lucidity, intending perhaps that his book should be read aloud to the illiterate.[111] Maurice Kyffin, like his brother, Edward, had it in mind to translate the Psalms into Welsh but never carried out his intention.

The other book to appear in 1595 was Huw Lewys's Welsh version of Miles Coverdale's *A Spiritual and Most Precious Pearl*[112] (itself a translation from the original German book by Otto Werdmuller). Lewys, an MA of Oxford and a cleric in Bangor diocese,[113] was the first author to publish a Welsh book in Oxford. A petition of 1584 to the earl of Leicester as chancellor of the University had given as one of the reasons for setting up a press there the need to disseminate literature in Ireland and Wales, though only three Welsh titles were published in Oxford and not a single Irish one.[114] Lewys, like Kyffin, had been sorely dismayed by the absence of suitable literature in Welsh, and was inspired by the example which Morgan's Bible had set. Although he paid Morgan a glowing tribute, he pointed out that even the Bible was not readily available. Most copies of it were kept locked up in parish churches and could be read only once a week, though many neglected even that opportunity. The result was that there were elderly men of 60 years of age and upwards who could no more give an account of their faith than new-born babes. Lewys claimed that he saw on all sides a great deal of 'false faith, idol worship, pilgrimages, and praying to dead saints and such practices' ('gaudduwiaeth, delw-addoliant, pereryndod, gweddio ar Sainct meirwon, ar cyfryw argoelion'). There

---

[108] *Deffynniad Ffydd*, p. ix.

[109] Ibid., introd.

[110] Ibid., p. x.

[111] Gruffydd, 'Religious prose', p. 73.

[112] Ibid., pp. 76–86; for the text, W. J. Gruffydd (ed.), *Perl mewn Adfyd* (Cardiff, 1929).

[113] Gruffydd, *Perl*, introd.; cf. also idem, *Llên Cymru*, pp. 97–105.

[114] Gruffydd, 'Religious prose', pp. 78–9; cf. W. Ll. Davies, 'Argraffu llyfrau Cymraeg cynnar', *JWBS*, V (1937–42), 114–19.

existed in addition a whole mass of 'pride, avarice, usury, lust, violence, wrath, quarrels, theft and despoliation' ('rhwysc, cybydd-dod, vsuriaeth, chwant, trais, lledrat ac ysbel'). They were 'too frequent and are nearly swamping our country' ('sy ry aml, ac agos a gorescyn ein gwlad').[115] It was in the hope of mitigating these evils somewhat that he had published his book.

When William Morgan published his Bible in 1588, at least two of the bards who praised him effusively for it – Siôn Tudur and Ieuan Tew – in customary poetic vein expressed their confident expectation that he would soon be elevated to the bench of bishops as his reward.[116] Not until 1595 were their hopes somewhat belatedly realized. The year before, Gervase Babington had been translated from Llandaff to Exeter, and Morgan was appointed in his stead. The bishopric to which he was now moved was a singularly uninviting one in more than one respect. In terms of remuneration it was the poorest bishopric in England and Wales, and almost the first thing Morgan had to do was beg Burghley that its temporal income might be restored from the date of his predecessor's departure, 'for', as he explained, 'the revenue is very small and the charge is very great'.[117] Another depressing prospect was that the cathedral and its surrounding buildings were in ruinous state; and to cap it all, Llandaff was the Welsh diocese where recusants were most numerous and influential. Morgan refused to be daunted. He gathered about him at his palace in Mathern a lively group of poets, scholars, and authors, constituting an enterprising literary and intellectual circle.[118]

The bishop himself continued to pursue an active role as translator and author. He pressed on with the work of revising his translation of the New Testament, into which, greatly to its author's dismay, far too many printer's errors had found their way. On a copy of his Bible which he presented to Westminster Abbey, he had inserted a message to the effect that he hoped to bring out an edition of the Testament which would contain fewer mistakes, be smaller in size, and sold at a lower price.[119] Unfortunately, no such version ever appeared. What did emerge from the press in 1599 was a new issue of the Welsh Book of Common Prayer, the first to be revised in accordance with the text of Morgan's biblical translations. All that remains of his intended New Testament is to be found in the epistles and gospels of 1599.[120] The two previous editions of the Prayer Book, those of 1567 and

---

[115] *Perl*, p. xxii.
[116] *W and R*, pp. 192–3.
[117] *HMC, Hatfield MSS.*, V. 290.
[118] *W and R*, p. 195.
[119] I. Thomas, *Y Testament Newydd Cymraeg, 1551–1620* (Cardiff, 1972), pp. 356–87.
[120] Ibid., p. 356.

1586, had been undertaken by Salesbury. They suffered from the usual shortcomings of the latter's texts and could hardly have been truly satisfactory for use in public worship. Morgan's new Prayer Book, however, represented as great a step forward in the field of liturgical translation as his Bible had been in that of scriptural renderings. It made an invaluable contribution to Welsh religious life and worship, for which its author has not received nearly as much praise as he deserves.[121]

The Prayer Book of 1599, like Morgan's Bible, was printed by deputies to the queen's printer, Christopher Barker. Much of the labour of overseeing in detail the printing and proof-correction may have been undertaken by the youthful John Davies, who was to be mainly responsible for the Bible of 1620. Bound up with the text of the 1599 Prayer Book was a revised version of Morgan's Psalter. Both were printed in black letter on an octavo-sized page, which must have made the book much more convenient to use than the folio volume of 1567 or the quarto of 1586. Nothing is precisely known of the print-run of the edition, though it can hardly have been less than 1,000 copies. It may have been larger, since there is some indication that private individuals acquired copies of it as well as incumbents and churchwardens of parish churches.[122] Morgan had revised and updated Salesbury's Prayer Book as thoroughly as he had modified the New Testament of 1567. The completed text represented a vast improvement on what had gone before. Morgan had succeeded in making his Prayer Book as functionally effective and as aesthetically appealing as his Bible. Just as his translation of 1588 was the bedrock of all subsequent Welsh Bibles, so his Prayer Book laid a similarly trustworthy foundation on which all future editions were to be based. This represented a striking advance in making Protestant services intelligible to the Welsh people and warmly received by them. It was a feat which has gone largely uncommented upon; possibly because the Prayer Book has played no part in the Nonconformist worship familiar to the majority of the population of Wales since the early nineteenth century, whereas the Bible was at the core of it. Consequently, Morgan's breakthrough in the liturgical field has tended to be unduly overshadowed by his accomplishments as a biblical translator. Yet there can be no doubt that the Welsh liturgy took firm root in the affections of generations of Welsh people in the seventeenth and eighteenth centuries. Echoes of it still reverberate outside Anglican worship. Parts of the communion service heard in the average Welsh Nonconformist chapel, for instance, still bear unmistakable traces of its origin in the Prayer Book.[123]

[121] *W and R*, pp. 217–22.
[122] Ibid., pp. 216–17.
[123] Ibid.

The example set by William Morgan, and the success he achieved, inspired a whole generation of Welsh authors to publish some forty to fifty Welsh books in the years down to 1640.[124] Most of them were translations into Welsh of very popular works by English authors. This might seem surprising at first sight, since it is notoriously difficult for translators to avoid following too closely the idiom and speech rhythms of the original authors. On reflection, however, it becomes more readily comprehensible. The prime motive of most of these writers was to safeguard the religious welfare of their readers rather than to enhance their own literary reputation. So they translated classics which had already won a secure place in the affections of the public – the Book of Homilies, or the writings of Jewel or Perkins – the output of men widely recognized as 'powerful and effectual workers in the vineyard of the spirit'.[125] Like the contemporary Catholic authors, they wrote chiefly in order to encourage their own faithful rather than to convert outsiders. Protestants and Catholics alike expressed their intention of writing in a plain, unadorned style so that the commonalty might understand without difficulty what they read.[126]

Welsh poetry, like Welsh prose, had its contribution to make to the Protestant literary effort. The classical *cynghanedd* poetry was difficult to exploit for the purpose, being hedged in by immemorial conventions of what patrons expected of the poetry and by the poets' own concept of their role. In so far as the fixed-metre verse responded to the Reformation, it did so in praise of clerical patrons, especially the bishops,[127] identifying the poets with their ideals and aspirations. Poets also continued to compose some poetry on the familiar themes of praise of God, the prevalence of human wickedness, and the terrors of death and damnation. But patrons seem not to have favoured that kind of verse as much as they had done in the Middle Ages. Possibly, too, it had lost much of its esteem as the result of humanist criticism. Much more serious was the failure of the classical poets to respond to demands for a new kind of religious verse. Critics, both Catholic and Protestant, called on the poets to abandon the mendacious flattery of conventional and insincere praise and become the mouthpieces of Christian learning through the medium of the printed book.[128] The bards, however, doggedly maintained their adherence to the old ways. They sensed that such revolutionary proposals, if acted upon, might have the effect of destroying the traditional bardic role. They may well have realized

---

[124] Ibid., pp. 158–61.

[125] *Perl*, p. xii; *Deffynniad Ffydd*, p. vi.

[126] *W and R*, pp. 160–1.

[127] *W and R*, pp. 161–5. For the bishops of St Asaph, who were the outstanding patrons, R. A. Charles, 'Noddwyr y beirdd yn Sir y Fflint', *LlC*, XII (1972–3), 3–44.

[128] Ibid., pp. 162–3.

what an extraordinarily expensive kind of poetic training, in time and money, such a new role would have demanded of them, and that at a time when there were already dire complaints of the effects of inflation, shortages, and penny-pinching patrons. They were also aware of the impracticality of replacing with the printed book the usual methods of diffusing their verse by oral declamation and manuscripts. So that stream of published books of verse called for by the humanists never appeared; possibly never could have been forthcoming in the circumstances of sixteenth-century Wales.[129]

Considerably more significant than the *œuvre* of the classical bards was that of the free-metre poets. By its very nature such poetry was far better adapted for religious teaching and far easier to remember than the verse composed in *cynghanedd*. Nowhere was this more convincingly borne out than in the various efforts to translate the Psalms into Welsh.[130] William Middleton (1603), Edward Kyffin (1603), and Siôn Tudur all tried to produce a fixed-metre version, but with virtually no success. It was not until 1620 that Edmwnd Prys published his metrical psalms in free verses that were eminently singable, meeting with immediate, immense, and enduring success.[131] They may have prospered all the more because of the widespread popularity of the earlier verses known as *cwndidau*. The authors of the latter enjoyed castigating the moral failings of society in general and the same sins among individuals as were denounced in contemporary sermons.[132] In fact, the censures being pronounced in the late sixteenth century were not very different from the medieval thunderings against the seven deadly sins. But there was one noticeable difference between the later *cwndidau* and earlier religious poetry, and that was the introduction of more frequent and detailed references to biblical teaching from the Old and New Testaments. The editors of the collections of *cwndidau*[133] were able to list a whole series of them from the writings of poets like Thomas Llywelyn or Hopcyn Twm Philip.[134] This would seem to indicate that other poets besides Thomas Jones of Bertholau were as deeply impressed by the merits of Morgan's Bible and just as keen to extend knowledge of it among the populace. These free-metre poems were

[129] Ibid., p. 163; G. Williams, *Grym Tafodau Tân* (Llandysul, 1984), pp. 63–86.

[130] W. Ll. Davies, 'Welsh metrical versions of the Psalms', *JWBS*, II (1916–23), 276–301; E. P. Roberts, *Gwaith Siôn Tudur* (Bangor, 1978), I. 625–60.

[131] C. Pollin, 'The earliest metrical Psalm-book of Wales', *NLWJ*, XXIX (1980), 276–301; G. A. Williams, 'Edmwnd Prys (1543/4–1623) . . . ', *TMHS*, VIII (1977–84), 349–68.

[132] J. W. Blench, *Preaching in England in the Late Fifteenth and Sixteenth Centuries* (Oxford, 1964), pp. 229–30, chap. 6; Williams, *Tafodau Tân*, pp. 51–62.

[133] *Hen Gwndidau; Hopkiniaid Morgannwg*, ed. L. J. Hopkin-James (Bangor, 1909).

[134] *Hen Gwndidau*, pp. xxxvii–xxxix.

particularly favoured by the common people – a later commentator, Erasmus Saunders, characterized the Welsh as being 'naturally addicted to poetry; so some of the more skilful among them frequently composed a kind of Divine Hymns or Songs'.[135] Their dissemination, orally and in manuscript, would appear to attest the slow but unmistakable percolation of the influence of the Bible among some even of the illiterate amidst the people.[136]

In addition to the literary drive spurred on by the appearance of the Welsh Bible, there were also signs during the last two decades of Elizabeth's reign of improvement in the overall quality of the Welsh clergy. The choice of bishops remained highly commendable. In 1591, following the death of William Bleddyn, he was succeeded at Llandaff by Gervase Babington,[137] a learned Cambridge graduate, who remained there until 1595, when he was translated to Exeter. Though not a native of the diocese or of Wales, Babington had kept a school in Llandaff for years and had become treasurer of the diocese. A protégé of Burghley, to whom he owed much of his preferment, he was chaplain to the earl of Pembroke, and a close friend of Mary, countess of Pembroke, and her sons. His 'Short Table of the Christian Faith' was translated into Welsh by Siôn Dafydd Rhys, though no copy of it is known to have survived.[138] He was followed at Llandaff by William Morgan, translator of the Bible and the most distinguished Welsh bishop of the Tudor age. Whitgift warmly commended Morgan as a 'man of integrity, gravity, and great learning', and Gabriel Goodman enthused about him as the 'most sufficient man in Wales', 'for his learning, government and honesty of life'.[139] Morgan remained at Llandaff until 1601, moving to St Asaph after the death of William Hughes. His successor at Llandaff was Francis Godwin, [140] an erudite student of Church history and close friend of William Camden, whom he had accompanied in 1590 on a tour of Wales in search of antiquities. In 1601 he had published his *De Praesulibus Angliae Commentarius*, a history of the episcopal succession in the Anglican Church and, as a reward, was made bishop of Llandaff.[141]

At the same time that Morgan was preferred to Llandaff, his Cambridge friend and contemporary, Richard Vaughan, who had helped him translate the Bible, was elevated to Bangor. An eminent scholar and a gifted

[135] *A View of the State of Religion* . . . (repr. Cardiff, 1949), p. 33.
[136] *Hen Gwndidau, passim*; T. H. Parry-Williams (ed.), *Canu Rhydd Cynnar* (Cardiff, 1932); D. Ll. Jenkins, *Cerddi Rhydd Cynnar* (Llandysul, 1930).
[137] *DNB*.
[138] Gruffydd, 'Religious prose', p. 35.
[139] *HMC, Hatfield MSS.*, XI. 132, 153; XIV. 144.
[140] R. G. Gruffydd, *JHSCW*, IV. 13–17.
[141] Williams, *GCH*, IV. 240.

administrator,[142] Vaughan was moved to Chester in 1597, and ended his career as bishop of London, 1604–7. His place as bishop of Bangor was taken by Henry Rowland, hailed as 'foremost among Tudor bishops of the diocese'.[143] A native of the diocese, Rowland was educated at Oxford, and served as dean of Bangor 1593–7. Bishop from 1597 to 1616, 'on a smaller scale he became a benefactor to his diocese no less than the great bishop of Winchester (William of Wykeham)'.[144] He founded the grammar school at Botwnnog, reroofed his cathedral, and won golden opinions for his piety, learning, and generosity.[145]

In the mean time, Anthony Rudd had succeeded Middleton at St David's in 1594. Rudd, a native of Yorkshire, had pursued a brilliant career at Cambridge, and had been dean of Gloucester before being raised to the episcopal bench.[146] He had a fine reputation as a preacher and was believed likely to be translated very soon to a more important see. Any hopes he may have had of promotion were wrecked in 1596, when he was chosen to preach the Lenten sermon before the queen. Alas! His lack of discretion in the choice of a text and the way he pursued his theme proved disastrous. Encouraged by Whitgift's comment that Elizabeth had now grown 'weary of the vanities of wit and eloquence', he was naïve enough to preach on the text, 'O teach us to number our days that we may incline our hearts unto wisdom'. Elizabeth, always touchy on the subject of her age, was all the more upset by the sermon because of contemporary speculation about the successor to the throne. She told Rudd in no uncertain fashion that 'he should have kept his arithmetic to himself'. 'I see', she added, with characteristic tartness, 'that the greatest clerks are not the wisest men.'[147] Rudd's personal loss was his diocese's gain. He remained there as bishop until his death in 1614 and established his family firmly among the minor gentry of Carmarthenshire.[148]

The improvement was most noticeable among the higher clergy. In each diocese there was a marked increase in the number of graduates being preferred. A gradual but significant shift was taking place, particularly from the 1580s onwards, towards the ideal formulated in the canons of 1571 and 1604 of an all-graduate, resident, and preaching clergy. Even in Llandaff, the most backward of the Welsh dioceses in this respect, the cathedral clergy, by the beginning of the seventeenth century, have been

---

[142] *DNB. Visitation Articles*, pp. xvii, xviii.

[143] A. I. Pryce, *The Diocese of Bangor in the Sixteenth Century* (Bangor, 1923), p. xxxii.

[144] Ibid.

[145] Ibid., pp. xxxiii–xxxiv; J. G. Jones, 'Henry Rowland, bishop of Bangor, 1598–1616' *JHSCW*, XXXI (1979), 34–53.

[146] *DNB*. E. Yardley, *Menevia Sacra (Arch. Camb.* Supplement, 1927), pp. 103–4.

[147] J. E. Neale, *Queen Elizabeth* (London, 1948), pp. 216–17.

[148] Yardley, *Menevia Sacra*, pp. 103–4.

depicted as being 'on the whole a credit to the diocese', 'a group who reflected the pastoral care shown by the bishops'.[149] The average length of service by members of the cathedral chapters has been calculated as follows: St David's, 16–17 years; Llandaff, 18.5 years; Bangor, 16.4 years; and St Asaph, 24 years. Such a fairly long average tenure provided continuity in the chapters and constituted 'an element both for stability and resistance to change'.[150] Most members of the chapters were themselves holders of parochial benefices and, because of their connection with the parishes, were able to spread the influence of graduates more widely throughout the diocese. The most serious handicap, however, was that men with a university background were unevenly distributed among the rural deaneries.[151] This was true of St Asaph which, *pro rata*, was the Welsh diocese best provided with graduates. Conditions were worse in the two southern dioceses. In St David's, although there was a perceptible trend towards the appointment of more graduates, the tendency in the counties of Carmarthen and Cardigan appears to have been to appoint a few well-qualified men in a select group of parishes. The more distant a parish was from the cathedral at St David's or the collegiate church at Brecon, the greater was the probability of its being overlooked or neglected. There may have been a suggestion that in the later years of Elizabeth's reign parts of the diocese were becoming run down.[152] This was especially likely during and immediately after the disastrous episcopate of Bishop Middleton. When Bishop Rudd arrived upon the scene, there was much for him to do, although within a few years he seems to have made some good appointments.[153]

Much the clearest picture of the ratio of graduates to the clergy as a whole in any Welsh diocese is derived from the Bangor registers, which cover the whole of Elizabeth's reign.[154] The number of graduates rose from about one in ten during the 1560s to approximately half forty or fifty years later. Whereas between 1560 and 1580 there were only thirteen appointed, between 1580 and 1599 this had risen to thirty-four. Tentative conclusions arrived at concerning graduates in the diocese are that there was a large, possibly over-large, production of graduates from north Wales. There were not enough livings for them in their own diocese, nor were a number of the livings that were available particularly lucrative, so some of the ablest graduates were always liable to look elsewhere for preferment – usually in

[149] B. Williams, 'The Welsh Clergy, 1558–1642' (Ph.D. thesis, Open University, forthcoming).
[150] Ibid.
[151] Ibid.
[152] Ibid.
[153] Ibid.
[154] Pryce, Bangor, *passim*; Griffith, *Learning, Law*, chap. 7; Gray, *JWEH*, V. 31–72.

southern England.[155] An examination of the seventy-one Welshmen who
were students at St John's College, Cambridge, between 1550 and 1642
reveals that twenty-eight of them became clerics, but only half of these
served in Wales.[156] Similarly, a survey of the clergy taken in 1586 showed a
number of students of Welsh origin holding benefices in Oxfordshire,
Buckinghamshire, Essex, and Warwickshire, though they were not always
resident.[157] Many owed their position to influence and favour. Some, like
Lewis Bayly, John Owen, Thomas Howell, and Griffith Williams were
royal chaplains; others, like John Williams (later archbishop of York), or
Robert Price, had been able to ensconce themselves in aristocratic
households.[158] By the beginning of the seventeenth century, education was
at a premium, and clerics without a degree, especially those without the
degree of MA were at a greater disadvantage then ever, even in dioceses as
poor as those of Wales.

The main object of appointing graduates to the benefices was to recruit a
body of clerics capable of preaching with some effect to their
congregations, though not all graduates preached. Not all preachers were
graduates either: only twelve out of fifty were in Llandaff, and sixty-nine
out of eight-four in St David's.[159] Others among them were seriously
handicapped by not being able to preach in Welsh. Nevertheless, the
number of preachers available in Welsh dioceses towards the end of
Elizabeth's reign was undoubtedly improving, even if unevenly. Thus, in
1592 one-third of the clergy in the diocese of St Asaph (54 out of 144) and
of Bangor (43 out of 154) were able to preach. Proportionately, both these
dioceses were better furnished with preachers than those of Hereford,
Worcester, and Coventry and Lichfield.[160] They also appear to have been
better off than the southern Welsh dioceses. Only 18 out of 155 were able to
preach in Llandaff, and no figures are available for St David's, although
George Owen, writing about this time, somewhat optimistically estimated
that there were a considerable number of preachers in the single county of
Pembrokeshire.[161] Ten years later, in 1602, the position was much
improved. St Asaph still had about one preacher in every three of its clergy;
but Bangor had gone up to more than one in two (thirty-seven out of sixty-
one), Llandaff now boasted fifty preachers and St David's eighty-four.[162]
Just how frequently and how successfully these preachers performed their

[155] Griffith, *Learning, Law*, pp. 296–7.
[156] Ibid., p. 300.
[157] Ibid., p. 302.
[158] Ibid., pp. 301–3.
[159] Ibid., pp. 316–17.
[160] Ibid.
[161] Owen, *Penbrokshire*, III. 98–9.
[162] Griffith, *Learning, Law*, pp. 317–18.

duties, it is impossible to tell with any degree of certainty. The surviving sermon notes of two among them, although learned and weighty, do not inspire much confidence in a modern reader that sixteenth-century congregations for the most part would have been able to absorb their contents without considerable perplexity, frequently interlarded as they are with Latin texts and learned references. Anxieties of this kind relating to the number and quality of sermons were not confined to Wales, but were encountered in many of the remoter areas of England as well.[163]

Even so, in every one of the Welsh dioceses at this time there were able and conscientious clerics to be found. They were generally graduates, preachers and, in some instances, authors, who devoted themselves with remarkable singleness of purpose, usually over a long period of years, to the task of implanting among the ignorant the essential doctrines of the Christian faith. In doing so, they were also more than ordinarily interested in furthering the interests of the Welsh language. There were some striking examples of the type in the diocese of St David's. Most notable of them was Robert Holland. One of the leading lights of a literary circle which included George Owen Harry, rector of Whitchurch, Humphrey Smart, rector of Pwllcrochan, and the laymen, George Owen of Henllys, and Griffith Toy, son of Humphrey Toy, Holland was one of the most fluent and prolific of early Welsh authors. Unlike most of his contemporaries, who were content with producing one or two books, Holland published no fewer than six. Included among them were Welsh translations of James I's *Basilikon Doron* (1599) and William Perkins's most popular work, *Sail Crefydd Gristionogawl*[164] (The Foundation of the Christian Religion). Holland's friend, George Owen Harry, was a protégé of George Owen and presented by him to the rectory of Whitchurch. It was Holland who encouraged George Owen Harry to embark upon his *magnum opus*, entitled in the manuscript as 'The Wellspring of True Nobility' and published in 1604 as *The Genealogy of the High and Mighty Monarch, James I . . .* This was a work designed not only to validate James's claims to 'British' ancestry but also to applaud the Protestant succession which his accession represented.[165]

Among William Morgan's group of bards and promising prose-writers at Llandaff were two who were to become major contributors in the field of Welsh translation and scholarship. The one was John Davies, best known as Dr John Davies of Mallwyd, and Wales's greatest grammarian.

---

[163] VCH, *Cheshire*, III. 26, 32; *Worcs.* II. 54, 56–8; *Gloucs.* II. 32–5; *Staffs.* III. 55, 58–9.

[164] Gruffydd, 'Religious prose', pp. 103–27.

[165] B. G. Charles, *George Owen of Henllys* (Aberystwyth, 1973), pp. 114–17.

He gave Morgan substantial help with his Prayer Book of 1599 and with his version of the New Testament, which was never actually published. He moved to St Asaph with his patron and was eventually to be primarily responsible for the Welsh Bible of 1620.[166] The other, also brought on by Bishop Morgan, was Edward James, who translated the Book of Homilies published in 1606, a classic text as celebrated for the power and grace of its Welsh prose as for the vigour of its religious content.[167] Both these authors were deeply indebted to William Morgan for his help and inspiration.

When Morgan moved back to the diocese of St Asaph, he knew that he was returning to a milieu uniquely congenial to him. Of all the Welsh dioceses, St Asaph could take pride in the richest and most varied literary tradition, which had made it the cradle of the urge towards scriptural translation. Whatever may have been Bishop Hughes's faults, he, too, had been a generous mentor of preachers, poets, scholars, and literary men, including Morgan himself at an earlier stage in his career. Among the notable clerics who graced the diocese during Hughes's tenure of it was David Powel (d. 1598),[168] eloquent preacher and gifted historian. His son, Daniel Powel, recalled how his father had intended to publish a series of Welsh religious books but had died before he could complete any of them. It therefore fell to the son's lot to publish the *Llyfr Plygain* of 1612, which was to have been the first in a succession of publications, though no others in fact followed it. It was a Welsh primer in general conformity with the English primer of 1580, and it proved to be extremely poplar in Wales.[169] A comparable figure was Richard Parry, later to be bishop of St Asaph and sponsor of the Bible of 1620, who had moved to Bangor as its chancellor by the time Morgan arrived at St Asaph. Another prominent member of the St Asaph confraternity was Edward Kyffin, the cleric-brother of Maurice Kyffin, and the author of *Rhann o Psalmae Dafydd Brophwyd* (Part of the Psalms of the Prophet David). Kyffin expressed in print his conviction that the Almighty, by having preserved the Old Britons and their descendants in freedom and security for so long, had in view 'some great achievement and supremacy for the enhancement of his own glory' ('ryw orchest-waith a goruchafiaeth tuag at amlhâd ei ogoniant ei hun').[170] A younger cleric, Robert Llwyd, vicar of Chirk, who was, in time, to become a successful translator of Dent's *Plain Pathway to Heaven, Llwybr*

---

[166] R. G. Gruffydd in *Y Traddodiad Rhyddiaith*, pp. 128–9.

[167] Williams, *Tafodau Tân*, pp. 180–98.

[168] I. M. Williams, 'Ysgolheictod hanesyddol yr unfed ganrif ar bymtheg', *LIC*, II (1952–3), 111–24, 209–33.

[169] Gruffydd, 'Religious prose', pp. 175–6.

[170] G. H. Hughes, *Rhagymadroddion, 1547–1648* (Cardiff, 1951), p. 106.

Hyffordd (1630),[171] must surely have derived encouragement and stimulus from the arrival of his new bishop.

In the diocese of Bangor, to which Richard Parry had moved, he had joined two other very well-known cleric-littérateurs, Edmwnd Prys[172] and Huw Lewys.[173] Attention has already been drawn to both. Lewys was a very conscientious incumbent of Llanddeiniolen, who later (1605) became chancellor of the diocese of Bangor. Prys had been made archdeacon of Merioneth in 1576 and remained there until his death in 1623.He was an accomplished preacher, a fine poet in the classical and free metres, and a literary critic of some distinction. He was, however, to become most famous for his metrical translations of the Psalms of 1620.

The general quality of the higher clergy of Wales, especially in the northern dioceses during this period, is aptly commemorated in the tribute paid to them by an historian of the Bangor diocese:

> The list of distinguished bishops and clergy was remarkable and cannot be equalled in a similar period of time either before or since. The age may called the golden age of the Church in Wales, not on the ground that the Church or its organization were free from imperfections, for such was certainly not the case, but because at a great crisis the Church inspired teachers who wrought their Church and their country lasting good.[174]

Nor was it only clergy who made up the constellations of Protestant intelligentsia emerging all over Wales during these years. Many laymen were no less energetic in the cause of literature and reform. More and more members of the gentry were seeking education at grammar schools, universities, and inns of court, where the atmosphere was predominantly that of Protestant humanism.[175] One of the most fascinating of them was Sir William Herbert of St Julian's.[176] An ardent Protestant who had spoken vehemently against Mary Stuart in the Parliament of 1586, he was a man of strongly intellectual bent, who corresponded frequently with his friend, John Dee. Herbert became a planter in Munster, where he showed his sympathy towards the Irish and was involved in the founding of Trinity College Dublin. Back home in Wales he encountered the same phenomena of inertia and Catholic residualism among the people, and a lack of

---

[171] *Llwybr Hyffordd yn Cyfarwyddo yr Anghyfarwydd i'r Nefoedd*, Hughes, *Rhagymadroddion*, p. 130; Gruffydd, *Llên Cymru*, pp. 12–16.

[172] G. A. Williams, *Ymryson Edmwnd Prys a William Cynwal* (Cardiff, 1986), introd.

[173] Gruffydd, *Perl*, introd.

[174] Pryce, *Bangor*, p. xi.

[175] *W 1415–1642*, pp. 429–35.

[176] *DWB*, s.n.

facilities for education. In 1589, to remedy the local 'backwardness in religion' he encountered in Wales, he offered the same solution as in Ireland, namely, a college supported from the income of impropriated livings. He also had it in mind to write a book intended to refute the Catholic Campion's writings; but his untimely death in 1591 prevented either project from being fulfilled.[177]

A number of his contemporaries among the Welsh gentry shared Herbert's interest in the acquisition of books and the reform of religion. They included men with such intellectual interests as Sir John Perrott and Maurice Kyffin, both of whom spent much time in Ireland, George Owen of Henllys,[178] Simon Thelwall,[179] and Edward and John Stradling.[180] All of them, and especially the last-named, acquired extensive libraries; but most of the books contained in them were, of necessity, works written in languages other than Welsh – English, Latin, or some continental language.

Of those who wished to extend publishing in Welsh, the most influential was Thomas Salisbury.[181] A member of the cadet branch of the prolific Salusbury clan, he continued in many respects the tradition instituted by his famous kinsman, William Salesbury. Thomas was admitted freeman of the Stationers' Company in October 1588 and thus began his career as a publisher and bookseller. The impressive increase in the volume of Anglican literary publishing in Welsh during the years between 1593 and 1604 owed most to him and Robert Holland. In 1593 Thomas Salisbury published the *Grammatica Britannica*, written by his relative, Henry Salisbury.[182] In the next year he borrowed £10 from Thomas Myddelton, a London-Welsh merchant of Puritan leanings, to publish a book called 'The Sick Man's Salve' in the Welsh tongue 'for the good of the poor people', though no copy of it is known to have survived.[183] It was in 1602, with the help of Edward Kyffin, and further financial assistance from Myddelton, that he began his ambitious campaign to extend Welsh literature. Authors with whom he was in contact were William Middleton (Myddelton), whose translation of some of the Psalms he published in 1603,[184] Bishop William Morgan, Robert Holland, and George Owen Harry. Unfortunately, however, this fusion of zeal for religious reform and the welfare of the Welsh language was brought to an abrupt end as a result of the confusion caused by the outbreak of plague in 1603. Thomas Salisbury refers in a letter

[177] Griffith, *Learning, Law and Religion*, p. 466.
[178] B. G. Charles, *George Owen of Henllys* (Aberystwyth, 1973), chaps. 6–8.
[179] *DWB*, s.n. Thelwall family.
[180] Williams, *St Donat's Castle*, pp. 17–54; Lewis, *Ysgrifau Beirniadol*, XIX. 139–207.
[181] Gruffydd, 'Religious prose', pp. 56–91.
[182] *DWB*, s.n.
[183] Gruffydd, 'Religious prose', p. 89.
[184] Ibid., pp. 91–3.

written about this time to the titles of five Welsh books which were lost. They included proverbs, psalms, translations of treatises written by William Perkins, and, most calamitous of all, William Morgan's revised version of the New Testament. Salisbury's business was not only disrupted by the plague, but he himself seems to have been completely disheartened by his experiences.

Serious a disappointment as this débâcle may have been, it proved to be no more than a temporary set-back. The momentum generated for reform and Welsh publishing in the last years of Elizabeth's reign would continue with growing vigour and confidence during the early Stuart era. All the signs were that, at least among the educated and literate minority, the Reformation was at long last really bearing fruit in Wales. The impact of the vernacular services in Welsh and English, the Bible, Prayer Book, and other literature, and the sermons being preached, is not to be measured simply in terms of the number of people involved, for they wielded a wholly disproportionate influence. They were, in general, the people who exercised authority and directed opinion in Wales. A member of this group at its best, Sir John Lloyd of Aber Llwyfeni, was later to be described as a 'man who served God chiefly and learned much from the books of divinity he possessed. He cared nothing for worldly wealth.'[185]

---

[185] G. H. Hughes, 'Cefndir meddwl yr ail ganrif ar bymtheg', *Efrydiau Athronyddol*, XVIII (1955), 31–41, on p. 34.

Conclusion

THE fate of religion was determined in many of the countries of sixteenth-century Europe as much by the operation of secular influences, if not more than by that of religious ones. It was the power of the State and the nature of its ruler's ecclesiastical allegiance which usually ordained the outcome. That was especially true of those polities where the sovereign's authority was, by contemporary standards, firmly established. Decision-making in this sphere was, in essentials, much the same in Catholic countries as in Protestant ones; in Philip II's Spain no less than Elizabeth's England, in the France of the Valois just as in the Vasas' Sweden. In most European states the ruling élites found it difficult, if not impossible, to separate religious authority from political jurisdiction. A Venetian envoy wrote of the subjects of the king of England,

> They follow the example and submit to the authority of the ruler in all matters; they esteem religion only in so far as it allows them to fulfil the duties of a subject towards his prince, living as he lives, believing as he believes, and, in a word, doing whatsoever he bids them to. This people would adapt itself to any religion.[1]

He may have been overstating his case somewhat, but he was not all that wide of the mark, and he could have commented along much the same lines about the subjects of other European rulers. One of Queen Elizabeth's most senior and experienced aides, reflecting on the delinquencies of Catholic recusants, accused them of 'failing their duties to God, can hardly be good subjects to her majesty, or true to this state'.[2] If the queen had the duty of maintaining true religion within the realm, her people for their part were expected to be under a religious as well as a political necessity of obedience to her.

---

[1] C. S. L. Davies, *Peace, Print and Protestantism* (London, 1977), pp. 299–308.
[2] *The State Papers and Letters of Sir Ralph Sadler*, by A. Clifford (3 vols. Edinburgh, 1809), II. 595.

Conclusion

Such loyalties were all the more compelling when religion became linked with patriotic associations. The ruler was envisaged as the focus of the people's allegiance, and national unity and destiny were achieved in and through him or her. In that cohesion, religion was held to be an indispensable element. It was what authenticated the king's authority as God's anointed lieutenant on earth and gave sanction to all his actions. Disobedience to him was tantamount to defiance of the divine will. Rejection of the royal command and disunity in religion led almost ineluctably to political disruption and social tensions. Not surprisingly, therefore, Elizabeth, like her father before her, held firmly to the conviction that religion was too important to be left entirely to the discretion of clerics. It must be an instrument in the control of the sovereign, to be wielded in the interests of royal power and the unity of the commonwealth. In this context, there were two vital principles to which Elizabeth adhered immovably throughout her reign, as has been seen. The one was unity, as a matter of religious as well as political obligation; and the other was authority, exercised by herself as Supreme Governor through bishops whom she herself chose. For nearly forty-five years she exerted her will in matters religious and ecclesiastical, and was, in general, supported in that exercise by her foremost councillors, lay and ecclesiastical. Before her reign was over, she had effectively prevailed over the main challengers to her authority. She had not, it is true, extinguished either the Catholics or the Puritans, but had brought both factions under her control.[3] She had deftly exploited her appeal as a woman as well as a ruler among the overwhelming majority of her subjects. For the most part she had convinced them – including many of the Roman Catholics in their midst – that the safety and stability of the kingdom and of their own lives and property depended on her.

One of the stoutest pillars of her regime was her Church; not only a buttress to the sovereign but also a guarantee of the self-interest of the governing classes. Therein lay an essential key to the role of the 'political nation'. What decisively mattered for most of them was the maintenance of a stable equilibrium in the social and political order, an intrinsic mainstay of which was the Established Church. That body gained in appeal because it was underwritten by the full authority of law and government, and, unlike the Protestant churches of, say, France, the Netherlands, or even Scotland, was not being contended for in war and tumult by dissident groups of nobles, merchants, or artisans. It was all the more attractive to many of the laity for being erastian, comprehensive, and undemanding. It

[3] P. Collinson, *The Elizabethan Puritan Movement* (London, 1967); W. R. Trimble, *The Catholic Laity in Elizabethan England* (Cambridge, Mass., 1964), chap. 8.

offered the incentive of a Church in which the landowners could apply an appreciable measure of influence over patronage and livings, acquisition and leases of Church land, choice and control of clergy, and enforcement of statutes regulating attendance at church. All these interests had been brought increasingly to their notice and thrown into sharper relief by seeming to be at stake in the protracted struggle with international Catholicism. In the course of this contest the gentry in Wales, like their fellows in England, had become completely integrated into mechanisms for the defence of the realm and on behalf of which they had had to make heavy sacrifices.[4]

By the end of Elizabeth's reign, the queen's unwavering steadfastness in religion had done much to underpin a sense of permanence and continuity. No one under the age of 50 (a considerable age in the sixteenth century) could remember any form of public worship being allowed other than that conducted according to the Book of Common Prayer. Whatever the inadequacies of the clergy may have been, custom and habit in themselves counted for a good deal in maintaining loyalty. The Church had become associated in the minds of the upper classes in Wales with constancy to the Tudor dynasty and the Tudor State. However tenuous the royal family's connection with Wales might by this time have become, among the Welsh it was virtually an article of faith that the Tudors were a 'British' (i.e. Welsh) dynasty, who, because of their 'great care and natural love and affection . . . unto their subjects of Wales above all others' (George Owen),[5] had set them free from ancient bonds and conferred upon them the status of full citizenry. Throughout the latter half of the sixteenth century, and beyond, poets, littérateurs, historians, and antiquaries, writing in Welsh, English, and Latin, had all united in choruses of praise to a royal family which had wrought such wonders for the Welsh.[6] Fidelity to the Tudors sprang not only out of sentiment but also as a result of the gains accruing from a growing participation in politics, government, and the economy. Such involvement led to an increasing attachment to a whole complex of institutions that, besides the sovereign and the dynasty, included common law and Parliament, the courts of justice great and small, and the whole apparatus of local government and administration.[7] Not least among these organs of authority at the disposal of the Crown were the Established Church and the Protestant settlement. Moreover, the successful transition

---

[4] *W 1415–1642*, chap. 15.

[5] G. Owen, *Description of Penbrokshire*, ed. H. Owen (3 vols. London, 1906), III. 54.

[6] G. Williams, *Religion, Language and Nationality in Wales* (Cardiff, 1979), pp. 17–20; G. Williams, *Henry Tudor and Wales* (Cardiff, 1985), pp. 93–101; *W 1415–1642*, pp. 352–3, 359–60.

[7] A. H. Dodd, 'The pattern of politics in Stuart Wales', *TCS* (1948), 20–7.

from Elizabeth's Protestant regime to another of similar complexion under the rule of James I guaranteed the victory of the Anglican settlement in Wales no less than England.[8]

Had Elizabeth been succeeded by a Catholic monarch the outcome for religion in Wales might possibly have been very different. There, as in other 'backward' regions of the realm, political and social conditions had indeed been sufficiently favourable for the Elizabethan settlement to be imposed. But a restored Roman Church under a Roman Catholic ruler might have found enough surviving adherence to the old faith and certainly plenty of vestiges of a conservative past to have restored the Catholic religion with conceivably not so very much more opposition than Queen Mary had encountered in 1553–4. Conversion to Protestant belief was still not sufficiently widespread, nor had it gone deep enough, for a Catholic reaction not to have been distinctly feasible. With the backing of State power and the force of law the will of a Catholic sovereign might have been enforced without any determined resistance, just as that of Tudor rulers had been. Admittedly, the change to Welsh as the language of religion had eased the path for a readier reception of Protestant reform, but it had not been used long enough to do more than begin the task of turning Wales into a genuinely Protestant country. The road ahead to implanting such beliefs and practices firm-rootedly among the mass of the population stretched far into the future and was strewn with obstacles.

Nevertheless, if the Reformation was to become accepted for religious as well as secular reasons, the face of the Welsh people had been turned in the right direction. At an earlier stage, under Henry VIII, Edward VI, and the first years of Elizabeth, there seems no doubt that the Crown's intention had been to compel all its subjects, whatever might be their natural tongue, to accept the Reformation in English. In Celtic-speaking areas such as Cornwall,[9] the Isle of Man, and even Ireland to a considerable extent,[10] it succeeded in its purpose. Nor is there any reason to believe that its object in Wales was any different, or that, if it had carried out its policy unchanged, it would not have been accomplished there also. In some limited areas of south and east Wales, and among the prosperous and educated classes throughout the country, there had been enough English-speaking people for the far-reaching modifications embodied in the Acts of Union, 1536–43, to be pushed through without any serious opposition or

---

[8] Idem, *Studies in Stuart Wales* (Cardiff, 1952), chap. 1; 'Wales and the Stuart succession', *TCS* (1937), 201–25.

[9] A. L. Rowse, *Tudor Cornwall* (London, 1941), *passim*.

[10] R. D. Edwards, *Church and State in Tudor Ireland* (Dublin, 1935); T. W. Moody, F. X. Martin, and F. J. Byrne (eds.), *A New History of Ireland*, III. *1534–1691* (Oxford, 1976).

rebellion.[11] Much the same could be said for the Reformation changes introduced by Henry VIII and Edward VI, in spite of some expressions of acute distaste for them. In towns like Cardiff, Carmarthen, or Haverfordwest, there is clear evidence that the English Bible and Prayer Book were widely read, and English sermons listened to with relish. Later, English books such as Foxe's *Book of Martyrs*, Jewel's *Apology*, Lewis Bayly's *Practice of Piety*, or William Perkins's writings were eagerly read by a minority. On this showing, the course of the Reformation in Wales might not have differed markedly from that which it followed in Cornwall. Although the Cornish language was not as commonly spoken as Welsh was in Wales, nor did it command as much literary pride as its sister language, it would be difficult to argue that the long-term consequences in Wales would have been significantly different from the Cornish experience, or that of the Isle of Man, i.e. the English-language church services would gradually have been adopted and the native language would have died out. In Wales, as in Cornwall, there were enough who understood English among those who were the decision-makers and exercised the key influence in the community to have ensured the eventual implementation of the Established Church among all ranks of society, even though its services were conducted in the English language. Wales, in respect of its social structure and the political values of its governing élite, was not notably different from any of the other peripheral regions of the kingdom, and the influences shaping acceptance of the Established Church were much the same.

Yet there were too few of these English speakers in Wales for the Reformation to be a popular success there in the sixteenth and early seventeenth centuries. With such a large proportion of the population speaking only Welsh, it would have taken far longer for the Anglican Church to win the affections of the populace through the medium of English, if indeed it would ever truly have done so. It would always have had to contend with deep-rooted prejudice against the language of the conqueror. From the outset, almost, there had always been a small but ardent cultivated minority who never had any doubt about the necessity for presenting the new faith to the Welsh in their own language, on cultural no less than religious grounds.[12] They feared that English-language services would inflict a mortal wound on the language and the culture of Wales, so greatly prized by them, as well as rendering Reformed religion an empty mockery and unmeaning farce to its people. The task of convincing many of their fellow-countrymen of the truth of such views, not to mention

---

[11] *W 1415–1642*, chap. 11.
[12] R. G. Gruffydd, *Y Gair ar Waith* (Cardiff, 1988), pp. 27–65; pp. 38–9, 65 for bibliography.

inducing the authorities in London to modify government policy in their favour, had involved them in a long and hard-fought battle. Successfully translating the scriptures and the service book into Welsh and producing a Protestant literature in the language had been a mortifyingly slow process. Earlier decisions to propagate the Reformation without using the Welsh language had been the primary reason for its abortive attempts to strike root in the country. Only in the last years of Elizabeth and the first four decades of the seventeenth century was it possible to sense that the Reformation was gaining ground among the Welsh-speaking population.[13] The combination of a Welsh Bible, Welsh services, and an improved clergy was beginning to take effect. Even then, the Reformation still had to overcome the twin obstacles of mass illiteracy and apathy. It would be the second half of the eighteenth century before enough of the Welsh had been taught to read and a sufficiently large number of books been published in Welsh for the Reformation to come of age.[14]

Before the end of the sixteenth century, however, the course of events had dictated that Wales, together with England, had become a member of the Protestant camp in Europe. Its place in the Reformed ranks was the more firmly entrenched because of the enhanced status the Reformation had given the Welsh language. Even before the sixteenth century was out, three short-term consequences could already be discerned. First, the scriptural translations had answered with a resounding affirmative a question which had been deeply troubling Welsh scholars and reformers for at least half a century: were the Welsh language and the Welsh literary tradition capable of rising to meet the new demands being placed on them by the Renaissance and the Reformation?[15] In both instances, successful scriptural translation was regarded as the supreme test. If that hurdle could be triumphantly surmounted, then all the others were at least theoretically manageable. William Salesbury's earlier efforts may have had shortcomings which laid their author open to criticism, but Morgan's Bible and Prayer Book were universally acclaimed as an indisputable masterstroke. No group received them more lyrically than scholars and writers, greeting them as much as a breakthrough for the Welsh language and its literature as for the Reformed religion.

Secondly, presenting the Reformed religion in Welsh meant a wider and warmer acceptance for it and also for the reinterpretation of Welsh Church history as put forward by the reformers. The Protestant minority in Wales

[13] *W and R*, pp. 41–7, 155–72.
[14] G. H. Jenkins, *The Foundations of Modern Wales* (Oxford, 1987), chaps. 9–10; *WRE*, pp. 27–30.
[15] *W and R*, chap. 5; G. Williams and R. O. Jones, *The Celts and the Renaissance* (Cardiff, 1990), chaps. 1 and 2.

were just as aware as their co-believers in other countries that nothing endeared Reformed teaching to the populace more than having it conveyed to them in their own language. Moreover, Richard Davies's restatement of Welsh history in Protestant terms had bonded the Reformation inseparably to some of the oldest and most tenacious instincts of Welsh patriotism. Henceforward, it could be regarded not as a new-fangled heresy imposed upon a reluctant nation only at the *diktat* of the alien English, but as the restoration of the pristine purity of early British belief as it existed during the immediate post-apostolic age. Indeed, it was presented as the consummation of the ancient prophecies of a rebirth in Wales of its golden age, ushered in by the triumph of the Tudor dynasty and fulfilled at its most sublime level by the 'second flowering' of true religion.

Thirdly, the Reformation helped to lock Wales more firmly into the orbit of the Tudor polity. The secular loyalties of the gentry to the monarchy and its institutions of government were now being reinforced by a more recent allegiance to the Established Church, which had earlier been received in Wales somewhat lukewarmly to say the least. The affection of the Welsh for their own language and history could now be perceived by them to be more fully compatible than ever before with adherence to the Tudor kingdom, its ruling family, and its religious settlement.

In addition to these more immediate consequences, the decision to use Welsh for public worship in all those parishes where it was customarily spoken had highly significant long-range implications.[16] Over the centuries, it was to make Wales a committedly Protestant country. Religion, it need hardly be said, was the overwhelming concern of that minority who had pressed for installing Welsh as a language of worship. The object which they had most at heart was the souls' health of their countrymen who could speak no language but their own. In the eyes of convinced reformers the Church would be a living lie until it could offer the Welsh the faith in their own tongue. But the Reformation was a religion of conversion and a religion 'of the book'. Wherever it took hold, it tended to appeal to those who could read and also added to their number. It stressed how crucially desirable it was that people should be able to read the vernacular version of Bible and service book – those detonators which were believed capable of releasing the most dynamic reforming charges. In addition, Protestants had confidence in the power of literacy to overcome what they identified as the most pernicious moral failings of the age: ignorance, superstition, corruption (including drunkenness and blasphemy), and idleness. Nevertheless,

---

[16] Gruffydd, *Gair ar Waith*; for its influence on the language, literature, mentality and national consciousness, see the chapters by D. S. Evans, D. Ll. Morgan, R. T. Jones, and J. E. C. Williams.

the spread of literacy and the publication of more religious books in Welsh were slow in arriving. In the seventeenth century it was only the most determinedly Protestant minority among Anglicans, Puritans, and Dissenters that pressed for more schools and publications.[17] It was comparable bodies in the eighteenth century, such as the SPCK, the Circulating Schools, and the Sunday Schools, which contrived to bring about the breakthrough to mass literacy and effective publication.[18] At last, the soil which for so long had lain fallow was ripe to yield an abundant harvest which made the Welsh the out-and out Protestant nation which they ultimately became.

To this agency of propagation and education an immeasurable contribution was made by Protestant clergy and ministers.[19] They were the only educated class which had a vital interest in publicly using the Welsh language, in teaching the people to read it, and in publishing books in it for them to read. At the time when most of the upper classes were becoming increasingly Anglicized in speech,[20] the clergy bridged the widening chasm in language and culture between the gentry and the people. It is necessary to try to estimate what the effect would have been if the clerics, instead of seeing it as their function to instruct, catechize, and preach to their parishioners in Welsh, had concluded that it was their responsibility to induce their charges to learn English as soon as possible. In that case it is not easy to envisage much scope for the charitable and philanthropic movements, or the Circulating and Sunday Schools, of which the clergy were the principal founders and sustainers, to have operated in Wales. It comes as no surprise, therefore, that the foremost pioneers of popular education and publication in the seventeenth and eighteenth centuries should have been clerics such as Stephen Hughes, Griffith Jones, or Thomas Charles. Or that the great – and not-so-great – writers of Wales in the same period were, almost to a man, clergy of the Established Church or Nonconformist ministers, whether prose authors like Morgan Llwyd, Ellis Wynne, or Theophilus Evans, or poets like Vicar Prichard, Goronwy Owen, or Williams Pantycelyn. If, from the realms of Welsh literature and education during these years, the names of clergy and ministers are removed, not much is left.

From early on, the protagonists of the Welsh language had been quick to seize upon the point that the Reformation had as much to contribute to

[17] Jenkins, *Foundations*, chaps. 5 and 6; idem, *Literature, Religion and Society in Wales, 1660–1730* (Cardiff, 1978).
[18] Ibid.
[19] There is no history of the role of the Welsh clergy in modern Welsh history but the nearest thing to it is G. H. Jenkins's excellent study, *Literature, Religion and Society*.
[20] Williams, *Religion, Lang. and Nationality*, pp. 159–63.

it as to religion.[21] What they did not, and could not, appreciate was just how decisive it was going to be in that respect. It would have been virtually impossible for them to imagine a situation in which Welsh was in danger of not being spoken by a large majority of the population. Indeed, one of the most compelling reasons why Salesbury and Morgan undertook their translations was that there was so little prospect of most of their compatriots being able to read the Bible or anything else in any language but Welsh. Yet there is a strong case to be made that if the Bible had not been translated, the language would undoubtedly have been gravely weakened, might possibly have become extinct. Not at once, naturally; it would have been a gradual process but an inexorable one. If English had continued to be the language of the Bible and the Prayer Book, and thereby, increasingly the language of worship, preaching, catechizing, and religious life generally, then every parish church in the Welsh-speaking areas, no matter how remote or inaccessible, would have become a focus for the dissemination of the English language, which otherwise might rarely or never have been heard at all. It seems highly likely that the same sort of fate might have overtaken the Welsh language as befell its sister-language, Cornish, into which no biblical translation was undertaken and which had died out by the early eighteenth century. The Manx language went much the same way. Even Irish and Gaelic, both spoken by many more people than Welsh in the sixteenth century, dwindled much more rapidly than Welsh. One of the principal reasons for this was that neither acquired the same status in religious worship as Welsh. A leading Scottish historian, commenting on the symbiosis of the English language and religion in the Scottish Reformation, gave it as his opinion that 'it is one of the most important facts in their history that the Scottish people never had a printed Bible in their own tongue'.[22] Without a Bible, Welsh might have lingered on only as an assorted mass of dialects, lacking dignity, correctness, or uniformity.

If the language had survived at all, if it had dragged out an existence as a debased peasant *patois*, it could hardly, by any stretch of the imagination, have continued as a fitting medium for literature. Such a crisis would also have been intensified by the sad and rapid decline of the bardic order in the sixteenth century. If the function of the bards in maintaining a single literary language of the highest quality throughout the whole of Wales, regardless of the many differences in dialect, had been extinguished without being replaced by an adequate substitute, then the outlook for

[21] Evans, *Gair ar Waith*, pp. 67–86.
[22] G. Donaldson in S. T. Bindoff *et al.*, *Elizabethan Government and Society* (London, 1961), p. 291.

Conclusion

Welsh as a literary language would have been catastrophic. Fortunately, the Welsh Bible, like the vernacular scriptures in a number of European countries, performed an invaluable service to the native literature as well.[23] By conferring upon the language an enhanced status and greater exactitude, and extending the range and diversity of its vocabulary and powers of expression, it served as the standard for future prose and poetry. It came at the critical point when the professional poets, for centuries the conservators *par excellence* of the literary language and tradition, were moving into a state of terminal decline.[24] Before the close of the seventeenth century their influence was at an end. It was the Welsh Bible, itself so securely grounded in what was best and most enduring in the medieval literary tradition, without preserving what was outmoded or irrelevant, that filled the breach. It did more than that; it achieved for Wales what Luther's Bible did for Germany: it became the touchstone of all later literary expression. In the following two or three centuries, the greater part of what was written in Welsh and published in the language, derived from a religious or moral purpose. Comparatively little of it was primarily motivated by literary ambition; its function was overwhelmingly didactic. The horizons of this literature may have been limited and its themes restricted, but within those confines a remarkably virile and accomplished output was maintained.[25] It was the only one of the Celtic literatures which successfully spanned the transition in the sixteenth century from an oral and manuscript tradition of the Middle Ages to a printed literature of modern times.[26] The bridge was the Welsh Bible.

Finally, there was the impact of this interweaving of religion, Church history, language, and literature on the overall sense of identity among the Welsh.[27] Even if there had been no such fusion, Welshness could almost certainly have survived. In other Celtic countries – Ireland, Scotland, Cornwall, or even the Isle of Man – a sense of individuality has been maintained, although in each instance the native language and literature withered to a greater extent than in Wales. But in such a sequence it seems likely, on balance, that Wales would have been much nearer to the model of Cornwall than that of Scotland or Ireland. That is to say, Wales would have been peaceably Anglicized over the long term but would have retained a distinctive flavour of regional awareness rather than a sense of separate nationality. It would be rash, all the same, to conclude that this was the only possible scenario. In the absence of a Welsh Bible and Welsh services,

---

[23] *Cambridge Hist. Bible*, III, *passim.*
[24] T. Parry, *History of Welsh Literature*, tr. H. I. Bell (Oxford, 1955), pp. 161–3.
[25] Ibid., chap. 8; *W and R*, chap. 5.
[26] Williams and Jones, *Celts and Renaissance, passim.*
[27] *W and R*, pp. 169–72, 238–9.

it is not entirely inconceivable that in parts of Wales, as in Ireland and parts of the Scottish Highlands, the native language and national consciousness might have become estranged from the Anglican Church and become identified with the Roman faith. If that had happened, parts of Wales, at least, might have been subjected to a repression not unlike that which fell to the lot of the Irish and some of the Highland Scots. But it would be a futile exercise to speculate at length on the might-have-beens. The fact was that the mixture of religion, history, language, and literature did take effect, and served as a most potent and active leaven in the Welsh consciousness. This pride in a blend of religiosity and Welshness, founded in the early modern era, continued for centuries subsequently. It encouraged among the Welsh a belief that they were an elect people, singled out by God, on a par with, and ultimately descended from the same stock as, the chosen race, the Hebrews themselves.[28] Nothing was better calculated to preserve among them their own sense of a separate identity.

[28] P. T. J. Morgan, *A Bible for Wales* (Aberystwyth, 1988), chap. 4; idem, *The Eighteenth-century Renaissance* (Llandybïe, 1981).

Bibliography

THESE lists are not intended to be an exhaustive bibliography. They do not constitute a complete catalogue of all the material consulted by the author. They are intended to include, in the main, such manuscripts, books, articles, and theses as are mentioned in the text, except that where a printed item is given no more than passing mention it has not usually been included in the bibliography, but details of place and date of publication will have been given in the appropriate note. The omission of any work from the bibliography should not necessarily be taken to mean that it has not been consulted or that it is regarded as being of slight value. The best general bibliography of Welsh history is P. H. Jones, *A Bibliography of the History of Wales* (Cardiff, 1989). Useful lists of current publications appear regularly in *Arch. Camb.*, *Studia Celtica*, and *WHR*. The relevant sections of *Bibliotheca Celtica* (Aberystwyth, 1909– ; new series, 1954–) are valuable. The best check-list of current publications on general British history is the RHS's *Annual Bibliography of British and Irish History* (London, 1975–).

I. Contemporary Sources

(A) Manuscripts

Balliol College
Balliol College MS. 353

British Library
Cleopatra MS. E. iv
Egerton MS. 2350
Harleian MSS. 280, 420, 563, 595, 604, 605, 4060, 6994, 6998, 7158
Lansdowne MSS. 5, 8, 45, 64, 111, 120
Stowe MS. 141

Cardiff Central Library
Hafod MSS. 19, 22

Corpus Christi College, Cambridge
CCCC MS. 1148

Jesus College, Oxford
Jesus College MSS., 18, 115

Lambeth Palace Library
Registers of Archbishops Cranmer, Pole, Parker, and Whitgift

National Library of Wales
Badminton MS. 1463
Brogyntyn MS. 6
Great Sessions Records
Llanstephan MS. 133
Plas Power MS. 1
Plymouth Deeds
Slebech Papers 3141
Vairdre Book
Welsh Church Records:
    Bangor Miscellaneous MSS.
    Brecon Probate Records
    Llandaff Chapter Records
    Llandaff Probate Records
    St Asaph Bishops' Registers (SA/BR/1)
    St Asaph Miscellaneous Book (SA/MB)
    Archdeacon D. R. Thomas's MSS. (SA/DR/39–40)
    St David's Bishops' Registers
    St David's Chapter Records

Public Record Office
C1 Chancery Judicial Proceedings (Early)
C3 Chancery Judicial Proceedings, Series II
C24 Chancery Town Depositions
E26 Exchequer Treasury of Receipt Miscellaneous Books. Renunciations of Papal Supremacy
E112 Exchequer, Bills and Answers
E117 Exchequer, Church Goods
E134 Exchequer, Depositions taken by Commission
E163 Exchequer, King's Remembrancer, Miscellanea of the Exchequer
E164 Exchequer, King's Remembrancer, Miscellaneous Books, Series I
E301 Exchequer, Augmentations Office, Chantry Certificates
E321 Exchequer, Augmentation Office, Proceedings of the Court of Augmentations
E322 Exchequer, Surrenders of the Monasteries

PCC Prerogative Court of Canterbury (formerly at Somerset House, now in
  PRO) Will register books of Alenger, Loftus, Pynnynge, Spert
Req. Court of Requests, Proceedings
SC6 Ministers' Accounts, Henry VIII, 5675
SP1 State Papers, Henry VIII, General Series
SP12 State Papers, Domestic, Elizabeth
SP99 State Papers, Foreign, Venice
Star Chamber Proceedings
      STA C 2 Star Chamber Proceedings, Henry VIII
      STA C 5 Star Chamber Proceedings, Elizabeth

(B) Printed Sources

Acts of the Privy Council (London, 1890–).
Barddoniaeth William Llŷn, ed. J. C. Morrice (Bangor, 1908).
Bateson, M., 'Original letters from the bishops to the Privy Council', *Camden Miscellany*, IX (1893), 11–23.
Beibl Cyssegr-lan (1588).
Bibl Cysegr-lan (1620).
Book of Common Prayer (1559).
British Museum Catalogue of Printed Books (London, 1881–).
Calendar of the Caernarvonshire Quarter Sessions Records, I. *1541–1558*, ed. W. O. Williams (Caernarfon, 1956).
Calendar of the Carew Manuscripts (London, 1867–73).
Calendar of Deeds and Documents. Coleman, Crosswood and Hawarden Deeds (Aberystwyth, 1921–31).
Calendar of Letters relating to North Wales, ed. B. E. Howells (Cardiff, 1967).
Calendar of Papal Letters (London, 1894–).
Calendar of Patent Rolls (London, 1891–).
Calendar of the Register of the Council in the Marches, 1569–91, ed. R. Flenley (London, 1916).
Calendar of the Salusbury Correspondence, 1553–c.1700, ed. W. J. Smith (Cardiff, 1954).
Calendar of State Papers, Domestic (London, 1856–); *Foreign* (London, 1861–); *Ireland* (London, 1860–); *Rome* (London, 1916, 1926); *Spanish* (London, 1862–); *Venetian* (London, 1864–).
Calendar of the Wynn (of Gwydir) Papers, ed. J. Ballinger (Aberystwyth, 1926).
Canu Rhydd Cynnar, ed. T. H. Parry-Williams (Cardiff, 1932).
Carolau Richard White, ed. T. H. Parry-Williams (Cardiff, 1931).
Cartae et Alia Munimenta quae ad Dominium de Glamorgan Pertinent, ed. G. T. Clark (6 vols. Cardiff, 1910).
Catalogue of Manuscripts relating to Wales in the British Museum, ed. E. Owen (1 vol. in 4, London, 1900–22).
Catalogue of Star Chamber Proceedings relating to Wales, ed. I. ab O. Edwards (Cardiff, 1929).

Bibliography

Catholic Record Society Publications (London, 1905–).

Clenennau Letters and Papers, ed. T. Jones Pierce (Aberystwyth, 1947).

Clynnog, M., *Athravaeth Gristnogawl* (1568; reprint, London, 1880).

Conran, A., *The Penguin Book of Welsh Verse* (Harmondsworth, 1961).

Correspondence of Robert, Earl of Leycester . . . 1585 and 1586, ed. J. Prince (Camden Society, London, 1844).

Davies, R., *Funeral Sermon preached at Carmarthen on the Death of the Earl of Essex* (London, 1577).

Detholiad o Waith Gruffydd ab Ieuan ap Llywelyn Fychan, ed. J. C. Morrice (Bangor, 1910).

Diary of Henry Machyn (Camden Society, London, 1848).

Drych Cristianogawl . . . (1586).

Early Chancery Proceedings concerning Wales, ed. E. A. Lewis (Cardiff, 1937).

Edgeworth, R., *Sermons Very Fruitful . . .* (London, 1557).

Edwards, C., *Y Ffydd Ddiffuant*, ed. G. J. Williams (Cardiff, 1936).

Ellis, H. *Original Letters, Illustrative of English History* (11 vols. London, 1824, 1827, 1846).

The Episcopal Registers of St David's, 1397–1518, ed. R. F. Isaacson (3 vols. London, 1917–20).

Exchequer Proceedings concerning Wales, ed. E. G. Jones (Cardiff, 1939).

Exchequer Proceedings concerning Wales in Tempore James I, ed. T. I. J. Jones (Cardiff, 1955).

First and Second Prayer Books of Edward VI (Everyman edn., 1949).

Foxe, J., *Acts and Monuments . . .* , ed. S. Catley (7 vols. London, 1837–41).

Frère, W. H., *Register of Matthew Parker* (Canterbury and York Soc., 1907).

—— and Kennedy, W. P. M., *Visitation Articles and Injunctions of the Period of the Reformation* (3 vols. Alcuin Club, 1910).

Geiriadur Prifysgol Cymru (Cardiff, 1950–).

Geoffrey of Monmouth, *Historia Regum Britanniae*, ed. Acton Griscom (London, 1929).

Giraldus Cambrensis, *The Journey through Wales . . .*, ed. L. Thorpe (Harmondsworth, 1978).

Griffiths, R. A. (ed.), *The Principality of Wales in the Later Middle Ages*, I. *South Wales, 1272–1536* (Cardiff, 1972).

Grindal, E., *Remains*, ed. W. Nicholson (Parker Soc., London, 1843).

Gwaith Siôn Tudur, ed. E. P. Roberts (2 vols. Bangor, 1978).

Gwaith Tudur Aled, ed. T. G. Jones (2 vols. Cardiff, 1926).

Gwssanaeth y Gwŷr Newydd: Robert Gwyn (1580), ed. G. Bowen (Cardiff, 1970).

Gwynedd, John, *A Declaration of the State wherein All Heretikes doe leade their lives . . .* (London, 1554).

Hen Gwndidau, Carolau, a Chywyddau, ed. L. J. Hopkin-James and T. C. Evans (Bangor, 1914).

Historical Manuscripts Commission: Reports on Manuscripts in the Welsh Language (London, 1898–1910); *Salisbury Manuscripts* (London, 1883–); *Wells Cathedral Manuscripts. 10th Report* (London, 1885).

Bibliography

History of the Gwydir Family and Memoirs, ed. J. G. Jones (Llandysul, 1990).

Hopkiniaid Morgannwg, ed. L. J. Hopkin-James (Bangor, 1910).

Hughes, G. H., *Rhagymadroddion, 1547–1648* (Cardiff, 1951).

Jewel, J., *Works* (4 vols. Parker Soc., 1845–50).

Jones, E. G. (ed.), 'History of the Bulkeley Family', *AAST* (1947).

Jones, I. G., and Williams, D. (eds.), *The Religious Census of 1851* (2 vols. Cardiff, 1977, 1981).

Journals of the House of Lords (London, 1846–).

Kennedy, W. P. M., *Elizabethan Episcopal Administration* (3 vols. Alcuin Club, London, 1925).

Kyffin, M., *Deffynniad Ffydd Eglwys Loegr*, ed. W. P. Williams (Cardiff, 1908).

Latimer, H., *Sermons and Remains* (Parker Soc., London, 1845).

Laud, W., *Works* (6 vols. London, 1853).

Leland's Itinerary in Wales, ed. L. T. Smith (London, 1906).

Letters and Memorials of Cardinal Allen, ed. T. F. Knox (London, 1906).

Letters and Memorials . . . by Sir Henry Sidney, ed. A. Collins (London, 1746).

Letters and Papers, Foreign and Domestic, of the Reign of Henry VIII . . . , ed. J. S. Brewer, J. Gairdner, and R. H. Brodie (23 vols. London, 1862–1932).

Lewys, H., *Perl mewn Adfyd*, ed. W. J. Gruffydd (Cardiff, 1929).

Lloyd, C., *Formularies of Faith put forward by Authority during the Reign of Henry VIII* (Oxford, 1825).

Lloyd Jenkins, D., *Cerddi Rhydd Cynnar* (Llandysul, 1931).

Llyfr Gweddi Gyffredin 1567, ed. G. M. Richards and G. Williams (Cardiff, 1967).

Mathew, D., 'Some Elizabethan Documents', *BBCS*, VI (1931–3), 70–8.

Merrick, R., *A Booke of Glamorganshire Antiquities*, ed. B. L. James (Cardiff, 1984).

Nichols, J. G. (ed.), *The Chronicle of Queen Jane . . . and Queen Mary* (Camden Soc., London, 1850).

Original Letters relative to the English Reformation, ed. H. Robinson (2 vols. Parker Soc., London, 1846).

Owen, G., *Description of Penbrokshire*, ed. H. Owen (3 vols. London, 1906).

Oxford Book of Welsh Verse, ed. T. Parry (Oxford, 1962).

Oxford Book of Welsh Verse in English, ed. G. Jones (Oxford, 1977).

Parker, M., *Correspondence* (Parker Soc., London, 1853).

Pembrokeshire Life, 1572–1842, ed. B. E. Howells and K. A. Howells (Pembrokeshire Record Society, 1972).

Penry, J., *Three Treatises concerning Wales*, ed. D. Williams (Cardiff, 1960).

Pilkington, J., *Works*, ed. J. Scholfield (Parker Soc., London, 1842).

[Price, J.], *Yny Lhyvyr Hwnn . . .*, ed. J. H. Davies (Bangor, 1902).

Pryce, A. I., *The Diocese of Bangor in the Sixteenth Century* (Bangor, 1923).

Purvis, J. S. *Tudor Parish Documents* (Cambridge, 1948).

Records of the County Borough of Cardiff, ed. J. H. Matthews (6 vols. Cardiff, 1898–1911).

Records of the Court of Augmentations relating to Wales and Monmouthshire, ed. E. A. Lewis and J. C. Davies (Cardiff, 1954).

Bibliography

Rees, E., *Libri Wallie* (Aberystwyth, 1987).

Rhyddiaith Gymraeg, I. *Detholion o Lawysgrifau, 1488–1609*, ed. T. H. Parry-Williams (Cardiff, 1954). II. *Detholion o Lawysgrifau a Llyfrau Printiedig*, ed. T. Jones (Cardiff, 1956).

Robert, G., *Gramadeg Cymraeg*, ed. G. J. Williams (Cardiff, 1939).

Roper, W., *Life of Thomas More*, ed. E. V. Hitchcock (EETS, 1935).

Rymer, T., *Foedera, Conventiones, Litterae, et Cuiuscunque Generis Acta Publica* (20 vols. London, 1860).

Sadler, Sir Ralph, *The State Papers and Letters of*, by Arthur Clifford (3 vols. Edinburgh, 1809).

Salesbury, W., *A Dictionary in Englishe and Welsh* (London, 1547).

—— *Kynniver Llith a Ban*, ed. J. Fisher (Cardiff, 1931).

—— *Oll Synnwyr Pen Kembero Ygyd*. . . (London, 1547).

Saunders, E., *A View of the State of Religion in the Diocese of St David's* (repr. Cardiff, 1949).

Statutes of the Realm (11 vols. London, 1810–28).

The Carmarthen Book of Ordinances, 1569–1606, ed. J. Davies (Carmarthen, 1996).

The Statutes of Wales, ed. I. Bowen (London, 1908).

The Stradling Correspondence, ed. J. M. Traherne (London, 1840).

Talbot, C. H. (ed.), *Letters from the English Abbots to the Chapter at Cîteaux, 1442–1521* (Camden Soc., London, 1967), 4th ser. IV.

Testament Newydd, 1567 (repr. Caernarfon, 1850).

Thomas, W., *The Pilgrim*, ed. J. A. Froude (London, 1861).

Three Chapters of Letters relating to the Suppression of the English Monasteries, ed. T. Wright (Camden Soc., London, 1843).

Tyndale, W., *Doctrinal Treatises* (3 vols. Parker Soc., London, 1848).

Valor Ecclesiasticus temp. Henry VIII . . ., ed. J. Caley (6 vols. London, 1810–13).

Visitation Articles and Injunctions of the Early Stuart Church, ed. K. Fincham (Church of England Rec. Soc., London, 1994).

Wilkins, D., *Concilia Magnae Britanniae et Hiberniae . . . 446–1718* (4 vols. London, 1737).

Williams, C. H., *English Historical Documents*, V. *1485–1558* (London, 1967).

Wriothesley, C., *A Chronicle of England*, ed. W. D. Hamilton (2 vols. Camden Soc., London, 1875–7).

Wynn, J., *History of the Gwydir Family*, ed. J. Ballinger (Cardiff, 1927).

Zurich Letters, ed. H. Robinson (2 vols. Parker Soc., London, 1842–5).

II. Secondary Sources

(A) Printed Books

Alcock, L., *Arthur's Britain* (Harmondsworth, 1971).

Alsop, J. D., 'Religious preambles in early modern wills', *JEH*, XXXVII (1989), 19–27.

Ashton, C., *Bywyd ac Amserau'r Esgob William Morgan* (Treherbert, 1891).

Ashton, R., *Reformation and Revolution, 1558–1660* (London, 1984).

Aston, M., *England's Iconoclasts: Laws against Images* (Oxford, 1988).

Ballinger, J., *The Bible in Wales* (London, 1906).

Banks, R. W., 'Brecon priory: its suppression and possessions', *AC* (1890), 209–33.

Baring-Gould, S., and Fisher, J., *The Lives of the British Saints* (4 vols. London, 1907–12).

Baskerville, G., *English Monks and the Suppression of the Monasteries* (London, 1949).

Bebb, W. A., *Machlud y Mynachlogydd* (Aberystwyth, 1937).

—— *Cyfnod y Tuduriaid* (Wrexham, 1939).

Bell, H. I., 'Translations from the Cywyddwyr', *TCS* (1940), 221–53; (1942), 130–7.

Beer, B. L., *Northumberland: The Political Career of John Dudley* (Kent, OH, 1973).

Bennett, H. S., *English Books and their Readers, 1475 to 1557* (Cambridge, 1952).

Bernard, G. W., 'The fall of Anne Boleyn', *EHR*, CVI (1991), 584–610.

Bevan, W. L., *St David's* (SPCK Diocesan Histories, London, 1888).

Bindoff, S. T., *Ket's Rebellion 1549* (Historical Association Pamphlet, London, 1949).

—— (ed.), *The House of Commons, 1509–1558* (3 vols. London, 1982).

—— *et al.* (eds.), *Elizabethan Government and Society* (London, 1961).

Black, J. B., *The Age of Elizabeth* (Oxford, 1936).

Blench, J. W., *Preaching in England in the Late Fifteenth and Sixteenth Centuries* (Oxford, 1964).

Bossy, J., *The English Catholic Community, 1570–1850* (London, 1977).

Bowen, D. J., *Gwaith Gruffudd Hiraethog* (Cardiff, 1990).

—— 'Detholiad o englynion hiraeth am yr hen ffydd', *Efrydiau Catholig*, VI (1954), 5–12.

Bowen, E. G., *The Settlements of the Celtic Saints in Wales* (Cardiff, 1954).

—— *Wales: A Physical, Historical and Regional Geography* (London, 1958).

—— *Saints, Seaways and Settlements in Celtic Lands* (Cardiff, 1977).

Bowen, G. (ed.), *Gwssanaeth y Gwŷr Newydd: Robert Gwyn (1580)* (Cardiff, 1970).

—— 'Canolfannau llenyddol y ffoaduriaid Catholig', *LlC*, III (1954–5), 229–33.

Bradney, J. A., 'The speech of William Blethin, bishop of Llandaff', *Cymm.* XXXI (1921), 240–6.

Bush, M. L., *The Governmental Policy of Protector Somerset* (London, 1975).

Butler, L. A. S., 'Leicester's Church, Denbigh . . . ', *Journ. Brit. Archaeol. Ass.* (1974), 46–63.

Cambridge History of the Bible, III. ed. S. L. Greenslade (Cambridge, 1963).

Carter, H., *National Atlas of Wales* (Cardiff, 1980–).

Chadwick, N. K., *Studies in the Early British Church* (Cambridge, 1958).

—— *The Age of the Saints in the Early Celtic Church* (Cambridge, 1961).

Chapman, H. W., *The Last Tudor King* (London, 1962).

Charles, B. G., *George Owen of Henllys* (Aberystwyth, 1973).

—— 'The records of Slebech', *NLWJ*, V (1948), 179–85.

Chaunu, P. (ed.), *The Reformation* (Gloucester, 1989).

Clark, D. S. T., and Morgan, P. T. J., 'Religion and magic in Elizabethan Wales', *JEH*, XXVII (1976), 31–46.

Clark, M. L., *Bangor Cathedral* (Cardiff, 1969).

Clay, C. (ed.), *Rural Society: Landowners, Peasants and Labourers* (Cambridge, 1990).

Cleary, J. M., *The Catholic Recusancy of the Barlow Family of Slebech* (Cardiff, 1956).

—— *A Checklist of Welsh Students in the Seminaries* (Cardiff, 1958).

—— 'The Catholic resistance in Wales, 1568–1678', *Blackfriars* (March 1957), 111–25.

Collinson, P., *The Elizabethan Puritan Movement* (London, 1967).

—— *The Religion of Protestants* (London, 1982).

—— *Godly Rule: Essays on English Protestantism and Puritanism* (London, 1983).

Constant, G., *La Réforme en Angleterre: Le Schisme anglican* (Paris, 1930).

—— *The Reformation in England*, II. *Edward VI (1547–1553)* (London, 1941).

Corish, P. J., *The Catholic Community in the Seventeenth and Eighteenth Centuries* (Dublin, 1981).

Coulton, G. G., *Five Centuries of Religion* (4 vols. Cambridge, 1927–50).

Cowley, F. G., *The Monastic Order in South Wales, 1066–1349* (Cardiff, 1977).

Crean, P. J., *Sir William Dai* (Dublin, 1958).

Cressy, D., *Literacy and the Social Order: Reading and Writing in Tudor England* (Cambridge, 1980).

Cross, C., *Church and People, 1450–1660* (London, 1976).

—— (ed.), *Law and Government under the Tudors* (London, 1988).

Cross, F. L. (ed.), *The Oxford Dictionary of the Christian Church* (Oxford, 1957).

Crossley, F. H., 'Screens, lofts and stalls situated in Wales and Monmouthshire', *AC*, XCVII–CVII (1943–58).

Daniel-Rops, H., *The Catholic Reformation* (London, 1968).

Davies, C., *Latin Writers of the Renaissance* (Cardiff, 1981).

Davies, C. S. L., *Peace, Print and Protestantism* (London, 1977).

—— 'The Pilgrimage of Grace reconsidered', *PP*, XLI (1968), 54–76.

Davies C. T. B., 'Y cerddi i'r tai crefydd fel ffynhonnell hanesyddol', *NLWJ*, XVIII (1974), 268–86, 345–73.

Davies, H., *Worship and Theology in England from Cranmer to Hooker, 1534–1603* (Princeton, 1970).

Davies, J. C., *Episcopal Acts relating to the Welsh Dioceses, 1066–1272* (2 vols. Cardiff, 1946–8).

Davies, R. R., *Conquest, Co-existence and Change: Wales, 1063–1415* (Oxford, 1987), repr. as *The Age of Conquest* (Oxford, 1991).

—— *The Age of Conquest* (Oxford, 1991).

—— *The Revolt of Owain Glyn Dŵr* (Oxford, 1995).

Dictionary of National Biography (63 vols. London, 1885–1900).

Dictionary of Welsh Biography (London, 1959).

Dickens, A. G., *Robert Holgate* (York, 1955).

—— *Lollards and Protestants in the Diocese of York, 1509–1558* (Hull, 1959).

—— *Thomas Cromwell and the English Reformation* (London, 1959).

—— *The English Reformation* (London, 1964).

Dixon, R. W., *History of the Church of England* (6 vols. London, 1875–1902).

Doble, G. H., *The Lives of the Welsh Saints* (Cardiff, 1971).

Dodd, A. H., *Studies in Stuart Wales* (Cardiff, 1952).

—— 'Wales and the Stuart succession', *TCS* (1937), 201–25.

—— 'North Wales and the Essex Revolt of 1601', *EHR*, LIX (1944), 343–70.

—— 'The pattern of politics in Stuart Wales', *TCS* (1948), 8–91.

Donaldson, G., *The Scottish Reformation* (Cambridge, 1960).

Doran, S., and Durston, C., *Princes, Pastors, and People* (London, 1991).

Dowling, M., 'Anne Boleyn and reform', *JEH*, XXXV (1984), 30–46.

Duffy, E., *The Stripping of the Altars: Traditional Religion in England, c.1400–1580* (New Haven, 1992).

Eagleston, A. J., *The Channel Islands under Tudor Government, 1485–1642* (Cambridge, 1949).

Easterling, R., 'The friars in Wales', *AC* (1914), 323–56.

Edwards, I. ab O., 'William Morgan's quarrels with his parishioners', *BBCS*, II (1926–7), 298–339.

Edwards, R. D., *Church and State in Tudor Ireland* (Dublin, 1935).

Ellis, T. P., *The Catholic Martyrs of Wales* (London, 1933).

—— *Welsh Benedictines of the Terror* (Newtown, 1936).

Elton, G. R., *England under the Tudors* (London, 1954).

—— *The Tudor Constitution* (Cambridge, 1960).

—— *Policy and Police* (Cambridge, 1972).

—— *Reform and Reformation, 1509–1558* (London, 1977).

—— 'Tudor government: points of contact', *TRHS*, 5th ser. XXIV. 183–200; XXV. 195–212; XXVI. 211–28.

Emmison, F. G., *Elizabethan Life* (Chelmsford, 1970).

Evans, A. O., *The Life and Work of Edmwnd Prys* (Carmarthen, 1923).

—— *A Memorandum on the Legality of the Welsh Bible . . .* (Cardiff, 1925).

—— 'Nicholas Robinson', *Cymm.* XXXIX (1928), 149–99.

Evans, D. S., *Medieval Welsh Literature* (Cardiff, 1986).

Evans, J. W., 'The Reformation and St David's cathedral', *JWEH*, VII (1991), 1–16.

Fisher, H. A. L., *Political History of England, 1485–1547* (London, 1913).

Fisher, J., *The Private Devotions of the Welsh* (Liverpool, 1898).

Fleming, D. H., *The Reformation in Scotland* (London, 1909).

Fraser, A., *Mary Queen of Scots* (London, 1969).

—— *The Six Wives of Henry VIII* (London, 1993).

Frère, W. H., *The Marian Reaction in relation to the English Clergy* (London, 1896).

Froude, J. A., *The Reign of Elizabeth* (London, 1912).

—— *The Reign of Edward VI* (London, 1926).

—— *The Reign of Henry VIII* (London, 1928).

Gairdner, J., *Lollardy and the Reformation in England* (4 vols. London, 1908–13).

Garrett, C. H., *The Marian Exiles, 1553–1558* (Cambridge, 1938).

Gee, H., and Hardy, W. J. (eds.), *Documents Illustrative of English Church History* (London, 1910).

George, C. H., and K., *The Protestant Mind of the English Reformation, 1570–1640* (Princeton, 1961).

Geyl, P., *The Revolt in the Netherlands* (2nd edn., London, 1958).

Glamorgan County History, IV. *Early Modern Glamorgan*, ed. G. Williams (Cardiff, 1974).

Gray, M., 'The diocese of Bangor', *JWEH*, V (1988), 31–72.

—— 'The last days of the shrines and chantries of Monmouthshire', *JWEH*, VII (1991), 20–40.

—— 'The diocese of Llandaff in 1563', *JWRH*, II (1994).

Green, F., 'Early wills in West Wales', *West Wales Historical Records*, VII (1917–18), 143–64.

Griffith, W. P., *Learning, Law and Religion . . . c.1540–1642* (Cardiff, 1996).

Griffiths, G. M., 'Educational activity in the diocese of St Asaph', *JHSCW*, III (1953), 64–77.

—— 'St Asaph episcopal acts, 1536–58', *JHSCW*, IX (1959), 32–69.

Griffiths, R. A., *Sir Rhys ap Thomas and His Family* (Cardiff, 1994).

—— (ed.), *Boroughs of Medieval Wales* (Cardiff, 1978).

Gruffydd, R. G., *Argraffwyr Cyntaf Cymru* (Cardiff, 1972).

—— *Y Beibl a Droes i'w Bobl Draw: The Translation of the Bible into the Welsh Tongue* (Cardiff, 1988).

—— (ed.), *Y Gair ar Waith* (Cardiff, 1988).

—— 'Dau lythyr gan Owen Lewis', *LlC*, III (1954–5), 229–33.

—— 'Dau destun Protestannaidd cynnar o Lawysgrif Hafod 22', *Trivium*, I (1966), 56–66.

—— 'Carol santaidd i'r Grawys o Waith y Tad William Davies', *TCHS* (1967), 37–46.

—— '*Yny Lhyvyr Hwnn . . .* (1546); the earliest Welsh printed book', *BBCS*, XXIII (1968), 105–16.

—— 'The life of Dr John Davies of Brecon', *TCS* (1971), pt 2, 175–90.

—— 'Dr John Davies: the old man of Brecknock', *AC* (1992), 1–13.

Gruffydd, W. J., *Llenyddiaeth Cymru: Rhyddiaith o 1540 hyd 1660* (Wrexham, 1926).

Guy, J., *Tudor England* (Oxford, 1988).

—— and A. Fox (eds.), *Reassessing the Henrician Age* (Oxford, 1986).

Haigh, C., *Reformation and Resistance in Tudor Lancashire* (Cambridge, 1973).

—— *The English Reformation Revised* (London, 1987).

—— *English Reformations: Religion, Politics and Society under the Tudors* (Oxford, 1993).

—— (ed.), *The Reign of Elizabeth I* (London, 1984).

Harrison, S. M., *The Pilgrimage of Grace in the Lakeland Counties* (RHS, London, 1981).

Haugaard, W. P., *Elizabeth and the English Reformation* (Cambridge, 1968).

Hays, R. W., *The History of the Abbey of Aberconway, 1186–1537* (Cardiff, 1963).

Head, R. E., *Royal Supremacy and the Trials of the Bishops, 1558–1725* (London, 1962).

Heal, F., *Of Prelates and Princes* (Cambridge, 1990).

—— and R. O'Day, *Church and Society in England from Henry VIII to James I* (London, 1971).

Hembry, P. M., *The Bishops of Bath and Wells, 1540–1640* (London, 1967).

Herbert, T., and Jones, G. E., *Tudor Wales* (Cardiff, 1988).

Hill, C., *Economic Problems of the Church from Archbishop Whitgift to the Long Parliament* (Oxford, 1956).

—— *Puritanism and Society in Pre-revolutionary England* (London, 1964).

—— 'Puritans and the "Dark Corners" of the Land', *TRHS*, 5th ser. XII (1963), 77–102.

Hirsch-Davies, J. E., *Catholicism in Medieval Wales* (London, 1916).

Hoak, D. E., *The King's Council in the Reign of Edward VI* (Cambridge, 1976).

Hodgett, G. A. J., 'The unpensioned ex-religious in Tudor England', *JEH*, XIII (1962), 195–202.

Hughes, P., *Rome and the Counter-Reformation in England* (London, 1942).

—— *The Reformation in England* (3 vols. London, 1950–4).

Hume, M. A. S., *The Wives of Henry VIII* (London, 1905).

Ives, E. W., *Anne Boleyn* (Oxford, 1986).

—— 'Faction at the court of Henry VIII', *History*, LVII (1972), 169–88.

—— *et al.* (eds.), *Wealth and Power in Tudor England* (London, 1978).

Jack, S., 'Dissolution dates', *BIHR*, XLIII (1970), 161–81.

—— 'The last days of the smaller monasteries in England', *JEH*, XXI (1970), 97–124.

Jacobs, H. E., *The Lutheran Movement in England during the Reigns of Henry VIII and Edward VI* (Philadelphia, 1908).

James, M. E., 'Obedience and dissent in Henrician England: the Lincolnshire Rebellion, 1536', *PP* (1970), 3–75.

Janelle, P., *L'Angleterre à la veille du Schisme* (Paris, 1935).

Jarman, A. O. H., *The Legend of Merlin* (Cardiff, 1960).

Jedin, H., *The Council of Trent* (2 vols. Edinburgh, 1961).

Jenkins, G. H., *Literature, Religion and Society in Wales, 1660–1730* (Cardiff, 1978).

Bibliography

—— *Hanes Cymru yn y Cyfnod Modern Cynnar* (Cardiff, 1983).

—— *The Foundations of Modern Wales* (Oxford, 1987).

—— 'Popular beliefs in Wales from the Restoration to Methodism', *BBCS*, XXVII (1976–8), 440–62.

Jenkins, P., *Modern Wales, 1536–1990* (London, 1992).

Jones, E. D., 'A survey of South Wales chantries', *AC* (1934), 134–55.

Jones, E. G., *Cymru a'r Hen Ffydd* (Cardiff, 1951).

—— 'The Lleyn recusancy case, 1578–81', *TCS* (1936), 97–123.

—— 'Anglesey and invasion', *TAAS* (1947), 26–37.

Jones, E. J., *Medieval Heraldry* (Cardiff, 1943).

Jones, F., *The Holy Wells of Wales* (Cardiff, 1954).

Jones, G. E., *Modern Wales: A Concise History* (Cambridge, 1984).

Jones, G. H., *Celtic Britain and the Pilgrim Movement* (London, 1912).

Jones, J. G., *Wales and the Tudor State* (Cardiff, 1988).

—— (ed.), *Class, Community and Culture in Tudor Wales* (Cardiff, 1989).

—— 'Y tylwyth teg yng Nghymru'r unfed ganrif ar bymtheg a'r ail', *LlC*, VIII (1964), 96–9.

—— 'Bishop William Morgan's dispute with John Wynn of Gwydir', *JHSCW*, XXII (1972), 49–78.

—— 'The Welsh poets and their patrons', *WHR*, IX (1979), 245–73.

—— 'Thomas Davies and William Hughes: two Reformation bishops of St Asaph', *BBCS*, XXIX (1980–2), 320–35.

Jones, N., *Faith by Statute* (RHS, London, 1982).

Jones, R. B., *The Old British Tongue: The Vernacular in Wales, 1540–1640* (Cardiff, 1970).

—— *William Salesbury* (Cardiff, 1994).

—— *'A Lanterne to their Feet'* (Drover's Press, Llandovery, 1995).

Jones, W. B., and Freeman, E. A., *The History and Antiquities of St David's* (London, 1856).

Jordan, W. K., *Philanthropy in England, 1480–1660* (London, 1959).

—— *Edward VI: The Young King* (London, 1968).

—— *Edward VI: The Threshold of Power* (London, 1970).

Ker, N. R., *The Medieval Libraries of Great Britain* (RHS, London, 1941).

—— 'Sir John Prise', *The Library*, 5th ser. X (1955), 1–24.

Kissack, K. E., 'Religious life in Monmouth, 1066–1536', *JHSCW*, XIV (1964), 25–58.

Knappen, M. M., *Tudor Puritanism* (London, 1965).

Knight, J. K., *Glamorgan County History*, II. *Prehistoric Glamorgan*, ed. H. N. Savory (Cardiff, 1984), chaps. 8 and 9.

Knowles, D., *The Religious Orders in England* (3 vols. Cambridge, 1948–59).

Lake, P. G., *Moderate Puritans and the English Church* (Cambridge, 1982).

Laurence, C. H., *The English Church and the Papacy in the Middle Ages* (London, 1965).

Lehmberg, S. E., *The Reformation Parliament, 1529–36* (Cambridge, 1970).

—— *The Later Parliaments of Henry VIII* (Cambridge, 1977).

Bibliography

Le Neve, J., *Fasti Ecclesiae Anglicanae, 1300–1541*, XI. *The Welsh Dioceses*, compiled by B. Jones (London, 1965).

Levine, M., *Tudor Dynastic Problems, 1450–1571* (London, 1973).

Lewis, C. W., 'Syr Edward Stradling', *Ysgrifau Beirniadol*, XIX (1994), 139–207.

Lewis, H., 'Darnau o'r efengylau', *Cymm.* XXXI (1921), 193–216.

Lloyd, D. T., 'Welsh pilgrims at Rome, 1471–1738', *Trivium*, VI (1971), 21–31.

Lloyd, H. A., *The Gentry of South-west Wales, 1540–1640* (Cardiff, 1968).

Lloyd, J. E., *Owen Glendower* (Oxford, 1931).

Loach, J., and Titler, R., *The Mid-Tudor Polity, c.1540–1560* (London, 1980).

Loades, D. M., *Two Tudor Conspiracies* (Cambridge, 1965).

—— *The Oxford Reformers* (London, 1970).

—— *Politics and the Nation, 1450–1600* (London, 1974).

—— *The Reign of Mary I* (London, 1979).

—— *Mary Tudor* (Oxford, 1989).

—— 'The theory and practice of censorship in sixteenth-century England', *TRHS*, 5th ser. XXIV (1974), 141–58.

Loomie, A. J., *The Spanish Elizabethans* (London, 1963).

Lupton, J. H., *A Life of John Colet* (2nd edn. London, 1909).

MacCulloch, D., *The Later Reformation in England* (London, 1990).

McGinn, D. J., *John Penry and the Marprelate Controversy* (Rutgers UP, 1960).

McGrath, P., *Papists and Puritans under Elizabeth I* (London, 1967).

McGurk, J. J. N., 'A survey of the demands made . . . for the Irish wars, 1594–1602', *TCS* (1983), pp. 56–68.

Mackie, J. D., *The Early Tudors* (Oxford, 1952).

Manning, R. B., *Religion and Society in Elizabethan Sussex* (Leicester, 1964).

Mathew, D., *The Celtic Peoples and Renaissance Europe* (London, 1933).

Meyer, A. O., *England and the Catholic Church under Queen Elizabeth* (London, 1910).

Morgan, P. T. J., *Beibl i Gymru: A Bible for Wales* (Aberystwyth, 1988).

—— *The Eighteenth-Century Renaissance* (Llandybïe, 1981).

Morison, S. E., *The Prayer Books* (Cambridge, 1949).

Muller, J. A., *Stephen Gardiner and the Tudor Reaction* (London, 1926).

Neale, J. E., *Queen Elizabeth* (London, 1948).

—— *Elizabeth I and Her Parliaments, 1559–81* (London, 1953).

Newell, E. J., *A History of the Welsh Church to the Dissolution of the Monasteries* (London, 1895).

O'Day, R., *The English Clergy: The Emergence and Consolidation of a Profession, 1558–1642* (Leicester, 1979).

—— *Princes and Paupers in the English Church, 1500–1800* (Leicester, 1981).

—— *The Debate on the English Reformation* (London, 1986).

—— and Heal, F. (eds.), *Continuity and Change: Personnel and Administration of the Church of England* (Leicester, 1976).

Ogle, A., *The Tragedy of the Lollards' Tower* (Oxford, 1949).

O'Sullivan, J. F., *Cistercian Settlements in Wales and Monmouthshire, 1140–1540* (New York, 1947).

Owen, G. D., *Elizabethan Wales: The Social Scene* (London, 1962).

—— *Wales in the Reign of James I* (RHS, London, 1988).

Owen, L., 'A seventeenth-century commonplace book', *TCS* (1962), 16–47.

Parmiter, G. de C., *The King's Great Matter* (London, 1967).

Parker, G., *The Dutch Revolt* (London, 1977).

Parker, T. M., *The Reformation in England* (Oxford, 1950).

Parry, T., *History of Welsh Literature*, tr. H. I. Bell (Oxford, 1955).

Pembrokeshire County History, III. *Early Modern Pembroke*, ed. B. E. Howells (Aberystwyth, 1987).

Peter, D., *Hanes Crefydd yng Nghymru* (Carmarthen, 1816).

Phillips, J., 'Glimpses of Elizabethan Pembrokeshire', *AC* (1897, 1899, 1904).

Pierce, T. Jones, *Welsh Medieval Society: Selected Essays* (Cardiff, 1972).

Pierce, W., *The Life and Times of John Penry* (London, 1923).

Pollard, A. F., *Thomas Wolsey* (London, 1929).

Proctor, F. and Frère, W. H., *A New History of the Book of Common Prayer* (London, 1914).

Pugh, F. H., 'Glamorgan recusants in the reigns of Elizabeth I and James I', *SWMRS*, III (1954), 49–68.

—— 'Monmouthshire recusants in the reigns of Elizabeth I and James I', *SWMRS*, IV (1957), 57–110.

—— 'William Griffith of Llanvithyn', *Morgannwg*, XXX (1986), 8–19.

Pugh, T. B. (ed.), *Glamorgan County History*, III. *The Middle Ages* (Cardiff, 1971).

Raleigh, W., *The English Voyages of the Sixteenth Century* (London, 1910).

Read, C., *Mr Secretary Cecil and Queen Elizabeth* (London, 1955).

Redworth, G., *In Defence of the Church Catholic: The Life of Stephen Gardiner* (Oxford, 1990).

—— 'A study in the formulation of policy . . . the Act of Six Articles', *JEH* XXXVII (1986), 42–67.

—— 'Whatever happened to the English Reformation?', *History Today*, XXXVII (1987), 29–36.

Rees, B., *Dulliau'r Canu Rhydd, 1500–1640* (Cardiff, 1952).

Rees, D. B., *Sir Rhys ap Thomas* (Llandysul, 1992).

Rees, J. F., *The Story of Milford* (Cardiff, 1954).

Rees, W., *The Order of St John in Wales* (Cardiff, 1947).

—— *An Historical Atlas of Wales* (Cardiff, 1966).

——'The union of England and Wales', *TCS* (1937), 27–100.

—— 'The suppression of the friaries', *SWMRS*, III (1954), 7–19.

—— 'The friars at Cardiff and Newport', *SWMRS*, IV (1958), 51–6.

Roberts, G., *Aspects of Welsh History* (Cardiff, 1969).

Roberts, P. R., 'The Acts of Union and Wales', *TCS* (1972–3), 49–72.

—— 'The union with England and the identity of "Anglican Wales"', *TRHS*, 5th ser. XXII (1972), 49–70.

—— 'The Welsh language, English law and Tudor legislation', *TCS* (1989), 19–76.

Robinson, W. R. B., 'Early Tudor policy towards Wales . . .', *BBCS*, XX (1962–4), 421–38; XXI (1964–6), 43–74, 334–61.

—— 'The first subsidy assessments of the hundreds of Swansea and Llangyfelach', *WHR*, II/2 (1964), 125–46.

Roderick, A. J. (ed.), *Wales through the Ages* (Llandybïe, 1959, 1961).

Rogers, J. R., *Slebech Commandery and the Knights of St John* (London, 1900).

Rose-Troup, F., *The Western Rebellion of 1549* (London, 1913).

Rowse, A. L., *Tudor Cornwall* (London, 1941).

Rupp, E. G., *Studies in the Making of the English Protestant Tradition* (Cambridge, 1949).

Savine, A., *English Monasteries on the Eve of the Dissolution* (Oxford, 1909).

Scarisbrick, J. J., *Henry VIII* (London, 1968).

—— *The Reformation and the English People* (London, 1984).

Schenk, W., *Reginald Pole* (London, 1950).

Seaborne, M. V. J., *The Reformation in Wales* (London, 1952).

Shiels, W. J., *The English Reformation, 1530–70* (London, 1989).

Skeel, C. A. J., *The Council in the Marches of Wales* (London, 1903).

Smith, H. M., *Henry VIII and the Reformation* (London, 1948).

Smith, L. B., *The Elizabethan Epic* (London, 1969).

—— *Henry VIII: The Mask of Royalty* (London, 1971).

Smith, Ll. B., 'Pwnc yr iaith yng Nghymru, 1282–1536', *Cof Cenedl*, I (1986), 1–34.

—— 'Yr iaith yng Nghymru'r Oesau Canol', *LlC*, XVIII (1995), 79–191.

Smyth, C. H., *Cranmer and the Reformation under Edward VI* (Cambridge, 1926).

Southern, A. C., *English Recusant Prose, 1559–1582* (London, 1951).

Starkey, D. R., *The Reign of Henry VIII: Personalities and Politics* (London, 1985).

Stephens, M., *Companion to the Literature of Wales* (Cardiff, 1986).

Strype, J., *Annals of the Reformation . . .* (4 vols. Oxford, 1820–40).

—— *Ecclesiastical Memorials . . .* (3 vols. Oxford, 1820–40).

—— *The Life and Acts of John Whitgift* (3 vols. Oxford, 1822).

Sykes, N., *The Crisis of the Reformation* (London, 1946).

Thomas, D. A., *The Welsh Elizabethan Catholic Martyrs* (Cardiff, 1971).

Thomas, D. R., *The Life and Work of Richard Davies and William Salesbury* (Oswestry, 1902).

—— *The History of the Diocese of St Asaph* (3 vols. Oswestry, 1908–1913).

—— 'Extracts from old wills relating to Wales', *AC* (1876), 220–6; (1878), 148–56; (1880), 217–21; (1882), 118–26.

Thomas, I., *William Salesbury a'i Destament* (Cardiff, 1967).

—— *Y Testament Newydd Cymraeg, 1551–1620* (Cardiff, 1972).

—— *Yr Hen Destament Cymraeg, 1551–1620* (Aberystwyth, 1988).

Thomas, J. D. H., *A History of Wales, 1485–1660* (Cardiff, 1972).

Thomas, K. V., *Religion and the Decline of Magic* (London, 1971).

Thomas, L., *The Reformation in the Old Diocese of Llandaff* (Cardiff, 1930).

Bibliography

Thomas, W., 'The Trinity College, Carmarthen, copy of William Morgan's Bible', *Carms. Antiq.*, XXIV (1988), 110–13.

Thomas, W. S. K., *Tudor Wales* (Llandysul, 1983).

Toussaert, J., *Le Sentiment religieux en Flandre à la fin du Moyen Age* (Paris, 1965).

Trimble, W. R., *The Catholic Laity in Elizabethan England* (Cambridge, Mass., 1964).

Victory, S., *The Celtic Church in Wales* (Cardiff, 1972).

Walker, D. G., *A History of the Church in Wales* (Penarth, 1976).

—— 'Religious change, 1536–1603', *Pembs. County Hist.* III (Aberystwyth, 1987), 94–125.

Walker, M., 'Welsh books in St Mary's, Swansea', *BBCS*, XXIII (1968–70), 397–402.

Wark, W. R., *Elizabethan Recusancy in Cheshire* (Manchester, 1971).

Waugh, E., *Edmund Campion* (Harmondsworth, 1953).

Wernham, R. B., *England before the Armada* (London, 1966).

White, F. O., *Lives of the Elizabethan Bishops* (London, 1898).

Whiting, R., *The Blind Devotion of the People* (Cambridge, 1989).

Williams, D., *A History of Modern Wales* (London, 1950).

Williams, D. H., *The Welsh Cistercians* (2 vols. Tenby, 1983, 1985).

—— *Atlas of Cistercian Lands* (Cardiff, 1990).

Williams, G., *Bywyd ac Amserau yr Esgob Richard Davies* (Cardiff, 1953).

—— *Welsh Reformation Essays* (Cardiff, 1968).

—— *The Welsh Church from Conquest to Reformation* (2nd edn., Cardiff, 1976).

—— *Religion, Language and Nationality in Wales* (Cardiff, 1979).

—— *Grym Tafodau Tân* (Llandysul, 1984).

—— *The Welsh and their Religion* (Cardiff, 1991).

—— *Recovery, Reorientation and Reformation: Wales, c.1415–1642* (Oxford, 1987; repr. as *Renewal and Reformation*, Oxford, 1993).

—— 'The episcopal registers of St David's 1554–65', *BBCS*, XIV (1950), 45–54, 125–38.

—— 'The collegiate church of Llanddewibrefi', *Ceredigion*, IV/4 (1964), 376–52.

—— 'Prophecy, poetry and politics in medieval and Tudor Wales', in H. Hearder, and H. R. Loyn (eds.), *British Government and Administration* (Cardiff, 1974), 104–16.

—— 'Wales and the Reign of Mary I', *WHR*, X (1981), 334–58.

—— 'The Stradling family', in R. Denning (ed.), *St Donat's Castle and Atlantic College* (Cowbridge, 1983), pp. 17–53.

—— 'Welsh authors and their books', in M. B. Line (ed.), *The World of Books and Information* (London, 1987), 187–96.

—— 'Poets and pilgrims in the fifteenth and sixteenth centuries', *TCS* (1991), 69–98.

—— and Jones, R. O. (eds.), *The Celts and the Renaissance* (Cardiff, 1990).

Bibliography

Williams, G. A., *Ymryson Edmwnd Prys a Wiliam Cynwal* (Cardiff, 1986).
Williams, G. J., *Traddodiad Llenyddol Morgannwg* (Cardiff, 1948).
Williams, H., *Christianity in Early Britain* (Oxford, 1912).
Williams, J. E. C., 'Welsh religious prose', *Proceedings of the International Congress of Celtic Studies* (Cardiff, 1966).
Williams, P. H., *The Council in the Marches of Wales under Elizabeth I* (Cardiff, 1958).
—— *The Tudor Regime* (Oxford, 1979).
Williams, W. Ll., *The Making of Modern Wales* (London, 1919).
Willis, Browne, *A Survey of the Cathedral Church of Bangor* (London, 1721); *Llandaff* (London, 1719); *St Asaph* (London, 1801); *St David's* (London, 1717).
Woodward, G. W. O., *The Dissolution of the Monasteries* (London, 1968).
Wormald, J., *Court, Kirk, and Community: Scotland, 1470–1625* (London, 1981).
Yardley, E., *Menevia Sacra* (*AC* Supplement, 1927).
Youings, J., *The Dissolution of the Monasteries* (London, 1971).

(B) Unpublished Dissertations

Bowen, D. J., 'Y Gymdeithas Gymreig yn niwedd yr Oesau Canol fel yr adlewyrchir hi yn y farddoniaeth uchelwrol' (MA, Wales, 1951).
Bowen, G., 'Llenyddiaeth Gatholig y Cymry, 1559–1829' (MA, Liverpool, 1952–3).
—— 'Rhyddiaith Reciwsantaidd Cymru' (Ph.D., Wales, 1978).
Carr, A. D., 'The Mostyn family and estate, 1200–1642' (Ph.D., Wales, 1976).
Cleary, J. M., 'Welsh recusant clergy' (MA, Liverpool, 1965–6).
Davies, A., 'The attitude of Wales towards the Reformation' (MA, Wales, 1911).
Edwards, T. J., 'The disposal of monastic property in the diocese of Llandaff' (MA, Wales, 1928).
Fitzgerald, G. J., 'The religious background of the classical Welsh poets, 1435–1535' (MA, Liverpool, 1964).
Gray, M., 'The disposal of Crown property in Monmouthshire, 1500–1603' (Ph.D., Wales, 1985).
Griffith, W. P., 'Welsh students at Oxford, Cambridge, and the Inns of Court, 1500–1642' (Ph.D., Wales, 1981).
Gruffydd, R. G., 'Religious prose in Welsh from the beginning of the reign of Elizabeth to the Restoration' (D.Phil., Oxford, 1952–3).
Jones, Emyr G., 'The Caernarvonshire squires, 1538–1625' (MA, Wales, 1936).
Jones, J. G., 'The Wynn Family and Estate of Gwydir: their origins, growth and development up to 1674' (Ph.D., Wales, 1974).
Kerr, R. M., 'Cywyddau Siôn Brwynog' (MA, Wales, 1960).
Mathias, W. A., 'Astudiaeth o weithgarwch llenyddol William Salesbury' (MA, Wales, 1949).
Morgan, G., 'Pregethau Cymraeg William Griffith ac Evan Morgan' (MA, Wales, 1969).

Bibliography

Owen, G. D., 'Agrarian conditions and changes in West Wales during the sixteenth century' (Ph.D., Wales, 1935).

Saunders, E. J., 'Gweithiau Lewys Morgannwg' (MA, Wales, 1922).

Williams, B., 'The Welsh Clergy, 1558–1642' (Ph.D., Open University, forthcoming).

Index

Abbreviations

Index

magic, magicians, 22, 27, 286, 324–7, 329
Mansel, Anthony, 379–80
Mansel family, 101, 136, 261, 379
  Sir Rice, 98, 134, 135, 174, 212
manuscripts, 15, 26, 48, 95, 145–6, 150, 252,
    261, 328, 367, 387
  copyists, 261, 274, 367
March, Marches of Wales, 7, 36, 42, 49, 98,
    105, 193, 271, 368
Margam, Cist. abbey, 11, 15, 46, 75, 77, 79,
    82, 89–90, 95, 96, 98, 99, 101, 134, 365
marriages, clandestine, 381
martyrs, 227
  Catholic, 366, 367
  Protestant, 174, 205–8
Mary I, Queen of England, 37, 62, 97, 104,
    143, 165, 169, 172, 173, 174, 179,
    180–222, 224, 225, 227, 229–32, 315,
    374, 400
  accession of Mary, 188–90
  clerical marriage, 194–200
  death, 218–20
  and death of Edward VI, 185–9
  Marian reforms, 209–13
    results, 213–15
  martyrdoms and exiles, 204–9
  Princess Mary, 51, 52, 57, 153, 157, 187
  reaction of clergy and laity, 200–4
  rebellions against, 192–4
  reintroduction of Catholicism, 191–2
Mary Stuart, Queen of Scotland, 219, 237,
    253–4, 257–8, 262–3, 270, 272, 273,
    275–6, 350, 361, 362, 372, 394
mass (es), 20, 21, 24, 28, 148, 158, 165, 169,
    179, 180, 181, 191–2, 223, 248, 261, 263,
    266, 269, 272, 324–5, 342, 360, 365, 370,
    373
Mathew family, 69, 379
  George, 168
  Miles, 128, 160–1
  William, 377
Mawr or More, William, 112, 142
merchants, 81, 107, 136–7, 138, 184, 205,
    321, 333
Meredith, Sir William, 380
Merioneth, 7
Merrick, Rice, 284, 299
Meyrick, Rowland, bp. of Bang. (1559–66),
    160, 164, 168, 172, 195, 200, 201, 208,
    221–4, 331–2
Methodist Revival, 16
Milan, 252, 267
Milford Haven, 130, 209, 262, 368, 369–71
Mirk, John, 26
Middleton, Marmaduke, bp. of St D.
    (1582–92), 228, 280, 289, 295, 296–7,
    298, 302, 307, 315, 330, 333, 334, 335,
    369–71, 376, 378, 380, 390

Middleton, William, 387
monasteries, 7, 8, 16, 72, 74, 85, 93, 363
  architecture, 99
  bells, 95
  churches, 96
  dissolution, 99, 109, 124, 127, 138, 159,
    299
  lead, 95
  officials, 81
  possessions, 101, 133
  servants, 94
  tenants, 88–9, 101
  worship, 103
monks, 14, 23, 56, 153
Monmouth, 256, 278
  Ben. priory, 8, 75, 78–9, 83, 86, 96
Monmouthshire, 70, 74, 99, 135, 136, 161,
    231, 261, 266, 270, 277, 278, 279, 315,
    319–20, 331, 368, 371, 372, 375–6
Montgomery, 96
Montgomeryshire, 268, 288, 364
More, Sir Thomas, 31, 45, 47, 48, 103, 105
Morgan family (Llantarnam), 104, 136, 262,
    266, 278, 331, 333, 363, 373, 375
  Edward, 373
  Sir Thomas, 204
Morgan, Henry, bp. of St D. (1554–9), 195,
    201, 205, 210, 212, 217, 218, 220
Morgan Henry, Lland., 128
Morgan, Thomas, conspirator, 258, 270, 273
Morgan, Sir William, 69–70
Morgan, William, bp. of Lland. (1595–1601)
    and St A. (1601–4), 146, 238, 291, 295,
    300, 302, 303, 318, 331, 341, 378, 382,
    388, 395, 396, 402, 405
  education and early career, 342–6
  influence on other authors, 383–5, 392–3
  qualities as translator, 352–7, 383–6
  reaction of contemporaries, 357–60
  translation of Bible, 343–6
Mostyn family, 331
  Sir Thomas, 269, 274
Myddleton family, 236, 395

Neath, 46
  Cist. abbey, 11, 46, 76, 77–8, 88–9, 95, 96,
    99, 100, 102, 112, 134
Netherlands, 263, 270, 291, 398; *see also*
    Low Countries
'neuters', 203, 235
Newport, 161, 256
  Austin friary, 91
New Testament, 236
  English, 63
  Welsh (1567), 15, 146, 149, 201, 241,
    242–5, 246, 302, 314, 329, 338, 340, 342,
    344, 347, 352, 355, 357, 358, 384–5, 393
Nichol, William, 206–7, 208

Index

simony, 298, 337
Siôn Brwynog, 38, 153, 180, 186, 190, 192, 212
Siôn Cent, 29–30, 325
Siôn Dafydd Rhys, 275, 289, 310, 314, 325, 340–1, 346, 365, 388
Siôn Mawddwy, 325, 359
Sion monastery, 31, 45
Siôn Tudur, 212, 315, 352, 359, 384, 387
Six Articles Act, 130–1, 141, 142–3, 158
Skeffington, Thomas, bp. of Bang. (1509–33), 43–4, 61, 66
Slebech commandery, 43, 86, 92–3, 134, 141, 204, 278, 363
Smart, John, abb. of Wigmore, 43, 67
Smith, Dr John, treas. of Lland., 128, 231
Somerset family, 38, 136; see also Worcester, earls of
Somerset, Edward Seymour, duke of, 122, 141, 154, 155–6, 157, 167, 168, 171, 173, 174
Spain, 27, 47, 48, 62, 84, 191, 248, 253–4, 255, 259, 267, 276, 277, 282, 350, 361, 370, 371, 397
Spanish Armada, 276, 277, 357, 361, 362–3
SPCK, 404
Spenser, Edmund, 276, 303, 383
Spes, Guerau de, 254
Standish, Henry, bp. of St A. (1518–35), 42, 46, 53, 56, 61, 67
Star Chamber, Court of, 43, 51, 120, 265, 294, 301, 309, 310, 317–19, 321, 367, 370, 376
Stationers' Company, 236, 239, 243, 395
Stradling family, 100, 136, 233, 313, 379, 395
Sir Edward, 290, 298, 313–14
Sir Thomas, 104, 174, 202, 232
Strata Florida, Cist. abbey, 11, 75, 80, 88–9, 94, 95, 96, 97, 99, 102, 103, 134
monk of, Richard Smith, 80
Strata Marcella, Cist. abbey, 44, 76, 79, 96, 97, 98, 134, 319
succession, royal, 52, 188–9, 216–17, 361, 371–3, 389
Sundays, 320, 322
superstition, 27, 28, 118, 129, 173, 182, 223, 234, 245, 247, 256, 272, 280–1, 282, 283, 297, 320, 326, 327
Supplication unto the High Court, 306
Supreme Governor, 219, 398
Supreme Head, 36, 40, 55, 106, 113, 114, 126, 147, 148, 219
Surrey, Henry Howard, earl of, 154–5
Swansea, 169, 174, 223, 242, 298, 351
Hospital of the Blessed David, 160
Sweden, 35, 84, 235, 397
Switzerland, 84, 249

Talachddu, Brecs., 381

Talley, Premonst. abbey, 73, 87, 96, 134
Talley, Thomas, 147
taverns, 26, 65, 149, 285, 293, 322
Teilo, St, 3, 10, 127–8
Ten Articles (1536), 115, 116
Tenby, 111, 161, 272
Ten Commandments, 22, 26, 116, 145, 239
Welsh, 147, 150, 239, 302
Tewkesbury abbey, 8, 97
Thackwell, Roger, 274–5
Thirty-nine Articles, 166, 284, 302
Thomas ap Ieuan ap Rhys, 109–10, 178, 191
Thomas, Dr Isaac, 243, 347
Thomas, Leyshon, abb. Neath, 76, 77–8, 79, 88, 89, 93, 100
Thomas, Oliver, 381
Thomas, R. S., 345–6
Thomas, William, 37, 192–3
Throckmorton, Job, MP, 305, 306
Throckmorton conspiracy, 270, 271
Tintern, Cist. abbey, 10, 43, 76, 79, 83, 86, 87, 95, 96, 98, 99, 133
tithes, 317
towns, 32
Toy, Humphrey, 210, 239, 242, 392
Griffith, son of, 392
Trefor, John, bp. of St A. (1394–1410), 14, 33
Trent, Council of, 27, 215, 221, 233, 249, 250, 252
Trillo, St, 365
Trojans, Troy, 1, 2, 5
Tudor(s), Tudor dynasty, 33, 38, 42, 152, 170, 185, 190, 216, 399, 400, 403
Tudor, Edmund, earl of Richmond, 90, 123
Tudur Aled, 50, 90
Turberville family, 233, 262, 278, 366, 367, 371
Christopher, 233
James, 371
Jenkin, 371
Lewis, 271, 371
Matthew, 367
Tye, Thomas, 142–3
Tyndale, William, 31, 32, 47, 48, 146, 243, 245
Tyndale's Bible, 32, 47, 146, 147

universities, 33; see Cambridge, Oxford
Urban, bp. of Lland. (1107–33/4), 7
Usk, Ben. nunnery, 73, 87
Usk, river, 280, 283

Vaen, Veyn, Andrew, archd. of Lland, 290, 319, 337
Valle Crucis, Cist. abbey, 11, 67, 79, 83, 87, 96, 99, 100, 102, 134
Valor Ecclesiasticus, 21, 69–70, 72, 74, 82, 102